Josie Dew has spent over fifteen years cycling in fits and starts, mostly alone, around the world. Now 200,000 miles, 41 countries, five continents, a lot of wobbly legs and a handful of punctures later, she is still firmly fixed in the saddle. She is the author of two previous books about her travels: THE WIND IN MY WHEELS (shortlisted for the 1992 British Books Travel Writer of the Year Award) and TRAVELS IN A STRANGE STATE: Cycling Across the USA. She has written for many magazines and appeared on television and radio discussing numerous aspects of the activity that has obsessed her for most of her life.

Also by Josie Dew

THE WIND IN MY WHEELS

TRAVELS IN A STRANGE STATE

A RIDE IN THE NEON SUN

A Gaijin in Japan

JOSIE DEW

Maps and drawings by Peter Wilson

WARNER BOOKS

A *Warner* Book

First published in Great Britain in 1999
by Little, Brown and Company
This edition published by Warner Books in 2000

All photographs, bar one, taken by the author, many with the aid of a ten-second self-timer and mini-tripod.

A CIP catalogue record for this book is available from the British Library.

ISBN 0 7515 1755 0

Typeset in New Baskerville by M Rules
Printed and bound in Great Britain by Clays Ltd, St Ives plc

Warner Books
A Division of
Little, Brown and Company (UK)
Brettenham House
Lancaster Place
London WC2E 7EN

For my *oya,* at last.
And for Tetsu

Why travel if you
know where you are?
One travels for the
pleasure of being lost.

Christopher Hope

Contents

Acknowledgements

I owe a very big '*domo arigato gozaimasu*' to Hiroshi Nagai and his wife Sonoe for all the immeasurable kindness and enthusiastic help they have given me both in Japan and in England. I would also like to thank:
Barbara Boote for her encouragement and remarkable patience and for not giving up on me; Hilary Foakes for ploughing through my weighty piles of untidily typed pages and giving me hope ahoy; Val Porter for unravelling my nonsensical words and thoughts and two-fingered typings in record time and for reacting so promisingly at the prospect of me ensconcing myself over the hedge; Herr Peter Wilson for taking my scratchily sketched melée of topsy-turvy maps and making them into something even more top-sidedly turvy; Taeko Oliver for providing assistance and a Claridges tea and a Matsuri supper and for putting me in contact with Noriko and Akitomo Imai and Sachiko and Kunio Igarashi; Toshiko Owaku for giving up so much time to answer my muddle of multitudinous questions; Hideko Martin for my Japanese lessons; Jim(my) Holmes and Mariko Inoue for being the first to alert me to the '*oishii*' joys of Japan and for circuitously leading me into an extended state of multi-paged confusion; Roger and Maggie Bellamy for putting me

in contact with the honourable Nagai-san; Ruairidh Alexander for boosting my antipodean sales; Trevor Beauchamp and Nigel Hamm at Liphook Cycles for tip-top service; Andy Brown for his Outwardly Bounding help and assistance; Lonely Planet for permission to quote from Alex Kerr's *Lost Japan*; Juliet Coombe for inviting me on board her La Belle Aurore *Intrepid Journeys*; all the countless *obaasan, o-kaa-san, mama-san, oku-san, ojo-san, okusama, ojii-san* and *otochan* who went out of their way to help me, house me, feed me, water me, *oolong-cha* me, wash me and scrub me – a combination which made my journey into Japan so memorable, so enlightening and so much fun.

My thanks too to:
1. Sue Lodge at Intermediate Technology (IT) – a British based charity and international development organization. IT's mission is to build the technical skills of poor people in developing countries, enabling them to improve the quality of their lives and that of future generations.

Intermediate Technology (Reg. Charity No. 247257)
The Schumacher Centre for Technology and Development,
Bourton Hall, Bourton-on-Dunsmore,
Rugby CV23 9QZ UK
Tel: +44 (0)1788–661100

2. Stefan Meigh at Sense (The National Deafblind and Rubella Association). Sense is the national voluntary organization supporting and campaigning for people who are deafblind, their families, their carers and professionals who work with them. The charity is the world's largest organization working with deafblind people.

Sense (Reg. Charity No. 289868)
11–13 Clifton Terrace
London N4 3SR
Tel: +44 (0)171–272 7774

N
RUSSIA
Vladivostock
HOKKAIDO
PACIFIC OCEAN
TOHOKU
SEA OF JAPAN
N. KOREA
Sado Island
Sendai
Niigata
Seoul
HONSHU
Tokyo
MT. FUJI
KOREA

JAPA

SHIKOKU

Nagasaki

KYUSHU

EAST
CHINA
SEA

Amami-Oshima

Tokunoshima

Yoron

Okinawa

Miyako

Ishigaki

Iriomote

No of miles* cycled 2,900

No of klix* cycled 4,640

Time taken to pedal the Jap... 4 months

no. of Punctures 1

Number of Typhoons that tied me up in their typhoons 1

Denotes where 70% of all Japanese live, die, cough, laugh, ponder the meaning of live & drink Pocari Sweat

400 Miles

*hot, sweaty, humid & usually lost

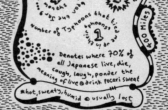

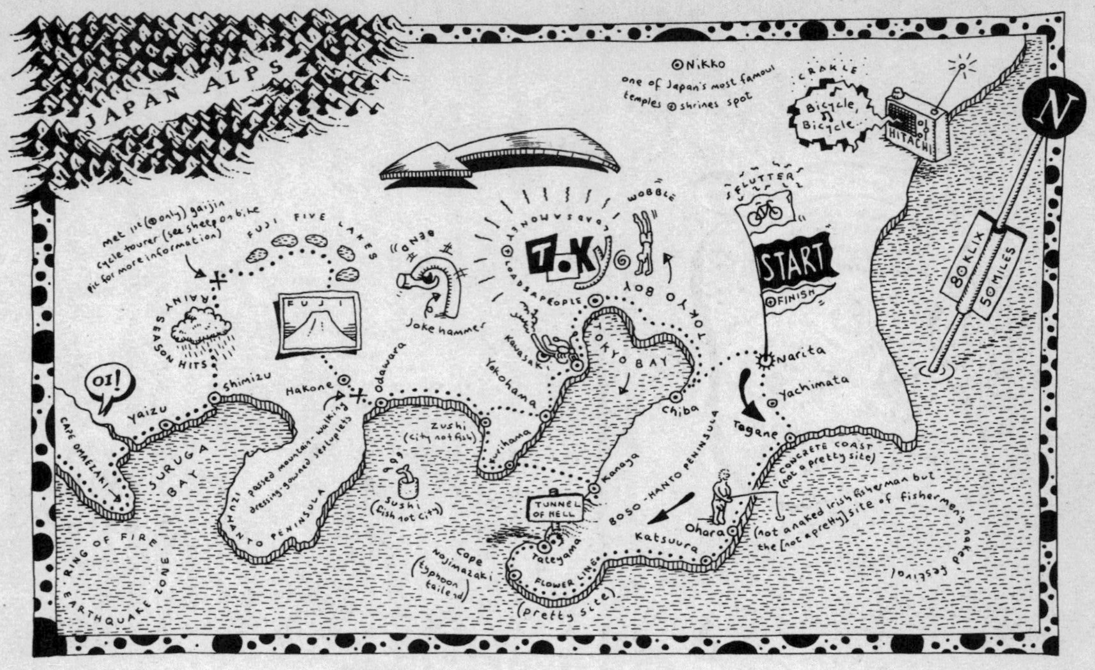
JAPAN ALPS
Nikko
one of Japan's most famous temples & shrines spot
CRAKLE
Bicycle, Bicycle...
HITACHI
N
80 KLIX
50 MILES
FLUTTER
START
FINISH
WOBBLE
LOADSAMONEY
LOADSAPEOPLE
TOKYO BOY
BEND
Joke hammer
met 1st (& only) gaijin cycle tourer (see sheep on bike pic for more information)
FUJI FIVE LAKES
FUJI
RAINY SEASON HITS
OI!
Shimizu
Hakone
Odawara
Kawasaki
Yokohama
TOKYO BAY
Narita
Yachimata
Chiba
Togane
Yaizu
CAPE OMAEZAKI
SURUGA BAY
passed mountain-walking dressing-gowned sextuplets
IZU HANTO PENINSULA
Zushi (city not fish)
Sushi (fish not city)
Kurihama
Kanaya
TUNNEL OF HELL
BOSO-HANTO PENINSULA
CONCRETE COAST (not a pretty site)
(not a naked Irish fisherman but the [not a pretty] site of fishermen's naked festival
Ohara
Katsuura
Tateyama
FLOWER LINE
(pretty site)
Cape Nojimazaki (typhoon tail end)
RING OF FIRE
EARTHQUAKE ZONE

CHAPTER 1

Lost

Don't look for the donkey since you're on it.
Don't look for your head, since it's on your shoulders.
The donkey, you and the universe are one and the same.
(Zen teaching)

There is something about being hopelessly lost that is strangely enjoyable. Flailing around in a vortex of unfamiliarity can give rise to a bout of what the Japanese so enchantingly call *doki doki* – that arousingly fluttery and faintly nauseating sensation that ricochets from heartbeat to stomach and makes pupils dilate and throats turn dry.

Doki doki can strike in moments of intense trepidation, expectation or unpredictability. Breathing becomes barely discernible as a sudden thrilling shiver surges through your system. Fear, bewilderment, confusion, passion – all have their finger on the *doki doki* trigger: while a part of you is longing to turn tail and run, another part is luring you into an enticing lair, to be encapsulated, uprooted and spun off your feet.

Dizzy from the heady heights of Oriental disorientation, I was struck by a lavish dose of *doki doki* as I found myself wavering with a growing sense of uncertainty while weaving my way around neon-flashing puddles amidst the meaningless melée of Tokyo.

I felt lost. 'One is never lost, just seeing new places,' the travel writer Hilary Bradt once said. Somehow I seem to combine the two fairly adroitly.

My earliest memory of becoming lost took place in Waterloo Station. I was about six. After a day out in London with my mother and two elder brothers we were hurrying – late afternoon, rush-hour sort of time – to our train. In one of my hands was my mother's. In the other was a fresh copy of *Dandy*. Up ahead my eldest brother clutched *Cor!* while the other clasped *Whizzer and Chips*.

It was my first day of being a *Dandy* reader. Until then my mother had only allowed me the embarrassingly sissy *Disneyland* and, although *Dandy* was definitely a breakthrough into a more rough-and-tumble read, I secretly pined for the *Beano*. In my eyes Dennis the unyielding Menace was 'naughty but nice', a rogue worthy of deification, but in my mother's he was irrefutably a yob, a no-gooder, a bad influence. He would have to wait, she said in a rather tantalizing manner, until I was older. So the exploits of Desperate Dan had to suffice before I could unleash myself upon the misdemeanours of the Menace.

Thus, it was Desperate Dan who diverted my attention as I was steered around a labyrinth of legs that Waterloo afternoon until I was suddenly aware that my mother's hand was no longer a part of mine. The warm, reassuring, pianist-strong palm had gone and so had she. So had my brothers. I stopped amidst a tide of commuting suits rushing past me. Fear. Heartbeat. *Doki doki.* I was adrift on a platform among a sea of knees. Alone. Lost. And Desperate Dan.

But I didn't stop for long. The stampeding, scurrying crowd saw to that. Caught in a rip-tide of churning train-rushers I was bowled along, knocked by the force of the flow, pitched, rolled, dragged under, breathless, flailing, drowning. Just me and Desperate Dan rolled into my tightly clenched grip. Lost. Unattached. Adrift. British Rail flotsam. Yawing wildly, I was tugged and turned over from one slipstream to another until I finally resurfaced at the knee-level of a pair of sturdy black trousers.

Raising my gaze, I identified the top-heavy helmeted head as that of a Plod from whom questions issued forth. Lost?

Name? Home? An alien leather-gloved hand wrapped tight around mine. More questions, more distortion. Unfamiliarity. No mother. Waiting and worrying and shiverings of spine. *Doki doki.* Noise, excitement, uncertainty, waiting. Then a face, a warmth, a soaring elation – engulfed by a tearful and loving form. My mother, shuddering with relief, squeezing our breaths, holding tight, not letting go. Found, with Desperate Dan.

CHAPTER 2

Confused

It was the bath that threw me. At least I took it to be a bath – either that or a very big sink. Cubular, compact and containing a seat, it was a far cry from the wallowing sort of tub that I was used to. Unlike many baths I have known, this one was not attached by umbilical cord to an integral shower unit. Instead the shower head lay severed from the bath and, coiled incongruously, sprouted from the wall at about calf-level, half-way between the base of the bath and the door.

The door, incidentally, was no great distance away as the bathroom was more cubicle than room, more bath than space. No sooner had you stepped through the door than you found yourself immersed in the bath. Elbow room was indeed at a premium. Floor space was about as generous as an unfurled broadsheet and consisted of an uneven mosaic of black and white glazed pebble-tiles the size of postage stamps set in concrete. The whole floor (or what there was of it) had a sink-like, built-in tilt enabling all the shower water and bath overspill to surge down to an open drainhole set in one corner. It was the sort of darkly ominous and bottomless drain from which you could imagine a host of alien livestock, sporting pincher-serrated proboscises, crawling in menacing style.

Apart from the bath, the only other furniture in the room was a pink plastic bowl inverted upon a toddler's pink plastic stool. Wedged into the corner sat a small, plastic, two-tiered triangular rack containing a used razor, remnants of soap and a dark wooden scrubbing brush in the shape of a hedgehog. Fixed to the wall just above the spiralling shower coil was a small mirror. There were no hooks, no towel rails, no shower curtains. Clothing was obviously not shed from within. I went back out before coming back in and stood naked, ready to begin.

It was by pure chance that I embarked upon my ablutions in correct Japanese fashion. Instead of running the bath and climbing in for a soak and a scrub in the Western way, I began by showering. This would have roused a round of applause in itself had any Japanese been watching, as Japanese don't actually wash in the bath but only wet themselves. To them, the peculiar foreign method of sloshing and wallowing in your own grime is quite repugnant and just goes to reinforce the widely held view that those big-nosed and hirsute foreigners are a smelly lot. And how right they are.

The reason I chose to shower first was because I wished to wash my hair. Having observed that the shower was situated outside the bath I concluded, without too much dilemma, that this operation could be conducted more smoothly before entering the tub.

The shower in itself was a novelty: I had never before had a shower sitting down. Perched on the small plastic stool I felt more in position to start milking a cow than shampooing my hair. And watching myself in the low-lying mirror through sudsy eyes as I washed was an innovative experience. Instead of just eyeing the repetitive curly-mazed pattern of bathroom tiles (as I did at home), here, when I sluiced away the steam, I was actually looking at something. Me. My reflection. It came as a bit of a shock: I looked absurd, stooped low on a milking stool with drowned features apparently sprouting from my knees. Through a shroud of suds and peach-scented lather I sat with a vacuous expression looking at a foaming form looking back at me. Odd. But then, as I was to discover, life was only to become odder.

Shower accomplished, it was time to adjourn to the bath. This had already been run for me by some unseen presence and kept steaming hot by a detachable, rollable cover; in effect, like a lid. I rolled it back half-way before hoisting an eager leg ready for the plunge. But this was no ordinary hoist, as the wall of the bath seemed of formidable height and to scale it was quite an operation in itself. This struck me as strange – it's not as though the Japanese are giants. Then, a flashing thought occurred to me. Perhaps that was what the milking stool was for: to ease elevation in the ascent of the mountainous face of the bath. Spurred on by this unexpected revelation, I drew up the stool and in tottering style embarked upon entering the bath from this novel standpoint.

Usually when I have a bath I blithely step straight into about six inches of water before turning prostrate, face uppermost. But this time, aware of the thick swirling clouds of copious steam arising from the water, some rare instinct told me not to be so hasty. It was an instinct for which I was most grateful. I felt it judicious for a tentative hand to turn guinea-pig and test the waters. Rapidly, an explosive heat registered in my brain as the roving rodent hand squealed in shrivelling pain and impulsively withdrew. Nursing a fiery extremity I reassessed the situation. Obviously I was faced with a boiling cauldron which logic told me to leave well alone but which a parlous but dogged curiosity lured me to pursue, come hell or hot water.

In such steamy circumstances I was confronted with an option: either add cold or burn. Had I been on home ground I would have simply turned on the cold without further ado. But this wasn't home ground, it was Japanese ground and Japanese bath and I fancied adopting Japanese practices. Why enter an exotic culture and yet live in habitual safe and cosy ways? How can foreign flavours be properly sampled if you carry a homely carapace upon your back? You may stick out your head but not your tongue. To taste an unfamiliar clime, shells must be shed, strings must be severed, habits must be loosened. Thus, I was doomed to fry. And fry I would, in true Japanese style.

So, still on stool and anxiously conceding that there was no turning back now, I once again hoisted an experimental leg in preparation for the plunge. If there is one cut-and-dried way of entering a hot and wet bath, it's slowly – painfully slowly. Steam billowed from ears.

Naturally when one enters a bath one expects to find a bottom. Inch by inch I continued lowering my hesitant foot, expecting to ground any moment. As I straddled the wall of the bath in ungainly fashion and clumsily clutched the sides, my boiled-lobster limb continued to be submerged and swallowed by what now appeared to be a bottomless bath.

Feeling faintly perturbed by the thought that what goes down might not come up, I continued to sink into this aqueous conundrum until my foot finally, and thankfully, ran aground. Seemingly, Japanese baths were as deep as European ones are long and, although now standing, I was virtually submerged and could scarce see out over the side. It was like being in a large saucepan on the stove and I was momentarily overcome by a few vague pangs of guilt for all of those carrots and parsnips that I have nonchalantly tossed into the boiling pot over the years. In a vicarious way I could now see (and feel) things through a brassica's pores and it wasn't altogether pleasant.

But compared with the fate of a lowly carrot, at least I had the benefit of a seat (or was it a step?) sunk into the side of the bath. Thus in a Japanese bath if one can't lie one can sit in style. So, with knees up and bottom down I sank to my neck, reclined back grandly and thought not of England but of the Land of the Rising Sun.

Finding myself in Japan had come as a bit of a shock. I had been planning on going to New Zealand and how I came to be some 6,000 miles off course is one of those things that I'm not altogether sure about. Sometimes, life can become hazily unsteady as the vacillating veil of vagueness lowers its shroud. One may strive to follow a steady course of clear intentions but sooner or later a straying elbow knocks you adrift and you find yourself reeling with both paddles out of the water.

But there's no getting away from it; 6,000 miles is a fair old distance to go astray. Fortuitously, for lesser mortals such as myself, so vast and discrepant a navigational misplacement generally incites no point-blank explanations, no painful tearings apart, no harrowing and interminable internal enquiries. Frankly, what I suppose I'm trying to say is that it's a good job I'm not a pilot or else I could have some serious, mealy-mouthed explaining to do.

I know it's no excuse to say that Japan and New Zealand bear a rough resemblance (at least in my Philips School Atlas) in shape and form and that they are both found to be stretching curvaceously in the same sort of angle afloat in the mighty Pacific, but it's . . . well, an excuse of sorts.

Then there's the fact that while New Zealand is renowned for bearing an inordinate number of sheep, Japan is renowned for bearing an inordinate number of people. That's a shaky comparison, but if one finds oneself 6,000 miles off course one has to dig deep to justify one's error. And dig deep I will. Sheep have an inherent tendency to cluster together in groups. It is a sort of homing instinct, and some say (with sweeping generalization) that the Japanese herd themselves together in similar style. To me, they are more like birds, moving in formation.

Some people travel with firm ideas for a journey: following in the footsteps of an intrepid ancestor whose exotic exploits were happened upon in a dusty, cobweb-laced attic containing immovable trunks full of sepia-curled daguerrotypes and age-discoloured letters redolent of bygone days.

Others travel for anthropological, botanical, archaeological, geological and other logical reasons. Some are smitten by a specific country brewed from childhood dreams. For others, travel is a challenge, a release, an escape, a shaking off of the shackles, and even if they don't know where they will end up they usually know where they will begin. For me, the opposite stands true: I tend to begin where I thought I'd end up.

I landed at Tokyo's Narita airport with a bump and a bicycle and a handful of clichés about Japan: swarming armies of identically sombre-suited businessmen; houses more like hutches, with no room to spare; pollution and Walkmans and yeses that mean no entwined among inscrutable smiles and impenetrable speech and an enigmatic people whose names sounded like makes of motorcycle.

Floating in my mind among these clichés were two indelible and disparate sounds that had spurred a sudden intrigue with Japan: *Madame Butterfly*, and a drum. Puccini's illustrious opera had always ruffled my feathers, tingled my spine and alluringly drifted in and out of my head. Then I set eyes and ears upon Kodo, a troupe of bewitching Japanese drummers powerfully unleashing themselves like coiled springs upon their traditional *taiko* drums, beating frenetically with a raw, naked and primal rhythm that resonated deeper than the heart and made me suddenly realize what the hairs on the back of my neck were for. These two contrasting sounds – Italian opera and Japanese drum – oscillated around my head until they inexplicably merged and grew into a haunting crescendo full of a nebulous titillation and a sudden stirring desire that led me impulsively to Japan.

My entrance into Japan was a decidedly unsteady one and saw me reeling last off the plane and lurching past spick-and-span satellite stations while clawing at thin air for support.

Had I been flung at midnight straight into the subterranean world of Tokyo's subway, then my apparently inebriated condition would have passed scarcely unnoticed among the surplus of semi-conscious 'salarymen' either recumbent or staggering home after a typical daily dose of after-work drinking with business companions. But no, I hadn't imbibed a cargo-hold of duty free during the twelve-hour flight, nor had I braved the notorious rubberized and creamy-blob globules that passed as airline food. I had touched neither solid nor liquid and yet, for the whole of the endless time on the wing, I had been struck down with a stomach that kept me doubled over like a Japanese rice planter and a head that felt embedded with blades.

My condition was marginally improved by a genial Finnish air hostess informing me that she had never seen a passenger so ill. A doctor materialized who dutifully doled out an impressive and unappetizing array of pills and potions, which I obediently threw down the hatch and swallowed hard. Moments later up they came. Nothing would stay down.

Scarcely conscious, I was dimly aware of being borne aloft and elevated to Business Class (being unwell has its advantages), where I remained a perplexity for the rest of the journey. Try though they might, none of the cabin crew could put a definite finger on the cause of my poorliness. Appendicitis, food poisoning, ruptured hernia, flight fear, motion sickness and pregnancy were all ideas mooted and batted to and fro. But despite these interesting suggestions I knew the cause was simple and, although not particularly practical at 33,000 feet, could be easily rectified by the mere opening of a window.

Needless to say, my self-attained and remedial diagnosis was pooh-poohed by the wary souls around me but I knew what was what and had suffered from it (though not as debilitating) in times of airborne past. Basically, it was nothing more exciting than an allergy to sealed windows and dead regurgitated air. That such an apparently innocuous but artificial atmosphere can strike with such incapacitating vengeance is understandably treated by many with sceptical bemusement. But stomachs are stomachs and, for mine, those pervasive air-conditioners spell sickness to a violent degree.

This dubious disorder has gradually built up over the years as a result of, quite simply, having spent too much time living in tents out of doors. It seems I'm one of those sorts who has to be constantly attached to a howling gale to be able to function efficiently. Hurling open windows wherever I go is not a particularly sociable way to conduct oneself in modern life. Most people like their train windows up and their vehicles well sealed. On those rare occasions when I'm permitted to be conveyed by car I find that fans tend to be for heating and windows for closing. 'Air?' enquires he at the helm when I'm suspiciously observed grappling with the multi-switch, electric-windowed door panel. 'Oh, yes please – if that's not too much trouble,' says I in eager ingratiating style, only to be quelled by an automatically opening fume-tinged side-vent or that lovely equilibrium-displacing, sweet dead-dog smelling air-conditioner. Turning pasty of face, I'm occasionally granted half an inch of real-life open window and sit pinned to the glass, neck askew – panting canine fashion with snout sniffing the breeze.

For a country which evokes the image of no room to manoeuvre, with everyone on top of each other and everything compressed together in compact form, it seems a trifle odd that Narita, Japan's main airport and Asia's busiest, is located a sizeable forty miles from Tokyo.

Vast international airports tend to be the same the world over – spectacularly ugly expanses of concrete and glass and massive phalanxes of fuselage that swallow the scurrying hordes of sky-borne passengers. Narita is no different, despite the translation of its name, 'Becoming Rice Fields', which in reality is quite the opposite. 'Concreting Over the Paddies' would perhaps be more apt although I doubt the Diet (Japanese parliament) would agree.

For ten years the proposed construction of two new runways and terminals was plagued by terrorist threats, riot police and political demonstrations involving 20,000 anti-airport activists (anyone from children to farmers to housewives to grandmothers) claiming to support the farmers of the area who had been dispossessed of their centuries-old homesteads by heavy-handed government tactics.

Iniquitous circumstances have kept heels dug in, temperaments volatile and, with the occasional eruption of violent protest, security stringent. Riots in the Land of Wa (harmony) and Peaceful People could come as a bit of a shock should the average newcomer to Japan happen upon them. But, as I discovered, they are kept mostly under cover, under wraps and out of sight behind bulwarks of sky-scraping fences, so that the freshly landed traveller is greeted by nothing more than the sort of scene that tends to embellish the average hefty airport anywhere: swathes of exhaust-churning freeway, ponderous towers of concrete hotels, wasteland and eyesores and billboards and buses.

Feeling of delicate disposition after my rocky ride on the wing, the prospect of cycling forty-odd miles through alien urbanization to the core of Tokyo (one of the largest and most polluted cities on earth) was a little daunting. So instead I opted for a more gentle approach and jettisoned myself a short distance down the expressway to Narita-shi (Becoming Rice Fields City).

By luck and by chance I found myself weaving along the colourfully narrow, winding and lantern-strewn streets of the Old City, as opposed to the featureless, wide and flavourless ones of the New. Neon pink and silver plastic cherry-blossom streamers hung like bunting from the telephone poles, fluttering brightly in the spice-laced wind. Weird pickled foods of improbable colours and textures lay unprotected in squelchy, stomach-churning style upon wooden racks that lined the bustling streets, the stallholders soliciting passers-by with untempting cube-sized samples pierced on cocktail sticks. Everything looked strange, felt strange, smelt strange.

It is a common assumption that the more a person travels, the less their feathers are ruffled on entering a new country. The worries, the waverings, the *doki doki* uncertainties when feet touch down on unfamiliar soil are thought to dilute, dissolve, disappear even, into a fruity and foreign air pushed aside by a cocky self-assured confidence that beefs up your mettle, intuitively telling you (with a dismissively insouciant wave of the hand) that experience has delivered you an impregnability such that no new sights or sounds are likely to sway you from your groundings. After all, you've done it and seen it all before – haven't you? Or have you?

I'm not so sure. Maybe for much-travelled travellers worldly experience eases the fretful pangs of being delivered into an alien culture, but for me this only seems to exacerbate it. Unlike others who may stride forth into the world with dauntless step, I find that the more I wave goodbye to green, grassy, asphalted England, the more my moorings are left afloat, awash with a growing unease.

I used to head off into the world with an unfettered and all-embracing gay abandon, my arms open, my ignorance a blessing. I didn't brood, I didn't ponder, I didn't agonize. I just went – come what may. These days I still just go but I tend to take with me a progressively burdensome baggage of gnawing fret that I drag along heavy-handedly, at least for the first few days.

Perhaps this is a good thing. Perhaps, having had a number of shaky close shaves and having read about more, heard more and seen more undesirable things and people, it's expedient to be wary, almost untrusting. Confidence, not diffidence, is a valuable trait with which to travel, but with a confidence too pumped up, too buoyant, too overt, too heedless, it can be easy to slip, to fall fast prey to a malevolence that creeps insidiously from the shadows, shaking you to the ground, or even the grave.

With senses bombarded by the cacophony of an unaccustomed land and still not yet reunited with a dicky stomach which had left me high and dry somewhere over Siberia, my first priority was to flop on a floor, a bed, a bench – anything, so long as I could turn horizontal out of the heat.

Some sort of hostel or guest house that wouldn't break the bank would of course be most welcome, but was this wishful thinking in the land of the rising yen? Indeed, what was I even supposed to look for, or for that matter ask for, when not a single Japanese word nor even a single piece of writing made a single piece of sense? Arriving so suddenly, so unprepared, into a land so enigmatic was the price I had to pay for my spontaneous switch from the plan to travel to New Zealand; and it left me reeling. I didn't even know the basics: hello, good morning, excuse me, toilet, thank you – I had planned on learning these on the plane, but then I should have known that me and plans on planes are not a promising mix.

The week before I had left for Japan (which, incidentally, was the same week that my cycling destination flipped hemispheres) I had the good fortune to meet Roger and Maggie Bellamy, who lived just a few hours' cycle from my home and had previously lived for a few years in Yokohama. 'Come for tea,' they said, so for tea I went and sat in an immaculate sitting-room containing a fine selection of large and sumptuous coffee-table books about Japan. Tea was poured, maps pored over and photographs of awesome splendour were pawed with a rapturous delight. Glorious pages of mysterious colour leafed before my eyes – pages and places that meant much to Roger but little to me.

On the turning of each glossy page Roger would effuse over an exotic array of meaningless places – the sounds so far-reaching that, had there been no images, they would have been enough in themselves: Izu Honshu, Kinki, Unzen, Matsushima, Miyajima, Amanohashidate, Fukuoka, Kumamoto, Miyazaki. Was I really heading for these places? They sounded too good to be true and floated deep in my head with an alluring thrill as I vigorously spun my pedals homeward after tea.

Before leaving, Roger and Maggie had handed me their well-thumbed copy of a small yellow phrasebook improbably titled *Japanese in 3 Weeks.* 'It'll get you out of a fix!' they said, as they waved goodbye. 'And good luck!'

Pausing alongside a seaweed stall, I stood in the shade of a long rippling banner and extracted the phrasebook from my handlebar-bag, opening it for the first time in the hope that it would shed some light on my search for accommodation.

Foreign phrasebooks are notorious for providing some of the most useless sentences in times of dire foreign need. Sometimes I have a nightmare in which I am on an operating table, still conscious, and desperately trying to tell the Urdu-speaking, knife-wielding surgeon to rummage in the murky depths of my bicycle panniers for the hypodermic syringes that I've lugged half-way across the world for just such an emergency as this. But, thanks to my handy phrasebook, the best I might come up with is something like: 'Help! My carburettors have blown. Let's bury the tomahawk!'

Although the circumstances were now much less fraught, I was still faring no better in my search for a bed. *Japanese in 3 Weeks – Revised 83rd Edition* was not a lucid read. The first rather bizarre phrase that caught my eye when I opened the book was: 'You kill my cat and I'll kill your dog.'

I read on: 'I should like to be taken full length. Don't shave against the grain. These are quite damp yet. Why don't you call oftner? I have been tolerably well. This is like carrying coals to Newcastle. There is many a slip 'twixt the cup and the lip. Every Tom, Dick and Harry was there. All roads lead to Rome. Bless me! How you happen to be here? Well, by gosh, I am from Missouri.'

A trifle stunned I looked up and blinked hard, believing (or hoping) that perhaps my state of sleepless disorientation was playing tricks with my sight and that the words before me had scrambled illogically in my brain. But no, as sure as eggs are eggs, I was provided not with the 'Excuse me, is there a cheap hotel nearby?' that I was searching for but with 'The mountains will be in labour; an absurd mouse will be born. Call me sweetheart.'

Was this a cruel trick? Was I being taken for a ride? Did the Japanese language revolve around idioms and proverbs? 'It is folly to be in Rome and strive with the Pope' said the useless phrase on page 172. What was I to make of this? Was this some sort of linguistic *Candid Camera*? 'Women and weather are not to be trusted', page 170 kindly informed me. Huh! I thought, and nor are Japanese phrasebooks – especially ones published in Japan and written by a certain S. Sheba.

In desperation I turned to the preface in the slim hope of finding a plausible explanation. This was a tall shot as the preface page title was a cruelly misleading 'Simple but Practical' ('Simple and Practical' ways to get tongue-tied and twisted maybe, but certainly not a 'Simple and Practical' way to speak Japanese).

I read on:

> The author's aim has been to make this little book as simple but as practical as possible . . . Remembering however, that those who use this book are not children but adults who know some language, the author was not forgetful of the vital necessity of constructive as well as analytic explanations – a sort of a grown up person.

I felt I was losing him already but things were only to get worse:

> The phrases in this book are like milk, of easy and speedy digestion, while the diagrams explaining the peculiar construction of Japanese sentences are comparable to a palatable and nutritious food in a solid form.
>
> The students may say, after going through a few Japanese sentences that Japanese talk backwards, that is to say, the head in English is the tail in Japanese, and vice versa. So it is, but please remember that you are on the opposite side of the globe when you are in Japan . . .

Gracious! But pray, forgive me for interrupting; is one to assume that one is on the opposite side of the globe even though one might abide in, say, Hong Kong? What an interesting concept!

> . . . America sees the setting sun before Japan bids welcome to the rising sun which again, after the few hours it goes down beyond our western horizon, rises up in Europe as the morning sun. It is the same sun whether it rises in the East or sinks in the West.

How encouraging! What a caring and sharing world to discover that the sun is there to burn not just my bum, but everybody's! What a revelation! S. Sheba continues to shed more light:

> If you always use your own standard of time, you are bound to mix up American P.M. with Japanese A.M. or Japanese P.M. with European A.M., as you get confused in other matters by measuring other people with your own standard. Forget the hour in New York or in London while you are in Tokyo: otherwise you might say '*Ohayo*' [morning] when you retire at night or '*Oyasumi*' [goodnight] at breakfast, in the Land, that stands just as much on a level as your own country but on the opposite side of the globe.

Ah, useful tip this one. After all, don't most people travelling overseas keep the hands of their watch firmly synchronized with those of the clock beside their bed at home, however many hundreds or thousands of miles away it might be? Does everybody who surfaces after being washed up in new time zones find themselves saying in the early morning air: 'Well, by gosh and be darned. I am from Missouri and although the locals may be taking breakfast the folks back home will sure as hell be eating dinner. Waiter! I'll have the steak hollandaise, medium-rare, double portion of fries, Caesar salad and a bottle of your best, I'll take the table on the back deck so make it snappy if you will – I wanna eat before sundown.'

Feeling neither wiser nor better verbally equipped to accost a local for directions to nearby accommodation, I thought that I would, to quote from page 140, 'Be done with it; there isn't a least chance of success [as] there are eleven houses all told and a cracking good show in town [where] curses like chicken always come back to roast [*sic*].' Tucking my *Japanese in 3 Weeks – Revised 83rd Edition* (ha! more like years!) back into my bag (I was sure that after a hefty 83 editions something *must* have come adrift in the translation), I headed off down the bustling street to see what came my way.

And what came my way was a quite unexpected but auspicious low-lying white plastic sign which peeked from behind a blur of scurrying knees informing me, with a rare splash of English, that here stood 'Hotel Ohgiya Japanese style, Cozy atmosphere'. Sounded good to me so, with buoyed spirits, I slid aside the sliding door (finding it strange to slide and not to push) and stepped into the air-conditioned interior where I was greeted by a perfectly aligned row of lime-green plastic slippers.

Despite my nigh-on complete ignorance of Japan, I did at least know that to enter a Japanese abode with one's shoes on is considered virtually sacrilegious. No sooner had I extracted a pair of sweaty feet from my trainers than they (my shoes, that is, not my feet) were whisked away by a sweetly smiling and nodding woman who placed them neatly on a rack, heels to the wall, toes facing out – and awarded them a small rectangular tablet of wood inscribed in mysterious Japanese characters. What, I wondered, could it say? 'Warning: smelly foreigner's pumps – approach with caution' seemed perhaps the most probable. After all, my shoes had not had a break from my feet since England as I had been in no fit state to remove them on the plane.

The woman smiled and nodded some more and emitted a trilling sing-song sentence that sounded very nice but meant absolutely nothing to me. Unable to reciprocate in a common tongue, I could at least reciprocate with a common smile and so attempted to reflect her beatific beam as she obligingly proffered me a pair of those lovely green plastic slippers.

I duly slid into them and shuffled in the woman's wake towards the reception desk. Uh oh! Asking the price of a room isn't going to be a bag of roses, I thought, as I grappled with my phrasebook sentences, churning them unconvincingly around my head: 'Hands off! The mountains will be in labour; an absurd mouse will be born. I don't care a fig. Don't tread on one's corns. You kill my cat and I'll kill your dog. Cut your capers!'

'*Ohayo gozaimasu*!' said the cheery-faced woman standing behind the desk. Plucking at straws and out on a limb I realized that she was issuing some form of greeting. Feeling that

I couldn't go too far wrong by attempting to echo her sounds, I bounced back a sort of slurred '*O-hayo*-murmur-murmur-*masu*!' and left it at that. Unbeknown to me I had in fact scored rather well by batting back a cropped form of 'good morning' and all this without even having to resort to the steadfast 'Don't shave against the grain' inanities of my tongue-tying phrasebook.

The verbal ball now being in her court, I stood swaying with slight trepidation as to what rat-a-tat-tat form of 'the Devil's language' (as Jesuit missionaries once termed Japanese) would be fired my way.

'Harrow,' she chirruped. 'May I help you?'

I almost swooned with relief on learning that Sumiko Oki spoke a little English. That at least was one hurdle overcome with ease.

Asking for a room I discovered that, yes, this 'Japanese style, Cozy atmosphere' hotel did have a vacancy and, yes, they did have a place to store my *jitensha* – bicycle. I imagined that the neat and tidy Japanese would tuck it in some nook around the back, preferring to have it out of their sight. But, astonishingly, it was respectfully wheeled into reception and allocated an honourable perch on a ledge beside the shoes. There in the window was my bike, standing proud for every Tom, Dick and Harry to see.

And it was not only my bike which was to receive such deferential treatment, but also myself. No sooner had I filled out the hotel's register than I found the receptionist, Sumiko Oki, calling me Jodie-*san* – ostensibly the 'honourable' Jodie (Jodie being the closest that most Japanese came to pronouncing my name correctly).

The Japanese unfailingly put family before self, so it is logical for them to put a person's family name before his or her given name – Bloggs Joe instead of Joe Bloggs. However, when it comes to the *gaijin* (foreigner, literally 'outside person') surnames and forenames can be a bit confusing, especially as it is common practice for many Japanese to reverse their own names for the benefit of the outsider by introducing themselves in the format with which the foreigner is familiar. This tends to add to the confusion as it can leave the *gaijin* never quite sure whether they are addressing someone with a familiar and disrespectful use of their forename.

Because *gaijin* tend to give and write their names contrary to that of Japanese tradition, many Japanese automatically assume that Joe Bloggs is Mr Joe and accordingly refer to him as Joe-*san*, who surely can't be offended at this slight slip, as the Japanese are so endearingly respectful in virtually everything they do – it is impossible to feel piqued.

The suffix *san* is an honorific and more or less means Mr, Mrs, Miss, Ms all rolled into one (at least *some* things in Japan are simple to grasp), but it is important not to adopt the *san* on to your own name because to introduce yourself as Bloggs-*san* is considered most arrogant.

At £36 a night Ohgiya hotel emptied my wallet faster than felt good, but compared with Japanese hotels on the whole, the price was a breeze. Ohgiya was also not a hotel in the Western sense of the word. It was a *ryokan* – a Japanese-style hotel and about as far removed from a hotel as I knew it as, say, a calculator is from an abacus or a knife and fork from chopsticks. My room was not a number but a name and struck me as consisting mainly of matting – *tatami*, the plaited rush floor covering that floats like liquid gold in the warm wavering rays of a setting eastern sun. Only feet that are bare or stockinged are privileged to touch down on *tatami*; shoes and slippers must strictly keep their distance.

Softly, I padded across the golden surface. The room so simple, so uncluttered, made me feel an awkward addition and my dusty, world-worn panniers an insult. Never before had I entered a 'hotel' room and felt so poignantly obtrusive. Usually I would cast aside my cares and various belongings haphazardly upon the floor before flopping prostrate to try out the bed. This time, however, there was no bed. Over to one side of the room crouched a heavy, low-lying table, beside which, as if standing to attention, was a generous pile of silky-covered *zabuton* – cushions. Instead of a cupboard stood a wooden skeletal frame, with a few hooks and hangers, on which I hung my cycling helmet – it clung there like a skull, naked and incongruous, so I added my jacket to make it feel more at home.

Brooding in the corner sat a plastic toy-town type of television with big clumsy buttons and dials. It was topped with a maelstrom of angular antennae, like an out-of-control hairstyle. I popped a switch but nothing happened, so I delivered a hearty thud on its side and it squawked into life. Some sort of games show blared out a meaningless clamour of squeals but then, as if to spare me the sight of the raucous and glaring screen, the picture died. Just sounds of howling laughter, clanging buzzers and clanking bells assaulted the simplicity of the room. Then I noticed that, sitting elegantly in quiet contrast beside the blind and booming box, there was a plain vase holding a serene and single flower. The simple and the ugly; the silence and the noise. These two opposites standing paradoxically beside each other were to appear to me time and time again as a stark epitome of Japan.

The door opened and a maid entered, balancing a big thermos of hot water on a tray of tea things. She shed her slippers with graceful alacrity in the *tataki* (the small carpeted slipper 'drop-off and pick-up point' of each room) before gliding across the *tatami*, bowing amicably.

Despite my complete ignorance and inability to speak a word of Japanese, the maid appeared a remarkably chatty soul and treated me to all sorts of intriguing tones from her delicate bird-like mouth, not in the least deterred by my lack of conversation. Smiling, I cocked my head in a bemused look of incomprehension and was surprised to hear myself stutter some short staccato sounds, which merely seemed to encourage her all the more. I could only guess at what she was saying – probably something about the weather (the weather in Japan, as in England, is always a handy topical standby and features prominently at the outset of conversation) and maybe something about having a nice cup of tea?

Tea sounded like a good idea so I cast my sights upon her pots and took a telepathic and gesticulative approach. A delicate handle-less cup of steaming green tea was borne aloft towards me.

Feeling rather encouraged at having got this far without either speaking a word of the maid's native tongue or resorting to an inane 'There is many a slip 'twixt the cup and the lip' phrasebook-type phrase, I produced my map of Japan (picked up for free in the airport) and proceeded to 'tell' her, by way of a smattering of haphazard utterances and rudimentary sketches of bicycles, that I was planning to cycle around her country.

This statement produced an impressive sucking in of breath between the teeth before being released with a long, throaty 'Ahhhhhh – so – *desu-ka?*' – Is that so? – an unfailingly popular response which I was to hear (as well as emulate) in every conversation, wherever I was in Japan.

By now we had quite a little rapport going. By means of depiction, I pencilled a couple of stick-people together with their attendant stick-offspring and, along with an abundance of map-plottings, I gathered that she had been brought up in Tohoku, the northern-most area of Honshu (Japan's main island), and that her father was a fisherman.

I was in the midst of illustrating what sort of family I had when we were interrupted in our sketchy communication by a fleeting beak-type tap at the door. It swung open and in stepped my bed. A tiny, frail old woman, with legs as fragile as chopsticks, shuffled in, almost hidden from view by a mountain of futon, over twice her size, that clung like a shell to her back. Somehow, despite being dressed in a bed, she still managed to execute a touching little bow before deftly shedding her protective cocoon on to the floor and metamorphosing into a maid.

Swiftly, my bed took shape upon the *tatami* and before I had a chance to fumble through the misleading leaves of my phrasebook for 'thank you' (wishful thinking) the maids had disappeared in a rustle of silk kimono and a ripple of bowing.

Alone once more, I proceeded to explore my room. The futon, being a newcomer, needed some careful investigating. So, sinking to my knees, I endeavoured to find out just exactly what my bed comprised.

The futon was in fact two narrow mattresses unfurled on top of each other, the upper one covered in a sheet. This I smelt, as I am wont to do when faced with an alien sheet, and, although smelling clean, it evoked a hidden trace of incense.

The next layer took me slightly by surprise. Spread directly above the sheet was a thick, woolly ochre blanket. Above this lay a covered quilt (which happily passed the smell test) the upper side of which had a large, cut-out square linked in a nylon mosquito-netting-like mesh. The misfit was definitely the blanket. What was it doing suspended between the sheet and the quilt? Had the maids overlooked a secondary sheet? I doubted it, as I guessed they had made a futon or two in their time and knew what was what.

On examining the blanket, I was a little disconcerted to discover that it passed neither the smell nor the bodily hair test. Had the unusual assemblage of this bedding been a one-off occurrence I would have let the matter rest, but the same bed-building format followed me throughout my time in Japan.

Baffled by this blanket-covering-skin method of slumber, I tried on numerous occasions to enquire delicately of some families I stayed with, in faltering Japanese, why their flesh favoured the feel of a blanket as opposed to a sheet. Lacking not only understanding but also the intricate innuendos of the Japanese language, I failed to unravel my blanketed conundrum until I received a letter from Mariko Inoue, a good friend from Kyoto, who shed not only the light, but the sheet:

> Japanese houses do not have heaters in night in winter time. So, the way is much warmer (I have found British body temprature [*sic*] is warmer than Japanese. (at least than me). We traditional never sleep with naked bodies or near naked, always with *nemaki* (nightwear Pajama) [*sic*] or yukata [an unlined, broad-sleeved cotton gown, worn after taking a bath or during the summer months]. That's true putting a blancket [*sic*] on top is not being hygienic. Yes. So, blanckets should be clean. But . . . bacicaly [*sic*], we do not mind about that kind of hygienic so much.

The *makura* (pillow) was another oddity. In fact when I first felt it I mistook it for a sack of potatoes – it was *that* heavy. Thinking that the maid had perhaps mistakenly picked up the 'proper' pillow, I almost took the 'sack of potatoes' to the kitchen lest the cook was on the point of boiling up a pot of pillows. Further investigation proved that it was filled not with potatoes, but with a curious mixture of buckwheat and rice husks. I tried it out and was not impressed. It felt like my neck was supported by a large, cold lump of concrete, more apt for sinking a ship than for sinking a head into. Only later did I learn why Japanese favour propping their slumbering heads on sacks stuffed with rice husks – keeps them cool, or so I'm told.

Having studied the idiosyncracies of Japanese bedding to exhaustion, I felt that my next best move was to sink into it to replenish the sleep that had escaped me over the past two days. But no sooner had I cast aside my husky head support and stretched out futon-flat than I was hit by a second wind, bounced back up and breezed out the door to explore.

The sky was cloudless but the street was full of waves of bobbing umbrellas, all chasing the shadows. Beneath this wild array of colourful mushroom heads were mostly women, all darting and scurrying with weighty bags of shopping from one side of the street to another.

Come rain or shine, umbrellas get a lot of airplay in Japan. Down come the drops and up goes the brolly: out pops the sun and up shoots your shade. Even when there isn't really any weather – grey days that just loll around doing nothing in particular apart from riling people's nerves – giddying swirls of umbrellas spore like fungi, burgeoning from the heads of crowds like a profusion of protective antennae.

I strolled the streets, floating along with the sort of illusory neither-here-nor-there feeling that assails the senses when dropped suddenly into an exuberant and outlandish world. The streets, narrow and winding, a colourful confusion of pedestrians, cyclists, mopeds and hand-pushed carts piled high with mountains of carpets or cardboard or rice sacks or fridges, were pressed to the edges by tidal waves of spanking shiny cars. There were no pavements as there was no room – just an ankle-twisting channel of concrete slabs that bridged the river of untreated drainage at the sides of the road. In some places they were missing altogether and I would hop the gap, thinking: lucky I saw that. Too bad if I broke my leg, swallowed by a drain on Day One.

Limbs intact, I followed the flow and passed on by a curious assortment of small stores and sights: 'Lucy In The Sky With Diemonds' [*sic*] (a type of cut-glass jewellery gift shop), a tiny tucked-away hole-in-the-wall shrine, swaying red-paper lanterns, noodle bars, rice cracker and seaweed stalls rubbing shoulders with the head-damaging din of pink-spotted mechanized yapping toy-dogs performing somersaults in front of a Japanese pop-song-pounding *pachinko* (pinball) parlour. Next door was a shoe shop crowded with slippers, then an open-fronted *tatami* workshop with an old man in long, baggy underwear asleep on the floor, and a *sushi*-bar with a woman in wellingtons skinning alive piles of slithering eels.

I stepped into a small family-run foodstore with a cement floor and creaking wooden shelves full of tins and bottles and packages labelled in dizzy colours and indecipherable script. Nothing looked or even smelt remotely familiar. I poked and prodded a bag of something that resembled dead jellyfish and was a bit alarmed when it moved. Bottles of vivid pink drink looked more like something to clean out the toilet than actually consume. I picked up a cellophane tube that would have passed for a brightly coloured sweet-sticky stick of Brighton rock had it not flopped in my hands like putty and reeked of fish.

I was fascinated. Everything looked so wonderfully weird – more the sort of thing you would expect to find in the experimental section of a science laboratory than a foodstore. At least things in the cooler looked a little more familiar. Tucked beside trays of tremulous milky-white bean curd was a token offering of fruit and vegetables. The only problem was that they looked as if they hadn't seen a glint of sun or a speck of soil in all their developing lives. Too good to be true. Too perfect to be edible. The carrots too suspiciously orange, too carrot-shaped for their own good. The apples as round and red as cricket balls, only bigger and shinier – an unblemished tribute, I feared, to the agrichemical industry as much as tender, loving care. To add to their look of artificiality, they were packaged to extremes. Each pack contained two ruby-red apples sitting regally on a throne of meshed polystyrene and copiously cocooned from the hazards of the outside world by being swathed in princely seals of plastic. After a moment of prolonged mental currency conversion to ensure I hadn't been over-enthusiastic with my application of zeros, I discovered that the shocking price for the honour of eating this supercilious, pampered pair of apples was hard to swallow – bid farewell to a fiver and the fruit would be mine. Hunger struck me as a more acceptable option.

The fruit and vegetables in Japanese supermarkets, all so unblemished and so perfect in colour, shape and form, can, in an oversimplified way, exemplify how Japan is found more often to value the exterior over the interior. That rosy red apple, so big, so seductive, so flawless, is nothing more than glossy appeal – an almost waxen parody of nature that deludes the anticipatory taste buds: a fruit that appears more the product of the lab than of the tree.

So too can the importance of the exterior seem to pervade Japanese society, which places so much emphasis on harmonious relations that this 'harmony' can result in an apparent discrepancy between what Japanese say and what they think. Japanese language, both bodily and verbal, has developed in such a way as to allow incredibly vague forms of expression. The concept is that by not making direct statements, the speaker has a better chance of not offending anyone. For Japanese people the priority is to maintain external appearances while suppressing internal differences. This can be seen continuously in the conflict between *tatemae* (the mask of the public face, the situational voice that forms the façade behind which one conceals and protects oneself) and *honne* (the true intention, the private face, the inner and honest voice). The exterior sheen of the apple may please the eye, but it's the bite of the interior that counts.

Stepping back outside I was washed along again by the oscillating wave of flurrying umbrellas. I resurfaced some distance down the road at the foot of a grand flight of stone steps that led to Naritasan Shinshoji ('Newly Won Victory') Temple – the main temple of the Shingon-shu Chisan-ha sect of esoteric Buddhism. Although Naritasan was founded some 1,000 years ago, the main hall, with its sweeping trilby-like layers of traditional Japanese roofs, is a fresh 1968 reconstruction.

I meandered along with the milling crowds, momentarily pausing beside a small troop of elderly Japanese tourists as they encircled a large burning cauldron type of urn. Clutching the ubiquitous umbrella in one hand, they reverentially waved hallowed clouds of incense over themselves with the other. Different groups had congregated at the top of the steps of the main hall; with wishful prayers for good fortune, they were tossing one and ten yen coins into a large wooden-grilled chest with such enthusiastic gaiety that their actions could have been interpreted as competitively lassoing a prize at the fair.

From some gilded and mystical corner of the temple stirred the deep reverberations of a muffled gong. Moments later, surfacing from a panchromatic processional sea of brolly-shaded heads, there emerged, in blood-red splendour, the 'Mother of all Umbrellas'. Resembling an inverted bowl, the parasol, big enough to shade a whole garden party, slowly skimmed, like a UFO, surveying the lesser mortals in high and haughty style. Hovering, then slowly advancing, it cut a dead straight swathe through the crowds, parting them as effectively as did Moses the Red Sea's biblical waves.

In the blood-red shadow was a shiny-domed and bespectacled priest in purple and golden robes, clopping along on clogs that looked like boats. Two steps behind him a fine-featured minion, topped with a full head of thick black hair, bore aloft the munificent umbrella that glowed like a rosette of rising sun. As the priest passed, the multitudes dropped from the waist like wilting flowers, in a show of obeisance.

Following in his wake clip-clopped an impressive entourage of clogged and hair-cropped acolytes, all dressed in robes of brilliant colour. Keeping scrupulously to a colour-coordinated crocodile-line they glided across the expanse of Naritasan's grey-gravelled courtyard, splashing it in their swaying cloaks of electrifying hues with a vividness that belied the monastic air of solemn simplicity. Down the sweeping flights of steps they floated, moving in perfect crescent-moon formation, before vanishing with a whisper of silk into the cool, dark recesses of the lower temple.

I spent hours happily pottering among Naritasan's many temples and pagodas. For a while I sat in the shade watching a few pilgrims transcend the bustle of the eddying crowds by shuffling their way, slightly bowed, in a state of meditation, a hundred times around the *hondo* (main temple). They moved like phlegmatic somnambulists, with an odd unconscious deliberation and purposefulness, and a strange entranced expression ingrained on each face. Round and round they went, deep in prayer and chant, while keeping careful tally on specially prepared and numbered strings.

Slipping back into the sun, I ambled past stone lions and lanterns and a medley of small figurines that sprouted from the earth among a high bank of severely cropped shrubbery. The pathways behind the temple led into the slightly undulating land of Naritasan Koen, a wonderfully wooded and flowering park entwined with a cornucopia of flowering-cherry, plum, apricot and maple trees. I walked past budding azalea bushes, waterfalls and fountains, and flowerbeds meticulously tended by sinewy workmen in baggy jodhpur-style trousers and curious split-toed canvas boots. At first these boots baffled me, much as the split-toed socks baffled early European visitors to Japan. Once the Westerners had become accustomed to the peculiar practicalities of flip-flops (something I now never leave home without), it wasn't all that hard for them to get used to mitten-shaped socks, each housing the big toe in its own little nook while allowing the other four to bivouac down together. Rumour has it that these pasty-skinned and furry-faced visitors, who arrived in monstrous ships, assumed from the local socks that the Japanese only had two toes. On the other hand (or foot) the Japanese, assessing the visitors' toe-less socks, thought that Europeans had none. That, in essence, is the enchanting legacy of Japan: mystery and misunderstanding.

I emerged from the woods beside a large, peaceful pond on which a couple of stately white swans were patrolling its green glassy surface. I wondered why it was so quiet: why everyone seemed to stay up at the temple. After all, it was Sunday, the busiest of all busy days in Japan. Surely the gardens should be packed with people? A few secluded groups were picnicking on rocks beside the water's edge, eating from their *bento* (lunchboxes), which displayed an aesthetic selection of multi-coloured food, cordoned off from alternating taste and textures by delicate wood partitions.

A small cluster of black-maned and lithe young mothers with porcelain faces and cherry-blossom lips sat in a perfect row on a bench, knees neatly together and hands delicately folded upon laps, watching their toddling offspring who played and romped in exquisitely mannered and muted form – no shrieks, no shouts, no fights, no tears, just an angelic synthesis of cherubic smiles. The mothers softly twittered and tittered in chattering bird-like tones, occasionally sweeping back tufts of wind-displaced locks or adjusting various items of figure-hugging apparel, pruning their plumage.

As a wave of weariness washed over me in the form of jaded jetlag, I decided a nice sit-down was in order. I spotted a pagoda-roofed open-sided shelter hovering above the water on the opposite side of the pond, trailing an arm of wooden walkway to the bank. As it looked peaceful and people-free I sauntered to the end, removed my shoes and trailed my legs over the edge, my feet dangling a foot or two from the water.

Submerged in a dreamy state I watched the swans sliding effortlessly across the barely ruffled surface, their long elegant necks extended and pivoting like periscopes. Mesmerized by their tranquil toing and froing I nodded off, retreating into the addling vagaries of the mind. Moments later, as I stirred back into consciousness, I found an old man in bare feet and worn baggy breeches, rolled up above his knees, sitting beside me. Wrapped in a rope-like roll around his head was a lime-green towel which cordoned off his glistening copper-coloured dome from the rest of his face. An intricate weave of grooves and furrows laced together the walnut-wrinkled skin of his bony physiognomy, and yet, despite his obvious age, his demeanour conveyed an almost youthful fervour. He was reading a Japanese newspaper which looked as if it had already been read a few times over; its pages were crumpled, food-stained and torn.

All of a sudden he looked up, looked at me and smiled. I smiled, albeit a little tremulously, because I was sure he was on the point of saying something of which I would understand nothing. His mouth opened and I braced myself for an onslaught of meaningless sounds. But then, just as suddenly, he turned away and embarked upon an enthusiastic and prolonged hawking session that culminated with a hefty projectile of phlegm sent scudding across the pond. Adenoids cleared, he again turned to me with a smile. Again I reciprocated. Then he started. Speech flew forth with an impressive rapidity; a speech gutturally drawn, the words flinging and mingling from all directions. Some slid from the tongue with an almost mellifluous air, others lay in wait sheltering behind a wall of front incisors or lurked in shady cavities before launching a surprise attack, while the rest ricocheted from the roof of the mouth, firing with uncanny velocity.

Although the actual words may have been wasted on me, the exhilarating form in which they were delivered was not. It was the most bizarre and exciting language I had ever heard; a language punctuated with a wonderfully disconsonant mix of Italian, birdsong and hedge-strimmer.

Despite my inability to understand a single word of what he said, the old man was not in the least discouraged from his chatty discourse. Somehow or other, by offering him a liberal supply of encouraging smiles and grunts and 'ahh sooors' we were able to engage in a hearty spot of convivial 'conversation'. He unfurled his newspaper while I whipped out my map (always a handy standby as a topical back-up) and together we compared notes on geographical plottings and newspaper weather charts – the weather charts being the only part of the paper I had any chance of understanding. At one point the old man became so animated that he slapped me on the back in jovial style – and this from the supposedly 'reserved' Japanese. It was baffling stuff.

When it comes to conveying comprehension in a language that one neither speaks nor understands, there is only a certain amount of appropriate sounds that one can muster. After twenty minutes of this conversational carry-on my supply of eager grunts and 'ahh sooors' was turning decidedly lacklustre and my attention flickered back to the still, reflecting surface of the water beneath my feet. As I searched for an appropriately polite way in which to conclude our cheery *tête-à-tête*, I was saved by a boy with clouds on his head shimmering upside-down in the pond.

'America?' he said.

I turned from the reflection to the real thing and looked up into a smooth, young, inquisitive face.

'America?' I repeated, thinking in a vague way that perhaps he was lost – looking for the 'new world'. Then, waking up, it dawned on me. 'No, not America,' I said, 'England. I'm English.'

'Ah so, *desu-ka*?' he said. 'Is that so? San Flancisco?'

'San Francisco?' I repeated, a trifle confused.

'Ahhh, you are San Flancisco.'

'Er . . . well, no I'm not. I'm from England. The UK. You know, bread and butter, Big Ben, fish an' chips?'

'UK?' Pause. 'Ahhh, UK is nearing LA city!' he chirped triumphantly, making it sound as if the UK was perhaps a suburb of Los Angeles.

'No, no,' I said, feeling as if I was sinking into sticky water, 'you've gone too far. You're on the wrong side of the world. Come on over a bit. England, you know, that damp place beneath Scotland. Europe. It's about half-way between here and America – that's if you start in China,' I said, beginning by now to confuse myself. I smiled, hoping he wasn't feeling embarrassed: after all, he was the bold one, dabbling in a foreign tongue. 'Are you with me?' I piped hopefully. 'Do you understand?'

An expression of total incomprehension spread across his face, and I thought what a lucky thing it was that I hadn't come to Japan to teach English. Then, as if he had been building up to save the best offering for last, he delivered his grand finale with an almost robotic confidence.

'Harrow! My name is Toshiharu Sasaki, I am junior high school student. Bye bye.'

The old man, still sitting beside me, appeared almost as lost as I felt, so, seizing the opportunity to make my departure, I bade good day before retreating into the woods.

I walked past a fountain and up some steps to the 200-foot-high Great Pagoda – an impressive green-roofed, red-beamed and gold-rimmed architectural representation of the view of the universe according to the mystiques of Shingon Buddhism. Propped up against a vermilion balustrade, I just had time to catch my breath before I was once again set upon by a Japanese male. This time, however, compared with the hit-and-miss conversational formulae of my past two encounters, all proved plain sailing.

Takuji Yamakawa, an engineer maintenance man for JAL, had lived for a while near Seattle working on aircraft and, as a result, spoke good English.

'America. Very fine country. Very free. Maybe sometime much danger, but I make very many good friend. But . . .' he laughed, patting his washboard-flat stomach, 'bad country I think for easy make fat!'

I presumed Takuji was referring not to himself but to the average rotundness of America's inhabitants. Fat was definitely something that Takuji carried in short supply.

'Naritasan. Very beautiful temple. I think here very special place. You enjoy I hope?'

'I'm enjoying it very much,' I said. 'It's a wonderfully curious place – just a bit too many people around the main temple.'

'Ahhh, that is so,' said Takuji, and he told me that Naritasan attracts up to 20 million visitors a year, including two to three million (or about ten times the population of Iceland) during the New Year festival alone.

'Do you come here often?' I asked, adopting that well-worn phrase which made me feel as if I was struggling for topical chat-up down at the local disco. I wondered if perhaps Takuji made an annual pilgrimage.

'Always all Sundays I come,' he said, taking me by surprise. 'Sunday my only vacation day.'

'So Sunday is your weekend,' I said, feeling guilty already as to how much time I had given myself for cycling around Japan. 'You are a hard-working man, Takuji. How much official holiday do you have a year?'

'Ettorrr . . . ,' he ettoed, emitting the Japanese equivalent for umm and errr, 'I have ten-day vacation in one year, sorrr . . . I come to Naritasan each vacation day. But sometime I not always have ten-day vacation because my duty to work in airport. But Naritasan very peaceful place for me. I like very much.'

'The gardens are beautiful,' I said, 'a world away from the airport down the road. I've never seen such explosively colourful cherry-blossom before.'

'Ahhh yes. Cherry-blossom season very special time for Japanese people. Everyone make very happy moment.'

Then, with a hint of diffidence, Takuji lowered his head and said, 'Please. Excuse me. I am hobby photographer. Maybe you like to look my many picture. I am seeing also you have very speciality camera.'

Takuji had spotted my Canon peeking from my bag.

'I've had it for seventeen years,' I told him, 'dropped it a hundred times and it still works. Made in Japan – none of that English rubbish! But yes, I'd love to see your pictures.'

With that, Takuji enthusiastically extracted from his shoulder bag a photograph album.

'Please, this my big pleasure for you to look,' he said, before bowing and offering it to me in both hands.

By now we had walked down from the pagoda, ambled along a path lined with cherry trees and stopped in a small, sunlit dappled glade overlooking another pond. I gazed out over the water feeling a bit baffled as to why I felt so completely at ease with a strange man in a strange wood who for all I knew could be about to give me a private viewing of some kinky snaps. Judging from past, none-too-favourable encounters with lone men I should by now be smelling a rat. Were this America I might well be tasting death. Instead I felt just fine, not in the least bit worried. Intuition told me Takuji was a good onion.

I looked down and turned my attention to the album that I held in my hands. Printed in English on the hard, glossy cover amidst a smattering of offbeat punctuation were the words:

STYLISH: ALBUM OF CHERISHING MEMORIES ALL
OLD TIMES ARE GOOD TIME
It seems as if so much time has passed
since we first met,
quite, by accident, on that cold rainy,
day; and yet, at times, it
seems, as if it were only yesterday.
Time deceives us.

It was the sort of rather mawkish ode you would expect to find inscribed in italic hand on a flowery, fluted ornamental plate displayed on the mantelpiece at Auntie Dorothy's. Definitely not something to appear out of the blue in some woods in Japan.

Opening the cover, I found the entire album to be full of pictures taken in the park in which I was now standing. Although every turn of the page revealed a different location, each double page had four photographs of the same spot – only taken at different times of the year.

'Japan very special four season,' said Takuji, as he pointed to a sequence of four pictures of the same scene caught at dramatically different times of the year. Spring was displayed as a rampant show of vivid pink cherry-blossom showering from the trees; summer a diffused, vibrant thicket of foliage in hues of a thousand greens; autumn ablaze and awash in a fiery riot of rusts and reds and golds; while in winter everything was seized by a white stillness, starkly silent, solid in frost. Sometimes Takuji appeared, framed by the differing seasons, always standing as straight as a sentinel, face set firmly impassive.

'Please. I take your picture for hobby collection?' he asked.

'Oh, all right,' I said in slight surprise, 'but it's a bit boring with just me. Let's take one of both of us. Do you have a tripod?'

'Today I am not tripoding,' said Takuji.

'That's okay, I've got a mini pod which should work,' I said, and screwed it into the base of his camera. A location was cleared, buttons were set and seconds sent counting.

'Okey-dokey,' called Takuji, using such an unexpected expression it made me laugh. '*Chiizu!*'

Takuji scampered back excitedly towards me, tripped on a root, laughed, picked himself up and spun round to face the lens. With two seconds to go I nudged him and laughed. Click! Seasonal Takuji caught on film – grinning.

'Thank you,' he said, 'that was very happy time.'

CHAPTER 3

Waiting for the Catfish

Monday morning. Day Two. Feeling fraught, with a train to catch to take me to an appointment in the centre of Tokyo with Nagai-*san* – a friend of Roger's and Maggie's, who said he would like to meet me, hear my plans, take me to lunch. On the phone he told me not to worry about trying to find his office: he would meet me off the train in Tokyo Central subway station. Fine – only trouble was I had to get the right ticket for the right train to take me in the right direction. And still not a word of Japanese to my credit.

What's more, how was I going to find Nagai-*san* who, standing at average height in a country of averages, would be wearing the average blue suit and average polished black shoes of the average salaryman? A rendezvous under the clock at Waterloo I'm sure I could have managed (if I didn't get lost), but in Tokyo Nagai-*san* would be one of a million suits blended in a blue-black haze submerged in one of the world's busiest railway stations.

'Nagai-*san*,' I said, a bit perturbed, 'how do I find you?'

'Ahh, I find you!' he exclaimed. 'Just step off train and stay, please. Don't move. I find you!'

Fortunately, thanks to a machine, I managed to buy my

ticket without opening my mouth. All I had to do was decipher some charts and timetables and destination boards, poke a few buttons and fumblingly feed in a handful of edible yen. This I did. Money was voraciously consumed, swiftly digested. Out spat a ticket.

The ticket made me happy. Not so much because I had managed to fathom out the alien machine and get what I wanted (though that was nice) but because the ticket was so pleasingly ticket-like. It was as tickets should be – a short stub of card, two inches by one inch, small, compact, simple. The sort of thing British Rail used to have before it started to issue annoyingly wishy-washy, flappy bits of paper. The sort of thing you might find marking the page of an old dusty tome in the attic: a hard card 1940s Great Western train ticket from Paddington to Weston-super-Mare. That's the sort of thing. Nice to hold, neat to store. Sturdy. Long-living. Able to survive a wash or two, forgotten in the pocket of your jeans. The sort of thing that (so I read recently) a Swedish doctor found lodged for over fifty years in the ear of a half-deaf man who, as a schoolboy during the war, had wedged a bus ticket into his ear – a move that caused him a loss of hearing, until the doctor restored it by simply removing the remnants of the offending article. That's the ticket.

But although my buff-coloured ticket may have looked good and felt good, it didn't make a whole lot of sense. The price was bold and obvious but the rest had me guessing. The boxed *kanji* characters that resembled headless stick-people with interesting stomachs, I interpreted as Tokyo. The rest of the *kanji* was printed in minute script and escaped me; looked nice, but meant nothing.

The date caused most perplexity. Vertically printed along the left-hand side of the ticket I found, by way of reading in reverse, the day, the month, but no year – at least not a year with which I was familiar, as it was represented not by the '94' I was seeking, but by a mere '6'. Funny, I thought, how can this be? A calendrical conundrum – battling with stupefied brain cells to determine a feasible solution. '6.5.23.'

My initial interpretations were reached by way of the familiar Gregorian calendar: 6th May 1923. 1923? I know that some may describe travelling to foreign parts less developed than those to which they are accustomed as 'travelling back into another age', 'entering a medieval world', 'still living in the last century' and so on, but standing puzzled beneath computerized screens at Narita station in the land of bullet trains, microchips and neon, I felt it a touch far-fetched to imagine I had boarded a time-capsule back to the 'twenties.

'6.5.23.' I stared at it, deeply perplexed as grey matter creaked and groaned under the strain. Three sets of numbers. The month in the middle was May. That much I was certain. May could stay. The day, I fathomed, was obviously the twenty-third: it may have been in the wrong place for *me*, but was fine for the right-to-left reading Japanese. And at least it was there. I leapfrogged back over May to 6. Why six? 1906? Somehow, this seemed unlikely. Maybe, I pondered, the Japanese calendar operated by counting down from the year 2000. Hence '6.5.23' should be read as the twenty-third day of the fifth month of the sixth year from 2000: 1994. This tallied, swung, but didn't sway.

Only later did I discover the calendrical light. Since being re-established under legislation in 1978 many things in Japan adopt the traditional *gengo* system of numbering years by Imperial era rather than Gregorian calendar. Thus that brain-taxing '6' embedded enigmatically upon my aesthetically pleasing train ticket represented the sixth year of the reign of Emperor Akihito. Easy really – when you know how.

The train came and I had a seat. This surprised me as I had always thought that there were too many people in Japan (126 million in a country not much larger than the British Isles) to be able to sit down. That said, the train was far from empty and by the next stop all seats were taken.

My entrance on to the train had proved a bit of a head-turner. Not because of anything I had particularly done, but because I was . . . well, different. A *gaijin*, an outsider, a big-nosed foreigner who used baths in which to wash rather than soak. No one stared outright, but just snatched furtive glances. All very polite, nothing nasty. Curious. That was all.

The train filled with salarymen, schoolchildren, women off to work, and, although it was hot, they all smelt nice. No odorous tropical pit wafted on the air-conditioned breeze. An agreeably pure and pleasant aroma pervaded the air. Me? I wasn't so sure and kept arms tucked tight to sides, worried lest a scent of *gaijin*'s slippery-pit should sully the fragrant air.

I stole glances at the schoolchildren when they weren't stealing them at me. All were uniformed. The girls wore navy-blue sailor suits, sensible 'matronly' black shoes and spotless white socks hoisted to the knee. But whereas the girls' clothing flared and flowed, the boys were tightly brass-buttoned up to the neck in black, scratchy-looking Prussian-style military tunics: hot and uncomfortable – an educational straitjacket. Many boys were plugged into their high-volumed tch-tch-tch-tch-sounding Walkmans – a sight and sound that presented a strange antithesis to the severity of their clothing: the harsh tunics conveying a shell of traditional compliance; the Walkman an almost rebellious symbol of escapism.

The choice of reading material for most salarymen took me by surprise. Comics. No flimsy little lightweights these, but weighty doorstops as thick as telephone directories. *Manga* (Japanese comic books) cover every conceivable subject: history, romance, eroticism, mah-jongg, hobbies, sport, sci-fi, war, gourmet cookery, sex, survival, sadism. There are even 'information *manga*' that spin spicy yarns of nail-biting drama out of such unlikely material as 'Trade Friction' and 'The Budget Deficit'.

But the suited salaryman was certainly reading no benign governmental policy or gastronomic manual. Blood spilled from the pages in scenes of savage sex: a man performing sordid acts on the half-mangled body of a car-crash victim. It appeared the perpetrator didn't bother at first to drop or even undo his trousers, using the barrel of a pistol to do nature's job just as well.

Interestingly, I noticed that the woman depicted, or what was left of her, was a long-limbed, pneumatic-chested blonde (all foreign women are fair-haired and lily-skinned in this fantasy world) – a Western woman gun-barrelled then sadistically slashed apart by the legendary and fearsome Japanese sword. Lovely stuff, I thought. What a promising introduction to Japan! And I felt myself instinctively shuffle a buttock a tad closer to the window, a tad further from the sword. There was nothing sheepish at all in the way the salaryman devoured his comic-strip (tease) pages of brutal porn – no shifty sideways glances or culpable looks of top-shelf skulking. Far from it. The subject of his lurid fantasy comic was overtly displayed on his knees for all those within close proximity to peruse with ease.

Manga is mega business. A young *manga* artist later told me that almost a thousand different titles are published every week and that the annual production is equivalent to fifteen magazines for every man, woman and child. That's a lot of comic: an almost insuperable amount to digest. It's a lot of trees, too – and they are not Japanese trees either.

Manga appear to be omnipresent. Streets, shops, stations, homes, hotels and bars are piled to phenomenal heights with teetering towers of these fat, gaudily-covered comics. They are avidly consumed not just by commuting salarymen and brass-buttoned schoolboys (although from their prominent fixation I would guess they are the main contenders), but by Japanese of all ages and all walks of life. At the beginning of the *manga* boom, back in the early 'sixties, the average reader was under fifteen years old. But those youngsters never put them down, never outgrew them, so that their generation and the ones that followed consider them to be a wholly acceptable (and almost essential) accessory to life.

The sight, at first, is astounding. Take the train. Whereas in Britain carriages of mute commuters shrink behind their wide walls of 'serious' broadsheet, the Japanese equivalents are openly engrossed in thick wodges of comics. No surveying of the latest share prices for them, thank you: a good bit of S&M, a tasty rape and a head blown off with proper panache are the order of the day. Company directors can be seen poring over *gekiga* ('strong' comics) wearing the same deadpan expression as when scrutinizing their business's balance sheets or making multi-million yen business deals that can affect the livelihood of people all over the world.

Some say this phenomenon is best explained in psychological terms – the subconscious desire of the overworked, overstressed, conforming Japanese adults to regress to their pre-school years when life was free from the strains and palpable angst of duty and obligation.

Suddenly the air-conditioning got up my nose, tickled the inner bridge, prickled my shoots and, lo, I sneezed. Once. Quietly. Nothing too major, nothing too violent, but enough to make me rummage in a pocket for a tissue. But rummage was as far as I got before I froze. Hadn't I read somewhere that to blow, or even wipe, one's nose in public is the height of bad manners? I looked at those around me: the strap-swaying schoolchildren, the *manga*-reading salarymen, the neat-kneed women – were any of them blowing their nose? No one. Anyone dabbing their nose? Ditto.

I sniffed. I looked again. This time I was cheered to notice a few handkerchiefs either in hand or in pocket. There was hope for a nose-blow yet. I sniffed again – inwardly reproving myself for sniffing: such an unpleasant pastime, but still I didn't yet dare blow.

Avidly, I watched those hankies to determine their purpose in life. Were they for blowing, were they for dabbing, were they for clasping or were they simply for show?

A young woman with sealed eyes and ram-rod back was perched on a seat across the aisle reclaiming some sleep. Above the waist her wafery frame was swathed in a pearly-white translucent camisole, while that below was bound in a tight little number from Yves Saint Laurent. With fingers like thread she steadied a Gucci handbag that sat clasped to attention upon her skirted lap. Well dressed. Well heeled.

This woman, with a face as serene as alabaster, would not have warranted quite such detailed scrutiny had it not been for something upon her person that shrieked, 'Anachronism!' Lying neatly folded in the dip of her thighs and partially smothered by the gold-chained fashion accessory bag was a handkerchief. Okay, so I know a handkerchief is no great shakes, but this was no ordinary handkerchief to pass unobserved upon the *savoir vivre* fabrics of Monsieur Yves Saint Laurent. For, embossed upon this fancy pink-frilled hankie was none other than – Snoopy. Snoopy! Snoopy and Gucci and the chic-covered thighs of a woman in vogue. A pooch and panache lying side by side. Strange.

But it became less strange as the strangeness of Japan enveloped me with a vague sense of familiarity. Women, I discovered, were often found to be clinging to their pre-pubescent years of cartoon characters and infantile fads. Women in their twenties still sported pigtails and school skirts and knee-length socks emblazoned with '*Kitty-chan*' ('Hello Kitty') and shared their beds with families of freshly purchased teddy-bears. Snoopy offered a welcome relapse back to early mollycoddled memories of a time before they were committed to duty and deferential compliance.

I sniffed. And even though I had read that sniffing in the face of a cold is considered an admirable sign of self-restraint in Japan, I couldn't go on sniffing: my attention span was beginning to home in only on my next sniff. Something had to be done.

By now I had sighted a number of handkerchiefs, but none were utilized for the unacceptable activity of nose-blowing. On several occasions my eyes followed the raising of a handkerchief facewards. Hopes would rise and then be dashed as the 'chief in question would bypass the nose, elevating itself to the station of upper brow. Here, it would hover momentarily, still folded in four, before delicately undertaking its sole purpose as perspiratory bead-blotter. Gently, bobbing along the brow, it would blot away beads of barely perceptible perspiration before returning to roost in a pocket, lap or hand. Clearly, a Japanese handkerchief was for blotting, not blowing.

This realization (sniff) struck me like a blow. Sustaining prolonged sniffing is hard work and I found myself weakening under the strain. Concentration wavered. All signs of sniffing self-restraint were crumbling fast. Yes, something had to be done. I desperately needed a blow but equally I was desperate not to fall foul in the eyes of the Japanese – and heaven knows, there were enough of those eyes around. A compromise had to be sought. Obviously, in order to avoid an aura of pervasive uneasiness it was imperative that I somehow disappear from view. Feeling that time wasn't on my side, I hastily devised a method whereby I could conceal myself (in a carriage full of faces) and be relinquished from the debilitating pursuit of sniffing. As I was wearing two T-shirts (the outer big and baggy, the inner sleeveless and light) and as it was hot, I felt that the removal of a garment should cause no major stir. So, with a tissue secreted in a cupped palm, I withdrew like a tortoise into the amorphous confines of my shell, whereupon, in the process of hoisting it over my head, I paused just long enough to stifle all sources of sniffing. As simple as that. Still loitering within, I suddenly felt ludicrously triumphant. Like I'd conquered some sort of mission impossible. No offence had been given, no *gaijin*'s behaviour sullied. Rejoice! I felt I could now rise to the occasion – bare my face – a stronger person. But no sooner had I resurfaced from my shirt-screen than I was to catch the eye of a standing salaryman quite unselfconsciously blowing his nose in hearty fashion. It was a shocking sight – a deflating discovery and almost so awful as to send me scurrying back for cover into the safe interior of my shirt. However, that said, during eight months of wandering in Japan, he was the only Japanese I ever came across performing the incredibly distasteful act of nasal clearance.

To reach Tokyo I had to change trains at Chiba, the Japanese equivalent of Crewe. Although I had boarded what I supposed was the Chiba train in Narita, I was still far from certain it would stop. The reason for this gnawing doubt stemmed not only from a sense of displacement since landing in a land where all seemed strange and sounded stranger, but also because I was still reeling with surprise from an 'incident' on British Rail only three days earlier.

Woking, a scheduled stop, was where I had to change trains, but the one I was on sailed straight through the station. Just like that. As if in runaway mode. All passengers for Woking, who had been clambering into coats, retrieving personal possessions or poised by the door, gawped at each other with similar expression: 'Hey!' it said, 'Wasn't that *our* station?'

Apart from a few random 'Well I'll be buggered!' sort of comments that were let fly, passengers were momentarily too stunned to say anything of much significance. Shortly, an almighty explosion of distortion heralded a faint and disembodied explanation that emanated from the roof. It was the train-driver – a relief in itself to learn there actually was one. 'I'm sorry,' he said, 'I have forgotten to stop. I don't usually drive this service.'

Fortunately, Japanese train drivers are a little more reliable. Chiba came, the train stopped, the doors sprung open and I spilled on to the platform with the crowds. So far, so good. My next move was to find the train for Zushi which, I hoped, would deposit me at Tokyo Central before disappearing off round the inverted horseshoe of Tokyo Bay.

I found what I presumed to be the right platform, but presumption is one thing, certainty another. So, sensing there was too much to go wrong, I felt it judicious to check. Flicking through a language pamphlet picked up at the tourist booth in Narita station, I found the sentence I was looking for. '*Sumimasen.* Zushi *yuki no ressha wa nanban homo kara demasu ka?*' ('Excuse me. What platform does the train to Zushi leave from?')

Not wanting to approach a Japanese and read my request in automated fashion from a booklet, I mentally practised the phrase in rapid succession until I felt it embedded fairly securely upon my tongue. Now for a victim upon whom to unleash it. With head swivelling in radar mode, my sights homed in on a middle-aged couple who looked fair game.

'*Sumimasen*,' I piped as best I could, 'Zushi *yuki no ressha wa nanban homo kara demasu ka?*'

Silence. An expression of impassivity prevailed. Undeterred, I tried again. Again silence, only this time I detected a faint twitching of the lip. On the third attempt I opted to precis my enquiry and coax it along with a mild dose of gesticulation.

'Zushi,' I said, pointing to the platform beneath my feet, 'Zushi train, please, what platform?'

Still nothing, so, feeling I had entered a territory of sticky water in which heading backwards would be significantly more tricky than heading forwards, I continued to garble semaphorically in a hit-and-miss form, more miss than hit, of abridged Japanese.

At last, something stirred.

'Ahh so, Zushi!' the man said, smiling, before breaking forth into a whirling labyrinth of language. Well and truly lost, I nodded and smiled and Zushi'ed some more while sinking ever deeper into the murky mires of communication confusion. Why did life have to be so complicated? Yes, this platform, or no, not this platform was all I was really looking for. But reality doesn't come that easy, all gossamer gists of conversation having now long been lost to the wind. The grinning man's rapid spiel was now enforced by the equally swift speech of his grinning wife, a combination that had me drowning in an overwhelming torrent of sounds. As I flailed around hopelessly, floating ever deeper into the depths of confusion, I flung a forlorn glance into the surrounding crowds.

Fortuitously, an English-speaking salaryman, recognizing a *gaijin* in distress when he saw one, said, 'Excuse me. It is pleasing my pleasure I may perhaps help you?'

Gratefully, I explained my platform predicament.

'Ah, just a moment please,' said my saviour, before proceeding to extrapolate information from the still-grinning couple. A confabulation of nonsensical sounds ensued which culminated with my benevolent interloper bursting, rather disconcertingly, into laughter.

'Ha! Ha! Excuse me please!' he said, 'but these gentleman and these gentlewoman say very funny your question!'

' Funny?' I said, surprised. 'But I was only asking if this was the right platform for the Zushi train.'

'Ha! Ha!' laughed the salaryman again. 'Yes, you see this persons say you ask for train to *sushi*!'

'Uh, yes,' I said, nonplussed, 'that's right. Sushi.'

'But excuse me. I am believing you mean Zushi?'

'Sushi? Yes,' I reiterated, thinking: is this really happening? Is this just a cruel ploy to befuddle a muddled *gaijin*? 'I want the train to Sushi.'

'No *sushi*, but *Zushi*,' he said again, smiling with infinite patience and obvious pleasure. 'You want Zushi. *Zushi*.'

Hell's teeth! I thought – how long can this go on? By this stage, believing anything was possible, it dawned on me that perhaps this much sought-after station was in fact called Zushi-Zushi rather than plain, old boring Zushi.

'Yes,' I proffered gingerly, 'I want the Zushi-Zushi train.'

'*Sushi-sushi*? No *sushi* – Zushi. *Sushi* is . . . you know? . . . *sakana*. How you say . . . fish?'

'Fish!' exclaimed I with furrowed brow. 'Fish?' What the . . . and then, with a delayed flash, the bright scales of light shone forth. *Sushi*. Fish. Of course! Blank expressions, see-sawing speech and prolonged confusion could all now be brought up for air in simple explanation. By way of a slight mispronunciation I had, in effect, asked for the Raw Fish and Pickled Rice train. Ah well, it was only Day Two after all – plenty of time for things to get worse.

Nagai-san, bless him, true to his word, found me. This was just as well because I would never have found him in a month of blue moons, never mind in a sea of black heads. In fact, how I actually made it from my brutally overcrowded fishy-bound Zushi train on to the even more people-packed platform of Tokyo Station was, in itself, an achievement. Wedged in by bodies on all sides and unable to move my arms, let alone my legs, it seemed I passed from overloaded train to overloaded platform by way of osmosis. Everywhere appeared to be one massive human coagulation, as if the entire population of 'Greater Tokyo' (all 20-odd million of them – 35 million if you include the other huge neighbouring cities sprawling over the Kanto Plain) had been shoved down the subway, bonded by superglue and moved as one. And this wasn't even *tsukin jigoku*, or Commuter Hell (one of the many hells in Japan) where, during rush-hour, people are packed in so tight that one's feet don't even touch the floor. 'If you find yourself travelling during rush-hour,' a *tsukin jigoku* veteran warned me, 'remember to keep your arms close to your sides so they don't get broken.' Later I learnt that injuries sometimes occur when passengers, jammed together, fall down like dominoes when the train stops.

One of the best examples of the extraordinary tolerance of the Japanese is to plunge into the subway during rush-hour in Tokyo to be pressed by a crowd of commuters so dense that breathing becomes a problem. Crushed underground on a platform packed with people is not for the claustrophobic and yet, despite the heat, the discomfort, and the density, no one shouts, moans, complains or turns nasty. Commuter Hell, however hellish, is a prime archetypal sample of indomitable Japanese tolerance. '*Shikata ga nai*,' people say, using an oft-heard phrase – 'What can you do? It cannot be helped, it has to be.'

When the train arrives and the doors fling open, the crowd surges forward and the infamous white-gloved *oshi-ya* (professional people-packers) set to work using force (usually with their backs) to propel and compress the silently suffering throngs into the already overflowing carriages. Happy with their fill, they then ease off the pressure and, with that contrasting quirk peculiar to the Japanese, turn to face the encapsulated hordes with a polite little bow.

The *oshi-ya*'s work is a thankless task, but I suppose their job satisfaction stems from an almost supernatural ability to jam in the seemingly unjammable without an assortment of limbs getting caught in the door or left on the platform. It seemed to me all a bit reminiscent of the fight to close an overloaded suitcase after cramming in another superfluous article of clothing – a blood-rising procedure that necessitates full body weight (including that of any willing passer-by) and a dogged determination to seal the sides and snap-shut the lid. Tokyo's people-packers are dealing with bulging suitcases on a human scale – it's just that those half-severed trousers that get caught in the closing could, for them, contain a human leg.

During winter the *oshi-ya*'s job is made even more strenuous by commuters wearing extra layers of clothing and so, to combat the effort of people-packing, JNR (Japanese National Railway) employs an additional task force of 'pushers-in'. To be manually forced so tightly into a space that appears solely illusory is, I discovered, a highly disquieting experience, but testifies to the exquisite proficiency whereby the Japanese can make room where there is no room to make.

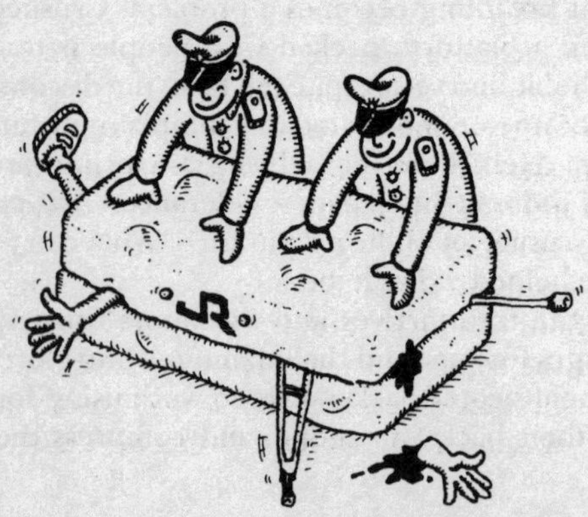

Although distinctly different as a people, I did at least share one thing in common with the Japanese: size, or lack of it. Having spent the majority of my life making conversation with the average person's kneecaps, suddenly to be among a whole nation living within such close proximity to the ground as myself was immensely reassuring. After all, there is only a certain amount you can say to a pair of knobbly patellas before words struggle, peter out, fizzle and fade. Generally, face-to-face conversation tends to be both visually and mentally more rewarding.

Nagai-*san*, a charismatic, fully grown, fifty-something salaryman, was exactly as short as me and, as a result, I naturally loved him immediately. But vertically challenged novelty factors aside, I would still have loved him immediately; he was just that sort of person: ardent, welcoming, informative, humorous and inordinately helpful, as well as modest almost to the point of self-effacement.

Although his leg length may have been on a par with mine, trying to keep up with him as he scooted so adeptly through the deep, dense crowds of the subway and the streets was no mean feat. Whereas Nagai-*san* seemed to navigate a smooth and streamlined path into the giddying masses without either ruffling a hair, knocking an elbow or stepping on a toe, I continuously swayed and swerved and altered course, tacking my ungainly way into the tidal waves of oncoming foot-traffic with about as much finesse as a hippopotamus on heat. As I pitched and tripped and bucked in and out of his wake, Nagai-*san* displayed a fine paradigm of the apparently congenital manoeuvring skills which the Japanese possess when tackling a crowd: whereas a foreigner is all arms and legs, a Japanese cuts as cleanly and efficiently as a samurai's sword.

The company for whom Nagai-*san* worked was situated on the ninth floor of a heavy, grey building that overlooked the gardens of the Imperial Palace. His own office was a claustrophobic and windowless box with scarcely room to swing a bonsai, never mind a cat, but the fact that he had an office at all wholly to himself was indeed a major privilege. Most of the rest of the floor on which Nagai-*san* worked was laid out open plan; everything happening, everyone watching, everyone doing everything else.

Nagai-*san* appeared touchingly concerned about me and insisted I send a fax immediately to my parents to let them know I'd arrived safely. I tried to assure him that as it was only Day Two they wouldn't be too worried about me just yet (more like glad to have seen the back of me for a while). I would contact them sometime over the next few days, when I could report back a few more newsworthy topics such as what raw squid and seaweed soup tasted like, along with a current update of my innards. But listen he wouldn't and he presented me with pen and office-headed notepaper, so I dutifully set forth and informed my parents of my inner workings anyway, even though I had not yet partaken of the pickled seaweedy culinary delights of Japan, and told them not to worry as there hadn't been an earthquake since I'd landed – at least not one that I'd noticed. Satisfied with my scribblings, Nagai-*san* smiled heartily and fixed the fax before introducing me to his continually bowing secretary, Kyoko Shimizu, whose head bobbed up and down with such incessant speed as to make me feel seasick.

Nods aside, Kyoko and the director's secretary, Kazua Yamazaki, were the pure embodiment of helpful concern. Before even meeting me they had bought me a wealth of books on Japan, utterly refusing any form of reimbursement, and paid my membership to the JYHA (Japanese Youth Hostel Association) even though, unbeknownst to them, I was already a member. Their English was fluent; their generosity was astounding. They were concerned for my safety, they said; they didn't think cycling alone in Japan to be a good idea at all. Kazua said she thought it would be dangerous, very hard, very difficult and 'may be many problems'. Kyoko nodded in full agreement. I was fairly prepared for hearing there'd be problems and difficulties but the fact that Kazua and Kyoko kept stressing the danger surprised me.

After all, wasn't Japan supposed to be one of the safest countries in the world? It's a country that has such strict gun controls that it's mainly only the fairly well-behaved *yakuza* (Japanese mafia) who are in possession of them. Despite Japan being the most technologically advanced country in the world, and despite its intense overcrowding, pollution, open pornography and materialism, it is still a country where they rob banks with cucumbers. Frankly, I was more concerned about traffic congestion, language barriers and the havoc that raw octopus might play on my vitals than I was about some undesirable giving me a karate kick in the spleen or knocking me over the head with a bike pump. But Kazua and Kyoku were insistent; there were many dangerous people, they said, especially further south, and perhaps it might be more advisable to travel by train. And where was I going to sleep?

'Don't worry,' I said, 'I've got my tent with me. I'm sure I can always find somewhere to camp.'

This idea caused grave expressions and much contention. Japan didn't have campgrounds, they said.

'Japanese people do not enjoy to live in tents,' said Kazua.

Again I tried to reassure them that even if there were no campgrounds I was sure I could find a small space to put up my tent – a park or a beach or speck of wasteland, or just knock on the door of a farmer. The thought of me, a *gaijin*, knocking on the door of a stranger caused Kyoko and Kazua to break in to a nervous fit of twittering giggles, their mouths shielded behind cupped hands. This is not the Japanese way, they tried to tell me.

'This could be very difficult – Japanese farmer will be having very much surprise.'

And how, they wanted to know, would I go about asking when I don't even speak or understand Japanese, and when there are so many different dialects in Japan that even Japanese people from Tokyo cannot make themselves understood in, say, Kyushu? In fact, the more they thought about it, the more they contested the notion of me alone on a bike with nowhere to sleep – a concept which I saw was inducing considerable signs of distress.

So solicitous were they that I was beginning to feel decidedly apprehensive myself – not for my own welfare, but for theirs. In such a short space of time I had unintentionally foisted a burden upon them. Inwardly I willed the swift return of Nagai-*san* (who had disappeared to finish some business) to clear the air. The whole situation had turned faintly ludicrous; everyone in an unnecessary state of worry for reasons that were merely hypothetical.

Finally, a consensus was reached whereupon Kazua and Kyoku carefully wrote down their full names, home addresses, home numbers, work numbers and lengthy instructions in *kanji* (a script of Chinese ideograms so wondrous to watch that it had me momentarily mesmerized). The idea was that, when I knocked on the door of the farmer, I was to hand him this artistic piece of paper which apparently explained my predicament: I was an English girl, travelling by bicycle, looking for a place to camp, and if he would be so kind as to telephone (reversed charges) to one of the given numbers, a Japanese friend of said cyclist would explain the circumstances in more detail. Furthermore, it didn't matter what time of day or night the telephone should ring.

I could hardly envisage myself mutely instructing a farmer to get on the 24-hour help-a-*gaijin*-hotline, pulling Kazua or Kyoko out of bed just in order to put me in one, but the fact that they were prepared to go to so much time and trouble and expense on my behalf was truly astounding. It was impossible for me to feel anything other than guilty gratitude, and Kazua's and Kyoku's actions only demonstrated the degree to which the bounteous and indefatigable Japanese spirit will go to help a somewhat frivolous stranger with half-baked ideas.

Meanwhile, Nagai-*san*'s 'business' that had pulled him away while I talked to the secretaries turned out to be nothing of the sort (at least not the sort of business I had had in mind). My mistake earlier had been to mention casually that one of my tasks when in Tokyo was to look for a detailed map of the Yokohama area, where the following week I would have to cycle my way to the home of some friends of a Japanese friend. For half an hour, while two Japanese were going out of their way to assist me face to face, another had been quietly helping behind scenes by diligently photocopying and numbering twenty pages of a Japanese map book, which he then nonchalantly presented to me. The maps were a most welcome gesture, even though the place-names were in *kanji* and to me totally unreadable. On top of this, Nagai-*san* revealed an obvious flare for the prodigious use of fluorescent markers: he had delivered an artistic squiggling array of flamboyant colours to the already perplexing lines and curves and whirls of the maps. As a result they looked more like a series of zip-zany paintings by a centipede on speed than a means by which to navigate.

While walking to lunch with Nagai-*san* down the main thoroughfare of (downtown) Marunouchi, I expressed surprise at seeing people scurrying and scarpering all over the road, with not a car in sight.

'Ah,' said Nagai-*san*, 'this is a very important moment in Japanese day. For twelve to one p.m. lunch hour this road is closed to traffic. In Japanese we call this most pleasant time Pedestrian Heaven.'

When Nagai-*san* had originally invited me to lunch I had automatically presumed that it would be a Japanese lunch with Japanese food. So it came as a bit of a blow to discover I was being taken to a sort of Westernized mish-mash restaurant in which I ate an odd mix of chilled pumpkin soup, tunaburger, pea omelette and chips. Despite this, I still thought that when I ordered Japanese tea it would arrive green, in a handle-less cup; instead, it came in a glass, milkless, and containing a limp Liptons teabag. Of course I had absolutely no reason to presume that, just because I was in Japan, I would automatically eat Japanese food – after all, were I to invite Nagai-*san* to a lunch in London, I wouldn't take him to a restaurant that specialized in steak-and-kidney pie, mushy peas and spotted dick.

In 1980 business had taken Nagai-*san* to London with his wife and two children and they had lived in Swiss Cottage for four and a half years. Over my tuna-burger and his lamb cutlets he told me how he found life in England so much easier compared with that in Japan.

'I like very much the British because they say what they mean. I think you call it "to speak one's mind" – we Japanese cannot be so direct. We cannot say what we think but we say what we think people would like to hear. Japanese people do not like to offend, or to stir the water. In Japan, "no" can mean "yes" and "yes" can mean "no" and you have to know which noes mean yes and which yeses mean no.'

'Ah, I see,' I said, not seeing at all, and thinking that if I can't even tell the difference between raw fish and the name of a city, how was I going to distinguish my yeses from noes?

Such an oblique method of communication tends to work well in Japan because, although a country of isolated islands, it has always enjoyed racial homogeneity and a common language, religion and value system. While vagueness is a quality held in esteem, directness is equated with sharp-tongued arrogance. To be frank is to be offensive. Life is all about beating around bushes and talking indirectly: brusqueness holds no virtue. Getting to the point is not the point in Japan as Japanese people prefer to slide slowly into a subject with the same degree of caution and dexterity that they display when easing into their steamy, searing baths. They go to vast and circuitous lengths in order to avoid giving a negative response, for to do so would most likely cause the other person to lose face. And to lose one's face is about on a par with losing one's head.

Time, nuances, innuendos, silence – all weave an intricate web over the idiosyncratic life of Japan. Just as members of a family can, the Japanese possess an intuitive ability to detect and anticipate the intentions and thoughts of each other.

The longer I spent in Japan, the more I became aware of the total and utter inanities I so often produce when in company. Ready with words, yet so shallow in meaning. Saying something just for the sake of saying it, to fill in, to plug the gap. When alone, silence is something I love. To cycle unaccompanied, detached and isolated in an unfamiliar emptiness is to me the height of happiness. You don't have to think, you don't have to talk, you just have to be. Wind. Silence. Birds. Heaven. Yet, when the silence occurs among people other than family or close friends, heaven can turn to hell. Happiness to awkwardness. Silence. Panic. Blurt. Poppycock. Verbiage. Death. But, Japanese people don't tend to experience this intense form of uneasiness when amongst themselves. To them, silence is a virtue. It is not seen as an emptiness to be filled. Silence is full of meaning in the context of the moment. 'Those who know do not speak' goes the proverb that illustrates how the Japanese so often mistrust verbosity. 'Speak only if it is better than silence.'

As we walked back down Pedestrian Heaven, in its dying minutes before it returned to a motorized hell, Nagai-*san* drew my attention to the headlines of the *Yomiuri Shimbun,* a broadsheet with a daily circulation of 15 million (the world's largest).

'Ah, very terrible,' he said. 'It is all talk about Koreans. This is very big news. A Korean schoolgirl has graduated extremely excellently but Japanese university do not allow her a place because she is Korean. This is very terrible news. Always Korean people have very much discrimination. Always they have to live in special Korean community and go to Korean shop and Korean school. It is great unfairness. Japanese newspaper are all supporting Korean schoolgirl. Stop discriminating, they say. This is very strong issue in Japan and much problems.'

I spent the next ten days wandering, mostly lost, around Tokyo. Sometimes I would recognize where I was, but the feelings of faint familiarity were only fleeting before I ducked into an alley or side-stepped a corner and became hopelessly lost again. Concrete. Neon. Crowds. Chaos. Towers of steel that scraped the sky. It doesn't take much to lose your way in the dynamic and spectacularly ugly sprawl of Tokyo. Take a taxi in Tokyo and the chances are you'll end up even more lost than when you started. Tokyo's like that. The average taxi-driver recognizes little more than the average stranger. This isn't because he (it's always he) necessarily suffers from a bad sense of direction but because Tokyo is just a hive of concrete confusion, an urban jungle of uniform scenery. Journey ten miles from one part of the city to another and it seems you've scarcely moved – more concrete, more steel, more neon, more chaos; a sameness like no other city on earth. It's a far cry from its lowly beginnings as a small fishing village called Edo (Estuary Bay.) For 400 years the face of Tokyo has been continuously changing. Nagai-*san* told me that buildings are torn down and rebuilt with such unseemly haste that to be absent from a major district for more than a few months is enough to render it virtually unrecognizable.

The constant activity and immense energy expended on construction continues unabated, no matter that the city sits on one of the most earthquake-prone zones in the world. Often the city sways, shudders and shakes as one of the globe's great plates grinds against another. Tokyoites, conditioned to such quakings, live their lives with an enviable philosophical equanimity despite experiencing as many as a thousand a year. The general attitude, even at such tremoring times when walls ripple and kink and jetsam slithers and skitters across the quivering floor, is one of habitual resignation – a phlegmatic shrug of the shoulders. Seemingly the earth rattles cups, not nerves.

Sometimes, of course, a 'big one' may strike, bludgeoning the city to death. Such a calamity last occurred as a result of the Great Kanto Earthquake in September 1923, which hit a titanic 7.9 on the Richter Scale. The destruction sparked fires that raced rapaciously throughout Tokyo and Yokohama, where nearly all buildings were wooden.

The earthquake struck at one of the worst times – noon, when in many households the *hibachi* fires were being kindled to prepare lunch. The strength of the initial tremor was sufficient to destroy many houses and other buildings, but far more damage to both people and property was caused by the fires that spread throughout Tokyo and nearby Yokohama. More than 100,000 people lost their lives, and the two cities lost more than 70% of their homes. As a result of such turmoil, public order completely broke down and a few thousand scapegoats – Korean residents – 'lost their skins' after the stricken populace, exploding in a rampant outrage, heard a rumour that the Koreans had poisoned the water supply.

To the Japanese, the massive fractures and fissures of their quaking land are put down not so much to temperamental plate tectonics as to a giant catfish that lives under Japan in the dark mystical depths. Legend has it that, when the catfish turns catty, it capriciously thrashes its tail, shaking the soil, the cities and the heartbeats of those above its head.

Despite the apparently philosophical attitude of the Japanese about the inconstancy of the rocks beneath their feet, there may be more to their unflappable façade than meets the eye. During the 'seventies the sensational novel *Japan Sinks*, a best-seller, hinted at a dark and morbid fear that lay behind the calm.

CHAPTER 4

A Face Behind the Façade

Tokyo, Supercity with its multiple millions of space-starved souls. Like a human ant-heap, it's expanding, moving, multiplying – an urban complex outlandishly vast, devouring the South Kanto Plain and even the sea – reclamation in concrete.

'Greater' or 'Metropolitan' Tokyo, or 'Tokyo-to' (Nagai-*san* explained that the suffix '-*to*' means the metropolis in terms of an official administrative district which includes twenty-three special wards, twenty-seven suburban cities, several towns and villages, and several detached islands such as the Ogasawara or Bonin Islands far out in the Pacific Ocean) is generally considered to encompass the three neighbouring prefectures of Kanagawa, Saitama and Chiba (including the three major suburban cities belonging to these prefectures: Yokohama, Kawasaki and Chiba-shi) and now holds more than one-tenth of the country's entire population. The area is so massively industrial and so hugely productive that, if it were an independent nation, it would produce more goods and services than the whole of Great Britain. With space at a premium, in real-estate terms the area is estimated to be worth more than the entire USA.

Needless to say, only the exceptionally wealthy can afford

to live within central Tokyo. People like the Emperor. At the height of the bubble-booming 'eighties it was calculated that the grounds of the Imperial Palace were worth more than the entire state of California.

The Imperial Palace sounded like an imperious place and it was. When I turned up one morning to have a little wander around I found it closed.

'Excuse me, what time does it open?' I asked in half English and half stuttering in-at-the-deep-end, trial-and-error Japanese to a man on the gate.

'In about six months, love,' he said (or words to that effect).

'Ahh so,' I said, using the only two words of Japanese I felt I'd mastered to perfection and thinking that perhaps I wouldn't wait but go and see something else instead. The Inner Palace, I discovered a bit late (or early, as the case may be), is only open to the public twice a year (23rd December, which is Emperor Akihito's birthday, and 2nd January, a New Year holiday). Supposedly it is possible to be granted permission to join a special guided tour (in Japanese) if you write in advance to the right place at the right time and arrive with the right slip of paper at the right gate with the right credentials (proof of an expensive hotel where you're housed and a passport in good nick). Distinctly lacking the necessary qualifications (apart from a tent, I was temporarily homeless, and there was a slight hitch with the entry stamp in my dog-eared passport) I felt disinclined to pursue permission for an inner viewing – which is, I suppose, another way of saying that, frankly, I couldn't be bothered. I mean, what a palaver! Get this, get that, go there, synchronize watches, synchronize days, and all for the pleasure of being herded with a Japanese tour around a twenty-six-year-old piece of ferro-concrete. It all seemed like too much of a performance to go and see something a bit . . . well . . . new. Its newness, though, couldn't be helped because the old palace was destroyed (like the rest of Tokyo) by the horrific firebombings of the Second World War.

The original palace was the impregnable fortress known as Edo-jo castle, the abode of the Tokugawa shogunate for 265 years. It had contained an intricate maze of moats, bridges, dead-ends and blind alleys all designed to confuse and deceive the enemy. (Most Japanese cities are, by all accounts, planned along the same haphazard lines.) Girdled by a wide moat, the immense and imposing stone walls spread for over ten miles and were so wide that it was possible for a troop of samurai warriors to march along the top, six abreast. In 1868 the last shogunate was overthrown and Emperor Meiji, taking a fancy to the palace, moved in with his court and trappings.

As a direct descendant of the Sun Goddess, the Japanese Emperor is referred to as 'Tenno' – the heavenly king – and until the end of the Second World War he was truly regarded as divine and treated as a living god. During Japan's wartime militarism (which, over fifty years on, is still a taboo subject) commoners were forced to make obeisance before his framed picture located at special altars set up in schools, stores, halls and other public places. On occasions when he stepped from the celestial shadows and revealed himself (so to speak) before the hoi polloi, all present had to bow to the ground with excessive obsequiousness and avert their gaze; children were warned that, should they so much as glance upon the god-king, their eyes would burn like coals.

As the course of the war turned increasingly against Japan, the mystique of the Emperor became even more essential in boosting the flagging and war-weary morale of the starving masses. Japanese troops were coerced into cheering the battlecry, '*Banzai*!' ('May you live 10,000 years!') and were issued with cigarettes printed with the nationalistic chrysanthemum emblem, while kamikaze pilots were plied with a 'specialized' and godly Imperial *sake* (rice wine) to spur them forth on their suicidal mission of death.

The summer of 1945 was one of utter humiliation for the Japanese people who, after eight years of fighting (which began with the second Sino-Japanese war), were dressed in little more than rags. As Japan was not only cut off from food supplies from its empire but also lacking an adequate force of farmers, most people in the cities (or what was left of them) had to survive on no more than a daily handful of beans or a bowl of millet gruel, as even the rice crops had failed. Diseases like beriberi were rampant and much of the population was reduced to eating seemingly inedible vegetable matter like grasses, weeds and pumpkin stalks right up until the end of the war.

The Emperor was still considered a demi-god when he made his famous broadcast on 15th August 1945, announcing the surrender of Japan. The majority of his people found his ambiguous Imperial language wholly unintelligible. To use a form of speech so impenetrable and alien to life outside his palace was a way of demonstrating his venerable inaccessibility. However, despite this 'speaking in tongues' there was no getting away from the fact that, once translated, Emperor Hirohito had delivered one of the greatest understatements in history. A couple of atom bombs had incinerated part of his empire, Tokyo had been carpet-bombed, every major city had been destroyed, and the Emperor blandly announced that 'the war situation has developed not necessarily to our advantage'. After his quivering, monotone speech, people wandered around in a state of shock, not so much because their country had suffered an ignominious defeat (the inevitability of which had been blatantly obvious for months) but because their Heavenly King had actually spoken to them.

After the war, so as to bolster the spirit of the new constitution established by the American Occupation, the Emperor plucked up courage and embarked on a series of walkabouts to meet the commoners of his land for the first time. Not surprisingly, there were moments of intense embarrassment as the Japanese discovered that their revered symbol of sovereignty and national greatness, their 'Royal Son of Heaven', was nothing to write home about – just one of the boys, really.

Face to face with the riff-raff, the Emperor, uneasy and at a loss for words, would utter the first phrase that entered his head: 'Ah so? Really? Is that so?' became his handy standby pat, which he repeated over and over again like a stuck record.

On New Year's Day 1946, in a radio broadcast, Emperor Hirohito came clean and formally renounced the concept of himself as a 'living deity', a concept which for the past decade had played a dominant part in government propaganda. What a dupe! What a wag! 'Okay, folks,' I imagined him saying, 'I was only kidding. I'm not really a celestial being. I mean, look at me – I'm just your average Mister Nice Guy, the boy next door, and you bunch of cuckoos believed I was something real special. A God-King! Jeez! I can't believe you guys really fell for it!' To add to this bombshell the new 'man about town', a mortal and terrestrial being in a Burton suit, had officially refuted the wartime belief that the Japanese people were superior to any other race and hence destined to rule the world.

Despite all his awkward formality, Emperor Hirohito was actually able to see the absurd position in which he found himself. When he returned to the remains of his palace after the broadcast he asked his wife, Empress Nagako, 'Do I seem any different now that I am no longer supposed to be a god?'

Opposite the American Embassy in Tokyo sits a building close to my heart and even closer to my rear. On its roof, standing proud, is a giant steel 36-spoked wheel. As I approach the entrance an incipient excitement creeps into my blood. I enter my element: a building devoted purely to the bicycle. A woman, in a grey-checked waistcoat, white shirt and black tassel-tie, bows to me behind the information counter. On the top of the desk is a kitsch penny-farthing clock – the sort of thing you'd steer well clear of at a car-boot sale. The woman smiles, says '*Irasshaimase* – Welcome,' and hands me a leaflet.

Fortunately it's in English. I read the first words: 'Have a close association with the bicycle.' Now we're talking!

This is the Bicycle Culture Centre which sensibly states that 'bicycles enrich our lives with their usefulness' and invites the visitor to [have] 'a new encounter with bicycles'. It's a nice idea and I'm all for trying. Only trouble is you need a doctorate in Japanese to make head or tail of the files and piles, books and maps and magazines and laser-disk screens of information. No one speaks English. But that's okay. There's enough to satiate a cyclist's appetite in the 'bicycle displayed hall', at least for the first two minutes. Under the spotlights and perched on stands is a medley of mostly modern cycles. Apart from the odd folder or HPV (human-powered vehicle) there's nothing of major interest. Mini pink Minnie Mouse bicycle baskets and Snoopy water bottles are pinned on the wall boards among a splayed garish cycling kit and helmeted mannequin – all a bit too reminiscent of the bicycle department at Halfords for my liking. In one of the five-sided glass display cabinets is a range of cycling paraphernalia: models of miniature bicycles with a fluffy puppy or pig or ubiquitous 'Hello Kitty' at the helm; mugs, cups, plates, thimbles, letter openers, clocks, key-rings – the usual sort of thing – some incorporating a bicycle or part of a bicycle into their design, the rest plastered in two-wheeled motifs.

The walls of the staircase are adorned with mural paintings that feature a velocipede in some shape or form. One mainly black-and-white picture depicts a man (raising his hat) as he passes two women in bonnets and voluminous skirts (*circa* 1900). Attached to each foot is a small pair of spoked bicycle wheels, enabling the wearers to propel themselves down the road in ice-skating mode.

Things start hotting up when a sign invites me to 'Come in contact with the history and culture of bicycles cycle museum' where 'you can also use the headphone survice [*sic*] which gives you clear and easy commentary on bicycles of historical importance'. But not if you're lacking in the lingo. However, there's a promising offering of old boneshakers, ordinaries, safeties, sociables and tricycles to consider. Perched on a satellite in one part of the room is a 'Panorama chronology and bronze sculpture' featuring an emaciated family, more stick-insect than cyclist. Standing indolently on the other side are a couple of bicycles 'presented to the Crown Prince and Princess' which are obviously more showpiece than thigh-firmer.

As I saunter over to view an appealing touring tandem, I'm reminded of the 'See Japan on Bicycle' pamphlet I picked up in the tourist office. Among the dubious list of special designated city 'cycling courses' (Sunday opening only), it informs me that riding a tandem is prohibited on all public roads in Japan. Odd. Just as well I haven't arrived in Japan with a Romeo and dual-controlled mount. However, all is not lost. If you do arrive in this far-flung land with a bicycle built for two or three or four, unaware of the quirkiness of Japanese cycling laws, you are still permitted to spin your pedals (or clash your wheels) with all the other millions and zillions of bicycle riders out for a stretch of muscle and scrape of metal along the handful of 'specially designated' cordoned-off cycling courses which, six days out of seven, are laden with bumper-to-bumper traffic. But remember: Sundays only, ten till four precisely. Don't be late.

And that's not all. Strangely, there is one prefecture – Nagano – where you can tandem to your heart's and better half's content. I know not why. Nor did anyone I ever asked know why, the majority not even being aware of such a peculiarity. Nagano is situated in the midst of the Japanese Alps, the 'Roof of Japan', with some of the hardest, hilliest roads in the country. Maybe that's why the anti-tandem crackpot who conjured up this curious law hit upon Nagano as a permissible two-stroke prefecture – believing that only the diehards would survive. Or maybe Nagano was home to some sort of Tandem Triangle whither tandem riders gaily ventured, never to be heard, seen or smelt again. And maybe, as far as some lycra'd backsides go, that is just as well.

For days I lost myself, wandering the streets of Tokyo. Each morning I would rise with the sun (which, smothered in smog and concrete, remained irksomely evasive) and set off with a spare roll of film and no specific mission in mind. There were certain places I wanted to see, sights to snap, smells to taste, but I wasn't particularly worried if none came my way. All I fancied doing was moseying along throughout the city in what I suppose others might consider to be a wholly unpurposeful manner. I had no map, no itinerary, no pin-point timed tour. Certainly I was a blatant paradigm of self-indulgence compared with the flurries of scurrying black-topped souls around me who all seemed to be hell-bent on their way towards a precise destination.

One of the wonders of Tokyo for me (small, lone female) was the feeling of uplifting liberty at being able to go virtually anywhere at any time without the fear of violence hanging heavy like a yoke around my neck. Few other major cities in the world can boast of such safety on their streets. To walk alone, unmolested, down a dark alley in an unsalubrious area of the city at two o'clock in the morning and pass a shadow that manifests itself as a lone drunk man who does nothing more than sing to the moon or bid a polite goodnight is a truly edifying experience. Of course there is crime and, as in most places in this progressively violent world, it's getting worse. But in Japan it's generally a crime of revenge that takes place behind closed doors and is brought about, paradoxically, by the pressures and constraints of living in a 'harmonized and homogenized' society. Behind the impassive mask there often lurks an irascible and vindictive nature just waiting to ignite. The stereotypical 'lost face' lover, the ostracized schoolchild, the tormented neighbour, the overburdened daughter-in-law, the humiliated husband – suddenly the bottled strains and pains and pressures explode into a spasm of catastrophic violence.

Squares, leafy avenues, parks, foliage, open space: ingredients surely essential to cities worldwide for maintaining normality. A place to breathe, to stretch, to dream, to read without exhaust fumes in your face. A place for the cork to pop. A place to swing your arms. A place to kiss. To lick an ice cream – together. Somewhere to lie on a bench on your back to watch the clouds. Space. A place of importance.

Often I found myself wandering through a cluster of Tokyo's dense, narrow streets where legions of people and cars jostled for the very air around them. No room to manoeuvre for either man or metal. That's Tokyo – a sprawling plantation of concrete and glass that, save for a parsimonious smattering of hard-to-find parks, is seemingly spaceless.

Look up, and even the sky is a riot of chaos, held together by a scaffolding of bulky, black telephone wires and utility cables as thick as creepers. An astral jungle of communication. Tokyo – a laser city, sitting at the hub of one of the richest nations on earth. Yet, even today, it still hasn't found time, let alone the inclination, to secrete its celestial web of creeper-cables underground, out of sight, out of mind. A mere one-fifth lie concealed beneath foot, whereas in London the cable world lies interred and has done for a century.

Maybe Tokyoites don't mind their sky cordoned off into portions. A paddy field of clouds. Maybe, when the catfish stirs, it plays too much havoc with subterranean wires. Maybe people don't mind living beneath a mesh, peering up to the light as if through the grid of a drain. *Shikata ga nai* – what can you do? Maybe they don't notice or maybe life is just too frantic to have time to cast an eye to the sky. And anyway, who needs the sun when there's neon?

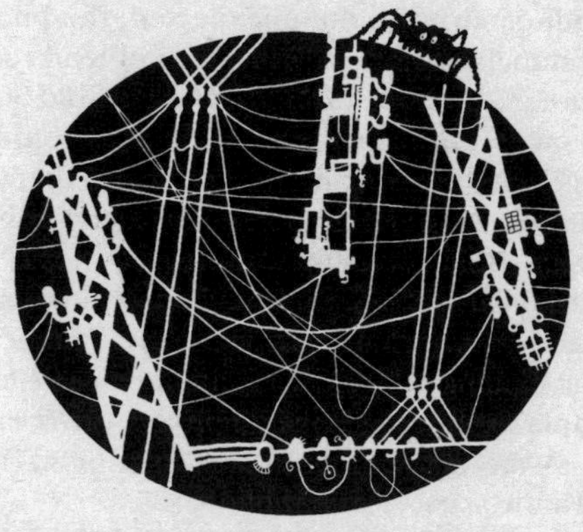

My wanderings through Tokyo's arid metropolitan landscape were purely superficial, skimming the surface of a complex and incomprehensible city that appeared to the eye spectacularly ugly and indiscriminately brash. I knew that behind the beefy concrete blocks that shouldered each other like a bunch of stocky heavyweights, behind the curtained and frosted sliding doors of corrugated enclaves into which men in blue suits swiftly vanished, behind the long bedazzling neon signs and flashy hoardings and boards that clung to every inconceivable space like the cloth banners that once hung in their place, there lay an inner heart, a *mizu shobai* – the 'water trade', an oriental Soho of geisha girls, love hotels, bars and cabarets. But I was in no position to penetrate that spirited *sake* world, where you needed not only the language but also the inherent subtle perception for innuendo. And that was fine by me. My world was the world at street level – a take-it-or-leave-it case of cosmetics; a slapdash frivolity that shone with glossy sheen. A spectacle of superficiality, maybe, but a spectacular one at that.

Tokyo is full of surprise, the unexpected, the bizarre. One morning I nonchalantly walked in front of Kyukyo-Do, a stationery store in the heart of snazzy Ginza (Gold Sovereign). I didn't know it at the time but I later learnt from Nagai-*san* that that morning I had walked across what is reputedly the most expensive piece of real-estate on earth. Should you fancy a morsel of this land you need more than a fat wallet, as about 9 million yen (£60,000) will buy only one square metre of land. Bit steep? Then slide across the Pacific to the Bargain Basement of Beverly Hills where a mere 80,000 yen will be ample for a square metre of Rodeo Drive. Bit rich? Then live in the Land of the Rising Sun. Semi-rich? Then mingle with the stars.

Not far from this dearest of spots in the heady razzamatazz of Ginza, where life sparkles and big money is spent, I passed a man in a starched white apron who was having a bit of a bonfire on the street. He wasn't homeless, wasn't trying to keep warm (on a hot May day) and wasn't, as far as I could tell, trying to send smoke signals. He worked in the small, dark noodle shop behind him and was simply burning some rubbish: cartons, boxes, polystyrene containers, tins and disposable chopsticks – that kind of thing. Impeccably clad shoppers, clutching big-name designer-wear bags of booty, stepped through the smoke, barely changing course around the smouldering, putrid heap. They moved with an air of insouciance, with no sense of surprise whatsoever, as if it was the most normal thing in the world for a shop-keeper to drag his rubbish out to the street and casually set fire to it. And maybe it was, but it certainly seemed strange to me.

In Japan strange things tend to get only stranger. There I was, sauntering along, lost as usual, head in the paddy clouds, loving every moment. Everywhere a blaze of activity. *Depaato*, shops, restaurants, coffee bars, *sushi* bars, beer bars, burger joints, *yakitori* (kebab) joints, galleries, cinemas, sex shows, night clubs. In short, neon! Signs! All shapes, all sizes, all over the place. All styles of scripts: *kanji, romaji, hiragana, katakana, furigama,* gymkhana (?!). Headcrunch. Overload. Brains blow. Zap.

Frazzled from the dazzle I moved on, I know not where. Over superhighway, underpass. I surfaced with the sun. Somewhere near a railway station. Strange scene. Surrounded by an industrialized hot-bed; traffic, fumes, cars, commotion and the can't-get-away-from-it concrete. Men fishing. Flippin' 'eck! Downtown-fishing men. Inexplicable Tokyo. Samurai city. Where well-behaved warriors make street fires at the feet of well-heeled shoppers. Where people fish beside a pool as life rushes around them in dizzying swirls. They stare, concentrating on the water, the float, oblivious to the blurring city and surrounds. Sitting Buddha-still. Waiting for the bite. Profound peace prevails amidst a cacophony of screeching and clattering city sounds. Sometimes there are stirrings – a catch, or someone gets up to shake a leg, drop 100 yen into the omnipresent Japanese vending machine for a can of tea or coffee, beer or whisky. The anglers can drink their drinks but they can't keep their fish – they're weighed, then thrown back in. Recycled carp.

I'm perplexed. Later my informant (Oki-*san*) tells me that this sport-fishing is based on the principle that the more carp caught, the less the fishermen pay. Catch a whopping seven kilo under the hour and your fishing is free. Free fishing near a fillet of the most expensive land on earth. Odd. But that's Tokyo.

Same city. Another time, another place. Of course, to air the platitude that there are a lot of cars in Tokyo is a bit like saying that there are a lot of ants in an ants' nest, or a lot of sand-grains on a beach or a lot of fat people in America. In short, stating the obvious. Think of Tokyo. Think of cars. Think of lots. But parking lots? Parking plots? Well, maybe not. Unless you have more money than space. Space in spacelessness. A personal plot for your wheels can cost an arm and a leg and all your viscera to boot – 13 million yen (£90,000).

A few years ago a law was passed forbidding car ownership unless the owner possessed proof of owning a parking space. But only a certain number of people can fork out such sums and there's only a certain amount of space, so the authorities triumphantly announced that, as a result of this new legislation, illegal parking and congestion had been reduced. It can still take ten hours to do 100 kilometres, despite numerous sky-suspended computers as big as movie screens and the 'unravel-me-from-this-mess' on-board car computers, both of which flash up-to-the-second updates on congestion and gridlock. Flashy warnings shuffle traffic here, shuffle traffic there. Is this really the way to tackle jammy horrors? I think not. I'm no mathematician, but then, I don't think I need to be. The equation is simple: put too much of something into too small a space and there's going to be trouble and snarl-ups. No amount of computerized wizardry is going to do much more than clog systems further and look flash.

There are other ways to clean and clear the streets – like, forget the car. But until they are forgotten, cars have to be put somewhere. During my urban ramblings around Tokyo I kept coming across tall, thin, flimsy buildings shaped like shoe-boxes. These city grain-silos are in fact garages, the Japanese equivalent of Britain's NCPs but far more ingenious. On the small street-level forecourt (constructed mainly of turntable) the driver hands over his car to an attendant, who transfers it into the up-ended shoe-box. The vehicle is then sunk down to a vertical conveyor belt and stored on a shelf. As simple as that. The snag? The price. But then, to own a car in Tokyo, you need money as well as patience.

So much for car parks; what I wanted was a real park. And on my eighth day I found one: Yoyogi Park. But this was no park of peace. I may have arrived on the wrong day (Sunday) for a spot of inner-city serenity but it was certainly the right one for a live, amplified, vocal-howling spectacle. Punks, rockabillies, hillbillies and heavy metal maniacs had converged in droves on a wide cordoned-off avenue of the park to rock 'n' roll, screech and strut their stuff. This was Tokyo's musical youth's equivalent of Speakers' Corner, only it was not to speak their minds but to sing someone else's. Sid Vicious, Johnny Rotten, Billie Holiday, Thin Lizzy, Jimi Hendrix, Elvis, Lennon, Dylan, in perfect carbon copy form, all shakin' and rattlin' and stridently vocalizing together in a clash of sound and earnest pelvic gyrations. Lofty towers of spiky mohicans mingled with aspic quiffs and lurid semi-headcrops. Studs, chains, buckles, pierced flesh, pins for safety(?), for pricking, for puncturing, for probing into another world. Tight leather, ripped jeans, torn egos, wire shades, woolly caps pulled low. Big-buckle belts, back-pocket combs. Faces. Grimaces. Grease-backs, slick backs, an image: reassessed, repositioned in the reflection of a gleaming Harley mirror. Cool bike. Heavy boots. Heavy looks. Get-a-blast of ghetto-blasters. An amplification of sounds and idols. Screeching feedback. Growls and writhing and pained expressions like those of torture victims. A twisting-turning release. Escapism? Ecstasy?

Gloss over the incongruous physiognomy of an Asiatic pink-maned punk or a quiffed-back rock-a-boy and you see a sublime duplication of the original rebels of pop-rock kings and shock-rock rebels. These are besotted fashion-following cults that, save for the odd perfunctory street-corner cluster or King's Road die-hards, have all but sunk in the West. An onlooker may laugh, may find it an absurd and satirical scene, but this is no spoof. It is deadly serious stuff: the dancing, oscillating, ersatz performer is The Business. It's weird and it's wonderful and way, way out. It's the post-war Economic Miracle personified; it's Japan, the innovative imitation taken to perfection. It's the supreme skill of superior duplication, be it videos, cinemas or cars. It's take something, make something and do it much better. It's brilliance *en masse*.

For hours I lost myself among the crowds – some of them happy-snapping tourists like me, others fanatical fans who mirrored their idols, following their every hip-twisting move.

A tap on my shoulder. I turn and a small Japanese woman, with a face as round and weathered as a walnut, wants to take my picture. My picture? But I'm no spectacle, I try to tell her, using my flappy hands to help; the picture is the performer, the metal-thrashing punk. No, no, she seems to say and steers me towards her grinning, camera-toting comrades who have spilled from the innards of a ticking-over tourist bus. There's a whole rank of them in identical colour-coordinated hat, badge and bag. None of them seems in the least bit drawn to the extraordinary facsimile rock-frolics that surround us. I am rolled down the line to have my picture taken by each and every one. All the same. Snap! A line of lenses point and snap. It's a long line. And it takes a long time. Smiling hurts. '*Chiizu!*' they call, again and again. Obligingly my face freezes into a cheesy grin. Snap! Arms cradle my waist. A man pinches my ribs. We're all in tight. A hat lands on my head. Snap! Shrieks of delight. '*Chiizu!*' they shout in unison, as if more can be pulled from a grin. I feel horribly conspicuous, but it's fun and I like them. More cameras. More snaps. More buffoonery. In every picture every hand sprouts two rabbit-ear fingers. The sign of peace. Peace. Peace in a park of noise.

Swifts copulate on the wing; one drops on top of another mid-flight. I picked up this tit-bit of plover while wading through one of the multitudinous hi-fi shops of Akihabara and tuning for a flash into the World Service on a three-inch Sony digital shortwave radio (10,000 yen). From this aerial snippet of life beyond the city it suddenly dawned on me (while surrounded by head-to-toe, wall-to-wall electronic digitation and soundwave gadgets) that it was time to get out. Swiftly. All this neon, all this concrete, all this urban insanity, wonderful though it was, made me feel hemmed in, detached from the earthy sounds of birdsong, wind in the trees, wind in my wheels. Space. Country. I needed to get cycling. Get moving. After all, I had come to Japan with my bike but a near fortnight had flown and still I hadn't got my leg over my crossbar. This was the longest I had been out of the saddle since I was eleven. Withdrawal symptoms had struck. I was pining. Sad state. I needed my bike: my life.

I found it where I had left it, dozing among the slippers of Ohgiya Japanese style, Cozy atmosphere hotel. Oki-*san* welcomed me back like a piece of long-lost jewellery while her husband gave me a hand-painted *boshu uchiwa* (a traditional flat circular fan made locally); a telephone card (1,000 yen – £6) that advertised Ohgiya with photo and number; and a free dinner of rice, *miso* soup (made from fermented soya beans, barley and rice) and *tempura* (fried fritters of giant prawns and aubergine). Touching stuff.

I planned to set off the next morning but before I did I needed a new notebook. Being lost in Tokyo for two weeks had resulted in me filling my stick-it-in-here, slap-it-in-there haphazard diary faster than ever before. I sent it off to Nagai-*san* to keep under a protective wing until I could retrieve it on my return journey.

Choosing a new notebook is not just a matter of swanning into a stationers and picking up willy-nilly the first thing that comes to hand. I wish it was that easy. The trouble is I'm ridiculously particular. It has got to be the right size, the right colour, the right paper, the right width of line. And the right price. Nothing else will do. But then a diary is a very personal thing, like a piece of underwear. Something close to you; something you show to perhaps only one other person – a person who knows you inside-out. And when it's not close to you in the physical sense, it's secreted away in a drawer where only a prying hand will discover its truths.

I spent a whole afternoon walking round Narita in search of an appropriate notebook. Dipping in and out of stores, picking through the shelves, flicking through the pages. Feeling. Smelling. My notebook was not coming easily. Usually I go for an A6, hard and black with lines spaced seven millimetres apart. Tends to fit snug in the pocket of my easy-access handlebar bag. Surely not too much to ask for? But in Narita, such a prerequisite proved perplexingly elusive. All the ones I touched and sniffed were either too soft, too small, too narrow, too big or adorned with too many mawkish motifs of teddy-bears or sunset scenes of silhouetted lovers. No black hardstuff came my way. In desperation I was forced to swing from the norm. Like buying a pair of silky crotchless knickers after wearing sensible, sturdy M&S cottons all your life. I felt not so much daring as swaying from the faithful. Not me at all. But it was that or nothing so I made my purchase of a flaccid-covered and lightweight offering before coyly slinking out of the door clutching a little something that didn't feel right.

Back in the privacy of my room I hoiked it out of the bag and tried it for size, turning it over in my hands and punctiliously writing the time, date, place. Thin, flimsy, grey with a sky-blue backing, it was (despite the initial disappointment) actually not too bad. The main stumbling block was the front cover with its peculiar choice of wording:

> College
> Enjoy lasting pleasure and satisfaction in using
> this notebook made of the best quality paper.

TITLE:
NAME:

> This is the most comfortable notebook
> you have ever run into.
> You will feel like
> writing with it all the time.

Surely words more apt for a piece of silky underwear than a decidedly nondescript school notebook? But the more I read this curious 'Ode to a Notebook' the more I warmed to it and, like a good conscientious student, I took considerable 'pleasure and satisfaction' in filling in the 'title' and 'name' with appropriate subjects. What I had at first taken to be a piece of incongruously maudlin Japanglish translated sentimentality was, I decided on reflection, actually quite endearing. And it struck me that, yes, I could perhaps mould to this pleasurable and satisfying theme after all.

I planned to leave in the morning. For where, I knew not, but go I would. As a result I was up most of the night sifting through the entrails of my belongings which were spread far and wide over the *tatami*. Camping equipment and bicycle impedimenta. Luggage is one of those uncanny things that, despite nothing more being added to it, mysteriously expands. For my forays into Tokyo I had left virtually all my equipment behind with Oki-*san* and yet, on my return, what had previously slotted very pleasingly into my panniers now seemed to have increased fourfold. I call this the Phenomenal Frank Syndrome after my rotund cat, Frank: the less I feed him, the fatter he gets.

Frankly, I know what's to blame. Me. I'll come clean, out of the closeted pannier: I am a plastic-bag queen. I have an addiction. Rare is the occasion I can venture out without a plastic bag secreted somewhere about my person. The prospect of finding myself utterly bagless in some location, be it half a mile or ten thousand miles from home, is almost enough to make me want to pull one tight over my head. I mean, what if one comes across a bushful of berries, and has nothing in which to house them apart from one's stomach? Or what if a bevy of ball bearings starts cascading out of a bottom bracket? Where to put them? The muddy verge? Perish the thought! What if it rains for five days and you have only one pair of shoes and no plastic bags in which to harbour your freezing toadish feet? What to wrap the wet tent in to prevent it from saturating the sleeping bag? What to wrap the toilet paper in? More to the point, what if the toilet paper gets wet and you have no other supply? Dock leaves are just not so efficient.

I fully admit I am the sort of person who has trouble passing through the fruit and vegetable department of a supermarket without collecting a few surplus-to-requirement plastic bags along the way. No doubt about it, I am a plasticized rogue. All shapes, sizes, colours have a worrying habit of attaching themselves to me like limpets, without even trying. As a result, I tend to rustle to extreme. I was once expelled from a hostel in Finland on account of my interminable rustlings. Virtually every piece of my equipment (utensils and the like) is stuffed into a polythene bag. Trouble is, as I can't bring myself to discard a bag unless it is severely soiled or holed, I accumulate a cache (pannier load) that involuntarily expands to the excessive.

And there you have it. Or, to put it another way, there in a bag you have me, a sort of self-confessed plasti-kleptomaniac, feigning perplexity at the expansion of my luggage. All it had taken was a mere fortnight for my squirrelling traits to augment an initially meagre supply to proportions of sheer absurdity: enough to stock the local grocer for months. After a hectic night spent shuffling cocoons of plastic bags from one side of the room to the other and bagging bagged bags in bags, I wriggled into my sheet sleeping bag to catch the last two hours of night. In the morning I was off with my bags to hit the road.

CHAPTER 5

Shiny Happy People

The same day I set off to see Japan, a pedestrian in America was robbed by a man who threatened him with a large black snake. A New Jersey policeman told reporters that it was the first robbery at snake point he had heard of. That's America.

This was Japan. 6.30 a.m. Radio on. In my room I was grappling with two small raw fish (variety unknown), a shoal of dried silver fish scarcely larger than plankton (eyes intact), a saucer of indeterminate pickled vegetables (sporting colours similar to those of the punks' Day-Glo hairstyles in Yoyogi Park), a hard pink ball (likewise pickled, only more slimy), a steaming bowlful of bean curd and kelp, an egg (in unappetizing and unadulterated state) and a dish of glossy white rice. A hangover remedy? A witch doctor's cure for a severe dose of the trots? No, simply bog-standard fare for a Japanese breakfast. And against all expectation, it was delicious. Cross-legged, with a chopstickful of seaweed in mouth, I reached across the low, brown table to my radio and twiddled the dial.

Radio Australia: 'matey joke'. Two policemen are driving along in the patrol car. The driver says to the other, 'Stick ya hid owt the winda, mite, to see eef the blipper's wairkin'.' So the other policeman sticks his head out the window and, looking up on to the roof, says, 'It eez, it eezn't, it eez, it eezn't, it eez, it eezn't.'

Oh dear, they'll have to try harder than that. Then the news comes on and I learn how the Australian tin can industry is breaking into the Asian market. Big demand. Trade and industry minister is interviewed, sounding happy and cocksure at some tin can conference in Victoria. Hmmm.

I return to FEN (Far East Network), the station that caters specifically for the copious US armed forces based in Japan. The ballgame report between the Blue Jays and the White Sox has just finished. The adverts come on and a low, slow, baritone twang tells the boys in the forces that 'you sure are an important part of the DOD team' before inviting us to hear what the spouses, girlfriends and mothers back home have to say. A woman's voice. Sounding crackly. 'Hi, Mac sweetheart. It's Annie. Kirsty misses her Daddy real bad but we're doing just fine with running the home. Hang on in there, hon, we sure are proud of you.'

More distant voices. More artificial sugary-babe morale boosters. A few swapshop announcements. 'Bobby G. has a six-month-old black Yamaha electric organ – in great condition – hardly used. Says a buddy talked him into buying it to develop a non-existent musical ear. Is looking to exchange it for a lesser-spotted dwarf-tailed parakeet. And a refrigerator.' Or something like that.

Then, the weather report, at the end of which the listener is reminded to 'gather together emergency supplies and secure outside items' in preparation for the typhoons which are possible throughout the summer.

I was a bit worried, not so much about what the weather might throw at me as about finding my way in a land of indecipherable signposts. I had been scrutinizing the maps

Nagai-*san* had photocopied for me for at least five minutes before I realized I was looking at them upside down. They appeared nothing more than a Daedalian mass of bewildering lines and coils and squiggles – a bit like peering into a telephone junction box, a chaotic network of intricate confusion.

One of my maps of the Narita area which I had picked up from the tourist office was equally astounding, but for a different reason: golf clubs – a profusion of golf clubs, surrounding the city. I counted at least seventeen green blobs ranging from the Caledonian and Narita Hightree Golf Club to the extortionate-sounding Privilege.

Few countries can be less suited to golf than Japan. Although the country is not much larger than Italy, three-quarters of its land surface is severely mountainous, rendering it mostly uninhabitable. The consequent pressure of the population on the plains results in those rare-as-gold tracts of land costing a billion bullion. Slightly incongruous, then, for a sport that needs space and gently rolling hills. Yet, since it was originally introduced to Japan at the beginning of the century, golf (much like baseball) has become an adopted national sport. Virtually everyone is at it.

Needless to say, in a country drastically short of space and seriously full of people, membership of a golf club is a million-dollar affair and requires an inordinate amount of patience: waiting lists can be years and years long. Once in, tolerance levels are further tested. Nagai-*san* (a keen golfer) told me that, owing to hopeless overcrowding, to play at a club at the weekend necessitated reserving a teeing-off time at least a month in advance. To play on a public course on any day of the week, reservations were necessary three or four months in advance.

'Of course,' he said, 'after waiting all that time, it is very possible to rain so maybe six month passes before reservation and weather circumstances are possible to play.'

Some clubs, unable to cope with demand, have stopped taking new members. As a result, memberships are often actively traded on the Stock Exchange – more for the challenging vagaries of an investment than for the satisfaction of the game. Golf revolves around business. A prime perk for a company executive is a club membership and so almost all the players are businessmen: the golf course is where clients are entertained and business is wooed. While the rest of Japan swirls around them in a frantic whirl, there's plenty of time for wheeling deals on the fairways, not to mention the two-hour break for lunch after nine holes and an *après*-golf communal bath.

For most golfers around the world, I suppose getting a hole-in-one is quite a happy occasion. But in Japan it's an excruciating experience – at least as far as personal funds are concerned. For the 'lucky' golfer, the repercussions of his (most of the golfers are men) spot-on hit are far more of a financial burden than simply buying a round of drinks for everyone. He is obliged to buy expensive presents for those he was playing with and also for anyone who witnessed the event, from caddies to other players to groundsmen. On top of that it's his duty to send gifts to business colleagues, close friends and family as well as take them out to dinner and hold celebratory parties. As the hapless-go-lucky player will be left with little change out of £8,000, golfers in Japan are now spending nearly £2 million a year insuring themselves against getting a hole-in-one.

As my own golf has never progressed further than the mini variety at Bournemouth Winter Gardens (it was the Doll's House that put me off – my balls went in and never came out) I was fortunately not tempted in the least to wield a club in Japan, despite being surrounded by a nation of batty clubbers. There were far more important things to be doing – like getting lost on Japanese roads. But I didn't panic, although I very nearly did. Instead I hung loose and told myself: well, if I get lost, I get lost, and the only thing I can do is find myself. Made sense to me. Sort of.

So I set out on a blazing blue May morning, helpless and clueless as to where I was going, but confident that at least it was somewhere and that somewhere was better than nowhere. And, despite this haywire approach, I knew that (at least for the first few days) I was a woman with a mission. Somehow I had to cycle into the environs of Yokohama and locate the address of some friends. Ah so, *desu-ka*? What I knew for sure was that I had a choice of routes. Either I could head west for fifty or so miles to be squashed into Tokyo's manic urbanity before bungling forty-five miles south-west to destination Higashi-Totsuka – or I could go on a roundabout way, hugging the coast of Chiba's Boso-hanto Peninsula, and nip across the bay by boat. Although I may not comprehend a map splattered in *kanji* characters, I can at least discern that a solid mass of colour spells more than a spot of congestion. On my freebie tourist map of Japan (scale 1:2,000,000) the Tokyo–Kawasaki–Yokohama conurbation appears as a very unappetizing solid yellow blob, the size of my thumbnail. Boso-hanto, on the other hand, is yellow-blob free. Thus, Boso-hanto it would be.

I left Oki-*san* waving goodbye to me from the sliding-door threshold of 'Cozy atmosphere' Ohgiya, wishing me '*ki-o-tsukete* – take care', and to ring if I had any problems. As I wobbled off down the narrow streets of Narita Old Town, heads spiralled and necks craned as curious eyes followed my precarious path. Strange sight – 'foreign barbarian' alone on a bike. I squeezed through a gaggle of identically sailor-suited and satchelled schoolgirls who giggled and twittered and nudged each other as I passed. I weaved around fast-moving forces of housewives out food-shopping, ducking the probing prongs of their eye-level brollies. I passed the recycled-cardboard-box street-collection unit comprising an old man in a T-shirt, cap and white gloves backed up by a dear old biddy in baggy pink floral apron and bloomers. Their vehicle was a heavy and rusted bicycle (*circa* 1870) coupled to a rickety wooden nose-diving trailer, a contraption straight out of the Bicycle Culture Historic Collection and piled improbably high with layer upon layer of flattened boxes. No small fry these boxes – they were boxes that until recently had spelt big business: Yamaha, Toshiba, Mitsubishi, Hitachi – containing the very latest wizardry of Japanese household equipment: freezers, fridges, washing machines, stereos. But now their carton armour was nothing more than cardboard coffins, stacked ignominiously one on top of another – coffins labelled with big names, big money, transported away to their burial pyre by a humble antediluvian pedalling machine. And a man in starched white gloves.

Opposite Narita *eki* (station) I turned left at McDonald's, or Makudonarudo, as the Japanese call it. The first time I saw McDonald's in Japan I was rather taken aback. And I don't exactly know why. Maybe it was seeing the harsh, fast, jarring food blended together unharmoniously with the graceful and aesthetic beauty of the Japanese script that adorned the walls, menus, bills and flags. It's not that I wasn't expecting to find it there; after all, it can land like a familiar extraterrestrial in some of the most unfamiliar and unlikely nooks and crannies of this world. Being surprised to see it in Japan is like being surprised to find it in America – because Japan, in a highly superficial and visual way, *is* America. At least, its cities are. Burger joints and fast-food emporiums (Wendy's, Denny's, Kentucky Fried Chicken, Domino's Pizza, Shakey's Pizza, Pizza Hut, Mister Donut, Taco Bell and Baskin-Robbins) are almost as numerous in Japan as in their country of origin. McDonald's alone has not much short of a thousand outlets (the largest number outside the United States) sprinkled liberally throughout the Japanese archipelago. The first hamburgers winged their way across the Pacific as soon as the war ended. The Occupying Forces brought them; the Japanese tasted them, embraced them – like they did most things American. Hence Japan was the first country in the world to import this commodity in bulk. From the McDonald's buildings flutter red and yellow flags bearing the familiar arched logo beneath which are the words in Japanese: 'Makudonarudo is the world's language.' These golden arches have been made so quintessentially Japanese and have infiltrated so extensively that Japanese children visiting America are often amazed to find McDonald's there too.

If the giant catfish beneath Japan was to lift its tail gently and pivot the country ninety degrees clockwise, the Boso-hanto Peninsula would resemble a foot, with Narita situated in the middle of the ankle. My slaphappy plan was to head for the arch of the foot before rolling on along the ball and round the toes.

I had no idea what to expect. In two weeks, the only scenes I'd seen outside of the city were through the windows of a train as it trundled past semi-rural Japan – paddy fields bordered and criss-crossed by an interminable network of roads. Mostly, though, the scene outside the train was all city.

Despite having been dazzled by an overdose of neon since my arrival in Japan, I had managed to drum a few basic Japanese phrases into my frazzled head. Finding myself in a spin after only ten minutes in the outskirts of Narita, I turned to one of these phrases – the never-leave-home-without-it '*wa doka desu-ka*?' ('which way is?'). Only trouble was, I wasn't too sure where to ask for as I wasn't too sure where I was going. So, if in doubt, pick a place at random and hope for the best. But of course, before you throw your random '*wa doka desu-ka*?' at some poor soul you need some soul at which to throw your question. Now that I had disentangled myself from the city centre only to entangle myself in the boisterous ring-roads, most people on whom I could unleash my experimental enquiry were spinning on by in cars, sealed from the outside world by glass and metal. Heads would turn momentarily to eye this forlorn figure standing astride a pink mount in the swirling Japanese equivalent of a couple of Birmingham's Spaghetti Junctions combined. Yes, there were a lot of roads. A lot of cars. And a lot of time for me to think: maybe I should have just kept to cycling round the Isle of Wight.

What I wanted was a person, or people – surely not too much to ask for when 125 million of them were milling somewhere around me in fairly close proximity? But I could not see any. Bit of a classic case of not being able to see the pod for the peas, or the cat for the fleas or . . . well, the people for the cars. I couldn't see the wood either, as there weren't any trees. Even the telegraph poles were concrete and looked indestructible.

In every bleak situation there usually arises some good and my bit of goodness came by way of a knight in shining armour, or, to be more precise, a sinewy old man on an ancient brown and rusted bike. From where he came I do not know. He just appeared at my side in a knightly puff of smoke (or lung-blackening haze of roadside pollution). His fatless, brown rustic face was crevassed in smiles. His eyes, narrow but not overly so, looked full of ebullient life. These features gave him a sprightly appearance of youth that belied his age. I guessed he could be anything from forty-six to a hundred and ten.

I bade him a confidently chiselled '*ohayo gozaimasu*!' good morning, followed by a not so confident '*Wa doka desu-ka*?' As I still hadn't ascertained a destination I simply asked him: 'Which way is *utsukushii*?' A ridiculous query, but as *utsukushii* (which simply means 'beautiful') was the first word that sprang to mind, it was not such a bad one at that, feeling as I did in need of some beauty.

I don't know whether the old man understood me but I for sure didn't understand him. However, my blank expression appeared no deterrent to him whatsoever. Quite the contrary; he embarked upon an animated one-sided conversation to which I could only offer a perfunctory 'Ah so, *desu-ka*?' – a phatic response that seemed to fuel him the more. For want of something more constructive to do, I showed the old man my somewhat senseless map, and was rather encouraged when he too looked at it upside-down. Despite that, he seemed to know where he was and, pointing at the map, kept repeating the word Yachimata which my disorientated mind told me must obviously be the name of a place.

Latching on to Yachimata I nodded enthusiastically: not only was it in the vague direction I wanted to go (I think), but also the three *kanji* characters for it looked fairly easy to decipher on signposts. The first resembled a 'road narrows' warning sign; the middle, a sort of railway track with kinks; the third, a crucifix wearing a skirt.

Still beaming, and blessed with the gift of the gab, the man seemed to be indicating for me to follow him. Dutifully and gratefully I did so. For an hour we rode along together, occasionally clashing wheels, along overpass and underpass, and eventually bypassed the worst of the traffic. All the time he chatted away incessantly to me as if I was a nearest and dearest. I was amazed how he could have so much to talk about with someone who could offer so little. But, like a good protégée, I smiled and nodded and half-head-bowed and, with a liberal dose of well-executed 'Ah so, *desu-ka*s?', made out I knew exactly from where he was coming. Or going, for that matter. But reality was all swings and see-saws. We came to a busy junction adorned with a wild array of signs, some of which had the more helpful *romaji* script written beneath the *kanji*. Hanging proud among this profusion was the much sought-after Yachimata. Hoorah! Now that I had been shepherded on to the right road from the wrong direction, I presumed this was where I would bid my sprightly companion farewell.

Not so. Apparently the old man was hell bent on coming along for the ride. Strange. I couldn't work this old codger out for toffee. I was also feeling a trifle guilty for having swayed him off beam and out of his way. But then, was it out of his way? Maybe, by chance, he too was bound for Yachimata and, thanks to my half-hopeless map, we had assisted each other in finding it. Unlikely. In fact, head-high-in-the-clouds unlikely. But, there again, maybe. You can't just cast possibilities aside like you can superfluous words. Anyway, to me, he looked like a man with a mission. We rode on together. And on and on together. He in his flip-flops and me in my Nikes. At one stage he extracted a small white towel from his wire-caged bicycle basket and, removing his hands from his handlebars (obviously a man with a trick as well as a mission), tied it in fetching fashion around his head.

Good idea. It was hot. Head-mop hot.

By now we had been riding together (in roundabout stop–start style) in the heat, in the fumes, in the hills, in the traffic, for most of the morning. And yet this emaciated old man with calves of elastic remained as fresh as a daisywheel. Meanwhile, back in the sinews of my muscles, things were beginning to flag. And complain. Bitterly. It was time for a pit stop; a drink.

In Japan, a drink is never far from hand or mouth, whether you be stuck out on a limb on the top of a peak or marooned on a highway and miles from a town. This is thanks to those omnipresent eyesores that are scattered with profusion around the land: vending machines. Japan's equivalent of New Zealand's non-eyesore sheep. They are everywhere, sell everything. Want a roadside hamburger? – a pot of steaming noodles? – a whisky? – beer? – an ice cream? – a book? – a lonely-hearts column? – a condom? – a bunch of flowers? – a two-kilo bag of rice? – a porn mag? – a disposable camera or, well, just a plain old can of pop? It's all yours, twenty-four hours a day, at the mere drop of a coin. Disposable income? Disposable goods, most of which land up on the verge. Big clean hearts the Japanese may have, but small clean land they don't.

These huge, gleaming digital monster-machines look as if they've just landed fresh from the production line. No bashed-in buttons or flaps, no booted-in windows or sides. No graffiti. No vandalism. That's Japan. Shiny happy people: shiny happy machines. Everywhere. Coca-Cola, the country's major purveyor of soft drinks, has 800,000 machines alone. Silly number. Hard to envisage. Unless you're in Japan. Like I say, everywhere: any table, any chair, top of piano, window-ledge; in the middle, on the edge. Everyone drops a coin.

Everyone drinks a drink. Thousands? Millions? No, billions. Stand by. Hold tight on to your figures. Big figures. On average (remember – a country of averages this) 20 billion cans of beverages are drunk a year, 85% of which are sold through vending machines. Let me see now . . . 20 billion divided by pop-ulation (125 million) multiplied by 0.85 (tap, tap, tap on the calculator – whoops, too many noughts – flown off the edge, pick them up, start again) equals, on average (of course), 136 cans of vending-machine drink per person per year.

Often, vending machines don't just deliver what they display through their windows or advertise on their sides but give the coin-popper a little added extra, for free: they give you sounds. A shrill, chirping woman's voice, thanking you for your custom. A repetitive stick-in-the-head sing-song tune so exasperating you'd gladly pay to have it removed. Take it away but don't take it home.

My pitstop came in the form of a lay-by lined with an illustrious parade of strapping great vending machines, all shouldering each other like a bunch of impenetrable sumo-kings. It was hard work, trying to persuade my aged companion to allow me to buy him a drink. He appeared a little ruffled and became intent on not only treating me to a *sushi* burger and beer but apparently a whole vending machine of my choice. It was even harder work, however, trying to choose what to drink. The selection was astronomical. There were over thirty different coffees and at least forty different teas: green tea, brown tea, black tea, sweet tea, bitter tea, weed tea, oolong tea, hot tea, iced tea, Far East tea, far-fetched tea, this tea, that tea, any tea. Don't fancy tea? Don't fancy coffee? Well, how about fifty different pops and sodas and vegetable juices and fruit juices and fruity vegetable juices and chemically vitaminized pick-you-ups (or put-you-downs) and dubious fluorescent-glowing concoctions of energy-boosters. Or maybe just a jar of *sake*, or bottle of wine or litre of beer. Ah yes, a beer. How about that huge silver can the size of a four-ball tennis container imprinted with the words: 'Hokkaido Beer – let your spirit run free and enjoy nature's rich bounty. Savour the taste of Hokkaido'? It's a nice idea but I think I'll keep my spirit under wraps for now – got a few more miles to get under my wheels before the day's out. I'll just let those Dydo juices woo me with the words:

Every satisfying sip a flavour experience
delicious refreshment is a DYDO tradition.
Relax and enjoy thirst quenching beverages at their best.
DYDO is your ticket to drink paradise.

Meanwhile, my towel-turbaned guide selected a can of Coca-Cola-branded iced Georgia Coffee. Judging from the number of slim, brown cans that littered the sides of the road more prevalently than any other dented, wheel-flattened ones, I deduced Georgia Coffee to be top of the most popular vending-machine drinks. Strange for a country renowned for its delicious green tea but, in Japan, coffee is associated with being quintessentially Western, the strong, black stuff of European street cafés and America's voguish Deep South. Follow the trend. Head West. Taste West. For Georgia Coffee, though, the essential appeal seems to lie in the design of its label, which depicts Scarlett O'Hara types in crinoline frocks and imposing gentlemen in august top hats on the sumptuous lawns of Tara, the celebrated great southern mansion in *Gone with the Wind*. A classic case of capitalizing on a fad. Most Japanese seem to have either read the book or seen the film. Now they can imbibe it too. So infatuated does Japan become with Western (mainly American) stars, Western myths, Western movies, Western nostalgia, that it seems immaterial whether the exploitative advertising used for a certain product actually correlates with the object (not to mention geographical location) that it's pushing to sell. A few years ago a Japanese importer marketed a California wine with a *Gone with the Wind* scene embellished on the label.

Drinks drunk and brows mopped, Towel-Top and I set off on the road again. While we had been drinking our way through the vending machines I'd attempted to ascertain just how far he was going. But, instead of extricating any facts or figures, my somewhat farcical and gesticulating form of Japanese had only encouraged the playful old boy to tie my head up like his in a spare towel. Larking around with a VOAP and entwined in a knot of oil-soiled towel, I thought: oh dear, if my mother saw me now she'd think there was no hope. But I saw myself, in the reflection of a hotdog-dispensing machine, and, finding that I looked rather fetching with a halo of stained rag wound round my head, I paraded, like a buffoon, up and down, cat-walk fashion, swinging my sweaty hips, much to the delight of Towel-Top One. So jovially pleased was he with this outlandish find that he showed me off to a car full of elderly husbands and wives who'd pulled up for a drink. Here we go, I thought, he's going to get me arrested. But, oh no. These old dears were so taken by this bizarre foreign spectacle, trussed up in a towel, that they eagerly draped themselves around and over me for a hearty and giggly session of camera-snapping fun.

Back in the saddle, the Towel-Top Team was spinning with gay abandon towards Yachimata. Owing to its elusiveness, we seemed to be approaching it in a very long-winded and roundabout manner. I still hadn't managed to establish how far I was to be chaperoned but, at this rate, judging from Towel-Top One's seemingly limitless energy, we ran the risk of shooting clean off the boot of Chiba and landing in the sinking sun. A nice idea, but not a correct one. Instead, without warning, my mad towel-hatted escort jammed on his brakes (an action that almost caused me to plunge up his rear) and dived into his bicycle basket for two chemically cultured rosy red apples the size of footballs. With a beaming bow he said *dozo* (please), gave me his fruity offering and disappeared with a wobble down a side road.

On my own again. Good time for the toilet, but where? I

rode on for a couple of blocks (busy block-like landscape this) until I came to Cosmo, a service station that resembled more a foyer of some fancy hotel than a forecourt of a garage. The gloss-painted ground looked polished to such an extent that I felt almost frightened to step on it lest I sully the surface with a smeary footprint. The pumps bore so brilliant a sheen they could quite easily have substituted for full-length dress mirrors. A young team of exquisitely neat and attentive attendants, dressed in fresh-pressed Cosmo colour-coordinated uniforms, were manning (and womanning) the services. And some service it was too, with no 'self' doubt about it. The customer, and even more so his vehicle, was pampered to extremes.

Dumbfounded, I watched the operation from the side-lines. A car would enter and, even before all four wheels had rolled upon the forecourt's ship-shape surface, a couple of attendants would scoot to greet it with a gratifying pack of lightning bows and high-pitched trills of *irasshaimase* (welcome). The car would then be waved and shepherded to a precise location in front of an appointed pump. Upon emerging from his vehicle the driver would be steered towards the garage's air-conditioned coffee bar where he would recline in black leather and chrome easy-chairs, in front of a large-screened television, and be plied with a lavish supply of complimentary strong black *kohii* and cigarettes by an obsequious attendant. Upon the polished, tinted-glass table, amidst a basket of boiled sweets and paper-packeted rice biscuits, lay a fan of *manga*, magazines and newspapers for the cosseted customer's leisurely perusal.

Meanwhile, back on the forecourt, it was all fast, efficient action. Two girls in Cosmo skirts, pop-socks and white sneakers had set upon washing, polishing and buffing the outside of his car with a fervent enthusiasm that beggared belief, while a team of zealous young men buzzed around, fine-tuning the engine, topping up the water, topping up the oil, emptying the ashtrays, wiping the steering wheel and polishing all windows from within. Each car mat was whisked away and fed into a special mat-cleansing machine that appeared to perform the car-mat equivalent of colonic irrigation. Buttons were pushed, time set ticking, motors turned on. Amidst a mass of wires and tubes and potions and brushes, the mats underwent a painful-looking procedure before being regurgitated fresh enough to eat.

In the 3.52 minutes it took for the driver to down his coffee and snacks and catch up on the sumo scores, the way-over-the-top beautification was complete. Scarcely acknowledging the frenetically bowing service team, he slid back behind the wheel and drove to the exit. Here, waiting like a sentry, in full Cosmo regalia, was yet another member of the kowtowing workforce who, with one swift, smooth move, fearlessly slipped straight out into the road to bow and stop the traffic. The dense procession of vehicles accepted this move without a murmur (after all, this was standard service-station procedure) and the mollycoddled driver accelerated off down the road, leaving a profusion of boot-licking bows in his wake.

Servicing my own stations, I found the toilets to be a far cry from the missed-target equivalent of garages in the West. Not a stain, not a smear, not a splash in sight. Polished pan. Polished wall. A musical toilet roll that unravelled to the strains of 'Greensleeves', the spare roll suspended beneath in a sort of pink towelling home-sewn sling embroidered with the words 'LOVE MY KITTY'. Toilet paper so soft it made Andrex feel like a loofah. A toilet paper you could actually find the end of, unlike those unnickable and unmanageable Western plastic dispensers the size of ferris wheels which are usually so stiff you end up clawing in frustrated desperation for a mere frayed sheet. Either that or drip-dry.

The marble-topped vanity unit with a light-bulb-bordered wall mirror was more the sort of thing you'd expect to find in a star's dressing-room. A vase of fresh flowers. A basketful of complimentary packets of Kleenex and Tampax. Toothbrush and toothpaste. Phials of free perfume. Automatic taps that provided water, soap and hot air in one and a high-twittering woman's voice emanating from some unseen orifice, thanking me for my custom. Odd. But all clean fun.

I spent the rest of the day cycling in various degrees of disorientation, lost in a continuous enclave of concrete, cars and corrugated iron. And litter. Everywhere. A far cry from the dreamy mystical mists and emerald green paddy fields of those glossy coffee-table picture books. But although I was passing through a scene of spectacular ugliness, it was for that very reason that I found it enjoyable. An ugliness so unlovely, so jarring, that it held a kind of beauty. That's the thing with sights that on first impression dismay. Because they may not be green, clean, architecturally 'Olde Worlde', historically eminent, scenically wholesome perfection, it's all too easy to dismiss them with a perfunctory glance as blemishes not worth exploring. Places from which to beat a retreat. But so often it's in just these very carbuncles that reality lies. Tourists like myself may flock to the camera-snapping sights (and very nice they are, too) but it is the insipid and insalubrious backstreets that can more often satisfy the expectations than a hounded and hoofed stereotyped attraction ever can. Yes, the Taj Mahal is an exquisite beauty, but there's something about a bill-sticker's worn-torn remains – the textures, the colours – that I see now on this heavy concrete Japanese backstreet which, in a funny sort of way, is even more impressive. The superlative Taj Mahal may aesthetically gratify the eye but so, too, can it leave an unfulfilled void, never for me comparing with the indelible impact of this poster's weathered detritus. The shard fragments of an indecipherable advert, with an abstrusely nebulous script, its jaded hues infused into an ashen-faced wall, are so unostentatiously startling, so accidental, so unexpected, so real.

That's one of the joys of travelling by bike: chance encounters; the practical weaving and varying speeds at which it's possible to stop, to notice, to feel. From the saddle there are no out-of-reach blurred walls, no glass-sealed barriers like that of a car. Catch a glimpse of a sight that intrigues, then brake, stop, turn. Easy. Find that wall, touch that wall, sniff that wall. Picture that wall. It's all yours. Yours to enjoy. There's no entrance fee. There's nothing about it in the guidebooks. It's just sitting there in its unloved beauty. Take a picture. Won't hurt. It's the only one of its kind. Click! Got it. Look at it again. It gets better. The light's changing. The shadows are longer. Click! Sit and look at the wall. It's okay, there are no buses to board, trains to catch, people to meet, time to keep. Remember, you're lost. On your own. Sit and watch the wall all day. If you want. I will. And it gets better. I sit in the shade opposite, on an upturned Coca-Cola crate with my dusty-lipped water bottle and camera. And I watch. It's the perfect stage-set back drop. Life unfolds in front of it.

Act One: an old man shuffles on to the scene, his ribs visible through his vest. He wears a towel like a scarf round his neck to soak up the sweat. (That's why I'm in the shade, but it's still hot.) On the edge of my stage is a cigarette-vending machine which has an advert on the front of a bicycle flying through the air. Smoke to cycle – is that what it's saying? The vending machine lies along the trajectory of the old man's course but, just before he reaches it, a white Noddy van pulls up which blots my man from view. The driver sits in his van a minute, shuffling through some papers on a clipboard. He jumps out, leaving the engine running, and trots off down the street. And then I lose him behind a long, flapping banner.

Act Two: now my scene is half wall, half van. Some young schoolchildren with yellow caps giggle and scamper along. But they're on and off the stage in a flash. A woman wobbles into my sights from the wings. She's on a bicycle, balancing two heavy-looking 'A-Coop' supermarket carrier bags on her handlebars. Her basket is full. More shopping. She wears a wide plastic-peaked sun-visor with a green hat on top and long lacy white gloves up to the elbows. She rides on the pavement, which isn't a pavement – the roads are too narrow for that. Instead, pedestrians and cyclists mingle together on an imaginary pavement – a strip of road over the drains demarcated by a yellow line. The A-Coop woman is on collision course with a young mother riding the other way on her 'Bike Queen'. She's carrying an even more awkward load – three children of various ages and dimensions, who are perilously balanced and suspended from various locations around the bike. No BS 1345982 government-approved child seats here. It's either hold on or fall off.

An old woman with a back bent parallel to the ground is the next character to emerge from the wings. Slowly she shuffles in front of my playhouse wall, pushing what looks like a bisected snub-nosed pram. Before she's had time to disappear behind the still-ticking-over parked van, she intercepts an identical pram pushed by an almost identical woman with an L-shaped back who approaches at a similar unhurried speed from the opposite direction. They stop and greet each other but, because of their set-solid angular spines, their heads are fixed in such a position that they can see little apart from the ground around their feet. The most their necks can manage is to rotate their heads forty-five degrees to either side, an awkward operation which they execute from time to time. Seemingly there's a lot to talk about – so much so that, after a few minutes, they opt to exchange their gossip sitting down. Although my stage offers no suitable props or chairs of any kind on which to sit, this oversight is of no concern whatsoever to my low-gravity high-street gossipers, who now reveal the ingenious use of their squat-square blue plastic prams. In one swift manoeuvre they have converted the stunted-growth cot of the pram containing their shopping into a seat, simply by releasing the lid. This in effect creates a perambulating wheelchair-cum-shopping trolley. And there they sit, quite at ease, bang in the middle of the street pavement, occasionally pivoting their heads to catch each other's face. The bypassing flows of pedestrians and cyclists seem to regard the old women's behaviour as nothing unusual and alter course accordingly around this impromptu WI coffeeless morning eight-wheeled obstacle.

An erratically driven moped with a red plastic box like a Unigate milk crate fixed to its rear buzzes suddenly into my frame, threatening to jettison the seated chinwaggers from their moorings as it slaloms recklessly among the shoppers and bikers. But, fear not. It's only the postman and, though he may look a peripheral hazard, he knows his nose from his brakes and whisks past the perambulatory traffic-island with a good two inches to spare. Meanwhile they gossip on. Sitting on their shopping on their wheels.

The Noddy van ticks on, ticks over. Then, quite forgotten about, the old man with the skeletal ribs and scarf-towel shuffles back on to the scene. Must have been hiding beside the obscured-from-view cigarette-vending machine all this time. He holds a packet of Hope in his hands while one of its contents hangs smoking from his lips. The Noddy van man returns, carrying a freezer nearly twice his height on his back by way of an agonizing-looking tump line suspended round his forehead. With surprising ease he slips his impossible load into the boot of the van and then jogs across to a liquid-dispensing machine to buy a blue can. He's about to climb into his van with his can when he looks up and looks out into his audience. All one of them. Me. I momentarily shrink. He smiles. Can't be smiling at me. Can he? Better smile back just in case. Then, like in Woody Allen's *The Purple Rose of Cairo*, he walks to the front of the set and steps out, into the road. Towards me. I stand up, surprised. He bows. Just a little.

'*Konnichiwa* – hello,' he says.

'*Konnichiwa*,' I reply.

'America?'

'No, I'm an English person,' I say in Japanese.

'By bicycle?'

'Yes, sort of.'

'Ah, Sir Goy!' he says.

(Sir Goy? I think. Who's he? Only later do I discover that *sugoi* is Japanese for 'great!')

'Please,' he says, beaming wide (nice teeth). '*Purezento.*'

And he gives me his chilled blue can. Pocari Sweat, it says on the side. The rest of the writing is in Japanese and it's only later, very much later, that I find an English translation:

> Pocari Sweat is quickly absorbed into the body tissues due to its fine osmolality and contains electrolytes for replenishing body fluids. Pocari Sweat is thus highly recommended as a beverage for such activities as sports, physical labour, after a hot bath and even as an eye-opener in the morning.

'Thank you very much,' I say to the van man.

'*Ganbatte*! – Good luck – have strength!' he replies cheerfully before trotting back across the road to his Noddy and driving away, with a wave.

I snap open the tab and take an exploratory and cautionary sip of Pocari Sweat, which tastes about as appealing as its name implies. It's very sweet, but it's cold and it's going down fast. When I reach the bottom of the can I wait with uncertain anticipation for the 'osmolating electrolytes' to light, take hold. They don't; at least, not in the way I had hoped they would. Bladder calls. The verdict? Not bad. The curtain falls.

CHAPTER 6

Black Ships Out of the Blue

I found the sea. Or maybe I should say, the sea found me, because I hadn't really been looking for it (too busy sitting in streets watching the world and his winkle go by). In fact it wasn't actually so much the sea as the smell of the sea that found me: seaweed, salt, sardines – that sort of thing – a tangy ocean aroma that mingled potently with the fumes of wherever I was, be it near the coast or further inland (Togane-shi, I believe the place was called). That's the nice thing about smells: maps don't matter, signs don't matter. Words don't matter. Just follow your nose, if you want to and have got the time. Time . . . funny thing, time. It ticks on the same as it has done for millennia and yet there seems to be less of it around. Time is malleable. You can do a lot with it. You can have it, bide it, make it, spend it, lose it. You can even have it high or half. And yet, you can't see it. So, if you've lost time, you'll never be able to find it because you don't know what you're looking for. It slips through your fingers and seeps through your shoes. It can even ooze out over the top of a pair of sturdy wellington boots. No refunds. No return to sender. It's an everywhere and nowhere syndrome. Delayed planes can make it up. They're fibbers then, because you can't. We all know that, really. And yet we continue to race around, trying to make better use of it. Like life.

The sea I saw was disappointing – depressing even. Not the sort of breezy, uncluttered coast that I had been naively envisaging. Firstly, it was filthy, much like the beach, and the piece of coastline where I had arrived was like one long trafficked, neon-strip mall of 'convenience stores', arcades, *pachinko* parlours and buildings with cosmic names like Rocket Man, Space Dragon, Orbit Daze and Neptunes Love Liquor Store. Not exactly the peaceful, wave-lapping ideal by which to pitch my tent.

I rode on into the evening, scanning the discordant landscape for a place to spend the night. I had abandoned the idea of trying to find a camp-spot. I felt in need of pampering myself for the first night or so, time to become adjusted, to gather a feel and familiarize myself with these alien environs. But finding a building with a bed was not easy. Apart from the odd neon-named words in English, everything else was in Japanese. In most countries, finding a hotel or motel or pension or hostel or guest house is a fairly straightforward business, the name of the accommodation being displayed on the outside of the building in a generally self-explanatory script. And a hotel tends to look like a hotel, much as a motel does a motel. But here on this shriekingly hectic, *kanji*-covered coast there was nothing remotely hotel-like and, moreover, every building had a disconcerting tendency to resemble every other building: raw and weighty lumps of faceless concrete.

From time to time I would try my luck and dip into one of these modern megaliths, testing the waters should they by chance be the providers of a bed. But they always turned out to be some sort of government administrative building, or prefectural hall, or school, or civic centre, or private office accommodation. At first people in reception would greet my sudden appearance with a look of surprise – a surprise that would rapidly dissipate into a smiling surge of bulleting rat-a-tat-tat questions, none of which I understood, but I pretended I did. Along with a profusion of undoubtedly ill-timed nods I contributed to the conversation by way of offering any Japanese word I had learnt so far. And in any order. Trotting off a steady stream of appallingly pronounced and meaningless sentences such as 'raining hot raw fish toilets sometimes maybe slippers please' (and in that order) is, I know, not normally the way to go about enhancing international relationships but these Japanese, bless them, seemed not to mind in the least. Somehow, among all the pickled slippers, I would manage to convey the point that I was in search of a hotel or similar establishment in which to lay my weary legs.

The word for hotel is *hoteru*, one of hundreds of European words that the Japanese have swallowed and assimilated with relish into their language after introducing an interesting spot of seasoning to suit their palate. Coffee is *kohii*, beer is *biru*, ice cream is *aisu-kuriimu*, cake is *keiki*, cheese is *chiizu*, mushroom is *masshurumu*, rhubarb is *rubabu*, honeydew melon is *honedu meron*, jam is *jamu*, fruit juice is *furutsu jusu*, beefburger is *bifubaaga*, hot dog is *hotto doggu*, curried rice is *kare raisu*, ham and eggs is *hamu eggu*, cup is *koppu*, card is *kado*, wife is *waifu*, shampoo and set is *shanpu setto*, department store is *depaato*, a glass is *garasu*, handkerchief is *hankachifu*, present is *purezento*, handicap is *handikyappu*, toilet (v. important) is *toiret*, necktie is *nekutai*, handbag is *handobaggu*, nonsense is *nansensu*. But just when you find you're getting in the swing of sticking a vowel on to the end of almost any word willy-nilly and hoping for the best, you discover that sexual harassment is *seku hara*, ear is *mimi*, woman is *josei*, bread is *pan*, apple is *ringo* and carrot is *ninjin*.

Discovering I was in search of a *hoteru* gave rise to a bout of convivial debate among the steadily growing crowd of receptionists, cleaners, delivery men, grandmothers and general hangers-on who had gathered to help me. I was miffed how a simple request, however poorly pronounced, could prove so taxing. Surely someone in this crowd knew of a hotel on what was supposedly, however ugly, a portion of coastline favoured by unwinding hard-pressed Tokyoites. Judging from the amount of heads and arms indicating various directions, I surmised that they did know. The only trouble was that this was Japan, where nothing happens (not even the simplest decision) without a protracted discussion in order to attain the much sought-after consensus. A consensus in which the ruffled waters are smoothed, the creased shirts ironed out. In short, a happy harmony in which no faces are lost. End of matter.

At least, it should be the end of the matter. Instead it is only just the beginning of the end of the matter, as now is the time for deliberating on the best route to get me to wherever I am being directed. An elaborate session of map-drawing ensues, everyone eagerly contributing their suggestions of landmarks, quickest route and so forth. Directions are being fast scribbled down in *kanji*, so much so that I haven't the heart to intimate that my grasp of their language (*handobaggu*, *sushi*, ah so, etc.) hasn't yet stretched to their intricate script – a script which, to understand the basics, requires a knowledge of at least 2,000 out of some 50,000 characters, making the English alphabet (in which I still confuse my p's and q's) seem like a piece of *keiki* in comparison.

At last I emerged from the cheery, confabulating cluster of crowds loaded down with offerings of *purezento* (*biru*, *aisukuriimu*, telephone *kado* etc.) and a wonderful wodge of cartography that looked more the sort of thing to frame and hang on the wall than lead me any the closer to a bed.

By now night had fallen, revealing a full neon-free moon that had turned the daytime sullied waters of the ocean into a glorious silver plate. Definitely the time for a spot of sea-viewing. So I pulled over and sat on a large lump of concrete on the beach to admire the shimmering scene. One of the nice things about the dark is that you can't see the dirt, so after a while I stretched out, head on a pillow of Japanese-drawn maps, and allowed another nebulous chunk of time to seep through my bones.

The following night I fared a lot better, having progressed from sleeping on a lump of concrete to sleeping actually inside one – albeit a somewhat larger one, with windows and toilets and baths and futons. And people. Lots of them. All sweeping around in identical plastic slippers and blue-and-white cotton *yukata.* It was a *kokumin* (citizens') *shukusha* (hotel with institutional overtones) which I had stumbled upon quite by chance when stopping near the entrance to refill my water bottles from the hose of a man who was watering the road. As he kindly altered the course of his flow into my three empty orifices, a tour-coach pulled up and ejected its contents of suitcase-clutching middle-aged couples who were sucked through the entrance. This was my first sighting of a troop of potential holiday-makers along this concrete coast. Things were looking up – especially when they were swallowed by the mouth of one of these ubiquitous concrete edifices and, more to the point, looking quite happy about it.

Curiously piqued, I followed in their slipstream, lurking in the shadows of reception until the way was clear. Once the hurly-burly of the coach tour masses had died down and the tourists had dispersed to their rooms, I disentangled myself from my pumps and slipped into the obligatory slippers before slip-slopping over to the front desk to make some enquiries in tentative Japanese. After a few false starts I was informed by a neat, shiny-looking man, pincering a cigarette between his fingers, that, yes, they did have rooms but, no, they had no room.

'*Ippai,*' he appeared to be saying, bowing and smiling apologetically. 'Full.'

'Oh, that's okay,' I said, or at least attempted to say, 'I just thought I'd try on the off-chance,' and gave him a reciprocative bow before retrieving my shoes and walking out. Preparing myself for another night on concrete as opposed to within it, I was on the point of mounting up after a swig of hose-water when, trotting out of reception, came the shiny man looking even shinier.

'Excuse me England lady,' he said in English (after all my struggles in Japanese), 'yes please room.' And then, slightly less urgently, 'Ah, very fine bicycle indeed.'

Surprised by this sudden turn of events, I thanked him for his compliments and trailed back inside with him. After another bout of shoe-untying and slipper-slopping, I fetched up at the desk again. Perplexed.

'Are you sure about this room?' I said. 'I thought you were full.'

'Excuse me please slowly,' he replied. 'My England is not so very understanding.'

'You could have fooled me,' I said. 'It's a whole lot better than my Japanese.' But I repeated my enquiry anyway in slower, clearer mode: 'Are you sure you are not full? Because I thought you were,' I said, carefully enunciating each word but beginning to confuse myself with just exactly what I was trying to say.

'No, maybe not.'

'Ah, I see,' I said, not seeing at all.

'You are one person?' he asked.

I looked around me with searching expression, just to make sure that, yes indeed, I was one person. Plain daft, I know, but I always tend to do this when a man asks me if I am alone and I don't exactly know why he's asking. I think it is because I'm listening to some sort of inner safeguard mechanism, just in case the man who has asked me gives me bad vibes. Weighing up my surroundings gives me a crucial moment for reassessment before breezily replying (should he be a bad onion), 'Oh, no, I've got forty-five burly boyfriends lingering round the corner.' I say you can never be too safe with all your chickens in one basket and an unbolted stable door.

But Mr Shiny looked like a good shallot if ever I saw one, so I said with complete confidence, 'Yes, just one person. And one bicycle.'

'Ah, yes, fine bicycle!'

He was obviously quite taken with my steed, so I said,

'Thank you. You can have a go if you want; we're the same size.' (And not often do I have the pleasure of saying that to a man.)

Although I was quite sincere in my offer, I wasn't in the least expecting him to take me up on it. But surprises are sent to surprise us and, after delivering a bit of rapid verbal to a deferentially nodding woman in an ante-room, he lit another Peace cigarette and took off on my bike for a lap around the car park. Fitted him perfectly.

'Good fit,' I said, when he'd delivered himself back to the entrance beside me.

'No please,' he said, 'I am bad fit. Too many smoke!'

After Mr Shiny had invited me in for a Suntory beer behind the counter with some of his pals, I realized I still hadn't yet established whether or not this Citizen Hotel had a vacancy. Two more beers, a lot of joviality and a few flushed faces later I found myself elevated to a tiny *tatami* room on the second floor. It was about half the size of your average garden shed. But it was luxury and, what's more, it was free. Strange how, in a matter of minutes, this hotel and its 6,800 yen (£45) rooms had gone from being full to issuing vacant and 'no charge' accommodation. A futon was stretched out invitingly. What with that and a low-lying table surrounded by two flat square cushions, there was precious little floor space left. Moving around necessitated a lot of hurdling over and stepping on things.

I like the feeling of being compressed into such a small space; a sort of tent with walls. It makes you utilize and appreciate every bit of space to its full. There are no useless areas like those in a conventional hotel room, such as unappealingly shadowy no-go zones under the bed – a treasure trove for overlooked and unidentifiable objects in transparent plastic bags. And beds are such ungainly and awkward things anyway, jutting out like a landlubber's piers, just asking to be sailed into, tripped over or fallen off.

My room contained no cupboards, no chest of drawers, no chairs and, save for the square fluorescent strip-lamp in the centre of the ceiling, no lights. And unusually, for a country of compulsive viewers, no television. There was a torch, though, fixed to a special bracket on the wall. Odd. I'd never before been to a hotel where a room had been kitted out with a torch and I was drawn impulsively towards it to switch it on. It worked. What's more, it was still there. Having such an easily stealable and useful object fastened to the wall of a hotel room obviously says something about the steadfast honesty of the average Japanese character.

On the table was a round lacquer tray of tea things: one handle-less cup, a wooden saucer, a tin of green leaves with a scoop, a small tea pot with a detachable plastic spout protector, a china saucer with two oriental sweet bean-paste cakes cocooned in wafery-thin paper wrappers, and a damp rolled-up *oshibori* – a cloth for wiping sticky fingers. Standing watch over all this was a stocky-looking thermos that delivered over a litre of piping hot water. On the floor at the head of the futon lay a wide-lipped brown wooden tray containing a perfectly pressed *yukata* with its blue-flecked cloth belt coiled tight like a giant woodlouse, a mustard-yellow towel, a newly cellophane-wrapped white *tenugui* (pronounced tay-nuu-gooey) washcloth bearing a blue *kanji* inscription, and a toothbrush.

In need of a good hose-down after two sticky days in the saddle and a sticky night on concrete, I swept up the ablutionary contents of the tray and slopped off in my slippers down the echoey, school-type corridors in search of a bath. First, though, I needed a toilet. After a few wrong doors I hailed a passing man (wearing an identical *yukata* to the one I had in my arms) on whom I tested out my Japanese for '*Où est la toilette*?' After a few cocked heads and mispronunciations, the man cottoned on pretty quick and led me back down an interminable corridor to a door at the end. As soon as I walked in I was confronted by the sight of a man urinating into a urinal.

'Whoops! sorry,' I said in English and backed out hastily. Funny, I thought: why had the *yukata* man led me to the gents? I tried the neighbouring door in search of the ladies but it was locked. The urinating man now appeared, giving me a quizzical look to which I returned a sorry-didn't-mean-to-catch-you-with-your-pants-down sheepish smile. He disappeared off round the corner and I was still loitering with discontented bladder when the door of the gents opened and out stepped a woman. Things were getting confusing. Was this a womanly-man or a manly-woman or was I just seeing double? Sensing my confusion, the woman set me straight. It was a gents-cum-ladies, so I ventured forth without further ado.

The first thing you do on entering a Japanese toilet is not to relieve yourself but to embark upon an elaborate process of slipper-swopping. As we know, life is never simple and the Japanese make it no simpler by spending half their day diving in and out of assorted footwear. Foreigners must of course follow in their footsteps. On entering most buildings (apart from offices, shops, banks etc.) it is imperative you disembark from your shoes into indoor-only slippers. Encountering any golden-padded fields of *tatami* along the way necessitates socked or de-socked feet only. Confusion arises in the toilet, where it all turns into musical slippers. Here one relieves oneself of one's corridor or carpet slippers for special toilet-only slippers. Sometimes a range of sizes and styles is provided so, depending on the state of urgency of one's water level, one can dither around playing shoeshops to find the right fit. Generally, though, as the average Japanese foot comes in standard size (small), only one choice is provided. This at least keeps things simple in a complicated business. Trouble is, sometimes the ladies slippers seem designed for dolls' feet which results in an ungainly webbed-style foreigner's foot being uncomfortably half-housed at the ball, leaving the heel and sole hanging over the back edge. And when it comes to slippers, it's all share and share alike in Japan, so if perchance you've become enamoured with a particular pair of communal corridor slippers which you have now exchanged for a pair of compulsory toilet slippers, anyone leaving the toilet is quite at liberty to slide away in your personally selected slippers before you've had a chance to retrieve them.

I never really warmed to this toilet-slippering game for two reasons. First, you have to have your wits about you (which I don't tend to have at the best of times, let alone on urgent, bleary-eyed nocturnal missions) when all this complex slipper-swapping can cut a fine line between whether you make it or don't make it to your golden goal. (I hasten to add that I always did, but at times it was a bladder-puncturingly close thing.)

The second reason is that it is a truth universally acknowledged that, when it comes to directional flow, not all men can boast of precise marksmanship. As a result it can be decidedly off-putting, when slipping into a pair of communal toilet slippers from whence a sloppy man has slid out, to discover a slipper's surface bearing witness to an unappetizing splatter. One last but crucial word: it is imperative never to slip up on those slippery matters; toiletry mission concluded, never forget to extricate yourself from toilet-only footwear back into general utility slippers, for to shuffle around in toilet slippers anywhere other than the toilet is tantamount to walking out of the lavatory with your knickers at half-mast.

I found the bathroom a lot more easily than I did the toilet, simply by following the sounds of happy sloshing. By now I had discovered that Japanese *furo* (baths) come in two sizes: either small, deep and private, or large, shallow and public. It's these big, communal ones which prove the most fun and, although most today are segregated, they are still an intriguing place to observe possibly the most important tradition of Japanese life.

Cleanliness is a natural obsession that manifests itself in a rigorous and vigorous daily bout of bathing. This infatuation with such regular long and lengthy soaks has been a solidly entrenched custom in Japan for hundreds of years because of the purification rituals, a paramount tenet of Shintoism (the native religion). The universal preoccupation with bathing dates from the seventh century when the first bath-houses appeared as part of Buddhist temples. Before long the religious habit had become a sensual experience enjoyed for its own sake.

When the first Western missionaries arrived in Japan in 1549, the scrupulously clean and sweet-smelling Japanese found the foreigners' odour to be utterly shocking. The puritanical visitors were equally shocked when they discovered the communal mixed-sex bathing habits of the Japanese. The missionaries, who saw the body as an instrument of the devil, found this Eden-like condition of non-inhibition and unself-consciousness deeply upsetting, running counter as it did to the best of their prudish doctrines. What was the point, they thought, of having a clean body if you've got a dirty mind? Better to smell like us and think pure thoughts. But they had completely misinterpreted the daily ablutions performed by men, women and children in the same public bath who happily washed themselves without prurience or embarrassment. For a while the missionaries did their best to prohibit mixed-sex bathing, but the Japanese, made of cleaner and more sensible stuff, felt that they'd had enough of being pushed around by these imperiously squeamish foreigners and kicked them out of their country.

The missionaries had blown it; and just when things had started so well, giving Japan a period of prosperous relations with the West as well as in neighbouring Asia. So, just under a century after the first Westerners (Portuguese) set foot on the Rising Land, the Japanese feudal rulers slammed shut their doors in 1639, bringing about a self-imposed quarantine that, apart from the odd chink in Nagasaki, hermetically sealed the country off from the outside world for over 200 years. The Japanese had a straightforward and effective way of dissuading any cocky foreigners from trying their luck at breaking the seal – they simply whipped off their heads with their swords. The same sort of rather unpleasant treatment awaited any foreign-tainted Japanese trying to return to their homeland after living abroad and also any Japanese trying to leave Japan. So, with those piously humdrum killjoys out of the way, the Japanese could once again lie back and soak up the blissful pleasures of mixed-sex bathing without being made to feel either guilty or sinful about it.

During these two centuries of deep hibernating isolation, in which the rest of the world felt that Japan had fallen asleep, if not completely off the edge of the world, the Japanese were in fact having a pretty good time. In spite of the fact that it was a period of repression and dictatorship under the firm tutelage of the shogunate military rulers, it was also a rich interval of peace and consolidation that gave them the opportunity of cultivating their popular art, literature and drama (*kabuki, noh*), tea ceremony, martial arts etc., developing their culture into one of the most distinctive in the world.

But an isolated Japan also fell technologically far behind the West. When, in 1853, the United States sent Commodore Perry and his navy of 'Black Ships' to knock sharply on Japan's closed doors with the object of bringing the 'nonsense of seclusion' to an end, the Japanese were thrown into confused consternation as they realized their feebly equipped defences were no match for Perry's steam-powered fleet. What's more, Japan had heard word of China's humiliating surrender after the First Opium War – sobering news that only reinforced their fears of the greater powers of the West and filled the Japanese government with a mood of sombre caution.

Perry made his demands known, saying that he thought it was high time Japan opened up shop. Giving them a few months to cogitate on this idea, he said he would be back the following year with a much stronger force to receive their answer. He then left to winter in Hong Kong. When Perry returned to Japan in 1854 he found little inclination to resist American demands. However refined its arts and however sophisticated its institutions might be, Japan realized it faced a fearsome prospect and was not able to compete with either Western military or economic technology. Also, the Japanese were by now well aware that far larger and apparently stronger Asian lands, such as India and China, had already been forced to bow to Western rule, or at least to semi-colonial domination. Eventually, Japan signed the Friendship and Commercial Trade Treaty that America had pressed upon it, opening up the country to diplomatic relations and preparing the Japanese for the shock of revealing themselves to the outside world.

Despite their reservations, the Japanese negotiators could not conceal the fact that they were mightily impressed with American technology. Before leaving for home, Commodore Perry, feigning an ingratiating appeasement, played a sort of game with the Japanese rulers in which he impressed them with a few of his 'toys': a model train that puffed its way around a track and an ingenious device with which Perry demonstrated how it was possible to send messages along pieces of wire. These Japanese 'warriors', who had had such a peaceful time over the past 200 years that they had taken up *ikebana* (the traditional art of flower arrangement) for amusement while much of the rest of the world waged war, felt that playing at trains and telephones was a piece of the pie they could well do with dipping their fingers into.

What with the legacy of the Industrial Revolution and all their fancy technology, the visitors from the self-professed 'developed world' found it difficult to perceive Japan as anything other than backward, however obliging and cordial its people and customs. Lengthy ceremonies in praise of tea were all very well but where, after all, were the imposing symbols, signs and structures that the cities of Europe and America were beginning to take for granted? Where were the bridges and viaducts, lightning conductors, cannons, steamships and (iron) towers that the Western engineers had made possible? Where were the trains and railway tracks that now cut great swathes across Europe and North America?

Six years after the treaty was signed, the first Japanese embassy was sent to Washington. Photographs still survive from this mission which show the Japanese ambassadors, dressed in their samurai finery, posing with a posse of formally jacketed, trousered and capped American naval officers. The Japanese, resplendent in kimonos, divided skirts, split-toed socks, shaved scalps and topknots and each wearing two swords, create an image that looks wildly outlandish compared with the somewhat staid and drearily clad Americans.

Western technology had hit the Japanese in such a rush that misunderstandings were inevitable. While visiting New York in the summer of 1860 the Japanese ambassadors acquired quite a taste for champagne. On one occasion they were much taken aback on discovering lumps of ice floating in their drinks. They couldn't fathom how ice could be procured in America, especially at the height of the summer.

There was further confusion in their hotel rooms when they discovered chamber-pots under their beds. Much baffled, they wondered what use could be made of such curious receptacles. It was only after extensive discussion that they finally agreed these peculiar objects must be special helmet-type pillows enabling them, while sleeping, to preserve their elaborate samurai top-knotted hairstyles.

By abandoning seclusion, Japan's shogun government in Edo (Tokyo) became embroiled in domestic political wrangling from which it was unable to extricate itself. In 1868 the conflict finally came to a head with a short, sharp civil war that resulted in the collapse of the government and restored the emperor back into the hot seat of the 'Chrysanthemum Throne' – a position which granted fourteen-year-old Mutsuhito (the new Heavenly God) power as an absolute and divine ruler. And so began the Meiji era (1868–1912), a period of huge change for Japan. The Japanese recognized that the 'foreign barbarians', with their technical and military superiority, were not going to go away, being far too strong to be pushed around let alone pushed out. They therefore set themselves a 'great national goal' that was simply 'to catch up with the West'. They embarked upon this goal with great zeal, cheerfully discarding the superfluous parts of their own 'primitive' culture and hurriedly embracing the curious (and often highly uncomfortable) accessories of Western civilization – including Western clothes, Western music and ballroom dancing. They even permitted the Gregorian calendar to be used alongside the traditional Chinese lunar–solar one. Japan's eagerness to learn during the last thirty years of the nineteenth century contrasted starkly with the pride and stubborn adherence to tradition that characterized China during the same period.

Although they had lacked the West's scientific advances, the Japanese were spared the humiliation and exploitation of colonialism. They may have lived a blinkered and ill-informed existence (as far as life outside their land's sealed doors was concerned) but they survived with pride and national integrity intact.

Japan's way of thinking seemed to be: well, if we've got to work with these 'foreign devils', we might as well have the best. Not a people for half measures, the Japanese chose, with scrupulous care, the most appropriate Western teacher for each subject. With a typically avid ability for learning fast, they made model students and before long they knew how to build a modern army and navy, a railway network and a textile industry and how to create an education system, a code of law and a solid constitution.

No country in history had experienced such a rapid and drastic transformation. At one point in their initial dire attempts to repel Commodore Perry's 'black ships', the Japanese had called out the fire brigade in the belief that a hefty shaking of firebells should be sufficient to deter and intimidate the Americans; within a few decades they had gained two victories in war against gigantic opponents – China in 1895 and Czarist Russia in 1905. (Incidentally these war 'successes' amazed the world, not only because Japan won, but also because of the civilized way in which the Japanese treated prisoners and civilians – a striking contrast to their behaviour in the Second World War.) Feeling like cocky conquistadors with their surprisingly easy victories, they then tore their way into Manchuria, Korea and Taiwan, where they proceeded to rule in a tough and brazenly arrogant 'European' manner.

But back on home ground there were plenty of Japanese who still felt that their country should never have opened itself up to the outside world and remained suspicious of the species from which the foul-smelling Westerners had descended. A bunch of anti-foreign fanatics in Kyoto warned people to preserve their land, sacred to the descendants of the gods, from being defiled by the barbarians, who were 'the offspring of dogs and cats'. (This was due to a group of Japanese scholars earlier in the nineteenth century who were earnestly deliberating whether the Dutch – the only Westerners then available for inspection in a tiny chink of Nagasaki – lifted their leg Fido-fashion in order to urinate.) These 'canine and feline offspring' were equally puzzled by the seemingly inscrutable orientals. Kipling expressed this most clearly when he wrote in 1900:

> The Chinaman's a native . . . but the Japanese isn't a native, and he isn't a sahib either.

Misunderstandings and misinterpretations. Where would we be without them?

When those pontificating missionaries and savants had expressed horror and shock on learning of the morally contaminating mixed-bathing tendencies of the Japanese, they had goaded the Meiji rulers (who were eager to bow in deference to the foreign spirit of the times) into taking remedial measures. The bath-houses (*sento*) were fitted up with 'his 'n' hers' entrances, giving the appearance of well-ordered separate-sex propriety. This, however, was where the segregation ceased. Once inside, the bathing area had indeed been divided into two areas but not quite in the way the missionaries had envisaged. In order to keep both the government and their customers happy the wily bath-house owners had simply suspended a piece of string across the middle of the bath. Amidst the hot and steamy atmosphere, the clean and sloshing bodies continued to follow the enjoyable traditions of association that suited them best.

There were no strings attached in the bath of the 'Citizens Hotel'. I passed beneath the *noren* (blue banner-style curtains at the entrance), slid open the sliding door and stepped into a small changing-room full of women laughing and chatting in various states of undress. They all bid me a cheery good evening but, as I shed my clothes into an empty pink plastic wicker basket stacked on a shelf, I felt quizzical eyes watching me with interest. Into this basket I also put, as everyone else had done, my *yukata* and towel, and picked up my *tenugui*. One more sliding door later and I had entered a sauna-like atmosphere of heat and steam billowing from the big kidney-shaped bath – more swimming pool than tub. A stone lion's head, the size of a sumo wrestler's fist, protruded from the wall and from its drooling mouth flowed a steady stream of scalding water. Sitting, crouching or floating in this pool-bath were six or seven women of various ages and dimensions, all engaged in some form of desultory discussion punctuated by bursts of raucous laughter.

Both of the walls leading from the bath were lined with a row of knee-high mirrors in front of which, perched on small, oblong plastic stools, were more women washing themselves or, in some cases, each other with earnest enthusiasm. Below each mirror were two pressure-releasing push-button taps. The washing women were busily filling plastic basins (taken from a pile stacked up in the corner) with a comfy mix of push-button hot and push-button cold water and then emptying the contents over their heads. By now I knew enough about Japanese bathing procedures to appreciate that marching straight from bath entrance to bath without first giving myself a proper sluicing would be as bad as spitting in the soup – disgusting, disgraceful behaviour. Definitely not the done thing.

For a moment I hovered in the doorway and surveyed the ablutionary scene. I swayed, feeling uneasily conspicuous and, although only among women, ridiculously English-shy. After the initial surprise of finding a lily-white skin in their midst, the women, in one way or another, rallied round to put me at my ease. Those steeping in the bath called out good-humoured words of welcome. One passed me her soap, another her stool. Yet another, a rather formidable creature of late middle years, laughed (not unkindly) at the shocking great bicycle-chain oil-stain ingrained on my inner right calf and, in a comical charade that had everyone in a fit of giggles, enthusiastically set about scrubbing it off for me. Never one to act my age, I soon got into the swing of things and, playing up to the fact that I was just a plain dumb foreigner, shaped my flannel into a rather fetching Tarzan-style loin-cloth and plonked an upturned plastic basin in jaunty style upon my head. More shrieks of laughter. This, I decided, after my initial misgivings, was turning into an unusual and clean form of fun.

Having vigorously scrubbed away my unsightly oil-stain, along with what felt like half my leg, the woman, with breasts swinging like pendulums threatening to knocker me flat, now set upon my back. Never before have I had my back scrubbed like this woman scrubbed it. I wasn't sure whether to laugh or cry. Using not so much a nail brush as a brush of nails, she ruthlessly worked her way down from my shoulders and across my blades using a circular scraping motion. Skin follicles which had seen me through since birth were being shed at such forceful speed that I feared any moment her scrubbing hand would come straight out the other side. But by the time she had reached my coccyx I was in such a pleasurable-painful state that I no longer cared. Tears pricked my eyes – tears fortunately camouflaged by a copious flow of water and suds.

By the time my skin-removing scraper had finished with me, I felt as if I had been left with the cat in the washing machine for a week, used as a test scouring-pad and dragged ten times through the local car wash. But this is the Japanese way. Only when de-follicled, and with every last trace of soap and bubble of suds rinsed from skin, is it then permissible to enter the scalding bath to be boiled alive.

The Japanese like their baths ferociously hot – anything from 35–60°C (95–140°F). The secret for entering such a fiery cauldron, I discovered, was not to hover on the edge and test the water with a tentative toe (as I was wont to do) but to plunge straight in and sit ram-rod still, up to the neck, without moving; for to flinch even slightly is to cause a flurry of water that scalds the skin. And there you sit, slowly cooking, turning lobster-livid red – a colour, incidentally, that the Japanese refer to as 'boiled octopus'. The searing heat seemed to shrivel my heart. Breathing faltered, then dimmed. My head turned giddy, ready to explode. A mere five minutes dunking, compared with the twenty or more endured by the locals, was quite enough for me and I dragged myself out, a red-wrecked cindering coal.

There was much joviality among my bathing and body-scrubbing companions. As some matronly, flabby fat forms flapped around me in a kindly effort to cool me down, they laughed and joked, calling me the Honourable Boiled Octopus while pouring basins of deliciously cold and revitalizing water over my raw and florid form.

The Japanese attitude to bathing is similar to that of the French to eating, the Spanish to bull-fighting and the Scots to kilt-wearing and caber-tossing; they do it with a heady mix of know-how and gay physical abandon. Bathing is a ritual which is just as much a way of relaxing and mixing socially as getting clean. Of course, a bath can be enjoyed alone and well over half the people in Japan now have their own private bathing facilities in their homes, but they still go out to visit the neighbourhood *sento*, not only for the all-together sharing of such a purely physical and sensual pleasure that rejuvenates both mind and body, but also to keep up with the latest gossip while scrubbing a neighbour's back.

Life in Japan revolves around rigid conformity where

individuals are generally brought up to sacrifice personal feelings and expression rather than fight against the flow of happy harmony. The priority of maintaining external appearances while suppressing internal differences is a value inculcated since birth. Virtually the only public place where people can shake off the shackles of such inflexible compliance is in the bath-house. Here the barriers are down. To shed ones clothes is to shed the constraints of the mind and, for a while, tongues and feelings can run free.

Swaddled in my standard-issue *yukata* I sloped off back to my room, clutching the remains of a body that hadn't (actually) been washed down the drain. Contrary to the desired effect after a Japanese bath, I felt drugged. Whereas, at home, a bath is for sloshing, singing and dozing off in, the purpose of a Japanese bath is quite the opposite. One of the main objectives of being immersed in such fiercely hot water is for it to jolt you awake so you leap out bright eyed and ruddy bummed, ready and raring to go.

After such a skin-shedding scalding, the only place I was raring to go was bed. Heroically I managed to summon just enough energy to wash out the sweaty residue from my particulars, hang them to dry from a bungee and eat a seaweedy *nori*-wrapped riceball before flopping on the futon, mindlessly steaming. To add to the excitement, I flipped on my radio and tuned in to the first English-speaking station I could find – Radio Australia: 'you can estimate a 'gator's size by the distance from his snout to his eyes. Whatever that is in inches is what length the 'gator will be in feet . . .' Ah so, *desuka*? And then I fell asleep.

CHAPTER 7

Of Tunnels and Tides

The following morning I awoke to find my radio still on and my skin still quietly smouldering, but at least an inkling of energy had returned. I was in the midst of packing up my bike when I heard a light flutter of footsteps behind me and a cheery '*Ohayo gozaimasu*!' I turned, pannier still in hand, to see a young woman in khaki shorts and sandals tapping her way across the tarmac towards me.

'*Ohayo gozaimasu*!' I replied, finding the words a bit too much of a mouthful first thing in the morning. Fortunately my tongue-tying trials with the language ended there for the moment, as the next thing the woman said was in English.

'You are, I am believing, a citizen of Great Britain on bicycle travelling?'

I confirmed that, yes, her statement was indeed correct.

'That is very great.'

'Thank you,' I said, thinking it would be even more great if I could actually get moving instead of being lost in baths and theatre walls and Tokyo.

'My name,' she informed me, 'is Meguni Kimizuka.'

'Hello, Meguni,' I said and then, rather idiotically, as I couldn't think of anything else to say owing to the fact I was still feeling a bit hot: 'Nice name.' Obviously my conversational skills had been washed down the drain along with half my skin.

Smiling, Meguni bravely persevered: 'Do you know can't belly England?'

'I'm sorry?' I said.

'Do you know can't belly England?'

'Do I know can't belly England?' I repeated slowly, brow furrowed. 'I'm sorry, I'm a bit slow. Do you mind saying it again?'

Still smiling angelically and, quite unruffled by my tardy uptake, Meguni said, 'Do you know can't-a-belly England?'

'Can't-a-belly England?' I said, wishing that I'd listened to my father and stayed on to take A-levels. 'Can't-a-belly?'

And then the dim spark registered a faint recognition. 'Oh, Canterbury!' I said, trying not to sound too jubilant. 'Do I know it? Well, not exactly. I've cycled through it about twice. It's got an impressive cathedral. Why?'

'I was for six month Can't-a-belly family exchange. I am having here very many happy memory.'

In my handlebar bag I had a small map of the UK and Ireland that I'd ripped from last year's diary. I dug it out and we sat on a pannier each, with the map on Meguni's white knees, for a spot of geographical name spotting. Along with Can't-a-belly she was familiar with Brighton (beach), London (Fortnum and Mason, Burberrys and Big Ben) and Liverpool (Beatles, of course).

We sat for a little while longer, chatting generally. Meguni lived in Chiba-city and was on 'one day vacation for beach-tanning'.

The beach, incidentally, was no great shakes – a dirty-grey and littered sand interspersed with large chunks of concrete and a couple of derelict warehouses with smashed windows. The weather fared no better – a murky and heavy humidity, threatening rain. But for 'beach-tanning' the weather is of no concern in Japan. What is important is the date. Today was the first of June, a day that signalled the onset of sun-worshipping time, even if there was no sun to be seen. In Japan the changing seasons are not seen as stages in the year that somnolently merge into each other, but are demarcated with a ritual precision that deeply influences the lives of most Japanese, including even the most urbanized soul. Their attitudes tend to be more ritualistic than realistic, their eye on the calendar rather than the actual weather. So, even if May has proved hot and cloudless (as it often is), you just don't go and lie on the beach because . . . well, it's not June and to lie on the beach in May is not the done thing because it's not officially summer. Nor in theory should you wear a short-sleeved shirt before the legitimate date . . . so, you don't do it. That's how Japan works. Precisely.

Before we went our separate ways, Meguni gave me a telephone card (worth £6) with a photograph of a puppy in a basket that bore the words PEACEFUL LOVE SCENE across the top, and four plain postage-paid (for Japan) postcards.

'Small *purezento,*' she said, handing me her address. 'Please to visit me. See you!' and then she was off, scampering across the car park to meet a pack of girl friends for a grey day of beach-tanning.

Now that I'd found the sea, I didn't really have a good excuse to get lost any more as my plan was to follow the coast south around the Boso-hanto Peninsula. Route 128 was the sort of road that is insensitively deceptive: on the map it leads you (or at least me) to believe that it will be an attractive, meandering route, clinging to the coast. Reality, as reality so often is, was another story – a story that unfolded through superhighways and not so super cities, clogged with trucks and cars and gaudy *pachinko* parlours and Japanized-Americanized fast-food joints. Very loud, very brash, very ugly. Very modern Japan, really.

The weather continued hot, clammy and oppressive, the sky so heavy that the weight of it produced a perpetual headache. Apart from the garish eye-jolting splashes of neon, everything else seemed to reflect the greyness of the sky: the sea, the beach, the concrete, the roads, the land, even my effusively sweating skin looked drearily ashen-laced; like dead meat, gone off.

To add to this happy scene I came across something that rates, along with ten-ton trucks, dogs and flashers, as my least favourite occupational hazard when it comes to cycling: tunnels. To plummet into a tunnel is to plummet into a nightmare; sucked into a giant black rectum of toxic effluvium – a murderous miasma of exhaust, of blundering into unseen damp-dripping walls. Tunnels are places to fall into, a death-dark abyss that has you blinded by the searching eyes of oncoming vehicles; to be crushed against sharp, wet walls or under wheels of thundering trucks; to be deafened, lost alone with only the sound of rats at your feet; to smell stench and fear. Your fear. Tunnels: dark shafts that burrow into an excavation of past recollection. A passage of time, of memory, of bleak penetrating experience. Not pleasant places, are tunnels.

Japan is a land of tunnels. A nation of moles. Dig it. Dig this. Dig that. Anything big in the way? Don't go over it. Go through it. Blow a hole. Blow a mountain. Blow a seabed. It blows your mind. No obstruction is too big or too small. Put on a helmet. Pick up a spade. And dig, dig, dig – until you see the light. But is it the light at the end of the tunnel or at the beginning? Ask Zen. He'll know because he knows who is walking towards you.

Had I known that Japan was tunnel-mad I think I would have made sure I found New Zealand. But there again, as I discovered on that first encounter with a Japanese tunnel, perhaps they weren't such fearful holes of horror after all. What's this? Beginning to see the light? But it's a light neither at the beginning nor at the end. It's on the roof – a legion of light. Praise be! I can see!

Japan has money, so Japan lights its tunnels, which lightens my way and lightens my mind. Sometimes it even gives preferential treatment to pedallers and pedestrians. That first tunnelling day I passed through twenty-one tunnels, some long, some not so long. Some directed cyclists to veer off course at the entrance to join a separate vehicle-free tunnel, like a big tube for walkers and wheelers. Some were brand-new . . . spanking clean, posing as art galleries with murals of marine life. No graffiti. No dripping. No rats. Friendly places – with jangling bicycles, people stopping to chat, children playing. Strange. In the space of one day my long-held view of tunnels had swung full circle. They were, I decided, perhaps not such formidable places after all.

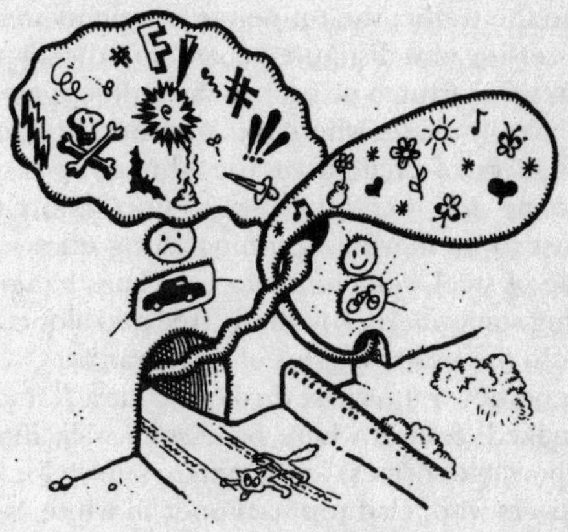

I rolled on south and passed paddling surfers bobbing on a grey flat-swell sea. Others carried their boards up the beach past frail old women collecting seaweed in baskets and sacks, hauled on their crooked backs. I sat on a sea-wall eating a lunch of tinned tuna and rice and bananas and watched them. They wore kerchiefs tied in a knot under their chins, with large conical hats and *jikatabi* (the traditional split-toed boots) and worn expressions. They never looked up. They couldn't look up. They looked only at the sea or pools or muddy sand around their feet. Mostly they worked alone but occasionally one would stop to help another load her basket upon her back. Slowly they trudged back up the beach, up the boat ramp, to spread the seaweed on the concrete quay to dry (if such a thing were possible) in the humid grey-skied sun. How long had they been doing this? All their lives? Had they been collecting the weeds of the sea as Japan grew and changed and forever expanded around them? Had they watched this once small fishing village expand into a chunk of America – a neon-lit, fast-food highway – while lean-limbed surfing boys in $2,000 wet-suits stepped nonchalantly from their CD-booming Toyotas and Nissans over the old women's weedy pickings? Probably.

Despite the traffic, the tunnels, the weighty weather, the unprepossessing and disfigured coast, and the all-pervading grey, it was wonderful to be back in the saddle again. It always is. Doesn't really matter where you are – nothing can seem to quash the surge of excitement, the edifying rush of adrenalin, the rising *doki doki* flutterings of uncertainty that filter within. Just to be moving, spinning along on a simple but useful pile of steel, your home in four bags hanging on all sides, going somewhere, anywhere, free and alone, sends me soaring into the heady heights of exuberance.

I spun on down the coast through Ohara (famous for its annual 'naked' festival where fishermen walk into the sea carrying portable shrines) and Onjuku, known for its '*ama*' – women divers who, clad top to flipper in white, resemble a marine version of the Ku Klux Klan (albeit substituting spectral witch's hat with a more practical balaclava) and, clutching burning torches at night, dive for abalone, lobster and other shellfish.

Then came a couple of tourist coach-trip hot-spots. Namegawa Island, which is not actually an island at all but a holiday complex of hotel and seaside villas surrounded by jungle-type animals – monkeys and guinea-fowl in a semi-tropical setting and where (so the brochure says) 'flamingoes and peacocks dance for you'. Sounds nice. And Kamogawa Sea World, starring those majestic beauties from the deep and natural world – dolphins, killer whales and Arctic beluga – performing not-so-natural stunts in not-so-natural settings.

I rode on, passing a small concrete and corrugated-iron dwelling, its front garnished with the skeletal remains of a white transit van that had been transformed into a greenhouse of glorious flowering abundance – the beauty within the beast. Nearby I stopped to replenish water supplies at a food shop curiously called 'Meet and Delica' which, presuming from its contents, was just the Japanese shortened and misspelt version of meat and delicatessan. The man behind the counter not only refilled my bottles but also thoroughly washed them out first, scrubbing the lids and enthusiastically rubbing them off with a drying cloth until they looked new. Seemingly all part of the service. Then he reached down into his refrigerated glass cabinet and, with a big smile, handed me two fried fish (species unknown) and a can of iced tea. On the house.

Route 128 continued across the peninsula but it was at this point that I could at last turn off on to a quiet and narrow-winding road that my tourist leaflet defined as the Boso Flowerline. This was more like it: small villages with slightly crooked houses made partially of wood. A profusion of vegetable gardens, all adorned with some bent octogenarian form working away, weeding or planting. Children playing in the street. Small squares of paddy fields. More *obaasan* (grandmotherly old women) pushing their blue pram-trolleys – some filled with shopping from tiny, dark, family-run stores, or with vegetables freshly plucked from their own gardens. Fishing nets, like giant spiders' webs, hung drying from upstairs windows or clung to fences and walls; they were even draped across the odd van or pick-up, camouflaging it in drag and fish-net stockings. More rice paddies, terraced towards the sweeping backdrop of high, densely forested hills.

Then, after days of steadily growing heavy grey weather, a drop fell . . . then another and another, exploding on impact. They smelt and felt delicious. As I pulled over under a thick umbrella-tree to put on my jacket, a little old granny shuffled towards me with her trolley, a brolly fixed to a metal bar that acted as a spare arm, leaving both hands free for pushing. As she passed me I bid her a cheery '*Konnichiwa*!' She rolled her head ninety degrees, looking a little startled, and kept on pushing. Moments later she performed a perambulating U-turn and returned to hand me a bunch of her earthy carrots freshly picked from her plot. She then reached for my arm and held it for a moment between her small fragile hands (like birds' feet) saying something that I didn't understand. She smiled a toothless smile; then, with a touching little nod of the head, she was gone.

By now the drops were dropping in earnest, coupled with a whipping wind. Out to sea sheet lightning flickered across the sky like a broken strip light, the thunder gradually shattering the sound of the wind in my ears as it steadily engulfed me. The narrow road turned into a rushing rivulet which had me aquaplaning on corners. By the time I'd passed Nojimazaki lighthouse and arrived at Tateyama Youth Hostel, I was well and truly soaked. Although it was only two o'clock I decided to call it a day as I fancied having shelter from the storm and somewhere to dry out, and the likelihood of finding anything cheaper within the next four hours before nightfall was very small. But, like most hostels, this one was closed from 10 a.m. to 4 p.m.

As I was already wet, I walked down to the beach, a mere skipping-stone's throw from the hostel. The sand, like most of the sand I'd seen, was dull and greyish and dirty. I kicked my way through the usual detritus of styrofoam, worn tyres, smashed bottles, rusty cans and cigarette packets and stood on a rock, bracing myself against a buffeting wind that tugged at my hood, ballooning my jacket. I scrunched up my face against the fiercely driving salt-laced rain and gazed out to sea like an old sea-dog. There is something immeasurably pleasurable about standing at the edge of the ocean in the teeth of a gale, especially when you know you're not going to have to wrestle with the weather to put up a flappable tent.

At three o'clock the hostel's owner, Yokoo-*san*, returned and, recognizing a bedraggled cyclist when he saw one, let me in an hour early. He lived there with his wife, who spoke a little English. 'Bath time is five o'clock,' she said. I wanted to get in there straight away to clean up and dry up but, in Japan, rules are not for breaking. Instead, I sat on a wet rump writing my diary and browsing through some of the hostel's books.

The place was pleasantly empty. Just me and Mr and Mrs Yokoo shuffling back and forth with piles of sheets in their arms. At five o'clock precisely I was stewing nicely in a pre-run piping hot bath and, ten minutes later, still wallowing, I heard the voice of Mrs Yokoo call from the corridor, 'Miss English, your bath is pleasing for taking now.'

By evening an angst-ridden young man had arrived, looking wet and unhappy, but, apart from hearing him slurping some noodles, I never saw him again. I was beginning to think I would have the dorm to myself when through the door walked Mieko, a young, dazzling, sylph-like beauty with long, raven-black hair. At first she was very shy, moving timidly about the room like a mouse, unpacking her bag and folding her clothes with infinite care and precision. When I offered her a pack of crisps she looked so momentarily stunned that I thought she was going to keel over, but happily she accepted it and her reserve began to thaw. She knew a few words of English but she spoke them in tones of such muted twitterings that I missed much of what she said. The most I could grasp was that she lived in Funabashi City (skirting Tokyo) and was off to Nanbo Paradise in the morning to see the famous flower nurseries with their extensive hothouses containing tropical plants, insects, birds and butterflies and 'Singapore Lion'.

Then she said, 'I love ballet ball.'

'Ballet ball?' I said, visualizing a team of tutu-clad players pirouetting around a football pitch.

'Yes, ballet ball I play one time in one month with many friend. Fine sport.'

Ballet ball, I realized, was not some form of choreographed football but was in fact volleyball. My confusion had arisen from my inability to distinguish between the way that most Japanese pronounce their V's and B's: to a Western ear they sound much the same.

Then, conversation over, Mieko lay back on her mattress and went to sleep, her face looking rigid and cold, like marble. I climbed on to my bunk, hooked into my mini-headphones and plugged in my radio – volume down, a twiddle of a knob. First stop was FEN, with two twangy stateside accents in the process of giving the Japanese an English lesson.

'Hi, you look great!'

'Wow, you look great too!'

'Haven't seen you for ages.'

'No, I'm living in Hawaii now.'

'Wow, where's the Opera?'

'Where's the Opera?'

'Hey, glad you could make it. Heard you been living in Hawaii. Like it?'

'Love it.'

'Seen Lenny lately?'

'He's here.'

'Hi, you look great!'

'You look grapefruit too!'

'I've lived in Hawaii for 800 years.'

'Like it?'

'Love it.'

Help! Save me! Knob twiddle. VOA: '. . . on average women cry five times a month compared to men, who only cry once'. I thought back to when I last cried but I fell asleep before I could remember. Probably just as well.

During the night an intruder with an umbrella made from the woodier parts of a carrot ran out from an unlit tunnel, smashed through the window, jumped on my bunk and, hissing menacingly, tried to throttle me with a long, strong strand of seaweed. I awoke from my dream with a start to find my neck tightly entangled in the wire of my frequency-distorted, whirring-sounding headphones and a raging gale banging and tearing at the window.

By morning the decidedly tempestuous conditions were still clamouring angrily against the panes. When I pressed my face close up to the glass all I could see of the sea was a melodramatic morass of dark and furious frothing waves detonating on the rocks in a spumescent show of wrath. The bleak, monotone sky had fallen low enough to join forces with the ocean, fusing as one to intensify its force. Back on my bunk I tuned into FEN just in time to catch the weather report, in which some annoyingly chirpy I'm-dry-in-here voice informed me that the goings-on outside the window were the tail end of a typhoon. *Arigato gozaimasu* – thank you, I thought. Just the sort of news I really needed for a sunny day's cycle.

Not one to be (completely) put off by a spot of wet and wind, I tugged on my well-worn waterproof gear (held together in places by gaffer-tape) and, harking back to the words of Ted Hughes ('There's no such thing as bad weather, only inappropriate clothing'), I made ready to do battle with the inclement elements.

Mieko watched me pack up my bike, asking questions like: Are you lonely? Answer: Not yet. Why don't you take the train? Answer: Because I like being outside (even in a gale) and a bike is more flexible and because there is less chance of knowing where you're going or where you're going to be and more chance of meeting the unexpected. Do you like Japanese food? Answer: So far. Can you use *hashi* – chopsticks? Answer: In a cack-handed sort of way, but I can manage as long as I've got time on my hands. Every now and then Mieko released a mellifluous resonance of extended ahhhhhs, emanating from deep in the throat before flowing like velvet up across the roof of her mouth and out to meet the ear. To me, these punctuations of speech signified a fusion of apprehension and incomprehension – a sort of safety-valve way of not giving offence. Then, along with her address and offers to come and stay, she handed me a 'typical Japanese purse' of comely shape and size, so small that it wouldn't have looked out of place in a doll's house. Mieko said it was for holding a spare set of earrings or a ring. As my jewellery collection doesn't extend much further than the pair of £1.99 silver sleepers *circa* 1991 that I bought from Ratners before it went bankrupt for selling what the director Gerald Ratner called 'crap', I used it instead for keeping safe a form of bicycle 'jewellery': a spare set of quarter-inch Campagnolo bottom bracket ballbearings – far more attractive and far more valuable than anything I'd ever worn in my ears.

I left Mieko about to catch the bus to her Butterfly Paradise and, with promises I would write getting lost on the wind, set off to try to find the ferry across the bay for Kurihama.

The weather was just the sort of weather that is so bad that it is enjoyable. Rain smacking against my face impaired my vision which, along with a furious wind that tossed me in buffeting gusts across the road, made for some eventful mountainous descents. At one point I remember just grabbing sight of a small hotel called 'Dear Friends – est. 1993' before plummeting somewhat out of control down a hillside.

Veering off unexpectedly, I detoured along a road called the 'Daiichi Flowerline' which, judging from the number of pylons marching through the hills, would have been more aptly named the 'Daiichi Powerline'. But these soon petered out, or at least the low-lying cloud level made sure they did, and the quiet, narrow road turned into a very pleasant ride to Cape Sunosaki (the very tip of the big toenail of

Chiba's foot) where waves sheeted across my path, thoroughly soaking me. By that stage, being wet doesn't really matter any more because, as you couldn't be wetter if you tried, you stop worrying about trying to plug the leaky spots in your shoes and start really enjoying the weather for what it is: appalling. To feel a pool of water tipping like the tide from heel to toes within your shoes is a pleasantly horrible sensation.

The fun ended when I rejoined the main road – Route 127 – at Tateyama City and was thrown back into the chaos of narrow roads clotted with churning streams of traffic.

I took a brief respite from the weather by sloshing around Odoya supermarket in search of affordable sustenance but instead only succeeded in scaring some children. I scared myself too when I caught sight of my reflection in the mirror above the bamboo shoot and beansprout department. Sodden, bedraggled, held together by gaffer-tape and with mini oil-slicks streaking down my cheeks (a result of scratching myself after touching my bicycle chain), I looked far worse than something the dog had brought in after the cat had chewed on it.

My condition was to deteriorate further when I continued up the coast along what rates as perhaps my least favourite cycling road of all time (along with the Esher bypass). For nearly fifteen miles it was almost one continuous tunnel – not the consumer-friendly sort of the east coast but truly nightmarish holes of blackness in which a non-stop procession of exhaust-churning dumper trucks crumpled me into the sides. Where the rain and sea had sprayed and pounded through the vent holes, collecting in the deep chasms and ruts of the road, the trucks sent filthy waves washing over me. How fast emotions can change on a bike! From a wonderful primal excitement a few hours before, when I relished whatever the weather threw at me, I had now plunged into a hateful state of revulsion, shrieking a tirade of colourful language at every filthy truck that passed and at every rut-roaded tunnel that engulfed me.

But that's another tantalizing thing about cycling: instead of travelling in a state of stagnancy such as is often the case in a car, bus or train in which you only see rather than feel what you're passing through, a bicycle is so much a physical form of transport that it instigates a wild assortment of powerfully emotive feelings which lift you up one minute and throw you down the next, hurling you along on a roller-coaster journey of see-sawing emotion. Variation not only keeps you awake – it keeps you alive.

I finally emerged from the last of the tunnels in an utterly terrible mood; a mood in which I hated everything: me, my bike, the tunnels, the trucks, the weather, the roads, the traffic, Japan. My veins protruded, pumping blue murder through a pent-up chest, piercingly tight, inwardly imploding. I was in a right old tizz. The last straw to make me shove my head through my spokes would be, having arrived in Kanaya, to find that there was no ferry and being forced instead to ride up the jammed and tunnelled coast into and through the concrete neon-clad mire of suburban Tokyo.

Fortunately, my spokes were spared. I arrived at the quayside just in time to find the ramp of the ferry being raised and the boat ready to sail. I'd missed it by a dragon's breath, or so I thought. A man wearing a walkie-talkie and white gloves, noticing my water-logged, filthy-faced looks of dismay, scampered up to me, smiling.

'Kurihama?' he asked.

'*Hai* – yes,' I said.

He shouted something very rapidly into his radio and the mouth of the ferry began to open.

'Please,' he said, 'this way. Please take care. It is wet.'

'*Domo arigato gozaimasu* – Thank you very much,' I said.

'*Do itashimashite – ganbatte kudasai*! – You're welcome, please do your best!' he replied.

And with that I rolled on to the roll-on roll-off in tip-top fine spirits, my rank-and-foul mood dissipated in a second by the thoughtful and spontaneous actions of a man in white gloves.

As I was wandering round my new buoyant environment watching people watching me, if they weren't watching the blaring television, a man in a white polo neck and gold medallion and gold watch approached me and introduced himself in English as Akira Yamamoto.

'Are you American student?' he asked.

'No, I'm an English cook,' I replied.

'Ah so. But excuse me, you are travelling one of many persons?'

'Er, no, I think I'm alone,' I replied, circuitously swivelling my head in well-worn sizing-up-the-situation form.

'Ah so.'

'Do you live in Tokyo?' I asked.

'I am a visiting gentleman only to visit my two daughter every weekend.'

Akira bought us both a can of chilled bitter tea from a vending machine on the deck and told me he was an orthopaedic doctor.

'You know Vancouver, Canada?' he asked.

'Sort of,' I said. 'I spent about two weeks there once, getting to know the bicycle shops when my bike broke down.'

'It is most charming city.'

'Do you go there for business?'

'Maybe sometime, but also there I have a house. I live there two months in summer season. A fine life!'

Very fine indeed.

'I hope to one day live always in Vancouver with my family. I think for my daughters life is more free, more opportunity. I think this important.'

'Is it not possible for you to live there now?'

'Mmm, not possible. I want my children to have Japanese education. To learn Japanese tradition I think this very important. Then they have . . . I think you say "the best of two world".'

By the time the ferry docked in Kurihama it seemed (at least for now) that I had left the worst of the tunnels and weather behind on the Boso-hanto Peninsula: it was now back to the hot grey mugginess, the sun trying to pierce a fiery tendril through the cloud. Out on the quay I leant my bike against a P&O sea container, bungeeing my jacket on to the back of the bike to dry, and looked out across the metallic sea – the mouth of Tokyo Bay whence I'd just come. This was a busy place for ship-spotting: over a thousand tankers, containers, fishing-boats, ferries and frigates came through this channel every day.

I had passed from one peninsula to another and was now standing in the heel of the Miura-hanto Peninsula – a ten-mile-long pocket-sized version of Italy. It was even kicking a shrunken Sicily – a tiny football of an island called Joga-shima. As I wanted to get to Yokohama, the most direct route was to ride up the calf, keeping the bay of Tokyo on my right. But from what I could make out on my map, I would have to pass through not only the industrialized area of Yokosuka (largest city on the peninsula and site of a major US naval base) but, gulp, a posse of tunnels. Feeling like I had already had one tunnel too many that day, I opted for the more roundabout route that ran up the shin.

I rode off in a south-westerly direction following a two-mile strand of beach which could have been nice if it hadn't been ruined. Judging from the number of surfers and wind-surfers, no one else seemed to mind the dirty sea and sand or the continuous jam of traffic that spluttered noisily along the front through which I was trying to thread my way. Seemingly this was something of a tourist resort for Tokyoites. Gaudy hotels abound. I stopped at one to ask, out of interest, how much it would cost for the night – 14,000 yen (£93) for a room far from special. But this didn't seem to put off the surf-boys, who were trotting barefoot back and forth across the road from beach to hotel in their masses.

I rode on, passing a family restaurant called 'Jonathon', a garage with a painted sign over the wall of the mechanics area inviting passers-by to 'LUBE HERE', and, sitting right on the road, a curious stone figurine dressed in a red bobble hat and a Snoopy apron.

Up the road – more fish in tanks but doing things with women. Welcome to Aburatsubo Marine Park, which offered 'syncronized swimming with girls and dolphins and laser light shows all put to music'. It's a lovely idea but I think I'll just keep going.

Once again I found myself asking directions for *sushi*'s close relation, Zushi – only this time I knew better and didn't end up being directed to the pickled fish shop. But I knew no better when I stopped at a Nisseki garage to ask for a *chizu* (map) and was offered a piece of *chiizu* (cheese) instead. Ah well, learning to stress syllables takes time and it could have been worse – I could have asked for a *komon* (adviser) and been proffered a *kōmon* (anus). Tongues in the right places – I suppose that's what it's all about.

Back on the boat, Akira had given me the address of a *minshuku* (cheap guesthouse) he knew of in Zushi. So, standing at six-thirty outside Zushi station swallowing a mouthful of *sushi* from a Zushi station's *sushi*-stall (and with not a she-sells-sea-shells shore in sight) I thought maybe I would try to find it. Actually, I didn't. I thought maybe I would try to get someone to find it for me – or more like point me in the right direction. The woman at Zushi station information looked blank when I showed her my *minshuku* address and even blanker after riffling through a few accommodation directories, which gave no clues. Never mind, I said – was there anywhere she could recommend that was cheap? Seemingly not. The best price she could come up with was a 'Business Hotel' which was equivalent in cost to a new Sony shortwave radio – and I knew which one I would prefer. Back outside, chewing over my next move with another piece of *sushi*, I decided to test my luck and ask someone.

In Japan there is at least no shortage of people to turn to for directions, whereas in, say, Iceland it's quite possible to solidify into a glacial stalagmite while hanging around at the roadside for the first person to come along. The only problem with Japan is that there are sometimes just too many people. The scene around Zushi station made Trafalgar Square on New Year's Eve look like a wet weekend in Warsop. Except that there were a few more bicycles. Although I was standing like a traffic island in the midst of this pedalling-pedestrianized melée, not one person crashed, bumped or tripped over me despite the furious flow rip-tiding past with merely a rice grain to spare. For Japanese crowds, it seems, push only comes to shove for the subterrestrial 'people-pushers'.

With darkness fast falling I hastily hailed one of a million salarymen streaming past and put my request to him for this particular *minshuku* whose address lay crumpled in my hand. A tall shot, I know, for a small person, but I like to shoot them big when I can. Studying my dog-eared piece of paper, the man's face registered a flickering of recognition.

Then, with a wide but slightly cock-eyed grin he said, '*Chotto matte kudasai* – Just a moment, please.'

To date, this was the one phrase that I could not only unfailingly understand but was actually capable of rattling off myself without fear of mispronunciation or misinterpretation. And it felt so good to say: CHO-TOE-MAT-TAY-KOO-DA-SIGH, a series of bulleting short, sharp sounds, fired with such striking rapidity that they seemed almost dangerous – too hot to handle – as if to shoot them furiously at someone in an uncontrollable fusillade would somehow be sufficient to gun them down. A sudden smash of glass. Scared, you wake to find a masked intruder crashing through your window one night. Quick! Turn to your weapon. Take aim. Fire! CHO-TOE-MAT-TAY-KOO-DA-SIGH! And watch them splatter against the bedroom wall.

Still intact, I waited a moment as the man had asked me. What he did next was interesting. Without warning he shot out his arm horizontally into the surrounding flurry of the crowd to form an instant barrier. The first person to be halted in his tyre tracks by this impulsive action was a bespectacled salaryman on a bicycle. Seemingly, this was exactly what my signalman had intended. The two men exchanged what appeared to be amicable words before the salaryman dismounted, lifted his attaché case from the front basket, handed his bike over to my still skewwhiff smiling man and, with a polite bow to both of us, walked at a smart pace off into the crowd. Hijack complete, my commandeerer then said something to me which I failed to grasp but his gestures were clear enough. They said: follow me.

I find it hard enough at the best of times to follow someone on a bicycle so that taking off in hot pursuit of a slightly manic black-haired man slaloming at speed through a black-haired crowd of confusion was no easy task. Recklessly we plunged through gridlock and people and arcades and markets, twisting and turning down an erratic coil of alleys and one-way streets (the wrong way) that doubled-up on themselves in a snaking and incomprehensible jumble.

These were the *ura dori* (backstreets) that, as in most Japanese cities and towns, were originally laid out and designed to mislead and baffle the enemy. Now all they do is baffle the not-so-locals and totally confuse the foreigners. Sometimes, in order to avoid cycling along a busier main road, I would try to be clever and peel off on to the quieter *ura dori* that seemed to run parallel. And that was the trick of it. The backstreet may have given me the impression it ran parallel, but in reality it led me astray. To add to the confusion, cyclists in cities tend not to cycle on the roads but instead mingle with the roving masses at the sides. Unlike Britain, where cycling on the pavements gives riders a tarnished image, in Japan pedestrians as well as bell-jangling cyclists swerve and scurry along in haphazard harmony. Swarms of light-footed monochrome-clad salarymen rub shoulders and elbows with everything from trolley-pushing grannies to brolly-haloed housewives laden with shopping. Add to this herds of satchel-backed schoolchildren, tottering towers of acrobatic *sushi*-balancing deliverymen alongside a maelstrom of mopeds for good measure. . .

All this makes for an eventful ride. Inevitably collisions occur, though surprisingly few, considering the heaving and seething mass of people – more than 20 million of whom commute into central Tokyo every weekday. Things can then turn even more lively as one small-scale clash rapidly develops into a full-scale pile-up – all arms and legs, saddles and spokes, baskets and bags and low-flying briefcases but strangely no shouts, no screams of abuse. Just smiles. Miles of smiles of embarrassment. Silently, the smiling victims of collisions pick themselves up, dust themselves off, realign a wheel or limb or hem, quietly apologizing to everyone else while the fast-flowing rivers of passing people, eyes set dead ahead, continue rushing by, never pausing to offer assistance, only diverting course around the obstruction in their path like torrents streaming round a rock.

Twenty minutes and a thousand turns later, I had been delivered outside the door of the *minshuku* which undoubtedly I would never have found alone even had I had the assistance of a GPS navigational aid planted on my handlebars. I wanted to thank my hijacking guide, buy him a beer or *sake*, but he was no lingerer. He didn't even stop. He just said '*Voilà*!' or the Japanese equivalent, smiled and bowed and biked off into the crowd.

The *minshuku* was more a traditional *ryokan* (inn) than a family bed and breakfast – old, dark, wooden with creaking polished corridors upon which glided two middling-aged hostess-type maids bound tight in kimono, their silken sashes fastened elaborately like giant butterflies settled upon their backs. One of these maiden butterflies took me under her wing and fluttered along in a rustle of silk to show me to my room. She slid open a flimsy and lockless door and we stepped up into a small, spartan room of *tatami*, having first reversed out of our slippers. It was dark. The Butterfly flitted noiselessly towards a dangling cord hanging from the usual square of stroboscopic light in the centre of the ceiling. I had already become familiar with these peculiarly discordant lights that are universally used in buildings and homes up and down the country. All look the same. All do the same. With each tug of cord comes a choice of three different settings: night-light dim; medium-brash shine; or full-blown garish glare that throws its cold and strident strobes inharmoniously upon the room's soft settings. How strange for a people who, in one sense, take so much aesthetic pleasure and care in their traditional surroundings – the golden regal reeds of *tatami*, the unelaborate bedding, the stark single flower, the simple paper walls – only to shatter all this with the jarring cold white wash of an incongruously grating fluorescent strip-light.

But, lights aside, one of the wonders of these rooms was the way in which they appeared rather like a stage setting, able to be transformed with the greatest of ease into a completely new scene by way of a procedure that seemed pleasantly theatrical. Swiftly the dextrous and delicate movements of the Butterfly transformed my initially dark and windowless ground-level room into an airy haven (once I'd flipped the light off) that merged with the moon. Deftly she had slid aside the *shoji*, a simple and beautifully primitive type of sliding screen with an open wooden grid covered on one side with semi-transparent paper, to reveal an adjoining wooden-floored room the length and width of an average coffin with a minute basin wedged at one end. That was all. Across this she flitted to another sliding screen – this one made purely of light wood which, once opened, revealed a miniaturized garden of tray-sized proportions laid with immaculately clipped shrubs, rocks and stepping stones and a floodlit pond ablaze with vividly coloured cat-sized carp.

When I turned round I caught sight of the Butterfly gliding softly from the room. But she soon reappeared bearing a large thermos and, dropping to her knees, crawled about like a chrysalis serving me tea. Although intrigued by her actions, being served on hand and foot made me feel slightly uncomfortable. After a day of being discreetly watched, I was looking forward to being left to my own devices.

But the Butterfly woman, more hostess than maid, hadn't

quite finished with me yet. It remained for her to reveal one more change of scenery. First she slid the table into the corner and tidied up the tea things. Then, from out of a flimsy wall cupboard, containing at least enough bedding for six, she pulled a futon and quilt, a sheet and blanket and a head-aching rice-husk pillow. Armed with such props she had, within moments, metamorphosed my general living area into a room for sleep. In the coffin room she lit a green mosquito deterrent that lay coiled and snake-like in the corner, slowly smoking. And then, with a colourful rustling bow, she swept silently from the room.

To save yen, I had declined the offer of meals and instead cycled off down the street in search of the OK Supermarket that I had passed earlier. A few enquiries later, I found myself outside the closer King Supaa instead, where a fruit stall had been set up by the main doors. The stallholders, a plump woman in a white kerchief and a skinny man with a silvery crop, seemed excited by my sudden appearance. As I leant my bike against the wall beside their barrow and proceeded to lock it up with a cable, they trotted over to me and rattled off a broad-beamed rocket of words. Far too fast for me, but I managed to catch the gist: that my bike was safe, no need for lock, they would watch. And innately I knew that they would. This was no scam. This was Japan.

For a few moments they jostled around me in jocular style, giving me two *gurepu furutsu* (grapefruit), feeling my tyres, smacking my saddle while adopting comical expressions of pain and joking at my freckles. They laughed even more when I stepped behind their stall and offered to serve a customer with a bunch of bananas on my head. Arms snaked round my waist for peace-poses and pictures amidst a gush of robust giggles from passers-by. Unfortunately I have yet to grow out of these school-like capers but it's just this sort of puerile and rollicking humour that the Japanese so relish.

Despite the façade of propriety, it hadn't taken me long to observe that within most Japanese lay an irrepressible hilarity. Given half a chance they would dissolve into fits of giggles – often at the most unhumorous things. Take television – a prime example. At peak viewing times at least one third of the output is devoted to quiz, game and amateur talent shows in which the ordinary, not-so-ordinary and plain odd (foreigners) interact directly, performing stunts of the most mindless frivolity. 'Endurance' tests are set in which participants lower themselves into tanks of snakes and lizards or crawl around on the floor, covering each other with dog food. Howls of raucous laughter, erupting even more so when grimacing participants are recruited from the audience. Foreigners are an essential ingredient – long lampooned for their weird and gawky ways. Some are dressed in nappies, blindfolded and, amidst scenes of hilarity from audience and viewer alike, fed samples of some of Japan's most celebrated and unappetizing cuisine which the foreigner is presumed to loathe: fermented bean paste, raw tendrils from squid-like creatures, congealed and slimy strands of an unidentifiable jellified substance.

One TV show, in particularly bad taste, shipped over a few members from a tribe of South African Bushmen to Tokyo after learning from a popular film show in Japan that these 'primitive' people worshipped a bottle of Pepsi. This caused much amusement but even more hilarious was watching the Bushmen's confusion when confronted with a pair of chopsticks and saucer of pickles. Long after the event, Japanese comics can still cause helpless fits of giggles simply by their crass impersonations of the chopstick-wielding tribesmen.

In a way I suppose that by my banana-headed antics I was only endorsing the fact that us *gaijin* are a strange lot. Larking about as I did (I'm ashamed to admit) was no put-on act or behaving out of character. I'm afraid that wearing foreign fruits comes quite naturally to me, even though most of my age group have been married for several years and given birth a few times over. Of course I could have acted staid and proper and said, 'Thank you very much, but really I'd hate to trouble you,' to the stallholders for offering to watch my bike, and left it at that. But despite leaving England with the widely held notion that the Japanese are a reserved, demure and unforthcoming lot, I found them (after initial appearances) to be quite the opposite. Any excuse for a giggle and they are with you all the way.

Opposite the fruit stall was a smaller stall shrouded in billowing clouds of blue smoke through which I could just make out a fat man with a towel draped round his neck who was selling charred portions of *yakitori* – little kebabs of grilled chicken served on bamboo skewers. He was doing a lot of shouting and a lot of sweating.

I entered King Supaa, picked up a basket and drifted up and down the aisles in search of an affordable supper. Since coming to Japan I had spent a considerable amount of time in supermarkets and food stores of various sizes, not just to stock up on sustenance to satisfy my shockingly voracious appetite, but also to appease my insatiable curiosity about food and what other people eat. I could easily visit a new country and be quite happy with scarcely venturing further than a food market. After my initial shock of discovering that two carrots could set me back over £1, four apples £8 or a melon £100 (I kid you not), I had discovered that it was still possible to eat cheaply in Japan simply by eliminating certain foods from my diet that I might normally have bought (apples, pears, oranges, salads, nuts, raisins, cheese, bread, crackers, honey) for those that I wouldn't have (tofu bean curd, fermented beans, tinned fish, dried seaweed, chilled pre-cooked noodles, beansprouts and unidentifiable sea creatures fried on street stalls). Together with bunches of blackened bananas sold off at a quarter of their original price, my new diet was a curdy-fishy-seaweedy-noodly-sprouty concoction that I enthusiastically stirred all together in a plastic container mixed with mashed bananas and a tin of tomato juice (real tomatoes being way too expensive), creating a strange-looking mix that would have made a dog's dinner look appetizing. But it was delicious and, intermingled with the odd riceball or rice cake, I ate it daily for breakfast, lunch and tea.

The only time I strayed from this inedible-looking formula was when I was either given food or offered meals by some benevolent passer-by. Sometimes it was more a matter of me passing them, which was the case while trawling the aisles of King Supaa. I came across a young lad in a white wedge cap standing behind a work-stand containing a couple of sizzling cauldrons. It seemed he was offering to customers free samples of some very odd looking fish-cakes that resembled more the sort of thing you'd expect to find in the U-bend of a public convenience. But never one to look a gift horse in the mouth, I altered course and sidled up to his pots.

'*Gaijin, ga*!' he blurted by way of greeting, evidently either agitated or excited by my sudden appearance from behind a pyramidal display of fermented bean paste. But he soon warmed to this foreign novelty, offering me some hefty samples (which I eagerly gobbled), clearly unaware that he had a gluttonous cyclist on his hands. After a few polite and timorous phrases in Japanese, he plucked up courage to try out some of his standard formula English on me: 'American?' 'Student?' 'You like Japan?' 'You eat Japanese food?'

Then, straying slightly from the textbook, he said, 'I am Japanese boy. I have nineteen years old. I am very unmarried.'

'That's nice,' I said, accepting another cocktail-stick-pierced piece of U-bend fish-cake, 'and long may it continue.'

He was an amiable soul and, in much the same way that he was testing the waters with his limited English, I experimented with my severely deficient Japanese. This worked out rather in my favour because, as we conversed in foreign tongue, he continued to feed me fishy morsels so that, by the end of our little over-the-counter *tête-à-tête*, I had (unintentionally of course) worked my way through half of his free samples. My replete (though ominously gurgling) stomach told me I need no longer make a purchase of provisions.

Nonetheless I continued wandering up and down the aisles, loitering over interesting foodstuffs that I came across such as chrysanthemum leaves, lotus root, curiously coloured roe, octopus suction pads, a collection of baking products generally labelled 'Mrs Bread' and a range of ready-made microwave meals ambitiously titled 'My Dinner'. In the cooler department I was intrigued by a series of packets of something that resembled giant Liquorice Allsorts, similar in size to a set of children's playing bricks. I touched, I poked, I prodded, but remained perplexed. Pliable, symmetrical, available in vivid fluorescent colours and patterned in psychedelic pink stripes, it could only be concluded that they might be some form of rubbery confectionery. I bought some to carry out a detailed investigation in the privacy of my room. And it was there that the bitter-sweet truth was revealed. It sliced nice – clean as a whistle. But so much for expecting some sort of exquisite oriental sweetmeat – the taste, though not unpleasant, came as a shock. They were fish, or, to be more precise, they were fish-flavoured – with the texture of plasticine, and no doubt containing more an EC mountain of E-numbers than real live fish – well, dead-live fish, if you know what I mean. I picked up my Fishy-Allsort and pondered on how it should properly be eaten. Did you serve it like pâté on toast? Did you slice it like salami or add it to risotto? Or did you simply peel back the cellophane and eat it in one go, like a banana? The answer came a few days later when I was given a bowl of *soba* (buckwheat noodle) soup. Floating on the surface like a solitary water-lily was a circular-striped slice of plasticized fish-swirl more commonly known as *kamaboko.*

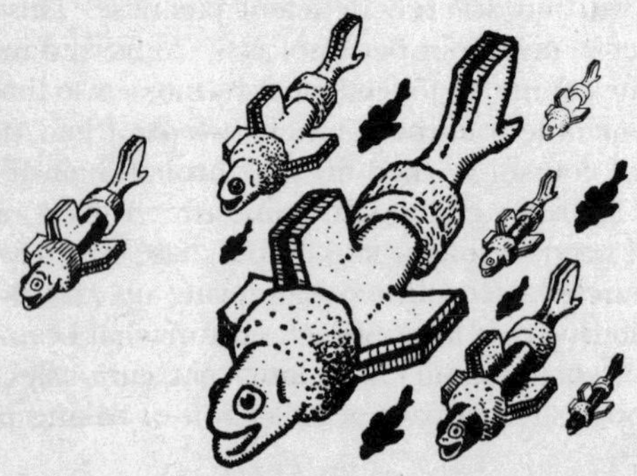

'There have been all kinds of ingenious ideas for futuristic engines that can run on hydrogen, nuclear fuel cells, bottled gases, sugarbeet or even chicken droppings. None has gained commercial acceptance.' So said the Voice of America when I awoke the next morning to hear a short debate about US vehicle emissions. My ears pricked further when the Voice remarked that the future looked bright for cycles. 'The Canadians have got the right idea,' said one. 'Why, at the lodge in Jasper National Park they even have cycling waiters!'

There are cycling waiters in Japan, too, though rather than meander through the sedate grounds of a Canadian lodge they must navigate with acrobatic expertise around an impossible course of jammed streets and packed pavements, all the time steering one-handedly while the other is platform to a teetering tower of perilously stacked dishes.

I cycled up the coast road to Kamakura – a road that the doctor on the ferry had recommended to me because of its beauty and beaches. Hard though I tried, beauty was not a word that leapt to mind. Being pinned to the side of the road by a constant cavalcade of passing cars and trucks pumping out their usual plumes of fumes does not help to create the impression of beauty. The beach fared no better. Lying thirty miles south-west of Tokyo, Kamakura beach has become a resort for thousands of Tokyoites who flock there to swim, sail, windsurf, sunbathe and pump up the volume. Faint wafts of sewer-smells greeted me as I stopped to 'admire' the scene. I trudged down across the dirty-coloured sand, picking my way amongst the litter and the mass of spread-eagled forms, to the water's edge and peered across its surface. So much for an azure sea – it resembled more a murky effluence pumped from the bowels of some industrial plant. I didn't even dare give my toes a dipping for fear of them turning black, shrivelling up and dying. I worked my way back up the beach, stepping on those few patches of murky sand that weren't covered with splayed bodies, broken bottles or crushed cans, wondering how anyone could lie on such a beach and still be able to look as if they've hit heaven. But, there again, I suppose having a lack of alternatives helps them to ignore the filth. For Tokyoites, time is short, travel is time, you can't go far and so you just make do and enjoy it while you can.

Beauty, though, was something I'm sure that the Kamakura coast had in plentiful supply way back when the town, facing the sea on one side and backed by densely wooded hills on the other, became the capital of the shogunate government at the end of the twelfth century. For just over a thousand years, Kamakura was not only the political hot-seat of power – populated by the new military class, the samurai – but was also a flourishing centre of religion (particularly Zen Buddhism) and culture. Because of this, Kamakura is lavishly endowed with enough temples and shrines to keep the average monument-lover happy until the camcorder battery runs dry. I intended to join the masses, daily disgorged at the station, and jump on the tourist-trail pilgrimage. But not just yet. I still had a Yokohama address to find and so, after pausing for a wipe of brow, I set sail again into a heavy coagulation of traffic on the road to Tokyo.

CHAPTER 8

The Neuro and Fuzzy Logic System

When Commodore Perry and his famous Black Ships landed in Japan a little over 150 years ago, Yokohama (today the country's second largest city, population three million) was a poor fishing village and was little more than a rank swamp. As the shogunate considered a smelly site worthy of a smelly people, the area was opened as a settlement for the new foreigners and an artificial island was built upon the mud-flats of Yokohama ('Horizontal Beach', though 'Horizontal Swamp' would perhaps have been more like it). As the Bullet had yet to take the bite or the Mitsubishi People Carrier to cart the masses, travel was still very much something undertaken on foot or on horse, and so the shogunate felt that Yokohama was far enough from Tokyo (about twenty miles) should they need to ward off any unsavoury 'surprises' that those unfathomable foreigners might just be storing up their strange flappy trouser-legs.

The fledgling settlement developed into one of East Asia's largest and busiest ports – consulates sprang up and foreigners descended upon the quayside, eager to learn more of this mystical country that had shut itself away for so long.

Now an urban colossus of consumer and commuter frenzy, Yokohama is a far cry from the days when it was the abode of Algernon Bertram Mitford, the first Lord Redesdale. Mitford was a diplomat-scholar who visited the court of the Mikado and presented the Emperor with the Order of the Garter (sent by King Edward VII). He witnessed the full ceremonial of a ritual suicide and left in his published memoirs some intriguing accounts of nineteenth-century Japan. In those days, with room still to roam, it was possible to see a real live creature of nature taking a turn where today there stands only yet another lump of concrete.

> One day as I was sitting at work, I saw a huge otter come sneaking into my little paradise [his home]. I cocked my Spencer rifle – but the enemy heard the click and bolted before I could get a shot of him. It was a strange invasion in a city of some half million souls!

And later, having become the wiser about these perambulating intruders:

> Miss Bamboo and another girl [put] the gold-fish to bed in a rock-covered hole, for fear of otters . . .

So much for a 'fear' of otters; for me, it was more a fear of having to navigate in an area littered with factories – Sumitomo Metal Industries, NKK, Nippon Oil, Tokyo Gas and Ishikawajima-Harima Industrial Plant, to name but a few. To add to the confusion I found myself syphoned off on to Route 1 – the heart-in-mouth clogged artery that sucks up traffic from some 300 miles away in Kyoto before regurgitating it all into the concrete conurbations of Tokyo – an area that appeared on my map like an angry haemorrhage of interlinking trunk roads and expressways.

Cycling into such an environment is something I generally try to avoid. I can think of more pleasant places to take a turn on two wheels than the lung-clogging, lane-clogging

Route 1. But a Yokohama address or, more to the point, a Yokohama family lay waiting for me to find. It was never going to be particularly easy because addresses in Japan seem to be made more for recognizing symbolically than actually locating. Firstly, the address is assigned to an area rather than a street; secondly the numbers are not necessarily in sequential order because, traditionally, numbers are allocated to buildings by date of construction rather than according to location. If you're looking for 64 Joe Bloggsushi Street and you've made it to number 63, then logic would tell you that number 64 must be either next door or across the road – in a word, close. In most countries this tends to be the case, but not so in Japan, a land that appears to work upon the premise: why make life easy when you can make it so difficult? Hence, because number 64 was built maybe five years after number 63, this could mean that the two addresses are in effect a blue moon away from each other. And nobody, but nobody, will know where it is unless they happen either to live or to work there. Even postmen and policemen get confused.

The trouble starts with the streets, as most streets have no names. It's like trying to find 10a Barley Mews Gardens, London W1 with no Gardens, no Mews and no Barley. Only 10a W1 – which could be Anywhere W1, unless you know where it is. After the war an attempt to instigate some system of street-naming was made by the Americans during the Occupation, but as soon as they left the Japanese reverted to their own system of anonymity.

An address is composed of parts which, like video instructions, are designed to confuse. They revolve around *ken* (prefecture, which is roughly equivalent to an American state), as in Fukuoka-ken. However, there are four areas in Japan that do not follow this rule: Tokyo-to, Kyoto-fu, Osaka-fu (those cities and their surrounds) and the northern island of Hokkaido. After the prefecture comes *shi* (city) so that Fukuoka City in Fukuoka Prefecture is properly Fukuoka-shi, Fukuoka-ken. It is not unusual for the prefecture and the city to have the same name. But in more rural areas there are also *gun* (a bit like British counties) and *mura* (villages). Large cities are subdivided first into *ku* (wards or districts,) then into *cho* (an area in a district which can also be a street or a village within a town) or *machi* (another sort of area but which can also be a town within the *ku*), and then into *chome* (an area of several streets or blocks within a district). The *chome* is the precise division (but, remember, not necessarily in sequential order) so that an individual address like 2-21-8 *chome* should in theory locate the actual address you're after. But it's not as simple as that as 2-21-8 *chome* can also be written 8-*chome* 2-21. For example, 2-21-8 Kasumigaseki could be 2-21 Kasumigaseki 8-*chome*. But don't forget that *machi* might be used instead of *chome*. The actual building number (or *banchi*) is either a simple numeral or a hyphenated double numeral. When there are three numbers interspersed with hyphens, the first one is the *chome* (or *machi*). Sometimes the proverbial pin in the haystack can seem a lot more simple to find than a Japanese address.

So I suppose it should have come as no surprise to find myself lost. But I was (surprised that is, as well as lost) because when I set out to try to find something, I like to find it – come what may. Everyone I asked either pointed me in totally the opposite direction from the next person I would ask or else just looked at me with a baffled grin. This slightly disconcerting reaction was, I hoped, because I had asked the impossible, like directions to an address, rather than because I was a small, squat, big-nosed foreigner.

It's funny that addresses can be so utterly disordered when the Japanese themselves are in general so orderly. It's as if they have a horror of revealing too much – as if they can show their ankles but not their face. Living with such elusive addresses gives the impression they don't want to be found. Or, there again, maybe they're just sentimental about their ways and don't like change – like some of us *gaijin* who cling lovingly to our pounds and ounces and fahrenheits and gallons and miles. Offer us half a kilo of kilometres and we don't give a furlong.

Trying to locate my Yokohama address I stopped at numerous *koban*. These small police cabins, or sub-stations, located at strategic corners in each neighbourhood, are worked by police officers in shifts twenty-four hours a day. Each is responsible for perhaps 300 households. They take turns patrolling their district, visiting and talking to the families and businesses on their 'beat', each of which they are required to call in on at least twice a year. They jangle their way along on bicycles or amble amiably, hands behind back, chatting to the shopkeepers, playfully pinching babies, helping drunks out of the gutter or cajoling them into their trains, aiding old women to gather in their aired bedding and acting as a sort of walking weather monitor, keeping abreast of the latest thermals and informing the locals whether anything 'unusual' lies in store. Along with this extraordinarily close and (mostly) friendly rapport they build up on their visits, they also keep a book in which they diligently record details of the family members, lodgers, businesses, employees and so on, the names of which are verified or updated on the map at the local *koban*.

One of the main jobs of these human surveillance cameras is to monitor people's movements and to keep track of their comings and goings. This struck me as an incredibly intimate and intrusive form of policing which I can't imagine being tolerated in many other countries, however effective it is at keeping the crime level low. In such an overcrowded land, where most people's lives already suffer from an outlandish lack of privacy, to have an official posse of Peeping Toms breathing down your neck and inviting themselves biannually to your home for tea and a snoop must be trying, to say the least. Yet only a smattering of residents spurn these tactics; the majority of the local population appear to cooperate with an exquisite equanimity. How can people seem not to object to such pry-eyed policing? I suppose some must cooperate because not to do so would make them immediately conspicuous and subject to stricter surveillance. And it must be quite reassuring to have such a high density of perambulating policemen. They go by the name of '*Omawari-san*' – literally 'Respected Mr Walkabout' – and they are undoubtedly looked up to. These benign-looking overgrown Boy Scouts with their rolled-up sleeves, creaking leather holsters and dangling 'night-sticks' are a far cry from the pre-war fascist police, who were regarded with suspicion, loathing and fear. But despite an air of faint comicality, which lies somewhere between *Top Cat* and *Trumpton*, they are not to be underestimated. Their unarmed combat training is second to none; step out of line and you'll end up sorry.

Mr Walkabout seems to tread the perfect line between approachability and respect – one moment chatting good-humouredly with men and women alike; the next, lecturing a gang of loafing youngsters, lolling around 'unJapanese-like' on street corners, about the anxiety and shame that their idleness must be bringing to their families. Instead of having to parry a fusillade of strident defiance and raucous abuse, the officers are listened to with bowed heads and shuffling feet. The police force even has an official song (as do most major businesses and corporations) in which they try to bolster the image that their job is one of neighbourly service, as this verse demonstrates:

> O we of the new day
> Filled with the love of gentle breeze
> Hold aloft the banner of freedom,
> Beautiful, flowing,
> Sacred, the duty of public peace;
> Genial, drawing close, smiling, truthful
> Friend of the people.

Not the sort of sing-song that is easy to imagine the boys in blue at Scotland Yard warbling at the start of every day.

However well they may trill their tunes, the smiling

'Respected Mr Walkabouts' I found sitting down in their corner boxes were not much help at locating my elusive Yokohama address. With hindsight I suppose this is understandable, considering the complexities of the street-naming system and especially as the address I sought was outside their patrolling area. It occurred to me that the most effective way of tracking down your precise location in a land that shies away from street-naming and logical numbering would be to have a compass bearing of the building you're trying to locate. All you then need is to resuscitate a few scouting skills, locate magnetic north and home in to the nearest degree. Life could be easy, after all.

But for me it seemed as complex as possible and it was definitely more luck than navigational skills that found me fetching up outside JR Higashi-Totsuka *eki* which I presumed must have something to do with the Totsuka-ku part of the address for which I was searching. The people I was trying to track down were the Imai family – friends of Taeko Oliver, a Japanese friend of my father's who is married to an Englishman and lives near London. The Imais had invited me to stay for the night, an invitation that had surprised me after what I'd read and heard about the Japanese tendency to avoid having foreigners to stay – not because they are wanting in generosity but because they are embarrassed to reveal the smallness of their homes.

I tried ringing the Imais but there was no answer, which didn't surprise me as it was much earlier than the time I had said I would ring. Next to the *eki* was a bookshop, outside of which high piles of breeze-block-thick *manga* books were surrounded by a row of men's and schoolboys' backs – heads bent, engrossed in their 'comical' read. The bookshop had a good map department so I took the opportunity of trying to find something to help me navigate my way around the country.

The only thing I found that wasn't covered in a swirl of indecipherable *kanji* was *The English edition of Road Atlas Japan 1:250,000 (Hokkaido Only 1:600,000)*, published by

Shobunska. Despite being a chunky and weighty tome of a map book it looked just the job – a good cycling scale, names of towns and cities were in both *kanji* and *romaji* (the readable Roman alphabet script, v. important), there were road numbers (though not as many as I'd have liked), minor roads were marked (though not in detail) as were those lovelies of all lovelies, tunnels (though, as I was later to discover, only a fraction of what there was in reality). Also I didn't have to 'read' the book backwards, as is the Japanese custom – something which I couldn't get the hang of at all. Complicated junctions were enlarged and there was a good wodge of city maps in the back. I spent a long time leafing through the pages, debating whether it was just too heavy (nearly two pounds – or about the weight of my sleeping bag) and just too expensive at 2,890 yen (nearly £20). Oh well, I thought, what's a bit of extra weight if I know where I am? So I splashed out.

Back at my bike I leant against a wall and perused my new purchase with pleasure. There is something so tantalizing about a map that I can quite happily stare at one all day. When I went cycling to Morocco with Mel (my brother's wife) I would spend such a long time studying the map that Mel would think I was learning it. Take a map, any map – doesn't have to be of some exotic far-flung place. I dip at random into my map box and pull out a pink Ordnance Survey 'Vale of Glamorgan and Rhondda' (sheet 170). Opening it up I'm faced with a feast of intriguing places. Enticing lines and shapes and squiggles weave their way through a host of wondrous names: Mynydd Maendy, Ty, N-y-Bryn, Nantyffyllon, Cowbridge, Monknash, Pricetown, Llantwit Major, Werfa, Muddlecross, Pontypridd, Pant-y-Gog and Peterston-super-Ely. There are people down there – maybe sitting in Tonna church or stretching their legs up in the heights of Fforch-Orky or collecting their pension in Tonypandy post office. Down there in those green woody splodges that splay themselves like amoebic pseudopodiam lies life – so too on those A's and B's and C's and M-roads of red and orange and yellow and blue all strung together amongst a whorl of thread-like contours. Very nice things are maps. And what's more, here, outside Higashi-Totsuka, in my hands lies a whole book of them – pages and pages (271 to be precise) which I will no longer observe just from above but into which I will step. Having stepped, names come alive, hills that will hurt, tunnels to fear. A piece of paper. A piece of land. A piece of life. Lost.

'*Sumimasen* – Excuse me.'

A small plump woman with a small plump daughter extracts me from my reverie. They appear excited to see me. Are they, by chance, members of the Imai family, I wonder. No, the woman's name is Hideko Nishikida and she hands me a business card. She owns a restaurant called Tokei Sou in Chiyoda-ku, Uchikanda, Tokyo. She chatters away – too fast – I can't keep up. Wants to know about me. Invites me to her restaurant. Am I alone? By bicycle? Ga! I thank her. Say I'm waiting for friends. Can I help you? she asks. Is there anything I need? No, I thank her. She is very kind, I say, but I'm fine. She keeps patting and shaking my hand – fondly. Here, she says while dipping into her purse, just a little something. The little something is a crisp 5,000 yen note (£33). I'm stupefied. No, no, I say, feeling florid of face, I can't possibly. She insists. I resist. Say I'm fine. I have everything I need. She holds my hand again – more patting. I wonder if I know this woman from a past life. Surely this is not normal behaviour to shower upon a stranger? But no, we are both new to each other. Feeling decidedly overawed by such attention I thank her again and say I must go to telephone. One last lingering pat, offer of help and she's gone. Lost in the crowd.

I wheel my bike over to the green phone protected by an open perspex hood. Reaching into my handlebar bag for my address book, my fingers fall upon a freshly folded 5,000 yen note secreted there with a deftness of digits other than my own. I hold it and think: the crafty devil – how did she manage it when all the time she had my hands in hers? Ah, the decoy daughter – must have snaffled it in behind my back. I am much touched and mystified and flabbergasted. What does it take, I wonder, for someone to foist such a lump sum upon a total stranger? I look downwards – at myself. Do I look a complete ragamuffin – such a sorry state that those with a big heart and big bill in hand feel motivated to lift me from my squalor? I don't think so. Not yet anyway. I haven't been on the road for more than a few days. My body has been scrubbed to oblivion; my clothes, though far from grand, are clean, holeless and torn-free. I don't feel ill, only a little lost.

I feed my puppy-decorated 'PEACEFUL LOVE SCENE' telephone card into the slot and again ring the Imais. Still no answer, so I have a wander before cycling off to try to find a park in which to sit down for a bit. But the only park I find is a paved-over space about the size of a pingpong table, sitting on a busy road junction. There's a water fountain so I go and drink my fill before flopping on a bench and watching two doll-like girls playing on their unicycles.

Back outside the *eki* I ring again.

'*Moshi, moshi,*' sings the voice down the line – the standard Japanese response which, on first hearing, evokes for a Westerner only a vision of tinned peas.

'*Moshi, moshi,*' I chirrup back before lapsing into broken English and very broken Japanese. It's Noriko, who, despite only learning a little English over twenty years ago and having never used it since, speaks it better than I speak French with my seven years of heavy-duty school learning.

She says, 'Too hard complication,' when I say I'll try to find her home. 'Please staying by station. Husband I come maybe ten minute, okay?'

Yes, very okay. I won't move. I attempt to describe myself for easy identification: stripy shorts, pink bicycle . . . but she breaks in and says, 'I think no difficulties to finding. Bye,

bye!' And, of course, she's right. In a sea of two-toned similarity I stand out like a flashing Belisha beacon.

Precisely ten minutes later Noriko slips from the passing crowds with her husband, Akitomo, who (having studied a little English at university) speaks slightly more of my language than Noriko. There are lots of smiles but no touching: no handshake, no kissing. They lead me back up the hill to their home, Akitomo bringing up the rear with a helpful pushing hand on my bike.

Akitomo strikes me as quite big as far as Japanese men go – broad-shouldered and sturdy. He has worked for the same steel company all his working life – about twenty years – and sometimes goes to Canada, the United States or Mexico City on business, where he says he uses his limited English. Noriko is the sort of woman who makes me feel not only tall but also a wide vehicle. She's tiny, maybe four foot ten, with a waist so narrow I fancy I could girdle it with the fingers of one hand.

As we walk back chatting, in a language full of misunderstandings, I think: lucky thing they met me, otherwise I would never have found them. We twist and turn along featureless streets of high blocks of identical buildings interspersed with identical patches of playgrounds in which seemingly identical clusters of children play. All very neat, all very sweet, all very well behaved. We come to rest at the entrance of one of these tall blocks of flats.

There's a bike-park lined with a long row of bikes. I glance down their ranks. They all look similar. No flashy paint-jobs, no flashy designs. No mountain bikes. No racers. They're all your average sensible roadster with integrated dynamo, wheel lock, basket, rear-rack and stand. Not dissimilar from Dutch bikes. Just what a city cycle should be. Akitomo says I can keep my bike here but he must have detected my slight hesitation at leaving my life-line out on a limb (coming from a culture as I do where honesty is in short supply) for he says I can put it in the corridor upstairs if I prefer.

Noriko and Akitomo live in a flat on the fourteenth floor with their two daughters: nineteen-year-old Umi, a university student who 'likes rugby football', and eleven-year-old Miki, who 'likes ballet and football'. The flat is modern – no *tatami*, but no shoes either, and there is a tiny cubby-hole in which sits, as Noriko puts it, 'Western-style toilet'. This is as opposed to the traditional and more prevalent squat toilets, which are small and narrow with a sort of splash-guard hood at the front shaped like a racing faring on a motorbike. Hunkered down on your haunches, there is also something very ski-dooish about them.

In the room opposite is a washing machine, a basin and, through an adjoining frosted-glass door, the short, deep, squat-like bath. Never in Japan will you find the toilet in the same room as the bath. This, quite rightly, is considered by the Japanese to be a disgusting set-up. At the end of the nineteenth century the Japanese, who wouldn't think twice about mixed bathing in 'nature's costume', were appalled when first exposed to the 'unnatural and unclean' American innovation of putting a toilet in the bathroom. 'A device that sets your own sewage out in front of your eyes,' a character in Junichiro Tanizaki's novel *Some Prefer Nettles* complains, 'is highly offensive to good taste.'

There are three bedrooms – a sign of a higher standard of living – so that Umi and Miki can both retire to the *puraibashi* (privacy) of their own rooms – a luxury that has come only relatively recently to a country in which traditionally three or even four generations live on top of each other with a total lack of inviolable individual space. As there is no traditional word for privacy in the Japanese language, *puraibashi* is in fact a word adopted from the West and tweaked just enough so as to slip manageably from a Japanese tongue. The concept of privacy had not been totally alien to the Japanese culture, but it had such a low order of priority that it was thought there was no obvious need to name it.

There is a small, narrow kitchen – with scarcely room to toss an octopus or chip a chopstick, never mind swing a cat – open at both ends, one of which leads into a modest eating and living area. The set-up of this room is very Western – a black glass dining table and chairs, a black leather sofa and armchair ('Akitomo's chair'), a mega-screen television, video, stereo, coffee table and a wall of window through which, on an exceptionally clear day, the mighty snow-capped cone of Mount Fuji can be seen shimmering gently in the haze.

The layout of this flat is common to most of the Japanese apartment blocks known as *danchi* ('collective zones' – high-rises rented inexpensively to low-income tenants, mostly nuclear families, by the local authorities) which arose as part of a massive house-building programme in the 'fifties and 'sixties as one answer to the crazy scramble for much-needed new accommodation. The *danchi*-dwellers, uprooted from the servile bonds of blood relations, family obligations and the village or neighbourhood community, became a mainstay of Japan's emerging bourgeoisie: well-educated, modest in their aspirations and apolitical. Vandalism was almost non-existent in the new high-rises and is still virtually unknown today. The social stigma attached to a failure to uphold standards proved an effective form of pressure. Japan's housing estates rarely became slum-like areas of squalid and intimidating decadence, such as those that cropped up in post-war cities in the West or in other parts of Asia where burgeoning populations were housed in high-rise buildings.

The rooms of these buildings were built in the traditional style, measuring between six and eight *tatami* mats (each mat measuring six feet by three). This is generally a lot less space than most Westerners are used to and it was this conception of being cramped that led to the 'rabbit-hutch' view of Japanese life – a prime example of the arrogance that prevails in the West. Precisely because space is at a premium in traditional Japanese homes, it has always been used economically and to maximum effect: the soft *tatami* and neat, square, stackable cushions in lieu of awkward and bulky immovable chairs and three-piece suites; the compact *kotatsu* – a table doubling up as a heater by way of an electrical element fitted to the underside of the table; the easy storability of the collapsible bedding that transforms rooms for living in by day into bedrooms by night; the fluidity and modularity of interior spaces partitioned with removable *fusuma* and *shoji* (sliding screens) so that rooms can be expanded (or combined) or contracted. These houses have no centre, no fixed walls – everything moves and slides, opens and closes. All is mobile. This gives an incredible feeling of freshness – of fragility and ephemerality. A stage-set of interiors and exteriors, forever changing. It is as if the room was a metaphor for the Buddhist belief in impermanence, which seems reflected as much in the disposable wooden chopsticks served at a restaurant as in the elaborate pieces of a kimono which are laboriously unstitched every time before cleaning.

But the Western notion that the Japanese live their lives in cramped and claustrophobic conditions continues to exist. In David Lodge's comic novel *Small World*, Akira, the Japanese academic, lives in a minute flat:

> He cannot actually stand up in it, and on unlocking the door, and having taken off his shoes, is obliged to crawl, rather than step inside . . . The apartment, or living unit, is like a very luxurious padded cell . . . four hundred identical cells are stacked and interlocked in this building, like a tower of egg boxes.

But Akira sees this with very different eyes:

> How much time people waste in walking from one room to another – especially in the West! Space is time . . . separate rooms not just for sleeping, eating and excreting, but also for cooking, studying, entertaining, watching TV, playing games, washing clothes and practising hobbies – all spread out . . . so that it would take a whole minute to walk from, say, one's bedroom to one's study.

Although it is becoming standard practice in modern Japan for children to have their own rooms (like Umi and

Miki), most older Japanese still live in this chop-and-changeable way. Since it is traditional in the older-style house for there to be no furniture determining that a room should be reserved for any particular function, those who live within regard themselves as 'one flesh' – their property belonging to all. This altruistic attitude has produced a remarkable nation of selfless people for whom nothing seems to be too much trouble when it comes to helping others. (There are, of course, some major exceptions.) But a more modern style of living, in which people are gaining more privacy and space in which to live (though still a long way off from Western wastefulness), is worrying the older generation, who feel that the younger generation is becoming increasingly selfish and egotistical.

When the multi-storey flats of the *danchi* started sprouting in the 'fifties and 'sixties, the running hot and cold water, family bath and flush toilet were all astonishing luxuries to their new occupants, most of whom arrived from run-down and draughty wooden houses. In the suburbs and countryside most homes still depended on the night-soil man who came to clear out the contents of the latrines into 'honey buckets' to be used as fertilizer in the fields. The smallness of the *danchi* meant that the limited space had to be meticulously organized in order to accommodate a range of household goods that were unknown until the American Occupation. Saturation advertising encouraged the idea that each family had to have a television, refrigerator and washing machine; by 1964, 90% did possess a TV set and more than half owned the other two items as well. These were known as the three 'sacred treasures' of the household, an ironic popular corruption of the phrase used to describe Japan's real 'sacred treasure': the mirror, sword and jewel which are the symbols of the Emperor's authority. Most Japanese women wanted these liberating gadgets immediately they appeared on the market; and as it has been customary for husbands to leave their wives in charge of the housekeeping, the women shrewdly made sure they got what they wanted.

Noriko's washing machine was soon put into action once I'd arrived on the scene. She said, 'Pleasure washing machine everything.' Never one to turn down an automated wash, I rummaged eagerly through the murky depths of my panniers, feverishly searching for anything washable whether it needed it or not, in much the same way as when my mother, having got her first washing machine, would rush around looking for things to load up into it just because it was there.

Noriko's machine was about as far removed from our old one as, say, a ten-ton thump-a-key typewriter is from a Worldwide Webbing Windows 98 PC. Instead of a chunky profusion of satisfyingly clunk-worthy buttons and dials, I was confronted with a touch-tone digital panel and LCD screen – all in Japanese symbols apart from the bizarre words informing me that I was using the 'Neuro and Fuzzy Logic System'.

While my washing was being illogically fuzzed I suddenly realized, mid-shower, that, owing to my ready eagerness to wash all my clothes, I had stupidly left myself with nothing to wear, apart from my sleeping bag. Nice though it was, I didn't really feel I could sit down to supper cocooned in my three-season goosedown North Face Kazoo, so I sheepishly poked my head out of the bathroom door and alerted Umi to my predicament. For five minutes I couldn't get a whippet of sense out of her, such were her giggles. Once they had subsided to some degree of normality she happily kitted me out in a pair of shorts and a T-shirt that bore a cartoon of some pooch, with the words CUTE DOGS FASHION.

Supper was truly a feast for eyes as well as for stomach, involving a dazzling array of bowls and saucers with *tempura* (giant fried shrimp and small whole fried fish with battered aubergine and onion and courgette), *onigiri* (balls of sticky rice that Noriko expertly formed into triangular shapes with her palms before wrapping in *nori* seaweed); *umeboshi* (pickled plums) and pickled radish and a salad of raw squid, broccoli and lettuce (surprisingly tasty). There was a cabbage soup topped with tofu and some curious smooth-moulded balls like putty that Noriko said were 'Japanese potato'. A profusion of confusion came in the form of condiments for dipping and drizzling, ranging from the staple soy sauce to mouth-blowing horseradish paste and sweet and fruity sauce. There were leaves that looked like nettles and tasted like flowers, and a fishy sort of fish roll that Umi told me she had made after 'seeing Demi Moore eating similar design food in mostly enjoyable movie *Ghost*'.

At the start of the meal I had been temptingly offered a knife and fork in place of chopsticks, but gallantly (foolishly) I waved aside such a clumsy form of cutlery with a reckless 'when not in England, do not as the English do' attitude. Because of my ineptitude with these seemingly impractical sticks I naturally paid the price in so far as I couldn't eat my fill, owing to my inability to keep up with everyone else's dexterity. Noriko, bless her, complimented me on my chopsticking skills anyway. Words of congratulation seem standard comment to any Westerner, no matter how uncoordinated, who manages not to drop them on the floor. However, when it came to filleting the fish no one could repress their giggles at my cack-handed method, by which the head was inadvertently jettisoned into Miki's soup. Heroically I battled on, determined to get to the fish-flesh of the matter. Once I had, I won an encouraging round of enthusiastic applause.

Umi and Miki took me under their wing and gave me some on-the-spot tutoring on *hashi* or *bashi* (chopstick) etiquette. Never *sashi-bashi* (spear your food with the tips of your *hashi*), they said, and never *mayoi-bashi* (wave your *hashi* indecisively over the food, as one might with a fork). Don't jam your *hashi* down into your rice to stand like masts and don't *hashiwatashi* (pass food back and forth via *hashi*), as this is the way dishes are served to the dead. Today *hashi* are made mainly in wood, the most common being *sugi* (cryptomeria), with bamboo a close second – either cured or fresh-cut, like ham. These fresh-cuts, or *aotake* ('green bamboo') have been found to closely resemble the earliest form of chopsticks, which probably originated in Southern China, except that the first *hashi* were not coupled together but consisted of a single, slender stick, curved at the end – more hook than rod.

In feudal days the aristocrats used *hashi* made of silver, both as an affectation symbolizing wealth and as a precaution against assassination: it was believed that any poison slipped into the food would cause the silver chopsticks to tarnish. Until relatively recently many were carved from ivory but this practice was finally made illegal – although, judging from Japan's notorious whaling record, I wouldn't be surprised if a few hapless elephants are not still paying a heavy price.

After supper everyone expressed amazement when I sat on the floor, Japanese style, to look at my map instead of on the sofa. This is my habit because, owing to a lack of leg-length, I tend to find floors more comfortable places to sit on than furniture.

'You are very good Number One England person for Japanese-style sitting!' laughed Akitomo. 'For self-comfy I am preferring chair!'

Not wanting to get in the way, I had planned on staying only one night with the Imais. So I was rather surprised when, despite not even knowing me, they told me I couldn't possibly leave so soon.

'Please you are many welcome to staying our home is you home. One week, one month is pleasurably our very okay!' said Noriko, touching my arm.

'Yes, fine time – all happy,' said Akitomo. 'We are considering you here is treat time!'

'Please staying,' joined in Umi. 'In two day I have University free day. I think this is best charming time to take you for visiting guest to Kamakura – many attraction city!'

Miki appeared so enthused at the prospect of me staying that she handed me her glass teddy-bear-shaped chopstick stand, saying, '*Purezento* special for you,' and changed into her bright orange tutu before pirouetting like a Swan from the Lake across the living-room floor. I didn't need much in the way of persuasion to stay with a family as welcoming as this and no sooner had I told them so than Akitomo had me on the floor (so to speak) with a large piece of paper. There he set about making me a five-day schedule with military precision, allocating specific hours for each activity (train to Kamakura; lunch in Yokohama; watching Miki in ballet class; morning for 'business transaction' in Tokyo, etc.) that resulted in a timetable resembling a worryingly regimented format which I hadn't experienced since my schooldays.

Schedules finalized, Akitomo settled back in his chair to doze off in front of some screeching TV games show while Noriko, stubbornly refusing all offers of help with the washing up, presented us girls with a bowlful of dark luscious cherries as big as tomatoes (supermarket price: about £25 per puny punnet) and slices of *nashi*, a yellow orange-sized pear that crunched like an apple. It was origami time and, kneeling around the low table, Umi and Miki went to great pains to teach me how to fold *chiyogami* sheets this way and that to make a paper crane, the national symbol of peace. Whereas I was all fumbling fingers and thumbs, taking at least ten minutes to form something that resembled a scrunched-up piece of wrapping paper that I might have found in the bin, Umi's and Miki's nimble fingers were a blur of folding perfection. In a flash they could turn their hand to anything – birds, dolls, boxes, balloons – while simulanteously eating cherries and watching television. When I sent my 'creations' home to my mother she mistook my cranes for elephants – which was actually more of a compliment than I had been expecting.

On arriving at the Imais I'd presumed that I'd be sleeping on the sofa, but not so: despite my protests that the sofa was more than luxurious, Miki had happily lent me her room while she moved in with Umi. Expecting a futon, I was surprised to find a bed, but I later learnt that beds are much more popular with today's teenagers, who regard them as something of a status symbol. I thought I could at least give the Neuro Fuzzy Logic System a rest by using my sleeping bag but Noriko wouldn't hear of it, telling me she actually enjoyed washing.

After bidding everyone *oyasumi-nasai* I slid shut my louvred-screen door before studying the framed photographs on Miki's walls. They were all of ballets – *Swan Lake, Cinderella* – but in one, taken during a performance of the *Nutcracker*, I spotted Miki, caught on camera, a dazzling and willowy tutu'd queen.

My window was a sliding glass door that opened on to a tiny ledge of a balcony that had the family's underwear hanging from an ingeniously collapsible, plastic circular contraption with integrated clothes pegs that resembled a cross between a toy chandelier and the Magic Roundabout – a contraption that no Japanese family is without: maximum drying capacity in minimum space. I stepped out of the door, slipping into a minute pair of special outdoor-only slippers, and looked out over a city of lights as the warm wind stroked my skin. Standing there I wondered what it must feel like (apart from shaky) to be up here during one of Japan's alarmingly frequent earthquakes. In between my *hashi* lessons we had talked about this during supper. Noriko said that earthquakes were such a common occurrence they hardly noticed them anymore. But a few weeks before there had been a bit of a big one during the night which had sent their high-rise flat rocking back and forth like a pendulum. That, she admitted, had been a little frightening. As I leant on the ledge-like balcony peering over the side at the headlights trailing below I had a sudden disquieting feeling that, should this teetering building start rocking and yawing like a ship, I would probably have to fight a distinct inclination to climb up on to the rails and jump overboard. But it won't happen, a voice from within told me – while another said that it might. Definitely maybe.

Earthquakes can't have been preying too much on my mind because I awoke at 3.10 a.m. in prancing mood, having dreamt I'd cycled through Tokyo in a tutu asking directions to the paper cranes of peace. Then, as coincidence would have it, I quietly switched on my radio (to, I believe, the

World Service's *Megamix*) and heard a distorted form of Morrissey's magically melancholy vocals crooning . . . 'Vicar in a tutu. I know – I know, it's serious . . .', refrains of which were still resounding round my head when I awoke again at 6.10 a.m. The World Service, having long been lost into the vagaries of the airwaves, I tuned instead to FEN: '. . . never swim alone . . .' some smooth State-side baritone warned, '. . . use the Buddy System – as advised by the lifeguard authorities . . .'. Right on. Then came a culinary morsel alerting me to the fact that some Australian chefs had come to Japan wanting to open up an Australian restaurant. Their idea was to serve such delicacies as water buffalo steak and crocodile pie but the Japanese authorities refused to grant them a visa because they said there was no such thing as traditional Australian cuisine – a comment, I'm sure, that wouldn't have gone down too well Down Under.

Breakfast was a strange mixture of crab salad, seaweed soup and Fortnum and Mason English Breakfast tea (the latter being a token offering I'd given Noriko the previous day).

As I had originally presumed I would be staying only one night on Floor 14, I had arranged for today to cycle to Asahiku, an outlying district of Yokohama, to meet up with Sachiko Igarashi, another friend of Taeko's. As it was Noriko's day off from her job (as a counsellor for pregnant women) she volunteered to drive me there, saying, 'Too much complications in address by bicycle.' Knowing all too well the impossibilities of Japanese address-finding, I readily acquiesced. But with Japanese addresses being what they were, or more like where they weren't, Noriko knew better than to search around indefinitely for an elusive street number and, ringing Sachiko, arranged to meet at the entrance of a park near Sachiko's house.

We drove through a confusion of streets in what Noriko called her 'familee car', a white Nissan Sunny, and, despite a traffic jam, met up with Sachiko who was driving an identical car. This coincidence is nothing unusual in a country where virtually every car is Japanese and every colour is white. The Japanese may like to flirt with foreign cars from time to time but it's obvious that, in their heart of hearts, they don't trust anything other than their own. When in 1985 the Labour Minister, Yoshio Yamaguichi, bought a Chrysler Fifth Avenue limousine in compliance with Cabinet guidance about ministers buying imported cars for their official fleets, he commented, after riding in it, 'It's rather like meeting a bride chosen by your parents. I prefer a Japanese wife and the same goes for cars.'

Sachiko lived in a smart house in a smart area with her well-built and jocular husband, Kunio. Although they had never met Noriko or myself, they greeted us both warmly and sat us down to coffee and biscuits. Having lived for five or six years in New Jersey before moving to Ealing for another five years, they both spoke English. Kunio, who said he was known as Gus in the States on account of his American friends' inability to remember his name, told me that the best time they had was in London.

'Ealing was so great place for living,' he said. 'Everyone had always many dinner party. Round table there was Polish, Jewish, Scots, Romanian, English, Japanese friend. Truly international neighbour! Ah so, England was really best time for us.'

Kunio and Sachiko went to live abroad because of Sekisui Polystyrene – Kunio's foam-manufacturing company, whose production base lay in Wales at Merthyr Tydfil (a town, I told him, which I was familiar with because of its high-spirited cycling club) and whose headquarters were in Windsor.

'Very excellent position,' said Kunio, 'because we were exactly next door to pub. Newcastle bitter – very fine!'

Along with British pubs, one of Kunio's favourite pastimes

when living in England was playing golf at the Richmond Club.

'So beautiful house,' he said, 'and fine 100-year-old green. Such history! Here golf is most impossible for playing – too many people, too much money. I enjoy very much club camaraderie. Always I was invited to join in with other group. In Japan this is not something we do. Japanese people like to keep themselves to themselves. I believe the Brits play more for club-house sociability time and after-game beer drinking than for actuality of the game. It is most agreeable attitude!'

Meanwhile Sachiko was busily chattering away in Japanese to Noriko amidst bursts of high-pitched giggles. After coffee Sachiko gave us a partial tour of her house, which was furnished in a mix of half Japanese-style and half Western: standing furniture and carpets here, *tatami* and *shoji* screens there. As we peeped into rooms and peeked around doors Sachiko told me she spent much of her time involved in organizing the OWC – Overseas Women's Club – in which the latest guests to visit them were the Lord and Lady Mayor of London. Her other great interest was painting – not the stark simplicity of traditional Japanese brush and ink but, as she put it, 'English typical still-life' of daffodils and fruit.

Before leaving, Sachiko and Kunio invited me to come back to their home for dinner that night, Kunio volunteering to pick me up from Noriko's flat and drop me back later. Suddenly my cycling tour seemed more of a motoring one – at least for the day. Back in the Sunny 'familee car' Noriko and I returned to her flat, where we picked up Miki before driving to lunch at, as she put it, 'American-style familee restaurant', where Noriko had chicken and fish pilaff while Miki and I ate spaghetti with chopsticks. This was followed by joining a two-hour traffic jam to Miki's ballet class.

Miki and I had so far communicated with each other in a monosyllabic fashion, a comical mix of her hesitant English and my hazardous Japanese. Here's a typical conversation:

ME: Miki, what fish this?
MIKI: Yes – fish
ME: Fish – yes. But name fish please.
MIKI: Good.
ME: Good fish yes. But what?
MIKI: Yes. Fish. Very good.
ME (adopting perplexed expression): Fish good yes. But name what? No octopus. No squid but . . . ?
MIKI: Yes. No octopus.
ME: And no squid but . . . ?
MIKI: Yes. No squid.
ME (by now feeling it might well be wiser to change the subject but doggedly determined to see this fishy matter through, come fish or high water): And fish, no salmon . . . ?
MIKI: Salmon? You like?
ME: Err, yes, salmon I like. But, fish here, what name?
MIKI: Yes.
ME: Yes? But fish name please.
MIKI: Best deliciousness.

And there my shrimpish brain would winkle out and I'd call it a day with the Best of Deliciousness.

So now, stranded in traffic in the Sunny old Nissan with Miki up front, it came as something of a surprise when, after a period of silence, she turned her head round to me and, without hesitation, said in perfect English: 'Please take a nap in my car.'

Miki's ballet class was an unexpected joy. I sat on a chair in the corner of a mirror-walled room with Noriko and a handful of other adoring mothers. The eight girls, all about eleven or twelve years old, wore identical marshmallow tights and navy leotards, beneath which signs of pubescence were beginning to bud. The dancers, black-bunned hair pulled tight from faces possessed of a lunar luminescence, resembled a sublime collection of miniature and orientalized Margot Fonteyns. They moved with a cat-like agility and grace that had me utterly transfixed. A vision of captivating perfection, their svelte-stockinged bodies launched in unison into thin air with an unbelievable weightlessness. Their expressions, set as if in the palest and purest of marbles, remained serenely unfaltering.

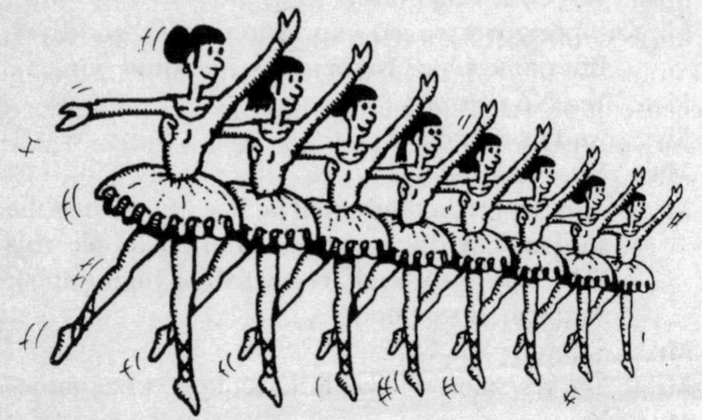

It was Sunday. Unlike the soporific Sunday of the Anglo-Saxon world or the long-drawn-out sun-and-siesta replete-with-lunch ones of the Mediterranean, this day was even more frenetic than any other day of the week. Sunday in Japan is no time for a snooze and a slob but *the* day for shopping. Unlike in, say, London which feels decidedly and delightfully deserted on a Sunday, Tokyo appears to fill up. Throughout Japan the cities' department stores resemble the consumer frenzy scrum of the first day of the Harrods sale. Packs of families turn out in force and although husbands who see little (if anything) of their families during the week are getting into the shopping swing of things, they still refer to this time spent with their wives and children as 'family service'. Sunday, it seems, is a day devoted to activity – to go, to do, to spend. A clockwork orange of impulsive furore, albeit on a modified, codified scale.

But this Sunday, Akitome was not so much servicing his family as entertaining *gaijin* and he whisked me off on an afternoon's brisk saunter which took us along a small section of the Tokaido Road, or 'Eastern Sea route', the old highway that led along the coast from Kyoto to Edo (Tokyo) on the Kanto Plain. This once scenic route (famously immortalized through Hiroshige's woodblock prints) is now an almost continuous industrial belt through which the *shinkansen* (or Bullet Train as we *gaijin* call it) shoots. At one point we branched off to visit a Second World War cemetery that Akitome seemed determined to show me, not so much because of the stark expanse of white crosses which bore the names of British, New Zealand, Australian, Indian, Pakistani and American servicemen, but because 'here exactly recently your Queen and Princess Diana visit'.

All I could think of to say in reply to that one was, 'Ah so, *desu-ka*?'

As we walked, we talked. Although Akitomo had worked for the same steel company for twenty years he still only had ten days' holiday a year. I couldn't quite gather whether this decidedly stingy allocation was the official amount of holiday his company gave him or was perhaps the most he felt it was feasible for him to take, due to company loyalty. Kunio had told me that this loyalty, which has been inherent in most Japanese companies, is diminishing and that, these days, there is more movement of employees than the well-worn cliché of lifetime employment suggests. Although Akitomo agreed that ways are changing and that the (mainly) younger generation is adopting the more Western practice of job-hopping, he didn't think it a good thing as the solid grounding, security, pride and respect that arose from such loyalty were being lost. Nonetheless he still felt that, after experimenting with modernization, Japanese workers would turn back to the more familiar 'lifetime employment' because 'it is in our tradition'. According to this tradition, when a new group of recruits enters a company they are put through a comprehensive and rigorous orientation, learning the corporate song, motto, philosophy, ways and whims and so on in a process which is intended to initiate a paternalistic bonding between employers and employees. Larger firms often provide housing in company-owned buildings along with transport and medical care, and even, in some cases, schooling for the employees' children. Office outings and team sports are organized and some corporations provide a computerized 'meet your mate' for in-house marriages, the notion being, I presume, that an incestuous workforce effectively makes for one big happy family. Another major incentive to stay with the same company is that, if the employee does switch jobs, it is rare for a successful salaryman to gain an equivalent job with a rival firm since poaching is often still frowned upon. As a result, his previous experience may be disregarded, so that he loses his place on the promotion escalator. Once cocooned within the bosom of the company, the employee's sense of security is enhanced by the knowledge that he's only likely to be sacked if he commits a flagrant crime or violates a company rule.

Instead of laying off in times of recession, it has been customary for companies to rally round and encourage the workers to tackle the 'bumping along the bottom' problems. To aid the business through rocky times, the high-flying bigwigs have their salaries cut and stall any pay rises or bonuses that may have been lingering in the pipeline. This seems to be a solicitous and civilized way of seeing out slumpish times while still keeping the company intact and is perhaps something that those Fat Cats on this side of the globe who favour kicking out a few hundred subordinate employees (if it means they keep their fleet of Porsches and Jags) could well emulate.

Whereas employees in Britain who know that their job is in jeopardy will understandably be wavering and worrying on the brink of uncertainty instead of concentrating on their jobs, it has long been the case (though the situation is now rapidly changing) that those in Japan will be working far more effectively with the reassurance and knowledge that they won't be gone tomorrow. Thus, instead of allowing the problems to defeat morale, traditionally everyone pulls together and the work group usually emerges stronger, having endured strenuous times together. Such fraternization produces ample loyalty on behalf of workers. As a result they often don't leave work before their boss does and, if their boss leaves early, they don't use this as an excuse to sneak off down to the pub or back to their wives, but stay much later. Seemingly, this is not only because they feel a sense of obligation to their employers but also because, unlike the average European who tends to keep private life out of the workplace, regarding a job as an income, the average Japanese regards the workplace as home.

The stereotypical Japanese dedication to work is legendary. A few years ago, when the Ministry of Trade and Industry (MITI) was involved in the annual budget hassle with the Finance Ministry, during which senior officials had to work so late on figures that they ate and slept in the office for several nights in a row, one of the men refused to go home even though his wife was dying of pneumonia.

Stress from overwork is still affecting Japan's workforce despite the majority of salarymen having (in theory) cut their twelve-hour day from six days a week down to a more reasonable five days. When a law was revised towards the end of the 'eighties and a committee was set up in an effort to encourage citizens to work a shorter week, the committee itself ended up working six days a week. After a year, finding that the new law was being mostly ignored, the committee, tired and overworked, was disbanded.

Since the end of the Second World War the Japanese have succeeded in giving the impression that, as a nation, they have less leisure time than people in any other industrialized country – a legacy of the relentless drive to 'catch up with the West'. In 1960 one of the government slogans was 'Double Your Income'. This money-making goal was meant to be achieved in ten years; in fact it took only seven. Such are the mesmerizing rates for which the beavering Japanese are known that, since the supposed implementation of the five-day week, it has been found that the average Japanese worker still puts in between 200 to 500 hours (or 25 to 62½ working days) a year longer than their European and North American counterparts. Even though the government has denied the figures, a victims' group has estimated that there are 10,000 cases of *karoshi* (death from overwork) a year. In a short item of 'Overseas News', *The Times* (30th March 1996) reported how Dentsu, a Japanese advertising agency:

> was ordered to pay £751,000 in damages to the parents of a twenty-four-year-old man who committed suicide in 1991 because of chronic overwork and lack of sleep . . . the man reported for work at about 8 a.m. and was required to work until 2 a.m. the next morning once or twice a week, and around the clock until 6.30 a.m. on other days. Worn down by this punishing schedule, he took his own life just sixteen months after starting his career.

The closest I've come to encountering a Japanese suicide occurred shortly after leaving school when I set up a somewhat haphazard bicycle-trailer catering business. One of my jobs was to cook for a company at the St James's end of Pall Mall. It was here that, one morning, at the top of the stairwell, the body of a Japanese businessmen was found hanging.

In a way, suicide is almost synonymous with Japan. Ask a random selection of British people what they associate with Japan, apart from cars and Walkmans, electrical goods and motorbikes, and the likelihood is that kamikaze and *hara-kiri* will feature at the top of the list. The English may have a grand old tradition of retiring to the library with a decanter of whisky and a well-aged Webley service revolver, but it pales into insignificance compared with the Japanese one of gory self-destruction. To traditionally minded Japanese, no crime is so heinous that it cannot be expiated by *hara-kiri*.

Hara-kiri (from *hara*, belly, and *kiri*, the root form of *kiru*, to cut) is more commonly known in Japan as *seppuku* – the act of self-immolation by ritual disembowelment with a sword. This gruesome rite evolved during the Edo or Tokugawa Period (1600–1867) when, after centuries of civil war, the samurai became the ruling class. These two-and-a-half centuries of Tokugawa rule were a time of frustrating peace for the samurai, who had little opportunity for displaying their courage, loyalty and military skills, except to cut a cocky peasant or merchant down to size – there are numerous stories of the notoriously savage samurai testing the sharpness of their blades on an unfortunate commoner's neck. This puts me in mind of a piece I tore out of the *Evening Standard* (28th September 1995) headlined 'Swordsman's Sharp Defence':

> A husband was discovered hiding a 3 ft Japanese sword in his trousers at his divorce hearing in Cologne. The man, who also carried a loaf, tomatoes and butter, said he was going to use the sword to make sandwiches while he waited for his case to come up.

Sarnies notwithstanding, the samurai had other things on their plate. No longer masters of the battlefield, the warriors' swordsmanship became bogged down in progressively useless theory such as laborious attention being paid to ensuring perfect footwork and stance, which depended not on wartime experience or effective combat but on what the teacher thought looked good. Bored with endless principles, the samurai, feeling in need of a little light entertainment to spice up their once stimulating lives, hit upon the idea of killing themselves excruciatingly painfully whenever they upset their masters. Such suicide was a privilege of the warrior class, definitely not something to be indulged in by mere commoners.

Hara plays an important role in Japanese life. The belly is considered, among other things, as a seat of intelligence and communication – the organ of thought. To cut it open was to bare your thoughts, revealing your pure motives and good faith. The strength of Japanese art before Western influence was its inarticulate emotiveness. The twentieth-century poet Kotaro Takamura once said, 'My poetry comes from my bowels.' *Hara-gei* – variously translated as belly play, stomach talk, visceral art or communication without words – is one of the keys to the Japanese personality. Like other parts of Japanese tradition, *hara-gei*-tummy talk is now under criticism owing to the growing 'threat' of individualism.

But *seppuku* has always had a respected place in Japanese tradition. In 1868 Mitford wrote:

> There are many stories on record of extraordinary heroism being displayed in the hara-kiri. The case of a young fellow twenty years old which was told [to] me by an eye-witness deserves mention as a marvellous instance of determination. Not content with giving himself the one necessary cut, he slashed himself thrice horizontally and twice vertically. Then he stabbed himself in the throat until the dirk [*wakizashi*] protruded on the other side with the sharp edge to the front. Setting his teeth in the supreme effort he drove the knife forward with both hands through his throat and fell dead.

Mitford later observed that:

> 16 March was fixed for the execution by hara-kiri of the twenty men guilty of the murders [of foreigners] . . . Some twenty Frenchmen were to witness the horror. When the first condemned man came out he plunged the dirk into his stomach with such force that his entrails protruded; he held them up in his hand and began singing verses of hatred and revenge against the detested foreigners who were polluting the sacred soil of the Land of the Gods till death stopped his ghastly song.

Following the Heian Period (794–1185) the samurai had developed a strict ethical code known as *bushido* – 'The Way of the Warrior', sometimes dubbed 'the road to death'. Along with this they had evolved homosexuality into a cult of the 'purest love', and glorified death. One of their many ideals was to avoid sex with women, who were thought distracting and impure. For centuries homosexuality was seen as quite normal and was enthusiastically encouraged. As part of the warrior tradition it was considered (or hoped) that gay lovers made good soldiers. At the height of samurai power during the Kamakura Period (1185–1333) women were despised as inferior creatures, 'holes to be borrowed' for producing children. Only manly love was reckoned worthy of a true warrior.

Japan has gone from glorifying homosexuality during the samurai years to stuffing it so far back in the closet that most gays now operate from within heterosexual marriages. Even so, it is much less of a taboo in Japan than in the West. Homosexual practices have never been regarded either as a sickness or as constituting a criminal offence. Although little discussed, homosexuality is treated as part of life, far from sinful and perfectly permissible if the rules of social propriety (getting married, for instance) are observed.

Perhaps one of Japan's most famous bisexuals was Yukio Mishima. Novelist, militarist, body-builder and flamboyant showman, he exhibited an exuberantly idiosyncratic personality. Concerned that Japan was losing its heritage and patriotic drive, he resurrected the *hara-kiri* tradition whereby unhappy samurai would resort to double suicides with their male lovers. On 25th November 1970, Mishima and four hand-picked lieutenants from his private army (known as the Shield Society) seized one of the country's military headquarters and urged the troops to restore the power of the Emperor. Mocked and jeered, Mishima and his boyfriend performed a sensational, suicidal disembowelment (*seppuku*), followed by decapitation by his most trusted lieutenant. Thus he achieved in death the fusion of art and action that he had sought in life. It was a nine-day wonder, embarrassing to the authorities and later relegated to the margins of history.

Mishima once wrote that 'men must be the colour of cherry-blossoms, even in death.' Before committing ritual suicide, it was customary to apply rouge to the cheeks in order not to lose life colour after death. The much venerated cherry-blossom, which only lasts about a week in Japan, is still compared with the sacrificial kamikaze pilots – few of whom made it past their twentieth birthday. Like the fleeting beauty of the blossom, the pilots died in the prime of their lives. And youth is beautiful precisely because it is so short-lived.

> If only we might fall
> Like cherry-blossoms in the spring
> So pure and radiant

wrote one kamikaze pilot moments before he departed on his suicidal mission. The term kamikaze was first used to describe a wind which was no ordinary wind and was thought to be of the Ise shrine which produced the *kami* (divine) *kaze* (wind).

The kamikaze was instrumental in defending Japan in the thirteenth century when the threat of invasion came from Kublai Khan, the first Mongol emperor of China (grandson of Genghis Khan), whose empire extended from the Danube to the East China Sea. A fleet of nearly 900 ships carrying 40,000 troops set sail from Korea, as most of the vessels, their provisions and the men on board had been supplied by Korea under duress.

Once the Mongols had landed, the Japanese at first suffered the worst of the fighting: the invaders had deviously scurried around in regulated groups skilfully using bells and gongs as signals, and terrifying the defenders with their use of gunpowder, unknown in Japan until then.

With no peculiar exploding devices to hand, the Japanese instead turned to their gods to save them. Obviously the gods were a force to be reckoned with for a gale blew up at night which wrecked much of the Mongol fleet, drowning up to a third of the troops.

Seven years later, in 1281, the second Chinese invasion loomed over the horizon, this time in the form of two fleets carrying a total of 140,000 men. (By comparison, when the Spanish Armada attacked England in 1588 it had less than one-tenth of the ships and manpower of the Mongol fleet.) At the outset the Chinese seemed to be in a winning position but the Japanese once again put in a good bit of heavy-duty praying. The elements obligingly whipped up a typhoon, causing huge loss of life that forced the invaders – or what was left of them – to withdraw. Undaunted, Kublai Khan prepared for a third invasion but it came to nothing. Japan had been saved by the kamikaze.

More than 600 years later, in June 1944, when Japan was facing something unique in its history – defeat – hopes were again pinned on the kamikaze; but this time, rather than leaving nature to do its work, the task was entrusted to the young suicide pilots. Unlike soldiers who are compelled to fight, these men – many not much more than boys – volunteered to die. Ironically, the single-manned missiles that slammed into American battleships like explosive coffins were called *ōka* or *sakura* (cherry-blossom), the flowers that the Japanese have long thought symbolize the nation. The *sakura* is mentioned in ancient myths and the way its petals fall while still at the height of their beauty was interpreted by the samurai as symbolic of resignation and grace in death – qualities that the warriors rated highly.

It is said that the pilots always cried the same famous last words before crashing: '*Tenno Heika Banzai*!' ('Long Live the Emperor!'). But, according to some sceptics, most of them instead screamed in anguish: 'Mother!'

Spiritual conviction, the papers told the people, had shown the way to vanquish material strength. Some of the kamikaze pilots who could not bear the tension and terror of waiting killed themselves the night before their mission. Most, though, were only too eager to volunteer. Many of those that belonged to the elite 201 air unit based in the Philippines and famed for their samurai spirit hoped to increase the chance of selection by signing their names in their own blood.

CHAPTER 9

The Sticking-Out Nail

At six-thirty Kunio picked me up in the Sunny and drove me back to his house for supper. As with my lunch with Nagai-*san*, I was for some reason once again expecting Japanese food in a Japanese atmosphere. But, instead of kneeling on *tatami* at a low lacquered table, I sat with Sachiko and Kunio at a fine polished dining-room table to the accompaniment of the soft strains of a Mozart string quartet as we happily worked our way through salad niçoise, cuttlefish with beans, carrots and mini corn cobs, brie (made in Hokkaido) with French bread, and finished off with a wide slice from a sweet and juicy cantaloup melon.

Kunio told me how he loved good British food – Welsh lamb, poached salmon and new potatoes. England, he said, made him a very relaxed person.

'Before I lived in London I was always very pushy to make deals. Then an Englishman gave me fine advice: "Don't worry," he said, "sit back – relax – see what happens." This is not good attitude to have in Japan,' explained Kunio, 'but now I am very much sit-back man. Life is much more happier time now.'

Conversation darted around from topic to topic in an enjoyable topsy-turvy style. One moment we were talking about the recession, with Kunio saying how it had hit Japan in a big way and that, although only 2–3% of the population were unemployed, this figure didn't include the farmers who were out of work. For some reason I couldn't quite grasp, the unemployment figures have never included the farmers. In the next moment Kunio was recalling the first business meeting he had in Glasgow with a Glaswegian and a Cockney.

'We made a most strange mix: me – Japanese man speaking American English; Glaswegian speaking heavy Scottish; and Cockney man speaking madness language from East End. No one understanding each other. Big confusion!'

Another time Kunio explained how he and Sachiko had always wanted a dog. Something like a terrier or a basset hound or Jack Russell.

'So we went to a dog shop,' said Kunio, 'but I ask too many question – like how many exercise, how many food, how many brushing – and dog-shop owner lost patience and said, "Look, Guv – you want this dog or what?" So we did not get dog. Ha! Ha!'

Kunio drove me back to Noriko's flat where, at 11.30 p.m., Miki was still up doing her homework despite having to leave at 6 a.m. for a one-and-a-half-hour train journey to her Mission Catholic School. But this is nothing unusual in Japan. The Japanese educational system is notorious for being one of, if not *the* most mercilessly competitive in the world, with the pressure being applied from kindergarten age to pass through the harrowing gates of *shiken jigoko* ('Examination Hell'), as the brutally competitive, fact-packed university entrance exams are known.

As pupils rise up the school system, the tough entry requirements set by the best universities – an essential route into the top jobs – force students to enter a neurotic rat-race. From primary school onwards most children attend the infamous *juku* (pronounced 'joo-koo' – private fee-paying crammers), of which there are an estimated 200,000 in the country, turning the whole crammer business into something of a multi-billion yen industry in itself. These 'after-school schools' (some are before as well as after) are all based on the much-maligned and ruthless regime of rote-learning, turning out people trained from infancy in feats of memory. Creativity is not something that is sought after in Japan; it is in fact actively discouraged. Classes work as a group – moving, working, thinking together.

I read an account of one Japanese who sat in on an American university politics class and was shocked to find the professor firing questions and the students firing back their own questions. 'I had never experienced debate,' he said. 'I thought how ill-mannered American students must be and how terribly disrespectful they were towards their professors.'

Another time I read of a Japanese student's complaints concerning his professors, saying that they 'impart knowledge without stimulating us to think'. He found his lectures 'far removed from actual problems . . . There is something in the atmosphere . . . that discourages discussion with our professors, who give us lectures as though they were disregarding our presence.' Increasingly, more and more professors approve of the use of discussion and debate but admit that it is not a method of teaching they can feasibly adopt because, as one professor frankly admitted, 'In Japan, we don't have time.'

The system in Japan is just to sit and take it in, memorizing piles of historical events and dates and formal grammar and so forth, and never to put forward your own point of view. Behaving as an individual will only cause trouble.

Most parents don't want creativity in their child as it is something that cannot succeed in the Japanese educational system. Instead they want them to be successful and pass exams. Tradition dictates that it is the mother's responsibility to bring out the children's best qualities and to motivate them to work hard for a successful life. These *Kyoiku Mama*, or Education Mamas, as they are known, take this role very seriously and devote themselves entirely to their children's success, much like the traditional Jewish Momma. If their child is sick, some mothers even sit in on their son's or daughter's crammer classes, taking notes to prevent them from dropping behind. So many mothers mollycoddle their offspring that only a fraction of the children help with chores around the house compared with their Western counterparts. The mothers feed them up with protein-rich foods which were either unavailable or unaffordable in former generations. As a result, these modern mother-spoilt youngsters are commonly called '*moyashiko*' (the Beansprout Generation) because, like beansprouts, they grow tall and fast in the dark but lack substance. Some department stores provide the ultimate accessory for *Kyoiku Mama*s to buy their children: a specially adapted desk featuring a call-button connected to the kitchen. Need a pencil sharpened? Or maybe a tea or *kohii* or light refreshment? Then give mama a buzz. You know she'll come running.

It is not thought unusual for a young child to be away from home chasing education from six o'clock in the morning until eleven o'clock at night. Most children around Miki's age go off to their cramming classes after school (and even during school holidays) only to return home at night for at least two hours of homework, which often they don't finish until well after midnight. For long periods the pressure is such that these students may get no more than five or six hours of sleep a night. Some who are both physically and mentally exhausted may pay a visit to the local nurse, who reputedly doles out catch-22 remedies. 'Try to rest more,' they say, 'but don't slacken in your studies.'

The Japanese education system is geared to success and respects only success, which has resulted in Japan having what amounts to the best-trained workforce in the world. For years the West has recognized the fact that Japanese schoolchildren regularly come top of the list in comparative international tests of maths and science. It seems this is due not only to more traditional teaching methods, including whole-class teaching, but also to the built-in respect for religious and cultural teaching.

The greatest influence on education comes from the Chinese sage, Confucius, who thought that the relation of a pupil to a teacher is like that of a subject to his king.

One reason for the harsh competition of Japan's educational system is that the country's class structure, one of the world's most rigid a century ago, has almost collapsed in modern times. Today well over three-quarters of the population consider themselves to be middle class. With a literary level of very nearly 100% (Japan has the highest newspaper circulation rate in the world), the scramble to get to the top of the heap must be undertaken remorselessly.

Before Japan's rapid modernization in the nineteenth century, the educational system was not very different from that of any other feudal nation, and only a relatively small percentage of the populace received any schooling at all. The privileged were taught literature and military arts and Neo-Confucian learning, while the less privileged studied mainly reading, writing and the abacus. Among the many reforms introduced by the Meiji Restoration in 1868 were those in education which made free elementary schooling compulsory. Thus, by the turn of the twentieth century, Japan was well on the road to becoming one of the most literate nations in the world.

From the 1920s the Japanese government had enforced strict conformity to the *kokutai* ('national structure') in schools, in workplaces and in people's homes; the dreaded *kenpeitai* (military police) had seen to this with thoroughness. School textbooks taught about the destiny of Japan to rule over Asia, the divinity of the Emperor, and complete obedience to authority. Schoolchildren were taught the myths about the divine origins of the Emperor and the Japanese islands as though they were historical fact. Teachers had been obliged to teach children that the Japanese were innately superior to all other peoples. But in 1947, the educational system was again reformed, this time under the auspices of the Allied Occupation authorities, and they adopted the American model of education – the so-called 6-3-3-4 system: six years at elementary school, three years of Junior High, three years of high school and four years of university. Classes in English and other languages were reintroduced after having been banned for many years.

Most Japanese teachers embraced the new order with apparent enthusiasm, brushing the militarist ideology discreetly under the *tatami* and turning to expound the virtues of democracy. Very few teachers resigned on grounds of conscience. Some were genuinely relieved to be free from the lies and oppression of the war years and openly admitted that Japan – superior as it was thought to be – had inflicted untold suffering on millions of innocent people abroad. Because of Japan's notorious wartime brutality, most countries in Asia have nursed a justifiable deep-seated sense of suspicion and mistrust of the Japanese but, by way of some sort of compensation, have looked keenly to Japan for economic assistance and investment.

Things gradually improved until, in 1982, the ghostly shades of war returned to undermine Japan's ties with China and other Asian countries: the Japanese government was bombarded with international criticism for its system of censoring school textbooks dealing with the Sino-Japanese War. Under a long-standing system of 'vetting' textbooks, government officials were pressing schools to delete the phrase 'Japanese aggression' and, instead, to refer to the army's 'advance' into China.

Today the greatest burden of all on Japanese schoolchildren is the pressure to succeed. Courses are set at the level of the ablest students, and there is precious little provision for the weaker ones – the opposite of what parents complain of in English state schools. And everything depends on what school you go to. Children at mediocre schools become sadly discouraged: they assume that they will never get anywhere in life, however hard they try. Teachers,

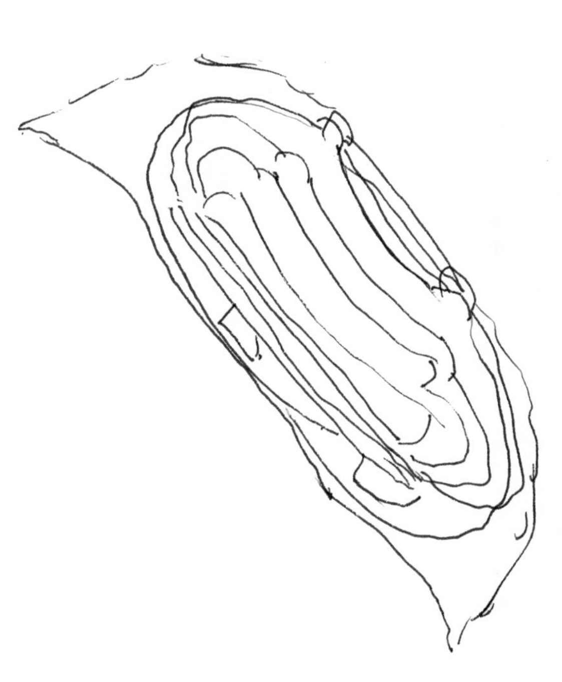

WELCOME

I am interested in joining St Martin's and would like to receive a special pack giving details of worship, activities, and how to get further involved.

Name ______________________________

Address ______________________________

____

Postcode _______________

Please hand this form to a steward or verger, or return it to 6 St Martin's Place, London WC2N 4JJ in turn, feel an immense sense of responsibility in making sure that their pupils will succeed at school – otherwise the pupil's prospects in life will be wrecked. The fanatical discipline, and even the violent excesses, come from the unbalanced sense of duty of some teachers who have carried their rage for order to extremes. I read about one schoolboy who took a hair dryer with him on a school trip, despite having been told that this was forbidden. A teacher hit him so hard that the boy died. Another time a girl arrived for school a fraction of a second late as the teacher slammed the heavy gate shut on her. She died of a fractured skull. These are of course extreme cases but the strange thing is that parents generally approve of severity in teachers.

With a schooling system that revolves around such pressure it's not just the teachers who explode with the occasional burst of violence. More and more children, unable any longer to bear the stress and strain or bullying and who are increasingly being beaten or kicked or stabbed are unleashing their anger upon teachers or family or classmates. One boy, desperate after failing his exams twice over and having been chided by his parents, picked up a baseball bat and bludgeoned his parents to death. On another occasion two boys of quiet disposition were arrested for murder. After being forced to commit an obscene act in front of their whole class, they had lured their tormentor to a secluded spot where they set upon him, shattered his skull with a hammer and gouged out his eyes.

The gruesome murder committed by these boys is an example of what the focus of relentless *ijime* (bullying or teasing) can lead to. Every year in Japan children are brought to the brink of mental breakdown and this leads to an increasing number of deaths. The usual format is depressingly consistent. A child only has to be a bit fatter or thinner or weaker or more intelligent or less intelligent, or have a slightly different shade of black hair or be a new arrival from another school, or to have lived abroad, to be singled out, picked on, victimized and turned into a living wreck.

The Japanese have a proverb that applies to those of non-conformist behaviour or those who don't fit in: 'A nail that sticks out must be hammered in.' Bullying is of course nothing unusual among children anywhere, but *ijime* is distinct from most other forms for its inexorable and mercilessly systematic quality. The victims have no chance of relief. Once the bullying has begun they will even be ostracized by their closest friends, who are forced to desert them in order that they themselves may avoid standing out from the crowd. The victim has no one. Most cannot turn to their parents for support, for to do so would only bring shame upon the whole family. They suffer alone – often for years – until either time or suicide or some angry act of violent revenge releases them from their anguish.

Doing your own thing is definitely not what Japanese education is all about. The most visible sign of this is that all Japanese schoolchildren wear uniforms: the boys in their black, brass-buttoned, Prussian-style tunics with standard black caps and gold braid trousers, which seem to combine a respectful reference both to the Emperor (military cadet) and to Buddhism (Shinto priest) and yet which end up looking not dissimilar from ill-fitting boiler-suits; the girls in white blouses and matronly long navy-blue skirts. And it seems these skirts cannot be just any old navy-blue skirt. Some schools' rules and regulations (in a pamphlet which can be as much as fifty pages long) state how many pleats there should be on a girl's skirt. Teachers may even be stationed at the school gates to measure the inches between a girl's skirt hem and the ground.

Interminably finicky rules apart, the fate awaiting almost all schoolchildren is the Examination Hell, which determines which university they will graduate from – a factor of crucial importance in the frenzied competition for the best jobs. There is a permeating anxiety in Japan: unless you can step on to the right ladder early on in life, you will never come to anything.

The rounds of Examination Hell for which children of Miki's age are being prepared at the crammers are for places in prestigious and mostly private middle schools. Children that fail to get into these schools have little chance of entering the sort of high schools that put them in a prime position for applying to the top universities – the most respected being Tokyo (Todai), Kyoto, Keio and Waseda. It is taken for granted that the golden goal for most children is university because, without a degree, there is almost no hope of a secure career.

In aiming to reach one of the prestigious private universities, the pressures of competition start early: most of these universities offer an *esukareta* ('escalator system') which virtually guarantees certain four-year-olds a place if a child enters the school's affiliated kindergarten. The entrance exam to Keio primary school is more competitive than the entrance to Keio University itself and is possibly the single most decisive event in a pupil's life. Once that hurdle is overcome, the child will be 'escalated' smoothly upwards through junior high, high school and then to the university. Keio calls this the 'integral system of education'. In order for her child to get a head start the Education Mama will strive her utmost to get her son or daughter in the right primary school. And, to make certain of that, she will put pressure upon her toddler by enrolling him into the kindergarten which has the best reputation for preparing children for primary school. Nor does it end there, as there are even pre-kindergartens that claim they can get children into the right kindergartens. And, just when you think you need a doctorate to follow these perplexing primary procedures, you discover that there is even one Tokyo maternity hospital that offers a remarkable package – or more like placenta-deal: privileged babies born there are guaranteed a place in one of the top-notch kindergartens.

The average Japanese schoolchild spends 240 days a year at school (which includes working three Saturdays in four – although the Ministry of Education is reducing this to two), compared with about 175 days in England. The diligence and perseverance that schoolchildren possess is astounding and puts my haphazard pea-shooting, catapult-making, paper-darts flying tomfoolery schooldays to shame.

The Japanese consider an ability to persist, even when the gains appear hopelessly small, to be one of the most admirable qualities in a person. This is the much esteemed *ganbaru* spirit, which enables one to hang on in there come examination hell or high water. *Ganbaru* is one of the major ingredients for success. The old adage '*Ishi no ue nimo sannen*' means that sitting on a rock for three years heats it up, implying that perseverance brings success – either that or piles.

The result of spending around twelve years of highly competitive and pressurized all-work-and-no-play time at school is that, by the time the students actually enter university, they are utterly exhausted – so they don't do much work. But this rapid decline in academic diligence is something quite acceptable. In fact, for most students, university signals a time in which to savour four years of unaccustomed freedom, leisure and fun. It doesn't matter what grades they come out with in the end, just so long as they get some sort of a degree. Companies are not so much interested in how much work their potential employees have done as they are in the name of the university. Find yourself in one of the high-ranking ones and you're well on the road to guaranteed lifetime employment.

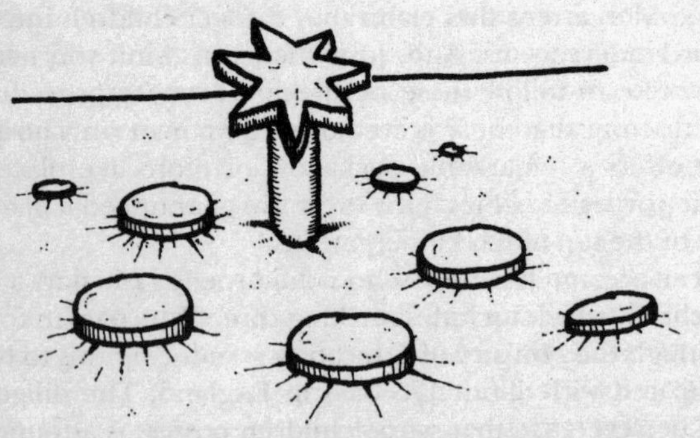

Lashings of rain fell all morning. The scene from Floor 14 was one of leaden greyness. As I got on with letter-writing, diary-writing, cutting bits out and sticking bits in from tourist pamphlets and learning my Japanese numbers, days, months and a medley of phrases which I would no doubt promptly forget, Noriko busied herself around the flat, hoovering and humming.

At eleven o'clock we braved the weather and scampered down the hill beneath brolly to the station to catch the train to Yokohama. Waiting for a train in Japan, you don't go and stand anywhere you fancy on the platform. Instead you find a person or people who are waiting for a train (there will always be someone, somewhere, no matter how early you arrive) and go and stand behind them. And wait. But not for long as trains in Japan seem to do more coming than going. The weird thing is that this queue, which starts out so neatly and politely, goes to pot once the train has arrived; as soon as the doors have opened, the queue fragments and breaks apart with a spurt and people are pushed on board. A queue of orderliness followed by a tidal-wave of packed confusion. All quite normal – for Japan.

Noriko and I spent the day ambling around San Diego's sister city, Yokohama. We did nothing in particular, just poked our way around the streets, dipping and delving in and out of shops in Chinatown (Japan's largest Chinese settlement), posing with the masses for snaps in front of the elaborately tiered roof of Kanteibyo temple with its super-sweeping eaves adorned with vibrant dragons. In one store full of curios and strange things in jars I picked up a leaflet entitled 'Japanese Home Cures', which listed a handful of tips that I thought might come in handy as part of my bicycling medical kit:

BURNS: apply egg-white mixed with *shoyu* (soy sauce)
RASH: rub with cucumber
MADNESS: ground monkey brains
LOVE POTION: charred lizards
SEX POTION: *akamamushi* (red snake)

What the instructions failed to reveal was in what manner the remedy should be administered – whether it should be a teaspoon of monkey brains in a glass of water three times a day or a whole snake on toast. And besides, just what is a love or sex potion anyway? Is a mouthful of burnt lizards supposed to make you more lovey and a suck on a snake more sexy? Who knows? But I packed the leaflet away with my waterproof plasters, pills, potions and lotions, just in case.

We nudged our way among the crowds past Yokohama Stadium – home to the professional team of baseball-batting Baystars – through Nogeyama Park, where a tourist pamphlet informed me that 'children can enjoy fonding the rabbits, guinea pigs and other animals', past the immense Yokohama Arena with its 17,000 seats (11,000 of which are computer-controlled and movable) and a giant four-screen projection system, before nipping up the hill past the Foreigners' Cemetery, containing the graves of more than 4,000 *gaijin*, past Christ Church on the Bluff (which elbowed rather fittingly on to the Toy Museum) and on to Harbour View Park. Despite the rain having now abated, Harbour View was perhaps a trifle optimistically named as it looked out over a haze of heavy concrete. I could just make out the stretched expanse of the Yokohama Bay Bridge spanning Daikoku and Honmoku Piers. With its two levels of highway the Bay Bridge looked not dissimilar to its earthquake-battered San Franciscan namesake.

Down at the harbour front, which was floating in filth, Noriko wanted to take me for a ride on the Sea Bass shuttle boat that, well, shuttles across the harbour from Yamashita Park to Yokohama Station. Although it seemed mostly to be pandering to the needs of sightseers such as ourselves, providing welcome light relief from the pavement-pounding of city streets, it also ferried a fair amount of salarymen who were obviously not just coming along for the ride. The difference between this ferry system and the one that was recently set up along the Thames (and which even more recently went out of business) is that it works. There is no waiting around on windy waterfronts thinking it could be quicker to walk, like I once did at Greenwich. The amphibious shoals of Sea Basses constantly flitted back and forth, picking up, putting down, turning round and taking off again. Fortunately, as we were among the last to board, we were saved from being cossetted in the air-conditioned, glass-concealed interior and, instead, hung out over the sides of the partially open aft deck savouring the breeze and the sights. From the sea, there were indeed sights to see as the sun shot its shafts through the haze.

As far as 'firsts' go, Yokohama must surely take some beating. It boasts the first settlement for foreigners; the first Western park in the country; 1860 – first bakery in the country; 1872 – first railway in the country; 1862 – first photographic shop and first *sukiyaki* restaurant (featuring beef newly introduced from the West); 1869 – Japan's first 'beef brewery' (as the tourist leaflet says); 1870 – Japan's first daily newspaper; 1871 – the first public toilets in Japan, built at eighty locations around the city; 1887 – the first modern water supply in the country; and so on and so forth. And now, from the decks of the sea-bussing Sea Bass, I felt that Yokohama could add yet another to its list: the first building to be built modelled on a grand piano. Perched on the waterfront of the 186-hectare development site of the Minato Mirai 21, 'New Port City for the 21st Century' (designed to be a model city of the future), was the vast white edifice of the Pacifico Yokohama – a convention and exhibition complex, conference centre and hotel which looked just as if a giant Steinway had fallen from the sky, crashing on to its own keyboard.

Once we were off the ferrying Sea Bass bus, Noriko whisked me underground – not to catch a train but to go shopping and eating. In most major cities in Japan, to plunge inward and downward for a spot of spending is quite normal. Plunging down deep beneath street-level Tokyo, Shop-City is like one huge consumer mall. You can walk for miles, shop for days, eat for months without ever having to come up for air. A mad maze of malls stretches like entrails through almost every subway arch, office block, department store, train station and hotel.

And now, in the shop-shape underworld labyrinth of Yokohama station (which led on to the Hotel Rich, the Hotel Cosmo and a complex called The Diamond), I floated along in Noriko's slipstream until we were washed up in the nether regions of Sogo Depaato, claimed to be the largest department store in Asia. Here, after much persuasion, I finally talked Noriko into allowing me to treat her to tea. Along with our pot of green tea Noriko selected a Japanese 'dessert' which, resembling some sort of raw viscera, looked more the type of thing you might expect to find on the floor of an abattoir than on the sweet-trolley of a tea room. Feeling in a dangerously adventurous spirit I decided to join Noriko in *keiki*-eating by choosing the best of a highly unappetizing looking selection. At least my choice didn't look like a lump of offal.

Somewhere along the taking-of-orders line there must have been a communication breakdown, for the dish that arrived in front of me contained a mountain of worms which struck me as more fitting for the compost pile than my stomach. What resembled a bowlful of cold, greyish-brown, rubbery spaghetti was in fact, thanks to Noriko's translation, a type of seaweed, boiled and now congealed and doused in vinegar. Slithering from my chopsticks it was, I can honestly say, the most disgusting thing I have ever tasted, but, spurred on by that strange thing called 'politeness', I was determined to make some brief inroads into the mass of tangled and gelatinous coils. The only way in which I was able to achieve this was to take a retch-worthy mouthful and time my swallow only when Noriko looked downwards to tackle her own food. In this way I managed to keep her from seeing the wrinkled-up face of disgust that I found impossible not to pull whenever a glutinous globule slimed its sickening way down my throat.

To take my mind off such an unpleasant and stomach-churning experience I consoled myself by elevating to a higher floor where, in the English-book department, I bought four books about Japan. I then went on to search out the bicycle department, where I found that a Bell helmet I had bought in England for £30 would cost me £120 here and where, despite being in the Land of the Rising Bicycle Component, a Shimano rear derailleur would make me four times worse off than if I was to buy it back home. In the light of that discovery, all I could hope was that nothing would go wrong with my bicycle.

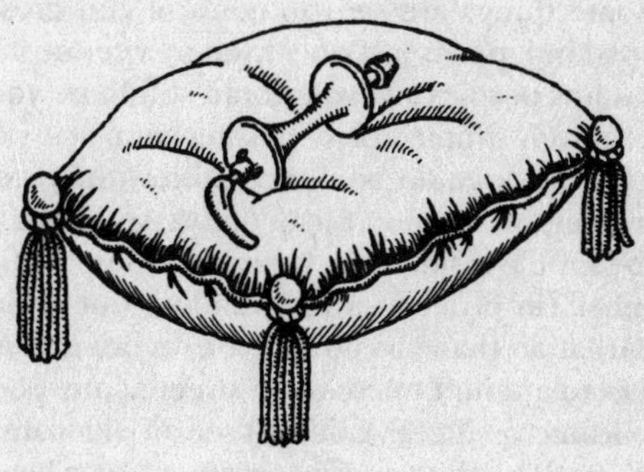

CHAPTER 10

How to Bow

Some things are sent to confuse and crossing the road in Japan is just one. Even in a country that is as peculiar as it is perplexing, you would still hope and expect that the relatively simple task of passing from one side of the street to the other could be undertaken without too much confusion. But, oh no, don't leap before you look. Nothing that can be simple is simple in Japan. In cities, the first thing to remember (in order to avoid standing out as more of a foreign barbarian than you already are) is not under any circumstances to attempt to cross the street at any point other than a pelican crossing. Even if you see an old woman dying of a heart attack on the opposite pavement, woe betide those who put the lives of others before their own and dash spontaneously across the street to aid the stricken dame. No, if you really feel you must help the helpless (most Japanese prefer to alter course just enough so as to avoid tripping over the collapsed obstruction) you must scurry down to the nearest set of lights and stand patiently, along with the placidly standing crowds waiting for the illuminated green man to give permission to cross, whether or not there is a car within sight.

And it's not just little green men who give the signal for

swinging a leg, but a clamorous concoction of clock cuckoos and repetitively discordant 'ditties' and high-pitched oriental nursery-rhymes which blare out their nerve-jangling refrains in identical style all over Japan every time the little men turn green.

I was back in the midst of the Impermanent City, as someone once dubbed Tokyo, the metropolis that permanently pumps with dangerously high blood pressure and which, thanks to earthquakes and war, has already had to be rebuilt twice this century. But I was only here for a day this time, to pick up some traveller's cheques, visit the tourist office and meet Nagai-*san* for lunch. It was during this lunch of omelette and chips that Nagai-*san* told me that he had found life in England considerably easier than in Japan.

'But,' he added, 'although many of my friends and colleagues want very much to live in England, they want to die in Japan because to "die on a *tatami* mat" is famous Japanese proverb which means traditionally Japanese people prefer to be buried in their own land.'

After lunch I mentioned to Nagai-*san* that I was off to the tourist office and, despite my protestations, he insisted on taking me there by taxi. There has been many a derogatory comment in the past about the dare-devil driving techniques of the average Tokyoite taxi-driver. An old and much regurgitated tale jokes that the former kamikaze pilots had become taxi-drivers but were hoping to get their old jobs back because, compared with having to do battle daily with the death-defying techniques of their fellow taxi-drivers, flying on a suicidal mission was far less dangerous. Today, grounded by Tokyo's infamous gridlock and unable to show off their notoriously erratic motoring 'skills', the white-gloved taxi-drivers seem to be a decidedly placid lot, more concerned with decking out their vehicles' interiors in fetching white lace or plastic seat covers than getting anywhere fast. To keep at bay the boredom of spending all day, every day, stuck in a bottleneck, some Tokyo taxis even come fitted with miniature televisions. But the most curious aspect of a Japanese taxi is the way in which its passenger doors open by remote control. Initially, this can come as a bit of a shock, especially for the uninitiated foreign male who, hailing a taxi from the kerbside, runs the risk of being bashed in the groin by the poltergeist phenomenon of these automatic doors swinging open.

Outside the tourist office I came across an exciting sight: a couple of touring cyclists. The two young men turned out to be Vietnamese refugees who had spent the past twelve years living in Denmark. They had set out about six months before and, by combining train and cycle, travelled through Eastern Europe. They had then flown from Istanbul to Thailand, which they found too hot so had taken a flight to Japan, which they now found too expensive. When I met them they were in the process of trying to buy a plane ticket to Hong Kong via Shanghai so as to be able to pick up a cheap flight from there to Bangkok, from where they could find a cheap ticket back to Denmark. I think they lost me somewhere over the South China Sea via the Gobi desert. From what I could make out it all seemed like an incredibly complicated and circuitous way to see the world after setting out on a particularly simple form of transport. Anyway, I wished them well and, after a bout of heavy handshakes, I watched them wheel off down the road before being engulfed in exhaust fumes.

I spent the rest of the day surfing my way in lost state through some of the department stores. On my last visit to Tokyo, before I had set sail on my cycling voyage around the Boso-hanto 'boot', I had spent quite a bit of time floating through the curiosities of these *depaato.* Tokyo, like London, is a network of 'villages' all glued together, although Tokyo struck me more as cities within a city. But cities aside, you take Tokyo by neighbourhoods – Shinjuko, Shibuya, Aoyama,

Akasaka, Roppongi and Ginza, to name but a few – all of which are as simultaneously different as they are similar, catering for every taste, fulfilling every need. But, above all, what binds them together (apart from a common tongue) is sex, *sushi* and shopping. For the latter, the bulky weight of *depaato* (never '*depaatoes*', like potatoes, as there are no plurals in Japan) rate high in this modern thriftless society.

Big buildings spell Big Spend. The aptly named district of Shibuya (if I can take the liberty of combining a spot of Janglish: *shi* = city in Japanese; *buy* = buy in English; stick them together and you get Spend City) is an area which resembles one vast shopping mall of consumer frenzy, full of hip and swinging, money-oozing fashion-followers in their twenties. *Depaato* feature heavily – and, for some, heavenly – on the agenda, offering a cornucopia of foreign goods. Seibu (which in the pecking order of *depaato* is as Selfridges is to Harrods), Parco and Marui are all *depaato* where the recklessly wealthy can have a field day. The fresh-of-face Tokyoite in their fêted *Comme des Garçons*, Issey Miyake and Yohji Yamamoto designer collections swill along among the well-heeled crowds of Chuo Dori in downtown Ginza, surging through the doors of the big and exclusive *depaato*: Matsuya, Waco and Mitsukoshi (the latter, which was established in Edo in 1673 as a dry-goods store, is the oldest department store in the world).

Most large *depaato* are set out along similar lines. Fancy a new kimono? – rise to the third floor. Need a handkerchief? – drop to the first (but remember, no blowing). Feeling peckish? – ride up to the sixth or seventh floor for a generous assortment of restaurants. Need to stock up on groceries? – plunge to the basement to be overwhelmed with free samples, choice and price.

Dropping through the floors of Matsuya *depaato* I passed through a number of clothing departments – the most notable ones being those that sold a silk suit for £3,500 and a £6,500 kimono decorated with fans, looking as regal and elaborate as a peacock's tail – until I arrived in the food basement where genial sales assistants plied me with a plethora of free promotional samples that were either pierced on cocktail sticks or delivered into my far-from-reluctant hands by *hashi* (chopsticks). Down my ever-eager hatch slithered titbits of *sushi*, tofu, *tempura*, dried fish (heads, eyes, tails and all), seaweedy cod's roe, circles of squid, and pickled this and slimy that.

Over in the 'naughty but nice' section I was asked by a sing-song salesgirl, '*keiki taberu*? – want some cake?' As delicately as a bird, she proffered me morsels of *zenzai* (steamed rice cakes with sweet soya bean paste) and *manju doryaki* (*keiki* made from the ever-adaptable soya bean). After loitering with tasty intent among the tantalizing stalls, sampling here and sampling there, I was no longer hungry, which was good news for the weight of my wallet because if I had fancied a bit of a sit down with a *keiki* and a coffee I wouldn't have walked away with much change from a tenner.

The first time I lined up at 10 a.m. outside a *depaato* waiting for the doors to open I received quite a shock. Unlike, say, John Lewis or the Army & Navy or Debenhams, where you wait impatiently biting at the bit while watching a gruff, slow-moving security guard unlocking the doors with a jangle of keys, the department stores of Japan have ready a formation of doll-like young women smartly turned out in uniform, hat and white gloves to greet the flood of customers spilling through the doors. The girls, operating like a rank of mechanical toy soldiers, make identical bows and pipe in perfect unison in artificial falsetto voices: '*Irasshaimase* – welcome.'

In many countries, despite the customer being considered as king, it tends to be true that the only time you get waited on hand and foot is when you get charged an arm and a leg. In Japan the customer is not so much king as God. The moment your foot steps through the doors of a *depaato*, you will undoubtedly find yourself being attended to by a series of shrill-voiced girls welcoming you in a manner of almost excruciating obsequiousness. Nip on to an automated escalator and a clockwork puppet-doll girl issuing the standard ritualistic bow and ballerina arm movements will greet you, pointing up, pointing down, while another, identical semaphoring girl will be waiting at the other end to greet you off.

Like the subservient tea-making and general odd-jobbing OLs (Office Ladies), the elevator escalator girls are essentially seen as just a piece of decoration. Take the lift, for example, which is yet another of Japan's curious juxtapositions of man (or, in this case, woman) and technology. A uniformed girl will bow you in through the automated doors and the same one, or another who looks the same as the first one, will bow to you continually as the lift (which is automatic and can run without an attendant) rises or falls through the floors. Keeled over at a precise 45° angle she will thank you for going up and down and explain in surreal and simpering tones what departments are on what floors. At least I presumed this was what she was saying but for all I knew she could be wishing me to 'have a nice trip' or 'keep fine health' or maybe even to 'stand up straight and pull your stomach in'. Well, whatever it was, elevator girls repeat it about a thousand times an hour with infinite patience as they stand there bobbing up and down, hands folded neatly in front of them, right over left. To be caught alone in a lift with an elevator girl and to find yourself the sole object of her almost sycophantic pose and patter is something of an excruciating experience. I wanted to say something like, 'look, please, take a breather, have a break, have a Kit-Kat. I'm just your average sweaty-pitted foreigner. It's very nice of you but I really don't need such honourable treatment. Please, feel free to give your smiling mouth a rest.'

I wanted to break her bows – stretch her spine – and offer her a brief respite to be . . . well, normal. But instead I remained uneasily silent, filled with an overwhelming urge either to burst out laughing or to die with embarrassment. I didn't know which was best. And anyway, just who did I think I was telling her to act 'normal'? Maybe for her all this simpering *was* normal behaviour. Surely *I* was the one with the problem, forever judging this alien life to be odd just because it was so radically different from the life with which I was familiar. In a sense those elevating girls were acting normal because, to be polite, most Japanese spend most of their time acting. It's the difference between wearing a mask and revealing what lies behind it. And simply walking through a *depaato* gives ample opportunity to see both sides. To happen unexpectedly upon some store girls is to witness a group of young women talking quite naturally to each other. But the gap between the public and the private persona is as noticeable as it is instantaneous. Turning to address you, the salegirl's pitch will rise several octaves while her body implodes and a shrill and servile pose and patter is, for as long as you stand there, the order of the day.

All *depaato* girls are drilled to perfect their back-breaking bows. In order for them to get in a good bit of 'bowing practice', some stores have even been known to put young employees on to a special machine whereby a metal bar pushes the girls' backs into the desired 15°, 30° or 45° angle – all of which are minutely registered on a digital screen. But it is not as if the salesgirls need some state-of-the-art steel contraption in order to practise: a Tokyo journalist, with true Japanese propensity for detail, once calculated that a young woman working a six-day week in a *depaato* bows an average 798,720 times a year. A Japanese consumer magazine conducting another survey (the Japanese like their surveys) revealed that a typical escalator girl may bow up to 3,000 times a day while greeting approaching customers. Once more, out with my calculator for a spot of tap, tap, tapping which means, on average of course, that salesgirls perform an astounding 375 bows an hour or 6.25 bows a minute which surely is enough to make even the most proficient and acclimatized bower seasick.

Whether in store or out of store, bowing is something of a compulsion in Japan. Before arriving in this Land of the Rising Up and Down Spine, I had always thought that a bow is a bow is a bow – in much the same way as I was once informed by British Rail that a bike is a bike is a bike and that they don't much like them in any shape or form on their trains (I was trying to board with a Brompton folder). All I thought a bow entailed was to bend over forwards a bit before bending back up again. But oh no! In the land where the precision of the ceremonial bow is a fine art, there is more to a bow than meets the eye.

For a start, there's the geometry. Fortunately it is not so much in the right-angled and triangular theorem of which the formulaic Pythagoras is made, but it's pretty angular nonetheless. And it can all get a bit technical. The most frequent bow consists of an informal 15°, held for just one or two seconds. Stoop a spot deeper and you find yourself performing a more respectful bow of 30° used for formal occasions, like a first meeting. But keel over into a radical 45° angle held for about three seconds and you show your lowly self to be in the humble presence of a superior. Having protracted your angles to a masterly fine degree I'm afraid you can't ease up yet.

First, it's important to remember that a bow is not a bob. Bows should be controlled and deliberate actions – not, as mine turned out to be, an erratic bobbing up and down like some demented clockwork chicken.

A bow also depends on whether you are male or female. Men usually leave their arms at their sides, penguin-fashion – ram-rod straight. Women, on the other hand, or more like arm, tend to turn their arms inward to place their hands on the front of their thighs with the fingers, if not overlapping, at least touching. Heels should be together.

The Japanese are a far from stingy race – a fact that is demonstrated not only in their excessive gift-giving but also in their giving of bows, which can come not in a measly one-off, like a handshake, but in a generous grouplet of twos or threes or fours or more, such as when saying goodbye.

There is a time and a place for most things, but for bows, things can get a little confusing as to the number of times and the number of places. I read in some guide book or tourist pamphlet which I picked up in Tokyo a list devised for *Uses of the Bow*:

1. FOR GREETINGS AND PARTINGS: introductions, welcomes, acknowledgements of another's presence, gaining attention.
2. FOR SINCERITY: offering assistance, food, presents etc.
3. FOR HUMILITY: requests, respect, apology.
4. FOR CEREMONY: onset of events such as negotiations, competition, closing of events.
5. To ACKNOWLEDGE or show AGREEMENT.

I will try to simplify this list by making it more complicated. Basically there are three types of bow, all of which are to be performed while silent. The first is the *saikeirei* or 'Highest form of Salutation' which, since the end of the war, has been abolished. This bow was made to express profound obeisance and used only as a sign of paying the highest respect towards the Emperor.

Then there's the 'Ordinary Salutation', which can be performed either sitting or standing. For sitting (on the floor Japanese fashion): place the hands on the floor, palms down, four to six inches apart and bow between the hands, bringing the head to within four to six inches of the floor. For standing: you should stand bolt upright, looking forward, before bending the body to 30°, holding your position for a short pause before rising back up.

Lastly is the 'Light Bow'. The newcomer to Japan may well think that the Japanese have a bit of a fetish for bowing. But today's busy show of bows is decidedly laid back compared with days gone by when people used to bow to each other after every few words. Not surprisingly, the Japanese came to view this giddy-making custom as just a touch too complicated even for them, so now, after the first salutation is made, only the light 15° bow is used at sporadic and appropriate intervals.

The ubiquitous bow is also fairly practical as it can be performed either while standing or, if one is sitting in a Japanese-style *tatami* room, while kneeling – thus avoiding all that unnecessary energetic jumping up and down for a formal shaking of hands as tends to be the case in the West.

Bowing may seem a bit finicky with all its precise angles, but compared with our dubious penchant for sloppy kissing and the 'just-where-has-your-hand-been?' handshake, it is at least (by being a non-body-contact pastime) hygienic. The trouble with kissing is that you're never quite sure who to kiss and when to kiss, or for that matter, how many kisses to deliver. Then there's all that farcical or embarrassing confusion about which cheek to aim for that tends to result in a mass collision of noses. Generally, given the choice of lips or a shake, I prefer a hand. But it's got to be a good dry hard one. No sweaty palms or flaccid wet fish, please.

These days, though, it's becoming more and more common in Japan to witness a clash of cultures: when greeting a Western client, a salaryman will often perform a bow and a handshake simultaneously. Another common sight, which for some reason can look quite amusing through the eyes of a *gaijin*, is to see a Japanese bowing while speaking on the phone. But I suppose that, in retrospect, this is no odder than a Westerner gesticulating with gay abandon down the line.

But the basic ingredient in a bow is humility, as you elevate or honour the other person by humbling yourself. The lower you bow, the more you honour the other party.

One of the first things I discovered about bowing was that it is spontaneously infectious. You only have to be in the country a few hours before you automatically start bowing yourself. But for a dumpy or gangling *gaijin* the graceful habit of bowing is impossible to imitate. No matter how hard you try or how often you practise you'll always end up doing it wrong: you'll either bow too deeply or not deep enough; or you'll bow to the wrong person at the wrong moment in the wrong place or for too short a time; or your fingers won't be touching or your heels won't be tucked together, or your bum will be sticking out and, well . . . frankly, by not being Japanese you will also look daft.

But the Japanese expect this. They don't believe for one minute that a foreigner can emulate their enigmatic and exquisitely respectful ritual of oblique bowing which every number of society practises towards people whose function is known to them. And quite right too. How can we non-Japanese have the arrogance to know what's right when there is so much to go wrong? The elaborate intricacies of a bow are not something which you can pick up in a 'How-do-they-do-that-in-three-easy-steps?' instruction manual. A bow is in the blood from birth and is infiltrated and improved through the years mainly by intuition. Just take, for instance, the complicated hierarchy in bowing: who bows to whom, how deep to go and for how long? One of the American states once had an early traffic law whereby if two cars met at an intersection, neither was to go before the other had gone. The same sort of leeway can be seen when two Japanese are locked in a bow, as neither should straighten up before the other has risen. How they manage this without eyes in the back of their heads is most perplexing, but they seem to accomplish it without difficulty while simultaneously conveying the most minute differences in age, rank, social position – all of which will be subtly reflected in one of the bowers' bows being a mere fraction of a second shorter than the other's.

However, should you rise from a bow only to find the other person still doubled over examining their shoes with unnatural and lengthy intent, then bend back over quick before you are caught failing to acknowledge the necessary expression of respect.

Compared with the hazardous handshake or the saliva-spreading kiss, the bow is basically a safe, if time-consuming, form of greeting. Danger occurs mainly when bowing farewell to another person from the confines of a people-packed lift, because if the back-bending formality is not wrapped up quick you run the unpleasant risk of losing your head in the closing doors.

Time, or more likely Tokyo (and its lack of breathable air), was getting to me. Before the war Tokyo used to be a relatively clean place. Nihonbashi, the heart of the old city, is located beside the wide Sumida River where, during the 1930s, people would swim and fish. Then along came the massive destruction of the war and the Sumida became an open sewer into which neither man nor fish dared venture. Geisha houses lay along the bank and it is said that the methane gas from the river was so powerful that it could turn the silver pins in the geisha's head-dresses black overnight.

The massive industrial expansion that followed the war turned Tokyo into one of the most polluted cities on earth. By the time the Olympics had come to town in 1964, the pollution was so appalling that policemen who tried to unravel the traffic congestion at intersections had to have small cylinders of oxygen to assist their breathing.

Three years later the Diet, realizing things had gone a bit too far, passed a law that launched not only Tokyo but the whole of Japan into a long and lengthy clean-up act. By 1970 it was possible to smell things other than the effluent of exhaust and industrial plants. Angela Carter, writing in 1970, remarked that:

> Tokyo's scents are the reek of a peculiarly acrid petrol and of food. Shrimp frying in deep fat, curry and spices, the hot smell of cinnamon candy and the sumptuous smell of marrons being glacéd while you wait. Now and then, though, a sudden sweet whiff or the moist freshness of a flower shop.

Today, although far from fine, Tokyo is one of the cleaner dirty big cities.

Freed from the frenzied grip of downtown Tokyo, I took a day-trip with Umi and her friend Jun Takahashi, who were keen to show me the sights of vibrantly historic Kamakura, a city that bulges at the seams with temples and shrines. Most of the sights to be seen (or, in the Japanese case, to be seen in front of) are connected with Zen Buddhism, since it was this sect that the early military rulers warmed to in a big way.

The Buddhism which arrived in Japan during the sixth century came from India and China via Korea and belonged to the Mahayana (Greater Vehicle) school. However, another five centuries had passed before the by-products of the established doctrine – notably Zen and the art of motorcycle . . . whoops, I mean meditating maintenance – had arrived on the scene.

In Japan, Zen comes mainly in two forms: Rinzai and Soto. Rinzai tends to rely on the *koan* (illogical stories used as a meditational tool to achieve enlightenment) and the *mondo* (a type of multiple question-and-answer session between the *roshi*, or master, and the *deshi*, or pupil). There are thousands of *koan* and the anecdote books make nothing of a man devoting seven years to the solution of one of them. *Koan* enshrines the dilemma of life. For example: 'All things return into One; where does this last return?'; 'How does it feel to feel the yearning of one's mother before one's own conception?'; and 'If a tree falls in the forest with no one around, does it make any noise?' Hmmm. Conundrums. Confusion. How do you hear when you have no ears with which to hear? Can the *roshi* teach you to hear the one-handed clap or the silent tree fall? Sit in a leg-seized up *seiza* (lotus position) for a few long hours or days or months, endure a thwack on the back with a bamboo cane when concentration turns sloppy, and meditate on and on and on and on and maybe you can. Nangaku, for instance, spent eight years on the problem, 'Who is it who is walking towards me?' At last he understood. His words were: 'Even when one affirms that there is something here, one omits the whole.'

Soto, on the other hand (the one that isn't clapping), depends more exclusively on meditation – meditation being the literal meaning of Zen.

Kamakura may be a centre for temples and shrines but the first thing that greeted me as I spilled off the train with the crowds was the sight of a none-too-enlightening McDonald's and a Love Burger joint that sat in a state of neon transcendence across from the station. But of course the quirky juxtaposition of modern and old, ugly and beautiful, is something that sits side by side quite happily in Japan, and Kamakura is just another prime example: many of its temples appear bang next to supermarkets, car parks or *pachinko* parlours, all of which reverberate with the wailing and grating sounds of Japanese boppy pop.

With Umi and Jun, my chatty and genial escorts, I marched up shady lanes and stone-paved alleys, crossing car-jammed streets or nipping in and out of crammed and curious curio shops. Temples came and temples went. Seen this, done that. We snipped snaps of each other amidst tidal waves of yellow-capped schoolchildren's peace-poses. We dipped into a noodle shop to slurp our way noisily (the noisier the politer – a custom in which I evidently failed when a laughing Umi hailed me as impolite for not making enough appreciative slurpings) through a mountainous mound of *soba* – buckwheat noodles with 'mountain vegetable', bamboo shreds and Day-Glo pink *kamaboko* swirls.

It was hard work trying to keep up with Umi and Jun, who had sloshed their way through their *soba* before I had even broken open my *waribashi* (cheap, disposable *hashi*). But speed-eating is nothing unusual in Japan. Most of the population seem to race through their meals with an urgency similar to that which they reserve for catching a train. Somehow they are able to conduct an acrobatic blur of chopsticks, consuming the most slippery and unconducive food imaginable, while simultaneously speaking fifty-six chopping-sticks to a dozen and still succeed in finishing a multi-bowled meal in record time.

So, barely ten minutes after I had collapsed temple-weary into my *soba* seat, I was clumsily clambering back on to my feet to give chase to the slipstreams of Umi and Jun as fistfuls of swallowed-whole strands of undigested *soba* slopped around in an unsatisfying swill inside my stomach. But there was no time for commiserating with my griping intestinal tract as there were still a dizzying myriad of temples to be viewed and snaps to be snapping in a space of time that I would usually reserve for blinking. Where was the time for contemplating that one-handed clap? Where was the time for straining an ear for the sound of a falling bough in a silent forest? Strangely, it wasn't here in the City of Zen. People didn't come here for their limbs to seize or for time to freeze. They came here apparently to race, to rush, to see fleetingly, to snap, before racing home again. The tourists flock to stick Kamakura in the album. That's me in front of Kencho-ji Temple, they will say to their friends. That's me beside the ancient Ohgane bell. That's me in front of the Great Buddha. And that's me too. Ah so, *desu-ka*? say the friends in cheerful but glazed-eye reply. And then the album will close, will be stored away and before you can say '*chiizu*' they will race off again along with the millions to record yet another piece of famous-landmark Japan on film. Same pose. Same grin. Same crowds. Done. The book falls shut. The celluloid snap-shots sleep. Forgotten. Maybe that's the time for silent applause.

In the end, we're all the same.

But faster, Jodie-*san*, faster. It's time to speed up, catch up – no time to dream. This is the Japanese way – the whirlwind way. Keep a racy pace with Umi and Jun – explaining this, explaining that and tirelessly teaching me more weird but wonderful words, more frazzling phrases, more rumbustious tales of tradition to add to my paltry worldwide web as the great sights come and the lesser sights go.

As we marched breathlessly along busy back lanes daintily dabbing at our perspiring brows with carefully folded handkerchiefs, Umi suddenly stopped and said, 'Listen – Japanese nightingale!' And Jun and I both obediently stopped, mid-dab, and listened to the nearby song of 'Japanese nightingale'. A pitch-perfect piece of paradise. For a moment I pondered, absorbing the exotic sound. But there was no time for even the merest of ponders and I was off again, accelerating after Umi's and Jun's fast dissolving forms in the swirling crowds ahead.

Down one alley we passed an array of impeccable homes, some bordered by elaborate fences of woven bamboo on the one side and not-so-elaborate tile-capped walls of concrete on the other. Sometimes I would break step in order to peep through the gaps or bounce up and down to catch a momentary flying view of the gardens within. Always, exquisite paradigms of raked gravel or the tortured and twisted shape of bonsai greeted my eyes – except once, when through a chink of the fence I espied a rare strip of miniature, manicured lawn as perfect as a pristine and sumptuous emerald-green carpet. Standing on the lawn was a woman, sweeping the grass with a broom.

Between temples and sights to 'be seen at' we perched on

a wall with our vending machine iced teas and pops and Umi told me about *otoshidama* or 'New Year gifts' whereby children are given money up until the age of twenty, an age which signifies their entry into adulthood – a time that permits them legally to smoke or drink (although eighteen is the age they can drive). The 15th January is the celebratory day of the year when these children become adults. 'We wear *furisode* kimono with long *sode*,' said Umi. And then, tugging at her cuff she said, 'Jodie, excuse me but what English name?'

'Sleeve?'

'Ah so, *desu-ka*? And when we have marriage kimono sleeve is cut for making short. Short sleeve show other man we no possibility available for them to marriage.'

'Ah so, *desu-ka*?' I said. 'So it's a bit like the effects of a wedding ring?'

'*Hai, hai.* Yes.'

'Except, Umi,' I said with a sort of raised eyebrow dirty-sort-of-devil smirk, 'I think married women don't wear their short-sleeved kimono often.'

'No,' agreed Umi with a knowing grin, 'most woman in fashion jean or fashion skirt and many boyfriend!'

One of Kamakura's main tourist pulls is the Daibutsu (Great Buddha), a hefty bronze statue (ninety-four tons and forty-eight feet high), which sits with thumbs pressed together (according to tradition, the Buddha's hands were in this position when he achieved enlightenment) on the western side of town. Cast in 1252 for the Kotokuin Temple, the meditating Buddha today sits open to the elements – to weather the sun and the storms and the trainloads and busloads of camera-toting tourists and pedestal-clambering schoolchildren.

But for the first 250 years or so the Buddha didn't have so much to look at as it was originally enthroned inside a giant wooden hall that was swept away in 1495 by a massive *tsunami* (tidal wave) which destroyed Kamakura. Despite the clamorous crowds that mob its base, the Buddha continues to sit in a state of peaceful repose surviving typhoons and earthquakes intact. The technical term for this illustrious and giant figure is said to be 'Roza' ('Seated Among The Dew') although today the bucolic idea of it being surrounded by pearly drops of morning moisture is a bit of a tall order.

With the Greatness of Buddha framed on film we sped equally snap-happily around the 'Five Great Temples of Kamakura' (Kenchoji, Engakuji, Jufukuji, Jomyoji and Jochiji) and charged round a picking of the rest.

Some of the grounds of these temples were shaded by an impressive array of cedar or cypress or juniper trees. Most were reached by climbing ranks of twisted or tilted massive stone steps. Each temple had a tale to tell, such as Engakuji which, founded in 1282, was virtually destroyed in the great earthquake of 1923 and is now, in true Japanese tradition, more or less a concrete replica of the original, but still reputed to house one of Buddha's teeth brought from China. Tokeji Temple is more popularly known as Enkiridera ('Divorce Temple') and is famed for having granted refuge to desperate women fleeing from the abuse of a husband or callous mother-in-law. But life for those who made it to its confines was still far from rosy – divorce was only granted to those who completed the rigorous training as nuns.

By now I was well and truly temple-weary and feeling in need of a good spot of meditation myself. But there was no time for a sit-down or a ponder as Umi and Jun were determined that my f-stopping finger snapped shut my shutter on as many 'send-to-sleep' photogenic album-fillers as possible.

However, I did manage to make them slacken pace momentarily as I dropped a few hundred yen into a vending machine for cold drinks all round – accompanied by a handful of sweetmeats and rice cakes eaten on hoof. Revitalized, at least for the next five minutes, I chased the blue 'fashion-jean' rears of my hypersonic consorts as we shot up a hill to the tongue-tying Tsurugaoka Hachimangu Shrine where Umi told me that *yabusame* (horseback archery) takes place during the shrine's September festival.

As we paused for the obligatory 12.25 seconds (and not a nano-second more) to contemplate the sweeping views of Kamakura's tiled rooftops and distant grey sea that the shrine presides over, Umi told me she was herself a keen student of archery – but strictly of the foot brigade rather than that of the hoof (there isn't much room for hooves in Japan). I had noticed that archery was a popular pastime among schoolchildren and students: I had often passed whole classloads of orientalized Robin Hoods eagerly attuning their bows and fixing their sights for a gallant rescue of a wayward Maid Marian.

'Where do you prac . . . ?' Before the rest of my words could come up for air they were sent spinning back down the shute as it was now time to make haste, to make our fortune in the Zeniarai-benten Jinja – a decidedly way-out shrine where you go to cleanse not your mind but your money.

Entering a welcomingly cool, if crowded, cave Umi turned to me and said, 'Metal money washing day!'

Feeling that perhaps the Japanese were taking their predilection for cleanliness a drop too far, I nevertheless knew better than to question the logistics of such a curious ritual at this stage and dutifully placed my paltry collection of coins in a small wicker 'laundering' basket to sluice and shake them around in the water of the cave's spring. It was an odd experience to cleanse one's change so devoutly and I only wished that, after a long day of temple-tramping, my pavement-pounded feet could follow suit. But of course such whims were well out of the question. This was neither the time nor place to be cleansing one's soles (or soul) as, quick march, there was money to be drying in the heat of an incense flame. It seemed that the point of all this money-laundering was a belief in high-interest-making gods who, acting a bit like a bunch of altruistic bank mangers (are there such people? If so, show me The Way), increased your offerings by three-fold. (Hallelujah! Oh eastern Natwest god!)

Back outside in the gold sovereign sun, Umi turned to me with a lucrative laugh and a glint in her eye and said, 'Now everybody rich!' Rich in laughs maybe, but not, I suspect, in funds.

Feeling just as poor as when I entered the wheeling-dealing Zeniarai-benten Jinja, we again marched off at a keen lick to yet another *jinja.*

It was up at the Egara Tenjin shrine (home to a wizened old gingko tree rumoured to be a ripe 900 years old) that the indefatigable Umi and Jun had another mission in mind. It appeared this *jinja* was something of a hot-spot with schoolchildren and students because of the shrine's perceived devotion to the god of education. Steady streams of young hopefuls visit the shrine to buy small *ema* (wooden plaques depicting divine steeds) upon the back of which they pen their scholastic aspirations. However, it seems not all of the inscriptions are strictly concerned with the students' academic wishes of good fortune. I asked Umi and Jun to translate the penned *kanji* of three at random.

1. Hope to enter NY Pennsylvania University.
2. Contentment. Peace. Balance.
3. Want to become slender.

Although temple-saturation was seeping out of my shoes, the ever stalwart Umi and Jun dragged me, whimpering, off to the hilltop of the Hasedera Temple where, carved in camphor by an eighth-century priest, reposes a whopping great (nine metres, or thirty feet to you and me), eleven-faced Kannon, the Goddess of Mercy. With staff in hand and lotus flower in the other, this great Kannon (said to be the largest wooden image in Japan) is a Bodhisattva – a Buddha who has altruistically forsaken enlightenment so as to aid others along the same path and, because of this, holds a high reputation for compassion and mercy.

Mercy me.

Wandering outside in the grounds I momentarily thought I had stumbled on to the forecourt of a garden-gnome production factory when I happened upon row upon endless row of thousands of identical small stone statues which, decked out in some fairly weather-beaten red crocheted hats, bibs and bonnets, stood rank like an army of street urchins. Although supposed to look beatific, there were no smiles here. These half-sneering, stony-face statues were representations of Jizo – traditionally the patron deity of children, pregnant women, travellers and guardians of the souls of dead children. Today, though, most of these little Buddhas are guardians of the *mizugo* – 'water babies' or 'unseeing babies', the lyrical euphemism for an aborted foetus.

Abortions are bigger than big business in Japan. Thirty or so years after the pill sparked the rampant sexual revolution in the West, the easy oral-popping contraceptive is still not freely available in the 'Land of Easy Going Sex', ostensibly for fears over its safety (Japan's powerful medical lobby has managed to maintain a ban on its use, citing its negative side-effects – both real and allegedly invented – as justification), along with the government's concerns over the threat of promiscuity and a declining birth rate. More recently they say that due to the increase of AIDS in Japan it is virtually impossible to obtain the high dosage pill unless through a doctor's prescription and a great deal of red tape bureaucracy. (Incidentally AIDS has long been rumoured to be a 'white man's disease', and thought to have been kept at bay simply by sticking 'No Foreigners' signs on brothels.)

It's this spectre of HIV along with the powerful influence of doctors fond of lining their kimonos with outrageously high abortion fees that have all conspired to keep the pill out of Japan's birth control clinics. An estimated two out of three Japanese women have had at least one abortion.

Family planning has had some interesting ups and downs in Japan. Up until the end of the feudal period, infanticide and abortion were socially approved methods of birth control. But as Japan modernized and industrialized as a result of the 1868 Meiji Restoration, both became illegal due to the country's shortage of factory workers. Despite the continuous ban, more and more women began to have abortions during the depression that followed the First World War. But the government remained opposed to any form of birth control, seemingly because of the threat it was believed to pose to the nation. Then, for a short while, condoms became openly available to troops in the hope of preventing the spread of VD. Then, in 1937, as a result of the escalation of the war with China and the subsequent increase in demands for able-bodied young men, a total ban on all forms of contraception was again enforced. The military drove through neighbourhoods in megaphone blaring trucks, exhorting women to '*umeyo fuyaseyo*!' ('bear children, swell the population!').

Following the war, the pendulum of opinion changed once more. Japan was a bomb-blasted scene of devastation struggling to feed those who had survived. What with a weak economy, a post-war baby boom and the haunting sight of mixed children fathered by the US Occupation troops, a law was passed in 1948 which legalized abortion for 'economic reasons'. Thus Japan's vacillating laws continued to swing up and down almost as often as the proverbial underpants.

During the late 'fifties and early 'sixties, family planners in some parts of the country conceived the idea of having 'love boxes' containing contraceptives among a selection of hygiene products which married women passed from one home to another tied up in a traditional *furoshiki* (wrapping scarf). Free from embarrassment behind closed doors, the women were now able to select what they needed in exchange for cash, which they placed in the box.

Today, door-to-door saleswomen are still doing the 'love box' or, more exactly, the 'condom box' rounds in Japan's more respectable neighbourhoods. With a lack of contraceptive alternatives, the condom reigns supreme, but more out of necessity than for any great love of rubber. Every year the Japanese buy some 600 million condoms – more per person than any other country in the world. Eighty per cent of couples rely on them and the condom saleswomen (or 'skin-ladies', as they're known), whose sex-based sales patter would probably surprise those foreigners who have stereotypical ideas of the timorously deferential Japanese housewife, equip themselves with a wide assortment of samples.

Of course, it's not just the roving condom saleswomen that are relied upon should you want to 'pick up a packet'. Condoms are available in all the usual places – chemists, supermarkets, corner stores and nightclubs as well as the never-far-from-reach vending machine. Sometimes I would work my way down a wall of vending machine this and vending machine that, starting off maybe with a chilled can of tea before moving on to a main course of pot-noodles before finishing off with a nonchalant window-browse of the sex-mag machine, which would display the covers of porn magazines and videos bearing photographs of naked and near-naked women and schoolgirls caught in absurd positions and poses. One step further and there would often be a condom-vending machine, the packets of which would always prove an entertaining read with names like: 'X-rated', 'Loveme', 'Tight', 'Passion', 'Passion Rose Z' (subtitled: 'For Your Lovely Tonight'), and the cryptic 'Three O SUGER'.

The firm of Sagami, which at first I thought was some sort of strongly flavoured Italian sausage, supply virtually all condoms sold in Switzerland and about two-thirds of those sold in France and Scandinavia. The picture on the packet depicts the head and bare shoulders of a woman with waves of yellow hair, blue eyes and thick, gleaming cherry-red lips. Perched on a large expanse of naked flesh (which is obviously a certain part of the male anatomy) is a glass of wine. A word-bubble lies suspended from the woman's seductively juicy mouth with the come-on: 'Excalibur – ULTRA THIN'.

No matter how zany the brand names, there's no getting away from the fact that the man controls the condom and that women (who are still viewed very much as inferiors in Japan) are denied the greatest single advance in women's control over her fertility – the pill. Synthesized from the roots of the wild Mexican yam, the pill has given women the choice to conceive or not to conceive: to love without fear or, if they are so inclined, without obligation. Originally intended to help population control in the over-crowded developing countries, the pill transformed life for women in the richer nations (except Japan), breaking what had forever been that permanent connection between sex and reproduction.

Paradoxically, although Japan is decades behind other advanced nations with authorizing the wide availability of the pill, it led the way in legalizing abortion: being, for instance, twenty years ahead of Britain and thirty years ahead of Italy.

For unmarried Japanese women, social pressure often forces them to have an abortion as an illegitimate child will dirty her *koseki* (household register of families) that any would-be employer or husband would most likely want to see. To look after the souls of their aborted children, mothers are virtually forced to buy one of those red-hatted gnome-like 'child-guarding' stone Buddhas (for sale in temples all over Japan), which can cost anything up to £1,000. Many of the temples have signs in their grounds that thoughtfully remind mothers who fail to splash out on a statue or, at the very least, decline to pay the temple to conduct a memorial service for the souls of their 'water babies', that they run the risk of falling heavy prey to lengthy bouts of bad luck. One of the temples' most popular ploys is intimidating a mother into thinking any subsequent children that she might give birth to will be born handicapped. So the guilt-ridden mothers buy the statues and the yen-spinning temples make a killing.

CHAPTER 11

The Honourable Gushing Out

It was time to get on my high horse – even if it was a small bicycle – and head off for Mount Fuji. The trouble was: how to navigate my way out of car-crammed Tokyo while engulfed by meaningless sights and sounds? Signposts more often than not bore a chaotic web of aesthetically pleasing but totally indecipherable *kanji* characters (the sort of thing more fittingly hung in an art gallery than as a mode of direction) and which led to a bewildering disorientating oriental way to get lost. Correction: very lost. But the reassuring thing about spending days, as opposed to hours, disentangling myself from Tokyo's manically confusing mesh of highways and byways and roads and alleys was knowing that, unlike (say) Los Angeles, where it's all too easy to be used for target practice by some patrolling trigger-happy street-gang, my chances of survival looked surprisingly high.

The majority of signposts in Japan are written in *kanji*. As I could make neither head nor dragon's tail out of these thousands of complex Chinese characters the chances of going to where I wanted to go were decidedly remote. Although spotting the occasional helpful *romaji*-scripted sign among the insane urbanity of the Great Tokyo Sprawl gave a welcome boost to my wavering navigational morale and sent me galloping off to where I had hoped to be heading when I had set out days before, it was alas only momentary as signposts were for the motorists and all roads ultimately led to one big road which, if not veering off in the opposite direction from the one I had intended, was prohibitive to cyclists. Then it was back to square one to go round in circles again, because every pedestrian I asked for directions seemed to be a motorist and knew only the car way and every motorist I asked said that they were really a pedestrian and knew only the walk way. Or something like that. Then, any bicycle person I asked who could actually understand me (or me them) said they knew only the car way as they had never had to cycle out of the city before – just in and around it.

So it was back to those whiffy, fishy and fumy backstreets and side streets that coiled up on themselves in flummoxing fashion, forcing me to dispense with the map, log a happy-go-lucky compass bearing and turn to the swirls of shining neon stars for a spot of guidance.

I rode on in befuddled state, overwhelmed by an interminable accretion of concrete and car, while the sun burnt a hole through a thick, hot haze of pollution. Moisture poured from every pore, coating my skin in a filthy, sweaty glaze. It no longer really mattered what direction I was going in; all I wanted was to find a way out – presuming there was a way out. Maybe there wasn't.

Curious sights came and curious sights went. At one point I passed a sign in English that said: NATURAL BOYS SCHOOL. As opposed to 'unnatural'? Another time I pulled over to watch a clutter of housewives crowding around a white pick-up van to trade piles of old newspapers for rolls of toilet paper. Catching sight of me one woman, clutching bagfuls of booty, peeled away from the pack and, with enough rolls to wipe an army, approached me with a winsome smile.

Checking over my shoulder to make sure she was smiling

at me and not a friend behind, I smiled a sort of raised-eyebrow 'are-you-really-smiling-at-me?' smile back. Strangely, it seemed she was.

'*Atsui desu-ne*? – Hot, isn't it?' she observed.

'Yes, that is so,' I said using the Japanese all-time favourite phrase.

'Alone?'

'Yes.'

'Gaa!'

She then tore off a strip of newly acquired toilet paper and curiously set upon giving my sweaty, dirt-stuck forearm a quick rub down. The tissue turned black. The woman, still smiling good naturedly amid little sing-song exhalations of breath, had now been joined by toilet-paper reinforcements. An elfin-faced woman, equally laden with bundles of lavatory rolls, and a woman with a silver-toothed smile peered with interest at the swipe of cleaner skin on my arm that Toilet-Paper Carrier No. 1 had hitherto wiped. Chattering away merrily together amid a swirl of raucous giggles, they tentatively poked my arm as if trying to goad a toad into action. Nonplussed, I thought: is this normal behaviour for the supposedly 'reserved' Japanese?

It took me a moment to work out just what was going on and then, like a bolt from the Bullet Train, it hit me. Freckles! Of course! The women were pointing out, or more like polishing up, my freckles – a form of pigmentation that is in decidedly short supply in Japan. Never one to shun the fun of being fussed over, I ended up being placed on display for the whole gaggle of clucking toilet-paper-bearing housewives who patted and pampered me with enchanting interest. When I finally managed to pull myself away by indicating that I had a spot of cycling to get under my belt, I was besieged by offerings of gifts – mostly rolls of toilet-paper (of which you can never get enough) but interspersed with a *sensu* (folding hand-fan), a lime-green sun hat and an array of freshly purchased drinks from the nearby vending machine.

Later, as I waited alongside a congealed knot of motorbikes, cyclists and pedestrians at the flashing gates of a level-crossing, I noted a boy in front of me wearing a black silk bomber jacket, the back of which was emblazoned with the words:

PROMINENT
The Privileged Classes
especially tested for your
satisfaction of life
SELECT ARTICLES
The best quality of this
wear us to guaranteed
you. Thank You
INTERNATIONAL FAMOUS

And just reading that made getting lost in Tokyo all worthwhile.

I continued riding – spending most of the time imprisoned by countless cars and buses and lorries in phantasmagorical traffic jams through an interminable city whose outskirts dwindled like a lingering infection.

Finally, I surfaced. It didn't much matter that I didn't know where I was. What was important was that the concrete and cars were slowly, if only momentarily, left behind. I saw hills, then I saw mountains and a surge of excitement, of hope, shuddered through my veins.

Then, I saw sea – a sea kept at bay not by an inviting beach or dunes or promenade, but ruined by a wall of concrete. But not just any concrete – this was a bulwark of colossal solid-set blocks piled on top of each other like thousands of giant knuckle-bone jacks erupting from the water to form a massive sea-break with the aim of taming the ever-threatening *tsunami*. The effect was an artificial mound of moulded coast floating deep in concrete kisses.

By now, having threaded through a weave of winding backstreets away from the motorized frenzy of the main road, I found myself bumping down a path alongside the Great Sea Wall of Concrete. Because of the size of the wall I could not actually see the sea, but it was at least nice to know it was there.

A sign loomed into view. I stopped to admire it. The metal face depicted a blue-curling wave beneath which, in both *kanji* and *romaji*, it stated in no uncertain terms: WARNING – TIDAL WAVE AREA.

Thinking this was as good a spot as any for a picnic I climbed up on to the top of The Wall – an advantageous vantage point, I thought, for noting a sudden oceanic surge – to tackle the *bento* (lunchbox) that Noriko had made for me many an hour (or was it days?) before we had said *sayonara*.

Far more exciting than a slab of sandwiches, my plastic *bento* consisted of a hive of tiny compartments, each containing a couple of mouthfuls of exquisitely tasty morsels. Slivers of smoked salmon lay alongside small chunks of roasted cuttlefish. A couple of leaves, like nettles, fried in batter were divided from a section containing three strips of Umi's leftover 'Demi Moore' omelette and a cluster of bright, round, firm fresh peas. The indispensable ingredient was a shining field of pure white rice, in the centre of which rose a red, plump pickled plum – symbolizing the inspirational glow of Japan's much-lionized rising sun.

Along with the food, Noriko had also packed a pair of new wooden *waribashi* chopsticks bound in a *kanji*-inscribed wrapper (that ended up Pritt-stuck in my diary) and a miniature plastic sachet shaped in the form of a fish containing the ubiquitous soy sauce. As I pincered my food with my chopsticks, I gazed out over a charcoal sea wondering just how effective this mountainous *tsunami* break upon which I was sitting would be in the event of a rampaging cataclysmic sea coming to town. It didn't take me long to reckon: not very.

By now I knew enough about Japan to appreciate that volcanic eruptions and earthquakes are endemic to the archipelago of islands on which I was perilously perched: the islands are part of what geographers call the 'ring of fire', a turbulently volcanic area that circles the Pacific Ocean. The capricious sea that faced me was Sagami-na da, part of the Bay of Shizuoka, situated just south of Mount Fuji, in which two of the earth's massive great plates meet beneath the seabed, grinding into each other at a rate of six inches a year. Such giant gratings create a springboard tension which will one day thrust up the surrounding soil and seabed in a forceful, and potentially calamitous, show of nature. These stirrings from the deep can give rise to the rapacious *tsunami* that are capable of devastating coastlines hundreds, or even thousands, of miles from their source. No wonder that Japan, so severely mountainous a country where the majority of the population are shoe-horned into the flat coastal plains, annihilates the beauty of so much of its coastline with monstrous walls of concrete blocks in a tenacious attempt to thwart the quaking effects of the voracious sea.

I continued on along the coast, bouncing through busy towns and cities comprising nose-to-tail traffic, concrete and corrugated iron, before bouncing back out again. I was heading in a somewhat long-winded, roundabout and lost fashion for Fuji – perfectly symmetrical conical queen of all mountains.

Finally I fetched up in the feudal town of Odawara, a rather nondescript place vaguely famous for being the base for development tests of the Bullet Train back at the beginning of the 'sixties. It was on 3rd March 1963 that engineers were at last given what they had long hoped for – the chance to bite the Bullet and pull out the stops – and the train set a new world record for rolling stock as it shot past the timing device at 256 kilometres per hour (159 miles an hour). A light aircraft, commissioned by a newspaper to photograph the train's run, couldn't keep up.

Bullets aside, Odawara still appeared to be a remarkably unremarkable place save for its old castle, a glorious and elaborately carved stone and wooden structure that harked back to bygone years of sabre-wielding samurai – or so I thought. In reality the castle, like so many of Japan's castles which once served principally as garrisons and fortresses, as well as being the residences of the shogun (military dictators) and *diamyo* (provincial warlords), was a recent ferro-concrete reconstruction of the original. The same fate is true of many of Japan's castles because at the time of the Meiji Restoration the government ordered most of the originals to be destroyed in order to break the power of the clans.

Despite its impressively heavy 'stone' walls and voluptuous wood roofs, the thought of it not being the real thing (like the Tower of London) where heads were sliced and battles waged nullified its initially inspiring presence. But this is so indicative of Japan – a country in which there are few actual manifestations of the past. Time and time again I would come across an 'old' castle or shrine or stirring historical sight only to discover that what I was actually looking at was nothing more than a perfect reproduction. The cake without the cherry.

There is something very special about bending over backwards eighty-three feet above ground to kiss a wall knowing that that very stone your lips have brushed is the true Blarney and not a recent ferro-concrete replacement trucked in from some stone-replica factory based in East Croydon. Or something like that. Obviously the devastation of the earthquakes and the ferocious bombings of the Second World War haven't helped to preserve buildings of historic wonder, but it seems so often in Japan that what is physically old is not valued as it is in other parts of the world. Out with the old and in with the new tends to apply not only to buildings (which are built and destroyed with unseemly speed – aided by the unpredictably rapacious forces of nature) but also to furniture, cars, clothes, cameras, televisions, hi-fi and so on. And most of these things don't even have to be old – just old-new. No matter that your Walkman bought last year still works just fine – turf it out with the *gomi* (rubbish) for no other reason than that it's not the Latest Model.

But as things turned out, it wasn't so much the age of Odawara castle that disenchanted me as finding a squalid, half-hearted attempt at a concentration camp-type zoo in the grounds. I passed some decidedly disconsolate macaques and moth-eaten foxes and bears. Crammed into a shabby-caged concrete corner lay a languid lioness with cheerless eyes. Over a wall in a grey and gloomy coffin-sized plot 'lived' an Asian elephant which was in the painful process of attempting a finely-tuned three-point manoeuvre just in order to turn round. Logging its pitiable progress through their viewfinding camcorders whirred a coachload of merrymaking Japanese tourists kitted out in full filming regalia, clearly having a hoot of a time at the elephant's truncated expense.

The castle had a museum. Usually, in days gone by, mention a museum and my eyes would rapidly glaze over and . . . zzzzzzz would tend to be my automatic reaction. But lately, as age creeps up through my bones, I find myself being drawn involuntarily towards a museum for no other reason than a genuine interest to see what's on show behind the doors. And more often than not I come away having actually enjoyed myself. It's a bit worrying.

Anyway, although far from outstanding, the museum of Odawara's castle had a curious jumble of exhibits ranging from a few fine showpieces, such as a fragile boxwood lute with two pearly slivers of ivory facing each other like a mirrored crescent of silver moon, and fine cedar chests inlaid with intricate marquetry of mother-of-pearl to a somewhat haphazard assortment of bric-a-brac reminiscent of the sort of thing salvaged from a car-boot sale.

Among the exhibits was a *yamakago* – a people-carrying vehicle carried by people and used by travellers for ascending and descending the Hakone mountain area during the Edo Period (1600–1867); a powder set for dyeing teeth; and peculiar cages made of pottery or china specially designed for listening to the raspy trillings and chirrupings of cricket-like insects. Even today, keeping insects as pets is a popular pastime in Japan. Many of the children of families I was to stay with later would proudly give me a private viewing of their *suzumushi* – small stick-like insects whose ringing bell-like songs could only be heard at night. Together we would sit on the kitchen floor and feed them by dropping morsels of watery foods like watermelon and cucumber through the cage's plastic or bamboo bars.

But the exhibit which really intrigued me and fired my imagination with gory thoughts of warrior days was the weaponry department. Along with the neck-breaking helmets topped with tufty plumes of horsehair, and the thick cloth armour reinforced with brass plates stitched on in overlapping layers like the scales of a fish, was a mindboggling assortment of spear heads, arrow heads, pikes, halberds, dirks, sabres, cutlasses, longbows, shortbows, and arrows with wonderfully ornamented heads. It seemed like a lot of hard work and effort had gone into something that was designed to lodge in an enemy's heart. Mind you, should the enemy survive, it would make an attractive souvenir. Above all there were swords: big swords, small swords, long swords, short swords, medium-sized swords, sharp swords, rusty swords, jagged swords, wide swords, narrow swords, curved swords, straight swords and swords with bits missing. But no matter what state the swords were in, one thing was clear: none of them were the sort of thing that you'd want to find yourself the wrong end of.

Having left my shoes in an obligatory plastic bag at the entrance to the castle, I climbed up the polished wooden staircases, passing through rooms which diminished in size the higher I rose. At the top I walked out on to a narrow walkway and, giving up on an unfocused thirty-yen-in-the-slot telescope, I surveyed the surrounding scene. In one direction I was greeted with a commanding view over the grey and unprepossessing roofscape of Odawara (the ninth of the fifty-three stations of the old Tokaido Road, where passing travellers once had to stop at the nearby Hakone Barrier and pay their compulsory toll to the castle lord) down to the waves of car confusion filtering and faltering along National Route 1 – the not-a-pleasant-ride coastal-hugging highway. Beyond this spread the vast swell of the Pacific, its breakers rolling in lugubriously upon a long, narrow beach of murky dark volcanic sand.

Behind me lay a quite different scene – the looming, rich green mountains of Hakone which would lead me up and over to Fuji-*san* – the almighty and 'honourable' mountain.

Japanese castles are very different from the permanent solidity and castellated battlements, severe cylindrical turrets and painful-looking portcullises of, say, Warwick or Caernarvon. Apart from sitting on foundations of massive stone walls designed to lean inwards in order to limit (if not escape) the damage from frequent earthquakes, they appear to be decidedly fragile affairs. Mostly in white, with storeys separated from each other by curvaceous eaves topped with heavy terracotta tiles ('stronger and lovelier than any we use in Europe', noted the sixteenth-century Jesuit, Luis Frois) they look more like beguilingly dainty damsels with voluptuous and layered skirts than the heavy, brooding and seemingly impenetrable fortresses of Europe.

But though Odawara castle, with its graceful layers of virginal walls as white as royal icing, may have resembled nothing more than an exotic, teetering wedding cake, it was, in its warrior-waging heyday, quite a sturdy stalwart at heart. When in 1590 a certain Mr Hideyoshi sought to seize it from the lord of the Hojo clan, it took a three-month blockade by 150,000 sea and ground troops to do the job. Not that those three months were all spent locked in savage combat, mind. Japanese battles at the time could, apart from a few unpleasant skirmishes fought out in the open in which swords swiped and heads flew, be a bit of a holiday. Mr Hideyoshi's technique seemed to be all about sitting tight, putting one's feet up and letting the old top-knotted hair-do down: in a word – having a bit of a party. This he achieved by supplying his troops of super-samurai with an army of entertainers, courtesans, shop and foodstall staff. All in all, it seemed waiting for war could be a right lark; most of the time was spent drinking, dancing, feasting and frolicking. And when the frivolities became a little heavy on the head – why, there was always a spot of gentle gardening to be done. The troops (who were obviously a bunch of pansies at heart), used to their leader's lengthy waiting-game war tactics, would mark out small allotments to grow a few vegetables. Those who fancied dabbling in something a touch grander than cultivating a plot of leafy greens would play at being early Capability Browns and set about designing and constructing a number of very fetching landscaped gardens.

And it wasn't just the Odawara waiting-for-war castle-cocooned samurai who revealed a softer side. John Casey wrote in London's *Evening Standard*: 'The mediaeval Japanese and samurai were expected to be brave, sometimes wild, and super-masculine. They were supposed to fight unquestioningly for their feudal lord and, if necessary, to commit the ritual suicide that involved ripping their stomach across and up. But they were also expected to enjoy incense-smelling parties, dress in exotic robes, go cherry-blossom viewing and write poetry.'

After my surprisingly enjoyable excursion to the castle I got back to more pressing matters by seeking out a supermarket to stock up on dwindling supplies. Inside the *supaa* I suffered a near hernia of ecstatic surprise when I happened upon a packet of porridge – a much pined-after foodstuff that I had been frenziedly scouring supermarket shelves for ever since I had set foot and mouth in Japan. I don't like to admit it but when I first realized that, yes, this really was the beguiling-smiling Mr Quaker Oats (albeit spouting Japanese) in front of my oat-hungry eyes, I could scarcely contain myself. Despite the price – 350 yen (about £2.50) for a poxy-sized box – I snapped up the packet lest it be a pure figment of my gruelling imagination. No matter that I had no means on board my bike by which to cook it – I would eat it raw on the rocks, on rice, on ice, on anything. Suffice it to say I had porridge. Hallelujah! Life felt good.

Wandering around the rest of the *supaa* in a happy sort of glazy daze, I stumbled across a stack of blue crates piled high and containing what looked like deep-fried bricks of bean curd soaked in tar. Intrigued to know exactly what it was I was looking at, I lolloped off in search of a sales assistant.

I found one – a sprightly dame sporting *supaa*-logo apron,

and bearing a typically eager-to-help demeanour, but understandably concerned at being confronted by a wild oat-eyed foreigner. Always looking for the easy way out, I asked her in Japanese if she spoke any English.

'No,' she said in English and hastily swallowed a curbed giggle behind cupped hand.

Thinking she was probably being just characteristically modest, true to Japanese form, I said in half Japanese and half English, 'Excuse me, but what exactly is on this tofu?' while pointing to the crates.

'I'll show you,' she replied in English, surprising me with her sudden and unhesitant fluency.

So, I waited for her to show me. But she didn't show me. Mrs Supaa-Woman just stood there with her hands clasped neatly in front of her and smiled a coy smile. I stood, not so neatly, and smiled an equally coy smile back. Waiting. Oh dear. Gulp. Major communication breakdown. What now? Keep smiling – maybe it will sort itself out – or, there again, maybe it won't.

Realizing that we were locked together in a Going-Nowhere-Fast zone, I made a head-in-the-dark attempt to find the key in order to try to unlock us. I fell back on a form of pidgin-dropping Japanese.

'Excuse me, sorry,' I said. 'This tofu – yes? This black what please?'

'I'll show you,' said Supaa-Woman, but now, wise to the occasion, I suspected she wouldn't. If at first you don't succeed then give up, I thought. But alas, I was in too deep to do that. Dive on, I thought. Don't pull the plug. So I asked exactly the same question in a sort of repeat-to-fade-to-die last-ditch-hope.

'Excuse me, sorry,' I said (while thinking: does it really matter?), 'this tofu – yes? This black what please?'

Showing remarkable reserve (I fully admit I deserved to be hit) Supaa-Woman said, 'Ahhh, *shoyu*,' which of course is exactly what she had said all along, only this time my creaking cogs of comprehension ground into action and I realized that the aforementioned 'I'll show you' was in fact soy sauce. But that's Japan – a mad chasing-your-tail medley of misinterpretations.

This little *supaa* episode, together with the new-old castle, is all I remember about Odawara, which is probably quite enough.

By now the afternoon was waning fast, along with my energy. Seventy sticky hot-lost miles were beginning to take their toll. Staring for days at concrete walls and consuming bowlfuls of Noriko's irresistible food is no great recipe for keeping fit. I needed a place to camp – and soon.

On the outskirts of Odawara I wearily sized up a rare six-foot flat strip of land lying sandwiched between a building site and a marshy paddy and encircled by roads. Though far from a camping nirvana it looked, to a lacklustre cyclist, pure heaven. And I would (and should) have stopped right there and then and erected my tent had I not been besieged by two conflicting voices within the one body: while wilted legs were beseeching me to turn horizontal quick, my mind was urging me on, to keep going, to find a more conducive spot for laying a weary head. Something was trying to tell me that better things lay ahead.

I knew that if I didn't stop now I was unlikely to find anywhere else to camp for at least another two or three hours of uphill riding, as I was about to enter the much-acclaimed and mountainous Fuji-Hakone National Park. But try as I might to prevent it, mind prevailed over jellified muscle matter – I had to keep going (when of course I didn't have to).

As the incline of the road turned progressively more vertiginous I couldn't help but berate myself for so imprudently continuing when I could by now not only have eaten my way through the contents of my two front panniers (food department), dining on a fine feast of tarred tofu, raw soaked oats, noodles and *ninjin* (carrots), a tin of tuna and a bunch of discount (black and bruised) bananas, but also be out for the count.

This is one of the troubles with travelling alone: you only have yourself to blame. Had I been travelling with someone else it would, of course, have been all their fault for putting us in such a sinking and muscle-whining predicament. After all, what's the point of going through all the trials and tribulations of travelling with someone if ultimately you don't hold them personally responsible for every disaster – be it major or minor – that comes your way? Sounds reasonable to me. This might explain why, for the past decade or so, I have found myself travelling alone. But that's not my fault, of course.

So there I was, trundling up the mountain off the saddle, off my rocker, with my knock-kneed legs whinging like a couple of whining toddlers while simultaneously feeling very sorry for myself because, tragically, I had no one else to blame for my woeful state. So, as you do, I started blaming the road, the mountain, the tour buses, my bike, my bags and finally, my mind, until I was so overwhelmed with moaniness that I actually began to enjoy myself.

Up I went, higher and higher – hairpin after hairpin. The higher I rose, the better I felt. Sometimes, that's one of the strange things about cycling: life starts to improve just when it gets even more horrible. Down at the bottom of the mountain I had been on my last legs but now, having embarked on scaling the slopes, my spirits had risen with the incline and I felt as if I had found a spare set of hamstrings. Things felt good. In fact, they felt better than good: they felt raging marvellous.

Of course I knew that I was peaking before my time and that sooner rather than later my sudden surge of energy would drain from my endorphins and a rush of lactic acid would shoot me once more into disarray. But before they did, I had a little incident. Not enough to write home about but a little something nonetheless. There I was, happily moaning my merry old way up a nigh vertical escarpment when, amidst a rush of inconsequential whirlpool thoughts, a car – I remember it well – a white Suzuki Pearaboo (I'm sorry, but this honestly was its real name), suddenly pulled broadside. The lone occupant, a middle-aged man with a bristle of hair, gave me one of those looks that you know is more than just a look. Then he drove off. A little further up the narrow ribboning road I found that the same man had stopped his peek-a-boo Pearaboo in perilous fashion bang on a steep, blind corner (playing safe, as far as motoring manoeuvres are concerned, is not a motorist's priority in Japan) and, as I pulled out into the oncoming lane in order to pass him, he leant out of the window sporting a rakish, devil-may-care type of grin and said, '*Sumimasen* – excuse me,' before, in his outstretched arms, flashing me with the sight of a porn mag's double-page spread.

I was so unprepared for this unusual roadside line of approach that instead of turning testy or delivering him a good solid thwack! with a swipe from my trusty bike pump, I emitted an oh-dear-poor-soul, you-need-therapy snigger. And then, ridiculously, I promptly felt embarrassed – as if *I* had been the one to throw the insult. After all, he hadn't tried anything nasty – hadn't threatened me or dropped his pants or anything like that. No, compared with 'the ones' that I've had the misfortune to meet who really do need therapy along with a heavy-booted kick, this flashy non-flasher had been your ideal host throughout – a prize model of manners, politely offering me the porno double-pager as one might a cup of tea. Thus, all I managed to come up with in reply was a very British, 'Not today, thanks'. Who on earth did I think he was – the milkman? 'No silver-top today, thanks.'

Anyhow, whoever I was and whoever he was, the whole little episode was over in a jiffy, and I carried on riding up the mountain.

As I inched my way upwards I began passing small rivulets trickling down the vertical roadside rockface. But no ordinary streams these: stained bright yellow from sulphur, they emitted, in the fading light, an eerie incandescence, as if radioactively aglow.

Then, rounding a bend, I came across an unusual sight – six elderly men ambling along the road in their dressing-gowns and slippers. Oh no, I thought, not more potential flashers, not more offers of tea. The men looked identical, like a gaggle of overgrown sextuplets – all the same size, all dressed the same in *yukata*, all clod in the same *geta* (traditional slipper-style clogs), and all bidding me a cheery, if somewhat surprised, '*Konbanwa*! – Good evening!' as I passed.

My immediate reaction was to think I was hallucinating – seeing double (well, three times double actually) and that maybe the day's excursions were taking their toll. After all, there was no reason, as far as I could tell, why these merry men should be dressed for bed and meandering high along the heights of a breezy mountain road as if it was the most natural thing in the world. Had I happened upon a similar sight of gowned cloggers emerging from a town's public bath-house, well, that would have been more understandable. But here? Most odd.

However, all was revealed around the corner. Entering a small village – the first since leaving Odawara a couple of hours earlier – I came across further dressing-gowned clog-hoppers all clacking excitedly like a gaggle of freshly preened geese along the road of what, I suddenly now realized, was a small-scale sulphur-smelling spa resort. The tantalizing idea of sinking into a bubbling and steaming hot-spring made the lower half of my body immediately grind to a halt but the upper department won mind over matter and kept the pedals turning. But not for much further. Feeling as wilted as a limp lettuce leaf, I arrived at a junction of buildings and thought, if I don't stop now I won't have enough energy to eat (v. worrying, albeit hard to imagine). It was while scouring the ground in the near-dark for a place to camp that as luck would have it for limbs though not wallet,

I collided with a signpost (in English!) for the Fuji-Hakone Guest House – a touristy-sounding place which I remembered reading about back in Tokyo. Despite the price (a rather gulp-worthy £24) it was just what I needed in my jaded state: no exhaustive lingual struggles as the chatty owner, Masami Takahashi, had travelled throughout Europe and Asia and spoke perfect English; copious information on where to go, what to do and how to do it (v. useful when you didn't have a clue); a *tatami* room called 'Nikko' (Sunshine) overlooking a lusciously green oriental garden and stream and distant mountains; and, the knees of all bees, a piping-hot *onsen* (spa) – the mineral water of which was pumped directly from Hakone's main source. It was here that I wallowed alone in a truly ecstatic body-dissolving state, dreamily listening to the sounds of contented sloshings and voices of two Japanese men in the next door bath.

That night, after dining in my room (to save yen) on a thermos of hot water (provided for tea) stirred into my Japanese Quaker Oats together with one handful of raisins, four squashed bananas and a generous dollop of rich, plum sauce to form a most unappealing-looking but extremely satisfying stomach-expanding gloop, I flopped on my futon in a fine but fit-for-nothing state and found just enough energy to turn on my radio. The Far East Network's CNN news was the first station I found that wasn't wreathed in static so I left the dial there. 'Shopping carts,' I was told, 'cost around a hundred bucks a piece. In California alone there are around one million homeless people in possession of one . . . Other folk steal the carts, peel off the store logo and stamp on another and sell them to stores in other states. The more carts that are stolen, the higher the cost of supermarket goods for the consumer . . .' The official term for this buck-spinning pastime? Why, the fine art of Trolley-Rustling.

My trannie was still rabbiting on at me when I awoke the next morning, just conscious enough to register the last few minutes of the Rush Limbaugh Show. 'Know what?' said Rush in comical tone. 'Been married thirty-four years and my wife used to say to me in the first years of our marriage, "Hon, I get the feeling you're using me." And I'd say, "Why sure, course I'm using you, because if I didn't have any use for you why the hell would I marry you?" You know? The sort of thing we once used to fight about benefits from a long marriage. At first I used to try real hard – brush my teeth just great every day, but now I can skip it once in a while. My wife's used to it – she does things automatically like picking my dirty underwear off the floor because she's not dumb – she knows that arguing with me to do it myself will get us nowhere.'

Thanks Rush, I thought, for sharing that with me.

The Fuji-Hakone National Park is the busiest park in the world, just pipping England's very own 31 million-visitors-a-year Peak District park to the post. I suppose this isn't really surprising: not only does it contain one of the most finely chiselled and famously photographed mountains in the world, but is also situated a mere sumo throw from the over-spilling milling masses of Tokyo.

Although the majority of the Fuji-Hakone region is designated as a 'national park', this is something of a misnomer in a country which is not known for the 'green-ness' of its policies on environmental protection or for its restrictions on commercial exploitation over its well-endowed assets of exquisite natural beauty. Just riding up over the mountain to Lake Hakone (properly known as Ashino-ko, pronounced Ah-She-No-Ko) I passed vast monolithic hotel blocks rearing their ugly heads like cement works out of the hillside.

Down on the other side, by the tourist-trodden lake, there were all the tourist trappings that all too often deface areas of outstanding natural beauty – souvenir shops, car parks, plastic giant-swan pedalos, loudspeakers competing with each other to produce the most ear-grating noise, and more large lumps of concrete.

Surrounded with verdantly forested mountains and with the mystical elegance of Fuji rising over distant hills, its symmetrical snow-clad slopes reflected on the lake's glassy surface, it's easy to see why the three-mile-long shimmering waters of Lake Ashino-ko are one of the most camera-trammelled focal points in Japan. A prime picture-perfect spot. That is, if you can see Fuji-*san*, otherwise known as 'Oh Venerable One'. I couldn't, thanks to a humid haze that hung heavy over the hills. It wasn't actually raining, but it reminded me of the only *haiku* (seventeen-syllable poem) that the seventeenth-century wandering poet, Matsuo Basho, ever wrote about the mountain:

kiri shigure	Misty drizzle –
Fuji wo minu hi zo	A day you can't see Fuji!
omoshiroki	Interesting.

Basho, who took his name from the *basho* (banana tree) because, so he said, 'I love the tree for its very uselessness', was the veritable great master of *haiku* – a form of poetry which in a sense is the literary extension of Buddhism. Basho's Fuji poem testifies to the ability of Buddhism to see further than what can be seen because, although Basho looked upon the glories of Fuji many times, the only *haiku* he wrote about it was on not being able to see it: thus he was able to find beauty in a famous sight that could not be seen – something to which I, for instance, am blind. If I go, camera in hand, to somewhere famous and then, because of weather conditions, can't see what I came to see, I think: oh, what a blow! Does this make me a shallow, superficial sightseer? Standing at the end of Ashino-ko on the 'famous camera-snapping spot', I thought:

Hazy and humid –
A day I can't see Fuji!
Disappointing.

Obviously I had a thing or two to learn from Oh Great Banana One. But not yet. After peering at a grey, mountainless spot through my lens I sauntered off, feeling a trifle swindled, to make do instead with gazing at Japan's most revered sight on the racks of the numerous postcard stands which littered the lakeside, and fingering through fetching displays of keyrings and trinkets that declared: MOUNT FUJI – GOD GIVE YOU JOY OK?, and: MOUNT FUJI – I EXPRESS HEARTY WELCOME TO YOU. They were what Basho might have called 'interesting'. But I doubt it.

Outside the trippery shop a stall had been set up and piled high with a pyramid of perfect, almost plastic-looking *gurepu furutsu* as big as beachballs. I loped on over for a poke and a prod – just the sort of annoying behaviour that our fine barrow boys in Berwick Street Market rightly give you short shrift for. 'Don't squeeze me till I'm yours!' they say. And I don't. But my poking stopped mid-prod when I discovered the price – 2000 yen (about £13) for two. I gulped hard and, incredulous, briskly turned away.

It was at that moment that a middle-aged couple, with smiles spread wide, trotted up to me enthusiastically. The woman was so tiny that even I had to crane my neck downwards – a rare but most pleasing experience. Bowing profusely she burst into an extraordinary and effusive torrent of Japanese, most of which jetted forth so fast that it washed clean over me. However, a few words sprang out, grabbing me by my eustachian tubes until I registered that, somehow, this woman knew me, though I not her. Before I had a chance to gather in the small herd of Japanese words and phrases that I had turned out to graze somewhere in my mind, formulating them into something that resembled woolly and stilted sentences, I had been swept off my feet by the two-foot woman and her four-foot husband into an adjacent lakeside noodle bar. Here my new-found friends bought me a bowlful of dangerously addictive seaweedy *soba* swimming in a *sake* soup, which I ate as noisily as possible in that curious gesture of true Japanese appreciation. The 'conversation' which ensued was an example of one of those peculiar situations whereby we were mysteriously able to conduct an animated dialogue, despite speaking scarcely a word of the other's language, but apparently understanding everything. Hence I deciphered the reason why Keiji and Shizuka Murai had so spontaneously come running up to me: they had spotted me a few weeks before, cycling through their hometown – Kamakura – and on recognizing me they immediately felt they knew me.

Keiji and Shizuka had two daughters. One of the daughters was married, lived in Vancouver and was about to have her first child. Shizuka, in her soon-to-be capacity as *obaasan*, would be flying out there to lend a nappy-changing hand for a month. She was, she said, very excited.

Half-way through our noodle-slurpings, Shizuka produced from her small backpack a plastic bottle insulated in a damp cloth which, once unwrapped, revealed a yellowy liquid reminiscent of the sort of sample that one sometimes finds oneself having to produce in a jar at the doctors. Shizuka sent Keiji off to fetch some glasses and then, declaring that the substance that we were about to receive was indeed homemade tea, poured me some. It was cold and very nice. Our *soba* meal took on the air of a bit of a picnic as, once the tea was drunk, Shizuka (obviously a woman in control) sent Keiji off to fetch some plates. Then, from out of her rucksack-larder, Shizuka produced a sharp, serrated knife and three big grapefruit. These she segmented with dexterity and piled some high on a plate for me. Despite the plastic appearance, the fruit was *oishii* (delicious), but I couldn't help guiltily thinking that each segment cost the equivalent of £1 – a price hard to swallow.

Back outside, Keiji and Shizuka announced they would

like to take me home with them to sleep in their absent daughter's room and stay as long as I liked. It was an appealing offer but seeing as I had just spent what felt like several months trying to extricate myself from the Kamakura area I felt, that with time leaking away, I would rather forge on forwards than backwards. Keiji and Shizuka took my decision well and didn't try to abduct me. Instead they gave me their address, together with a generous offering of grapefruit reinforcements which Keiji, the crafty devil, had slipped off to buy. I did my best to say that I couldn't accept them, that they had spoilt me quite enough already, but my protestations fell on deaf ears. The 'unwanted' *gurepu furutsu* were tossed back and forth amid much farcical '*Dozo-dozo*, please-please' (Shizuka) and 'No, no, really not' (me), until on the third offer I put on my best face of feigned reluctance and relented. Phew! It was hard work, all this gift-giving or, in my case, gift-accepting. But, as far as I knew, I had carried out the ritual in the appropriate manner. In traditional format, if the giver offers the gift once or only twice then they do not genuinely want you to have it. But, should the whole little charade proceed to the third offer, then this is the indication that the present is yours to be taken with grace. Thus, from a very early stage in my Japanese gift-accepting career I became adept, as well as adapted, to the ping-ponging ritual of:

GIVER: Please, please
GAIJIN: No, no, really not.
GIVER: Please, please.
GAIJIN: No, no, really not.
GIVER: Please, please.
GAIJIN: Oh, all right then – if you insist. Thanks. (While thinking: Great! Yeah! More presents!) (P.S. Sorry, God.)

So, with a bagful of juicy booty, I bid a fond *sayonara* to Keiji and Shizuka and sallied forth by bike to attempt a reconnaissance loop of the lake. The north shore of Ashino-ko was hugged by a busy road, which had its pleasant parts, but it was the south side that I was interested in: apart from a small cluster of fishermen, it looked enticingly empty. From the noisy bustling hubbub of Hakone town I swiftly accelerated past a knot of souvenir stores and a cascade of tourist buses and out on to a rocky track, which petered out into a path – and then suddenly I was alone. Just like that. No one. Alone. Wonderful.

I carried on, half-pushing, half-riding, half-carrying my bike along the narrow, rutted, jungle-like way studded with pockets of strange wild flowers. For two hours I didn't see anyone apart from a couple of fishermen who were banging out their buckets over the side of their small wooden boat. Nearby I sat on a rock overlooking the soft lapping shore and ate another *gurepu furutsu*. After a while the fishermen saw me and waved. Behind, in the deep, wide greenness of the overhanging trees, weird-sounding birds hooped and whooped and cackled. I looked up to the mountains, down to the lake, over to the fishermen (who waved again) and felt very happy. Japan was working its charm.

But the tourist frenzy was never far away. In the distance the shrill and restless whistles and the irritating bleeting megaphones that the tour-bus girls used to round up their herds drifted discordantly towards me over the water. Every now and then, in complete contrast to the soft murmurings of the fishermen now sitting quite still watching the end of their lines, a rip-roaring chauffeur-driven speed-boat would blast past, the £50-a-go fun-seekers shrieking with delight from the stern. Then a true paradigm of a corny tourist anachronism glided across the lake in the form of a replica seventeenth-century galleon – the sort of thing you might expect to find on display in Portsmouth Harbour rather than at the foot of Fuji. All I need now, I thought, was for a coin-operated Napoleon to limp from out of the lake saying 'Not tonight, Josephine.' But fortunately I was spared.

I awoke the next morning to find that the sun had melted a

hole in the clouds so I leapt aboard my bike, rode back up over the mountain to Lake Ashino-ko and, on the spur of the moment, jumped in a landscape-scarring cable-car (or what the Japanese strangely refer to as a 'ropeway', even though there isn't a rope in sight) to be winched up towards Mount Sounzan, passing through Owakudani ('The Valley of Greater Boiling') where the air was steamily gaseous and fumaroles flourished. Squeezed into the glass-sided 'hope-the-cable-doesn't-snap' car (or what the Americans refer to as a gondola, even though Venice is nowhere in sight) I found myself competing for window space with Jake and Barbara, a flamboyant couple from Florida. Jake or, as his business card informed me:

CAPT. W.K. 'JAKE' WEHRELL
Chief Pilot – Logistics Aircraft
Riyadh

was a 'born-again Harley – Davidson biker' who had spent the past six years with his wife, Barbara, in Saudi Arabia, where he trained pilots.

As the car cabled to a halt we clambered out on to a mountainside avalanching with yellow-capped schoolchildren. The ground was bubbling, volcanic, alive, the air a potently sulphurous and reeking brew and, as a steamy sea of bobbing heads momentarily parted, I caught a mesmerizing glimpse of distant Mount Fuji mysteriously floating above a skirting of cloud. Then the yellow-heads closed back in, blotting out Fuji in an instant, and I turned to be offered by Jake a blackened hard-boiled egg he'd bought that had been cooked *al fresco* in the bubbling mud and boiling sulphurous steam that spewed from the ground. I looked at it a little dubiously but Jake told me it would be good for an immediate health-tonic as the eggs reputedly contained certain medicinal turbo-boosting properties extracted from the earth's boiling cauldron. Dutifully I peeled and swallowed, pausing in anticipation of some unknown life-enhancing symbiosis, but I felt nothing more from my sulphurous volcanic pick-me-up than a mild eruption located somewhere down in the lower recesses of my alimentary canal.

Way up on top of this great seething mountain, covered with some of the earth's fresh lacerations of nature, there was still all the usual non-close-to-nature assortment of tourist trappings: restaurants, junky shops of trippery, noodle bars, museums, and a generous array of toilets.

Rather than cable-car it back down the mountain, I fancied attempting to battle my way through thick undergrowth on a trail I couldn't find as it had been washed away by recent rains. For over an hour I scampered around trying to gather information about another trail that no one seemed to know anything about. I was contemplating whether I should forge ahead into the foliage come what may, feeling that I surely couldn't go far wrong if I simply headed down, thus breaking two Golden Mountaineering Rules in one:

Rule No. 1: Know where you are going before you go.
Rule No. 2: Know that you can go very far wrong if you simply head down.

I suddenly caught sight of a small party of professionally kitted-out Japanese rucksacked hikers in hats, plus-fours and sensible sturdy boots disappearing with a purposeful air up the steaming mountainside, bearing bodyweight-transmitting three-section telescopic trekking poles in hand. Thinking they looked as if they knew what they were doing (breaking Golden Mountaineering Rule No. 3: Never presume other climbers know what they are doing just because they look as if they do) I hurriedly set out in pursuit, fighting my way back through the milling hard-boiled-egg crowds. In mid-scrum I bumped into Barbara and Jake, who expressed interest in joining me (breaking Golden Mountaineering Rule No. 4: Should anyone express interest in joining you on your crack-brained expedition, give them a hard-boiled egg instead – better that than they drop off a mountain). Happy to be accompanied on my possible Journey to Death I considerately encouraged Barbara and Jake to join me. But no sooner had I taken my first step when, glancing behind me, I realized that I had already lost two-thirds of my team before they had even started. I saw them excitedly diverting course towards an old man who was doing a swift trade in carved wooden walking-sticks. For 650 yen (£4.30) Jake made his purchase, declaring it as something of a 'buck-saving bargain'.

By now the fleetingly-sighted party of trail-blazing trekkers had long since vanished and, judging from the ferocity of speed with which most Japanese undertake their tasks, had most likely scaled a score of peaks by the time the ill-equipped Anglo-American trio leaving behind the pleasant reassuring tarmac of the bus park, had set a tentative trainer-clad foot upon the unpredictable muddy mountain.

For two hours we slipped and tripped our way upwards (it appeared we had first to go up before heading on down) dressed in totally unsuitable attire: me in broken-laced trainers, knee-grazing cycling shorts with a bicycle pump and tool-laden handlebar-bag throttling me around my neck; blonde and braided Barbara, looking like a Parisian catwalk Cindy Doll – curves in all the right places, who was looped through her *handobaggu* handle and clad (for a long and muddy ramble) in immaculately impractical butt-hugging white-stretch jeans; and Jake, who kept declaring, 'Hey honey, these son-of-a-gun pants are real uncomfy.'

More and more chunks of skin were scraped from various parts of our anatomies as we battled through the jungle-like hills, colliding with various lethally jutting rocks and sharp-spiky foliage. Jake was telling me how he had met Barbara ten years before while she was working as a teller girl in an East Coast bank.

'I went to cash a cheque,' he said, 'and I thought: Wow! Now that's one cute blonde. And, well, I guess we just kind of clicked. Ain't that right, sweetheart? Hey honey – you doing okay back there? C'mon, I'll carry your purse.'

The result of their capital-bonding was that they now had eight children between them – six of Jake's and two of Barbara's. Jake went on to tell me how he was a Vietnam Vet and had just been back there for the first time since the war – an experience which he found 'real sobering'.

At one point in our mountaineering mission, as I found myself embedded upside down on a near-vertical, stumpy tree-studded slope dangling from a root which had entwined itself around my ankle, Jake told me how he was 'looking for a religion and it sure as hell's not Islam after living in Saudi'. Jake seemed to have quite a lot on his agenda because he was also in the process of writing a novel, to be published in six volumes, called *I Guess I Just Wasn't Thinking*.

Five hours later, after having divided a ration of two boiled sweets between us (thus breaking Golden Mountaineering Rule No. 5, which should really be Golden Rule No. 1: Never embark upon a mountain descent without at least two boiled sweets *each* – preferably strawberry-flavoured), we finally, and thankfully, toppled battle-scarred and dehydrated from out of the tangle of shrubbery and on to a road at the bottom of the mountain.

'Holy-moly!' Jake exclaimed hoarse of throat. 'Well, sweetheart, I guess we're going to live after all!'

Parched, we marched along the road for a while until we found what we had been pining for over the past four hours – a drinks vending machine. I would never have imagined such a coin-draining ugly lump of a machine could bring so much joy, but it did, and together with my bonny florid-of-face Floridans we managed without hiccup to drain the whole thing dry. Having survived a good day's rough and tumble and handful of near-death experiences we had by now, so said Jake, 'bonded real good'. Addresses were swapped, hearty hugs exchanged and I rode away with invitations to 'come lie on our beach some day soon' suspended on the wind.

The Honourable Fuji, Japan's highest mountain at 3,776 metres (or a higher-sounding 12,399 feet), remained stubbornly elusive. Occasionally an alluring flank would be revealed, or a disembodied halo of conical snow would hover radiantly for a flash in an arresting spoke of sunlight, but mostly it (or more like 'she') chose to remain under wraps – veiled, curtained and mystical.

In the language of the Ainu, the original inhabitants of Japan, who are said to have witnessed the eruption that created Fuji's cone 10,000 years ago, 'Fuji' means 'gushing out'. Being one of approximately 250 volcanoes that shape Japan (a number of which are still active), Fuji, although having remained dormant for nearly 300 years, is still classified as alive. Such was the fury of the fire goddess who is said to reside in the mountain that during the last eruption, in 1707, Tokyo was covered with over a foot of thick volcanic ash despite being more than sixty miles away.

In Shinto (the polytheistic indigenous religion of Japan), all mountains are sacred and the enigmatic Fuji-*san* is the most sacred of all. Together with the ensign of the red Rising Sun on a field of white rice, Fuji is a national emblem, a symbol of Japan, held in lofty awe. Such is its hold on the nation that whenever the Bullet Train sweeps along the mountain's lower flanks the driver, as a mark of respect, reduces speed and the guards turn towards the goddess's gracefully curving slopes to perform a neat and reverential bow.

Until the Meiji Restoration women were forbidden to climb Mount Fuji as it was held that the fire goddess would be struck by jealousy if she was trodden upon by another woman. Today, though, her mysterious ways have been either eroded or pounded into oblivion by the footsteps of the thousands of women who annually climb her matchless cone heavenwards. Even though the view from the top on a clear day is undoubtedly magnificent, Fuji is, in a way, a mountain best viewed from afar. Up close the goddess looks barren and broken-headed, dishevelled and scraggy – a pile of volcanic debris, battle-scarred from a billion battering boots.

The official climbing season lies only between the generally bare-of-snow 1st July and 31st August, but around 400,000 litter-prone hikers annually amass on Fuji's prize symmetrical slopes to pound, both day and night, the pilgrim path to the top. Millions more climb at least part-way up, aided by coachloads of tour buses which deposit their highly animated and chattering contents in a car park at 7,600 feet – less than 5,000 feet from the sacred summit. In the true Japanese spirit of nature conservation, there are plans to turn the parking area into an appealing four-storey garage with room for 500 cars – just the sort of thing you would want to find halfway up one of the most beautiful mountains in the world. No wonder Fuji looks so tired.

Fixed to a wall in the reception of the Fuji-Hakone Guest House had been posted a note with the words: 'The foolish man has never climbed Mount Fuji, but he who climbs it twice is a fool.' Although I was here a month before the official climbing period began and although the rainy season was almost upon me, I thought: well, it's not often you find yourself standing at the foot of Fuji, so I decided foolishly to be a semi-fool and to give it a go.

At first things went well. After loitering within tent at a lakeside campground for a couple of days hoping the weather would clear, I set off one bright and breezy dawn with my mission in mind and a kilo of fast-bruising bananas in pocket.

According to tourist-traipsing tradition, the true goal of

scaling the heights of Fuji-*san* is to make it to the top in time for the earth-moving experience of *goraiko* – mountain sunrise. But, for me, catching this reputedly spiritual moment was not going to be easy. For a start, most 'pilgrims' for the peak take the bus up to what is known in Fuji-climbing-speak as the Fifth Station – one of five fixed points up the mountain (which are divided further into ten stages) from where you can begin your assault to the top. There used to be four Fifth Stations, but that's another story. However, only three out of the five Fifth Stations can be reached by road, thus offering a handy half-way-house launch-pad to catapult you to the top rather than having to hike all the way from the bottom because, heavens, who in this day and age wants to exert themselves more than is absolutely necessary? To be honest, I was a bit disappointed to find that there wasn't some sort of bulleting escalator service whisking us see-sunrise-or-die touristy troops to the top. After all, I had already discovered that in Japan it is possible to find escalators in the most unlikely places: only a couple of weeks or so before, when riding through Enoshima on the Shonan coast, I had passed a shrine, or more like a trio of shrines linked by an escalator – a sort of automated veneration.

So, with walking not an option, I was left with a choice: take the bus or bike. As buses aren't really my cup of tea (talking of tea, the Fuji area produces terraced acres of green tea which was once only used medicinally but now happily is the addictively delicious national beverage along with, it seems, the not so delectable Pocari Sweat) and as I couldn't find a bus anyway because it was out of season, and as I am quite keen on cycling, I went by bike.

It was, as to be expected, hard work. Up and up I went, hour after endless hour, making painfully slow progress by road but pretty good progress by banana – so much so that by the time I arrived at one of the Fifth Stations I had only a pile of peels to jettison me by foot to the top. Things were not looking good. In fact, they weren't looking anything at all because by now, true to Fuji form, the mountain was once again enveloped in cloud – a thick, wet and surprisingly chilly cloud, though seeing as I was standing at 2,305 metres I suppose I shouldn't have been surprised. I probably would not have been surprised had I planned properly, but then who wants to plan properly and miss out on the chance of being surprised? It's fun to have life's vicissitudes and serendipities and long words lying in wait around the corner – keeps you on your toes. But what I really wanted now was sun and views, like the ones I had perused on the postcard rack. Instead, slowly it dawned on me that if I hung around for much longer I would not so much experience the rising sun as the rising damp. So, after pottering around for a bit, colliding into car parks and vending machines that I couldn't see for the fog, and after bumping into an exhausted party of professional-looking ice-pick and crampon-kitted Japanese climbers who told me that they had had to turn back because of 'dangerous weather', I opted to play safe and plunged back down the mountain in the rain.

Back at base I crawled dripping and weary into my tent wondering whether, having partially attempted a Fuji ascent, I now qualified as merely half a fool as opposed to a complete fool for not trying, and whether if I was to endeavour to be a 'he who [attempts] to climb it twice' would make me a fully-fledged fool. But rather than spend time pondering over such ruminations I opted to get on with the more important things in life, like wringing out my socks and bailing out my shoes. In short, life had turned wet.

CHAPTER 12

Supper with the Stars

On arriving in Japan I had felt more than a trifle apprehensive about how lost I might get (answer: very); how I would make myself understood (answer: not easily but dive straight in with a hearty smile and a pretence that you understand what you hear and all is well); how I would afford such heart-palpitating prices (answer: easy – just don't buy anything expensive); and how I would cope with eating raw squid and pickled seaweed for breakfast (answer: also easy, by dousing the lot in liberal lashings of 'I'll show you' *shoyu* and by not thinking too hard about just what you're swallowing).

Initially I had also fretted about where I would sleep. Accommodation was mostly of the yen-eating variety, but that was okay as I had my tent. The problem was: where would I put it? After Nagai-*san*'s secretaries had made it clear that camping was not a wise move and after the woman in the Tokyo tourist office had quite firmly stated, 'Camping in Japan? There is no room', it was perhaps understandable that I had felt a bit apprehensive. Others did little to boost my wavering confidence; their words varied little from Takuji's (the 'Japan very special four season' photographer I met in Naritasan). 'We are small country,' he had said, 'many people, many mountain. No space for tenting.'

Camping, I deduced, was definitely not a popular pastime in Japan, which was hardly surprising seeing as most of the masses who spent their time frenetically beavering away long hours for a handful, if that, of holiday a year didn't particularly want to spend it sweating away with rocks in their backs during the distinctly horrendous summertime humidity, or being washed well away by the very rainy rains, or swallowed whole by a tumultuous typhoon or sucked to smithereens by squadrons of hell-bent mosquitos or poisoned by a posse of Okinawan deadly poisonous snakes. Not when they can afford air-conditioned pamperings – and who can blame them? But as far as the question of space went, that was easy: there was plenty of it, just so long as I didn't mind camping in a less than pitch-perfect spot. There were lakesides, riversides, roadsides, harboursides and seasides. There were temples, shrines, schoolgrounds, stations and parks. Lots of parks. And there were even a few bolt-out-the-blue official campgrounds, like the one I had planted myself on now at Shoji-ko lake.

Despite my initial happy surprise at actually coming across a real-life Japanese campsite together with a meagre cluster of real-life Japanese campers (a bunch of boys on trailbikes and a jeepful of windsurfers), it was a bit of a dismal offering – especially, I thought, in a country which is not only oozing with yen but prides itself on its cleanliness. More gravel site than campsite, it was situated on rock-hard stony ground glinting with broken glass. I sauntered into a shelter of trees with escaped plastic bags flapping, torn and entangled in their branches, where a few cheerless and mouldy old caravans stood on unsteady feet: rusty and empty shells brooding in the moist mountain air.

Dotted around the campsite like molehill mounds rose small cairns of rubbish that previous campers had thoughtfully left behind. The toilet block was derelict and bare, full of cracks and cobwebs and large scuttling insects and cisterns that didn't flush. Strangely, in the midst of the dish-washing area (an open but roofed slab of long sinks with plugs blocked with matted black hair, plastic bags and slithering remnants of week-old noodles) sat an enormous tropical fish-tank containing a few forlorn fish and a scuttled shoe.

Ignoring these slightly unappealing features as best I could, I decided to stay and camp as it was located on the shore of Shoji-ko, one of the famous Fuji-go-ko (Fuji-Five-Lakes) that loop themselves around the northern skirts of Fuji. Before arriving at the campground (the first official site I had yet come across) I had cycled around the other four lakes: Yamanaka-ko, the largest and also most spoilt, with much of its shore blighted by a strip of Kentucky Fried Chickens, Denny's and 7-Elevens; Kawaguchi-ko, in whose waters float (when the clouds have blown) the best reflection of Fuji; Saiko-ko, whose name (pronounced sigh-ko) conjured up visions of Hitchockian murders in showers; and Motosu-ko, the deepest.

Shoji-ko was definitely the least spoilt and, despite the swilling rubbish, it had made a good basecamp for my aborted excursion up Fuji. It had also been free. One of the windsurfers had told me it cost 750 yen (a fiver) per person per night but when I bumped into an ancient woman who seemed to own the place and lived in a house on the site she waived aside the fee and gave me a dried fish instead.

Another evening she invited me over to join her for a bowl of *miso* soup. As we sat on a low plank outside her door, slurping and smiling and generally misunderstanding each other, a car drew up and out sprang a lively couple who raced into the lake. They splashed around in frolicking fits of giggles for about thirty seconds and then promptly ran out again. Then they fell asleep in the back of their car and were still asleep when I left the next morning after a breakfast of leftover noodles.

I followed the quiet and narrow lakeside road passing Hotel She Who (she who did what? I wondered) and the Trendy Business Training Center and the small curious-sounding Curry and Cake Take Out shop. At the far end of

Shoji-ko I stopped at a petrol station which promisingly no longer sold fuel, the pumps having been converted into vending machines and selling, among the usual array of teas and beers and coffees, such carbonated delights as Mucos and Pocari Sweat.

Up the road and round the bend lay Fugaku Fuketsu Lava-Wind Cave and Narusawa Hyoketsu Ice Cave, which were both formed from one of Fuji's prehistoric eruptions when internal pressure forced back the flow of lava. Plunging into Narusawa (a natural ice-box where a sign at the entrance warned: 'NOTICE – this cave has low ceiling or slippery floor in several places please be care fie') my sweat rapidly turned to shivers as I 'care-fie-ly' slithered my way along dimly lit tunnels full of giant icicles and ice pillars and other naturally sculptured oddities that clung in weird and eerie contorted shapes to the glaciated walls.

I arrived just before a siege of 'COOP BUS' coach parties marched as one into the mouth of the cave, their guttural 'ahh-so-ings' and '*hai-hai*-ings' reverberating excitedly around the icy chasms. Before being engulfed (and photographed by the COOP BUS troops) I made a hasty exit and clambered back out of the tunnel. I was immediately hit by the enervating heat and humidity. To reacclimatize I made a bee-line for the air-conditioned souvenir shop which was doing a brisk trade in *o-miyage* – intricately wrapped gifts that, true to custom, tourist-trippers were snapping up to give to family and friends and co-workers back home.

No Japanese worth their weight in yen who venture away, if only for a day, on holiday or business trip, would dream of returning home without a lorry-load of expensive *o-miyage* to dish out to both loved and non-loved ones alike. To arrive home giftless is considered unacceptable and shameful – definitely not the done thing unless you fancy sticking out like a nail to be hammered down. Pressure-purchasing is all the rage in Japan.

That night I pitched my tent in the thick of the Aokigahara Jukai ('Sea of Leafage') primeval forest, an area famous not only as a popular location for committing suicide (averaging 60 victims a year) but also for its parasitic trees: various types of trees such as pine, azalea, akebi, hinoki cypress and Japanese hemlocks all cluster by growing together on a parent tree of Japanese oak more than 300 years old. All night I was surrounded by a cacophony of strange scratching and squawking sounds emanating from the thicket of forest which darkness, along with an imagination running wild, somehow always manages to amplify out of all proportion. Feeling a strong sensation that there were a thousand long-fanged cyclist-eating creatures prowling around outside my tent, I tried drowning out the troublesome shrieks by tuning into a distant Voice of America news report, and learnt how a war veteran returning to Normandy for the D-Day 50th anniversary visited a war cemetery only to discover his own name on a grave. On that cheery note, I fell asleep.

The next morning, after removing a long red snake as thin as a pencil from my shoe, I fell, for about ten miles, from the dizzying hair-raising hair-pinned heights of Fuji's flanks back down towards the built-up bustle of the coast.

Half-way down I came across a strange species – a cycle-tourer, on his way up. A born-and-bred Scouser from Kirkby, Alan Gardner had emigrated first to South Africa and then to Perth, Australia, after living and teaching in the north of Japan for five years. He was now on a six-week tour, riding from Kyushu to Tokyo before flying to Liverpool to see his folks (who, he said, were soon to follow in his transplanting footsteps to 'join me in Oz') before heading back to Perth. We spent a few animated moments straddled across our top tubes comparing notes and then, deciding we had far too much to say, ambled across the road to sit in the shade of a small shrine, avidly exchanging news and views for over three hours.

In countries where cycle-tourers are a bit thin on the ground, rare is the occasion that I pass a fellow tourer by. Not only is it a good excuse for a rest but, being by nature inquisitive, it tends to get the better of me (as fortunately it does them) and an intriguing barrage of hows and whens and whats and wherefores is enthusiastically lobbed back and forth. Tips are taken, routes discussed and ideas shared. Never mind those guide books – it's these spontaneous and unexpected encounters and snappy snippets of information that spice your life and freshly fill you in.

Alan had been travelling on and off for over two and a half decades. At first he had always hitched or campervanned his way wherever he was in the world and it wasn't until he had read Dervla Murphy's *Full Tilt* that he felt inspired, as she had been thirty years earlier, to take off for India by bike. As his journey progressed more slowly than anticipated, he decided instead to fly to Egypt due to the onset of winter in Turkey and the worsened war in Iran. From Cairo he flew to Bombay, spending four months in India and Nepal from where he flew to Singapore, and my diary seems to have lost track of where he went from there.

Calling himself an 'itinerant welder', Alan had had over 200 jobs in his time. When he'd been living in Sapporo in Hokkaido he'd had a Japanese girlfriend ('now past history') and as a result spoke fluent Japanese, which he demonstrated on a good-humoured disabled man who had appeared erratically weaving down the road on an electric cart seemingly oblivious of a sudden life-snuffing cavalcade of thundering dumpertrucks which careered from around the corner, threatening to flatten him into the black and bruised bitumen.

Alan had what looked like the remnants of a sheep attached to his saddle. He told me he had bought a lead-hard Brooks saddle twice and didn't know why he had as they didn't agree with the more tender contours of his nether department – left him all numb and all that. So to try to combat this somewhat distressing symptom he said he cushioned his Brooks with a fluffy covering of sheepskin padding which, I discovered, was hastily whipped off whenever a camera appeared. 'That's because I don't think it looks too tough perched on a fluffy bit of padding!' he said.

Tanned, muscular, sweaty and with a Liverpudlian-cum-Ozzie accent, Alan – lone, alluring male in what I guessed to be his mid to late thirties – was one of those faintly feather-rustling types as far as I – lone, late twenties female – was concerned. Sometimes there comes a time when travelling alone out on a shaky-legged limb can rapidly lose its attraction if faced with a possible appealing alternative. Trouble is, pipe-cleaning dreams are usually better than the real thing and, anyway, Alan was heading up the mountain that I had just dropped down. No matter how pulsating his pectorals, I just didn't have an exhausting ten-mile retrace-a-track ascent left in me that day.

I hit the fast-flowing Fujigawa River and, in order to avoid the truck-laden Route 52, turned off on to a quiet riverside road through Minobu-cho, a small town whose outskirts had weed-free verges of flowers and tidy round bushes on one side of the road and a paddy field backing on to a car-corpse scrap-yard on the other.

I needed a flat little nook to camp but the land was all taken up with waterlogged rice fields, railway tracks, rivers, roads or homes. I decided to knock at random on a door to see if the occupants had any bright ideas as to where I could lay myself to rest. Sheepskin Alan had taught me some nifty phrases in times of need, one of which I now turned over and over in my head as I gingerly tapped on the glass sliding-door of a house. A shuffle of slippers, a woman's voice calling out something unintelligible and then, after a few more shuffles and interesting sounds the door slid back to reveal a small, round woman wearing a *yukata* and a face of surprise.

'*Sumimasen, kono hen ni wa koen ga arimasuka*? – Excuse me, is there a park in the area?' I piped as best I could before explaining I was travelling alone by *jitensha* and looking for a place to camp.

The woman, now joined by her husband bound in identical *yukata,* said something that was lost on me but I smiled and nodded and half-bowed anyway which resulted in them both breaking into fine and silver-toothed grins and, from what I could gather, urging me to enter their home. A pair of sloppy slippers was offered to me so, after reversing out of my shoes and sliding into my slippers, I eagerly followed in their shuffling slipstream into a cluttered *tatami* room: a room that gave the lie to Japanese minimalism. There were trinkets and ornaments and paraphernalia everywhere: fishing rods and bottles, flowers and jars, shrines and monkey nuts, comics and ceramics, dolls and dogs, silk cushions and shells, books and boxes and socks and washing lines and tea things. As we knelt on our cushions, sipping green tea, Mr and Mrs Yukata chatted away to me with great gusto as if Japanese was my native tongue. Although I did my best to pretend I knew where they were coming from by dutifully nodding and 'ahh-so-ing' in any available slot, I really only understood about one word per mouthful.

But it doesn't take that much turn-of-tongue to ascertain when the use of a bath is being offered, so I trotted off to my bike to extricate my wash-bag feeling rosy from the glow of warm-hearted hospitality.

Back inside, it was their toilet that first took me by surprise. After fumbling around outside the door for a while trying to find a light switch I stepped inside, thinking: oh bugger the light – I'll do it in the dark. A dazzling spotlight automatically shot on which not only momentarily pinned me to the spot by surprise but also triggered off some jauntily jazzed-up strains of 'Waltzing Matilda' emanating from a small speaker concealed in the ceiling. As the toilet was 'Western-style' I lifted the lid – and discovered a puzzling pink stretch-towelling cover pulled across the seat. At first I mistook it for some unhygienic drip absorber and it wasn't until later that I discovered its true purpose: a bum warmer. Owing to the Japanese dislike of sitting on a hard, cold lavatory seat (toilets generally being situated in a part of the house which is rarely heated) a layer of not particularly tantalizing lower buttock-warming towelette is stretched over the rim to make one's sitting more conducive to the matter in hand – or even, matter in bottom.

However, there I was, enthroned upon a pink-towelled toilet seat providing a few hazardous and misplaced *sotto voce* '. . . and I'll go a-waltzing Matilda with you . . . Waltzing Matil . . .' refrains to the all-enveloping melodies when, on reaching the toilet paper course, I tugged on a sheet only to be taken aback by yet another unexpected harmonious din: a musical toilet roll, which burst into a synthesized version of 'Greensleeves' whenever the wiping stage was reached. So much for a nice, quiet and reflective sit-down on the pan – instead all orifices were rudely bombarded by a clashing cacophony of 'Sleeves on the one buttock and Matilda's Waltzes on the other.

Things were fortunately a little more sedate in the bathroom, although I felt a trifle nervous about flicking a switch, turning a tap or basically just moving lest I trigger off further mind-numbing melodies that were lurking in wait in the most improbable places. But the cleansing process went without hitch or high water, the only noteworthy encounter being with the bath, in the bottom of which lay a cluster of hefty rocks (for inducing some authentic *al fresco* spa experience?) and on the surface, huddled together in a net bag, floated six oranges emitting a most appealing aromatic scent to my lingering ablutions.

Scrubbed from scalp to sole and wafting faintly of neroli, I slippered my way back to Mr and Mrs Yukata who had gone out of their way to lay on a lavish supper of slippery delights for me. We chatted and chortled our way through pickled this and slimy that, with me never quite sure what they were rabbiting on about but rolling along on the rollicking ride of misinterpretation anyway.

One thing I did manage to grasp out of all the peculiar sounds emanating with rapid fluidity from the Yukatas' lips was the almost venerated phrase (at least to its millions of British viewers): *Coronation Street.* The Yukatas were seemingly addicts. 'The Street', which struck me as being as out of place in Japan as Yorkshire Pudding, is in fact a firm favourite. Intrigued by this, I later discovered that *Coronation Street* rates up there among the Top Five British TV exports which include the likes of *Cadfael, Band of Gold, The Private Life of Plants,* and *Cracker.*

The Yukatas were all for me staying the night, but not wanting to be more of an imposition than I had already been and as I was also keen to get a few more breezy miles under my expanded belt-line before the sun slid down behind the hills, I thanked them heartily while trying to explain that I fancied getting as far as possible before the imminent arrival of the *tsuyu* (so-called 'plum' rainy season).

My winsome hosts appeared, perhaps understandably, a trifle perplexed at my decision to head off into the evening to find a place to camp (they recommended a school playground about fifteen kilometres down the road) instead of sleeping on a nice comfy futon in their nice safe home. And, in retrospect, it's one of those things where I'm not quite sure why I did it. Of course, it would have been far more sensible to rest a weary limb and stay cocooned within the sliding walls of the Yukatas' home. But the Big Outdoors was calling and I couldn't resist a bit more of a pedal that day, if only to move a pointless ten miles in order to lie in a playground. I scooped up my wash things and made some appreciative farewell bows.

Mr Yukata however, still dressing-gowned in his *yukata*, insisted on mounting his moped and joining me for part of the ride. With his blue-and-white *yukata* robes flapping wildly in the wind, he buzzed alongside waving merrily to copious neighbours who were either bent double in their miniature vegetable patches or hauling in their well-aired bedding, which had been draped for most of the day out of windows and over balconies and walls.

Mr Yukata was in fine spirits, urging excitedly for me to grab a hold of his rear rack so that I could be dragged along at daredevil speed. This was not quite the sort of sedate and meditative evening pedal I had envisaged back at his house, but, feeling game for a disaster, I grabbed a tight hold around a tail-light with my right hand while clinging with my left on a handlebar for a haphazard ride along the riverside road. Just what the neighbours made of this mad and unruly scene – a bicycling foreign barbarian flying by attached to a wild, dressing-gown-flapping moped man – I hate to imagine, though undoubtedly it must have added a little spice to their evening chatter.

Then, all of a sudden, midflight, we ran out of petrol, drifting to a slightly ignominious put-puttering stop. We both laughed as I tried to motion to Mr Yukata that it was now his turn to grab a hold of me for a whirling-dervish tow. But running out of petrol in Japan is not such bad news as it might be in other parts of the world (the Sahara springs to mind) – at least it's not in Mr Yukata's oriental neck of the woods, where no one is far away and where everyone pulls together to give a helping hand.

Before we could say 'Ah so, *desu-ka?*' we were inundated with offers from all directions for an instantaneous refill from at least fifty different sources, most of them delivered by tiny wizened old-age pensioners. No money exchanged hands – just bows and guffaws of laughter, with a few old dears daring enough to come and stroke the hairs on my arms.

Spluttering back into life on his nippy little scooter, Mr Yukata made a comical 'Hey-ho and onward-go' sort of gesture to me, but feeling he had truly gone quite far enough out of his way for me already I tried to urge him to abort his mission and head on back to Mrs Dressing-Gown who I felt might just be wondering what her jolly old husband was up to. But it was like trying to send a loyal and frisky dog home – Mr Yukata wanted to play. 'Oh, go on, be a devil, throw me one more stick,' he seemed to be saying. But I stood firm, assuring him I would be *daijobu* (just fine, all right, safe) and, after a bout of protracted bowing, sent him scooting back to his *oku-san* (wife).

A few wrong turns later I found the children's playground tucked behind a cluster of corrugated iron houses, each one adjoined to about two square feet of neat and prolific vegetable patch. It was a perfect camp-spot – it had everything I wanted: grass, trees, a tap in one corner and a solitary plastic sentry-box-like cubicle containing a low-lying squat toilet. Feeling happy of heart and weary of leg, I set up my tent and crawled inside and, after propping myself up on an elbow to scrawl illegibly upon a few pages of my 'Enjoy lasting pleasure and satisfaction' diary by fast-fading head-torchlight, I flipped on to an aching back in preparation for a good night's sleep.

But I had only been asleep for about an hour when the amplified whirring sound of an electric hair-dryer entered my dreams, jolting me back to a bleary-eyed consciousness. The ear-grating racket grew ever louder and, coupled with a spot-light beam bouncing erratically across my tent, seemed about to engulf me. Something was revving its engine and threatening to flatten me. A moped. It was a sound I felt I recognized but I couldn't be sure. Probably a couple of local likely lads, I thought, as I hastily tugged on a sweaty T-shirt and shorts. Cooped within the confines of my tent I lay in wait on hands and knees, which struck me as a faintly ridiculous position – more apt for scrubbing the kitchen floor than for fending off any possible interloper. Finally the engine died, the silence revealing an eruption of excited chatter preceded by a woman's voice softly calling my name. Taut muscles relaxed, my breath came back and, like a tortoise, I popped my head out of my protective shell to find Mr and Mrs Yukata, still cocooned in their *yukata* dressing-gowns, peering eagerly with toothy grins into my face. They were so sorry for disturbing me, they said – was I asleep? No, no, I lied, just having a lie down. We were worried, they said, maybe bad directions, maybe you lost. Maybe hungry. Rain is coming. You cold? No, really not, I said, it's hot. (And it was – clammy hot.) Please, this is for you, they said, handing me a plastic carrier of tasty-smelling goods. We batted back and forth a few more niceties as best we could with my more miss-than-hit grasp of the language and after they had risen to their feet and said something about telephoning them if there was trouble at mill (or words to that effect) they clambered – dressing-gowns, slippers, smiles and all – back on to their buzzing and flying hair-dryer and bounced off, waving, into the night.

By now it was 10.15 p.m. (no night-owl am I) and so, well weary after all the excitement, I again lay myself to rest, instantaneously drifting back into dream-mode. But not for long. Soon after 11 p.m. I was awoken once more with a start, this time by the sound of men's voices approaching. Instinctively I felt an uneasy ripple of fear up my spine. Lying alone 'protected' by a sliver of nylon gives no great reassuring shakes for safety, especially when, judging from past experience, men will be men (or, more like, some men will be flashers) and approach with an up-to-no-good ready-for-action weapon loitering with intent within their pants.

The voices grew louder and the footsteps more fishy as I lay in an advanced state of rigor mortis sensing that, sooner or later, all would be revealed. A path of erratic torchlight flashed across my bow but, fortunately, the torch was to be the only thing flashed that night. As the men made their advance, rustling and calling around my tent, I had little option but to unzip a small portion of door. Gingerly, with my old battle-worthy pump at the ready, I peered out of my porthole upon three small silhouettes stumbling around in the tufty grass outside my tent. I directed a feeble beam of torchlight their way, which picked up three moon-dazzling smiles. Instinct told me they were more friend than foe and, indeed, my three wise men were schoolteachers – one a good *tomodachi* (friend) of Mr Yukata who, it appeared, had been on the blower to keep a check on the playground-camper. Thus, my chirpy posse of nocturnal visitors had not so much come to bare their 'wares' as to bear their offerings: an icy can of Pocari Sweat (that all too ubiquitous pick-me-up pop), two large bottles of Sapporo beer, an apple the size of a grapefruit and a grapefruit the size of my head, a hot foil-wrapped bundle of *onigiri* (seaweed-covered riceballs), a chilled can of Dydo Java Coffee ('There's a gallon of deliciousness in every drop. Reach for the taste of good taste, reach for DYDO – DYDO DRINCO INC'), a short fat stunted cucumber, a pack of candied nuts, a pair of 'Hello' socks (did I, I wondered, look like a 'Hello Kitty' person?) and, most perplexingly, eleven six-inch pieces of string. Just what the string was for I never discovered, but I put on a fine show of charades to convey to my visitors that eleven, and definitely not ten or even twelve, pieces of string were the order of the day. Amid much laughter and misunderstanding, beers were popped and cameras flashed and then, with a polite little bow, they were gone.

I had been asleep for all of 2.4 minutes when, on the dot of midnight, the dreaded rainy season struck with unnerving vengeance. Although I had had a few wet days up at Fuji, that was a mere dainty sprinkling compared with what hit me now. Being sucked ten times through a car wash would have been kinder than what the heavy skies threw at me that night. It was pointless even contemplating packing up in search of more heavy-duty shelter, as I would undoubtedly end up worse for wetter as well as for wear than if I weathered the storm *in situ*. So I protected myself as best I could against the wild and the wet by putting everything that was already in plastic bags into more plastic bags – me and my sleeping bag included. Towels, cloths and T-shirts soaked up the fast-flowing leaks. A terrible sinking feeling overcame me when I thought: I didn't have to be here. I could be dry and content at the Yukatas'. But it was too late.

For days before this rainy onslaught, the air had grown increasingly and menacingly thick and clammy – the sky obviously building up for something big. The trouble with following in the slipstream of spontaneity is that I tend to be particularly adept at ending up in places far from home in not the most desirable of seasons. What's more, these undesirable seasons are inclined to have the most ungracious habit of being unseasonably bad: the coldest winter for 97 years; the iciest spring for 105 years; the rainiest summer for a century; the snowiest snow or the wettest rain or the worst of all worst and . . . well, that sort of thing.

Although Japan's latitude lies somewhere between Cairo in the south and Milan in the north, June, and part of July, are not the sunny type of summery months that one might associate with these climes. For six long saturated weeks the waterworks gush forth for the very rainy season.

For hours I fretted as the water-level rose up from beneath my groundsheet, threatening to play havoc with my moorings and send me floating off into Oriental oblivion. At about 4.30 a.m. I finally fell asleep but at 4.55 a.m. I suddenly surfaced from a drowning dream, woken by cries of '*Ohayo*! *Ohayo*! Good morning! Good morning!' from somewhere up-prow. Feeling like death's doornails and still lying prone, I one-handedly manhandled my front door zip to discover, in the dim, damp light of dawn, Hajime Sano, one of my three wise men, beaming into my tent far too beamily for this time of day. He was half-submerged in fishermen's waders and sheltering beneath a massive black brolly as big as a satellite. This was wise wear as it was still raining – hard. Hajime spoke a little English.

'Rain,' he said, 'very raining.'

'Yes,' I replied, 'it's very much raining.'

'Rain,' he repeated.

'Yes, rain,' I agreed feeling in no mood to dispute the fact which of course was indisputable – it was indisputably raining. Even I, in my heavily saturated soporific state, could tell that.

'Big raining okay?' he enquired.

Still lying prostrate in my plastic-bagged sleeping bag and feeling a little too much like an aqua-slug for my liking, I said, 'Yes, very big rain and thank you, I'm fine.'

'Today you bicycle? No check-out time.'

With half a head still asleep and unable to tell whether I was sinking or swimming, I said, 'No check out! You mean I can stay here later than 10 a.m.? Thank you. You're very kind. Maybe later I'll bicycle – if it stops raining!'

'Big raining today and similarity day tomorrow day. Big raining,' said the Bringer of Good Tidings.

'Oh dear,' I sighed, 'sounds wet.'

'Yes, one month maybe more much wetting.'

'Oh dear,' I sighed again, 'sounds unpromising.' And then, as a hopeful afterthought: 'Does the sun ever shine in rainy season?'

'Yes. Sometime sun no shining maybe.'

'Ah so, *desu-ka*? That sounds like it could not maybe possibly be hopeful.' With water addling my swampy cranium, intelligible speech was failing me fast.

'Yes please my pleasure guest breakfasting?' asked Hajime, still beaming.

'Breakfast?' I said, surprised, feeling my stomach reel at the prospect of dealing with raw eggs, pickled fish and seaweed at five o'clock on a soaking wet morning.

'Yes please location with my pleasure house and wife.'

Deep damp, a flooded home, a sleepless night and inertia are not the best bedfellows for producing an enthusiastic mood, never mind a hearty appetite. Despite Hajime's kindness, all I wanted to do was withdraw back down my aqua-bag and to wake up a day, a week – hell, maybe even a month later – with the sun. Feeling like a valiant skipper of a sinking ship I said, 'Thank you. You are a very kind man but I am unable to have breakfast with you as I fear I must stay with my tent lest it go down.'

'Extension invitation today tomorrow okay please.'

'Thank you. If I'm still here tomorrow I would love to have breakfast with you.'

'Fine deal! Excuse me big rain very much.' And with that Hajime handed me a rain-streaked piece of paper upon which, prepared before the programme, he had slightly unsteadily written his name and address in *romaji* script. Then, having risen to leave, he bent forwards in a bow – an action which caused what felt like half the contents of Niagara suspended on the roof of his umbrella to filter most inconveniently down the neck of my sleeping bag. On rising from his unfortunate genuflection to discover what mischance had occurred while he'd been over, Hajime leapt back with a start – apologizing profusely.

'Please don't worry about a little wet,' I said in jaunty tone, trying to make light of the fact that my dear down sleeping bag would take at least a good decade to dry, 'it's all good practice for the weeks to come.'

After a little more peripheral chatter Hajime sloshed off across the flooded field, leaving me to slither back down my swimming-bag for a last damp ditch at a submerged snooze. Miraculously I succeeded, but only for about half an hour as, on the nose of 6 a.m., I was rudely hoisted aloft from my dreams by a shockingly loud air-raid siren that shrieked offensively from loudspeakers fixed to the tops of telegraph poles up and down the village. The shattering racket reverberated across the otherwise quiet valley floor, rebounding quite hideously off distant mountain walls. I lay there, or to be more precise, floated there in my tent, stuffing T-shirts into my ears in a horrified state, unsure as to whether the caterwauling siren was a signal for the local firecrew to spurt into action or whether it was a warning that World War Three had just begun. Both musings were incorrect. For the

Japanese, who appear to have a strange love affair with noise, this brain-splintering siren was just a piece of everyday life that usually recurred at noon, 5 p.m., 6 p.m. and 9 p.m. in many towns and villages throughout Japan, dividing up the day and alerting in socialist style workers and residents alike to the fact that it was time to get up, time for lunch or time to stop/start work.

Sometimes the air-raid siren was replaced by jarring Big Ben-type chimes preceded by blaring and tinny melodies wailing to high-hell from loudspeakers strung along the streets. These speakers doubled up as PA systems from which anything from political announcements to the price of fish or vegetables or some imminent event or festivities would nerve-gratingly screech.

As time went by I found many things in Japan to be either irritating or offensive but which I gradually came to accept because they were necessary (eating seaweed on a daily basis was one, lack of privacy was another), and equally there were various things that were unacceptable because they were offensive without being necessary. By far the worst of these was noise: unbearable and all-enveloping noise. I usually like to think I'm quite temperate by nature but if anything stirred my hackles to severe explosion point it was the continuous bombardment of totally unnecessary noise that life in Japan seems to revolve around. In the cities I expected noise – after all, for several million people living cheek by jowl on top of each other, to move around noiselessly in a serious lack of space is not, in this engine-growling, music-blaring world, too easy. But out in the Japanese countryside or in small towns or villages, I felt that my eardrums would at least find a degree of respite. If anything, though, it was worse. It was not uncommon to find whole communities of houses which had a loudspeaker attached to an outer wall through which early morning calls, local announcements, advertisements, wailing ditties or various warnings and instructions were communicated by the district government to local residents on an hourly basis.

Although in theory the volume on the loudspeakers could be turned down, they never seemed to be switched to anything but full-blown distortion mode. Worse, the residents on whose house the speaker was fitted were unable to turn it off. Despite it not being compulsory to have a wailer on your wall, it was unlikely that, in a community which had such a system, anyone would refuse as the system was seen on balance to be a token of belonging to the local community rather than as a strident invasion of privacy. As Ronald Dore once observed: 'The lack of what in other societies might be valued as "privacy" is part of what it means to be a "member" of a community.'

And if it's not a speaker on a house, a shop or a lamppost then it's a megaphone on van-patrol vehicles competing with each other for noise output which, for instance, approaching local or not so local election time boom out, in the most effusively courteous language, supplications like: 'We humbly beg your honourable support, we humbly beg your honourable support, we humbly beg . . .', as if adopting such ingratiating courtesy might somehow atone for the bawling head-damage they produce. And then, just when at last you think you have got away from it all – maybe by climbing high into the soundless mountains, save for the wind and the birds – a low-flying megaphone-aircraft will suddenly screech from the clouds shattering in an instant the peace of the peaks by exhorting their insufferable messages to the few and the far between.

Whenever I expressed my exasperation about the insufferable racket and asked people how they could stand it, day in and day out, their answer was always the same: '*Shikata ga nai?*' – 'What can you do?'

It was still raining heavily when I surfaced at about 7 a.m. for an urgent sprint through a slicing downpour to the port-a-loo bobbing around in the corner of the waterlogged play/swim-ground.

I lived in hope – hope that it would stop raining, if not properly then at least long enough for me to pack up. But despite managing to spin a breakfast of rice-rolls and apples out for four hours it was still raining, if not harder than before. Although I would have been quite happy to slosh around in my tent all day (I'm a lazy sod at heart) I was fidgety to get on – get moving.

So I moved. And once I had conditioned myself to the fact that I was wet and couldn't get much wetter even if I was to swim the Pacific twenty-seven times, the rain no longer worried me. In fact I began to enjoy it. As ever, there is something strangely pleasing, hypnotic even, when togged up in wet weather gear, to have, hour after mesmerizing hour, sharp shards of splicing rain zinging off your legs, your arms, your head – to watch them leap a foot off the road.

When I finally emerged from my sodden sleep-spot (ha! some sleep!) to roll off down the riverside way, who should I meet but Hajime, still in waders, still beaming and still seeking refuge beneath the bulbous dome of his big, black *kasa.* He was standing as stiff as a sentinel in the middle of the road – albeit a quiet road. I don't know if he had been waiting a minute, five minutes or five hours, but undoubtedly he had been waiting for me as he was holding a large plastic carrier containing *bento* of fresh *sushi* and *sashimi, onigiri* rice wedges, *tempura,* fruit, dainty cakes, nuts and crisps and sweets and teas and pops and a salmon pink T-shirt (did I look like a salmon-pink T-shirt person?) with the words 'TASTE THE CANDY LIFE' pasted upon the chest. There was also a hand-painted card inside which Hajime had written in his faintly unsteady *romaji* lettering:

JODIE – STRENGTHY AND HAPPI TIME BICYCLE JOURNEY JAPAN
PEACE AND HEALTHFULL CARE
Hajime Sano.

As I sailed off down the underwater road, Hajime, bless him, stood bowing and waving and smiling triumphantly – a tiny forlorn figure dwarfed by the bulbous dome of his big, black umbrella.

The rain wasn't so much fun once I had crossed the Fujikawa River to join Highway 52 – it never is when regiments of thundering trucks are involved, covering you in oily spray and filthy fumes. The road surface did little to raise my dampened spirits either: it was full of long, corrugated gullies that channelled my tyres in haphazard directions through grooves and ruts and potholes awash with greasy water.

I toiled up and over the green and misty Fujimi Pass, skirting lay-bys that resembled mini landfills (hurling litter willy-nilly out of a vehicle's window appeared to be a favourite national pastime) which, come noon (lunchtime), with lorry drivers who were either nonchalantly peeing in full (frontal) view of passing traffic (not an appetizing sight), speed-eating their way through their lunchbox or else asleep, reclined in their driving seat – white-socked feet resting haughtily upon the top of the steering wheel.

Back down on the congested Shizuoka side of Suruga Bay I splashed along a spectacularly unpleasant road – built-up, busy and grey and awash with traffic and petro-chemical plants. Entering the city of Shimizu my mission in mind was to try to locate the youth hostel at Cape Masaki – a bit of a long shot, this, seeing as the Japanese youth hostel guide I had on board was printed purely in Japanese and offered a map about the size of a postage stamp, crawling in *kanji* characters. No matter which way I held it, it all looked just the same: a highly confusing web of meaningless squirls and whirls and hieroglyphics.

After drifting for miles along an interminable industrialized wharf, I veered off down an alley and dripped into a small, dark, creaking wooden store which sold slippers, marbles, fishing tackle, white gloves, seaweed and gumboots. Stringing together a few random words of Japanese I asked an old man behind the counter directions to the *yusu hosuteru* at Cape Masaki and in reply I was offered a pair of fluffy slipper inner soles. This wasn't quite the answer I was looking for and after a number of futile attempts, which resulted in me being offered sheets of sugared *nori*, lead weights, feather flies and boots, we both grinned and bowed and uttered a few verbally incomprehensible sounds before I left him to rehouse his tackle and boots and slippers and seaweed back on the shelves.

The next store I scampered into out of the rain proved a little more promising. The man behind the counter was still old, his floor still wooden and creaking, but miraculously he managed to grasp a word or two of my faltering Japanese. The only trouble was he seemed uncertain as to just what the devil a *yusu hosuteru* was, never mind whether one existed or not on the tip of Cape Masaki (wherever that was). But undeterred by his sketchy knowledge concerning the two crucial combining factors as regards my search for that night's accommodation (What is a *yusu hosuteru*? Where is Cape Masaki?) he was nonetheless quite determined to rustle up a series of elaborately detailed hand-drawn maps which he kept scrunching up, throwing away and starting again until he was satisfied. How the old man managed to draw a map of a place in an area he didn't even know was most perplexing and was not something which promised success. However, I applauded his efforts effusively and after he had voluntarily towelled down my jacket for me (a quite unprovoked and unexpected operation, especially as I was still wearing it) and given me a gift of a hand-held paper fan (for a rainy day?) I reversed, bobbing and bowing, out of his shop.

Back outside, in the darkening deluge, I peered at my new, interestingly composed map of squiggles and wiggles and thought: looks good, but means nothing. Still, I was determined to decode it as I was too wet and the land too concreted-over to contemplate camping.

Later, much later, soaked to the core and having suffered through a number of major navigational errors, I arrived in not the best of moods at Cape Masaki *yusu hosuteru* more by chance than any particular skill at map-decoding. I squelched through the doors, was hounded by a scrum of far too boisterous 'Harrow America! Harrow!' junior high schoolchildren from Osaka, and went to 'sleep' on the top bunk of a mosquito-infested dormitory called 'Liverpool'. Next door eight hyperactive adolescent bodies 'slept' amidst screams and hysterics and crashes and thuds in a far from peaceful 'Copenhagen'.

At 5.30 a.m. sharp I was torn from my mosquito-sucking slumber by a preposterously incompatible musical medley incorporating, among other tunes(?) amplified beyond anything remotely decipherable as music, a lyricless Tom Jones's 'It's Not Unusual', Jimmy Nail's 'Crocodile Shoes' and something annoyingly head-sticking from Andrew Lloyd-Webber's *Cats.* This early morning brain-crunching alarm, which automatically heckled my hackles, appeared to be emanating from a point just outside my window. Peeved, I stumbled out

of bed and peered through the finger-smeared glass into the grounds below to see a battalion of shrieking schoolchildren performing excruciating ritualistic exercises to the amplified caterwauling of Tom Jones and Co. All quite normal for Japan.

It was another gloomy grey day. Slicing rain (the sort that hurts) greeted me the moment I stepped outdoors. As I sluiced my way along the fast-flowing Route 150 past the 'Lounge Napoleon' restaurant, a 'Liquor and Rice' store and the ever-popular computer bowling, it grew steadily – and then very suddenly – wetter.

Not many urban areas in the world are improved by rain and traffic and Route 150 was certainly no exception. Everywhere and everything was stunningly ugly: concrete and corrugated iron (Japan's two favourite building materials), litter and cars. Fed up with fighting with my handlebars to prevent being sucked into the swaying underbellies of the growling trucks swooshing past my elbow, I peeled off down a side road that ended in an alley which took me on to a track leading me down to the sea. This was more like it. For miles I bounced along a coastal rubbish-strewn path behind the backs of houses, shops and garages. Apart from the massive tidalwave-break, the beach could have been nice. Instead, as in so much of Japan, it was used as a giant dustbin for bottles and cans and old tyres and fridges, mangled bikes, rotting furniture and abandoned cars. Every so often someone set to, attempting to burn a pile of it away but merely creating a thick black plume of noxious gases and charred eyesores.

Frail old women in bonnets and aprons and baggy floral pantaloons toiled away untiringly with bent backs in small compact patches of land behind their far from resplendent homes. Under the corrugated eaves of most of the houses hung clusters of fat golden onions. The people who lived in these shanty-style abodes were a world away from the money-spinning and computerized wizardry that I had always associated with Japan. Undoubtedly they were yen-stretchers, growing vegetables not so much as a happy hobby but as a means of survival.

I bumped my way along the gravel track, swerving round broken glass, crab shells and, at one point, a litter of dead kittens strewn carelessly across the path. Fishermen in airy conical straw hats sat on tottering heaps of wooden pallets beneath awnings of tarpaulin. They smoked and chatted and waved a sort of surprised wave when they saw me. Behind them on the shore, a tangle of boys shouted to each other above the noise of the breaking waves while they dragged up the beach a couple of small fishing boats that bore the names of 'Lone Lone' and 'Dissemination' painted gaily on their bows.

Finally the coastal path petered out and I merged with a narrow strip of road that bowled me along into some backstreet alleys of a small village where a model class of primary children, dwarfed by large rigid red satchels strapped to their backs, were trotting along, happily unsupervised, on their way home from school. All the children had large hazard triangles stuck to the rear of their satchels and on their tiny black heads perched identical white pudding-bowl helmets that, from a distance, made them look like a Boer battalion of toy soldiers marching off to war.

The road ran into some cliffs and it was tunnel time again – nothing too traumatic, just a lot of dirt and dark and sweat – before finally emerging into the open on the top of a hill that overlooked the flat, pollution-cloaked urban sprawl of Yaizu city.

I swooped down the hill, slaloming at speed through the thick knots of traffic, catching glimpses of bewildered expressions on the faces of oncoming motorists as they spotted a wild-eyed devil hurtling towards them aboard a heavily pregnant bicycle. Life, at moments like this, felt good.

Route 150 had done me in so I veered off on to a quieter alternative as soon as one appeared which led me back closer to the coast. I passed alongside wharfs – hives of manic activity – and twisted through an intricate webwork of narrow backstreets full of the heady aroma of fish. Most of the stores along here were part of people's homes: the front room the shop, the back room the *tatami* and television-blaring living quarters. Lined up outside on the roadside virtually every store displayed identical small, pale blue or pink plastic wicker baskets containing a selection of various fruit and vegetables: strictly four oranges or onions or fat tomatoes to a basket – never five.

At one shop I stopped to buy a supply of surprisingly cheap (for Japan) apples and bananas, but the shopkeeper, an old man whose head was crowned with a twisted towel, refused to let me pay. In return I delved deep into the bottomless pit of my panniers to extricate a packet of biscuits and a bag of nuts which I handed to him, but no sooner had I vacated the space in my bags than he lobbed in a basket of oranges. Swiftly, like a trained retriever, I dived in after them and tossed them back but the towel-crowned man simply batted them once more into my panniers followed by a *daikon* – a carrot-shaped radish the size of a small hoover. Then he told me to *chotto matte kudasai* (just a moment, please) – my favourite gun-splattering expression – and disappeared behind a sliding door for just long enough to give me time to scoot across the road to a vending machine to buy him a couple of Kirin beers.

When I returned the man had reappeared with his wife in tow, who smilingly offered me a bowl of steaming noodles and a pair of Mickey Mouse socks. (Did I look like a Mickey Mouse socks sort of person? And, hell – what was it with socks?). The usual farce ensued: No, no; Please, please; No, no; Please, please; No, no – oh, all right then.

After much appreciative but unappetizing slurpings on my part and much happy beer-swilling on theirs, I finally managed to make my departure, lumbering off unsteadily down the road with panniers loaded to the gunwales with half the contents of their fruit-fronted store.

The land flattened out into a head-on windy expanse of chequered rice paddies criss-crossed with a network of narrow roads. Submerged at sporadic intervals upon small-holdings of drained ground floated houses among their square moats of watery paddy.

Fighting into the teeth of a small-scale gale I crossed the wide, and surprisingly dry, river bed of the Oi River – which I felt was bereft of an exclamation mark somewhere along the way and should really be the Oi! River, in similar ejaculated style as England's very own Westward Ho!

My sodden, wind-blasted mood was in no fine form to look forward to merging once more with the truck-laden Route 150 and, just before I did, I spotted a small sign in both English and *kanji* pointing the way to the 'Pacific Coast Bicycle Route Path'. I couldn't believe it! Oi! River, I thought, a Bike Path! Westward Ho! It is stumbling upon little unexpected joys like this that can rocket your spirits to lofty peaks, causing you to forget the wretched weather for at least two minutes.

Onward Go! – I went, following the Bike Path! which was bordered on one side by a river (not the Oi!), the other by some small square fields containing not only vegetables but bent people busy at work. At one point I stopped to watch the chemical-spraying process: no beefy and state-of-the art mechanized farm equipment here – just a woman bundled up in aprons, elbow-length cotton gloves, bonnet and bows with a large plastic receptacle strapped to her back like a rucksack. From this snaked a wide rubber tube peppered with spraying holes which, with the aid of six other women supporting it at intervals across the field, stretched across the crops. The women walked slowly and methodically between the rows, the woman with the chemical back-pack activating a hand-pump that sprayed the plants with a fine mist of killer-chemicals. Two men stood smoking on the sidelines, seemingly only galvanized into action by a shout from the pumping woman whenever her cargo needed a top-up.

That night, as I threaded my way through a rainy confusion of coastal backstreets, I washed up at a hotel called Pink

River. From the outside it looked odd: mock crenellated battlements and a cryptic sign saying OK/NO (the OK was illuminated so I ventured within). The inside was even odder: there was no reception, no receptionist, no people – just a dingy booth with a wall-mounted door-phone beside which, contained in a gold-rimmed picture frame, was a display of room prices (3000 yen or about £18 for the cheapest room). As the prospect of sleeping in a flooded tent for another night was not an appealing one, I, for want of something better to do, removed the flimsy receiver from the wall-phone and placed it against my port-side ear. All was silent. Then I saw a knob on the handle which, hesitantly, I pushed. I heard a buzz followed by a woman's voice which emitted a short staccato of incomprehensible speed-splattering speech which shot clean out my non-receiving ear.

Telephones are frightening things at the best of times but trying to converse on one when you don't know what to say, never mind understand, in an alien whiplash tongue is enough to make me, if not you, panic. I panicked and slammed down the receiver. After a few moments of cogitation I thought: this is silly. I'm wet, I'm hungry and I want a room. So I put the receiver once again to my ear. Another buzz and the woman's voice returned. Again my eardrums were assaulted by a shot of rapid fire which this time I unflappably allowed to wash clean over me before I launched myself into the best of my worst Japanese, explaining that I needed a cheap room for one night. Please.

Once again I had no idea what the woman said but I must have put one word right because suddenly a key, sent from above, shot down a shoot to arrive in a chrome recess in the wall beside me. Finding this all rather strange behaviour for a hotel, I called '*Arigato gozaimasu*!' into the receiver, before placing it back in the socket. I then wandered along an unsettling mirrored corridor (unsettling because it had been a while since I had caught a reflection of myself and the sweaty, oil-stained, rain-sodden sight that greeted me was not a promising one) to my room.

Laden down with waterlogged panniers in hand I fumbled with the key and flung open the door with my foot and stepped into a rocket. No kidding! Westward Ho! Confronted with a 'room' that bore a striking resemblance to a stage set from *Close Encounters*, I felt I had landed on Mars. It was all curving space-ship, Captain Spock-style control panels and flashing lights. In lieu of a window stood a vast video screen recessed into the wall which, by flipping a few digits and dials, doubled up as a television or *karaoke* (literally 'empty orchestra') machine. In its stand-by position the screen, awash with flickering stars, conveyed the impression of travelling through space among other orbiting spacecraft. Earth looked a long way away.

Hanging in a pink-spangled cupboard I found a couple of space-suits, His 'n' Hers, with unzippable openings in places which were surely more revealing than necessary for a simple rocket-ride through space. Highly perplexed, and fretting that maybe I had downed a Pocari Sweat too many, it wasn't until I had investigated the large rocket-shaped bed where I discovered a 'love-pack' (a sealed and heart-shaped plastic pouch containing a small bottle of 'Erotica' scent, a set of Betty Boo folded paper towels, and two condoms) that it suddenly dawned on me that I had unintentionally stumbled upon a Love Hotel.

From the end of the twelfth century to the mid-1950s prostitution was legal, licensed and a hugely popular pastime in Japan. Then, from midnight on 31st March 1958, an Anti-Prostitution Act came into force. Although prostitution became technically illegal it went mostly overboard underground, growing into a gigantic industry run by a distinct class of pro-gangsters to whom the police turned a blind eye. Brothels continued to operate simply by masquerading as *toruko*, short for Turkish bath, which, due to the Turkish government giving vent to some vigorous fulminations in the mid-'eighties, are today known as *sopurando* – Soapland.

The architecture of these massage parlours tends to reflect the illusion of fantasy for sale within the steamy walls.

Some *sopurando* have façades resembling hospitals – the girls dress up as nurses to administer to their patient's every need (so long as the price is right). Others may have a foyer built to look like the cabin of an airliner, automatically simulating the sounds of 'take off' the moment the 'passenger' steps on board. Air hostesses clad in tight and scanty uniforms bend over backwards to tend to their passenger's every requirement which, needless to say, stretches a touch beyond fetching an extra blanket, handing out a headset or demonstrating the use of the emergency oxygen masks.

If an exchange of small change and a titillating teller girl is more your scene, then other *sopurando* pose as banks. Anyone for tennis? Then 'Young Lady' schools with girls kitted out in whites greet their players bearing smacking good rackets under arm. Perhaps turning a little more primal is the order of the day? Then any wannabe Tarzans can enter a creeper-swinging jungle, home to a hundred game Janes squeezed into skimpy leopard-skin skirts and leotards. Nuns and school-mistresses and chamber-maids are hot stuff too.

In other *sopurando* the frilly thrills may be swept aside in order to get down to the *furu kosu* (full course) on offer: a steam bath, a hot-water bath and then a lengthy sudsy massage by a girl dressed in precious little who goes on to act out the customer's every desire by providing an elaborate menu of sexual acrobatics.

Although *sopurando* are mostly for men, some are for mixed sex and a few for women only. But back in the 'fifties, with the onset of illegalized prostitution, along with the 'Turkish' bath-houses there sprang up on the outskirts of every city a host of special Love Hotels (or Lovetels). Originally seedy back-street operations, these 'hotels' (extravagant candy-cake edifices that offer gadgetry eroticism on a short-stay basis) have become folk art. At first I thought that the idea behind Love Hotels was like the equivalent of Mr and Mrs Smith meeting up for a dirty weekend in Brighton. In Japan, most people who patronize a Love Hotel need no such alias – they really are married – but to *each other*! They are not so much elopers on the loose but married couples simply seeking a rare few hours of intimate *puraibashi* which, owing to paper-thin walls, crowded conditions and inquisitive children, cannot be found even in their own homes.

Despite the fact that many countries have hotels that rent rooms by the hour for purposes other than sleeping, it is usually a bit of a knowing-look, hush-hush operation. In Japan, Love Hotels openly proclaim their function on television with regular adverts luring couples with the promise that a few hours spent together in a room technically equipped for an exotic sojourn of luxurious fantasy will put a spot of Oi! back into their marriages.

Love Hotels follow a theme: they are designed to resemble the QE2, grand palaces, medieval castles, European cathedrals, New York City, Hollywood, Disneyland or ten-tiered wedding cakes iced in pink, and so on. The rooms, like my futuristic space station, are pure kitsch: fantasy palaces with medieval banqueting halls and suits of clanking armour; ocean liners and ships sailing on artificial seas for the nautically inclined; small-scale basketball pitches with hoops, crowd cheers, score boards and plenty of balls; jungle settings with creepers, gorilla costumes and full wildlife and Tarzan-cry sound effects; pop-star status stages complete with microphones, dry-ice and drum-set.

Beds can come shaped like luxury cars, conch shells, elaborate surfboards, chariots or the Queen's coronation coach. There are beds which oscillate and toot their horns or launch into an earth-moving rendition of Beethoven's Fifth at the first movement or detection of the slightest sexually stimulated moan or groan. Others will rock and roll and rotate to help proceedings along. Many are equipped with closed-circuit TV cameras to record one's activities for posterity – or maybe so that one can improve one's technique: 'Whoa! Not such a great idea, that backhand swipe . . . must remember to follow through . . . perhaps give the old balls a bit more top-spin . . .' One Lovetel even has a space-shuttle bed which automatically slides down a launching rail, RNLI lifeboat-style, when a concealed microphone detects a climactic moment.

The high point of my spaced-out stay came when I was enthusiastically chopping up an onion on the bed for my noodle and porridge-based supper. One of the aforementioned concealed sensors must have mistaken the sounds of my culinary endeavours as pipping the peak of sexual ecstasy because all of a sudden the lights went out, screens started flashing, a Cape Canaveral baritone launched into a 10. . .9. . .8. . .7. . .6. . .5. . . countdown followed by a 'We have lift-off!' and, after a mildly disconcerting explosion which caused half my hard-worked-for noodles to slurp and spill on to the bedspread, I was overcome by the faintly sea-sick sensation of being ejaculated into space.

Needless to say, neither sleep nor sex was something I had a lot of that night but at least I managed to drip-dry my tent and wash out my socks with the stars.

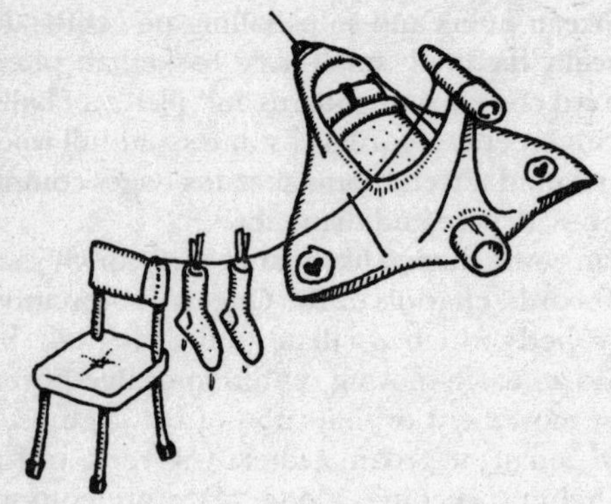

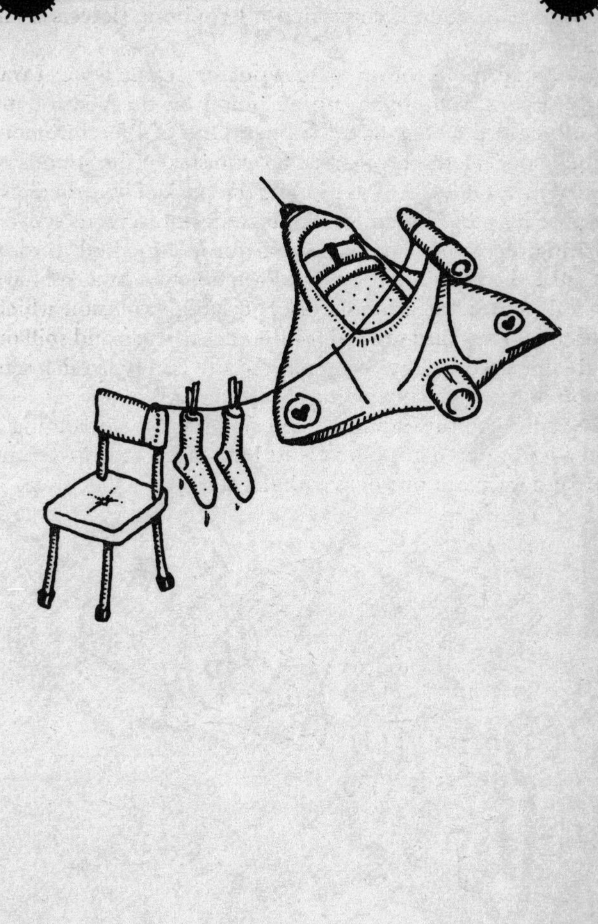

80 KLIX
50 MILES
RIDE RIDDEN THIS DIRECTION
HUGE INDUSTRIAL BELT
Himeji
kobe
kyoto
BIG TEMPLE CITY
lake Biwa
SUZUKA MTS
NAGOYA
N
Toyota
INDUSTRIAL AREA
Hi!
the inland sea
the outside land
OSAKA
Nara
Suzuka
ISE BAY
Komatsushima
wakayama
yuasa (birthplace of soy sauce)
KII HANTO PENINSULA
Ise shrine
site of cultured pearl
Toba
Nanto-cho (where I was submerged with presents)
Miyama-cho where I had 27 Baths
Hiwasa
HO
HA, HA
HE
Kawabe (laughter festival)
sea turtles (look there)
DORO-KYO
JAPAN'S TALLEST WATERFALL
ATSUMI PENINSULA
Hamamatsu
where I o.d.'d on watermelon (very odd!?!)
where the rain gods filled my panniers
Shirahama
Give me fight!
Octopus town
Shingu
PACIFIC

CHAPTER 13

Breakfast with the Rain Gods

The day after the night before, I didn't get very far: with the headwind and the rain so heavy, the road so awash, it felt as if I was fighting a constant battle with the elements to avoid being sucked down the plughole.

By late afternoon I had given up the slog and started to size up a potential spot to camp. The area was so peopled that the coast resembled one continuous lava-flow of concrete. Away from the dreaded Route 150 I twisted and turned my way through narrow, writhing streets until I came across a brand new park (not much bigger than the perfectly planted offering of flowers that are sometimes found adorning the centre of mini-roundabouts in some British towns) with a bit of path, a bit of bench and a bit of a lean-to rain/shade shelter. There was a toilet, too, and as I tend to be of the opinion that one should never pass a toilet by lest one lives to regret it, I went to deliver what little superfluous-to-body-requirement products I had on board.

But I got no further than opening the door because, there, splat on the floor of an otherwise spic and span squat toilet, lay a phenomenally large heap of severely misplaced human excrement. Like a Good Samaritan I swiftly closed the door in retreat and thought: poor person who has to clear that up.

Soiled toilets aside, I probably would have camped in the pin-prick of a park had it not been for a clutch of rumbustious schoolboys in short white shirt sleeves, black trousers and white trainers balancing on bikes and generally just loitering, shouting 'Harrow! Harrow! I ruv you! I am Japanese boy!' with tiring repetition. Undoubtedly they would peel away at some stage, leaving my 'bedroom' vacated, but as I don't like dilly-dallying I set off in search of a fresh space to sleep.

I passed another candy-cake edifice but not feeling up to another rocky night in a Love Hotel I kept going and had the good fortune to happen upon a long, grassy pine-tree-endowed central reservation lying between two back streets and a row of houses. Camping in the middle of a central reservation is, I admit, not an ideal location but then this was grassy-flat-land-starved Japan so you can't be too picky. Before I set to with tent erection I felt that I should perhaps go and make my intentions clear to someone lest I find the police on my doorstep at some unearthly hour of the night.

Across the road sat 'Snack Gorgeous' so I wandered on in and asked the *mama-san* behind the bar if she thought it would be all right for me to camp on the central reservation opposite. Her first reaction was to look rather surprised but I suppose this was only to be expected, seeing as my request can't have been an everyday occurrence. And then, because consensus is the name of the game for decision-making in Japan, she recruited every member of staff, plus a few inquisitive customers, for a protracted head-to-head discussion, the result producing a hearty and universal cry of 'But it is wet! You must sleep inside!' *Mama-san*, the proprietor of the Gorgeous Snack bar and a woman as wide as she was short, and who lived in an adjoining room behind the bar with what appeared to be approximately sixty-seven members of her family, warmly invited me to stay the night with her. As

Japanese life-expectancy is the highest in the world and as people never seem to die, and as there is no space to live elsewhere and as it is tradition for great-great-great-great generations of this to live with great-great-great-great generations of that, they still do in many places and Snack Gorgeous was a case in point.

Suspecting that a sixty-eighth body (a foreign body in all) might just be a body too many and spoil the broth, and not wanting to cause more of a stir than I had already, let alone drop my dripping-wet belongings all over her *tatami*, I politely declined her invitation. *Mama-san* then asked if I might like to use the *benjo.* Never one to look a gift-toilet in the mouth, I trotted off gratefully only to find waiting for me on my return a flask of iced tea and a 'Snack Gorgeous Special' – a packed supper of fishy rice and slippery comestibles – on the house. Thus my night stretched out upon the central reservation may have been a wet one, but it was well-fuelled and my stomach went to sleep replete.

I awoke before dawn the following morning and wasn't surprised to discover it was still raining. Rain is all very well (if you like that sort of thing), but I was having trouble getting used to the death-defying humidity. By 5.30 a.m., and having done nothing more strenuous than open my eyes, I was already hot and sweaty. Little did I know that this was decidedly cool compared with what was to come.

Waiting for the dark to dissolve, I lay in my altogether upon my sheet-sleeping bag (a good and easily washable sweat soaker-upper) thinking: wet with sweat within; wet with rain without. Producing another gallon of sweat simply by twisting my neck and lifting a shiny arm in order to turn on the radio, I tuned into the Rush Limbaugh Show on FEN. Rush's motor-mouthing tongue was in full swing: 'Hey all you lazy fatsos – grab a hold of this. Yesterday Clinton was visiting Oxford England to pick up some university accolade, and you know what? Those who went to college with him say he was no fun because he didn't inhale!'

Rush went on in jesting tones to describe the recent events of how Clinton had been filmed strolling along Omaha Beach, Normandy, as part of the D-Day 50th anniversary, with a well-rehearsed meditative expression fixed upon his fleshy features, when lo! just out the blue he came across a pile of stones. Stooping down, he took the stones and formed them into the shape of a cross. 'Is that likely or what?' ribbed Rush. 'I mean, jeez, talk about a staged PR ploy to boost those ever-plummeting poll-ratings of popularity!'

A twiddle of dial and Radio Netherlands (catchphrase: 'We've got the world talking!') was in the midst of a tasteful report about bestiality. Apparently this was once a widely popular activity. 'For example,' explained a professor of bestiality (or something like that), 'for a shepherd boy who would have spent all day every day out in the hills with his sheep, his first most likely sexual encounters would be with his animals.'

The professor then went on to inform the 'talking world' that having sex with animals of course still goes on, but that these days it tends to be a touch more awkward due to the fact that in most countries most people live in busy, populated urban areas where, like it or not, you just don't often find yourself alone for a quiet moment in an inner-city meadow with alternative sexual motives and a bunch of streetwise sheep. Desperate or not, it seems that, given the choice, beast can still rule over man – or woman. The *Sun* (October 1996) ran a survey of its readers and asked: 'Who would you rather date, Fergie or a goat?' The goat won hoofs down.

At about six a strange thing happened: the rain stopped. But no sooner had it stopped than a conical straw-hatted force of doze-shattering grass-strimmers and mowers fired up their engines and set about slicing their way through the grassy strip of my central reservation with typical Japanese speed-efficiency. Blades of spiky grass and sharp shards of pine cones were sent zinging and pinging and scudding off my flysheet. I wondered what this elderly workforce of strimmers must make of a tented foreigner housed on their patch, but despite a momentary flicker of intense shock (which even my mother would reveal if she saw me crawling in a dishevelled and sweaty state on all fours out of the mouth of my tent in the middle of a central reservation) they took it remarkably well.

Above the whining din I apologized to the chief strimmer – an old man with a short towel draped like a scarf round his neck while another was knotted around the cone of his hat – for being in the way and that I would be packed up and out of his firing line in just a tick. But the man, appearing even more apologetic than I, made it clear that he wanted me to 'please, please, stay, stay'. Feeling that lying as an obstruction in the path of the bionic strimmers was hardly conducive to enhancing the local community spirit, I hastily rolled up my mat, stuffed in my tent and packed up my panniers within a ten-minute personal best all-time record. But such was the furious speed of the geriatric strimmers that by the time I looked up they had already strum and gone, leaving just a small tent-shaped tuft of unstrimmed grasses where my nocturnal home had lain.

I rode a few streets down to the sea where, after climbing upon a mountainous mould of concrete sea-blocks, I watched a straggle of wet-suited boys on boards bobbing around on their stomachs in the swell of the dismal surf.

The rain considerately held off just long enough to fool me into thinking that it would remain dry for at least another half an hour – time enough for an *al fresco* breakfast – and then as soon as I had settled myself nicely on a bench surrounded by an array of open jars and panniers, it let loose its dastardly deluge. It has to be said that if ever a drought-ridden region of the world was in dire need of a raindancer, then I feel that, owing to an apparent inherent aptitude for galvanizing the rain-gods into action whenever I stop by the roadside for an elaborate spot of sandwich-making (a process which tends to involve the uprooting of the entire contents of my panniers in a chaotic plastic-bagged detritus around me), I stand as a strong contender for the job. Before I rejoined the unlovely Route 150 I had tried two more times to stop for a benched breakfast and both times, right on cue, on my first bite of sandwich, the waterlogged heavens had let loose their offerings.

Owing to a severe inability to open my eyes beyond a squint due to the splicing sheets of blinding rain, I saw very little that day. This wasn't such a bad thing, mind, because Route 150 was not blessed with scenic sights. Everything looked very wet and very grey and very trafficky. But one sight does stand out crystal clear or, I should say, one sight repeated several times: these were bundled up forms of solitary women sitting in the wet and the wind looking dejected on the edge of the greasy spray-lashed road beside enormous piles of ears of corn, and melons (costing £30 *each*), for sale. I never once saw anyone stopping to buy anything from them, so towards the end of the afternoon, I pulled over and bought a very corny cob from one woman, who looked so happily surprised at my purchase that it well made up for the fact that it was not only the most expensive corn (£3.50) I had ever bought but also that I had no means by which to cook it. So I scraped off the kernels with my deadly Kitchen Devil (the same one which had once severed a forefinger nerve in the Forest of Fontainebleau) and ate them raw. And, apart from the intractable strands that I found up to a month later still lodged in my teeth, it was a surprisingly enjoyable experience.

That evening, looking for a place to camp, I found myself in the wrong place at the wrong time: entering the fringes of Hamamatsu-shi as the little watery light that had been shed on me that damp day was fast draining from the sky. For mile upon mile every single speck of ground was either lived on or built over. I should have suspected as much but the trouble was I allowed my map to deceive me into believing that I would find camp-spots aplenty. The map showed what looked like great swathes of emptiness divided up by small, meandering minor roads; the sea was a mere quarter of a fingernail away; and ahead was the wide Tenryu River beside which I was hoping to camp. But reality was a different piece of pie rudely awaking me to the fact that Hamamatsu-shi blended into Hamakita-shi which blended into Iwata-shi which blended into Fukuroi-shi which blended into Kakegawa-shi – one mighty massive conglomeration of *shi*'s.

Faced with this none-too-rosy revelation, I rode on and on and on, quietly humming to myself to make me feel happier in an increasingly motorized and grey concrete world. The thought of space and hills and green pastures and invigorating crisp mountain air seemed to me to be unreachable and dim distant dreams.

For hours I kept plunging off the main road into side streets and alleys to try to find a six-foot patch of lie-able, tentable space, but there was nowhere – no parks, no shrines, no temples, no mildly conceivable plots. I tried looking for a *minshuku*, but it all seemed so complicated – I couldn't read *kanji*, I didn't know where to look and I didn't like to stop anyone to ask them for help as it was as good as dark and they all seemed so busy racing through the rain with umbrellas or diving into cars or disappearing like apparitions behind walls of sliding doors.

I stopped at a Nisseki petrol station to use the *benjo* before asking the attendant at the cash-till if he knew of a *minshuku* in the area. After a lot of collating of information with his colleagues and after a lot of sucking in of air through teeth, they were very sorry, they said, but knew of nowhere. Instead of directions I was offered a pack of Lucky Strike cigarettes and was given a road atlas printed in *kanji* of the Hamamatsu-shi area (which only made me more confused) and a can of orange pop from a vending machine that invited the passer-by to 'Drink Paradise'.

I rode on through a wet, flat cityscape of bleakness until, all of a sudden, my eyes hit virtual visual meltdown when, out of all the grey, I crossed a very big and shockingly pink-painted bridge.

For about the fiftieth time I took a sweeping swoop down a side street in search of sleepable land (I told myself there surely had to be some) and this time I struck a Lucky Strike when I came across a small wooden shrine tucked just back from the roadside. Beside the shrine I found just what I had spent the past five and a half hours looking for – a small flat patch of public unbuilt-upon land.

Feeling that I had better ask permission before planting myself upon a sacrosanct site, I wandered off in search of an appropriate person to ask. I tried the two closest houses that bordered the shrine but there was no reply. Back on the street I saw a salaryman in a car pull into his driveway. He'll do nicely, I thought to myself, and followed him in hot pursuit.

When the salaryman stepped out of his car, I felt that he took the shock of being confronted outside his home by a dripping, wild-eyed foreign cyclist remarkably well: he neither looked startled nor ran away and, after patiently giving time to decode my trial-and-error Japanese, he proved most helpful. Instead of shunting me off in the wrong direction before slinking safely away indoors out of the rain away from the stranger (as I fancy I would have done had I been faced with a shocking sight such as myself), he was all full of the genial and typical 'nothing-is-too-much-trouble' Japanese attitude.

Leaving his briefcase at the entrance of his driveway in full view of the passing masses (being honourable Japan it would still be there on his return), he led me to a small store down a narrow alley where he said some interesting-sounding words to a woman behind the counter. He then smiled and bowed and wished me *ki-o-tsukete* (take care) before heading back to his home.

The woman, it seemed, lived in a house beside the shrine

(one of the empty ones I had tried earlier) and, after presenting me with a Japanese tomato the size of a squash, she led me across the street to the shrine telling me it was no problem for me to camp.

'But,' she said, 'it is rain!'

'That's all right,' I replied, 'I've been wet for two weeks so I'm getting quite used to it now.'

Four drunken workmen in *jikatabi* and baggy jodhpurs appeared lurching around the corner taking a short cut home through the shrine. As the woman seemed familiar to them they stopped for a spot of raucous banter, which turned even more high-spirited when their wavering focus found me in their midst. There was much jovial poking of tyres, slapping of saddle (coupled with exaggerated grimacing) and total disbelief that I was English and not American. One of the men – the drunkest – called Toshi (Sloshied Toshi) tried fuddle-headedly to explain to me that half the world was Japan, the other half America. Then the oldest of the workmen, Hiroshi (who was toothless save for a solitary single fang clinging like a stalactite from his upper front gum), began theatrically patting the earthy wet ground with a whimsical look of dismay before suddenly disappearing through a gap in the wall. Shortly he reappeared, sweating beneath a gigantic pile of rolled-up rush-reed mats. He then proceeded to separate each mat, carefully laying them down on the ground – one on top of the other – as if preparing a giant filo-pastry pie. Then he nimbly (for a man so stewed) removed his boots before stepping lightly upon his layered creation. Promptly he turned prostrate, coaxing me (amid peals of laughter from his inebriated chums) to join him.

My first instinct was to consider Hiroshi just a dirty old drunken fool and to cast his invite aside to the windy rain. But it wasn't so much he that was at fault as I: a result of having misinterpreted his suggestion to join him on his woven bed of reeds as a bawdy move (too many dubious encounters with Western men). Instead he was merely inviting me to appraise a mattress of comfy groundsheets upon which I could sit my tent: no stones to dig the spine; no mud to seep through the floor – an act of spontaneous solicitousness rather than salaciousness.

With cheery encouragement, my merry old entourage watched intrigued from the sidelines as I raced to put up my tent in the rain while sheltering me and my belongings as best they could beneath the dome of a large umbrella. But the rain, having spotted my open panniers and tusslings with nylon fabrics, came on hell for weather by letting loose a head-hurting deluge for which a solitary umbrella and farcical cheers were no match. Then, well awash, I had no sooner hammered home the final guyline with Sloshied Toshi's monkey wrench when, in typically considerate meteorological style, the rain suddenly stopped. Just like that.

'Nice timing!' I said, with a heavenward shrug and a what-can-you-do-with-sod's-law sort of smirk.

'Ahh so. Very fine indeed!' came my pie-eyed audience's reply. And we all laughed.

The rain held off all night. Every time I woke up and heard the unfamiliar sound of silence (as opposed to watery patterings upon my fly) I thought: great – maybe rainy season is over!

Feeling encouraged by the prospect of being able to dry my socks out properly for the first time in a fortnight, I arose at 4.45 a.m. to greet the grey day with vigour. But, true to form, no sooner had I cleared up from breakfast and embarked upon tent dismantlings than, spot on 5.30, the rain returned. My mood spontaneously slumped and I looked to the heavens and thought: hell!

It was a horrible ride along National Highway 1 – an even more loathsome route than Route 150. The traffic was truly appalling, all funnelling towards the chaotic sprawl of

Nagoya, Japan's fourth largest city which, owing to its role as a major manufacturer of aircraft and munitions, led the US into bombing it into oblivion during the war.

The cycling improved (though the rain didn't) when I veered off on to the Atsumi Peninsula where, compared with what I had been battling against, the roads were relatively empty. Then the wind changed and bowled me along at tremendous speed and I felt like living again.

I passed clumps of women knee-deep in mud, stoically weeding the paddies (and I had thought I'd had it bad). Some would look up, see me and wave. Others, despite their considerable discomfort from stooping for back-breaking hours in the rain and the thick gloopy seas of mud, cried out '*Ganbatte*! – Please you have big strength, please! Good luck!' as I passed – a dazzling moon-smile shining from an earthy face. '*Dozo oki ganbatte o kudaisai*! – And you have bigger strengths!' I would whoop back in a string of illogical words before laughs were lost on the wind.

So in this lighter spirit I sallied forth aquaplaning along roads which didn't drain. Rain on me, I thought, I don't care – this is fun.

Giant greenhouses covered the land that wasn't riced over. In some, tomatoes were growing, but most seemed to be full of melons. Every so often a melon greenhouse would be part melon-house, part visitor centre with signs luring passers-by to come and have a taste (and hopefully a purchase). Needing no encouragement, I stopped at each and every one I passed, frequenting the *benjo* facilities where I would shake myself dry before surreptitiously grazing my way through platefuls of samples – at about £2 a marble-sized melon mouthful and of course having no intention, let alone the means, to buy a £50 melon, I was just the sort of visitor the melon staff could well do without. But because they kept offering me their freshly sliced produce and because the fruity flesh was too juicy and delicious and because I was severely lacking in self-restraint, I just couldn't stop. It was terrible – albeit a very tasty form of terrible. By the time I had ridden the entire length of the melon-growing area I calculated I must have swallowed the equivalent of at least £400 of free melon. My stomach was a melon-bomb waiting to explode.

Entering a small village I passed one of the ubiquitous Bridgestone garage-cum-banger-bike stores before stopping at the Circle K convenience store, thinking: what's a Circle K doing over here? It seemed so odd, so out of place to find sitting among an alien surround of paddy fields a store which I frequented at home for its new post-office counter – that lamentable and decadent state of affairs sprouting up in supermarkets and chainstores all over Britain whereby customers queue up for stamps and pensions among the aisles of Cornflakes and Jaffa Cakes and Rich Tea Biscuits of their local (in)convenience store.

Feeling hungry again (it doesn't take long on a bike) I dripped through the doors of the Magic Circle in search of something cheap to eat. Moments later I emerged with a not particularly inspiring 500-gram pack of 'finger' carrots from New Jersey (for half the price of Japanese ones), a rice-ball and a large bag of stale 'Special Sale' monkey nuts. Waiting for the rain to stop (which was like waiting for the cows to come home on a sunny Bank Holiday) I leant against my bike which was propped against the window and, for nearly an hour, hypnotically shelled and munched my way on automatic pilot through the entire bagful of nuts while dreamily watching the traffic sluice by in the rain. And the strange thing is that I don't even like peanuts. Obviously the rain was to blame.

At Cape Irako, the Atsumi peninsula ran out of land and dropped into the sea at the mouth of Ise Bay. I was planning on camping at the cape but the Ise-wan ferry to Toba on the Kii *hanto* (peninsula) was, as luck would have it, about to depart so I nipped up the ramp, last to board along with a women's team of professional surfers from Osaka.

I spent the hour-long crossing 'exploring' around the decks, day-dreaming over the rails into a leaden and rainy pockmarked sea and stocking up on plentiful supplies of blue sick-bags that I salvaged from various free-dispensers located around the ship (v. useful for containing anything from copious carrot peelings to dangerously potent, sodden pairs of mouldy socks).

Sprouting plastic bags from every orifice, I emerged back on deck and narrowly missed being caught in the phlegm-ridden firing line of a seaward-spitting sumo-shaped man. At one point off to port, or there again, it could have been starboard, lurked a murky submarine eyeing us ominously, like a semi-submerged crocodile. And then, just as my sealegs were getting a real taste for the ocean wave and wishing I was on board for a journey into the night, Toba appeared at the bows. After reclaiming my cycling legs, I spun out on to the quay.

With a mere half an hour left before dark, I splashed along the harbour front as sharp rods of rain smacked off the road. Finding it hard to get enthusiastic about looking for a place to camp in this dark, wet city, I instead rode up and down the streets for a while trying to recognize the *kanji* sign for *minshuku.* Finally I found one, situated over a garage, but it was closed.

Consoling myself by thinking that the money I would be saving could be put towards more food, I hastened off in search of a not too squelchy campspot. A fisherman directed me to a park overrun with shrieking peacocks. I felt I could put up with their raucous and strangulated cries just so long as it didn't last all night, but when I caught sight of a man peeing against a tree before turning to watch me rather too intensely for my liking, I decided both peacock and mancock were not a promising combination for a good night's sleep and retreated back out of the park.

Following the harbour wall (whose base was awash in the usual dreary detritus of floating polystyrene, bags, bottles, cans and plastic detergent bottles) I spotted a miniature square patch of grass on a high bank above the water. It looked perfect – protected from the squally wind and away from the busy swoosh-swooshing of the main road. The only trouble was that it was the front 'lawn' of somebody's house and I wasn't too sure if that somebody would relish the prospect of a strange dripping foreigner knocking on the door requesting to turn their garden into a spontaneous campground.

One of the advantages (out of many disadvantages) of travelling alone as a five-foot female is that most people I seem to meet fortunately don't regard me as some sort of psychotic serial killer on the loose. Instead of sweeping up their children in a state of severe agitated distress and disappearing in a spasm of wild panic behind slammed and heavily bolted doors, they tend to view me as an unthreatening and rather innocuous soul who is obviously lost far from home and scoop me tenderly under a protective wing, where, once under, I discover hearts too huge to be believed.

Hesitantly, my knuckles rapped upon the frosted glass and moments later the door was answered by Motoharu Nakashima. I had hardly to open my mouth before Hiromi, Motoharu's dazzling wife, appeared at his shoulder and I was swept inside, fed, watered, tea'ed and beered. My body was washed, my clothes were scrubbed and a futon was mine. But my original mission was to camp in their garden and feeling that I shouldn't press my luck too far, I insisted I sleep in my tent. I think they must have misheard and thought I was off to Antarctica because they armed me with enough blankets (for a wet and sultry night?) to bed a hospital.

The last thing I heard before I went to sleep that night (apart from the hammering rain) was a high-flying piece on AP Network News. A man in Kentucky who had worked in a fireworks store had recently died and been cremated and his next of kin, discharging the man's final wish before death, dutifully packed his ashes into a big firework to enable him to go out with a bang. Me? I went out like a light.

By morning the rosy glow from the night before had waned somewhat as I lay on my back listening to a brand of rain which drummed even harder than the previous day. Unzipping six inches of outer tent I peeped through my weather window to survey the watery scene. It did not look auspicious – definitely not the sort of thing to make me want to immediately shake-a-leg, saddle-up and cycle off. Pummelling stair-rods pounded the heavily misty grey harbour as mountains lay cloaked in cloud. A low-flying cormorant skimmed into view past the neighbouring warehouse of the TOKAI SALVAGE CO. LTD before swooping towards a fishing boat where two men were gutting fish. With impressive agility the bird plunged just low enough to snatch a catch before vanishing into the mist. The fishermen continued their work unmoved. Obviously pilfering cormorants are no big shakes round here. To complement my spontaneous scene of *Wildlife on One* a rather rattled-looking heron suddenly came in to land with an unceremonious bump, bang outside my weather (now nature) window, all gangly legs and no arms. For a moment it cumbrously flapped its wings so close to my budding ornithologist's beak that I could feel the breeze it made on my face. It's jaunty little moments like these that make sleeping for days in a deluge so worthwhile.

My next visitor was not of a feathered nature but was no less enthralling for that. She was Mieko Kawai, the tiny enchanting mother of Hiromi, who lived in a room next door. She approached my tent with light, slippered steps and bid me *ohayo gozaimasu* in soft, lyrical tones. In her bird-sized hands she held a bowl of steaming *miso* soup. Mieko was the sort of wrinkled, yet spry-faced and fragile-boned *obaasan* whom you immediately wanted to hug. Her gentle manner, her beguiling smile and her encapsulating radiance combined to such an effect that, apart from a brief fluttering of Japanese utterings, all I managed was to nod like a demented puppy with a daft, beatific grin.

Motoharu was a manager in the engineering department of the Toba Shinko Electric Co. Ltd. Before he sped off early to work he trotted beneath brolly round to my tent with rice-balls, coffee and cup-cakes. 'Badly wetting rain,' he said, speaking an English which he was too shy to reveal the previous night. 'You are speciality guest please pleasure stay today tomorrow day maybe one hundred day. Ha! Ha! Thank you.' And with that he revved off into the rain.

I spent two wet days in Toba – visiting shrines or museums of pearls. Ever since 1893, then Kokichi Mikimoto injected a grain of sand beneath the shell of an oyster to produce the world's first cultured pearl, Toba has proved a gem as a crowd-puller. If ever there is such a thing as pearl overkill, then Toba comes up trumps. There are pearl museums, Pearl Islands and pearl women called *ama* (women divers) who, clad in pearly-white suits, were once heavily employed in pearl-farming. Although a shellful of *ama* still dive off the coastal islands for what the local tourist authorities valiantly try to persuade the visitor are pearls, they are in fact only after a catch of humble seaweed or abalone.

But past the *Brazil Maru*, a former ocean liner that once shipped Japanese emigrants (mostly rice farmers) to Brazil but which had now been converted into a floating entertainment centre, I was told by a woman at the tourist office that, over in Toba Aquarium, *ama* could still be seen – performing in an aquatic tank with frolicking dolphins. 'Ahh so, *desu-ka?*' I said, while thinking: crying shame.

Instead of searching for pearls or watching with delight the acrobatic dolphins, I rode off into the mountains along the Ise-Shima Skyline, a leg-quivering vertical road which led me up Mount Asamagadake to Kongosho-ji Temple with its vermilion Moon Bridge and vast Buddha Footprint (seemingly one of many prints Buddha has left all over Asia). Here a ceremony of coin-tossing was taking place, the party-mood participants being a bus-load of hopeful tourists from Kobe merrily lobbing their yen towards their target: the Revered Footprint. Score an inner-soul hit and a year of luck is yours. All a bit like being at the fair, really, except that you have a prize piece of golden-Buddha fun instead of a goldfish.

One lobber, a bespectacled man with shiny black strands of hair swept Arthur Scargill-style across a hairless dome, sidled up to me. Revealing a smile of buck teeth, he said, 'America?'

'No, English.'

'New York?'

'Err, no.'

'Ah so.' And then, withdrawing behind his protuberance of teeth for a momentary sucking in of air, he said with a flourish, nodding towards Buddha's Footprint, 'Now I lucky man lucky year. Bye bye.'

Before leaving I tossed high a coin but missed.

I continued riding upwards until I arrived at the Grand Shrines of Ise – the most sacred of all Shinto shrines in Japan. Along with the Imperial regalia, this is where the spirits of the dead emperors are enshrined. The Ise shrines consist mainly of two fine wooden shrines: the Geku (Outer) and the Naiku (Inner). Having spent several hours slogging wheezily in the rain up a vertically unfriendly mountainside, the discovery that the Grand Outer and the Grand Inner are not situated a simple saunter across the way from each other, but a bumper big six kilometres apart, came as no leg-smiling matter. And to be informed by a happy, sing-song tourist-bus attendant that the shrines are linked by a convenient air-conditioned shuttle-bus service did little to boost my flagging enthusiasm for the shrine. Hold on, I wanted to say, these shrines date back to the third century, when air-conditioned shuttle-buses can't have been in such convenient supply, which surely meant that anyone who fancied a spot of Inner and Outer shrine worship must have had one hefty hike between the two. Maybe I was just missing the point, but from this momentary snippet of cogitation I concluded that even the early Japanese had an affinity for making life harder for themselves than was necessary. Still, this was no great sweat compared with what the beavering Japanese have done ever since. For centuries, Shinto tradition has dictated that the wooden shrine buildings at Ise (over 200 of them) possess an immortality defined by being dismantled and virtually rebuilt, in a ceremony called *sengu-shiki* ('shrine-removal'), exactly as the original every twenty years. In the paradoxical way that is so peculiar to Japan, the shrine is simultaneously both ancient and new.

Within the sacred enclosures are two adjacent sites, used in turns. The labour-intensiveness, not to mention the expense involved – the last (sixty-first) *sengu* in October 1993 cost in excess of five billion yen (£33 million) – is truly phenomenal. It has to be remembered that the Grand Shrines of Ise are no mere log cabins thrown together in haste when someone somewhere suddenly realizes that the twenty-year expiry date is nearly up for renewal. Each rebuilding takes years for the specialized craftsmen, who are kept in constant training in using ancient techniques, to carry out their much hallowed and intricate work. In respect of the renewal ritual even the tools and equipment must be replaced for each *sengu.*

The shrine buildings are constructed from unpainted *hinoki* – Japanese cypress, specially harvested from the Imperial forests in the Kiso Sanmyaku mountains. The simple style of architecture is of pure Japanese design (a style that prevailed long before the arrival of Chinese influence in the sixth century) based originally on prehistoric storehouses and granaries and must not be emulated by any other Shinto shrine.

Set in a small forest of towering columnar cedars, the Outer Shrine – which is dedicated to Toyouke-Omikami, the Goddess of Agriculture (which I imagine translates more in favour of the Goddess of Abundant Earth rather than the goddess of Agrochemicals, Set-Aside, Massey Ferguson and Bovine Spongiform Encephalopathy) – lies mostly hidden and out of reach behind a barricade wall of wooden fences through which the milling masses can only peep: the revered building is strictly out of bounds to all but the Imperial family.

This revelation could come as a bit of a bitter blow if you are looking forward to a close encounter with divine intervention. But fret not, as one can console oneself by doing what I did and saunter off in search of the famous tree whose lowest branches are prohibited from being less than ten metres from the ground. This may strike you, as it struck me, as a trifle excessive seeing as the average height of the millions of Japanese tourists who annually flock here to pay homage to their spiritual roots is not exactly head-bumpingly tall. But legend has it that a twelfth-century Imperial messenger from the Tiara clan had his hat ripped off by a lower branch of the tree as he was passing through the south gate. And that's it. One presumes that he was either on horseback or on stilts. Or possibly even on super-human growth steroids. Well, whatever; the fact is he banged his head on a branch.

I looked around for the tree but I wasn't sure if I was looking at the right one as all the trees in the immediate vicinity appeared to have had their branches lopped off below the ten-metre mark. Then, as I was peering at these trees feeling spiritually unmoved, I thought: what am I doing looking for a tree with a sawn-off limb (which is not exactly the sort of sight you come half way across the world to Japan to see) when I could be looking at the Inner Shrine? So, off to the Inner Shrine I lolloped.

This is where a guidebook is useful. The trouble was I didn't have one (took up far too much potential porridge space), but if I had I would have been forewarned that the Inner Shrine (which is dedicated to Amaterasu-Omikami, the Sun Goddess, one of the two fundamental Shinto deities, the other being the Goddess of Agriculture – just a little fact I thought I'd Set Aside) is, like the Outer, out of bounds to anyone but the Imperial family. Thus, once again, an obstruction of wooden fences keeps the lowly riff-raff out. But then this is hardly surprising: in the Oriental eyes of the Japanese, it is the Inner Shrine that is the bee's knees.

The Sun Goddess, who is the mythical ancestress of the Imperial family and the guardian deity of the Japanese nation, is represented in the Inner Shrine by the melted remains of the *yata-no-kagami*, the 'Eight-Pointed Mirror', one of the Three Sacred Treasures of Imperial authority.

But tourists (and tourists there are: one million alone at the New Year celebrations) need not necessarily turn away from Ise disappointed. Should you be wondering (as I was) what happens to all the venerated wood of the shrines when they are dismantled every twenty years, then wonder no more: the redundant wood is chopped up into nifty bite-sized bits before being distributed as talismans to the hundreds and thousands of pilgrims (tourists) who attend a 'Shrine Removal' ceremony. Only trouble was, I still went away disappointed because in order to claim my piece of shrine I was in for a long wait – nineteen years to be precise. Never mind, I thought as I rode away, what's a piece of dead-weight wood in your panniers when it could be a piece of cake? Peace of mind?

Some things fall from the sky: rain, dead birds, meteors, the odd fish and the occasional ill-fated aircraft. Japan once fell from the sky too. Or so legend has it.

A long time ago, before the beginning of the Beginning, there were no gods at all. Instead there was an egg. A big egg. No doubt free-range. When it cracked, out popped seven generations of gods and goddesses, among which were the brother and sister, Izanagi and Izanami. One day, things (as things tend to be after having spent a tedious time cooped up with dull relations within the world of an egg) became a little enlivened when Izanagi and Izanami (who at the time were romping around together on the hot-bed lava of Chaos) picked up the 'Jewel-spear of Heaven'. Now, as we lesser mortals all know, Heavenly Jewel-spears are not to be messed with lightly lest an impaling into the netherworld is on the cards. But being very much of a godly nature, Izanagi and Izanami were quite at liberty to spear-frolic without detrimental effect. So, there our godly two were, left to run riot with the 'Jewel-spear of Heaven' when it suddenly became all too much for the goddess Izanami and the laval games of Chaos turned rapidly to tears. As Izanagi comforted his sister a droplet of briny tear fell from the tip of the Spear into the sea, whereupon there arose an island.

Izanagi and Izanami descended upon this island to erect a phallic pillar dividing Heaven and Earth. In the new light of day the siblings then noticed that his body had something that hers did not, so, after a spot of investigative trial and error, they decided to put two and two together. The art of kissing was picked up after observing a pair of lovey-dovey doves and the rest of the happy union was inspired by watching the enlightening movements of a wagtail. Thus from every fruitful Earth-moving encounter, there was born a Japanese island.

The fertile Izanagi and Izanami were so impressed with their offspring that they descended from heaven to live on the islands. The happy incestuous couple then gave birth to the gods of the sun and the moon, of wind and of fire and finally to lesser *kami* (gods) who became the ancestors of Japan.

As I returned to Toba along the coastal road from Ise-shi, I stopped off to see a simple Shinto shrine that lies just off the craggy shore of Futami Beach. Meoto-Iwa is two large 'Wedded Rocks' jutting out of the sea which represent Izanagi and Izanami – our famously fertile creators of Japan. Standing at a sizeable thirty feet tall, Izanagi was topped with a *torii* (entrance gate to a Shinto shrine) and the solid-as-a-rock marriage to his petrified thirteen-foot wife is symbolized by a thick rope of plaited rice-straw connecting the two love-rocks like a giant umbilical chord. Every year, on 5th January, a Shinto ceremony takes place as the *shimenawa* (sacred rope) is ritually replaced in a show of great solemnity.

On my way back to my bike, I passed a coach party taking peace-pose pictures of each other beside the Kaeru Jinja – Frog Shrine (a shrine dedicated to fishermen and representing a safe return from sea). As I was looking at the Frog, a man peeled away from the chattering crowd and, with a springy gait, sprung breathlessly towards me. Bespectacled, buck-teethed, with the remains of his hair flowing across a smooth cranial tide, he looked familiar.

'America?' he asked.

'No, English.'

'New York?'

'Err, no.'

'Ah so. Thank you. Bye bye.'

And I thought: stark, raving bonkers.

I arrived back at Toba basecamp late afternoon. Hiromi, who had finished her day's work at the bank, was waiting for me.

'Jodie-*san*,' she said, 'today my husband telephone to make my house open invitation to conversation 6 p.m. Okay?'

'Err, yes, thank you,' I said, thinking I had got the drift but not quite sure.

I looked at my watch: 5.40 p.m. Plenty of time for a spot of tent-tidy (rearranging plastic bags from one plastic bag to another – that kind of thing) but, more importantly, the toilet. Along with my grassy, harbour-front location and genial 'campground' hosts, one of the many fortuitous things about having pitched up by lucky chance in Mr and Mrs Nakashima's garden was that I had my own *en suite* bathroom to boot. Tucked into a wall beside a small, inverted wooden-hulled fishing boat sat a stainless-steel sink garnished with various fishing paraphernalia (buckets, brushes, knife, scaler) along with an unfortunate resident plague of scuttling sea-water cockroaches, which I was to subsequently find haunting every sea-wall in Japan.

Creepy-crawlies aside, the sink was a boon for water supplies and ablutions and avoided my having to bother Motoharu and Hiromi by knocking at the house. Behind the boat stood a sentry-box-sized shack inside which sat a decidedly decrepit gravity-drop squat-toilet. The shack was in such a wonky state that whenever I clambered gingerly up on to the platform of flimsy floorboard in order to conduct my business, the whole toilet would disconcertingly shunt backwards a fraction, threatening to topple the out-house (me included) over the wall and into the sea. To add to the fun, the toilet housed two of the biggest and most unpleasant-looking spiders that I have ever set eyes (and, nearly rump) upon. Although they had commandeered exclusively the whole of the out-house as their domain, they spent most of their time doing nothing particularly useful (as far as I could tell), lurking menacingly in a strategically located thicket of tangled webs in a corner where the toilet-pan platform joined the wall. This meant, in effect, that when precariously poised for action, the spiders would size me up a mere arachnophobe's breath from my exposed behind. This might have just been bearable had they frozen on the spot (like me) but instead they would accelerate alarmingly towards my quivering rear before suicidally diving in a flash down the depository shoot beneath me.

So, at 5.45 p.m., having survived yet another terrorizing sixteen-legged encounter in the shanty privy, I embarked upon a momentary task of tent-housework reorganizing the aforementioned plastic bags and sweeping all the crumbs under the (Karri)mat. That done, I reversed back out of the mouth of my tent on the stroke of six (which in Toba was no stroke but a wailing great siren) just as Motoharu arrived at my door to escort me beneath brolly for the mere twelve-and-a-half steps to his house.

My 'invitation to conversation' consisted of sitting cross-legged on a *tatami* floor facing Motoharu on the opposite side of a low, lacquered table as he assayed his knowledge of English on me. He was fifty, he said, though he looked late thirties; his wife Hiromi was forty-seven but looked about thirty. They had two sons (nineteen and twenty-three), both at university.

'I am life-long engineer manager salaryman for Toba Shinko,' he said. 'Car motor part. Tomorrow I take *shinkansen* [the Bullet Train] to Tokyo – business meeting with many Italy gentleman from Fiat.'

Hiromi padded in bearing not exactly traditional Japanese fare: a trayful of white-bread egg sandwiches, thick black grainy coffee and a large, flat, rectangular unopened tin of very expensive-looking biscuits. I asked if she was going to join us but she just smiled with diffidence – a very different Hiromi from the one I had joked and chatted with alone that morning before she had left for work. Had I made a major *faux pas*? Had I outstayed my stay? Had she and Motoharu had a row? Did she not like egg sandwiches? No, none of these things. She was merely fulfilling her expected role as a traditionally subservient Japanese wife: her husband's wish was to be served a light meal while partaking of a soupçon of conversation with his foreign guest and Hiromi was to comply with his requests whether she liked it or not.

Every now and then Hiromi swept in as soft as a shadow to top up our coffee. To be served on hand and foot by a silent apparition filled me with a gnawing unease. 'Come on, Hiromi,' I wanted to say, 'forget the coffee, forget the food, forget your place round the corner out of sight, out of mind. Give it a rest, put up your feet, come and sit down. We urge you to join us.'

But Motoharu did not want his wife to join us. That much was clear. He continued to ignore her. Meekly I said nothing, for fear of causing a scene – for standing out as a nail to be hammered down. This was Japan. This was the Japanese way. *Shikata ga nai*? What can you do? It can't be helped. My lips remained sealed.

'Jodie-*san*,' said Motoharu, 'explain please GB-UK. I believe all same exactly?'

'Not quite,' I said. 'Great Britain consists of England, Scotland and Wales whereas the United Kingdom consists of Great Britain together with Northern Ireland.'

'Ah so, *desu-ka*?' Momentary thoughtful silence. 'But all Ireland is not special separate country?'

Feeling I was drifting out of my depth I adopted my best geopolitical analysis voice and said: 'Although Ireland is an island geologically separated by the Irish Sea from the rest of Great Britain it is still part of the British Isles.'

'Is that so?' said Motoharu..

'Yes, that is so.'

Motoharu then remained silent and I could see he was waiting for me to elaborate. But I wasn't too sure that I could elaborate on a subject about which I felt decidedly shaky. After all, Mrs Outlaw (my leave-more-than-a-little-to-be-desired 'O'-level geography teacher) had never taught me about distinguishing the difference between GBs and UKs and islands of Ireland (or was I just too busy folding paper darts?). Why couldn't Motoharu ask me something easy, like how many ballbearings did I have in the fixed cup of my bottom bracket? (Answer: eleven.) Anyway, doing my good overseas ambassador bit for paving the way towards exacerbating international misunderstandings, I struggled on and mumbled something about Ireland being a separate country up until the sixteenth and seventeenth centuries, when us English did the dirty and stirred up trouble by conquering the island – which resulted in Ireland being ruled as a dependent state until about 1800, when it was united with Great Britain.

'And,' I said, rather enjoying my newfound role as the Very-Confusing-Issue Overseas Correspondent, 'around 1920 Ireland divided into Northern Ireland (as part of the United Kingdom – although it has a separate parliament at Stormont, near Belfast) and Southern Ireland, which is also called the Republic of Ireland or its Gaelic name, Eire.'

'Ahh so, *desu-ka*?' said Motoharu, with a dazed expression.

'Yes, that is so – I think. Or something like that,' I said confidently.

Fortunately, having gone adrift somewhere back in the Irish Sea, topics turned less geographically brainstorming, albeit still choppy. Motoharu was inquisitive to know my travelling plans. Gulp! Plans? Have I ever had any plans that have gone to plan? What's more – have I ever even had any plans?

'Oh,' I said, thinking: plans? before blurting with a breezy plain-sailing sort of sinking confidence, 'my plans are to cycle round Japan.'

'Ah so, *desu-ka*? But always one person?'

'I'm sorry . . . ? Oh, yes – always alone – unless I find a husband *en route*.'

'But, Jodie-*san*,' said Motoharu, 'how long time you plan journey trouble in Japan?'

'Err, do you mean how long do I intend to spend cycling around Japan or how long did I spend planning my journey?'

'Yes.'

'Yes? . . . oh.' This was beginning to get somewhat baffling. Help, Hiromi! I wanted to say. Come and rescue us! Instead I said, 'Sorry, Motoharu, I'm a bit slow on the uptake. Do you mean how much time did I spend in England planning my journey to Japan?'

'Yes.'

I was beginning to suspect that Motoharu might have said 'yes' to anything. However, I thought: oh dear – here we go. Do I take the bull bars by the trumpet and own up and say: 'Well, actually, Motoharu – zilch.'? Do I come clean and admit to him that I never even planned to come to Japan – that I 'planned' to go to New Zealand? Do I confess that I became a touch disorientated, a trifle confused? Do I? Do I? Do I heck.

'Ohhh,' I ohhhed breezily, 'it took months of preparation. Always does.'

'Yes. But, Jodie-*san*,' said Motoharu, looking rightly concerned, 'why you trouble rainy season?'

'Errr,' I errred, feeling I was losing the drift of the thread, 'Why do I trouble with rainy season?'

'Ahh so, *desu-ka*? Yes. Excuse me.'

'Pardon?'

Whoa! Major communication breakdown. All systems blown. Quick! Get the maintenance man round – stick him up top in the upper skull department – get me sorted out. He turns up, as quick as a flash and now he's up there digging around with his tool box in my cerebral matter. I call up my spinal staircase to him offering him a choice of teas, coffees or light refreshments. A voice calls back: 'Tea please, luv. Milk and two sugars.'

He's up there for what feels like a good long rainy season, tinkering around before I finally hear him clodding down the back spinal disc-case. 'That should fix it,' he says, rubbing his heavy-duty maintenance hands on an oily cloth. 'The old grey-matter fuse box had blown. Don't often all go like that at once mind: must have been one hell of an overload. Anyways, should give you no further trouble. I replaced them sockets too so's as good as new. Takes a while to settle in though. Just give us a ring if it plays up and I'll be round in a jiffy.'

Systems reconnected, I'm back on full beam with not a dipper switch in sight. Suddenly: bright spark! – I realize my mistake. I had once again misinterpreted the Japanese pronunciation of a 'V' for a 'B'. Motoharu had not asked why did I *trouble* in rainy season, but why did I *travel* in rainy season? Having (supposedly) put so much planning into my trip, this was a good question. Didn't I know that I could skip rainy season altogether simply by propelling myself straight to Japan's most northerly island, which is amazingly rainy-season free? And didn't I know that this faraway island of Hokkaido not only escapes the six or so weeks of wet in which its southerly siblings wallow but also, compared with the stiflingly hot and humid months of July and August which sear the land that June has drowned, Hokkaido is a happy humidity-free zone? Well, umm, frankly, no I didn't.

Evidently, to summer in Hokkaido was to enter a pleasure zone of relative climatic comfort. Just to bring home the unsettling realization that (not for the first time in my life) I was in the wrong place at the wrong time, Motoharu and I adjourned from a room of *tatami* and low-lying tables and flat cushions to one of television and stereo and black leather sofas. The set was switched on, the weather channel flicked and . . . it was not a happy scene: Hokkaido sat basking in sun while the whole sodden southern rest of us lay sinking under a deluge of umbrellas.

'Jodie-*san* – see!' grinned Motoharu, far too enthusiastically for my liking, 'Hokkaido now fine trouble time bicycle. All time sun! Ha, ha!'

'Ha, ha!' I laughed, while thinking: fine 'trouble' indeed.

Six o'clock in the morning and it was still raining plums. Feeling unmotivated at the prospect of heading off into an interminable storm cloud I instead remained lying inert in my tent and reached for the radio. I turned the dial through the gauntlet of Japanese FM stations but, as usual, could take no more than a couple of seconds of each. Any more than that and my generally fairly placid levels of tolerance would be liable to give way to the unleashing of some unsavoury act of uncharacteristic violence – such as possibly smashing my radio to smithereens in a frenzied attack with a tent peg to silence it, which of course would have been a terrible waste of my favourite luxury. With the exception of the NHK public broadcasting station, which occasionally played tingle-worthy pieces by the likes of Pergolesi and Pachelbel, every other station was as inexorably awful as the other, revolving around streams of (even at low volume) shriekingly berserk adverts, shrill and exasperatingly over-excited presenters and, worst of all, an endless, nauseous gush of jangly Japanese pop songs which, more often than not, would break into a sugary semi-English chorus of infantile puppy-love lyrics. I was amazed to discover a distinct lack of Western bands played on Japanese radio. Only the Far East Network could be relied on for that, although this was equally disappointing as most American servicemen's requests were abysmal and the same tired old bands were played again and again: ELO, the Eagles, Dire Straits, Elton John, Abba, Status Quo . . . urgh! I mean, honestly, where were the likes of

Pulp, Portishead, Gomez, or for that matter the wonders of The Waterboys, The Bunnymen, The Smiths, The Blue Nile, New Order, Joy Division and co? Seemingly not on this side of the planet.

Occasionally I caught a sound of sing-along country or smoky sax jazz but it tended to be just a brief respite in a meaningless melée of trash. Astonishingly, foreign acts account for only 5% of the total Japanese music market. In the swinging 'sixties a generation of Japanese copycat bands imitated, like car and wireless manufacturers, whatever the Americans produced on the music front. Oriental Elvises, mimicked to perfection, scored hot hits. But these days, like automobiles, like videos, like cameras, imported products are tepid business in Japan. The Japanese prefer their own teeny-bop pop idols so the airwaves are bursting with mawkish-sounding bands with names such as The Bubblegum Brothers. And like bubblegum, it takes just one pop and you've had more than enough.

As usual, shortwave saved the day, although I kicked off on dubious ground, seeing as all I could pick up was Monitor Radio International Christian Science Radio (broadcast from Boston) on which some proselytizing ranter was raving in unearthly tones about the Mighty One. Praise be Lord Monitor, but not just now.

Twiddle, tweak and turn and . . . Hallelujah! – the World Service could just be discerned through a cackle of crackles. Newspapers were the subject: '. . . more newspapers are read in Scotland than anywhere else in Europe,' so I was informed. As a Japanese in Scotland might say, 'Oh-ki-da-noo!' And, what's more, 'the *Glasgow Herald* had been in continuous publication longer than any other paper in the world'.

From newspaper circulation to bodily circulation: '. . . one person dies every four hours from asthma in the UK . . . asthma generally only affects the Westernized developed world . . .' The World Service then died on me but there was more death on the waves on the Voice of America where an American Voice revealed that in the United States there are on average 99,000 gunshot wounds a year (about 270 a day) and that fatal wounds from guns have now overtaken automobile deaths. Over the past five years firearms use increased 64% and the highest risk group for gunshot wounds were black American males between the ages of fifteen and twenty-four. To top this cheery news, the Voice explained that it was no wonder society was turning so violent when, for instance, it takes only thirty seconds on the Internet to find instructions on how to build a bomb.

After this snippet of dispiriting information, the Voice suddenly went dead. Imagining that an Internetter's homemade incendiary device had perhaps found its way into the VOA studio, I hopped stations until Radio Netherlands reared its head telling me that in the seventeenth century the average Dutchman drank one litre of beer a day, not only because it was so cheap, but because water was so bad – especially in Amsterdam.

And so an hour passed and the plums kept falling. Remaining cocooned, I wrote my diary and letters and sewed strategically located patches on to my shorts. I then turned horizontal to give my aching back a rest and, as I lay there staring upwards, I devised a method for inner-tent clothes drying. Rummaging through my panniers I found just what I needed – some spare webbing, and a few small curtain rings which I had been cycling around with for the past ten or so years and had come close to turfing out on several occasions but never quite did so, just because they 'might be useful'. Thus it now gave me great pleasure finally to find their vocation and, in fine spirits, I set forth sewing them with a loop of webbing into various seams of my tent. By stretching a medley of bungees from ring to ring I formed a pleasing array of clothes lines on which to dry my smalls and not-so-smalls.

It was 7.30 a.m. A tap on my tent-flap door – Motoharu, about to leave for work.

'Jodie-*san,*' he said, 'journey trouble safety message,' and with that he handed me a folded piece of blue paper. I opened it up to find half a side of beautifully formed *kanji* characters.

'Motoharu,' I said, 'it looks interesting – but what does it say?'

'*Hai, hai!* Yes. Excuse me. Ettorrr . . . I am in conclusion that maybe Japanese people think confusion to see you journey one person *gaijin* on *jitensha.* Japanese people are no one person journey. Always many people. I think maybe understandment of your journey for Japanese people is much difficulty. Maybe little danger and problem and Hiroko worry and me also for you safety sleep.'

'Well, thank you, Motoharu,' I said, 'but really, you must not worry. I'm sure I'll be fine. So far Japanese people seem very friendly and helpful.'

'Ah so, but Jodie-*san,* if maybe problem situation and language many difficulting here paper *kanji* explanation for you give Japanese person understandment and my telephone for help, okay.'

'Well, yes, thank you very much, Motoharu. You are very kind.'

'No, no – always my home you welcome open time day time night time please pleasure,' and with that Motoharu climbed into his car and drove to work.

CHAPTER 14

Mr Hijet

Soon after 8.30 there was a strange silence: the plums had stopped. In disbelief I unzipped my weather door to survey the scene. All of a sudden a wind whipped up, sending days of stagnant clouds scudding across the sky. The long-forgotten sun broke through the gaps and, for the first time since arriving in Toba, the mountains were revealed. Their greenness was dazzling. The heat was on – both land and flesh began to steam. Within moments I was packed and, after Hiroko and her mother had filled my panniers to overflowing with edible offerings, I was on my way.

It was a fantastic feeling to be riding with the sun again, unrestrained by waterproofs, the welcome breeze whisking across the surface of my sweat-saturated skin.

I followed a virtually traffic-free road that wound round narrow inlets and bays sprinkled with oyster rafts and seaweed poles. The area has some weird-sounding festivals such as the *Ise Ebi* (Lobster) Festival, which involves the locals dancing around a giant paper lobster, and the *Warajihiki* (Straw Sandal) Festival, which takes place in September – typhoon season – to protect the local villagers and fishermen and involves floating a vast *waraji* (straw sandal) out to sea to scare the typhoon-stirring sea-monster.

The Kii Peninsula, which embraces the prefectures of Wakayama-ken, southern Nara-ken and southern Mie-ken, forms part of the Kinki District, a geographical division in the heart of Kansai (literally 'west of the barrier') that, in itself, comprises the core area around Kobe, Osaka, Kyoto and Hyogo. Because this area abounds in historical relics and legends, it celebrates several hundred festivals a year, among which are the curious *Kemari Matsuri* (Ball-kicking Ceremony), *Geita* (Fake Sun) Festival, *Yamayaki* (Grass-burning) Festival, *Shishimai* (Lion Dance), *Uchiwamaki* (Fan-throwing Ceremony), *Tanabe* Festival (Cockfighting), *Ya-Ya Matsuri* (Naked Festival), *Kaeru Tobi* (Frog-hopping Ceremony), *Shika no-Tsunokiri* (Ceremonial Antler-cutting), *Nakisumo* (Crying Babies Sumo Festival), *Hina Nagashi* (Doll-floating Ceremony), *Hagi* (Rice-cake Pounding Dance) a dance which imitates rice-cake pounding to the accompaniment of drums, and *Warai Matsuri* (Laughter Festival) which involves people gathering in festive costumes to laugh before the Niu Shrine. And who said the Japanese are a dull lot?

I passed small squares of fields bursting with a brilliant green, almost every one of them containing at least a couple of diminutive busily working bent-backed figures half-buried by the lush and prolific crops. Panting to the top of one mountain I came across a family of freshwater crabs sedately crossing the road. It looked odd seeing crabs so far from the sea – as if they were well and truly out of their depth. But as I embarked upon the descent I discovered that they were not alone. The road was littered with hundreds of fist-sized crabs, many of whose shells were cracked with bodies pulverized into the bitumen by the unmercifully bulldozing wheels of lorries and cars. While some froze in terror as they caught me in their stalk-eyed sight, others scuttled in sporadically ludicrous spurts all over the road making my navigation of a crustacean life-saving course something of a perilous task. At one point there were so many crabs crossing the road that I was forced to dismount in order to pick a safe route slowly through the crowds of crabs. It was the first mountain I'd ever been where it took longer to cycle down than up. But I made it, with not a crumpled crab to my name.

As I stopped at a ramshackle family-run garage in a small town to refill on water supplies, a man pulled up in a Toppo QZ – a bizarre-looking vehicle which bore a striking resemblance to a couple of Minis piled on top of each other. The man was obviously something of a sticking-out nail, as he wore a suit and sandals and a hideous pink and orange tie with elephants on it. He hopped out of this Toppo and scampered towards me like an excited puppy.

'Ah, this is much magnificence!' he exclaimed in English. 'I believe foreign legs to be strong – ha! ha! America?'

'No, England,' I said, 'I'm English.'

'England? Ah, how fine country I believe today.'

'Have you been there?' I asked.

'Ah certainly. Boston City. Many one time only.'

'Boston? The American Boston in New England or the English Boston in Lincolnshire?'

'Yes.'

'Yes?' Before we slid off track completely I felt it safer to change the subject.

'Are you a businessman?' I asked.

'Excuse me?'

'Are you a salaryman?'

'Yes, twenty-four-year road-machine equipment salaryman.'

'Road machines? What type of road machines?'

'Yes.'

Wanting to get to the bottom of this, I persevered: 'Road machines for driving on roads or machines for making roads?'

'Yes.'

One more try. 'You are a salaryman for a car company or for a company that makes something like road diggers?'

'Yes. Pleasurably I am bulldozing style salaryman.'

'Ah so, *desu-ka*?' Well, what could I say?

Hiro Nishiyama, my bulldozing friend, was apparently well familiar with the family who ran and lived in the garage. As no one had yet appeared (unlike the giant conglomerates, where you have at least half a dozen overly attentive assistants to service you) we walked straight through the cramped shop-cum-sales area, slid back a door and entered a smoke haze. Here an assortment of family and friends were lying on a *tatami* floor which was pockmarked with cigarette burns, drinking beer in front of a wailing television that no one appeared to be watching. Apart from people, the small six-mat room was full of clutter and nicotine-embedded grime. Within moments of my entrance, a bottle of Asahi beer was put in my hands followed by a cold can of *oolong-cha.*

Although I could understand little of it, the conversation seemed to revolve around raucous merriment. No one appeared in the least bit ruffled that there was a *gaijin* in their midst. They all acted as if it was the most natural thing in the world for a foreign devil to join them unannounced in their back room. Finally, when I asked '*Dozo o-mizu o-kudasai?* – Do you have any water, please?' a corpulent woman in aprons with a jolly, round and ruddy face scrubbed my water bottles in an oil-engrained sink before filling them with *kori* (ice) and water. After she had given me an iced coffee and three fancy-wrapped cup-cakes 'for the road' I was on my way.

A few mountains and a handful of tunnels later, I rolled into the small fishing town of Nanto-cho. As I rode alongside the foot of a vast stained concrete sea-wall I looked up to the walkway on the top and saw a small fleshy woman hanging up row upon row of large, brittle-looking brown socks from drying lines fixed to the sea-wall. Stopping to investigate this multi-socked phenomenon, I climbed up a bamboo ladder strapped to the side of the wall where I discovered the socks were not socks but fish. The woman, once she had overcome her initial surprise at finding a foreign face looming up over the wall, burst into laughter when, in halting Japanese, I told her I mistook her *sakana* (fish) for *sokkusu.* Suddenly her husband popped up over the wall holding an armful of fishy-socks and, when his wife explained to him the foreign fool's mistake, he too burst out laughing, more than perhaps the occasion warranted. Then, with a comical grin, he said, '*Dozo, purezento,*' and gave me two of his semi-dehydrated catch. I took them and mimicked putting one on my foot (as one would a sock) which set both husband and wife off again into peals of laughter. Back down by my bike at the bottom of the wall I lobbed the old dears a couple of cans of *kohii* from my on-board larder and they dropped down another foot-and-a-half-long fish-sock before I rode off down the road wondering what the dickens I was going to do with three whacking great dried fish.

The answer came a few pedal revolutions down the road when I pulled up outside a small supermarket to buy a few supper supplies. I had just propped my bike up against the shop window when a disabled woman in an electric wheel-chair buzzed up to me. She was wearing the usual floral-print smock and baggy trousers that most countrywomen seemed to wear, along with puffy over-sleeves which stretched from her wrists to her elbows. On her hands were white gloves (not for warmth but sun-protection) while her head was encased in a Bo-Peep bonnet. After only a few words and bounteous smiles she surprised me by being the second person within only a few weeks to try to press upon me a 5,000 yen (£30) note. Abashed and genuinely astonished, I took part in the usual pantomine and the overly generous offering was foisted back and forth. Finally, for once, it appeared I had won the battle and the woman good-humouredly whirred on her wheelchair through the doors of the supermarket.

Rather than risk bumping into her and repeating a similar charade inside, I thought I had better make my escape while the going was good. But before I had a chance to sally forth I was set upon by another lavishly benevolent assailant: a nut-brown and brawny old man in his underwear (white vest and three-quarter-length baggy white longjohns) who pulled up on his creaking black bike. On his head he wore the ubiquitous sweat-absorbing turban of towel. On discovering a foreigner standing outside his local store he became highly animated and offered me a 500 yen coin (about £3.50), insisting I keep it. No matter how insulting to the Japanese custom of 'three offers, then it's yours', I continued to refuse, assuming that the old man, who was anything but rich, needed the money more than I. Realizing he was up against *gaijin* stubbornness he reached into his wire-meshed bicycle basket and gave me a long cellophaned multi-pack of mini Yakult yogurts instead. In exchange I insisted he have my sock-fish, which he accepted, not without some trouble. No sooner had he disappeared through the door of the store than the wheelchair-bound woman nipped back out laden with groceries which, it turned out, she had bought especially for me. With an exuberant smile she handed me two carrier bags bulging with food and, after patting my hand with a tender little tap, she buzzed off at speed round the corner and down an alley, leaving me completely bemused.

I felt a conflicting mix of both intense happiness and awfulness: happy because I was utterly overwhelmed at a stranger's generosity; awful because I felt guilty for accepting her gift and not having a chance to be quick enough to get her address so I could thank her properly. Nor were the bags full of cheap packets of noodles or biscuits. Instead they contained five *bento* boxes of *sushi, sashimi* and *tempura* (total cost about £28) along with *onigiri* rice-triangles, sweetmeats, a can each of tea, coffee and an energy vitamin drink, two immense apples (costing £1.80 each), four *mikan* (tangerines), a *nashi* (apple-pear), a bag of cherries and a sealed polystyrene tray of perfectly formed pea-sized seedless black grapes. At the bottom of one bag was a small envelope containing a 5,000 yen note and a card with a short *kanji* inscription which a friend later translated as 'take care'.

Still somewhat stunned, I was on the point of swinging a leg over my crossbar and cycling away when a girl who worked in the supermarket knocked on the inside of the shop window and waved. I waved back and seconds later she whipped through the door, her face a crease of smiles, and handed me two sticky cakes before running back in to wave to me again on the opposite side of the glass. Help, please God, no more, I thought, but God had obviously turned a deaf ear because two tiny schoolgirls bounced out of the store and, nervously giggling, gave me a huge ice cream before scampering off down the road.

Before my stupefaction hit a point of no return I took off out of town with a bikeful of edible booty. What with all the excitement, I realized I had forgotten to fill up on water supplies so I pulled off into another small family-run garage on the edge of Nanto-cho. Compared with my stereotyped image of Japan I was discovering that life doesn't move fast for everyone. Slumped on a wooden chair at the back of the forecourt was the garage assistant – an old man with a bottle of *sake* and a glass eye. Sitting on the ground beside him was a pixie-faced old man wearing light cotton pyjamas and singing what sounded like a very drunken rendition of a folk song. On a chair in the corner in the shade was a truly ancient woman who looked about twice as old as Mother Teresa, with an equally angelic and lovable face creased with an intricate network of love and laugh lines. After I'd apologized for interrupting them, the glass-eyed man staggered to his unsteady feet and refused absolutely to allow me to fill my water bottles from a hose spiralling from the wall. Instead, between spasms of drunken laughter, he insisted it was his honour and duty to tend to the foreigner himself. Dragging me inside he polished up my bottles in the sink, filled them with iced water from a fridge and gave me two homegrown onions (each the size of my head) and four earthy potatoes. Back outside, his ruddy-faced friend gave me a jar of *sake* and a good-humoured smack on the back as the old woman smiled on sweetly. As I left, the men performed a series of bows – not the most proficient bows that I had witnessed but, considering they were up to their necks in *sake*, a pretty good display nonetheless.

By now the sun had slid down the sky so, rather than tackle a hurdle of mountains so late in the day, I thought it far more important to embark upon eating my way through my absurdly over-burdened panniers crammed to the hilt with tasty offerings. But before I could do that I needed a place to camp, so I veered off down a narrow lane to the harbour where, in front of a small *minshuku,* I found a piece of scraggy wasteland that bordered on the quayside where a straggle of fishermen were sitting and smoking and picking over their nets. One elderly fisherman who emerged from the rickety gravity-plop toilet in the corner, still pulling up his trousers, wandered over to say hello and offer me a cigarette from his pack of Larks. When I thanked him but refused he said 'Ahh – *jitensha*!' and walked up to the vending machine beside the *minshuku* and bought me a Pocari Sweat instead. I asked him if he thought it all right for me to camp here for the night and, expecting a lengthy debate with his fellow fishermen for a Japanese-style consensus to be reached, I was pleasantly surprised when, stamping his Lark butt into the ground, he replied spontaneously with a 'Why, sure' – or words to that effect. For the next ten minutes he went to unnecessary trouble clearing a patch of rubble and roots for me to pitch my tent. Then, adding a furrowed brow to his smile he said in Japanglish, 'Cars, cars very bad.'

Despite agreeing that yes, yes, cars were indeed very bad, I was a bit mystified as to what prompted this sudden outburst. Was it that I had arrived by *jitensha* or was he a strong supporter of Greenpeace? Maybe his dislike stemmed from an incident when his wife or child or friend or dog or, hell, even his fish, had been run over by a car. He reiterated his declaration but this time added a clue: 'Tonight, car, car very bad?' Tonight the cars were going to be bad? Was some event or festival going to take place after dark whereby this wasteland would be converted into a car park? Maybe neighbourhood fishermen piled in here in their pick-ups at some deadly hour of the morning, or maybe this was the local wide-boys' joy-riding territory for practising their figures-of-eight in their beefed-up, CD-blaring, spoiler-sporting four-wheel drives.

I was wrenched from my reverie by Kohji, the fisherman, alerting me to the fact that a car had just landed on top of me. I had never had a car landing on top of me before and, funnily enough, I didn't even notice it. This was not so much because I was made of indestructible metal, or mettle, nor was it because a Nissan Fairlady (yes, there really is a Japanese car with that name) had just fallen from the heavens to land on my head, but because the car in question was not so much a car as a *ka* – a mosquito. Within minutes I was beseiged by a thick and ferocious mist of Formula One-style *ka,* racing laps round my head in deafening drones before driving their loathsome blood-sucking needles into my fast-turning-anaemic flesh. Kohji, my *ka* attendant-cum-chauffeur, fanned the skin-invaders away as best he could with a towel that had been draped round his neck, before he was called away to board his vessel and head off fishing into the night.

The *ka* became so intolerable that, despite the humidity, I was forced to don my wet-weather gear to combat the possibility of the motor-mouths draining my blood department dry. Within my hooded hell I was vaguely aware of someone calling and I turned to see the *okusama* (madam) of the *minshuku* trotting across the compound towards me, flapping her arms above her head in a futile attempt to swipe a *ka* or two.

'Aargh! *Osoroshii, desu-ne*? – Terrible, isn't it?' she exclaimed, referring, I presumed, to the deluge of blood-sucking blighters rather than the state of the world.

'*So desu-ne,*' I replied, '*osoroshii*!'

'You cannot sleep here,' she said, 'the *ka* will kill you! Please be my guest of honour in my *minshuku.*'

'Thank you but I'm sure I'll be fine here,' I said, knowing only too well that I wouldn't be but not wanting to take her up on her tempting offer on account of possibly causing offence to Kohji, who had gone to so much trouble to smooth my ground.

'Ga! You are a mad foreign fool, are you not?' she said, laughing. 'But you cannot say no to a bath. Come, please.'

Gratefully, I scampered after Okusama into the *minshuku*, where I sank for a long and exquisite soak in the *ofuro*. On surfacing I re-emerged into the *tatami* corridor, at the end of which lay the clattering kitchen containing the ever-cheerful Okusama and a handful of chattering helpers. Espying me through the open door and despite being in the hectic midst of dishing up a vast variety of foods in a multitudinous selection of bowls for a party of workmen, Okusama beckoned me into the kitchen. My bathed and florid-faced appearance had the understandable effect of causing the girls to dissolve into fits of high-pitched giggles. Placed in my hands was a prepared-before-the-programme take-away menu of *sushi*, rings of octopus, *tempura*, hot rice and seaweed balls stuffed with a sweet dark sea vegetable, fried tofu and a can of iced *oolong-cha*.

Semi-dazed from a day of such insuperable generosity, I sloppily slippered my way back down the corridor clutching a trayful of food. I was intercepted by Okusama's round and jovial husband, Tomo, who gave me two beers and insisted I park my 'fine British cycle!' in his pink-glazed garage that overhung the house. A neighbour clopping along the street in his high-heeled wooden *geta* sandals spotted me and Tomo and came over to pick up some details on this strange foreigner in town. After much laughter and back-slapping and bowing the neighbour got away on his *geta* to get a jar of *sake* for me from the vending machine. By now I had hit such an overheated state of disbelief that so many people – total utter strangers – could be so kind that paradoxically I felt myself turning into a nervous wreck.

Echoing round my head was the lovable and neurotically distraught voice of Woody Allen: 'Oh my Gaad!' said the voice, 'why is everybody being so nice? This . . . this just cannot be normal. I mean, hell, what is this – some kinda conspiracy or whaat? Can't somebody shout at me – you know – get real normal? Is . . . is it that everybody is being so nice because they know I'm about to die. Ohh Gaad . . .'

To bring me back to the real world all I needed was to come across someone, anyone, giving me that sort of reassuringly apathetic pissed-off-with-life British Rail attitude. Instead I was surrounded by smiles and boundless generosity and people who could neither do enough for me nor be friendlier and I found it all rather overwhelming. Feeling I could take no more for that day I hurried back to my mosquito-impregnated den of nylon to zip myself in before any other huge-hearted soul could unleash their awesome generosity upon me.

Inside my tent I could scarcely move for food. I had accumulated so many edible offerings over the day that my tent was literally bulging at the seams from the multitude of packages crammed into every available space. I even had some hanging from my freshly fashioned internal clothes line. It was truly marvellous, like sleeping on a supermarket shelf. I had scarcely to move for another sackful of food to fall in my face. Food, glorious food was everywhere. It was a glutton's paradise, a cyclist's nirvana, a slimmer's worst nightmare. At first I was a trifle overwhelmed by the prodigious amount, especially as most of it consisted of perishable goods. If I didn't want to waste any (which I most certainly didn't), it would mean I would have to eat everything in one fell sitting. This is one of those instances when it pays to be travelling by bike as appetites tend to be insatiable. It took just under two hours of continual eating (save for the momentary break to rest my jaw) in order to polish off the entire load of *sushi* and such like and, if I hadn't been overcome by exhaustion, I'm afraid I could have done a pretty fine job on my dry supplies too.

After a mad feverish battle in which I finally succeeded in swatting and exterminating every single bleeding *ka* from the concealed confines of my tent, I flopped on my back and went to sleep. During the night I was woken up by what felt like a sticky chipolata sliming across my face but was in fact a large slug.

I arose at five the next morning not only because the heat

in my tent made further sleep impossible, but because I wanted to sneak out of town before anyone could be nice to me. But I wasn't quick enough: within moments Okusama was clopping towards me with a trayful of breakfast and drinks for the road.

Up and over a few passes and through a series of tunnels, I swooped down into a small fishing community where a man waved and excitedly ran up to me. Apparently Kiyoshi had driven past me the previous day as I was toiling up some mountains and, on account of this, he acted as if he knew me. I was shown off to his wife and friends and given my second breakfast. Everyone wanted to know where I was going so I pulled out my map and said, 'Round Japan.'

This was greeted by a great chorus of air being sucked through teeth together with expressions of disbelief. '*Kyo*?' I was asked – 'Where to today?' Rather than tell them the truth and say, 'I don't know – I like to keep my options open,' I hurriedly cast an eye a little way southwards down the map and picked a place at random.

'Owase-shi!' I announced which, despite it being only about thirty miles down the coast, prompted more sucking of toothy air. There followed something of a debate as to which road I was to take. Kiyoshi and his enthusiastic entourage were all for me taking a less mountainous route that wound its way inland before joining National Route 42 to Owase-shi.

But I was all for sticking to the more arduous route – not because I wanted to wear off the inordinate amounts of food I had consumed over the past twelve hours but because I felt certain that the more mountains, the fewer cars and the more beautiful the scenery. This road on my map so resembled a red worm of hairpins that drivers, like Kiyoshi, were bound to boycott it for faster alternatives.

For once, I was right. After passing through a spate of tunnels the road suddenly narrowed into a winding lane which for hours led me up towards the Nishiki Pass, through forests of pine and bamboo and thick, vibrant green jungles full of strange whooping birds and exquisite-smelling blossoms. About once every twenty minutes a car passed. The descent was truly tremendous. This was not only because of such stupendous scenery and rare isolation but because on every hairpin corner stood a symbol, testimony to Japan's excessive wealth and minimal vandalism: a near-as-new orange-rimmed convex mirror positioned to enable road users to see oncoming traffic. Thus, instead of having to brake on every blind bend in order to avoid a possible head-on collision, I could now go hell for leather at maximum speed output, charging like a wild-eyed wildebeest around the ribboning corners on the wrong side of the road. Here comes a sharp one – quick, flash a glance in the mirror – nothing – cut across the road, hands off the brakes – lean into the corner – straighten up – shoot back into the right lane – hurtle into another hair-raising hairpin – look, lean, up and over. Within seconds I'm upon another. I'm getting the swing. Still alive and with confidence soaring, I'm feeling dangerously cocky. I turn more prone – lean lower on my drops: the speed creeps up. I career into another succession of tight hairpin zeds but suddenly and quite unexpectedly I come upon a large monkey sitting in the road. I swerve to avoid it, brake, hit a patch of gravel as lethal as ice and feel myself going, losing control, flying towards the unbarriered edge, and the deep green valley. A tight knot of fear spasms into my stomach, obliterating all joy into oblivion, but somehow I regain my balance and miss the edge by a whisker. Hell's teeth! – this is the life!

Further down the mountain, in all this empty, wild green beauty I suddenly came across a depressing sight of inane activity: a battalion of bulldozers, earth-movers, pile-drivers, dumper trucks and helmeted beavering men – everywhere – carving and blowing up the pristine valley floor by building a fat, ugly, straight swathe of a road through the mountains. A prime example of excess yen and limited thought for the land.

At Kiinagashima-cho I was plunged back to hell after joining the horrendously busy Route 42 – just the road that Kiyoshi and friends had recommended I join much earlier. Sometimes it pays to ignore advice. Feeling well and truly overheated I pulled off to sit in the shade of a small pavilion at a riverside rest-stop where three workmen in baggy trousers and split-toed boots came and sat on their haunches for a smoke.

'*Konnichiwa*!' they greeted me.

'*Konnichiwa*!' I replied.

'Where are you from?' asked the youngest of the three, a waspish and pimply youth with a kamikaze-style bandanna tied round his head.

'England,' I said, which I half anticipated would prompt the response 'Ahh – New York?' But I was wrong.

'Ga! *Igirisu* – England!' said the youth, 'Winnie Poohsticks ha! ha!'

I was impressed. He had hit the right country bang on.

'You know Winnie-the-Pooh?' I asked, surprised, when really I shouldn't have been surprised because why shouldn't a Kiinagashima-cho pimply-youth workman smoking his way through a pack of Hopes know Winnie-the-Pooh? Of course there is no reason why he shouldn't but, I'm sorry, Winnie-the-Pooh and Japan just struck me as, well, odd. Like Japan and toad-in-the-hole. A weird kind of mix.

Anyway, brushing my narrow-mindedness under the bed of my head, I smiled as the pimply youth said, 'Hai! Hai! Winnie Pooh – *sugoi*!'

Not wanting to stir the water under the bridge I agreed that, yes, yes, Winnie Pooh is great, while thinking: what a strange place to be praising him – in Japanese to a Japanese in Japan.

But I later discovered that an oriental love for 'Pooh-phernalia' is nothing out of the ordinary for Japan – a country where *Winnie-the-Pooh* is a set book in many Japanese schools. In fact the obsession with A.A. Milne's bear is such that scores of Japanese fans make a 'Pooh Pilgrimage' to the original 'Poohsticks Bridge' in the East Sussex village of Hartfield. Nearby is Cotchford Farm where Milne once lived and which is only a short walk from other Pooh landmarks such as the Hundred Acre Wood, North Pole, Enchanted Place, Galleons Lap and Roo's Sandypit. The village's Pooh Corner souvenir centre even provides directions in Japanese to the ninety-year-old twenty-foot by ten-foot wooden bridge.

More tunnels came and went – most, fortunately, providing a separate pedestrian-cum-cyclist tunnel alongside. In one of these tunnels I came across an old, cackling mad witchlike woman who chased me on her bicycle. Running out of water again I stopped at a roadside building called the 'Old Fashioned Casual Restaurant' where a short, stocky man in bifocals and a *happi* coat (a sort of cut-off *yukata*) said, 'Ga! You are fine England Beatrix Potter!'

Back on the hellish Route 42 I happened upon a tasteful and timely reminder (as if I needed reminding) that I was riding along a potential death trap of a road: in a lay-by stood a glass-fronted hoarding displaying a spread of black and white photographs showing the aftermath of horrendous-looking car crashes. One pictured a crumpled driver at the wheel.

Late that afternoon, as I was paying for my groceries in a supermarket in Miyama-cho, I asked the checkout girl if she knew of a nearby *koen* (park). She did and directed me down what sounded like about fifty different twists and turns until I reached a river where I was to turn inland for some way until I came to the *koen*. As I was packing my supper supplies into my panniers outside the supermarket the checkout girl came running up to me complimenting me (of all unlikely things) on my Japanese. Then, in English, she said, 'I am New Zealand home-stay student for two month summer yesterday year.'

Home-stay, where parents send their children off to a foreign family (usually based in California or Australia or New Zealand) for English-speaking experience, is popular in Japan. As the host parents can be paid over £2,000 a month for board and keep of the Japanese child, the Japanese parents have obviously got to have a bob or yen or two to spare. But home-stay also has uses other than educating the child in foreign ways: more and more Japanese parents with a 'problem child' (i.e. one who bumps off school, gets caught up in drugs, gangs, all night sex – in a word, sticks out like a nail waiting to be hammered) solve their embarrassing problem by sending him or her off on a home-stay. Far better to have your child flown off to some distant land, under the pretext of 'home-stay', than to sully the name of your family by having the neighbours discover that your son or daughter has been banished to an inferior school or is languishing in a juvenile detention centre.

To me, Michiko, my park-directing checkout girl, looked like a genuine fresh-of-face home-stay.

'Where did you stay in New Zealand?' I asked.

'Ah Auckland fine city! All persons are so kind. One day I hoping sincerely to take my home New Zealand. So happy memory place!'

I found the river and followed it along its northern bank, passing through a series of tiny cluttered hamlets all dissected by an intricate weave of pathways and narrow lanes. The park was still in the process of being built, the pristine toilet block was locked and most of the unlaid turf and paving stones were cordoned off. Two fishermen, who were perched on the concrete banks of the river, gave me a funny look so, not wanting to draw more attention by putting up my tent in a no-go area, I back-tracked to the hamlets to see what I could find. Up an alley I came across a couple of pairs of husbands and wives busily laying a strip of concrete path at the side of the road. I asked them if they knew of any little space where I could camp for the night. This question prompted a colourful array of laughs, debates and misinterpretations. Finally they propelled me up a hill to a large-stoned grey-gravel car park which belonged to part of a shrine that lay situated higher up on top of the hill. Tucked in a corner bordering the road stood a small concrete-floored and covered garage-like outhouse, open on three sides.

'*Koko wa daijobu desu-ka?* – Here is all right?' I was asked.

'*Hai, hai* – yes, yes,' I said, 'here is certainly all right,' while thinking: lucky thing I've got a free-standing tent.

As I set about erecting my home on the hard slab floor my merry party of concrete-layers stayed to watch – the men volunteering to give me a helping hand with the poles but each putting a foot wrong when tripping comically over the guys, much to the amusement of their wives. A diminutive *obaasan* cycling slowly past on a creaking bicycle caught sight of this unusual shrine car park activity and, executing a spontaneously nippy U-turn which belied her advancing years, came to join us. Every so often another local villager passing by either on foot or on bicycle would do a double-take before coming to add to the increasingly enlivened audience. Everybody seemed to know everyone – bottles of beer and *sake* appeared which inevitably sparked off inebriated conversation and raucous laughter. Then the rain began to fall and, before you could say 'the plums are back with a vengeance', I was inundated with offers to come and sleep inside a multitude of homes. Not wanting to offend my original concrete-laying hosts by neglecting my car park camp-spot, I politely refused all offers of overnight accommodation saying I would be just *daijobu* out in my tent.

However, this assembled group of solicitous spectators would not accept that I was *daijobu* for food and bodily cleansing so I ended up being 'honourably' passed around the village from door to door, home to home, bath to bath.

By the end of the evening I had been fed so much and scrubbed so many times that I returned to my tent feeling like a pregnant glow-worm.

I was awoken the following morning by Norio and Nobuyo Hatauchi (a husband and wife from the concrete-laying team) who brought me a breakfast of rice, fish and green tea: room service 'on the tent'. Despite heavy rain and an early hour, groups of villagers gathered beneath brollies beseeching me to stay dry with them. They watched with interest as I reduced my surprisingly spacious home into a compact pack not much bigger or heavier than a three-pound bag of flour. As I left I was besieged by gifts of food and drink and given a cheer as I rode up the road in the rain.

Climbing up towards Mount Binshiyama I passed a uniformed and helmeted team of roadworking women clearing ditches at the side of the road. There was not a man in sight. It was strange to see middle-aged women doing such strenuous work which in the West would be work considered fit only for a man. I stopped for a chat, which gave them a surprise and a moment's rest to stretch their backs. They appeared incredulous to see me: travelling by bike! – all alone? – so far from home? Ga! I used the opportunity to dispense with some of my bulging ballast (the vast assortment of bottles and cans that had been piled upon me over the last twenty-four hours by the generous souls of Miyama-cho) and showered the women with an assortment of teas and coffees and pops and juices, which only made them even more surprised. What, they laughed, was this mad *gaijin* doing emulating a mobile vending machine while riding in the rain up a mountain?

I carried on in an upward direction, feeling good that I had dispensed with such surplus weight to such a worthy cause. Just after being passed by a lorry emblazoned on the rear with the words 'Caution – Fragile Fish on Board' I was waved over by a man who had stopped in a lay-by. He had climbed down from his 'people packer' – a white Daihatsu

Hijet MPV – and stood smiling at the roadside, holding an umbrella with one hand while mopping up beads of perspiration from a glistening brow with the other.

'You are No. 1 example of strong mountain-climbing leg!' he said, greeting me in English. 'You have I believe fine sporting body-tuning muscle!'

'Well, thank you,' I said, 'but it feels like I've only got legs of jelly for this mountain.'

'Excuse me?'

'My legs are not so strong.'

'Ah so, *desu-ka*? But may be problem cycle up mountain. There is much large tunnel.'

Earlier that morning, while studying the finer details of my map, I had noted Route 42, depicted as a red swathe of road, disappearing into a white dotted line of mountain – indicating a lengthy tunnel. As there was no alternative route, other than taking a several-hundred-mile detour inland which no doubt would be even more tunnelled and mountainous, I felt I would be able to get through on Route 42. But maybe not. This was Japan and so far I had seen no one (apart from Sheepsaddled Alan the Ozzie Scouser) cycling in the mostly uninhabited mountains.

With a sinking feeling rising upwards from my calves, I asked, 'Are bicycles not allowed in the tunnel?'

'Yes, maybe possible not.'

Oh dear. None the wiser, I replied equally cryptically, 'Ah – good news! Then maybe not I'll continue fine with problem bicycle tunnel.'

I wasn't trying to be difficult – it was just an automatic reaction to feeling uncertain as to what I should do. However, Mr Hijet made up my mind for me in an instant.

'Please be my no obligation guest bicycle in travel car no problem tunnel.' An offer which immediately set the inner alarm bells ringing.

'Thank you,' I said with a sudden assertiveness, 'but I would like to try by bicycle.' These days, lifts for me, no matter how beguiling the driver, were no-go areas. Having once fallen prey to one, I was determined never to fall to another as I knew that, once they've got you in, they've got you.

I thought Mr Hijet might be more pressing but instead he said, '*So desho*? – Is that so? You are Number One fine decision of strength!'

And with that he gave me a can of green tea, grasped my hand in a meaty clasp and shook it energetically before bowing and waving and driving away. And I was left thinking: oh – there goes my chance.

An hour or so later I hit the first tunnel. As there was no cycle-friendly pedestrianized alternative running alongside, I braced myself and took a deep lungful of mountain air before plunging head first into the dark and weaving two-kilometre tunnel along with a racketing rush of trucks. Although in theory two kilometres sounds not a long way, stuck cycling inside a traffic-reverberating tunnel while gasping down lungfuls of filthy fume-filled air and trying to steer a steady course through the crepuscular shadows only inches from a procession of thundering wheels – it's a nightmarish two kilometres of interminable length.

I finally emerged back out into the day, so jubilant at having made it that I even welcomed the rain. But my jubilation was short-lived because, before long, I was upon another upward two-kilometre tunnel. Owing to internal tunnel works this one was even darker than the previous one with its bilious glare of a temporary sodium-style lamp fixed every 100 metres or so. Arriving mid-way at the ear-splitting and drilling one-laned site of the tunnel repairs, I was waved over by a most surprised but genial workman, who climbed into his on-site vehicle indicating that he would follow me slowly so that I could ride a safe route out by the beam of his headlamps. So as not to waste his time I tried to cycle as fast as possible. All pistons were pumping, lungs were heaving and head so pounding that, with just over 500 metres to go, I thought I was hallucinating when the silhouette of a large monkey lolloped across my path.

Back out in the real world the workman lobbed me a rice-ball, wished me 'good strength', did a U-turn and disappeared back into the black, yawning mouth of the tunnel.

It was now downhill but no sooner had I embarked on my descent than the rain, which I had thought was heavy enough before, turned utterly torrential. Within seconds the road was a fast-running torrent. With no shelter around I could only continue, but at a downhill speed of no more than a quick walk. Any faster and I couldn't see where I was going, the rain was that hard and that cheek-stinging. Fortunately, I came across a sprinkling of houses bordering the road, one of which had an empty garage alongside with an open door, and without further ado I sailed straight in to take shelter from such unconducive cycling conditions.

As I stood with my bike, dripping, in the garage in a steadily growing pool of water, I thought: hope the owners don't come home. Then, after having probably been away for hours, a white Noddy van with the letters 'NIFTY' embossed upon the bonnet swung round the corner on course for the garage. And me. At the helm was an old man sitting alongside his elderly wife. Catching sight of me, the man braked sharply at the mouth of the garage. All three of us glared at each other with expressions of momentary surprise – mine out of embarrassment for being caught 'trespassing' and for causing a wet puddle of rain water; theirs because . . . well, finding a drowned rat of a foreigner propped against a bicycle in the middle of their garage can't have been an everyday occurrence.

For a few more moments they sat in their Noddy Nifty peering out at me, probably trying to decipher from which planet I had landed. In an attempt to allay their fears I flashed them a whoops-sorry-but-I'm-really-not-looting-your-garage sort of raised-eyebrows grin, but before I had a chance to move a saturated step they were bowing before me and apologizing for the terrible *ame* (rain), as if Japan's funereal rainy season was their own personal responsibility. Stay,

stay, they urged me and then, as suddenly as they had arrived, they disappeared – into their house. Five minutes later the Noddies resurfaced, Mrs Noddy bearing a trayful of tea things served in what looked like the best bone china, decorated with a delicate design of mauve flowers. Alongside was a small heart-shaped gold spoon and a jar of powdered milk with the appetizing brand name of 'Creap'. The Noddies climbed back into their Nifty, apologizing that they had to go out but insisting I stay sheltering in their garage as long as I liked.

For over an hour the rain continued to drum deafeningly on the tin roof of the garage. It fell with such force that I could scarcely see the house across the road, even though it was a mere ten or so strides away from me. There are certain words in Japan which are given a honorific prefix: *o-cha* (tea); *o-kome* (uncooked rice); *o-mizu* (water), to name but three. But rain is such a personality in its own right that there are more than twelve words for it in all its moods. I was beginning to discover only too well that it rains three times as heavily in Japan as it does in Europe. But the Japanese try to mitigate this fact by declaring that in Japan the heavy rain falls only at fixed seasons; therefore they know the sun and the snow as well as the rain. The trouble was, I found myself fixed in the wrong sort of season with the wrong sort of weather.

Waiting for the rain to ease, I sat on a box in the garage and practised writing a few shaky *kanji* characters so that I could at least leave a note, even if it was illegible, to Mr and Mrs Noddy Nifty, thanking them for their *oishii* tea, before I set sail.

The road was a river and for miles I aquaplaned downwards, passing through villages where wooden roadside shelters had local people's garden vegetables for sale. I stopped to buy a huge bunch of parsley for fifty yen (30p) and a *daikon* (giant white radish at least two feet long) for 100 yen, not because they were particularly practical things to eat in a tent (let alone lassoed to the rear of a bike) but because they were about a quarter of the price in the shops and I don't like to let a bargain slip me by.

Back down on the coast I stopped at the tourist booth in Kumano-shi and asked the man at the window if he had a map of the Shingu-shi area where I was heading. It wasn't that I needed a map but as I had washed up at the tourist booth by chance I thought I might as well ask for something in case it was interesting. The man bobbed down and rummaged for a moment through some drawers before resurfacing again at the window, apologizing profusely that he had no map of Shingu-shi. That's okay, I said, which as I didn't really want one in the first place was just that: okay. But the man, feeling a failure, told me to *chotto matte kudaisai* – that firing favourite, 'just a moment, please' – before nipping across the street into a stationery shop. Seconds later he bounced back out with a triumphant grin, bearing a 750 yen (£5) map of the Shingu-shi area aloft in his hands.

'*Dozo* – please for you *purezento*,' he said.

'No, no, you really mustn't,' I replied, which I really meant.

'Yes, yes,' he said.

'No, no.'

'Yes, yes.'

'No, no – really not.'

'Yes, yes – really yes.'

So I cycled away with a feeling of embarrassment and a map that I didn't really need.

Later that afternoon, as I was crossing the Oroshi River, a car coming towards me beeped its horn in amiable style, the driver raising a clenched fist of triumph out of his window. It was the Mr Hijet man who had offered me a lift through the elongated tunnels. It took me a moment to recognize him and, by the time I'd turned round to give a thank-you-yes-I-made-it-through-the-tunnel sort of wave, he had already been swallowed by the traffic.

As I reached the outskirts of Shingu-shi it was growing dark and still raining. Not wanting to get caught up in the frenetic whirr of the city, and fancying my chances of finding a place to camp were higher if I remained lingering on the fringes, I turned myself to seek-a-tent-spot mode. I was becoming quite good at espying from afar a possible campsite to install myself in for the night – places at which, during my first weeks in Japan, I would scarcely have batted an eyelid. The feeling of being instinctively drawn towards a place along with the ability to size it up immediately and take stock was a good one. In a way, it was a reassuring feeling of security and familiarity in a totally alien culture.

So I continued riding along busy Route 42, which was turning progressively more and more urban, while glancing down the side streets and thinking: 'That one? No. That one? No. That one? No. That one? Yes!' Swinging down a narrow and meandering alley to see what I would find, I passed yellow-capped doll-like children playing in the street, chirruping 'Bye bye, bye bye' as they spotted the funny-looking *gaijin* spinning on by. Old women stood gossiping beneath the essential umbrellas while others laboured along with dustbin-sized baskets strapped to their backs overflowing with spring onions or greens or weeds. A cat ran out half-way across the street, saw me, arched its bristled back, then darted away. After twisting here and twisting there I found a small shrine adjacent to a compact slice of rocky land – perfect for an urban tent-pitch spot. As the shrine was bang in the midst of a busy residential area I moseyed off to a nearby house to see if there were any objections to my shrine-camp. The first house was empty, the second was home to a horrible ankle-snapping yappy dog, while the third revealed a startled looking woman wiping her hands on her apron. I asked her if she thought it was all right for me to camp in a corner of the shrine. The woman's startled expression opened up to an exuberant smile. Never mind the shrine, she seemed to be saying, come and sleep in my school. Although she was on the point of going out, she walked me round the corner to show me where a small one-roomed port-a-cabin type nursery school was standing.

'But I'm sorry,' she said, 'the school is not empty until *hachi-ji* – eight o'clock.'

'That's all right,' I said, 'I'll go and have a look around for a couple of hours.'

So I cycled off, feeling buoyant of spirit in the knowledge that I wouldn't have to put my tent up in the rain. But, of course, no sooner had I allowed this happy thought than the Rain Gods thought: Ah ha! Think you've caught us out, do you? And they promptly readjusted their cockstops whereby the rain stopped and the skies cleared. The first perfect night for camping for days and days, but I was to sleep inside.

I cycled through the spiralling alleys and darkening back-streets, passing homes where the happy grunts and sloshing sounds of the traditional six o'clock bath-times could be heard emanating from open windows. Outside a small family-run store I suddenly spotted a basket of four beefy tomatoes for a bargain price of 100 yen (60p). Such was my excitement at the thought of snapping up these 'love apples' that I screeched to a halt without first signalling or checking over my shoulder for traffic. My emergency stop resulted in a man on a bicycle behind having to swerve to avoid me. He gave me a 'bloody-women-drivers' glance before stopping himself.

'Excuse me, sorry,' I said in my stilted Japanese, 'but it was the tomatoes,' and duly pointed over towards them. The man looked from me to tomatoes to me again and said, with puzzled expression, '*Hai, hai* – tomatoes.'

To which I replied, 'Yes – tomatoes,' mainly because I didn't know what else to say.

Seemingly nor did the man because he just smiled an embarrassed sort of smile before riding away.

Inside the tomato shop, which wasn't really a tomato shop but a bit-of-everything shop, I had to wake up an old man who was asleep on a mat behind the counter before being served. Along with the tomatoes I bought a tin of tuna, a packet of noodles and some new shoelaces – the latter two items looking remarkably similar. To add up the bill, the old man tapped some numbers into his calculator before squinting uncertainly at the total. Then he reached for his *soroban* (a small wooden abacus) on which he checked his answer. It was neither the first nor last time that I saw this. In the Rising Land of Computerized Wizardry it is possible, for instance, to buy a robot, video telephone and a digital dog, and the sales assistant will calculate the cost with a *soroban*. It is obvious that, in their heart of hearts, the Japanese don't really trust calculators.

With food supplies packed I spent the rest of my time until eight o'clock by drying out my tent on a fence, watching two small girls playing on their unicycles (in the dark, near a road with not a grown-up in sight) and sitting on the sea-wall beneath the sodium glare of a street lamp writing my diary.

I arrived back at the school-cum-hotel just as the last of the impeccably behaved children were filing out. The woman, Kiyoko Yamasaki, had told me it would be unlocked and to walk straight in. So I did. Inside I kicked off my shoes at the entrance and stepped up on to a floor of vivid green carpet which was covered with rows of shin-high tables. Books and paper and pens were stored neatly along the sides and tiny-tot-like green overalls hung from pegs on a wall. In the corner on a table lay a Rolex watch. It was a great feeling to be honoured with such trust.

Not long after I had planted myself on the floor surrounded by a spread of my sleeping bagged bedding, a knock came at the door and Kiyoko stepped in, apologizing for disturbing me before inviting me home for supper and a shower. Despite having already eaten a bowlful of tomato and tuna-flavoured shoelaces, I eagerly adjourned to Kiyoko's house for my second supper. There I met her husband, Yoshiro, a taciturn but perfectly friendly man, who worked in a hotel in Shingu. Kiyoko told me she worked in a car factory making something that my Japanese dictionary translated as 'harnesses'. Seatbelts, I presumed. As I was leaving I handed her a box of chocolates which I had bought earlier for her kindness along with a pack of Fortnum and Mason English Breakfast Tea that I had been cycling around with for weeks for just such an occasion. Kiyoko, embarrassed, then delighted, scurried away before returning to give me two pairs of stretchy pink and blue socks (did I look like a stretchy pink and blue socks kind of person?), a 'Hello Kitty' *hankachifu* (from surplus gift supplies?) and a can of Pocari Sweat.

CHAPTER 15

Goofyfun Time

'Women do everything, men do the rest,' goes an old Russian proverb which seems to ring true in Japan. As I wheeled along the highways and byways I never failed to be amazed at the huge amount of manual labour being done by women, from sloshing their way for hours, doubled over, knee-deep in muddy paddy fields during the season of rains, to sweating and staggering beneath the weight of steel girders as part of a road-building team during the overwhelming heat and humidity of the summer, while men often squatted on the sidelines having a smoke and a smile.

I came across a prime example of this when leaving Shingu-shi behind: a drove of women workers with conical hats and bonnets and shovels were busily digging ditches in the rain at the side of the road while the only man I saw on site activated a button on the back of a cement-mixing truck.

But by saying that the women (who still seem to be treated as second-class citizens) work hard isn't to say that the men don't. Virtually everyone in Japan works at fever pitch, darting and scurrying and beavering their way around the clock as if there was no today, let alone tomorrow.

Despite the dull and gloomy sky – the rain falling heavy and intense – it was an exhilarating ride, heading south past the 400-foot Nachi-no-Taki, Japan's highest waterfall (deemed to be a Shinto god), and on along what my map described as a 'Scenic Rocky Coast' past Taiji-cho, a small town with the dubious reputation of being one of the first seventeenth-century communities in Japan to organize its whale-hunting into a full-scale industry using hand harpooning. This was quite a step up from the pre-seventeenth-century methods which had relied simply upon the odd hapless whales becoming either beached or trapped in bays. Now, of course, Japan is infamous for its unnecessarily extreme whaling practices, which have led to the virtual extinction of numerous species of these magnificent mammals of the deep.

I arrived at Kushimoto-cho, where the impressive rock columns of Hashikui-Iwa rose out of the sea like, so it is said, 'a line of hooded monks'. As I stood contemplating these impressive rocky outcrops the sun suddenly came out to complement the scene. Having felt so little of the sun I was not going to let these welcome rays (even if they were melanomic) pass me by, so, feeling a trifle drowsy, I stretched out on the bottom row of a stack of bench seats. With the soporific effects of the sun, I was asleep within moments, launched into dream mode. Strangely it was not a Japanese-flavoured dream. Instead, I found myself running two steps at a time up the steel staircase of the Eiffel Tower, pushing past people in my furious attempt to reach the top to stop a woman with long black hair who was about to throw herself from the highest level at 1.30 p.m. With my heart knocking like a pile-driver I made it to the *premier étage*, screaming at people to stop the woman from jumping. But everyone just smiled and waved at me and continued taking photographs. Desperately I charged onwards, upwards to the *deuxième étage* where, on looking up, I saw a black silhouette launch itself, like a large bird, into the sky. Everything went silent: there were no cries, no screams, no sounds and then, literally out of the blue, she landed at my feet. Strangely there was no messy splatter like there should have been. Instead, the woman picked herself up and dusted herself off before making a sudden dash towards the edge to try again. Racing after her, I just managed to grab her dress as she stood swaying gently on the edge. But then, inexplicably, I remembered I had left my bike unlocked in a phone box and let go of the woman. The next thing I knew, I was looking up into a smiling sea of Japanese faces.

'*Konnichiwa*! *Konnichiwa*! Harrow! Harrow! America? Excuse me! Harrow! *Konnichiwa*!'

With half a head on the Eiffel Tower, the other half feeling sun-drugged in Japan, it took me a moment or two to come round but, when I did, I realized that I was being engulfed by an excited bus party of sightseers. Being disturbed in the midst of my dreams by such a rackety gaggle of people made me feel a little edgy and annoyed. Why, I wondered, do they have to come and chatter and natter right on top of me? Couldn't they see I was asleep? Couldn't they see that there were a hundred other spaces to go and stand and high-pitch yatter? Couldn't they . . . couldn't they . . . could not they just . . . ? But hell, no, they couldn't. Why? Because the bench that I was lying upon just so happened to be part of tiered layers of seats specially designed to seat the entire contents of a tour bus. Had I been more observant I would have noticed that forty or so feet from where I lay stood a wooden sentry-type box (like a workman's port-a-loo) to which I had not paid much attention, dismissing it as nothing more than a boarded-up attendants' booth for the car park. But now, its true use was revealed: it was a specially constructed stand for a professional photographer, who positioned his subject (the bus-load of nattering-yattering tourists) on the grand multi-tiered seat-stand (my bed) which itself was positioned to reveal the object (the 'hooded monks' Hashikui-Iwa rocks) as a perfect backdrop for the '*chiizu*!' Peace-Pose Picture which everyone would take home to stick in the album next to another famous multi-tiered bench site and say: Look! That's me! There! Ha! Ha! before rushing out to do the same sort of thing all over again. Not that there's anything wrong with this, mind; it's just that I get a bit peeved when woken up in a heated moment of a nonsensical dream.

That said, everyone was very full of fun and very fine and very charming (are they ever anything but?) and I was bought *aisu-kuriimu* and drinks and included in a hundred different snapshots, with a medley of arms draped amiably around my shoulders and waist. It was fun – they were fun – they always are.

Outside the Okuwa supermarket (a kind of bigger but better Japanese Sainsbury's) I was just standing peering at my *chizu* – map (as one is wont to do when one's not sure where one is) when a slightly gormless-looking young man sidled up to me.

'Harrow America!' he said, 'I am yes please English speaking man at hand.'

Then, pointing seemingly willy-nilly to a place on my map, he said: 'Oto-mura.'

Naturally I had never heard of Oto-mura, so I said, 'Oto-mura? Oh, is it nice?'

'No of course indeed,' he said, which indicated that I was once again groping along on that slippery slope of misinterpretation. Then, in similar vein to my own method of (non-)navigation, the Harrow-English-Speaking-Man-At-Hand plucked another name at random from my map.

'Hongu-cho!' he chirped.

'Hongu-cho?' I said. 'Is good?'

'Ha! Ha!' he staccatoed, a response which naturally left me none the wiser.

Tiring of this game, I felt it was time to make a move, but the mad map man obviously felt otherwise as he lifted another digit to land in reckless style upon my map. This time I decided to beat him to it, so, peeping beneath his print I read the nearest word.

'Ryujin-mura!' I said triumphantly.

'Ah so, you *kanji* read?' said the man, overlooking the fact that this peculiar map was printed in both *kanji* and *romaji* characters.

Not one to give the game away, I said, 'No of course indeed!' because sometimes it's nice to give as good as you get.

From Kushimoto-cho I diverted course to Cape Shionomisaki – the southern-most point of Honshu (Japan's main island) – which was part of a small podule of land hanging by a thread of an isthmus from the mainland. I followed a pleasingly quiet and scenic road that skirted this mini-dangling 'island', passing a small fishing harbour beside which I stopped to watch a group of mostly bonneted OAPs playing gateball (*gatta-ballo*), a game which is said to be similar to croquet but without the excitement. All over Japan the gateball 'pitches' (which are usually either a dusty or damp-grey area about the size of a tennis court) are to be found in abundance from the smallest village to the largest city.

Compared with Europe and America, Japan provides precious little in the way of special amenities for the aged: government-run old people's homes are non-existent and the handful of private institutions are exclusive and exorbitant. As dying does not seem to be high on their list of priorities (they currently achieve the highest life-expectancy stakes in the world) and because Japan is well on its way to becoming a nation of old people (albeit extremely fit and frisky old people) the Japanese authorities have relented over the past few years and have cordoned off the burgeoning armies of spritely 'wrinklies' into their gateballing corrals. The result? The government is happy that they have got away with providing a cheap means of gratification for the oldies, while the oldies are cock-a-hoop with their hoops to such an extent that they have embraced gateball with a fervent

So where is Japan anyway? *Space wall, near Naha, Okinawa*

Trying to make head or tail of Japanese signpost.
Near Cape Namikesaki, Amami-Oshima

The wheelings and dealings of a neon-flipped *pachinko* parlour in downtown Tokyo

The recycling cycle man. *Narita Old Town, Honshu*

Bed of Roses. (Roadside statue in commemoration of lost children.) *Honshu*

Statues in memory of aborted babies. *Hasedera Temple, Kamakura, Honshu*

Local lasses, waiting for their lift home from the fields. *Kyushu*

Tumpline and tea. *Aha, Okinawa*

'Mother of all Umbrellas'. *Naritasan Shinshoji Temple, Narita, Honshu*

Shopping for seaweed. *Boso-hanto Peninsula, Honshu*

Drums of *sake*. *Kumamoto temple, Kyushu*

Drumming for *sake*. *Kumamoto festival, Kyushu*

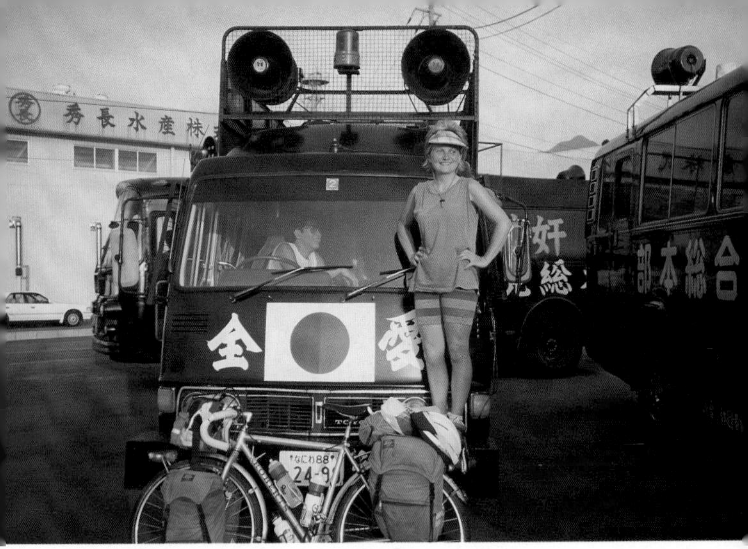

Swept up by a bumper crop of bellowing buses.
Political rally, Susaki-shi, Shikoku

Keeping firmly seated
beneath fantastical
phallus.
*Taga-jinja Sex Shrine,
Uwajima, Shikoku*

Storm in a Japanese teacup. *Tail-end of a typhoon, Ibaruma, Ishigaki*

Peace and *chiizu* with Tetsu's family. (Tetsu, the zippy Autozamming son, is taking the picture.) *Kametsu, Tokunoshima*

Standing small with tall wall. *Kumamoto Castle, Kyushu*

The bonny bonnetted threesome preparing for a game of Japanese-style croquet.

Geothermically cooking in Ibusuki's volcanic sands. *Kyushu*

Out on a limb. *Tojinbaka Chinese monument, near Cape Kannonzaki, Ishigaki*

Air-conditioned hat man. *Amami-Oshima*

A riot of roofs. *Kumamoto Castle, Kyushu*

A glorious people-less, car-less Japan. *Okinawa*

Mushrooming rocks. *Cape Hennamisaki, Miyako*

Taking a breather. *Half-way up Mount Kaimondake, Kyushu*

Turning loopy in camp-spot heaven. *Overlooking Mount Kaimondake, Kyushu*

Camouflage camping. *Gahama Beach, Yoron*

Stone lantern bike-stand. *Fusaki Kannondou, Ishigaki*

Tree-point turn. *Mount Kaimondake, Kyushu*

A taste of the good life with Mr and Mrs Baba and guests. *Higogi minshuku, Kumamoto, Kyushu*

A taste of the raw fish life while bound in a post-bath *yukata* with the Miyazaki family. *Near Nanako Pass, Shikoku*

The barbarian and the beauty. *Fisherman's boat, Koniya, Amami-Oshima*

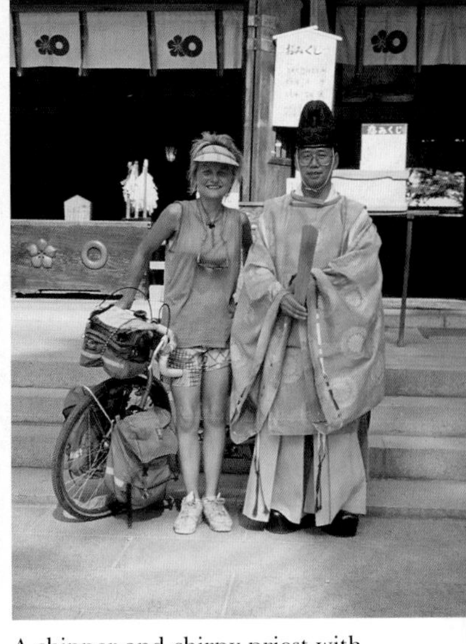

A chipper and chirpy priest with tool in hand. *Kumamoto temple, Kyushu*

Waiting for the dog's dinner. *Naritasan Shinshoji Temple, Honshu*

The grass is always greener on the other side. *Suizenji-Koen Garden, Kumamoto, Kyushu*

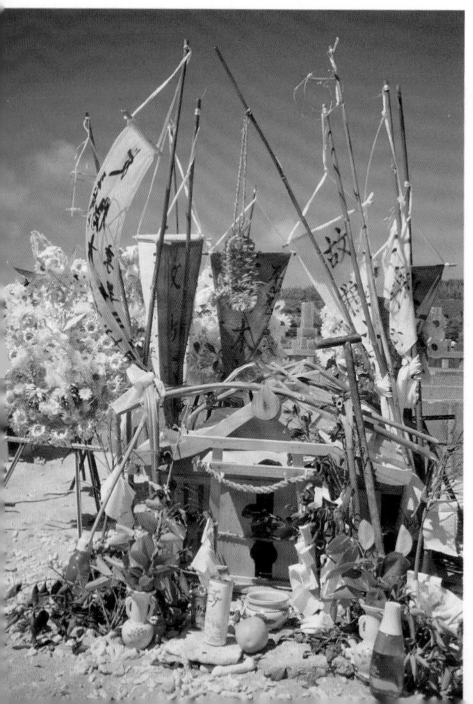

Japanese spirit set to sail. *Cemetery near Cape Chichisaki, Yoron*

Japanese obsessiveness and competitiveness, investing this gentle pastime with the full paraphernalia of league tables, gruelling practice sessions and expensive uniforms and equipment. The downside is that suicide – that other Japanese popular pastime (17.2 per 100,000 people compared with 7.5 in England) – has occurred from time to time as a result of players being ashamed of their poor performance.

As I stood on a hill looking down upon a fraternity of Kushimoto gateballers, I thought: what an endearing scene. A row of bobbing bonnet-heads sat on a board-bench at the edge of the pitch, cheering and gossiping and laughing and joking. In the middle, among hoops, stood a sprinkling of players wearing colourful bibs. After much lining up of his sights, a man with a towel on his head knocked a ball slowly but perfectly through his chosen hoop.

'Nice one, Cyril!' I called down in English in a Cyrilly English sort of way for no other reason than I couldn't stop myself. The sound of ball hitting bat and the croquet of hoops was so reminiscent of a rose-budding, tea-in-the-garden, English summer type of day that I was momentarily overwhelmed at the sight of it all. It was so Japanese to do something so foreign and so touchingly well. The gateballers, surprised and then seemingly honoured to have a *gaijin* in their audience, bantered an array of cheerful comments up to me, urging me to join them. But, not wanting to cause a total upheaval, I stayed up on the sidelines offering the occasional word of encouragement and enthusiastic round of applause. When I made to leave, the man with the towel on his head ran up to me and gave me a beer.

'Have strength!' he said and I went on my way.

Youth hostels can behave a bit like London buses: having not come across one for several hundred miles, what should I discover at Cape Shionomisaki? Not one hostel, but two – bang next to each other. After a recce of the two I ended up checking into Shionomisaki Yusu Hosuteru, simply because it was a sprinkling of yen cheaper than Misaki Lodge Hosuteru and, as we all know, a little sprinkling here and a little sprinkling there can all add up to quite a substantial sprinkling in the long run. Save for me and a miserable-looking boy on a moped who was mopeding around Japan for a year, the hostel was empty. It was wonderful. I hate full hostels – the bunks a scrum of screaming schoolchildren, the corridors a nightmarish tangle of heaving brats who can't do the simplest thing like brushing their teeth without shrieking the roof off the place.

Before it got dark I walked down across a wide expanse of green lawn towards Shionomisaki lighthouse, which didn't look to be anything particularly exciting so I walked back again. The only people I saw on the way were a couple of salarymen who drew up in a car to take identical straight-faced pictures of each other standing in front of the Cape Shionomisaki sign before getting back in their car and driving away. For some reason, the sight of that made me feel sad.

The view from my hostel window could have been nice – sea, sky, space, that kind of thing – but, as so often in Japan, a beautiful spot had been obliterated by a concrete monstrosity: in this case a massive grey lump of a tower.

That night it was so hot and clammy and the mosquitoes were so thick and thirsty that I ended up sleeping on the floor within the inner netting of my tent in order to escape them – another advantage of having a free-standing tent and an empty *hosuteru.*

The next morning it was raining so hard it would have been laughable had it not been so depressing. It was blowing a ten-ton gale, the rain slicing off the sea in diagonal torrents. I found the miserable-looking boy on the moped looking even more miserable and staring out of the window drinking a can of coffee.

'*Genki tenki*!' I said. 'Fine weather!'

But I think my sunny comment was lost on him because he just continued staring forlornly out at the rain. Apart from Mr Misery, there were no other signs of life in the hostel. I walked around for ages trying to find someone to pay (such an honest soul am I) until I finally heard some groaning emanating from a small *tatami* room in which I found the owner, flat out on her stomach on the matting, undergoing an excruciatingly vigorous massage. It didn't seem quite the time or place to thrust my hostel card under her nose so I left a couple of bills on the counter.

Not long after I had set out to do battle with the elements my bike started making some highly dubious grinding noises, arising from somewhere in the location of my block. As my bike had been living out in the rain for weeks now, I suppose such off-putting sounds were only to be expected. But they still made me fret.

The continual wet had made me concerned for the welfare of my steed particularly when I had to leave it outside at night (which was virtually every night). Hating the thought of the derailleurs, bearings and super-smooth hubs deteriorating in such cycle-unfriendly conditions, I rigged up an elaborate system of plastic bags as a cover to protect the moving and more delicate parts from the intrusive and detrimental effects of the rain. Such namby-pambiness made me liken myself to those sissy old samurai of the nineteenth century who, owing to an absence of war, had turned their focus from lopping off heads to polishing up on their vanity: in one notorious case, the wimpy warriors went about practising their horsemanship skills indoors on wooden horses on rainy days because they were afraid of getting their armour wet. Fortunately I hadn't turned quite that bad – I still favoured the prospect of riding *al fresco*, no matter how wet the weather.

Sluicing through the small village of Tako (Octopus) a man on a Suzuki trailbike overtook me and waved, before pulling off to the side of the road. Lifting his Oakley goggles on to the peak of his open-faced crash helmet he burst into an exuberant torrent of Japanese, most of which was lost on me. All I managed to glean was his excitement at finding a *gaijin* girl alone on a bicycle. And in such terrible rain. Ga! A few miles down the road I found the same man waiting for me outside a cliff-top restaurant where he invited me in for a slap-up meal of *soba.* There can't be many countries in the world where a lone female can take a motorcycling stranger up on his offer without sizing up the possible dangers. But such is the atmosphere of both safety and honesty in Japan that all I needed was my instantaneous instinct that all would be fine. And, fortunately, so it proved to be.

At one stage of this rainy, rocky, sea-lashed ride I came upon a vista point overlooking the minute island of Okinokuroshima where there stood a sign saying:

SAN FRANCISCO	10,000 km
HONOLULU	6,500 km
OKINOKUROSHIMA	900 m

More intriguing was another sign, just along from this one, that displayed the following snippet of curiously punctuated information:

LOVERS CAPE

KAREKINADA BEACH PARK. appointed by Wakayama Prefecture MEOTONAMI (the name of a married couple) THE SEA IS VERY BEAUTIFUL PACIFIC OCEAN. THE EARTHS LARGEST BODY OF WATER, BETWEEN ASIA AND THE AMERICAS. See these waves. They are just like holding a woman and a man. They, waves are rolling from both east and west. So, I NAMED, IT'S MEOTONAMI.

After riding a road of tunnels, trucks and ferocious rain I arrived in Hikigawa-cho, soaked and oil-stained and not in the chirpiest of moods. As I stood outside Okuwa supermarket sheltering temporarily from the weather, I sighed a rather long and lugubrious will-it-ever-stop-raining sigh. I was just in the process of building up for a second sigh of hopeless dampness when a small girl in pigtails and a T-shirt with the words 'GOOFYFUN TIME' emblazoned on the front skipped brazenly up to me and said in perfect English, 'I like tennis do you like tennis?' But before I had a chance to answer she added, 'You are my friend,' and gave me a bar of chocolate.

Wishing I could be such an instantaneous hit with the boys, I said 'Thank you' and gave her the can of Pocari Sweat that Kiyoko had given me. I then asked my little winsome admirer what her name was but I think she had exhausted the extent of her English on me as she suddenly turned shy and ran away.

As I stood surveying the scene and the weather outside the Okuwa store, a car pulled up close to me, the wife getting out to disappear into the supermarket, the husband into the neon-lit and bulb-flashing *pachinko* parlour across the road. Rather than face the rain just yet, I decided to follow him through the doors. I entered a smoke-filled world of noise and neon and row upon row of gaudy pinball machines. In front of these sat people, mostly men, their faces lost in a vacuous look. Blaring, taped martial music competed with high-pitched announcements over the tannoy that in themselves fought to be heard over the dense metallic cacophony of thousands of cascading silver steel balls. The scene resembled a disorientating cross between a Las Vegas casino and a ball-bearing factory.

Pachinko has become Japan's national obsession. The game was first introduced into the country after the Second World War as an inexpensive form of amusement. With typical post-war enthusiasm, the Japanese embraced and developed the game with a fervour so that, today, *pachinko* is considered 'theirs'. No one else in the world plays it – except Japanese Americans in Hawaii, of whom there are many.

The choice of recreation for more than 30 million Japanese is to sit riveted to a seat, firing a torrent of shiny steel balls around a clamorous vertical board with pins banged into it. More than 70% of men and 30% of women play regularly in one or more of the country's 20,000 or so neon-lit temples spread nationwide. The revenue generated by the *pachinko* industry was a phenomenal 17.6 trillion yen for 1993, outstripping the auto industry – which means that it is Japan's biggest business. (I tried to convert this sensational sum into more manageable pounds on my mini calculator but I lost all the noughts when they fell off the end and on to the floor.)

Thanks to Japan's strict laws on gambling, *pachinko* parlours are prevented from giving monetary prizes; instead, the winning players receive gifts consisting of cigarettes, chocolate, canned fruit, rice, detergent, electric razors, teddy bears and other such thrilling produce. Around 70% of players illegally exchange their prizes for cash with a nearby broker, who sells them back to the parlour for a profit. *Pachinko* is so popular that there are even *pachinko* magazines, *pachinko* widows and *pachinko* 'pros' – the latter earning hundreds of thousands of yen a month simply by hanging around outside the parlours waiting for them to open in order to hot-foot it to their favourite winning machine. Should anyone get a little bored with shooting their balls – why, some machines come with a miniature television implanted in the centre to keep boredom at bay.

Whenever I stopped by a parlour to use the *benjo* or fill up on water I was always amazed that the hall was invariably at least half full, whatever the time of day or night. Because *pachinko* has always suffered something of a seedy image, due to its gambling connections and the assumed dealings with the underworld, the industry has worked hard in recent years to clean up its act. Like the horse-racing industry, it has focused on wooing young women, creating more cheerful and cleaner parlours and luring housewives on their daily errands to drop in by installing refrigerated lockers for their shopping.

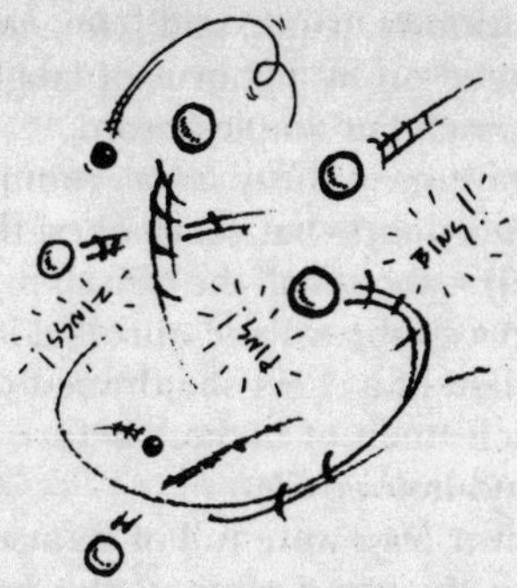

Leaving Hikigawa-cho I headed off into more rain and tunnels. But I didn't make it very far because, passing a sign painted in the *kanji* for *minshuku,* the thought occurred to me that I would far rather be lying in the dry on a futon than fighting with the incessant trucks thundering through tunnels and rain. Dismounting my grinding steed I went and knocked on the door but there was no answer. Then I noticed a sort of elaborate garden shed behind me with steamy windows. Sliding open the door I stepped into a sizzling noodle bar where a short, roly-poly *okusama* in white cap stood behind the counter busily launching fried eggs on to mountains of tangled *udon* and *ramen* swilling in soupy balls. Hunched on stools at the bar were a handful of workmen, some noisily slurping up clumps of quivering noodles into their mouths. All fell quiet as every head turned to look at me in various states of surprised shock. I felt like the Lone Ranger swaggering into town but, instead of shooting everyone in sight, I chirruped '*Konnichiwa*!' before asking Noodle-*san* if she knew whether the *minshuku* was open – because it was terrible *tenki* (weather) and I was on my *jitensha* and I fancied a futon. The change was instantaneous. Within moments I was offered a stool at the bar and given a swilling mound of steaming *ramen* to contend with.

'*Hai, hai*!' declared the sweaty Noodle-*san.* 'The *minshuku* is mine!'

One man, obviously drunk, said '*Hai, hai*! The *minshuku* is hers!' and, egged on by a chorus of laughter, crawled up over the bar to pinch her ample bosom.

Noodle-*san* gave me a dusty *tatami* room, with tear holes in the sliding *shoji* doors that overlooked the storming sea, for 1,500 yen (£9) – about half the official price. She dragged out a futon from a cupboard and unrolled it onto the centre of the floor. In lieu of a sheet she draped over a pink wrinkled towel (which smelt of bodies) before covering the lot with a stained and holey quilt.

The squat-down *benjo* were full of huntsmen spiders, the three urinals (in the same room as the *benjo*) were full of splash marks, the bath was full of hairs. Noodle cooking, as opposed to pernickety housework, was obviously Noodle-*san*'s preferred skill.

The *minshuku* was part of a hamlet of houses dotted either side of the road beside the sea. From what I could gather they belonged to a wide assortment of Noodle-*san*'s family – children, cousins, nieces, nephews, parents, grandparents, that sort of thing. The tiny *obaasan* (grandmother), who lived over the road in a rickety house in which she'd lived all her life, shuffled across Route 42 in the rain with a trayful of *tempura* and rice she had made specially for me. No charge, of course.

One of Noodle-*san*'s sons, a chatty teenager called Hideji Kasanaka, told me he had spent 'one year New Zealand working in Kiwi South Ltd near to cathedral'. Just which cathedral he was alluding to, or just what Kiwi South Ltd exactly was, I was naturally unclear about and, before I had a chance to ask him, he asked, 'Jodie-*san*, you like Earl Grey tea?' When I said, 'It's all right, but I prefer a cup of *o-cha* any day,' he was much tickled: 'Ah so, *desu-ka*? Ha! Ha! England drinker prefer Japanese tea! Ha! Ha!'

My room was across the narrow corridor from the kitchen and that night I lay on my futon listening to the rain hammering against the window on one side and the tumultuous clattering emanating from the kitchen on the other. At one o'clock when I got up to go to the *benjo* the kitchen was still a hive of activity – full of various laughing, drinking and eating members of family. I spotted Noodle-*san* amidst a whirl of smoke and pans, frying up circles of octopus. In the *benjo* there was more activity – albeit of a six-legged variety – as plagues of fat cockroaches scuttled for cover. Soon after 3 a.m. the kitchen clatter finally came to a halt, leaving me to drift into a stormy, cockroach-laden dream.

Noodle-*san* was evidently something of a dynamo because, barely three hours after she had scrubbed the last pot clean, she was busy making them dirty again. By 6.30 a.m. she had rustled up an elaborate breakfast for at least twenty-five hungry mouths – one of which I was pleasantly surprised to find was mine. She slippered her way into my room to deliver an unordered but very welcome breakfast of bean-curd seaweed soup, grilled fish and a shiny mound of rice.

Noodle-*san* alerted me to the fact that it was still raining (not that it was possible to ignore, with a forceful and clattering rain rattling the panes of the window and hammering away on the roof like a drum) and invited me to stay the day in her *minshuku* 'to sleep and eat'. I didn't need much persuading.

No sooner had I finished brushing my teeth than *obaasan* arrived on the scene and caught me washing my socks in the sink. For a moment she appeared most distressed, not because I was breaking any *minshuku* rules (of which there appeared to be none) but because I was putting myself to undue trouble. After encouraging me to round up all my dirty laundry (much of which I was wearing) she steered me across the road to her house where she dropped my soiled offering through the hatch of an antediluvian, rusty, lime-green top-loading machine which sat by her front door. (I had noticed that, outside the cities, most people installed their washing machines – all lime green, all top-loading – out of doors simply because there was not enough room to keep them in the house.) *Obaasan* must have taken quite a shine to me because she later brought me a pile of clean rags (when she saw me tinkering around with the greasy innards of my bicycle), a steaming bowlful of *soba*, a can of Pocari Sweat, two pink and white polka-dot *hankachifu*, a pair of 'Hello Kitty' socks and a large bar of 'Cow Brand-Beauty Soap'.

My bike was a worry. Despite dissecting my bottom bracket and rear derailleur and re-greasing my hubs it was still making dubious knocking noises, which I suspected were radiating from the block. I decided the best (i.e. laziest) thing to do was to ignore the problem until it got worse.

The rain was still pummelling the *minshuku* when I woke at six the next morning. Noodle-*san* told me I would be a mad *gaijin* to leave in this weather but a mad *gaijin* I would have to be as, that afternoon, I had arranged to meet for the first time a fellow *gaijin* who lived further up the coast in Inami. My mother was responsible for this rendezvous. Over a voice-delayed trans-global telephone line she told me how she had met a woman, Mrs Clausnitzer, in our village who had recently started up something called the Friday Lunch Club that took place from time to time in the village hall. From what I could gather my mother had on one particular occasion been invited along to play the honky-tonk piano for a sing-along session in the hall. The upshot was that my mother, who had so far been unable to track down any addresses for me of friends or of friends of friends who lived in Japan, suddenly discovered that Mrs Clausnitzer had a twenty-four-year-old daughter, Krista, who was working for a couple of years in Japan teaching English. Mrs Clausnitzer gave my mother Krista's address, telling her to tell me that I must drop by on Krista if I happened to find myself anywhere in the area.

'So are you anywhere in the area?' my mother asked, once I'd written down the address and looked at my map. Out of all the places where I could have been in Japan, I discovered that Krista's home in Inami was not much more than a day's ride away.

So I set off in dire conditions up Route 42 which, because of the rain and a surplus of trucks and tunnels, had turned even more diabolical. Splashing into the outskirts of Shirahama I passed a large sign in English which said:

TRAFFIC SAFETY DECLARED TOWN

No sooner had my eyes dropped from the sign back to the road than I witnessed the car in front shunt into the back of another. Traffic safety town indeed.

Along with Atami and Beppu, Shirahama is considered to be one of the three best spa resorts in Japan. Although I have a hot-spot for hot-springs I have a very cold-spot for resorts and, what with a seafront crammed full of plug-ugly plush hotels, golf courses and amusement parks where you could 'enjoy' such delights as 'Future City', 'Pirate's Cave', 'Dinosaur Land', 'Jumbo Tomato Tree', 'Adventure World' and 'Mystery Zone', I felt little inclination to give 'Accident Black-Spot Town' my custom.

I met Krista outside the railway station in Inami and my first reaction was one of slight shock at seeing a *gaijin* again. Sheepsaddled Alan, the Ozzie Scouser, had been the last Westerner I had seen and that had been weeks ago. More of a shock was having to make coherent conversation in English again – something that has never come easily, even at the best of times.

Krista lived in the ground-floor flat, or what the Japanese call an *apaarto*, of an old wooden house down a weave of narrow back streets and alleys, crammed with a higgledy-piggledy array of corrugated iron and wooden homes and smiling people. She slept on a Western-style bed in a room of *tatami*. The rest of the *apaarto* consisted of a pit-toilet (lots of flies), a *tatami* entrance hall by the door (where I slept on my camping mat) and a small kitchen with no hot water and three mega-pots of Marmite. Krista obviously had something of a 'growing spread' soft-spot. 'I always ask friends to bring me some over from home,' she said. 'I'm mad on the stuff.' Ah so, *desu-ka*?

To reach the shower (shared, I believe, with a neighbour) you had to go out of the door into the street where it was situated in a lean-to on the right. As the shower was electric and the heater gas, the whole contraption looked as if it could electrocute you with ease. Beneath the plastic matting dwelled a toe-snapping freshwater crab.

Krista, who was training to be a lawyer, was an interesting mix of nationalities: her grandmother was Japanese, her father half-German, half-Japanese and her mother English. She was part-way through a JET programme of teaching English in a local school – something that seemed to be a popular pursuit for *gaijin* in Japan. Not far away, in Osaka, she had a big bunch of expat friends, all teaching English, with whom she appeared to lead a hectic social life. The restless ringing of the phone was enough to indicate she was in hot demand and she would lie on her bed chatting for hours.

I asked Krista about the bicycles upon which I had seen schoolchildren flock to the station or school. What had surprised me was that they were all the same: regulation standard, black sit-up-and-begs. Were British children to cycle to school in their masses, such as they do in Japan, instead of being chaperoned unnecessarily in vehicles, the bike shed would undoubtedly be a wild jumble of multi-hued mountain bikes, racers, roadsters, chopper-styles, folders, shoppers and such-like. Why, I asked Krista, wasn't this the case in Japan, which after all manufactures some of the widest range of bicycle components for use around the world?

'Schoolchildren aren't allowed mountain bikes,' said Krista. 'It's to prevent them from outdoing and competing with each other for flashy models and paint-jobs. Everyone has to be the same – like with so much in Japan. Everyone must ride the government-approved style, dark sombre roadsters. It's the rules.' So that was that.

With a friend, Dana Mumford, Krista edited *Back of Inaka*, a newsletter which was circulated throughout their expat community. It was full of little snippets of information: what was happening where, school-teaching tips, Japanese news, as well as random cuttings such as a section of filmstar quotes called 'Sex on Screen'.

> Everyone moans about them, but it's a chance to have a jolly good snog!
>
> Emma Thompson

> They're a pain in the ass – like scrubbing the toilet!
>
> Lara Flynn Boyle

> They are a natural part of the story. I'll do whatever's right to portray the character.
>
> Richard Gere

After scouring the *Back of Inaka* I moved on to the *Daily Yomiuri*, a fairly unexciting English-printed newspaper in which I found only two stories of interest. One was headed:

> 39-YEAR-OLD RUNS JAPAN, TIP-TO-TIP
>
> Sapporo – A 39-yr-old hotel manager Saturday evening trotted out to Soya Point, the northernmost land point in Hokkaido, reaching his goal of running the length of Japan, a 3,000-kilometre trip.
>
> The feat took Norio Wada of Edogawa Ward, Tokyo, 42 days. He left the southernmost point of Kagoshima Prefecture on May 8 and reached the 'finish line' at Soya Point at 5.30 p.m. The trip totalled 3,153km.

Reading this, I felt somewhat dispirited with my progress – Mr Wada had run about three times further than I had managed to cycle in as many days.

The other *Daily Yomiuri* article of interest was a piece by Shunsuke Iwasaki about Japan's unsustainable logging industry:

> Japan consumes massive quantities of timber, importing 40% of the world's total production of tropical wood from broad-leaved trees and 80% of trees exported worldwide for paper production. Japanese savings, which have accumulated by the sweat of our brow since the end of World War II, have been loaned to developing countries in the South. The people in those countries however are so deeply in debt now that they cannot help but sell their trees and grow crops in a previously forested area, despite the dangers of the soil being washed away there. And, no matter how hard they work, their debts continue to grow.

I had planned on staying with Krista for one night only but, because of my bike playing up, I stayed nearly a week. After diagnosing a dodgy block and trying, to no avail, to find a replacement in the local bicycle-cum-moped shops (the insides of which, along with the equipment on offer, seemed not to have been updated since the War) I rang a number of more hi-tech bike shops in Osaka, Kobe and even Tokyo. The eye-opening outcome of this was that, in this Land of the Shining Shimano Components, it would work out cheaper for me to have a replacement Shimano block sent to me from England than to buy one in Japan. So I rang Jeremy Yeo – the good, tried and trusty owner of Weald Cycles, my local friendly bike shop at home. Jeremy was one of those rare breeds in the trade who was obviously more into giving tip-top service than getting rich quick. Whenever I rode through his door with a problem – which was more often than not – nothing seemed to be too much trouble for so little money, if anything at all. What's more, he would not only set me right but provide me with a good hour's chinwag covering any topic from Outer Mongolian archaeology or David Guterson's phenomenal *Snow Falling on Cedars* to his opinion of a good crunchy nut chocolate-chip biscuit cake.

While I was waiting for my package to arrive I spent my days walking around Inami and into the hills beyond. I liked Inami; it was a cosy little town, with its tight cluster of houses squeezed around a tidal river that ran through the centre. There were fishermen's moorings, and narrow humpbacked bridges crossed the river at intervals.

The first time I stood on one of these bridges, peering down into the river below, I got a bit of a shock: the water was filthy – little more than a murky, polluted sludge. But this was hardly surprising. For a country so advanced in technology, Japan has hundreds of thousands of homes still not connected to a main sewage system and Inami was no exception: raw sewage flowed directly from homes into the river and out to sea.

The beach was strewn with rubbish – dead fish, old tyres, bottles, bags, aerosols, cans, boots, shoes, polystyrene and a million plastic containers. This was not just the random remnants of flotsam and jetsam but had been deliberately tipped on the beach. One morning, as I sat on top of one of the thousands of monstrous concrete blocks rearing out of the sea as part of the *tsunami* break, I watched the dismal sight of a man struggling down the steps on to the beach with two large bags of household waste which he emptied on top of the existing rubbish before setting light to the lot. The beach was littered with putrid smouldering fires like this along with the mangled and tortured shapes of charred remains. It was a sight that made me feel decidedly gloomy. On one of my walks I passed another 'beach' entangled in barbed-wire incarcerating the smashed wrecks of cars and vans. Sitting on a crumbled wall nearby was a clutch of rumbustious schoolboys who shrieked hysterically as I sauntered past.

'Ga!' they cried. '*Gaijin* ga! Harrow! A-B-C-D-E-F-G! Bye Bye!'

Round the corner I was seized by a drunken mad-eyed woman with a soiled bandage wound round her arm who dragged me past another catastrophic barbed-wire beach back to her home. This was a ground floor *apaarto* sandwiched between the repugnant Route 42 and an ear-splitting, constantly drilling building site. The *apaarto* consisted of one tiny *tatami* room with two small shrines tucked in the corners, the whole being tacked on to a miniature kitchen. The place looked as if it had been ransacked. It was filthy: discarded clothes, crumpled magazines, overflowing ashtrays, empty bottles and piles of plates of uneaten food strewn about the room. The general miasma whiffed of a malodorous mix of stale smoke, sweat and decomposed fish.

The woman, who was ranting and raving in a continuous inebriated slur, tried to make me a coffee but this involved having to heat water, scrabble around for a jar of instant and extricate a non-existent clean mug – a process which her intoxication clearly rendered her incapable of carrying out. Apart from her repeatedly calling me 'America' I could understand little of what she said and I doubt whether any Japanese could either. For a moment she became preoccupied with rummaging around in a large box full of jars of pickled plums and radishes and packets of noodles until she found what she was looking for: a bottle of whisky. As she unscrewed the top, the bottle slipped from her hands, smashed on the table and flooded the *tatami*. Her reaction was to dissolve into hysterical laughter before spitting, and then cramming a couple of Hope fags into her mouth. After mopping up the whisky I didn't know what else I could do so I left.

On the way back to Krista's I came across some jaunty workmen who bought me a beer, posed comically for pictures and gave me a ride on their fork-lift truck. I didn't tell them where I was staying or who I was staying with but, after diverting course to the post-office to send some films home (the cost of which was calculated on an abacus), I arrived back at Krista's who, somewhat mystified, told me a bunch of workmen had dropped by to deliver a gift of four cream cakes.

Waiting for my bike parts from Jeremy Yeo to arrive I became fidgety and inwardly irritable. I wanted to get back on the move, to spin in the wind with my wheels beneath me. When, on the fifth day, the local friendly moped-riding postman pulled up on his standard issue Yamaha Towne Mate Deluxe with a parcel from England, I was overjoyed. Along with the new freewheel Jeremy had sent a new chain and block remover. Borrowing a hefty monkey wrench from a nearby mechanic I removed the offending block and screwed on the new one. After tinkering around, realigning the chain and adjusting the rear derailleur, the job was done. Following a fine-tuning test run I stood back and felt absurdly happy. I was ready to go.

It was Friday and Krista had planned to go to Osaka for the weekend for a splurge of parties and socializing. But when I returned from my test run I found her at home feeling miserable.

'Osaka's out,' she said, 'my tonsils are up.'

Just what tonsils being 'up' signified I wasn't entirely sure but they were 'up' enough to send her packing to the doctor. When she came back she wasn't clutching a jumble of pills and potions as I had envisaged but a £10 watermelon.

'The doctor gave it to me,' she said, 'instead of a prescription. We get on well.'

Her other remedy was to stay in bed all weekend with five videos which, in a Florence Nightingale sort of moment, I offered to pick up for her from Today Video in Minabe – a horrendous eighteen-mile round-trip cycle back down that loveliest of lovelies, Route 42.

While grounded in Inami with dry socks and a roof over my head I notified the weather that now was the time to flush the rain out of its system and to pour as hard as it liked. Think it listened? Think that snakes have earlobes? The sun shone strong and long.

Even if it was raining *neko* and *inu* (cats and dogs) it was good to be moving again. For a brief respite from the treacherous Route 42 I veered off course, skirting inland into the mountains along a narrow, empty road that weaved its way through quiet hamlets and steep hillsides stepped with paddy fields. The air smelt delicious – of fresh grass and oranges.

Crossing the Hidaka River at Gobo-shi, I followed a coastal detour that led me past the lighthouse at Cape Hinomisaki where, above the Bust of Knudsen (a memorial to a Danish seaman who had died in 1957 when attempting a heroic rescue of a Japanese ship which had caught fire off the Cape in a raging storm), the bruised skies were awheel with legions of black-tailed gulls.

The racing wind blew me to Yura-cho – home to Kokokuji, the main temple for mendicant Zen priests who wear sedge hoods and play the *shakuhachi* (bamboo flute). Kokokuji was founded many a blue moon ago by Hotto Kokushi, a Japanese priest revered in culinary circles who, having returned from a visit to China, brought with him the techniques for making *miso* and soy sauce (which is eaten with everything). Up the road was Yuasa-cho, known to Japanese as the Birthplace of Soy Sauce, complete with the obligatory museum where the wafted rich aromas of the home-brewed sauce drifted redolently on the wind.

That night, after filling all available pannier space with food supplies from 'Delicious Hirooka' supermarket, I rode out to a tiny fishing village near Semuiji temple where I hitched up at a wonderfully homely *yusu hosuteru* tucked away down a straitened alley near the seafront. It was run by a genial and doughty woman who had a large fat cat called (of all exotic names) Michael. As I was the only female staying I had a whole dorm to myself, which meant that I could festoon all the other bunks with my washing and throw open the windows as wide as possible without making myself severely unpopular, as I am wont to do. There were about eight males of various ages staying at the hostel, three of whom invited me to take iced *oolong-cha* with them. They were friends from Osaka, all with a few words of English and all in their early thirties. One was a security guard, another a computer games salesman and a third, with glasses so thick his eyes looked like ET's, was a 'mechanical electrian', which made him sound decidedly robotic.

Clinging to the wall of my dorm was an old banger of an air-conditioner. Although I didn't want to turn it on despite the clammy heat (I prefer to sweat to death in real air rather than freeze to the bone in artificial), I was intrigued to read a sun-faded curling-at-the-edges English-written notice stuck to the wall beside it explaining its use:

> Cooles and Heates: If you want just condition of warm in your room, please control yourself.

That night I went to bed and managed to 'control myself' very nicely indeed. There are some things in life which are best done alone.

Strange. It was sunny. A gloriously sunny Sunday – the day when husbands 'service' their families. That morning, after petting Michael goodbye, I set out thinking: what a wonderful day for getting lost. So I just let my wheels lead me anywhere they fancied and I ended up drifting along a road – too miniature for my map – that swung its way in a happy sort of swinging style along a rocky outcrop of a coast where fathers were 'servicing' their families by playing in the astonishingly pellucid blue waves of stony bays.

Rather than lose myself for weeks in the elongated industrialized jungle of Osaka and Kobe (which on my JNTO – Japanese National Tourist Office – map of Japan appeared almost as offputtingly large a yellow blob as Tokyo) I decided to give it an extremely wide berth by sidestepping to the island of Shikoko. But to do this first entailed getting lost in Wakayama-shi, until a jolly little man on a moped, with a yappity Pekinese dog perched on the handlebars, led me through the suburbs, down miles of Americanized concrete shopping strips and along endless docks lined and loaded with log saw mills to the ferry. Wakayama-ken is the primary region for producing *washi* (handmade paper) and the ubiquitous *waribashi* (disposable chopsticks) made from mountain cedar, found in every noodle shop and *sushi* bar in Japan.

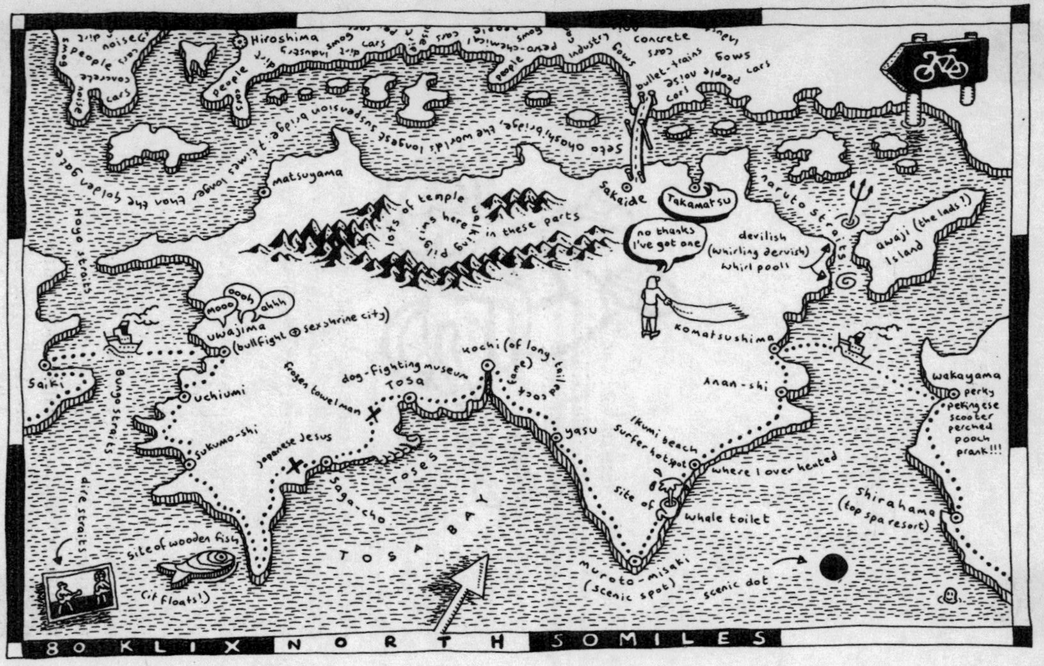

Hiroshima
Seto ohashi bridge, the world's longest suspension bridge: 7 times longer than the golden gate
matsuyama
lots of temple walking pilgrims here in these parts
Sakaide
Takamatsu
no thanks I've got one
devilish (whirling dervish) whirl pool!
naruto straits
awaji (the lads!) Island
Hoyo straits
mooo
oooh
ahhh
uwajima (bullfight ⊙ sexshrine city)
komatsushima
kochi (of long-tailed cock fame)
dog-fighting museum
Tosa
frozen towelman
Saiki
uchiumi
Bungo straits
sukumo-shi
Japanese Jesus
Saga-cho
Tose
Anan-shi
wakayama
perky pekingese scooter perched pooch prank!!!
yasu
Ikumi beach
surfer hotspot
where I over heated
site of
whale toilet
Shirahama (top spa resort)
dire straits
site of wooden fish (it floats!)
T O S A B A Y
muroto-misaki (scenic spot)
scenic dot
80 KLIX NORTH SO MILES

CHAPTER 16

Funnel of Tunnels

The Nankai ferry took just over two hours to cross the fifty-mile Kii *suido* (straits) that separated Wakayama-shi on Honshu from Komatsushima-shi on Shikoku. Outside it was hazy and hot. I was the only person on deck; all the other passengers were being air-conditioned inside as they lay shoeless on the carpeted floor (there were no chairs) in front of a blaring television games show.

Finding a strip of shade, I sat on the deck and opened my map to find out just where I was going. Shikoku, the smallest of Japan's main islands (about the size of Sardinia), floats in the revered Seto Naikai, or Inland Sea. Curled around its northern and eastern flanks lies Honshu, with Kyushu forming its western wall.

Shikoku takes its name from its feudal past when the island was divided into *shi* (four) *koku* (provinces), which today have become four prefectures: Kagawa, Tokushima, Ehime and Kochi. Most Japanese have always regarded Shikoku as something of a backwater – and, despite being linked up to Honshu in 1988 by the Seto Ohashi Bridge, it is still a place of relative remoteness, with a population smaller than that of the San Francisco Bay Area. The bridge took ten years to build, at a cost of five billion pounds, and just happens to be the 'longest double-decker car and train suspension bridge in the world'. Although large sections of Shikoku's northern coast are over-industrialized, like so much of Japan, this leaves the rest of the island predominantly rural, with the southern part concentrating on citrus production, lumber and fishing.

For this reason very few Japanese have ever set foot on Shikoku, perceiving it as being too underdeveloped, too out-of-the-way and too uninteresting to warrant a visit. And, I suspect, too *takai* (expensive): should you fancy motoring across the six miles of six bridges of Seto Ohashi (anchored by three small islands) it's *sayonara* to some £40 per trip.

A crew member walking past saw me studying my map and asked me where I was going. As I was not entirely sure I said, '*Minami* – South,' not only because it embraced a potentially limitless area but also because, being a cold-blooded northern-clime type, I've always thought 'south' sounds like a good place to go: a place to warm the cockles. But, with cockles already warmed, they felt like they could do with a freeze. The crewman, being of a nautical nature, looked like a good weather-fish to me so, concerned about how many wet days lay ahead of me, I asked him when the rainy season might be over. My understanding of this amiable oriental seadog's Japanese was as follows:

'Rainy season ended last night at 24 hundred hours.'

And he was right. Just as I had been seriously contemplating buying a wet-suit to cycle in, the rainy season had ended on exactly the day forecasted. Just like that. It was as if everything is so regimental in Japan that even the weather complies. Ahh sun, I had ahhed, as the first radiating rays of summer spread across the land. But, within moments, my ahhs! changed to arghs! when I discovered that the sun was the wrong sort of sun. It was not that luxuriously placid northern European kind that sends rosy-glowing tentative tingles into the wintered blood, but was more the stuff of merciless fiery tentacles that not only burns and blisters the skin but frazzles and fritters the mind. About to enter Japan's hottest summer for fifty years didn't help matters. Nor did the humidity. In fact, it was the appalling humidity rather than the searing temperatures that nearly knocked me for six.

My first night in Shikoku was spent camping at the roadside within the urbanity of Anan-shi between a noodle bar and a miniature shrine – so much for the rural Four Provinces. By midnight the temperature within my tent was registering 43°C (or, in Fahrenheit a mighty 110). I slept as if in a fever: restless and drenched in sweat. By my second night I had given up on my tent and booked into a surfers' hostel which I came across on Ikumi beach, just outside Shishikui-cho. With a room temperature of 36°C (92°F) this was little better. But this time I brought on the discomfort myself: my wilful aversion to air-conditioners kept me from switching it on. Instead I had ten cold showers that night.

By 5.30 the next morning the surfers were trotting down the beach, boards under arm. The weather pressed so heavy with humidity that the appeal of the sea (even if it was of a murky nature) won an easy battle over setting sail up a mountain by wheel. So I walked downstairs past a poster of the Wailer's Bob, past the behind-closed-door strains of

No wo-man no cry,
No wo-man, no cry . . .

past a shaggy-haired peroxide-blond Japanese youth at whom I had to stop myself staring, and up to the laid-back reception desk where there was sometimes to be found a long-haired chain-smoking surfer, but more times not. Up on the counter was stuck a sticker that told me Life's a Beach (well, at least for this part of Japan), while the cover of the signing-in book advised me to:

Keep stoned and Smilin'
Love Peace and Smoke.

It seemed that on Ikumi beach, even if the surf was not high, the surfers were. Apart from a dog there was nothing stirring at reception so I sauntered down to the beach and entered the waves. And that's more or less where I stayed all day. It was the only place where I felt my body temperature drop to anything near normal. Every now and then I dipped back to my room, where I collapsed on my bed to drink something and eat something and read another few pages of Kazuo Ishiguro's *A Pale View of Hills.* I had little energy for anything else.

I rolled on south, to the Cape of Muroto-Misaki – a perfectly inverted triangle of land hanging down off Tosa-wan Bay which my tourist leaflet of the area noted as 'one of the eight most scenic spots in Japan'. Interpreting this as 'one of the eight most tourist-trodden tips in Japan' I feared a cavalcade of tour-buses. But I was to be pleasantly surprised. After passing over the None River (of which there was some, albeit not a lot) the only vehicles I came across were two VW split-screens and a jumble of rusty old Toyotas and pick-ups parked at the side of the road whose occupants were surfing the waves. This palm-treed, wild black-sanded cliffscape strip of coast with geologically some of the youngest mountains on earth is plainly not dubbed 'Little Hawaii' for nothing.

At one point I came across a massive whale and, like Jonah, I was sucked straight in. But whereas Jonah had various viscera to contend with, I had toilets. I was merely passing by to pass some water in these most unusual roadside public conveniences shaped in the mould of a whale.

As I entered a cubicle with a hooded-spray squat bowl, the toilet suddenly flushed. That's funny, I thought, as I hadn't gone anywhere near the flusher – a silver button seated in the wall. Feeling I was maybe just imagining things I carried on, unperturbed. Poised for action, hunched down on my haunches, the toilet took me unawares by flushing again – only this time I noticed that, rather than a full-flung flush, nothing had happened – no water was involved. It just sounded as if it had. Presuming I had mistaken my flush for that of a neighbouring cubicle, I was in the process of hoisting up my shorts when, lo! – the lavatory automatically flushed again. And yet, it hadn't. Not a droplet of water had issued forth from the secreted cistern. This was getting too much. Was I sun-stoned and smilin' or had endless weeks of rain simply drowned my mind? Had water infiltrated my ears and affected my hearing? Was Japan beset by a lavatorial poltergeist who revelled in flummoxing sweaty cyclists with their shorts at half-mast? No, I discovered it was none of these things. Instead, by adopting a Sherlock Holmes air, I detected a small concealed speaker embedded in the corner at the top of the wall which, containing an electric eye, intermittently emitted a recording of a flushing toilet.

There are a lot of things in Japan which perplex, not least its toilets. Public conveniences appeared to be great sources of embarrassment to Japanese women. In order to cover up any undesirable noises which might issue forth from below decks (even the sprinkling sounds of a tinkle), I found that women tended to flush the lavatory constantly throughout their toileting stay – thanks to fast-filling cisterns. It was no wonder that, despite the rainy season, Japan had long been suffering from a water shortage. To combat this, most Japanese toilet systems offered a choice of flushes. For a big, full-blown flush, push the lever towards a symbol that resembles a headless stickman:

For a snappy flush, push it to the symbol that faintly resembles a disconsolate face:

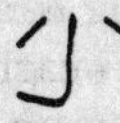

What's more, most toilets contained a water spout and mini basin integrated into the top of the cistern where the water that ran to fill the tank could be used to wash your hands. In this ingenious way it conserved water as well as space.

So I discovered that, owing to the amount of times Japanese women flushed a public WC per sitting (or squatting), the latest toilets had installed recordings of flushings in order to save water.

To save more flushed faces I found that, if I entered the Ladies at the same time as another woman, she would inevitably remain concealed in her cubicle until I had completed my business and left so as to avoid a possibly embarrassing encounter with a *gaijin* who might, heaven forbid, just have *heard*.

Then there is the endearing method Japanese women adopt in establishing whether the toilet 'stall' is occupied. Whereas we uncouth Europeans tend to go about this sensitive issue by pushing or, depending on urgency, rattling the door or calling 'Hullooo-hoo – anybody *in* there?' or, if all else fails, stooping down to check for signs of feet, the Japanese adopt a far more courtly (and anonymous) approach: two light taps on the door is all it takes. These are immediately echoed by the occupier, thus conveying simply and effectively to the outer tapper that, yes, the toilet is engaged. Hence, toilet door taps can be interpreted as follows:

OUTSIDER: Tap, tap (read as: 'Is anybody *in* there?')
INSIDER: Tap, tap (read as: 'Yee-es, so soorrry, *I* am.')

This little ritual took me a few visits to the toilet to pick up. The first time there came a knock on my door, I said:

'*Hai, hai*?'

Silence, followed by retreating panic-stricken heels – heels which said, 'Yikes! A *gaijin* in the *benjo*! I'm out of here!'

More shocking than any automatic fake-flushing toilets were the Western-style WCs I came across which, complete with an on-board control-panel of digital this and flashing that, resembled more the sort of thing you'd expect to find beneath the hindquarters of space-encapsulated Captain

Spock than in a mere earthling's private, or even public, convenience. The first one I came in contact with was situated in a *yakitori* restaurant: it had a most peculiar state-of-the-art, electronically heated lavatory seat that adjusted to my personal body temperature. To be faced with such advanced technology was, for someone who had just got to grips with an electronic typewriter, enough to make me quite forget what I had sat on the toilet for in the first place. I gingerly flicked a few switches and twiddled a few knobs and dials, half expecting to be either ignominiously swallowed by the pan or jettisoned through the roof. As it was, an over-enthusiastic ejaculation of warm water hit a certain nook in my anatomy with bull's-eye accuracy. Startled by this surprising type of enema I flailed around again for the control panel, flicked another switch and was promptly delivered a blast of hot air so strong that it almost propelled me through the lavatory door back into the restaurant.

One lavatory I was fortunate enough to be reading about rather than sitting upon used the latest microchip technology to monitor the user's waste products, weight, temperature and even blood pressure. Research was underway to develop this model further by possibly instigating a direct link between these advanced 'conveniences' and nearby hospitals so that suspicious symptoms of anything amiss could be instantly reported and the patient appropriately treated before anything untoward would have time to develop. Personally I prefer the idea of Mother Earth monitoring my offerings rather than men in white coats.

The RSPCA could have a field day in Shikoku. This somewhat rogue island plays host to the bloody sports of not only cock-fighting, but dog-fighting and bull-fighting as well. In the southern prefecture of Kochi there are bred, not without cruelty, the rare and highly bizarre *Onagadori*, or Long-Tailed

Cocks, which can produce tail feathers up to a sensational ten metres in length. Until setting foot in Shikoku, I had never heard of such a peculiar bird.

But then, as is the way coincidences go, I had not long been home from Japan when I found myself ambling along with the crowds at Milland's Rural Fair. Among the llamas and pigs and recalcitrant sheep I bumped into a man with a beard. His name was Dr Joseph Batty and, as coincidence would have it, he was something of a bird boffin. Amidst a lorry-load of books he'd written about poultry (e.g. *Keeping Jungle Fowl*) was one called *Japanese Long-Tailed Fowl.* Discovering my surprise and then interest, Dr Batty, being of a kind and generous nature, gave me the book, an A4-sized hardback that he had published himself and which today lives on my bookshelf, sandwiched in a randomly unclassified section between a 1966 edition of Arkady Leokum's *Tell Me Why – Answers to hundreds of questions boys and girls ask* and the Treasure Press's *Complete Book of Tools and How to Use Them.* (I have to admit that ever since making a letterbox and a cat coffin I really do get pleasure from looking at pictures of round-nosed chisels, pricking-iron punches and spiral-ratchet screwdrivers.)

But back to birds. The following is a taster of the sort of information that can be found in Dr Batty's intriguing book:

The Long-Tailed Fowl
Basic Definition

The long-tailed fowl is so named because its tail continues to grow to great lengths, thus making the species and associated breeds quite unique. The tail of five species may reach up to 30 feet.

The Tail

The tail of the fowl is the appendage at the rear end of the bird, which supplies balance and adornment. It comes in varying shapes and sizes and in one bird (the Rumpless) there is no tail at all. Between male and females there are differences [Ah so, *desu-ka?*], the males having 'hangers' and sickle feathers.

The origin or source of the original type of tail is difficult to determine with certainty. With conventional tails the style of the Red Jungle fowl can be seen . . . Possibly the missing link, the Gallus Giganteus is the origin, but we cannot be sure . . . There is the added problem that so far nobody outside Japan has shown ability to achieve the long tail growth. However, this may be due to not having the basic mutation stock rather than failure to be able to breed.

Current Position

The position is that outside Japan there are no known species with the really long tails. Growing these requires great skill, patience and understanding. Special boxes or cages are used and the breeder must remove certain feathers so they all grow in harmony . . . Feathers trailing on the ground are never very practical . . . to avoid damage to the feathers of the tail the cock-bird is taken from his cage and given exercise, with an attendant to watch that the train is held up away from the very clean floor.

Early History

[Long-tailed fowl] have a very long history, although the oldest breed or race is known as the Shokoku.

Artificial Stimulation and Patience

Factors which allow the tail to be grown to the phenomenal length are as follows:

1. Special, high protein food;
2. Pulling out tail feathers to stimulate further growth;
3. Wrapping feathers in special papers;
4. Provision of a special box or cage to allow the tail to be protected and folded – there can be no question of allowing these birds freedom.

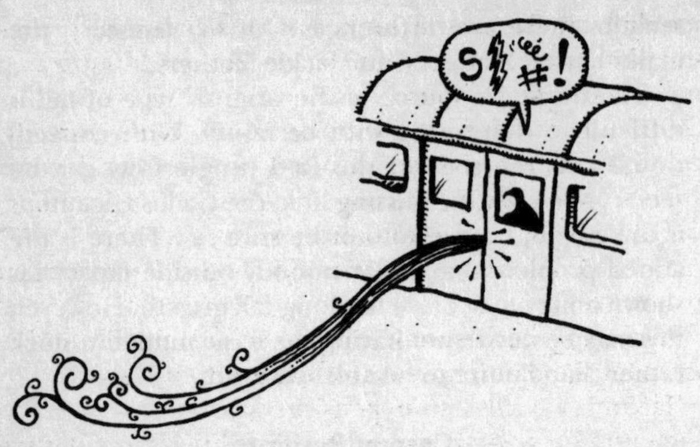

I rode down to Katsurahama, or what my map called Beautiful Beach. Down past the Tosa Token dog-fighting museum I came to a strip of dirty, gravelly sand which I'm sure not so long ago was indeed a Beautiful Beach. Now it resembled a building site as armies of dumper trucks, their backs heaving with massive boulders the size of cars, rumbled up and down. All around was the unseaside sound of a score or more of noisy bulldozers and diggers and pile-drivers that appeared to be re-designing the wilds of the beach into a seafront of concrete.

A grinning man holding a child in one hand and an *aisu-kuriimu* in the other came scurrying up to me.

'America?' he said.

'No, England,' I replied.

'Ah so. England fine city.'

And then, totally unprompted, he looked at the sky and said, 'Yes. Today rain 4.30 p.m. – bye, bye.'

It didn't rain; it just got hotter. I cycled past a small harbour in which a squadron of schoolchildren were swimming in circles, marshalled by three men with megaphones in three separate boats. The children behaved perfectly – none of that tomfoolery which I remember dominated my swimming lessons in the pool. As I watched the children clamber up the ladder over the harbour wall I was struck by how incredibly similar they all looked: same hair, same costumes, same skin, same stature, same beauty, a sleek homogeneous line of sylph-like nymphs.

Opposite Sunnymart two men ran up to me excitedly. I was surprised by their faces, which looked very un-Japanese. The men smelt of fish and oil.

'Hi! I am Felix pleased to meet you!' said Felix.

'Hi! I'm Thomas!' said Thomas 'Wow! Foreigner sure great to see!'

Felix and Thomas were Filipino ship-engineers and had just spent the past few weeks sailing up from Manila.

'Japan – aargh! – so expensive,' said Felix. 'Where you sleeping? You want to sleep on our fishing boat. Big party time!'

I said, 'Well, thank you, Felix, but maybe another time.'

That night I found a small park in which to camp, situated in a dip between a river and a line of houses. I tucked myself away in a corner among a small jungle of spiky yucca-like plants that appeared to be strung together in a tangle of thick sticky spider webs. A hungry cloud of mosquitoes descended on me with ravenous glee. It was not a good spot, but I was too hot, too tired to care. After washing my face and hands and feet as best I could in a bottle of water before squirting the contents of another one over my arms and legs and down my back, I crawled exhausted and already sweating again into the airless pocket of nylon that served as my tent. Despite having spent eight hours cycling over seventy sweaty miles and during which time I had eaten no more than a banana, I didn't feel hungry. The oppressive heat was so draining that it sapped away all appetite, replacing it with a giddy nausea. My head, pulsating with an over-heated and thunderous ache, felt fit to explode. When I flopped backwards on top of my sleeping bag and closed my eyes, my flashing-visioned world spun sun-drunkenly within my head. I lay there, clothes-less, occasionally swiping the air in a futile attempt to swat the mosquitoes I'd failed to cull within my tent. Sweat oozed from every pore, coursing from my temples and sticking my hair to my neck. I wet a flannel with water and laid it over my eyes. Brief relief for fifteen seconds before it radiated heat.

Drugged into a fiery exhaustion, I found just enough energy to hold my water bottle above me with my left hand, slowly squirting its contents over my wilted form while, with my right switched to auto-pilot, I swept the air with a small paper fan.

I fell into a fitful and feverish sleep, the exasperating whine of mosquitoes ricocheting down my ear. Later (was it one hour, was it ten hours, was it two?) I became aware of a light and lyrical voice calling at my door.

'*Konbanwa, konbanwa* – good evening,' it sang. Unsure whether I could find the energy to stir myself, I lay on my mat, like a flaccid wreck uncharitably hoping the voice would go away.

'*Konbanwa, konbanwa,*' repeated the voice, evidently intent on finding me. I flung a reluctant arm upwards to peel open the zip-door, allowing a cloud of eager mosquitoes to flood into my clammy den.

The voice belonged to Saki ('Blossom'), a young mother accompanied by Kozo, her five-year-old son. In her hands were three huge tomatoes whose stalk-tops in the torchlight resembled the spiders in the trees.

'*Dozo,*' she said, as her son stared incredulously into the *gaijin*'s face.

'Tonight it will rain,' said Saki. 'Please come and stay in my house.'

With a reeling, heavy head I wanted very much to go and stay in Saki's house but my lacklustre body seemed unwilling: the thought of going through all the palaver of packing up in the dark, being bitten to pieces by mosquitoes, having to be nice and make conversation when I could barely lift my head, seemed like an ordeal I could well do without.

I mustered up as much appreciation as I could for the tomatoes and Saki's kind offer before muttering that the rain was no problem – my tent was waterproof and that I was sure I would be fine. Saki, obviously recognizing a lying wreck when she saw one, would hear none of it. She sent Kozo cantering off back to the house to rouse 'Papa'.

Just as the first fat drops of rain splashed off the fronds of the yucca, Papa appeared in a white transit van, headlights blazing, blinding Saki and me like rabbits. My nylon home was lifted virtually intact into the back of the van, whose walls were lined with boxes of books. (Papa, it turned out, was a sales rep for a publisher.)

Back at the house a great fuss was made over me as friends had been invited over to 'view' the *gaijin*. With a pain splintering inside my head it was hard work putting on an air of smiling happiness. My face felt as if in a furnace – burning with a pulsating heat. I'm neither myopic nor hyperopic (not yet, anyway) yet everything turned blurred. Despite air-conditioning, sweat still trickled. I felt sick but I managed to laugh and play with little Kozo, who giggled like a toy.

Trays and trays of food appeared: soups, seaweeds, fish and plates of pickled oddities. My stomach rebelled at the sight. Somehow a bowl of *miso* and rice went down and stayed down. But it was a close thing. Finally, come midnight, the blissful moment arrived and Saki steered me to the shower. I sat on the little pink plastic stool staring with burnt eyeballs at my reflection in the knee-high mirror while spraying a continuous jet of cold water over my head. The sensation was . . . well, sensational. I could have stayed there all night, all day, all bloody year. I never wanted to sweat again. I wanted to shiver and feel chilled to the bone. But it was not to be: life was only to get hotter. By the time I turned off the shower my focus cleared enough to read the tropical beach-depicted bath mat:

> Oh, to lie beneath the gently swaying palms,
> to feel the cooling ocean wind
> brush across your body – that is HEAVEN.

That night my heavenly wind came in the form of a *senpuki* (electric fan) which Saki placed at the bottom of my futon and, as I lay splayed in the dark in its glorious draught, the summer rain drummed down.

As hard as I tried I couldn't stop people being nice to me. I only had to stop at the side of the road to check my map or wipe my brow for offers of help and assistance to come flooding my way. Drinks were placed in my hands, meals before me, futons beneath me. Japanese generosity knew no bounds. It was so overwhelming that it made me feel guilty – that people could go to so much trouble, just for me. I began to learn not to ask for certain foods I couldn't find in supermarkets (i.e. porridge), so as to avoid the entire workforce dropping everything to help me out good-naturedly.

Sometimes when people approached me or addressed me or called at me to stop I would feign incomprehension and just wave and keep cycling, because I didn't want them spending their time and money being kind to me. Also, finding myself the focus of such continuously effusive generosity was almost as exhausting as cycling in the unforgiving heat in the mountains of the rising land. Returning smiles and niceties in a foreign tongue was immensely draining. And, if I had stopped and accepted every offer that besieged me, I frankly wouldn't have got anywhere.

Skirting Uranouchi-wan (bay) I diverted course along a hellishly mountainous but exhilarating road where towering and craggy clefts plunged into a sparkling sea. Everything was so green, so blue, so *utsukushii.* Yellow stripe-winged butterflies as big as birds flapped across my flight path. Crickets whirred, snakes slunk beside the bitumen and strange song-birds whooped in the deep lushness of the forests. As I ground upwards in a suffocating sun up one vertiginous mountain, a car – a rare sight on this quiet road – overtook me and stopped on a hairpin corner in the middle of the road, all signs of safety having evidently vaporized in the heat. A woman with a perfect silky jet-black mane lowered her electric window and gave me not one drink but a whole insulated picnic-bag full of iced teas and pops and juices. Wiping sweat out of my eyes I tried to explain that, really, one or two cans would be quite enough, but neither she nor the other grinning occupants of her air-conditioned car would listen to me and, calling '*Ganbatte*! – Have strength!', they took off round the bend.

Later I came across an army of workmen in hard hats, harnesses and split-toed boots, dangling like insects from ropes up the sheer wall of mountain beside me. To prevent potential car-crushing rock-falls they were taming the shaly mountain by covering its face with massive square slabs of cement and steel. From a distance these adulterated mountainsides resembled severe landscapes of concrete eggboxes. Man meddling with nature – it was the same sorry sight all over Japan – mountains of concrete. I feared some day Japan would sink beneath the sheer weight of cement that smothered its surface.

Part of the road at the bottom of the cement face was cordoned off behind a temporary barrier of steel girders and sheet metal. Where the road had been reduced to a single lane a set of traffic lights had been set up. But no ordinary traffic lights these. Instead of staring impatiently at an intransigent red light and edging ever closer, challenging it to change, I was offered a digital count-down system discouraging me from straining at the leash by sharing with me the fact that there were 20, 19, 18, 17, 16, 15 . . . seconds left to green (or, as the Japanese say, blue) and GO! It said: Hey! Look! Traffic lights can be fun!

I had also noticed how acres of roadworks and building sites always attempted to make their scenes of bulldozing destruction and concrete construction as pretty a picture as possible for the public by dressing up and festooning the surrounding worksite with miles of squeaky-clean plastic banner-type barriers bearing happy smiling cartoon elephants or rabbits or monkeys or teddies or 'Hello Kitties' or cheerful dinky flowers and bees and trees. What was this? A grand-scale setting for a children's tea-party? The makings of a theme park? While the real raw beauty of the land was being bulldozed and sandblasted and detonated and concreted into oblivion, you were being offered a placation: plastic nature on a plate.

Every now and then I came across other roadside attractions: policemen. But these 'boys in blue' lying in wait in the shrubbery to curb a speeding motorist were of an unusual breed – the sort you could knock on the nose and yet not face arrest. This was because they were the equivalent of Milton Keynes' cows: cardboard cut-outs. For years Japan has maintained a comical force of life-size wood, fibreglass or metal models of policemen who stand to attention at the side of the road or sit in strategically located stationary patrol cars.

It was all action in Susaki-shi: the city was crawling with police – real live ones, too, and definitely not the sort to rub up the wrong way. These were Japan's élite riot police, noted for their discipline, toughness and restraint whose advanced training, along with judo, kendo and karate, includes the delicate arts of *chanoyu* (tea ceremony) and *ikebana*.

Resembling samurai, these riot police were shaped like inverted triangles in a protective uniform of hefty blue padded tunics. Helmets with full-face visors covered their heads while a heavy cushioning of armour protected their necks. Attached to their belts were substantial black sticks, more stave than baton, which, thanks to kendo, could kill in a flash. White-gloved hands clutched long curved shields of metal. Their demeanour said: don't mess with me.

At first I couldn't see why the streets of Susaki-shi were lined with such men. There were no protest marches, no riots, no anarchy. In fact, the public were behaving as if they hadn't even noticed them – they were shopping in A-Coop, eating in Hungry Tiger or filling their white family saloons up on petrol in the Cosmo station like they always did. Life was being lived as normal.

But then, above all the usual noise of the city I heard a new noise. An awful distorted megaphoning din of martial music and screeching voices amplified beyond belief. Slowly this deplorable bull-horned wailing crept ever closer until the source was revealed: a cavalcade of black buses and cars and trucks, their sides bearing the old national motif of a radiating rising sun. It was election time but no one seemed to care. Far more important was to eat and shop and spend. The riot police stood redundant with a samurai stance in the torrid heat beneath their thick, cumbersome uniforms of armour. There was nothing doing today so, leaving them to stew, I rode on.

But I only made it to the suburbs, where the midday heat forced me to take a break. In a spic-and-span housing estate I found a small concrete area with a bench and a lattice shade shelter. Despite being overlooked by four blocks of flats, its windows full of inquisitive faces, it looked like a good place to flake out for an hour. Beside the shelter stood the ubiquitous and very welcome water fountain which I found of the same design all over Japan: a push-button fountain seated on the top of a small concrete obelisk, with a low-level tap spouting out of its side into a neat gridded drain bordered with gravel. I had developed a ritual on arriving at these fountains. First I would remove a water bottle from my bike, refilling it at the tap before drinking my fill. Then I would pour a couple of bottles of water over my head. If I was sure no one was watching me (a rare occurrence) I would stoop down, whip off my T-shirt and soak it under the tap before speedily donning it again. For a few brief seconds the cool tingling damp rippling across my skin was a sensation of utter exquisiteness. I would tie a wet folded bandanna round my head which I repeatedly re-wetted. Then I would wash my feet and drink again.

Although I knew that in hot conditions it's possible to lose up to two litres of sweat a day simply by doing nothing, I didn't even have to try to make myself drink. Cycling over mountains in such stupendous humidity, my body was taking on board over two litres of water an hour. I was constantly drinking, both on and off my bike. Even at night I would drowsily sit up and down a litre with ease. And yet the sweat still poured.

After I'd finished my lunch of riceballs stuffed with seaweed, tin of tuna, cucumber and banana, I stretched out on the bench, lay my soaking wet bandanna over my eyes and tried to dream of snow. It's always the same: when you fry you want to freeze; when you freeze you want to fry. Travelling in a happy medium seemed a hard cookie to crumble.

Tunnel time again. Monster tunnels these. For mile upon mile the road burrowed black through the mountains. My record tunnel day to date was fifty-two in *one day*. Sometimes the tunnels were so choking in lung-clogging exhaust fumes that I nearly keeled over and died. The worst was cycling out of Susaki-shi: the tunnel was so long, so hot, so fume-filled, so up-hill that I turned dangerously light-headed. With legs of lead I forced myself onwards, upwards, chanting a mantra of 'I mustn't faint – I mustn't faint – I mustn't faint.' For to do so would have spelt disaster – capsizing into the path of one of the multitude of trucks grazing past my elbow. Sweat and fumes stung my eyes, my head pounded and throbbed with heat and noise, and yet there was still no sign of light.

I made it, but only just. I collapsed at the side of the road panting like a dehydrated *Tyrannosaurus rex* and poured two litres of water down my rasping, fume-filled throat. The third I sprayed over my head.

Needing to refill my bottles again I stopped at a family-run petrol station up the road. When I asked the man if I could use the *benjo* he looked at me as if I had handlebars growing out of my ears. When I looked in the mirror, I saw why: my face was a filthy wreck – streaked with sooty particulates from the exhaust-ridden tunnel which had stuck to my sweaty face in a blackened film. My eyes, bloodshot and raw, stared back with a glazed and distant emptiness. My hair, plastered with perspiration, stuck in straggles to my neck and brow. What a mess! I sunk my face into the sink and the paper towel on which I dried it looked as if I'd cleaned a chimney with it. But it was an improvement.

Back outside the owner, on discovering I was in fact human (albeit one of those funny foreign ones), said, 'Ah so, you speak King's English!'

Correctly deducing I must be hot, he plunged into his freezer and re-emerged with a frozen fillet of lime-green towel.

'Please,' he said, 'for you souvenir!'

Freezing one's hand towels, I discovered, is a popular culinary delight during a Japanese summer. It's a very practical and ingenious way of wearing a lump of ice round your neck. As it slowly thaws a delicious stream of steady, cold drops drips down your clammy over-heated skin. And, as a bonus it doubles up as a sweat-swipe.

The frozen-towel man, having obviously warmed to me, had more offerings in store; he filled all my water bottles up with iced tea and gave me a bowl of seaweed-wrapped tofu and fermented beans – the latter proving surprisingly tasty.

In dire need of a shower I was aiming to reach the hostel in Kubokawa-cho. The trouble was that daylight was on the wane and the temperature was on the rise (the afternoon had a dispiriting habit of growing hotter despite a sinking sun) and I still had several mountains lying off-puttingly high ahead. But, miraculously, life returned to my legs and as I cycled up and up I began to feel stronger and stronger. These Shikoku mountains, their voluptuous hillsides thick with a lush and carefree green, were so *utsukushii* that they filled me with a vigour that just kept me going and going.

Once over the Nanako Pass I was well on course to reach the hostel, with only another sixteen or so kilometres to go. With the sun sinking into the mountains making the evening (as Thomas Hardy once wrote) 'pinking in a ready', I thought: life's too short to sleep indoors, and so started scouring the land for somewhere to camp. I passed a farmer in a field, herding a handful of cows (the first cows I'd seen in Japan), who looked up and waved a spontaneous wave – there was something about that wave that was more than just a wave and which told me I'd be a fool to ignore it. So, listening to my instincts, I pulled on the brakes, did a U-turn and bumped down on to a track and over the field towards him. The farmer, young and lean with a friendly and rustic face, probably thought: do all *gaijin* think a wave means 'come and say hello?' But, if he did, he responded well to my request to put up my tent in his field. As we were talking three inquisitive faces popped up from behind the back of the barn – not cows, but girls: Michiko, 12, Akiko, 10, and Yuriko, 6 – all the bubbling offspring of young farmer, Tutomo Miyazaki.

After overcoming their initial shyness with Michiko's first sentences of standard text book English ('Harrow! my name is Michiko Miyazaki. I am junior high-school student') things soon loosened up and I was excitedly hand-led by little Yuriko into the barn to watch Tutomo's forty cattle being milked. A tall glass of udder-fresh warm milk appeared in my hand which went down a treat.

Tutomo told me I couldn't possibly camp when they had

room in their house for me just down the road and he rang his wife, Emiko, telling her to expect a visitor. Waiting for Tutomo to finish milking the cows, the girls steered me outside to the wildflower meadow and sat me on a milking stool while they played and romped around me like kittens. Yuriko caught a baby stripe-backed *kaeru* (frog) in her hands and placed it on my knee. Then they asked for an English lesson, so first I read the motto printed on Michiko's tracksuit bottoms:

WHALE POP
Somedays I feel like
smiling at everyone

followed by the motif on Akiko's T-shirt:

GIRLS SPEND MUCH
TIME ♡ DREAMING
BY NATURAL FRIEND

The tricky part came when they asked me what it meant. Was the whale popping, or was it a drink? Maybe it was something to do with whale population or maybe whales are just poppits and make you feel like smiling at everyone. But as for girls spending 'much time (heart) dreaming by natural friend', well, I'm sorry, but I failed on that one.

The Miyazaki home was an attractive old rambling wooden farmhouse – a single-storey collection of compact buildings surrounding a small higgledly-piggledy courtyard. Emiko was warm and welcoming and later admitted to me jokingly that she had been worried when Tutomo rang from the barn saying he had 'charming young lady'. Having deposited my bike and bags, the daughters animatedly announced it was bath-time and trotted me back across the yard to the outhouse bath-house. Michiko handed me a towel and a *yukata* and then I presumed they were just going to leave me to it. But, oh no! The girls speed-wriggled out of their clothes in the 'changing area' – a room lined with black wellington boots – before charging through the glass sliding door into the shoe-box-sized bathroom, dragging me with them into the tiny tiled room.

Before submerging ourselves we perched on plastic milking stools outside the bath as basins of bath water filled and emptied and soap-suds flew. It was wash-anyone-within-sight time and we all set to with giggly enthusiasm, scrubbing each other's back and neck and hair and feet. The colour of my skin caused much merriment and Yuriko became obsessed with trying to wash off my freckles. Meanwhile Akiko could not get to grips with my two-toned skin colour, otherwise known as the undesirable cyclist's sun-tan: a uniform of white shoes, white socks, white shorts and white T-shirt. The rest? A peculiar blend of murky brown and lobster pink.

Scrubbings complete, I dived after my minor charges into the sociably intimate squat-deep blue plastic bath. This was so small that most Europeans would consider it inadequate to wash their feet in, let alone their body, but size, as I discovered, is of no consequence to the ever resourceful-with-space Japanese, and we all soaked and joked together.

Back in the boot room I tied myself up in my light cotton *yukata*. On turning round, Michiku took one look at my gown and raised her cupped hands to her mouth with an expression of exaggerated horror. No, no, no. I had done it all wrong. Always tuck the right side *under* the left because, if it crosses *over* it, this symbolizes death or mourning. Ah so, *desu-ka*?

Yuriko crammed my feet into a pair of terry-towelling slippers whose tops were embroidered with the words:

LOVERY FRIENDS
good life : good sense

Outside in the courtyard the girls introduced me to the rest of the family: Taeheme the dog, Mi the cat and Kozo, the *ojii-san* (grandfather), a skeletal figure clad in a worn-white vest and *suteteko* (the below-the-knee baggy cotton underpants which are much favoured by Japanese men during summer). Kozo spoke no English but, aided by my compact dictionary, shaky understanding and Michiko's odd English-worded help, Kozo explained how he had worked and lived on this farm all his life (although well into his seventies, he still rose at dawn every day to hand-weed or sow or harvest the rice crops) apart from a stint as a fighter pilot during the Second World War. He brought out a musty old album full of slightly grainy black-and-white photographs.

'That's me there . . . and there . . . and there . . .' he said while smiling and pointing to a fine, lean, uniformed young man standing to attention in a row of similarly dressed pilots in their jumpsuits. Behind their heads reared a phalanx of war-planes. I was shockingly intrigued. All I could think of was kamikaze, but I didn't want to mention it. Instead, because I didn't have the words to say what I wanted to say, I said, 'You must be a *yukan* man.' Kozo cast me a look of perplexity as Michiko burst out laughing.

'Excuse me, no, no,' she giggled, 'it is *yukan*, not *yukan*,' which sounded exactly the same to me, and more or less was. But, from what I could gather, I had slightly mis-stressed something somewhere along the line and, instead of telling Kozo he must be a 'brave' man, I told him he must be an 'evening newspaper'.

Turning a few more pages of the album Kozo launched into a rapid burst of Japanese – all words lost on me save for a whip of syllables which hit me with a jerk: Pearl Harbor. Did this gentle grandfather sitting beside me play a part in the out-of-the-blue attack on the American fleet? Were his bombs perhaps responsible for catapulting the US into entering the Second World War? Only a couple of years before I had stood at Hawaii's memorial to Pearl Harbor among mostly American tourists – some quietly weeping – thinking: those cold-blooded Japanese; and now I had just bathed and romped with three of them and I was sitting next to another in his capacious underwear who could very well have been on that catastrophic mission. I asked Kozo if he went to Pearl Harbor and he said, '*Hai, hai*!' along with a lot of other things that I didn't understand and, because Japanese often tend to say 'yes' when they really mean 'no', I couldn't really grasp whether he had or not. Anyway, I didn't really want to know. I wanted to accept and enjoy him as he was now: the good-natured, hard-working *ojii-san* of Michiko, Akiko and Yuriko.

Over a supper of homemade tofu-type cheese with *katsuobushi* (shaved flakes of dried tuna resembling pencil sharpenings) and soy sauce, pickled *kyuri* (Japanese cucumber) salad adrift with scores of miniature silver fish with staring eyes, *suimono* (clear soup), *unagi* (eels), cold *ramen* and the indispensible rice, the television chatted away inanely in the corner. Another games show was followed by another games show – a *gaijin* buffoon sinking himself into a bath of slimy noodles. This was followed by a cookery programme and Tutomo changed channels. Football – World Cup – Switzerland v. Spain. Michiko jumped up and pressed a bi-lingual button on the television which gave me a running commentary in English. Most modern televisions came with this unusual bilingual facility. It was even possible (though pretty pointless) to listen to your programme in both English and Japanese simultaneously, with English coming out of one speaker and Japanese out of the other.

At the end of the football highlights (Spain 3, Switzerland 0) the impeccably suited Japanese presenters bowed traditionally to each other before bowing to me and the Miyazakis, sitting in the kitchen with our mouths full of eel. How Japanese, I thought: to present such a traditional element by such an ultra-modern means of communication – the TV bow.

That night was no great night as far as catching sleep was concerned. I had presumed that I would spend it stretched out on a futon on a small spare space of floor somewhere, but instead I was offered Michiko's bed, along with an added extra – Michiko! It was her honour, she said, to share her bed with a *gaijin* so, despite foreseeing a bad night's sleep ahead of me, I pulled on a brave face along with a clean T-shirt and climbed into a saggy bed surrounded by posters of androgenous young Japanese males posing with their sugar-pop bands.

I knew from the start that sleeping with Michiko would be a disaster. She spent the first hour in fits of giggles at the novelty of having a sun-burnt and freckled foreign devil tossing and turning beside her. Then, excitement over, she promptly fell asleep with a robust snore. Not so me. Every so often a stray slumberous limb would land on top of me together with a wide assortment of airborne livestock of a particularly vicious, blood-sucking variety. The room was so hot and airless that even my tent would have felt like a fridge in comparison.

How, I wondered, could Michiko stand it? Tucked into a pair of thick pyjamas and curled up beneath heavy covers, she looked as if she was hibernating for the winter. If I stayed there for a moment longer I knew I would expire so I quietly rolled on to the floor, tugged off my clammy T-shirt, rummaged in a pannier for my sheet-sleeping bag and then splayed out on top of it – by now too tired to care about the easy feast I presented to the multitude of winged insects. Through the thin *fusuma* paper-walled partition drifted the low soft tones of Tutomo and Emiko talking in bed before they too fell into a partition-penetrating snoring sleep.

CHAPTER 17

The Wooden Fish

The hot days got hotter and the mountains more mountainous. The humidity was so great that my sweating hands kept skidding off my handlebars. To minimize this I wound a flannel on to the tops of my handlebars and had to keep stopping to wring it out. The wet towel which I'd been given was bungeed on to the top of my back panniers. Whenever I reached a source of water I would soak the towel before draping it over my neck and shoulders or twisting it round my head. It had been wetted and dried in the sun so many times that wiping my face with it felt like trying to dry myself on sandpaper.

At Saga-cho another beach was being bulldozed. I found an open-sided wooden shelter with benches so I sat in the shade with a Pocari Sweat and watched a procession of diggers and dumpers and tipper-trucks reorganize the sandy beach into one of concrete. At exactly midday seven workmen joined me in the shelter to speed-eat their *bento.* They looked hot, which was hardly surprising as they were wrapped up in a pale grey uniform of jacket and trousers, boots and belt and suffocating helmet (some of which featured an ingenious detachable sun-brim shaped like a frisbee). If these workmen had been the typical British construction worker they would most likely have been sporting a pair of boots and shorts and I'd be looking at broad backs burnt bronze. But in Japan I never once saw a workman without his shirt on. They may have looked a little sweaty but they were always impeccably turned out – so neat and compact and, well, so tidily similar.

Riding up a mountain pass I was so hot and tired that, at one point, out of the shimmering heat, I saw Jesus walking towards me. I stopped, wiped the cascading sweat from out of my eyes and looked again. Along the road – so hot it looked as wet as the Sea of Galilee – shuffled a sandalled man in white robes. In his right hand he clasped a long wooden staff; on his head he wore a domed straw hat. Praise be! I thought – a Japanese-faced Jesus!

'*Konnichiwa*!' I said, as I paused to swig some water.

'*Konnichiwa*!' he replied with a smile and carried on walking.

He looked exhausted, but he had good reason to be. He was an *o-henro-san* – a devout pilgrim – making a two-month, 1,000-kilometre pilgrimage (called the Shikoku Henro) between the eighty-eight Sacred Temples of Shikoku. This, Japan's most famous pilgrimage, was made in honour of Japan's most revered Buddhist saint, Kukai, who became known as Kobo Daishi after his death. In 807, after a visit to China, Kobo Daishi founded the Shingon sect and his teachings became instrumental in spreading Buddhism throughout Japan. In the spring of 835 Kobo Daishi decided it was high time he passed from this life in order to emigrate to another where he would live with Buddha in the pure Land of Miroku (Miroku being the future Buddha and saviour of the world). So, on 22nd April, after announcing his intentions, he bid *sayonara* to the Emperor and sealed himself into his 'Tardis' tomb. 'Fret not,' he had said to his perplexed disciples, 'I'll be back just as soon as Miroku appears on earth.' And with that he zapped off into his other life, leaving behind him his legacy of eighty-eight Sacred Temples – eighty-eight being the number that is thought to symbolize the eighty-eight worldly passions identified by Buddhist dogma.

Now, over 100,000 pilgrims (many of them, like my oriental Jesus wearing their *kasa* sedge hat and *hakui* white robes bearing the calligraphic motto: 'Daishi and I go together') make the pilgrimage annually. These days, instead of taking to foot with *otsue* (staff) in hand for the full-blown two-month hike, most 'pilgrims' tend to opt for the less demanding two-week bus tour.

I once heard of a man who undertook the pilgrimage in a Tokyo department store skipping among an array of eighty-eight symbolic stepping-stones, each one exhibiting an object from the appropriate temple, before being blessed by a high priest at the end of the whirlwind 'course'.

Outside Nakamura-shi I passed the PIN PON PAN dance hall and the Stone House Joint Café before riding alongside the Shimanto River and entering the city itself. Although

Nakamura is yet another city of concrete, with scarcely an old building remaining, it is still known as 'Little Kyoto': its founder, Norifusa Ichito, a Kyoto nobleman, in 1468 modelled the town after Kyoto. Nakamura itself is just one big breezeblock, but the narrow valley in which it sits can claim to be home to the greatest number of dragonflies in Japan. What's more, one of the sixty-eight species which patrol the valley landed on my handlebar bag as I cycled along, and very splendid it was too.

Because I was hot, thirsty, hungry and tired and because my bicycling wherewithal was wearing-within, I decided to call it a day and sleep in Dragonfly City.

Near the *eki* (railway station) I found a *minshuku* where a rotund *okusama* showed me to a small *tatami* room the size of a coffin and as hot as a furnace. Even standing for ten minutes beneath a cold shower brought little respite. As soon as I'd dried myself off I was sweating again. Back in my coffin-sized sauna I ripped off all my clothes and sat on the futon, panting, as I tried to write my diary. But I didn't have much success: not only was my hand so sweaty I couldn't get a grip on my biro, but, as it inched down the page, it left a dampened sheet of paper in its wake on which my pen refused to write.

A knock on the door, a quick scurry of clothes-donning and a man walked in. (*Minshuku* rarely have doors with locks, which makes life a bit dicy for wandering around with precious little on.) The man was Jun Yokoyama, a workman who was staying at the *minshuku* and with whom I'd had a quick chat at the long communal basin in the corridor where I'd washed my shirt, shorts, socks and smalls. Jun, who already looked decidedly drunk, stood in the doorway and invited me to join him downstairs for a *biru* with his friends.

While we sat in a smoky haze on the floor around a low table with a couple of Jun's colleagues, he told me he was an engineer for KUTV and was spending a few days up a nearby mountain installing new aerials and telecommunication masts. At this point we were joined by Akio, a quiet and slightly bashful young man who worked for Jun and who had just lost 1,600 yen at *pachinko*, which Jun and his workmates thought highly hilarious. Jun spoke a little English because twenty years ago he had spent two years living in Texas, at Fort Bliss air force base.

'But, Jodie-*san*,' said Jun, 'one day I take plane for morning flying and suddenly I thinking my life not made for pilot. Too many responsibility!'

At the drunken insistence of the KUTV team, the gold-toothed and boisterous *okusama* was encouraged to join us. At first she was fascinated by my freckles, before becoming concerned that I would waste away to nothing by cycling over mountains in this heat. Her remedy was to fatten me up with a multi-bowled feast of rice and noodles and *tempura* and pickled octopus tentacles and lashings of iced *oolong-cha*.

That night, although I was utterly exhausted, it was too hot to sleep. So instead I lay in a feverish pool of sweat listening to the radio. At one stage I heard a programme on VOA about plane crashes, one of which was particularly memorable having occurred only three or so months before. It involved a Russian Airbus which crashed near Novokuznetsh, killing all seventy-five people on board. It emerged that the pilot had left his seat to talk to the passengers, handing the controls to his fifteen-year-old son who fancied trying his hand at flying an airliner.

Veering off on a mountainous detour along a coast of dazzling white beaches and hefty cliffs, I saw the first cycle-tourer I had seen since Sheepsaddled Alan. He was Japanese and had what looked like DIY panniers made from sacks which he had strapped over a rear rack in somewhat hazardous fashion. I had stopped at the crest of a small mountain to take a snap of the fetching scene just as the cyclist appeared. I gave him a cheery wave, thinking he might stop to compare notes, but, apart from acknowledging me with a minimal nod of the head, he just kept on going.

Before I rejoined the multi-tunnelled Route 321 I stopped for a midday rest in a small fishing village. The only sittable shade I could find was a low concrete wall that bordered a quiet alley. A woman in a dark store across the way had filled up my water bottles for me and I now sat spraying the contents of one of them slowly down my neck. I was too hot even to eat and anyway I had no appetite for any food I could afford – noodles, rice, bananas, tinned tuna and so on. I tied my small wetted towel around my head while trying to imagine I was lying naked in an igloo and asked myself: what would I really fancy eating now? The answer was easy: a massive great slab of watermelon. But this was wishful thinking – watermelon was way out of my price bracket. Instead I took another few swigs of lukewarm tap water.

A woman, carrying her umbrella for portable shade, came shuffling in her slippers down the street. Espying me sitting on the wall, she slippered over for a chat.

'*Atsui desu-ne*? – So hot, is it not?' she said.

'Ah, *so desu* – that is so,' I replied.

'You are one person?' she asked.

'Yes, that is so – just one – one hot person!'

'Ah so, *desu-ka*? Are you not frightened?'

'Frightened? Frightened of what?'

'Of being one person only. Japanese people do not travel as one person.'

'I feel much safer travelling alone in Japan,' I said, 'than I do in England.'

'Ah so, *desu-ka*?'

The woman lapsed into silence for a moment – not an uneasy silence, just a thoughtful silence, and it gave me a chance to read the motto on her long-sleeved button-down T-shirt:

An honorary
ELEGANCE
Poetic Circles Royalty
Member since 1976
Century Girl

Mrs Century Girl saw me reading her shirt and asked me what it meant.

'I've no idea,' I said, truthfully.

'Ah so, *desu-ka*?'

We passed the time of day for a few more minutes before Mrs Century Girl ambled off around the corner. No sooner had I written her T-shirted motto of honorary ELEGANCE down in my sweaty-paged diary than she re-appeared in front of me bearing an ice box.

'*Dozo* – please – for you,' she said, before removing the lid. Inside were fat ruby-red wedges of *suika* (watermelon), sitting on a bed of ice. It was seventh heaven on a plate and Mrs Century Girl sat smiling and chatting away to me as I sunk my teeth into the sweet, chilled *suika* flesh.

Moments later an *obaasan*, bent double at the hips, slowly pushed her pram-of-produce up the street. She saw me and stopped to exclaim, 'So hot! – is it not?' before asking me if I was alone, if I was frightened, and if I had any children. I replied, 'Yes,', 'No,' and 'None that I know of.' After giving me a tender little pat on my shorted thighs she resumed her shuffle, edging up the street with her trolley-pram.

Before I had managed to summon enough energy to head on my heated and mountainous way, the *obaasan* came shuffling back along the street. Parking her pram at my feet she opened up the seat compartment and pulled out a bag of shopping.

'*Dozo* – please – for you,' she said, 'to give you fine strength.'

I opened the bag. It was a *bento* full of food: *sushi*, riceballs, *tempura*, grapes, cherries, biscuits, cakes, drinks. Before the *obaasan* disappeared she gave me one more thing: a silk fan as fine as a butterfly's wing. 'For making wind,' she said and then she was gone.

Wending down the narrow and virtually traffic-free roads to Cape Ashizuri-Misaki, the southern-most point of Shikoku, was quite unexpectedly stupendous. This small compact peninsula, hanging by a mere sliver of land off Shikoku into the Pacific, is part of the highly impressive Ashizuri-Uwakai National Park and, being subtropical, is a voluptuous tangle of banyan and bamboo, vibrant mosses and vines, ferns and blazing camellia. The road, barely more than a single track in places, twists and turns in excitable extremes, following the rough and rugged coastline of cliffs and clefts that plunge with severe drops into the frothing blue sea.

Once again, after failing to come across a *yusu hosuteru* for days and days, I found not one hostel but two at the top of the Ashizuri Peninsula. I went to investigate and discovered that one of the hostels was in the grounds of Kongofuku-ji Otera, the thirty-eighth temple on the circuit of the eighty-eight Sacred Temples and dedicated to the Thousand-handed Kannon, goddess of Mercy. Kongofuku-ji was surprisingly quiet. Apart from a Japanese couple videoing themselves in front of the gates, I wandered alone in the cloyingly humid evening air beside the pond, pagoda and gently rustling palms that surrounded the temple.

Outside the Kongofuku-ji *yusu hosuteru* hung a rank of stiff, starched, T-shaped *yukata*, their arms threaded on to a long bamboo pole so that, from a distance, they resembled a uniform line of crucified clothing. The hostel looked like an interesting place to stay but, although a shower would have been nice, I didn't want to sleep inside. So instead, I pegged my tent on top of a wild and windy cliff that plummeted down into a cove strewn with rocks washed by crashing seas.

It was so hot the next morning that the road was blistering, causing melted gritty tar to stick to my tyres. Every now and then I had to stop to try to scrape it off as it was starting to clog up between the tyres and the mudguards. As I rode along tarred chippings flicked up, sticking to the back of my T-shirt and legs – some becoming lodged in my hair like hard pieces of chewing gum.

I stopped in a small fishing village to buy a can of tea from a vending machine. The neighbouring machine was for cigarettes and fixed to its front was an advert displaying a sporting-looking cyclist with the words: CLEAN SMOKIN'.

Round the corner I came across the strange sight of a man in a pair of black, calf-high wellington boots raking a sea of chocolate-brown, edible wood. At least, it looked like wood, but when I asked him '*Kore-wa nan-desu-ka*? – What is this?', he said '*Sakana*! – Fish!' Hundreds of thousands of petrified fish were being raked at the roadside and dried in the sun. The man handed me one – a whole fish about the size of my sole and as hard as stone. Across the road was a small old rickety-rackety open-doored fish-factory full of fish and motherly women in black wellies, white aprons and puffy-type shower caps. Looking out of the door and seeing me with a fish in hand and quizzical look on my face, they came trotting along excitedly to sort me out.

'People really eat this?' I asked a moon-faced woman who smelt of fish.

'Ah, that is so!' she said and, after a bit of sifting through my dictionary, I discovered that I too had eaten this fish. These hard lumps of wood were tuna (*bonito*) – the dried shavings of which I had on many occasions eaten as *katsuobushi* with tofu and soy sauce. Amid a profusion of high-spirited giggles the women patiently explained to me (one woman going so far as to draw diagrams in my diary) how the fish were shaved like a fat pencil in a special wooden box made of cedar which slotted together with a sharp blade set at an angle at the top. By grating the *bonito* back and forth across the blade, shavings of fish were produced which collected in the boxed compartment below.

On another mountainous brow the Japanese cyclist passed me again, this time acknowledging me with a quick wave along with the initial nod, but he still didn't stop. And this time he overtook me going the opposite direction, which made me think: is it me or is it him who's cycling in circles?

A crocodile of toddler-sized schoolchildren, topped with white pudding-bowl helmets, their backs strapped into the rigid standard black-leather rucksack-style satchels, were walking unsupervised back from school along the pavement outside Tosashimizu-shi. A group of these lovable little cherubims had stopped to watch with intense fascination a family of dragonflies sunning themselves on some leaves. They were so absorbed in their nature studies that they didn't even notice me stopping to see what they were looking at. It was so heartening to see such young children walking back and forth to school like this – sometimes alone or with just a friend or two – without having to be shepherded by an adult or, as is sadly the case in most parts of Britain, ferried hither and thither in motorized lumps of metal.

After stocking up on food supplies in Sunnymart I went to the bank to change some traveller's cheques. I found Japanese banks to be highly curious places. The first time I walked into one I promptly walked out again because the open layout was such that I thought I had mistaken it for just a normal office. There was no protective wall of glass dividing the customer from the teller-staff; no segregated windows or high-security recessed cubbies in the counter in which your money transaction slid back and forth; and, surprisingly, there was no great air of efficiency. Indeed, most Japanese banks, even those sitting in the rich heart of Tokyo, did not give the impression of being the largest financial institutions in the world.

Behind an easy-to-hurdle (i.e. easy-to-rob) chest-high counter (Japanese chest-high, that is) would be a usually rather cluttered and cramped open-plan office, full of staff flurrying back and forth with armfuls of bureaucratic paper-work. Rare was the occasion when I could be in and out of a bank within five minutes. The general procedure for being served was reminiscent of a doctor's waiting-room. You would join a stack of people piling up on rows of soft-plastic easy chairs leafing through a vast assortment of magazines and explicit *manga* which the bank provided. Although it could take anything up to fifty minutes to be called up to the counter by a sing-song teller girl, I would usually be served within half an hour. However, at one bank in Naha I had to leave my 'papers' for four hours to be processed through the antiquated system and return later – just to change $150 in traveller's cheques.

One of the main reasons why banks are such bottlenecks is that Japan is very much a cash-in-hand society. Personal cheques are rarely used, which means that every hefty purchase necessitates a separate visit to the bank and a separate wait – a curiously old-fashioned and time-consuming exercise for such a forward-marching country. Paying by credit card is still rare: my Mastercard was only recognized once and I was forced to apply for a Visa card, which resulted in slightly more success. Cash was definitely the preferred medium for transactions. Real money is held in great respect. It is never creased or torn or scrawled on or so insanitary-looking that you want to scrub your hands after handling it. *O-kane* (money) is one of those hallowed words which automatically acquires the honorific '*o*' prefix no matter what the relative status of the speaker.

Another oddity was that nobody ever seems to sign for anything. In fact, your signature is as good as useless for getting into your account, or for that matter anyone else's. All that is needed is a *hanko* (personal seal) – which every Japanese person carries and uses to sign legal documents – plus the bankbook.

But lengthy queuing and inconvenient service tills could all be forgiven because I found Japanese banks to be a bit like the end of a children's birthday party. Once my transaction was finally complete I would be presented with a going-home gift: tissues, towels, pens, pads, plasters, sweets, soap, bacofoil, socks or even company-motif toilet-paper.

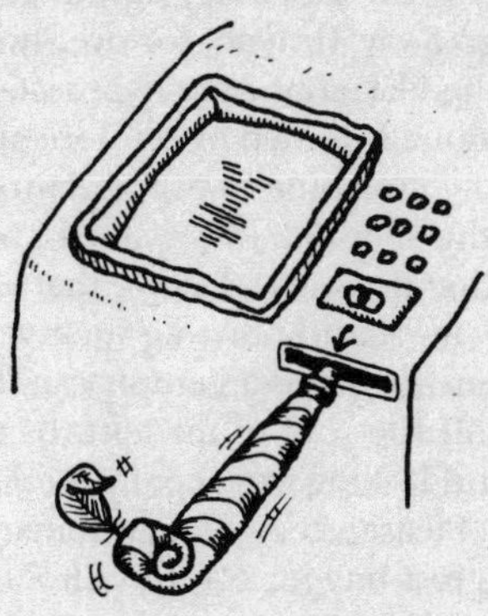

That night I spent just outside Sukumo-shi, camping in a pristine park jutting out to sea on a windy promontory. In order to avoid the frying rays of the rising sun I pitched my tent in the shadow of the only structure that would provide me with a modicum of shade the following morning: a large, wooden-slatted children's climbing frame. As it was almost dark by the time I stooped under the frame to put up my tent, I didn't think my choice of sleep-spot would be a hindrance to any potential children at play the next morning as I planned to be gone by dawn. All went well, for a while. I washed myself under the public tap, rinsed out my clothes, ate a tea of tuna, rice balls and bananas, drank three litres of water, wrote a letter, wrote my diary, listened to 'We get the world talking' Radio Netherlands, oiled my chain, patched up a pannier, met a woman who gave me a packet of *bisuketto* and a dainty Japanese purse, brushed my teeth, marvelled at a highly spectacular sunset and crawled into my sauna in preparation for another sweaty slumber. I had fallen into an over-heated sleep for about an hour when I was suddenly woken up by the sound of several pairs of footsteps clambering up the climbing frame and on to the ramp above me. The feet belonged, not to children, but to a group of high-spirited and giggly friends in, I guessed, their late teens, early twenties. I lay very still, listening, thinking: please go away. But they didn't go away. Instead, for over two hours they sat yattering, sounding like a bunch of hyperactive chimpanzees, their troop occasionally joined by reinforcements, clattering up the ramp to the gossiping hot-spot platform on top.

Tucked into the shadows in my small green camouflage tent I could tell that no one was aware that a mere foot from their feet a *gaijin* lay silently cursing their very existence. At one point someone dropped an empty can through the slats and it bounced off the roof of my tent. By this stage, tired, peeved, sweaty and lacking in sleep, my initially polite pleading thoughts of 'Please go away' had metamorphosed into 'Aaargh – please just bugger off, the whole splattering nattering lot of you!' When an empty bottle bounced off my home I had to hold myself back from raging like a mad woman, semi-naked, out of my tent, storming up the ramp and screaming blue murder at the top of my pent-up voice. But feeling that such a reaction would do little to help make the world a happier place I resigned myself to eating a banana instead.

After another hour of listening to their incessant clamour, the fireworks started. Boomph! Pow! Phroooom! Gaa! Although the *hanabi* (literally, fire-flowers) were being set off at least fifty yards away it still sounded as if I was under aerial attack. The fiery explosions were not the sort of noise to induce a good night's sleep but they did at least have one advantage: they attracted the attention of the chattering chimps, who all clattered off the climbing frame to get a closer taste of the action.

By now, desperate for a pee and feeling my way was clear, I was about to extricate myself from my tent when I realized that there was a couple who were still left on top. The trouble was that it soon became evident that this couple was not just any old couple of this or that but a copulating couple. Purlease, I thought, this is all I need – incarcerated in my tent in a state of urgency while being besieged by the too-close sound effects of a fumbling sexual encounter in stereo. Why hadn't someone like the *bisuketto* lady warned me that this was Lover's Park? Why hadn't there been a sign attached to the climbing frame saying: 'Midnight Caution: Coition in Progress'? And what's more, to add to my discomfort, the love-doves above were not quick workers. The more I listened, thinking, 'Come on – get a bloody move on,' the more urgent my intended toilet mission became. I felt a strong urge to crawl out suddenly from beneath them and remark, 'Oh, good evening! Did you by any chance drop these?' handing back the empty beer bottles. But this was not quite the moment to adopt a public-spirited persona nor to disclose that they were carrying on in such close proximity to a barbarian's nigh-exploding bladder. When I had hit danger level, there was nothing else for it but to fill any available receptacle, and fast. It was a very strange sensation to be on my knees, peeing into my lunchbox with a couple of lovebirds going hammer and tongs just above my head – it was the sort of faintly ludicrous situation that makes you think: if only my mother could see me now!

By now I was fairly well conditioned to coming across strange sights on a daily basis. But one sight I was most certainly not prepared for appeared on a hill on the outskirts of Johencho. Just before a tunnel a car overtook me, slowed and stopped. The driver's door opened and out stepped a solid, red-headed *gaijin*. In my world of slight, black-headed people, this was a very strange sight. I stopped and stared.

'Boy!' he said. 'It sure ain't every day you see a foreigner on the road. Had to stop. You from the US or Oz?'

'UK,' I said.

'Jeez – a European! Well, hi! The name's Red. Real pleased to meet you.' And he offered me a big sweaty hand shaped like a shovel. 'You got a moment? Be great to talk.'

'Yes,' I said, 'I've always got a moment for a rest.'

'Yeah? That's great.'

So we stood in the sun, sweating away, having a chat. Red, whose business card said Clarence (Red) Stoltfus, was an Amish senior quality engineer from Milpitas.

'That's the Bay Area,' he said, 'California.'

His company, Quantum, had sent him overseas for a two-year stint in Shikoku. Having digested this sudden surge of information (which, for someone who hadn't been spoken to in English for several weeks, almost sent my brain into immediate overload), I latched on to the interesting mention of the Amish.

'So you're originally from the East Coast?' I asked.

'You got it,' said Red. 'Pennsylvania. Lived in an Amish community till I was twenty. My folks – in fact most of my family – are still there. But I was getting kinda bored. Fancied seeing a bit more of the world. So I headed west – California. Jeez – talk about a culture shock! Put me in good stead though for Japan!'

'How do you like it here?' I asked.

'Well,' said Red, 'it's a kind of love–hate relationship. More love than hate, though. Wouldn't mind staying another two years. It's a good life. Know what? Back home I get two weeks' vacation. Here, its two-and-a-half months! Now you can't beat that!'

'No,' I said, 'that sounds pretty good.' I asked Red how easy it was to slot into the Japanese workplace. Were there many misunderstandings?

'Sure,' he said. 'It's taken me about a year to be accepted into the company. For months I was treated real cold. Still am in many respects. A day's work is full of misunderstandings. You know, you've got to conduct business from a completely new approach. It's a new world. You can't go direct. You've got to work round the sides. Gently. It takes time and, boy – patience! Move too fast or get too pushy and the Japs can get real mad. But they don't express it in an explosion of anger like us guys from the West. Instead your ratings plummet and you're treated like ice. It's not nice. I'd prefer someone to scream in my face. At least that way you know what you're up against. But I guess you've got to respect the Japanese way. After all, it sure works well for them!'

'Are there many women in your company?' I asked.

'Just the OLs – you know, Office Ladies. Doing all the hum-drum jobs – teas, coffees, photocopies, that sort of thing. Not so long ago we had a lady engineer from the States come over to work as a regional branch manager. She knew her stuff all right. In fact, she was a whole lot better than the guy from home she'd replaced. But the Japs – they just couldn't stick a woman holding such responsibility. Japanese life is still very segregated. Know what? One of my colleagues came up to me and said, "Red, do you honestly think a woman can be as good as a man?" I mean, jeez, what do you say to that?'

By now we were both sweating profusely – Red's blue sweatshirt stuck to his portly paunch. It was time to get moving.

'Say,' said Red, 'you ever find yourself in the Bay Area, make sure you look me up!'

'Thanks,' I said, 'I will.'

Not long after leaving Red I saw the Japanese cyclist again. This time he stopped. He spoke no English but I managed to glean he was a policeman taking his annual eight-day leave by cycling around Shikoku. But he wasn't getting as far as he wanted because of the heat. Up close I noted that his panniers were indeed made from pieces of sacking, covered in plastic and tied on with twine.

Route 56 was another road of tunnels. These days, though, it was so hot that, despite hating tunnels, I also rather welcomed them for the shade, albeit polluted shade, which they offered. If I wasn't competing for space with a multitude of dumper-trucks then the shorter tunnels could almost be described as enjoyable – certainly more so than plunging back out into a dazzling fireball of heat.

Sometimes I even stopped in a tunnel to eat my lunch and put my feet up. Not a motor-traffic tunnel, but the pedal-pedestrianized ones which I sometimes found alongside. They could always be guaranteed to provide two much sought-after conditions: complete shade and a welcome racing draught.

Not far out of Uchiumi-mura I stopped at a roadside noodle-shop to fill up on water. Being mid-afternoon the place was empty save for the *okusama* and a stocky dumpling of a cook who were perched on stools watching sumo on a television suspended from the ceiling. My apologies for disturbing them were rapidly waved aside and I was offered a stool at the bar as my request for water resulted in a free mountain of *udon* – a tangle of chilled white tapeworm-shaped noodles, served with separate small, dainty bowls of soy sauce, spring onion and chopped ginger. *Okusama* kept my liquid levels topped up with lashings of iced greeny-brown tea.

When I finished eating I made ready to leave but *okusama* insisted I stay for longer, telling me it was far too hot to go cycling up mountains. 'Ah so!' she said when I told her of my plans to cycle around Japan. 'You *gaijin* are all *baka* – foreign fools!'

What with *okusama* playfully fussing over me, keeping me lubricated to a tee, I was certainly in no great hurry to leave this air-conditioned haven for the mind-numbing, sweat-pouring heat outside. So I sat back, propped my elbow on the bar, my head on my hand and spent an hour watching sumo.

The size of the *rikishi* (wrestlers) beggared belief – massive mounds of flesh thrashing together momentarily like mountains of rippling blancmange. Their girths were so gargantuan that their tree-trunk sized arms, unable to hang vertically down their sides, were forced into an elevated curve. Most *rikishi* weigh between 250 and 350 pounds (110 to 160 kilograms) although Konishiki, the legendary six-foot-two Samoan–Hawaiian heavyweight, reached a crushingly phenomenal 576 pounds (261 kilograms). A man of cartoon proportions, his waist (if you could find it) measured six feet. He was not nicknamed the Dump Truck for nothing. He required two first-class seats with the middle arm-rest removed whenever he flew home to Hawaii.

During the early 'nineties it was widely rumoured that Konishiki (born Saleeva Atisanoe) would be the first alien to attain *yokozuna* (grand champion) status. But the all-powerful Japanese Sumo Association decreed that, while his results were acceptable, he lacked the necessary *hinkaku*, an intangible quality encompassing the dignity, prestige, humility and spiritual purity demanded by the Shinto gods.

Instead the accolade went to Akebono, another mammoth Hawaiian (six foot eight, and 470 pounds) who became only the sixty-fourth wrestler (and the first foreigner) to have been awarded the title of *yokozuna* since records began in 1750.

As a result of his success Akebono (whose name means 'dawn' – although his real name is a slightly less romantic Chad Rowan) was rewarded with a basic salary of £120,000 a month, around £1 million a year in gifts from his stable-master (the stables, or *beya*, being the abodes where sumo wrestlers sleep and train), private fan club and corporate sponsors, a choice of six slaves to wait on him hand and foot and the pick of the most beautiful Japanese women who, oddly, find such leviathans irresistible. Never are *rikishi* in want of a wife or a date: their prestige and glamour triumph over their unprepossessing and exaggerated bodies. Indeed, Sumika, the Dump Truck's wife, was not only stunning, but also slimmer than one of her husband's legs.

Sumo, pronounced '*s'mo*', is the oldest and most popular sport in Japan, dating back as far as the third century, and began as a religious exercise when young men wrestled in the courtyards of Shinto shrines to amuse the gods.

The wrestling takes place on a raised ring, or *dohyo*, made of packed clay which, despite having twenty small rice-straw bales sunk into it, is as hard as concrete. The wrestler's goal is to force his opponent to touch the surface of the *dohyo* with some part of his body (other than the soles of his bare feet), or to set foot out of the ring. This happens fast: the average round lasts between six and ten seconds.

Like *tatami*, the *dohyo* can never be trodden upon with shoes but, unlike *tatami*, it must never be stepped upon by women because of their impurity.

Although encrusted with centuries-old ceremony, sumo transmits perfectly on Japanese television. Wherever I went during the fourteen-day *basho* (tournaments), televisions in restaurants, bars, shops, garages and homes or, in some cities, massive screens rigged up in parks or shopping centres, would be switched on to sumo.

Cameras would home in on the huge near-naked men (their only garment being a *mawashi* – silk loincloth) performing their pre-wrestle ritual of stamping and squatting and puffing and throwing-of-salt (for purification) before the actual addictive-viewing massive collision of flesh.

One of the many curious things that struck me about sumo was that, compared with the West's form of wrestling, which seems to inevitably attract a somewhat bawdy crowd, the Japanese audience sits politely and neatly, either intent on the happenings of the ring or busily tucking into delicate subdivided trays of food and *sake* served by boys who resemble the extras in a *kabuki* drama.

Every Japanese schoolboy with a spare bit of flab fantasizes about a sumo career, but most of those who pursue their dreams find that the reality is, apart from all the eating and drinking, a hard and monastic existence, full of injury. They live in their own castle, in the special stables, segregated from daily life. They grow long hair. When they're not sleeping or training, they achieve their elephantine size by eating . . . and eating . . . and eating . . . and eating. Not McDonald's, *keiki* and *aisu-kuriimu* but special dustbin-sized cauldrons of *chanko-nabe*, a hearty 'wrestler's stew' of beef, pork, chicken, fish, shiitake mushrooms, Chinese cabbage, carrots, tofu, spring onions and Popeye's spinach, accompanied by assorted side dishes of thick buckwheat noodles, aromatic pickles, deep-fried shrimps, a private mountain of boiled rice and a constant supply of beer and *sake.*

But beneath all this blubber (or, as Lord Mitford called it, 'monstrous mountains of adipose tissue') lie muscles of steel. The wrestlers train by striking at a *teppo* – a bare wooden pole, which acts as their punching bag – until their hands and forearms are as solid as rock and as damaging as bludgeons.

It was while I was in mid-flight, hurtling down one of many mountains that graced the splendid Uwajima coastline, that a large and particularly unpleasant stinging winged insect flew down my shirt and got lodged in my bra. Now, trying to negotiate hazardous hairpins at a speed of forty miles per hour with a heavily laden mount is one thing; trying to do it while simultaneously attempting to extricate a potentially lethal biting insect crawling over your mammaries is quite another. The main concerns are not to go to pieces by flapping the invaded item of clothing around in a hysterical panic and, of course, not to come to grief in the sudden pandemonium by flying off the edge of the mountain. Although I failed on the first, I fortunately succeeded in the second. Plummeting down the mountain with a car up your bum and your head down your chest monitoring the said interloper's movements, while attempting to bring yourself to a safe halt at the side of the road, is not easy but I managed it, much to the bemusement of passing motorists. My next preoccupation was trying to hoick the hornet-like blighter out before it deposited its fearsome ammunition into a sensitive bosom. Turning my back to the road I lifted my T-shirt up to my neck and tried to flick this alarmingly large, proboscidean insect out of my portside 'cup' but only helped it to become lost in the clammy folds of my shirt.

Now I know removing one's shirt at the side of the road in full view of passing motorists is not the best way to blend unnoticed into the landscape, but when you've got a bloody great hornet lost in your clothing, such concerns tend to take a back seat. Thus, off came my T-shirt, which I vigorously flapped and shook around to try to dislodge the blessed beast. Heaven knows what the passing traffic thought of a topless (save for brassiere) *gaijin* hopping from foot to foot like a wild thing at the side of the road. I felt as if I was marooned on the proverbial desert island semaphoring my wherabouts to a passing ship with my rag of a T-shirt. Anyway, the outcome was that Japanese suspicions that all *gaijin* are buffoons were probably confirmed, while the *gaijin* in question succeeded in avoiding being stung on the breast, but not on the hand. It was not a sting to be recommended but, as they say, better your mitt than your nip.

Just as I was climbing back into a safely vacated T-shirt, who should come swanning round the corner but the cycling policeman. Without stopping he held a disposable camera to his face, aimed in my direction – snap! – and then, with a nod and a smile, he was gone.

I was about to enter a long, hot noisy tunnel outside Uwajima when a truck driver tooted as he overtook me, prior to pulling over and stopping at the side of the road. As I approached he leant out of his window and offered me a ride. Not particularly keen to entrust myself to the whims of a lift-giving trucker, I called back the Japanese equivalent of 'Not today, thanks!', a reply that didn't deter him from lobbing down from his cab a pack of three thin strips of sweat-absorbing hand towels (a similar model of which he wore tied round his head) and two cans of iced Asahi beer.

'*Ganbatte*!' he shouted over the noise of his engine, before being swallowed by the tunnel.

I arrived in Uwajima early evening. As I had planned to camp that night, I cycled along to Warei Koen to find a little nook in which to install myself. But the park was packed with people sitting and playing and smoking and drinking and thinking.

As I sat on a stone bench eating my supper and waiting to see if the place would quieten down, four boys – maybe about twelve years old – set upon two smaller boys who were playing together on their bikes. The older boys laid into their victims by kicking them off their bikes and shouting aggressively. Then one of the older boys, a particularly nasty looking piece of work, spat in the small boys' faces before jumping up and down on the front wheel of one of the bikes until it buckled. The boy whose bike it was dissolved into hysterical tears while his friend delivered a couple of thumps to the aggressor. This all happened very fast but, out of the large crowd of people (me included) who were sitting around or walking on by and had witnessed the attack, not one person intervened. I vaguely thought a Japanese parent would resolve matters, but when I realized no one was going to do anything about the boys who were still tugging and kicking at each other, I felt I had to do something before the smaller boys or their bikes sustained any further damage. Feeling (rightly) that every face in the park was staring at me, I sidled up to the scrum and, acting as international peace-maker, I said, 'Don't fight; have a biscuit,' and offered them a pick of fancy *bisuketto* from a pack I'd been given. Judging from the expressions of the boys, not to mention the spectators, what I had done was very un-Japanese and I couldn't have felt more like a *gaijin* if I had tried. Not wanting to attract even more attention to myself, I then aborted all plans of camping in the park and went to look for a place to stay.

After a lot of cycling around in circles I found what I was looking for – a *minshuku.* But the *okusama* who answered the door said it was *ippai* (full). Feeling hot and sticky and sweaty and tired, this was not a welcome answer, so I turned on my woeful-lost-alone-and-far-from-home look of despondency and asked her if she knew of anywhere else in the area. The *okusama,* a kindly-faced dame in her forties, told me to '*chotto matte kudaisai*' before disappearing behind a sliding screen. So I dutifully waited, and waited, until I began to think that maybe, rather than saying an out-and-out 'no' (out-and-out noes being very un-Japanese), she was shyly hovering behind the sliding walls, willing me to go away. Just as I was about to retreat the *okusama* reappeared with a smile, inviting me to, please, come in. She had a room for me, she said, if I didn't mind it being the one where her guests ate their meals. She slid open a door to reveal a small box of a *tatami* room where about half a dozen workmen were on the floor at low tables spread with a plethora of small round dishes. They all bid me a hearty welcome. Okusama chided them good-naturedly and told them to hurry up so that the 'honourable *gaijin*' could have some peace.

Instead of waiting to clear the room she invited me to take a bath and use her washing machine, which I happily and readily did. On my return downstairs I found my room with a futon rolled out and a tray of tea-things laid on the table. The words on the tall fat flask of hot water were:

PRINCESS FLOWER
There are nice goods nearby.
Come hither, come hither, come hither.

The room was windowless save for a small paper opening which looked into a concrete garage containing a white Nissan Sunny 'Fam-i-lee car' and another of those daft-looking Toppo Minica QZs.

Usually, the thought of sleeping in a windowless air-conditioned box would put me in a very edgy state indeed but here in Minshuku Mihara it didn't bother me in the least. Sick of sweating and wanting to experience the unusual sensation of feeling cold again, I dispensed with my scruples and switched on the air-conditioner, bringing the temperature rocketing down to a blissfully chilly 12°C. I revelled in the fact that I had goosebumps. For the first time since arriving in Japan I wore my fleece, thick socks and woolly hat. All I hoped was that *okusama* would not walk in as I would find my attire tricky to explain. Then, also for the first time since being in Japan, I eagerly wormed my way into my downy sleeping bag, tucking the hood around my head and pulling the drawstring tight. I was almost too cold to sleep but this rare freezing sensation brought me great pleasure.

The following morning I was gone by 10.30, but not before I had caught the televized weather forecast. The weatherman, as always, was waving his long, slender pointer over the enlarged map of Japan looking more in a position to conduct an orchestra than to reveal the whereabouts of the sun. He was announcing how Japan was currently a country cut in half: while the south was sweltering in the hottest summer for fifty years, with temperatures scorching into the high thirties and humidity 100%, the north was awash in a quagmire of severe storms and floods. For once I felt I was in the right place, even if it was at the wrong time.

As I folded up my washing (there's nothing like a bundle of clean clothes to give you a buoyant boost) and packed it tight into a pannier, I heard on the American airwaves of Monitor Radio International how a radical and obvious Francophobe English MP was trying to ban all French words from the English language. 'He thinks they're bastardizing our speech! The guy's gotta be crazy!' spluttered the presenter with understandable distaste. 'If he gets his way, this means we'll have no *à la carte*, no *nom de plume*, no *café*, no *brasserie*, no *baguette*, no *croûtons*, no *coup de grâce*, no *nouvelle cuisine* – though that could be no bad thing – and no *rendezvous*.' How was the MP going to go about prohibiting the use of thousands of English words derived from French ones? One bright idea of his was to enlist traffic wardens to keep not only 'an eye open', as they usually do, but also 'an ear open' on the streets for anyone heard using French, and issue them with a ticket accordingly.

A Cockney traffic warden was interviewed and asked what he thought of this brainwave of enrolling him to rid the English language of French idioms. He said, 'We get 'nuff abuse as it is for doling out parking tickets. The bloke's a nutter!'

There were two things I wanted to see before I left Uwajima. One was a *togyu-jo*, or bullfight, and the other was the Taga-jinja – a shrine totally devoted to sex.

For Japanese bullfights, you don't have to be a bloody-sported supporter as no blood is spilt. Instead, the *togyu-jo* is more like bovine sumo where a *seko* (trainer) goads the bulls into 'wrestling' together until one has forced the other out of the ring. Anyway, I never got to see a *togyu-jo* because the vividly colourful posters stuck to walls and lamp posts and shop windows around the city told me I was two weeks too early.

I had more success as far as the sex shrine was concerned. This really was a most extraordinary place and included a three-storey museum packed with a bizarre collection of erotica from all over the world. It came into existence many a blue-movie ago when Shinto shrines were tied up with fertility rites. But following the Meiji Restoration, the puritanical killjoys from the West were so shocked by what they found that they set about systematically purging the shrines of all sexual innuendo. However, a steadfast smattering of shrines remained, Taga-jinja being the main survivor.

The courtyard around the shrine was filled with phallic carvings – one, fashioned from a tree trunk, was so large that it had to be displayed on its side on a sturdy support. Dotted around were statues of decidedly penile-looking Buddhas and immense vaginas carved and chiselled out of wood and stone.

I followed a clutch of sheepishly giggling young women through the doors of the museum. Here I was greeted by a ludicrous collection of phallic this and vagina that. Dainty *geisha* dolls gaily slid down hills on penis-shaped sledges beside small models of masturbating Buddhas lost in Seventh Heaven. There were leather cushions with strategically positioned holes and pictures of mating frogs and platypuses and hippopotamuses. A photograph of a woman showed her hard at it with a large fluffy dog, while another showed a cat licking a woman's clitoris. There were modern porn mags and early Japanese *shunga* (pornographic prints) and Tibetan tantric sculptures and explicitly moulded South American pottery, and even suggestively shaped clothes pegs designed to represent coupling couples.

On top of all that was a most unappetizing exhibit of pubic hair, collected at the turn of the century by a certain Dr Kato, who had gone to all the trouble of cataloguing the details of the provider by name, age, occupation and region. It was all most bizarre and, by the third floor, saturation point had well and truly set in so I headed back out into the heat, foregoing the temptation of purchasing an assortment of phallic key rings and sexual aids from the souvenir shop to send my mother, preferring instead to save my money for a banana and a packet of seaweed.

KYUSHU
TSUKUSHI MOUNTAINS
Saiki
site of Jools Holland cardboard cut-out
&
Italian Tomato Cakeshop
Mt. Aso
Kumamoto
Gokase River
KYUSHU MOUNTAINS
Nobeoka
PETRO CHEMICALS
Hyuga
POP
Furue (site of first & only puncture in this whole Japanese Jaunt
wild(ish) horses area
Kagoshima
Miyazaki (real lips coffee Bar)
Aoshima (mountain products man Island)
OSUMI PENINSULA
home of Coca-cola roller skating mother
Cape Toi-misaki (Asia's largest light house & horse-head telephone box*)
Cape Satamisaki (southernmost point of main Islands)
north
50 MILES
80 KLIX
* Maybe the largest H-H-T-Box in Asia

CHAPTER 18

Realips Realife

It was time to hop on a boat and switch islands again. I liked places which were made up of so many different bits and pieces scattered about the seas or lumps of land severed or subdivided by multiple clefts of water. Hawaii is like that; so too are Norway, New Zealand and Iceland, the Hebrides, the Faeroes and part of British Columbia. All awe-inspiring watery islands for a cycle.

I had booked myself on the 3 a.m. ferry to Kyushu. Although there had been sailings at 7 p.m. and 11 p.m., I chose the most undesirable hour of 3 a.m. for two reasons: I would arrive in Kyushu at 5.30 a.m. – a better time to arrive in a new city than the middle of the night; and I would save the worries of having to find a night's accommodation. And, anyway, I simply fancied a pre-dawn voyage.

I spent the evening before the boat set sail sitting on the long narrow strip of concrete pier eating my supper, writing my diary and watching the sunset-streaked fishing boats chugging out to sea. Slowly, I was joined on my three-sea-sided perch by an assortment of fishermen dressed in an interesting combination of clothing: one, a salary-looking man, wore an office shirt and tie, blue suit bottoms and a pair of flip-flop slippers. Another, an elderly man, arrived in his long, baggy white underwear; while another sat fishing in a kimono garment alongside a couple of lads, eighteen or nineteen years old, wearing immaculate polo shirts tucked into expensively belted, lightweight check-flecked trousers that well-to-do Frenchmen always seem to favour – but this whole Parisian effect was knocked for a burton when I spotted their footwear: a pair of traditional clip-clop *geta* clogs.

This was one of the reasons why I found Japan so appealing. It was such an enchantingly topsy-turvy place, with imported ideas flipped inside out and back to front, all rubbing shoulders with century-old traditions in such beguiling ways.

After a while two old *yukata*-clad women came clacketing along in their high-heeled wooden *geta*, out for their evening's perambulation of the pier. All the fishermen seemed known to them as they paused at each one in turn for a spot of good-humoured banter. Finding a foreign fish in their midst came as something of a 'Gaa! *Gaijin*!' surprise, but being full of warmth and curiosity they hitched up their *yukata*, revealing knobbly-veined legs, before squatting down on either side of me, sandwiching me between their soap-smelling skins.

Was I America? No, England. Is that England near America? Am I alone? Yes? Gaa! Where do I sleep? Am I not afraid? Where am I going? Kyushu? The land where the hot-tempered people are from – ha! ha! By now a group of the oddly clothed fishermen had joined us and opened bottles of beer and a hefty five-litre container of *sake* which was rapidly doing the rounds. After a while the two swaddled *obaasan* announced it was time to hit their futon and rose to leave, but not before one of them offered me her silk *sensu* (hand-held fan). 'Japanese *o-miyage* – souvenir,' she said, before adding, '*Ki-o-tsukete* – Take care. Bye bye.'

I stayed another two hours sitting with the fishermen, who were by now well and truly flushed with *sake*. There can't be many countries where a lone female can sit out on a limb on the end of a pier into the night with a bunch of raucously drunk men and not have to worry about her safety. The fishermen's collective honour and duty were so innate that I never once feared things could get out of hand.

I would have slept a couple or so hours on the pier while waiting for the ferry had not the salt-water cockroaches appeared, scuttling all over the concrete in fast jerky movements. Definitely not a promising nightcap for a pleasurable few dreams, so I rolled up my groundsheet and pushed my bike back down to the ferry 'terminal' – a flimsy, claustrophobic port-a-cabin of a waiting room. The 11 p.m. ferry had come and gone, which had caused a small flurry of activity before it emptied again. All was quiet. The only person around was the night-watchman who was locking up the port-a-cabin's doors. When he saw me he thought I'd missed the 11 p.m. ferry.

'No,' I said, 'I'm waiting for the 3 a.m. boat.' I was hoping I could wait in the waiting room.

'Mmmmmmm,' he mmmmmed. 'People are not allowed to wait in waiting room.'

'Ah so, *desu-ka*?' I said. 'So what is allowed to wait in waiting room?'

'Mmmmm,' he said, looking slightly uncomfortable. I didn't want to make him feel uncomfortable but then, I also didn't want to sleep among the cockroaches.

'Go on, be a devil,' I said, as best I could in Japanese.

And a devil he was: he let me stay – but he locked all the doors (please God, don't let there be a fire), closed all the windows, turned out all the lights and told me not to tell anyone. So I gave him a beer and he gave me a map and then he locked himself into a little dark cubbyhole whose tiny window looked out into the waiting room. It was through this window that the only light shone – dancing shadows from his television screen.

I lay down on one of three 'Enjoy Coca Cola Coke' red benches with only a cacophony of mosquitoes for company. After a lot of swatting I was launched briefly into dream mode – trying to deliver packs of TDK tapes by Chinook helicopter into a highly active war-zone. Lots of guns, lots of bombs, lots of near hits, but I managed to land and was immediately surrounded by friendly troops who applauded my attempt at getting their TDK tapes to them – but then it was discovered I'd left them behind and I suddenly found myself at home, in the small churchyard of Iping Marsh where there used to be a church before it was demolished (lack of funds), and I was standing beside the gravestones at the top of the slope looking down to the gate, where there was some stock-car racing taking place and a van was continuously careering up and down, skidding all over the place, and the driver was laughing and I knew he was going to crash so I shouted at him to stop but it was no good as the van lurched into the air, landed on its roof and rolled over and over down the hill, and then there was an earthquake and the next thing I knew the boat had arrived from Kyushu and I felt exhausted.

The first thing I saw when I rolled off the ferry into a rosy red dawn was Jools Holland. Only instead of exercising his phenomenal fingers on the keyboards, he appeared as a cardboard cut-out advertising something outside a chemist shop for Yunker Kotel Solution – whatever *that* was.

Wanting to extract myself from the city before it got too busy I rode out of Saiki-shi past the Italian Tomato Cake Shop, past bent forms working in the paddy fields, over a hundred mountains and through a thousand tunnels, until just outside Kitaura-cho I arrived at Official Campsite No. 2 – the only one I'd seen since Fuji. Compared with the litter-laden, smashed glass-gravel ground of Fuji this was a joy: white sand, blue sea, big waves, tall pines, tufty grass, shade, showers, no cars in camping area – all for a very nice 100 yen (60p) a night. There were flying-fish, too.

Kitaura Shimoaso Beach Resort was definitely not a place to pass on by so I rode back to the town, stocked up on food supplies in a small family store (they wouldn't let me pay), rode back and stayed three nights. The first night, apart from a couple who had rented one of the seven spanking new two-storey air-conditioned wooden cabins for 10,000 yen (£60) a night, I was the only one staying so it was wonderfully quiet: just the sound of the wind in the pines and the surging wash of the waves. But, come the weekend, the masses appeared. One group of campers – all workmates from the Miyazaki ferry company – planted their marquee tent virtually on top of me and set up an elaborately pounding music system powered by a hefty great generator.

Others followed in much the same vein, all in groups, lots of shouting, lots of music, lots of raucous laughter, lots of fireworks all through the night. I felt I must be getting old when I found such rowdy behaviour grating on my nerves – all I wanted to hear was the soothing songs of the sea rather than the gushing wishy-washy wails of Japanese puppy-love pop reverberating out of the mother of all sound systems.

It surprised me to see such inconsiderate actions emanating from a people who, up until now, I had mostly found to be full of faultless thoughtfulness. Was I guilty of stereotyping, I wondered? Did I think I could pigeon-hole the Japanese into something that I imagined them to be rather than what they actually were? Maybe I did. Their behaviour wouldn't have hit me with such a jolt had every camper been in wild party spirit (after all, why shouldn't they let their hair down as surely, of all people, they deserve to, coming as they do from a supposedly conformist society) but there were clutches of more elderly Japanese too who didn't look exactly cheered by the actions of their fellow countrymen.

To confuse matters more, I then became part of the problem when I was inundated with invitations to join barbecuing groups here and well-inebriated drinking parties there for fun and food. Hypocritically I took everyone up on their offer and entered the fray.

The food was delicious – lots of skewered octopus and squid and barbecued cabbage and onion and peppers and aubergines with a sweet *shoyu* sauce, all washed down with immeasurable amounts of beer and *sake* and a *shochu* – a potent spirit made from sweet potatoes.

No one spoke English, apart from one very sumo-shaped character who came up to me and said, 'Hi there! Where you from?'

'England,' I said.

'Cool, man.'

Kel was a Hawaiian–Japanese from Oahu teaching English in Japan.

'It's sure real strange to see foreigners round here, you know – most keep to the cities. I guess you're having a kinda hard time of it all.'

'Well, no, not really,' I said, 'apart from having to speak Japanese – but that's no bad thing. In fact I really like it that there are no other foreigners around. If I kept bumping into *gaijin* everywhere I think it would put me off.'

Kel introduced me to his Japanese friends, all of whose names I promptly forgot apart from one whom Kel nicknamed 'Superman'. But Superman was being Superquiet.

'He's not feeling so great,' explained Kel, 'been drinking too much – so today he's on milk!'

Some of Kel's friends were laughing at one girl who they said was Chinese.

'Have you always lived in Japan?' I asked her, but she didn't seem to understand.

'She's not really Chinese,' said Kel. 'The guys are just kiddin'. But because she's a bit stupid they all call her Chinese . . .' Kel broke off to translate what he'd just said into Japanese and the boys all guffawed with laughter.

'They think it's the best joke to insult a Japanese as being Chinese – but then the Japanese sense of humour can be real weird.'

'Yes,' I said, 'I'd noticed.'

I carried on down the coast and merged with Route 10, an appallingly over-trafficked highway which carved its way relentlessly through industrial wastelands and concrete cities apparently modelled on the main strips of American drive-in fast-food joints.

Life turned into one sweaty concrete blur: McDonald's, Kentucky Fried Chicken, Mister Donut, Hungry Tiger, 'Mens and Ledys Permanent' hairdresser and the 'Cake Cooky – Hand made cake Factory' where a large sign outside informed me:

> 'Cake made by your wife's hands are the best. But I have prepared these for your wife who is busy and pressed for time.
>
> presented by Patisserie.

In Miyazaki I paused for breath at the Hotel Bigman where I filled up my bottle in the Realips Coffee Bar and where I met a man who appeared so impressed at my attempts to cycle round his country that he gave me three packets of tissues, a two-litre bottle of iced tea, a pair of 'Hello Kitty' socks and a small kit of grow-your-own cherries (v. useful for cycling).

Leaving the bulk of the traffic to cut across Kyushu on the Miyazaki Expressway I continued south, hugging the coast, which turned rocky and blue and spectacular with big black-and-white butterflies flapping in my face.

I paused for thought and a look around the tiny island of Aoshima (*ao* – blue; *shima* – island) which, strictly speaking, is no longer an island, being connected to the mainland by a causeway. Betal palms abounded, as did over 200 varieties of subtropical plants which, due to the prevailing warm currents, flourished in the balmy air. I cycled past a glut of souvenir stalls which had rooted themselves on the causeway, past part of the interesting washboard rocks of the 'Oni-no-sentaku-ita' or Devil's Washboard Shoreline, through a large red *torii* gate and into Aoshima Shinto Shrine. This shrine is dedicated to a lot of hard-to-pronounce deities such as Toyo Tamahime no Mikoto, Shio Tsutsu no Ookami and Hikohohodemi no Mikoto – the latter also known as Yamasachi Hito, or 'Mountain Products Man'.

Easier to get my mouth around was the name of a monk who came to talk to me.

'Hi!' he said, 'I'm Al.'

Al, or, to go the whole hog, Albert Nango, was in fact Japanese but had lived for a while in San Francisco twenty-seven years ago, where he'd worked in a school.

'It was great time experience certainly,' he said, 'but I decide, mmmmmm, maybe not great time country to long-time staying.'

'Why not?' I asked.

'Mmmmmmm, because certainly I find Japanese people have not so rude.'

Aoshima Shrine, so Al said, is supposed to give a divine blessing, especially to those who want to be married.

'You are with husband travelling?' asked Al.

'No,' I said, 'I'm husband-less.'

'Ah so, *desu-ka*? You want marry time?'

'Not now, but maybe sometime.'

'*So desu-ne?* Then you come back honorary guest for blessing wedding Aoshima *jinja,* okay?'

'Okay – *tabun* – maybe,' I said. 'Maybe' always being definitely a good word to keep up a sleeve.

Blue Island has an interesting winter festival. Legend has it that when the Mountain Products Man returned from the Dragon Palace in the Sea Country, he was met by delighted naked people who ran out into the sea to meet him. Now, every year on a day in mid-December, people scamper into the sea dressed in their next-to-nothings. That night I camped at the foot of the causeway but it was so hot I had to go and sit in the sea.

Liquid levels were replenished the following morning when, cans in hand, I propped myself up against a vending machine emblazoned with the words:

Enjoy Coca-Cola
'Soft Drinks' enjoy refreshing
taste while having a good
time chatting.

A man walking past bid me a cheery '*Ohayo!*' before disappearing into a small souvenir shop and emerging with a Fuji disposable camera which he said was a *purezento* for me. A battle ensued in which the said offering was lobbed back and forth between us: me saying really no, no; he saying really yes, yes; until he relented when I pulled out my cameras and reiterated, 'Thank you but no, no – I have two already.'

Phew! I thought, wiping the sweat from my brow; this gift-giving lark is no mean feat. And I set off up the Horikiri Pass feeling exhausted before I'd even begun. Half-way up an arm was extended from out of a car window. Attached in the grip at the end was a bottle of 'Carotene Energy Drink'. I took it gratefully, without argument.

At the top of the pass I met a boy in psychedelic baggy shorts and vivid green sneakers. He said he was a surfer on holiday from Tokyo.

'In Tokyo,' he said, 'all persons is mad because the airs and waters is very dirty.'

'So in Miyazaki,' I said, 'you have clear sea so clear mind.'

'*Hai, hai*!' he laughed. 'Satisfaction life indeed!'

More roadworks. More children's tea parties; more banners and awnings of pandas and rabbits and roses and whales and fish. Smiling fish. Here the workmen are all workwomen – bonnets and frilly elbow-length gloves and calf-high gumboots. The road has been narrowed to one lane, the traffic being halted not by flashy fun-to-count-down traffic lights, nor by big red/green lollipop Stop/Go signs, but with strange hard-to-see hand-held batons; roadworks like a relay race – only it's not. Instead it's all hard-to-interpret signals. And bows. Bows to the traffic. Bows to bicycle-riding *gaijin*. As I pass I call to the baton lady (keeled over in a spine-hinging bow), 'Please, save your back!' But I don't think she understands.

Cape Toi-Misaki is a sight to see, but a bugger to climb. It was so hot and the climb in parts so steep and the flies so big and stinging that, in an exasperated sweaty exhaustion, I swore at everything under and over the sun. Why, I wondered, was I putting myself through all this het-up, head-hot effort? Was it because here on these green-grass bald-domed hills roamed Japan's only wild horses (which in Japan are hardly wild)? Was it to reach this much-famed cape of cliffs from which rises Asia's largest lighthouse? Was it to reach the end of another pointy peninsula? Was it to see the sea, which I could more or less see from anywhere? Was it . . . was it . . . was it . . . was it what? It was because I just wanted to be there. Nothing more. Did it have to be?

And when I got there I looked at a telephone box with a plastic horse growing out of the roof (typical tasteful Japan); I looked at busloads of peace-posing camera-snapping tourists ('*Chiizu*!'); I looked at a lighthouse, which was not bad as far as lighthouses go but not so good as a certain Peggy's Cove, Nova Scotia; and, once I'd drunk enough water to fill a swimming pool, I felt good. Content. Happy. And I thought: I'm glad I came.

Down at the bottom, at a junction in a village with no name, I stopped at a small petrol station (was it Cosmo? was it Nisseki? was it Stork?) to fill up on water. The pump attendant took me by surprise. Her name was Meredith – an American from New York, though she'd lived in Maine and Connecticut and for nine years in LA.

'So, what brings you to this nameless village so far from home?' I asked.

'Well,' said Meredith, 'I was working in Noo Yawk when I won a place as a roller-skater girl for Coca-Cola and . . .'

'Excuse me, Meredith,' I said, 'but just what is a roller-skater girl?'

'Oh – right – okay. Well, I was put into a tutu and had real pretty bows in my hair and it meant skating around as an adver-tise-ment for Coca-Cola. It was so neat. The company sent me to Fukuoka . . . you know Fukuoka?'

'Fukuoka in the north of Kyushu?'

'You gottit. And, well, Fukuoka has this really neat festival every year and this was where I first worked as a Coca-Cola roller-skating girl. The company wanted me in Japan for six months – at $5,000 a month. It was unreal. Anyway, I just fell in love with Japan – never went home, been here five years now.'

'So how did you go from a Coca-Cola skater to a gas station attendant?'

'Well, I fell in love with a Japanese man – he's seven years younger than me! And we got married, had two kids. This place has been in his family for years. I'm an artist by trade but last year I took over my father-in-law's job of running the gas station. His family didn't accept me at all at first. It was real hard but I was determined to show them I could do it. My Japanese got pretty good, I improved and refitted the fittings and . . . well, things are kinda easier now. They're good people. We get on fine. It just takes a lot of perseverance to win yourself into their ways.'

There were more cyclable capes in store for me – this one, Cape Satamisaki, famed for being the southern-most point of the main four islands of Japan. Here stood another lighthouse which, despite being the 'oldest in Japan', was not that flashy.

Rejoining Route 220 I passed through Kanoya-shi – one big, ugly, fast-food strip of a city which my map identified as 'Accident-prone area'. Amongst all the traffic and neon I spotted an elderly woman pushing a large rusty wheelbarrow overloaded with a sky-scraping pile of futons. I watched her navigate the crowds, the cars, the cuckoo-sounding traffic lights, before wheeling straight into a dry cleaners. Well, I thought, that's one way to do it.

Despite my aversion to Japanese cities, they have their uses by providing a vast assortment of supermarkets. It was in Kanoya-shi's Sunnymart that *doki-doki* struck with a vengeance – my heart missing a beat when I was united with five 350-gram boxes of Quaker Oats. I snapped up every one of them in a state of feverish excitement. I felt like crying out something like 'There's sugar at Sainsbury's! There's sugar at Sainsbury's!', as I recalled a frenzied woman doing during a sugar shortage in the 'seventies.

After passing through the checkout I stood at the grocery-packing counter and set about carving up my boxes of Quaker Oats; in Japan you don't clog up the queue by loading your purchases into carriers at the checkout but move with your basket on to special counters which, by providing Sellotape, scissors, string, marker pens, and damp cloths to aid bag-separation, resemble a Blue Peter prepared-before-the-programme studio. My mission in mind was to decant the contents into plastic bags (lighter and more pannier-friendly to store) before cutting the cardboard from the front of the box to make a pleasing supply of free post-cards – a process which may well have saved paper and money but which caused a series of bemused sidelong expressions from the cluster of neighbouring housewives as they packed up their shopping. From out of their heads popped thought-bubbles, each of them filling with the same quizzical words: 'What on earth is that strange *gaijin* doing?'

Filling up on water at Mister Donut, I read the long-winded advertisement banner suspended above the door:

> World's best coffee and fresh donuts – could some of San Francisco's fog be caused by the steam of dim sum? A woman from San Francisco told me: 'Dim sum is healthy and trendy. It's just like Japanese food.' I asked a lady. Who had just paid her bill: 'When you go out with your boyfriend what do you prefer, dim sum or Japanese food?'
>
> 'Well I'll think about it while I have some dim sum,' came the reply.

Careering full pelt down a mountain near Furue I was hit all of a sudden by puncture No. 1. The cause – a one-inch nail, embedded in my back tyre, which I extracted with the pliers of my mini Leatherman. Fortunately I had ground to a bumpy-rimmed halt right beside a fat bank of vending machines, which meant that every motorist who pulled in to buy a drink bought me one as well, making up for the fact that, because of the humidity, my patches refused to stick. In the end I had to walk down to a sea-scape restaurant where the owner not only allowed me to mend my puncture in the air-conditioned coolness (where patch stuck to glue with ease) but also gave me a mountain of noodles on the house. Sometimes, just sometimes, it's worth getting punctures after all.

That night I camped behind a small shrine that sat in the shadow of the almighty Sakurajima (Cherry Blossom) volcano. This smoking, belching, brooding giant is far from dormant and constantly billows out black-grey plume-clouds of ominous smoke. There have been many eruptions, the most tumultuous lasting more than a month in 1914, during which the volcano spewed out over three billion tons of lava that buried eight villages. Its ash was found to cover land as far away as Siberia. But the most remarkable effect of the explosion resulted in a massive flow of lava: it filled in the

400-metre-wide, 70-metre-deep channel of the Seto Strait which had, until the eruption, separated the island of Sakurajima from Kyushu's Osumi-hanto peninsula.

It was across this landbridge that I cycled, past a sign advising me not to venture into the 'Danger Blast Zone' and on into a lunar landscape where I climbed up torturously shaped lumps of lava as big as bungalows. Ash-dust stuck to the sweat of my skin in a filthy blackened film. This ash may not please the people but it pleases the land. The mountain soil is so fertile that Sakurajima has become famed for producing both little and large edible oddities: sweet, juicy minute *mikan* – tangerines the size of marbles; and giant *daikon* – radishes which, with a circumference of four-and-a-half feet, can weigh anything up to seventy-five pounds.

I caught a music-blaring reverberating ferry for the far-from-peaceful fifteen-minute ride over to Kagoshima, the prefectural capital and centre of industry, economy, culture and communications in Southern Kyushu, where some unusual annual events take place – such as the 400-year-old Kaijiki spider fights, which feature *kogane gumo* (large striped spiders), and the post-rainy season umbrella-burning festival.

With the restless activities of Sakurajima as backdrop, not for nothing is Kagoshima called 'The City where you can see the Earth on fire!'

One of the first *gaijin* to step off a ship at Kagoshima arrived 450 years before me. He was the Spanish missionary of the society of Jesus – St Francis of Xavier – who, on arriving in 1549, brought to the Japanese the first contact with Christianity.

I pedalled off the ramp and on to a pier lined with palm trees on an oppressively humid late July afternoon. The air was so weighty with moisture and the sky so grey with ash that even the fierce blades of the sun were unable to penetrate this sinister layer of dark war-clouds pressing ever closer around my head. Although I knew the smoking Cherry Blossom (huh! some cherry!) was to blame, I felt the atmosphere so charged with storm that it made my blood tingle and pupils dilate. I wanted to find accommodation before the sky caved in, but even more urgent than that was first seeing to a matter that was causing me to fret. My visa was about to expire and as I had now planned, somewhat on the spur of the moment, to head further south to the subtropical islands of Okinawa, I needed to be granted a hefty extension in order to stay in Japan. I was fretting because things I'd read and tales I'd heard confirmed my concerns that Japanese immigration officers were a stringent lot and were far more in favour of *gaijin* leaving the country than staying. Also, I was told you needed good reasons, substantial funds and an air ticket out of the country to attain the much sought after stamp – none of which I possessed.

The immigration office was not easy to find. When I didn't even know what to ask for (my dictionary had no word for immigration) how did I know what to look for in an alien city of *kanji* and neon. The girl at the railway station's information booth took a while to grasp what I was talking about and when she did she said I would need to go to Fukuoka (sitting about 200 miles north on the opposite end of Kyushu) as no such place existed in Kagoshima. In an attempt to ask directions I showed my passport to some taxi drivers imitating a stamp with my fist. This only resulted in my receiving cans of coffee and jars of *sake* and you're-a-mad-*gaijin* grins. Out of the four policemen I asked, the first looked at my passport upside down, the second directed me to a hospital (did I really look a sick case?), the third directed me to the Vie de France Bakery (a nice idea but not quite what I had in mind) and the fourth gave me a riceball.

I was sure an immigration office existed in Kagoshima because at the Japanese embassy in London I'd managed to acquire a list of immigration offices throughout Japan in which, despite being solely in *kanji*, I deciphered the characters for Kagoshima. There was no address but there was a telephone number, which I rang. The conversation with a woman's voice went something like this:

'*Moshi, moshi.*'

'*Moshi, moshi,*' I replied, before adding in Japanese, 'Do you speak English?'

'*Hai, hai*!'

'Is this the immigration office?'

'*Hai, hai*!'

'Please could you tell me exactly where in Kagoshima you are.'

'*Hai, hai*!' (Long pause.)

'Hello?' (Silence) 'Hello? *Moshi, moshi*? Your address please?'

Then a man's voice sounded in my left ear, saying something so fast in Japanese that the words shot clean out of my right. The result? I panicked and apologized ('*Gomen nasai*!') and slammed the phone down. Hmmm! I thought as I stared dazedly at the receiver; not much luck there.

Short for time before my visa expired and not wanting to be forced into taking a yen-eating train ride all the way to Fukuoka and back, I was determined one way or another to track down this elusive bureau of bureaucracy. Okay, I thought, trying to think rationally, where would you most likely find an immigration office in a port-side city? The port? Sounded a fair bet to me. I sought out the old port, the new port and the in-between ferry terminals, all to no avail. People I asked either had no idea what it was I was looking for or else denied that such a place ever existed. So, in a somewhat exasperated last burst of effort, I decided to ride around a few streets with the hit-and-miss idea of seeing whether any building I passed looked as if it could be the office of officialdom. Off I lurched, up and down a myriad *dori* (streets), finding myself on the surprisingly named Perth-*dori* and Naples-*dori* (I later learnt that Italy's Naples and Oz's Perth were sister-cities to Japan's Kagoshima). Still no joy, until back down on the fast thoroughfare of Route 226 that rushed its way along the coast I found a heavy, unprepossessing, browny-grey lump of a building with big *kanji* letters plastered to its front wall. If not immigration, it looked like something suitably official.

Parking my bike beside the front steps I walked into a stark, shabby entrance with clunky run-down lifts and echoey stairs. It looked like school and smelt of authority: a bureaucratic building where papers got shuffled and lives got stamped.

After trying several doors on several floors I eventually found the one I was after with a sign on the front giving the office's opening hours: 9 a.m.–12 p.m.; 1 p.m.–4 p.m. It was now 5.05 p.m. I knocked anyway and was surprised when the door was opened by an official-looking man who spoke no English.

'Oh, hello!' I said. 'Are you open or closed?'

'*Hai, hai*!' said the man.

Taking the liberty of interpreting this answer as being 'a little bit open and a little bit closed' I flapped my passport in his face and, together with a few illustrative fist-stamps on the appropriate page, explained the situation as best I could in Japanese. Expecting the door to be slammed in my face, I was pleasantly surprised when he invited me in for a cup of green tea. This was not the usual bureaucratic behaviour.

The office was long and narrow and cramped, full of battered grey filing cabinets and unpeopled desks. A small timid woman, who I took to be the OL, brought me my tea and bowed before silently retreating. I stood on one side of the high desk, the immigration man on the other, as I tried to answer his questions in Japanese. Not the usual sort of questions, mind, that one might expect to be asked by an immigration official but ones such as: did I know Beatrix Potter and *Miss Saigon* and had I read *Anne of Green Gables*? To which I replied *hai!* and *hai!* and *hai!*, because, after all, when it comes to securing vital stamps in your passport, one aims to please. After a while the questioning proceeded into more familiar territory; Was I alone? Was I scared? Where did I sleep? Did I have children? before the actual reason for my visit to his office was tackled.

I was presented with a couple of forms to fill out, full of the usual tedious immigration sort of questions, before I had to provide Mr Fan of Green Gables with an address in Japan. I scribbled down Nagai-*san*'s, bless him, who in Tokyo had volunteered his address to be used in such a case. Next I had to show proof of sufficient funds which, thanks to Mr Gables' negligence, I managed to inflate wildly by 'accidentally' slipping an extra 'nought' on the end of what I really had without him noticing and by padding out my traveller's cheques with a pack of cards, which when flicked fast in front of his face looked like quite a sizeable wodge. My newly acquired Visa card looked impressive, too, even if what it represented of my behind-the-scenes dwindling funds didn't.

Trouble arose when I was asked to show my air ticket out of Japan. Air ticket? Gulp! Air ticket there was none. Hoping this wouldn't be my downfall, I blathered something about not having an air ticket as I was planning on leaving Japan by boat to Korea, and that I could not buy a ferry ticket in advance as I was travelling by bicycle (totally irrelevant but always a good one to drop in for the incomprehension stakes) and that this was why I was at this moment ticketless. Simple, really.

Much telephoning ensued while the OL refreshed me with a top-up of green tea and black-haired men in blue suits flurried in and out clutching my passport and armloads of paperwork. I stood at the desk looking as pitifully hopeful as I could until nearly two hours after the office was supposed to be closed (I felt a bit guilty about that). Mr Fan of Green Gables answered the telephone for about the hundredth time, did a lot of nodding and a frenzy of short, sharp, stuttered *hai*! *hai*! *hai*-ing before putting down the phone and beaming triumphantly. Expectantly, I beamed back as it's always nice to reciprocate with an expression of happiness. Did I have 4,000 yen (£26) in cash on me? he asked. *Hai, hai*! I replied, after which he wrote something in *kanji* on a scrap of paper and directed me to plummet down in the lift several floors to the office canteen, where I was to show this chit to one of the kitchen staff. Suspecting this was some sort of elaborate hoax or perhaps a form of unusual bribery whereby I was to buy the immigration staff a free meal, I dutifully dropped to the basement. There I found an empty canteen but a steaming kitchen in which worked a couple of spritely, albeit geriatric, old dears. I passed them my note through the hatch and in return they handed me two stamps to the value of 4,000 yen (for which I paid them) along with a mountainous bowlful of piping-hot noodles, which the smiling wrinkly-faced cook indicated were for me – a *purezento* from Mr Green Gables upstairs.

After I finished slurping I returned to the immigration office where my 4,000 yen stamps were stuck into one of the forms I'd filled out and my passport, complete with its ninety-day extension permit, was handed back to me with a bow.

'Happy pleasuring season!' exclaimed Mr Gables in English and I skipped down the stairs two at a time, feeling happy of heart.

After riding around the post ash-storm streets of the city for a while looking for a place to stay, I found the 'Young In Kagoshima' – a *minshuku* tucked behind a neon-blinking *pachinko* parlour run by the Hondas – not Goldwings or CBR 900s but a friendly family of three. My room, with its Western bed, pile of futons, carpet, *tatami*, *yukata* and locking hinged door, was a peculiar blend of East hitting West. A small sink unit sat wedged in the corner which, I later discovered, must have housed at least half the entire force of Kagoshima's cockroaches. Downstairs in the *ofuro* I was forced to forgo the large communal L-shaped bath, owing to its skin-scorching heat, and instead perched on a milking stool, level with the shin-high shower, scrubbing a layer of ash off my body. Mrs Honda intercepted me as I exited from the *ofuro* and invited me next door into the bar. Seating me on a stool at a long table carved out of a log, she presented me with a pot of green tea, a bowl of stew (carrot, sweet-potato, tofu and seaweed) and a peculiar mound of rubber rice paste with the mouth-feel of a squash ball. Mr Honda, who was wheelchair-bound, sat hunched and silent in front of a rabbiting television.

That night, after stamping on a few cockroaches, I sat on the *tatami* in my room surrounded by open maps and books, plotting my next day's plan of action. I was off to Okinawa.

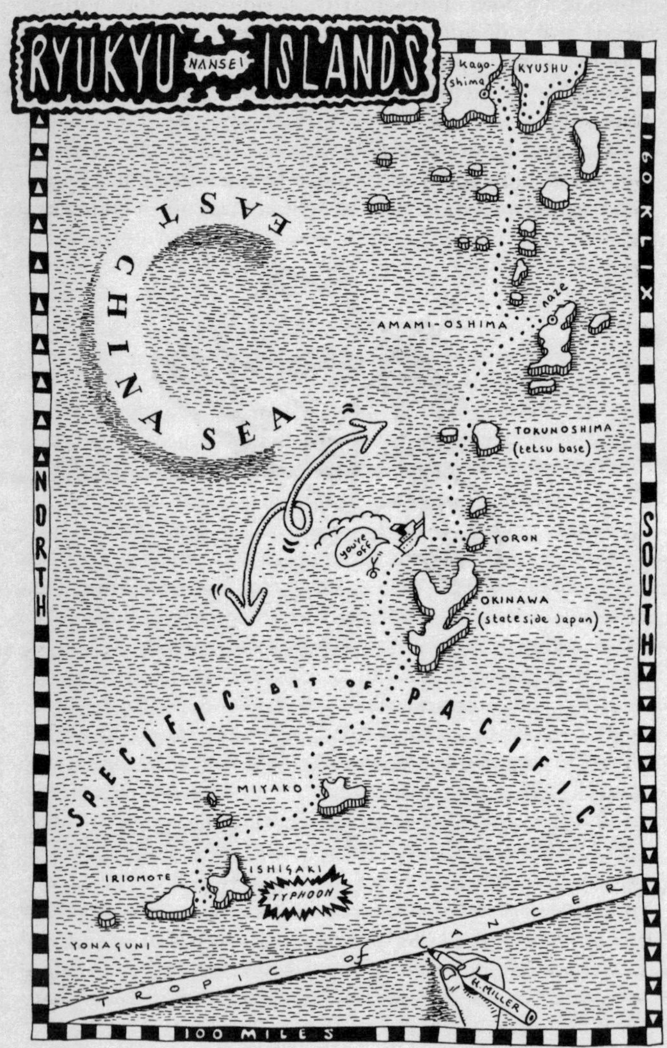
RYUKYU NANSEI ISLANDS
kagoshima
KYUSHU
EAST CHINA SEA
naze
AMAMI-OSHIMA
TOKUNOSHIMA
(tetsu base)
you're off
YORON
OKINAWA
(stateside Japan)
SPECIFIC BIT OF PACIFIC
MIYAKO
ISHIGAKI
TYPHOON
IRIOMOTE
YONAGUNI
TROPIC of CANCER
H. MILLER
NORTH
SOUTH
160 KLIX
100 MILES

CHAPTER 19

Smiling Hurts

Okinawa – or, to be more precise, the Nansei Shoto (South-West) Islands – stretches out in a crescent like a Japanese sword between Kyushu and Taiwan. This thousand-kilometre archipelago, dangling from the Japanese mainland, separates the Higasi Sina Kai (East China Sea) from the Taiheiyo (Pacific Ocean) and is divided into two major prefectures that belong to Kagoshima-ken in the north and Okinawa-ken in the south. The Nansei Islands are further subdivided into various groups. The islands which belong to the prefecture of Kagoshima are also known as the Satsunan-shoto area, comprising the lesser archipelagos of Osumi-shoto, Amami-shoto and Tokara-retto. The southern half of the Nansei Islands is part of the prefecture of Okinawa and encompasses four groups of islands, the most visited of which are those of Okinawa-shoto (a name commonly given to the whole group, also known by its former name: the Ryukyu-shoto Islands), while further south lie the island groups of Miyako-retto, Yaeyama-retto and the isolated Daito. Okinawa-jima, being the largest of these islands, is referred to as the *honto* while the other islands are the *rito*. *Rito*? Right-oh? *Hai*! *Hai*? No! No? I was getting confused, which is why I stayed up half the night in my Young In room of cockroaches trying to make head or tail of where I was heading, or even tailing. Because, when it comes to taking boats, it's nice to know where you're going.

The Nansei Archipelago comprises about sixty-five islands (forty-five of which are inhabited) along with hundreds of islets and alluring atolls. Because Japan's western-most island, Yonaguni-jima, is only sixty miles from Taiwan, it formed for over 2,000 years the first of a natural series of stepping stones that linked Kyushu and the other main islands of Japan with the rich mother culture of China. For centuries Okinawa and its outlying islands formed an independent kingdom, described by the Chinese as either Liu-Chiu (Land of Propriety) or Shurei no Kuni (The Nation that Keeps the Peace). This wasn't so much because the kings of Ryukyu were a bunch of peace-loving hippies, but more down to the fact that Okinawa was sandwiched between the formidable might of China on the one side and the rampant neck-slicing clans of the Japanese shoguns on the other – a combination that would make anyone think twice about throwing their weight around.

So, with no wars to be waging, Okinawa drifted along quite happily between the fourteenth and seventeenth centuries in its Golden Age of Prosperity, developing a distinctive culture in which its theatre, dance, music and arts flourished. Okinawan ships plied the seas of the Far East and merchants were sent to trade with Thailand and Indonesia. Lying at the hub, Naha, the capital of Okinawa, became a prominent entrepôt for medicines, metals and silk from China; swords, armour and gold from Japan, and spices and textiles from elsewhere in Asia. Okinawan seamen became known and respected throughout the Far East.

The Golden Age came to an abrupt end when, in 1609, the expansionist Shimazu clan from the Satsuma Kingdom of southern Kyushu invaded Okinawa, bringing it under the heavy-handed control of Japan. To add to sour feelings the Ryukyu dynasty, reduced to puppet status, was compelled to pay taxes to China as well as Japan. The Japanese, considering the Okinawans to be a backward and inferior race, treated them with such contempt and exploited them so voraciously that traces of bitter anti-mainland resentment continue to this day.

When Westerners started appearing on the scene towards the end of the nineteenth century the Japanese, fearing that they might lose Okinawa to these big-nosed barbarians, officially annexed the islands as a Japanese prefecture. At the same time Okinawa's connections with China were completely severed when sixty-six Okinawan fishermen were executed by Chinese authorities after they had drifted off course and accidentally landed on the island of Taiwan. From then on Okinawan culture, including its unique language, was severely suppressed, although a distinct dialect, almost completely incomprehensible to Japanese mainlanders is still spoken.

As I was planning on coming back through Kagoshima I left a pile of possessions I wouldn't need (books, maps, extra T-shirt, film, old diaries, and so on) with Mrs Honda, who happily said she'd look after them until my return, which I told her would probably be in no more than a couple of weeks. After all, the islands which looked mere pin-pricks on the map could be nipped round pretty quickly by bike, I thought.

It had been another impossibly heavy and sultry grey ash-cloud sort of day which considerately culminated in an explosive storm just as I was racing through the rush-hour streets to catch the evening ferry. Such was its ferocity that at first I thought the Cherry volcano had Blossomed and blown its top, spewing the innards of the Earth into this eastern-most world. The storm clouds were so thick that a dreary daylight turned instantly to night. Headlights crawled through the ominous gloom as the roads turned to filthy black torrents of ash. By the time I arrived at the ferry terminal I resembled a drowned rat that had been dragged backwards several times through a coal scuttle.

A flurry of activity erupting from the crowd gathered around the ticket desk revealed that the Marix Line ferry might be delayed, due to a typhoon lurking somewhere in the direction of where our boat was headed. During this lull, I sauntered off to the *benjo* to clean myself up as best I could and wash my clothes in the sink. By the time I'd emerged word had it that the typhoon had undergone an unexpected 90° about-turn so we slid out into the night, leaving the ash-blown lights of Kagoshima to flicker in our wake.

A grandmother wearing a Walkman and a girl in a 'We Love Sunny Day' T-shirt were my immediate neighbours in the 'Lady's Room' – a long rectangular compartment which held at least thirty other women. This cheapest of accommodations contained no bunks or sheets or chairs but consisted merely of a raised expanse of carpeted floor (strictly no shoes) upon which lay rows of orange-brown blankets and plastic brown block-pillows shaped like bricks. The windows were sealed and the air was conditioned. A television gabbled away inanely from a corner of the ceiling. It didn't look like a recipe for a good night's slumber so, using the 'Lady's Room' as base camp, I extracted my ground sheet, Karrimat and sleeping bag and laid myself to rest in a leeward nook on deck beneath the stars. The next thing I knew it was early morning and I was being rudely jolted from my dreams by a head-splitting rendition of 'I could have danced all night . . . I could have danced all night . . . until you asked for more . . .' blaring forth from the onboard PA system. This was followed by a kinder-on-the-ear-drums but totally out-of-place recording of the dawn chorus trilling and tweeting away. I half expected a blackbird's dropping to splat on me at any moment. This was the Marix Line's method of saying, 'Wakey-wakey, *ohayo gozaimasu,* land is nigh!'

The land in question was the forty-mile-long volcanic island of Amami-Oshima. Just as the first spokes of an early morning sun lit up a splintered pink sky, I scooted off the ship's ramp, weaving around a buzzing army of cargo wielding forklifts, and entered the island's principal city of Naze. All was shut and all was quiet. I had the streets to myself. Had this been mainland Japan, the city would have been a cacophonic blur of activity – even at this sun-rising hour. I felt as if I'd left frenetic Japan behind and entered a laid-back land. Palm trees rustled above my head and the warm air smelt exotically tropical.

When it comes to islands and countries where people drive on the left, unless I have a very good reason not to do so, I will always cycle clockwise around their shores for no other reason than that it means I'm riding right on the sea-side. To miss out on cycling inches away from precipitous cliffside drops that plummet into a raging and foaming ocean just because you're tucked to the inside of the road across two lanes of asphalt is not my idea of fun. In my view, if you're on the sea, you might as well be on top of it.

I rode along the wharf, past a park and the closed doors of DAIEI (one of the few chains of supermarket that sells *doki doki* Quaker Oats) and past a petrol station offering Car Foot Surgery – presumably for calloused and bunioned tyres. I turned off on to an empty road that looped its way over the mountains. Despite being only 7 a.m. it was so hot and so humid that I felt dead. The severe gradient didn't help matters either: hauling my bike was like trying to drag a tank up the mountainside.

But, as we all know, mountains have their upsides as well as their downsides and for most cyclists the downside is

AMAMI OSHIMA
DEADLY SNAKE ISLE
12 MILES
20 KLIX
wild seas wild land wild beaches
CORAL
Naze (port/city)
Yamoto-cho
NORTH
Koniya
Cape Namikesaki
② Moped Hell's angels
① where I spent the night in toilet sheltering from a semi-typhoon
③ Big horn jeep journalist interviews me on sea wall
⑥ Tricycle-riding women town (night ride)
④ where I met the non sexual 'arass-ment, round the world-sailing-Frenchman
⑧ where I was saved by a cool swimming pool school teacher
⑦ Lots of squashed snakes
⑤ where I jumped in to the harbour

the going up; the upside the going down. The upside of the mountain to Ata was the truly thrilling down that spiralled to a small fishing village full of bright blue tin-topped houses.

With brilliant cobalt seas, coral reefs, palms, and crops of sago, papaya, bananas and sugar cane, it was not difficult to see why this subtropical archipelago had been labelled the 'Hawaii of Japan' (it seems that Japan has several Hawaiis). The whole place felt and smelt as if it belonged more to the easy going ways of Polynesia rather than the robotic arm of Japan.

But however different these islands, the inhabitants still like to dig. Just after passing a small rural factory that smelt of molasses, I came across a brand new tunnel boring its elaborate way through the mountainside. Now, tunnels come neither cheap nor easy to make. The obvious expense and effort put into the construction of this one would perhaps have been understandable had the road been a frenzied two-laned highway. Instead, it was a sleepy backwater – a single-track lane where the only traffic I'd seen in two hours was an old man bumping along at about ten miles per hour on a time-worn tractor, another old man on a back-firing moped with a front basket full of fish, and an *obaasan* wearing on her back a basket loaded with brittle shrubbery and pushing a wheelbarrow piled with what looked like desiccated pineapple stalks. The narrow road hugging the rocky coast around the mountain was more than adequate to handle this scanty supply of road-users, so just what was the tunnel for? To practise a spot of digging or to squander funds? Or maybe the locals just want to peer through from one side of the mountain to the other, which I suppose is as good a reason as any.

I was enjoying a peaceful pedal beside the shore – the only sounds being the gentle wash of the waves and the rustling of the palm fronds – when four boys on 50cc mopeds, with engines sounding like cans of nails, shattered the dreamy scene by haring up and down the road, zigzagging back and forth and shrieking insanely at the tops of their voices. I smiled at them meekly, thinking: well, maybe if I lived on a small sleepy island on the edge of the world I too would burn rubber at the sight of an out-of-the-blue *jitensha*-riding foreign barbarian.

I stopped by at a small rural post-office – not to do the usual post-officey things, but because I had discovered post-offices to be one of the best sources of chilled water; in virtually every Japanese post-office I called at stood a metallic water-fountain machine that provided me with bottle-loads of refrigerated water. Some post-offices even provided a help-yourself counter of iced tea.

That night a sago farmer let me camp beside his *taka kura* – a traditional Amami thatched-roof wooden store-house set on stilts to keep rodents and vermin from eating the harvested grain. The farmer said I was welcome to sleep inside the *taka kura.*

'Look,' he said, sliding open the heavy wooden door and flicking a switch, 'there is *denki* – light – and also no danger from *habu*.'

'*Habu*?' I asked. 'What are *habu*?'

'*Abunai*! *Abunai*! – Danger! Danger!' he replied, rather dramatically. '*Habu* are dangerous poisonous snakes!' And sweeping his arms in an elaborate arc to illustrate his point he added, 'Take care, *habu* are everywhere!'

Had I known then what I know now about *habu* I would not only have jumped at the chance of sleeping in the snake-free storehouse but most likely have hot-footed it to the port for the first boat out. Deadly poisonous snakes are not my cup of tea, especially Okinawan ones, which can grow up to six feet long – definitely not the sort of tent mate with which a lone female wants to share her sleeping mat.

There are three kinds of these pit vipers found throughout the Nansei Islands: the Okinawan *habu* is either a solid dark green all over or has a colouring similar to a Western diamondback rattlesnake; the Sakishima *habu* is brown and the Hime *habu* is dark green. Although both the latter can be only two to three feet in length (mere tiddlers compared with the almighty Okinawan six-footers), they are just as dangerous.

All varieties of *habu* have slender necks, broad heads and a pattern of erratic diamonds. Nowhere on the Nansei Islands apart from Mikayo and Yoron is *habu*-free, the snakes being found anywhere from the interior mountains to the coastal mangrove swamps, from dense vegetation to small caves, from pineapple to sugar-cane fields to sleeping bags and boots. When it comes to that potentially deadly bite, a *habu* has a main set of fangs and a second set of five spare fangs on each side of its mouth. All of the fangs, including the reserves, are stock-piled with venom. If a *habu* gets punched in the face (so to speak) and loses one of its main fangs, a new one slides into its place within three days. Then a replacement fang for that spare starts forming within a week or so.

Testicularly speaking, *habu* are quite something. Due to their double set of genitalia they are able to mate continuously for twenty-four hours, which is probably why Okinawans use all parts of the snake for everything from creams and pills to powders and potions. They admire and respect the *habu* (why can't they leave them alone, then?) and believe that if a person takes in part of the snake, the snake becomes part of them. When it comes to venom, a *habu*'s is haemotoxin, which destroys the human bloodstream and muscle tissue. Not good news. Worse news is that a *habu* has a 360° striking range, so if you think you can cautiously retreat unawares behind its head – beware! When it strikes its prey, it doesn't shoot its venom but injects it via the puncture wounds of its bite. Although an estimated 200–300 people are bitten by *habu* each year, only about five will actually die. Some local information about *habu* told me that, if I was bitten, I would have between one to four hours (depending on the location of the bite) before death became a possibility. Bad places to be bitten would be above the jugular and elsewhere above the waist – or anywhere if jogging or cycling, as a fast-beating heart would spread the venom more rapidly.

Although hospitals are all equipped with anti-venom the likelihood of my being able to get to one within the one-to-four-hour danger-zone would not be great, unless a lot of luck was on my side. If there was no hospital nearby, I was told, I should apply a not-too-tight tourniquet, three or four inches above the wound (which will first feel hot, then numb, becoming red before discolouring to green and blue – what a show!), which I was to loosen every fifteen minutes for fifteen seconds. During this time (presuming I was still alive) I should make two small slits next to the puncture wounds – vertically rather than horizontally so as not to add fire to the frying pan by slicing across a major vein or artery. The slits could be made with anything sharp (Swiss Army knife, razor blade, shard of broken glass etc.) as long as it had been sterilized in the flame of a match or lighter, or boiled in water. This done, one would then supposedly be able to push the venom out slowly. Next move: hot-tail it to the hospital. Easy. No sweat.

Knowing little of the horrors of the '*habu*' at the time, I politely refused Farmer Sago's offer of sleeping in a snake-free zone and merrily pitched my tent in the sandy dust across the path from the *taka kura* storehouse. However, I did take the half-hearted precaution of performing a rapid ten-second war-dance, stamping heavily on the ground in the

hope that the vibrations would be sufficient to scare any deaf, vibration-sensitive snakes well away. I then went to sleep with my outer tent door open as usual (the mosquito-netted inner tightly zipped, mind) and peered up at the wonder of a clear, star-spangled subtropical sky. Soon the glory of a gibbous moon slid into view, working its way slowly through the gently whispering fronds of a palm until it hung suspended above my head. As I lay there, I was reminded of a story about the Buddha.

One day, the Buddha was walking through the woods and lost his way. A hare appeared and said he would show the Buddha the way but the Buddha said, 'I am only poor and would never be able to repay you for the favour.' But the hare said, 'In that case I will instead provide you with a sacrificial meal,' and promptly leapt into the fire. Shocked, the Buddha hurriedly pulled him out by his long ears and threw him into the air – up and up to the moon. The dark lava plains (the maria) seen on the moon today are parts of the sacrificial hare.

The meandering road up around Cape Kasarizaki was mountainous, sparse of life and truly spectacular. The first vehicle to pass me after a long time was a woman on a moped, her standard white-peaked, open-faced helmet worn on the back of her neck in similar carefree style to the myriad mopeding youngsters I'd seen in Kyushu. She motored alongside me for a couple of miles laughing animatedly, shouting above the spluttering strains of her engine, until she gestured me to follow her down a bumpy track, its edges crowded with a windbreak of wild *fukugi* trees.

Her house, virtually hidden beneath a glorious tangle of cascading bougainvillea, hibiscus, ruby-red poinsettias, camellias, strings of white moon pearls, trumpet lilies and papaya trees, was in cluttery disarray. A muddle of books and comics and *manga* and papers lay open upon the *tatami* among telephones and teapots and photos and socks. One whole wall was covered in an assortment of calendars from bygone years.

Mrs Moped saw me looking at them and said, 'I like calendars!'

'Yes,' I said, 'I can see.'

She then wrote her name on my map: Minami Toshiko. Minami, I knew, meant 'south', so I told Mrs South that in England we have Mr North and Mrs West but no Souths, as far as I know.

'Ah so, *desu-ka*?' she said. 'And East? Is there East?'

'No,' I said. 'In England there is no East, which explains,' I added, speaking mainly for myself, 'why us Westerners are always lost!' Mrs South threw back her head in a very un-Japanese manner and laughed loudly.

I stayed with Mrs South for a couple of hours as she plied me with various edible delicacies and several litres of liquids. She told me she lived alone (she was either divorced or a widow – I couldn't quite gather which) and her three children had flown the nest to work in Kagoshima. And indeed, her house was a nest, with an assortment of twelve budgies and parrots and mynas. Oh, and one very sniffy dog. Before I left, Mrs South gave me a little drawstring bag her mother had made, one melon, a doggie-bag of fried eel, six riceballs and four cartons of fruit juice. Then she climbed on her moped and followed me at about five miles per hour all the way to the top of the mountain before bowing on her bike, smiling and waving and heading back home.

I hadn't been on my own again for long before a gun-metal Isuzu Big Horn jeep overtook me and stopped up the road. A man in his thirties with black wavy hair and a face more Polynesian than Japanese gestured excitedly for me to stop. Iwai Kouichiro was a journalist from the island's daily paper and said he had briefly spotted me yesterday riding out of Naze and had been driving around the island looking for me ever since. A lady *gaijin* alone on a *jitensha* – on Amami-Oshima – this is very strange sight! he said. He asked if I could spare a few moments for him to interview me. A few moments? Of course. I have plenty of time – what with time oozing out of my shoes. So he drove to the nearest vending machine just down the road and returned with several cans of chilled beers and teas and coffees and juices and we sat on the sea-wall drinking Hokkaido beer as I tried as best I could to answer his questions in Japanese – an effort which caused much merry confusion. At the end of it all he handed me his *meishi* (business card, printed in the alluring nonsensical swirls of *kanji*) and invited me out to dinner on my return to Naze that night. But thanks to the tail-end of a typhoon whipping the island into a palm-tree-bending frenzy, I never made it back to Naze. I slept in a tunnel instead.

If I thought people had been overwhelmingly generous with their gift-giving up until now, then the next day was something else. As I travelled back through Naze and then on over the mountains into the south of the island, virtually everyone I met – shopkeepers, fishermen, petrol station attendants, roadworkers, and lorry drivers – lavished upon me a phenomenal succession of gifts because they had seen a picture of a *jitensha* riding *gaijin* in the paper. As I was heaving myself and my bike, by now a veritable mobile vending machine of refreshments in itself, over Mount Torigamine, a pick-up truck bursting with camping equipment and excitedly shrieking chattering couples pulled over, the youngsters waving a picture of the *gaijin* in the paper and inviting me to join them that evening for a barbecue on the beach down near Cape Namikesaki.

Everyone was all for lassoing both me and my bike on

top of their piles of gear – something I didn't feel quite up to, so I said, '*Domo* – thanks – but I think I'll cycle instead.'

By the time I arrived in Koniya (a bustling fishing town tucked into the magnificent Setouchi Coast), exhausted after a day of mountains, humidity and gift-accepting, it was almost dark. The location of my barbecue rendezvous was still some miles off. When a fisherman told me that Koniya had a typhoon warning it wasn't a difficult decision to abort all plans for camping and start looking for a *minshuku* instead. The *minshuku* of Koniya proved elusive: after I'd cycled in circles for a while and found nothing that remotely resembled the accommodation I was after, a petrol pump attendant sketched a map on a page in my diary showing where he thought one might be. After a lot more circles and wrong turnings up and down narrow streets lined with festive, bobbing, lighted lanterns, I found what I thought was the house marked on my muddling *kanji*-sprinkled map. There were no signs or boards indicating it was a *minshuku*, but I walked up the steps and tapped at the door. A small boy appeared, took one look at me and hastily scampered back inside. Hmmm, I thought, a promising reaction. The sounds of excitable shuffling ensued from within and, shortly, a dumpy *okusama* came to the door, looking mightily surprised. She wore a red apron emblazoned with the words:

Other one long-time apron
Taste-the-Fairyland

'*Konbanwa*!' I said cheerily. 'Excuse me, but is this a *minshuku*?'

Long pause, accompanied by a look of incomprehension. Obviously my Japanese was not having the desired effect on Mrs Fairyland. Undeterred, I pressed on.

'*Heya wa arimasu-ka*? – Do you have a room?'

'*Hai, hai, arimasu*,' she said, her expression creasing into a smile.

Speaking very fast and excitedly she led me upstairs to a *tatami* room full of wall-to-wall washing suspended from lines of cord. Mrs Fairyland continued chattering away at a nonsensical speed, into which I continued to interject sporadically '*Hai, hai*!' for good measure, just to show her I was with her even if I wasn't.

Mrs Fairyland shuffled around me busily dragging a floral nylon-covered futon from out of a flimsy-doored wall cupboard. When I helped her to shake out a sheet and cover the mattress, she burst into fits of giggles – it doesn't take much to be a comedian in Japan. A concrete pillow of beans and rice husks completed my sleeping arrangements. Mrs Fairyland then made a start at taking the washing down and I did my best by gesticulating and saying, 'No! no! Please leave it to dry – it's fine!' She promptly dissolved into peals of laughter.

She then said something else to me very fast, to which I '*hai hai*-ed!' (wondering if I should perhaps have 'no, no-ed!') before she stepped out of the room with a bow, sliding the paper-screen door shut behind her. Wiping the sweat from my gleaming collarbone, neck and face, I stood for a moment swaying gently in a bit of a hot humid-daze, wondering: Is this a *minshuku*? Is it a private house? Is it a laundrette? Before I'd even had a chance to have a shower, my door slid open. It was Mrs Fairyland, together with her two young sons peering shyly from behind her aprons, urging me hurriedly to follow her.

'*Ima*?' I said. 'Now?'

'*Hai, hai*!'

So, despite my weariness and feeling in no position to argue, I obediently followed.

We all tumbled down the steep, narrow, dark wooden stairs and into the kitchen, where a small party of people were noisily throwing back tumblers of *awamori* – a *sake*-type of local brew that islanders often drink with a raw egg and sugar. Mrs Fairyland then handed me a cling-filmed stainless steel oval platter displaying exquisite bundles of *sushi* and *sashimi*.

Gathering themselves together, the two couples and their children, Mrs Fairyland and her boys each picked up another platter of food or bag of something and we all hurried out into the hot humid night. The pink-paper-lantern-lit streets were alive with activity: people, some dressed in kimono and *happi* jackets, happily clattering along in their *geta*. After dodging for some way across small hump-backed bridges and busy alleys, our *sushi*-carrying convoy arrived at the harbour front. Here, *otochan* (papa), a round jovial man already well lubricated, was waiting for us on board his small fishing boat. He heaved on the mooring ropes, pulling the bow closer to the quay, and giggling, we all leapt unsteadily on board with our booty of gastronomic delights.

Otochan and a couple of his friends took to the wheelhouse while the rest of us crowded into the cockpit, where there stood two huge plastic dustbins filled with ice and scores of cans of beers and pops and teas and coffees and Pocari Sweats. Slowly, we motored out into the bay.

By now, I realized that I'd arrived in town just in time for Koniya's exuberant summer festival and tonight was the night for the spectacular show of *hanabi* fire-flowers.

Out in the bay we joined a flotilla of other small vessels that bobbed around on the gently rolling swell. Their riggings were festooned with a myriad of kaleidoscopically flickering lanterns and lights, the oscillating reflections dancing off the face of the sea. The warm tropical breeze swept like silk across my bare shoulders, bringing with it faint odours of cigarette smoke, beer-breath and fish. Captain Otochan cut the engine and the sounds of chattering laughter drifted on the wind across the water. A sense of heightened expectation hung in the air. My stomach swilled with a mixture of *sushi* and *sake* – a combination which, when united with the rousing distant deep beats of the traditional drums emanating from the shore, made me feel recklessly in love with Japan.

Then the fireworks started, set off from a barge moored

off the shore. The sky exploded into wildly scintillating flowers of fire. Shrieks of delight erupted from boat to boat as continuous bursts of *hanabi* discharged and bloomed with a boom into an incandescent shower of radiating shapes that splintered the sky.

Not long after the grand finale the wind whipped up and, with word of an approaching storm, everyone hurried for home.

Compared with the cooler breeze of the sea the intense, sultry torridity of my *minshuku* room was almost intolerable. Sweat continued to flow, my head pounding with feverish heat. Mrs Fairyland, on coming to bid me goodnight, realized she had a florid-faced foreigner on her hands and scuttled off to fetch me a life-enhancing electric fan, the base of which was embossed with the words:

AIRY FOR JUST LIVE
made by NATIONAL

Gratefully, I positioned the fan at the foot of my futon, switched it to high-wind mode and flopped naked on top of the sheet, relishing the Force 8 gale blasting up the wreck of my body.

In this way I fell into a cyclone-sleep until, some hours later, I awoke with a start when I felt a stinging sensation followed by a 'something' crawling over my stomach. Springing bolt upright, I yanked on the long dangling cord of the square fluorescent centre-light just in time to see a fat cockroach the size of a small mouse scuttling to the edge of the room before vanishing through a crack in the floor. I was so alarmed by the size of the creature I had seen that I tried to console myself by putting it down to nothing more than an over-heated imagination running wild. Too exhausted to do anything about it other than putting on a pair of knickers (made me feel more protectively sealed against any unwelcome invaders), I turned prostrate once more and drifted into a crawling commotion of dreams.

Half an hour later I was again wrenched from my slumber by another nipping cockroach scurrying over an upper thigh. This time there was definitely no case for a stretched imagination because at least half a dozen mice-roach were racing for cover between the ominous livestock-breeding cracks of the *tatami*. To add to the fun a gecko ran out from under my sheet to join his strange clucking family that was suction-footed to the wall.

Determined to carry out a cull of cockroaches I picked up a solid book (unfortunately, thanks to the Japanese tradition of no outdoor footwear indoors, I was severely lacking in a walloping, certain-death, cockroach-crushing shoe) and switched off the light, awaiting the return of the partial-to-dark, armour-suited, claw-pinching creatures.

About five had re-surfaced by the time I again turned on the light, but they vanished back down the floor cracks far faster than I could annihilate them. That is, all except one, to which with book in hand, I delivered a crashing blow. Well, for all the damage that it did, I might as well have tickled it with a feather. It shot off completely unharmed under the gap of the sliding door and out into the long wooden corridor. Ha! I thought, I've got you now, and, throwing on a T-shirt, gave chase. With nowhere to go the cockroach scuttled along at a keen lick, keeping close to the wall. Despite beating and battering the brute with my book at least a score of times, the indestructible carapace careered onwards intact before disappearing into the toilet.

Fraught with agitation at the thought of 'sleeping' in a room crawling with these apparently imperishable horrors, I thought: well, there's only one thing for it – erect my tent on the *tatami*. This, though, was not quite the simple operation it might sound. My room was so small that, in order to slot together the three ten-foot lengths of shock-corded poles, I had first to feed them out of the window to give me sufficient space before sliding them through the sleeves of the inner tent. Thankfully I accomplished the task without either waking the Fairyland household or puncturing a hole through the delicate sliding paper-covered walls of my room or, more importantly, without smashing the nearby neighbour's window with an out-of-control pole.

Fortunately, as the free-standing part of my inner tent was made almost solely of 'no-see-um' mosquito netting, lying inside it was not that much hotter than lying outside. And anyway, I was so relieved at being safely zipped up that I felt at that moment I could have put up with a temperature twice as hot as long as my sleep remained cockroach-free.

As there were no locks on the door I made sure I woke up especially early the next morning in order to pack up my tent, in case Mrs Fairyland should come wandering unannounced into my room to reclaim some of her washing. The trouble was that, unbeknown to me, she had arisen early to hang out some more washing on a line that stretched along the bottom of the upstairs windows. As I dismantled my tent, sliding a length of pole back through the sleeve and out of the window, she chose this most inopportune moment to raise her washing line. My pole simultaneously speared a pair of her bloomers, which then hung suspended over the street like a flag.

Still holding the lightweight trembling pole, I peered out of the window to try to deduce what had happened. Glancing sideways, who should I see peering out of the adjacent window but a very quizzical Mrs Fairyland. Our eyes locked – mine with embarrassment, hers with bemusement. How, I wondered, reddening fast, do I explain in foreign tongue just exactly what I'm doing hanging out of the window at 5.45 a.m. holding a ten-foot pole with her ample underwear attached to the end?

Well, I couldn't. Instead, I did the only thing I could think of doing at that moment which was to give her a sheepish smile along with a cheery '*Ohayo gozaimasu*!' morning greeting and pretend that hanging out of windows at dawn harpooning people's underwear was quite normal behaviour for a *gaijin*. Thankfully, when I next saw Mrs Fairyland, the matter was never even raised.

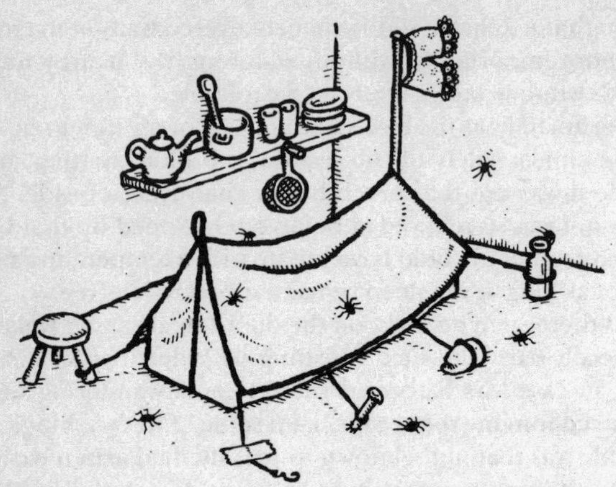

I stayed in Koniya for over a week. It was one of those sort of places where you occasionally arrive when everything feels right. Despite the shenanigans with my tent pole, Mrs Fairyland kept insisting I stay another day whenever I said that I felt I had best be moving on – after all, I was supposed to be cycling around Japan, was I not? Mrs Fairyland appeared to have taken quite a shine to me. I think she found me fascinating. She told me she had never spoken to a *gaijin* before, let alone had one sleeping in her house. She seemed utterly intrigued and amused with everything I did, whether it be washing my clothes in the sink in order to save a small wash in her washing-machine, eating Japanese food and actually enjoying it, making my own postcards out of food cartons or seeming quite content to travel alone.

I just wished I could explain myself better to her. I became frustrated that the extent of my Japanese could go no further than the superficial face of things – basic niceties were just about manageable but I was totally incapable of probing any deeper. And that's really where I wanted to be: under the skin. I knew she saw me – like all *gaijin* – as a comical character, a funny foreigner with deeply perplexing habits. But, at the same time, I also recognized that she too wanted to go beyond all that; she kept finding any excuse to come shuffling into my room – would I like *aisu-kuriimu, oolong* or *mugi-cha*, a shower, watch television, eat supper with them . . . ? Genuine generosity but, at the same time, questions acting as a sort of decoy in order to ask me more searching questions about feelings and thoughts and hopes and doubts and susceptibilities. Questions that needed answers way beyond the realms of my stunted Japanese or limited dictionary.

Despite the short time I had spent at Mrs Fairyland's it felt in a way as though I'd lived there for weeks. Sights and sounds and smells became very familiar: the early morning exercise music of the post-office across the road – the workers (many with cigarette poised between lips) synchronizing their stretching movements in the loading yard; passing beneath my window, the dustcart painted with swirls of bright flowers and playing loud, volume-distorted Chopin sonatas and Bach preludes from its exterior speakers – the rubbish collectors, all women in dainty floral bonnets and frilly gloves, more the sort of garb you might expect people to wear to the theatre than for collecting odorous piles of refuse; the sounds of the gossiping neighbours – mostly women – with their high-pitched chatter sounding like birds; the constant nonsensical yattering strains of television drifting through my windows, seeping through the walls (Mrs Fairyland alone would leave her three televisions, located in various parts of the house, all competing with each other, switched to their different channels); the wafts of frying fish floating on the air and the six o'clock sounds of a man across the alley breathing out luxurious moans of contentment as he sunk himself into his deep and indubitably scalding bath.

Most days I would go on mini expeditions into the hills and mountains where I would walk for hours feeling ridiculously happy.

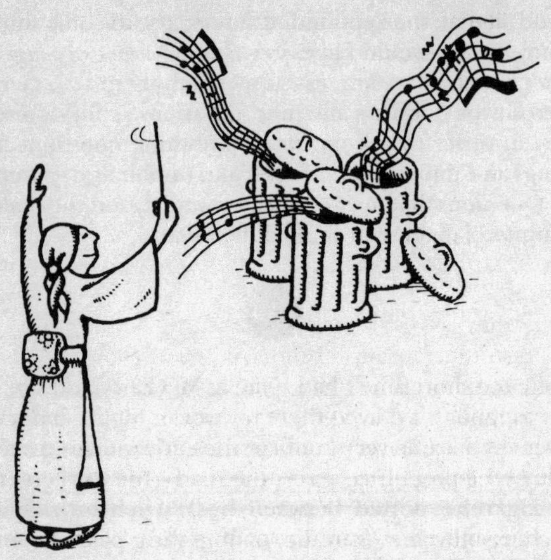

One morning I wandered down to the harbour, where I found the quaysides crowded with a lively chaos of people and stalls and flags as music and commentating machine-gunning voices screamed from a multitude of loudspeakers. I was at the races – the boat races, where teams of men and women with colour-coded kamikaze-style bandannas tied around their heads raced each other across the harbour in six-man traditional wooden canoes. Back and forth, back and forth they skimmed, careering around anchored poles before the powerful frenzy of their simple single-paddled strokes heaved back the water again. It was a fine and fun spectacle and I sat on the sea-wall, legs dangling over the edge, wedged into a small space a local family had made for me, and watched and cheered and laughed with the happy crowds around me.

A man beside me introduced himself as Kozo and placed a can of Hokkaido beer in my hand ('Let your spirit run free and enjoy nature's rich, bounty. Savour the taste of Hokkaido. That Good Hokkaido Taste').

Kozo nudged me and pointed over towards the crowds on the adjoining harbour wall.

'Your *tomodachi* – friends?' he asked.

I followed his gaze, which rested on the first *gaijin* I had seen for weeks and weeks – a small group of both black and white, some preparing themselves to take part in the boat race. Kozo, convinced that they must be my friends, kept urging me to take him over to meet them.

'But, Kozo,' I said, 'I have never seen these people before in my life.'

'But they are your friends!' he replied with a grin.

It wasn't just because I didn't know them that I was reticent about going over to say hello but also because I felt exceedingly bashful – I wasn't confident that I would know what to say to them or whether I could actually string together a coherent conversation in English as I had grown used to talking in a sort of willy-nilly, hit-and-miss form of Japanese, a form of desultory conversation with which I felt comfortable.

Also, I didn't want the added attention. I knew I looked odd enough as it was without having to go and increase the number of eyes upon me by joining the group of equally odd-looking *gaijin*, who were causing quite a stir. In fact, I was enjoying far more the pastime of staring at their seemingly eccentric ways than being a part of them.

Inevitably, though, we met – not all of them but a small breakaway faction who came over to talk to me. My unsociable ways moderated into intrigue as I found them fun and somewhat unusual. The two English sisters, Caroline and Diane (originally from Glastonbury), had flown in specially from Osaka as part of a performing pantomime – something to do with an international set-up – which explained their participation in the boat races. Caroline, wearing a long, loose, tie-dye cotton wrap-around mini-skirt, told me sheepishly that she was divorced and not far off forty. She had lived in Australia for five years, and after her marriage had broken up she had felt she 'needed a new life' and became involved in working for various conservation and rainforest groups. For the last two years she had lived in Kyoto, teaching English.

'But right now,' she said, 'I'm really pissed off with Japan. Do you know – the place where I work has no photocopier so I'm made to write out a hundred copies of whatever my boss needs.'

Diane, who lived in Totterdown, Bristol, had been working for a brewery before being made redundant – which gave her the opportunity to think: great! – now's my chance to travel.

'I'm going to Vietnam next,' she said, 'although I wish I had longer in Japan – I've only been here a few days. After Vietnam I'm going to Thailand and all that South East Asia bit before heading down to Australia. I'll be away for a year.'

Nour Rashied was an imposing black man, flamboyant beyond belief. He was cloaked in a fine white jellabah and wore a green-brimmed white hat upon his head.

'I am maybe thirty-four going on thirty-five,' he said, his face set in a perpetual and dazzling grin. 'I do not know the date of my birthday exactly because I was born in a small village in Sudan near to the border of Egypt. There was no hospital.'

'Is that anywhere near the Nubian Desert?' I asked.

'Yes, my language is Nubian – and of course some Arabic. Nubian people are fine people! You know, we have a 5,000-year-old history. My name Nour means "light" and Rashied means "straight", although I am not a straight man – I like to waver off line sometimes!'

After watching a few more boat races, Nour gave me an Asahi beer and said, 'I am a great man! Just like Margaret Thatcher – my girlfriend. In fact I have 2,000 girlfriends as I like to live illegally!' And, not for the first time, Nour threw back his head with a marvellously rollicking laugh.

When he learnt that I was cycling he said, 'I have never learnt bicycle travel as I went to school by donkey or camel.'

One of Nour's brothers was a rich and successful businessman working for the UN. He had two wives and eight children and lived for some of the year in Kenya and the rest of it in Birmingham.

Nour, a civil engineer by trade, said his home was now in Japan where he lived in the Orange House in Osaka working for the Community Village as part of an international programme.

'I would like to go to Britain,' he said, 'but your very friendly government does not allow me a visa.'

'Even though Margaret Thatcher is your girlfriend?' I said.

'Ha! Yes – some girlfriend! Sometimes I go to the Philippines to live for a while in Manila. A few years ago I was living in Kuwait and I found myself agreeing with Sadam Hussein by saying "no" to the USA, but then, when I felt Sadam took things a little too far, I left for the Philippines.'

That night there was singing and dancing and drumming and multiple heats of tugs-of-war taking place in the festively noisy and bustling streets. Caroline and Diane had invited me to join them in a parade of street dancing but, preferring the idea of spectating to prancing, I lay low, mingling among the crowds, hoping I would remain hidden from my fellow *gaijin* in case they should lure me into the 'show'. I weaved my way through the streets, peeping here and poking there, intrigued by the strange foods and games available on the lines of stalls, listening and watching various groups of traditional Japanese dance and music and costume. At one point I came across the *gaijin* contingent dancing wildly in the street and before I had time to lose myself among the crowd I was spotted by Caroline, who beckoned me to join them. A gaggle of grandmothers in festive mood couldn't have timed it better for expressing an interest in me, taking me under their wing and back to one of their houses where a party of drunken fishermen had gathered. Here I was clucked and fussed and giggled over and fed a feast of fish and chunky crescents of iced watermelon.

By the time I'd gone back out into the streets to watch some more dancing there wasn't much point in going to bed, so instead I decided to return to base to collect my bike, telling Mrs Fairyland that I was off to catch the dawn ferry over to Kakeromajima Island and that I would be back later that night. Cupping her cheeks in her hands, she looked a little shocked.

'But Jodie-*san*, you cannot go there!' she said. 'The island is a dangerous place – full of *habu*.'

The ferry took only thirty minutes to glide over the glassy sea between the bays and it was such a glorious sun-rising crossing that, had I been bitten by a *habu* the moment I stepped of the boat only to drop dead, I think the ferry ride alone would have been worth it.

Kakeromajima appeared to me to be not so much Habu Isle as Yama (mountain) Isle: severely graded mountains appeared to cover the entire length of the island's thirty-odd kilometres. There were definitely more *yama* than people, that was for sure. Occasionally I would plummet down to a tiny fishing village where the liveliest thing I would see might be an old man in a conical hat sitting on a bench in the shade beneath a tree, or a bent-backed *obaasan* pushing a loaded wheelbarrow along the road.

Near Nominoura I stopped at an interesting beach-side building with a big bright fish mural painted on an outside wall. Needing some water, I walked inside to find it was a hip café – the type of place you might imagine finding in Hawaii, full of surfers. But here there was no one to be seen. I called, then waited a while, then called again before wandering round the back and into a large kitchen. Here I found Patrick, a truck driver from Basel who had also worked for some years as a chef in France. I asked him what had brought him to Japan.

'I 'ave just sailed around zee world,' he said, quite matter-of-factly, as if sailing round the world was no more arduous a task than brushing your teeth. 'Zat eeze my boat in zee bay. And now I 'ave no money and I meet zees man who say I can work in 'is kitchen so today eeze my first day for working.'

For a moment Patrick resumed his job of scraping off encrusted layers of black grease from the oven. He looked disgusted.

'Ahrgh! Deez-gusting. You could make a meat ball from zees stuff – I don't sink zees oven 'as ever been cleaned!'

We were silent for a moment as I watched him chiselling away at the burnt grease and grime, his deeply tanned and muscular shoulders and forearms layered in a thin film of sweat that covered elaborate tattoos.

Then he stood up, stretched his back, wiped his face on a short towel that lay on a work top and said, 'You want to talk or you in a 'urry?'

'Hurry?' I said. 'No, I'm in no hurry. I was just coming to see if I could fill up on water.'

Patrick went to the fridge and pulled out a large glass jug of iced tea.

''Elp yourself,' he said.

He asked me what I was doing on Kakeromajima.

'Oh,' I said, 'I thought I might try and cycle around the island. I wasn't bargaining on quite so many mountains, though.'

Patrick slowly scratched his stubble, looking at me with a sort of neither-here-nor-there expression. A cockroach broke the ice, scuttling down a crack behind the sink.

'Those things make me feel sick,' I said. 'I think they're my least favourite organism on earth!'

'I 'ad zem for months on my boat,' Patrick said. 'Finally, zay leave me in Tahiti only to pick zem up again in Japan. Japanese cockroach not only bite but zay fly. Zay say zere are even cockroach on zee moon.'

I asked Patrick how long he had spent sailing around the world.

'Ergh, maybe for two years now.'

'And have you been alone all that time?'

'*Non, non,* I 'ave a Japanese wife.'

'Oh,' I said, 'well, that must have improved life considerably.'

'Ergh, you know, but you cannot love weesout 'ate,' said Patrick, a touch enigmatically.

'Are you referring to your wife or your boat?' I asked.

'Bose!' he said. 'Sometimes it eeze I love zee sailing and other times I 'ate so much. My feeling eeze zee same weeze my wife. She say I fuckin' swear too much. But, you know us Europeans speak our mind. Japanese people, zay never scream out in anger – always . . . 'ow you say? . . . I sink zay keep anger in zair *bouteilles.* I tell my wife: you 'ave to shout or else you get cancer.'

I was about to point out that maybe shouting has nothing to do with it, as Japanese people have a far lower incidence of cancer than Europeans, but by now there was no stopping Patrick in full flow.

'We 'ad many fight – always I shout at 'er but she never shout at me; always she just go quiet. I say to 'er "I can't understand you why you don't shout at me." I 'aven't seen 'er for . . . maybe now three month. She live on Yoron-jima weeze our three-year-old baby.'

'So you don't see your child much either?' I asked.

'*Non.* When I try to bring zee baby to live weeze me on zee boat my wife . . . aargh . . . she cry so fuckin' much I worry for zee baby – my wife eeze working so zee baby is looked after by zee grandmother. I don't like ziss idea – for zee baby to grow up like typical Japanese. I want my baby to 'ave open mind.'

'Are you going to continue living in Japan?' I asked.

'*Non, non,* I go to France. I love France – it eeze my 'ome. I work in Switzerland for zee bigger money and zen I cross zee border to live in France for cheaper life.'

'How soon will you leave?'

'Ergh, first I make some money and zen I must mend zee boat.'

'You do that yourself?'

'Of course. Zee Japanese don't do anything – always zay pay someone else to do zee dirty work. But us poor Europeans we 'ave no money. We must do zings ourselves. Tonight, where you sleeping – you want to sleep my boat?'

Detecting my raised eyebrows he added, laughing for the first time, 'Eeze okay. I give *non* sexual 'arassment. We can 'ave maybe a bouteille of wine under zee stars okay?'

'Well,' I said, 'it's a nice idea, but I've got to get going – got a few mountains to get under my belt.'

'Okay, okay, 'ey you are going to Yoron?'

'Probably,' I said, 'but at this rate I'm not going anywhere.'

'So you give my wife a ring – maybe she can give you some 'elp. Okay?'

'Okay, maybe,' I said, '*merci*.'

'*De rien*,' said Patrick, scribbling a number on a napkin. After filling up my bottles I walked back out into the searing heat.

I carried on over mountains and through silent hamlets – Ikenama, Ankyaba, Shodon, Akitoku, Sachiyuki. Reaching a small, quiet harbour I was so hot and so tired from exertion and lack of sleep that I dropped down a wall into the deep and crystal clear blue water and swam out past the moored fishing boats, where I floated on my back feeling as if I'd gone to heaven. As I swam back to the harbour wall the only sign of life was an old man sitting perfectly still in the shade, gazing out towards me. At the opposite end of the wall, sitting in exactly the same position, was an old woman also gazing out towards me. They probably sit there every day gazing out to sea, I thought; and as I swam towards them I wondered what they must be making of a *gaijin* head, bobbing in and out of the water among the gently rocking fishing boats.

The road then turned into a narrow dirt track and the only people I saw over the next couple of hours were a woman with a wicker basket on her back who, dipping inside it, gave me a bunch of what she called 'monkey banana' – the smallest, sweetest and most tasty ones I'd ever eaten; a man in a small wooden store who filled my bottles up with iced *oolong-cha*; a bunch of workmen in a tipper truck who stopped and, without prompting, handed me a thermos of their iced tea to finish; and a couple of *obaasan*, their heads wrapped in sun-protective towels, sifting through seaweed in the heat on a narrow strip of beach dressed in knee-length coats, gloves and wellingtons while keeping a watchful eye over their grandchildren splashing around in the sea on a truck's large inflated inner tube.

I arrived back at the ferry after having seen only a handful of *habu* all day, some tyre-squashed, others slithering silently into the overgrown verges. Later that night, back with the Fairylands, I collapsed utterly exhausted into the safe haven of my cockroach-free zone of tent. I had only been asleep about an hour when, shortly before 1 a.m., Mrs Fairyland (who rarely seemed to sleep) came shuffling into my room to ask me if I would like some *aisu-kuriimu*.

This was the first time she had caught me sleeping in my tent in her house. She looked more than a little startled. I didn't quite know what to say – after all, I suppose it must have been a bit like inviting an Eskimo to come and stay, only to find later that the comfy bed you had provided had been ditched in favour of an igloo. The only thing I could think of to explain this ludicrous situation was to mumble in a comatose state something about the 'dangerous *habu*'.

Despite the fact that, in Mrs Fairyland's eyes, I was becoming madder and madder by the minute, she continued to shower me with edible gifts and come on regular visits to my room to talk to me at high speed in her well-nigh incomprehensible Okinawan dialect. Always though she would end up in fits of giggles; I don't think it was because of anything I particularly said but more because of what I did. She was fascinated by my expressions and actions and habits. The one thing that was usually guaranteed to set her off was when she found me sitting on the futon in my bra and knickers, writing letters or postcards or diary at the low table. She couldn't seem to understand how I could find it so hot to have to sit in my room in my next-to-nothings and not be embarrassed.

'But no one's going to see me except you,' I told her.

'But the *rinjin*! the *rinjin*! – the neighbours! the neighbours!' she laughed.

I told her I positioned myself so the *rinjin* couldn't see me and that, when I looked out of the window, I always put on a shirt. But I could tell she didn't believe me. Holding on to her ample sides she would dissolve into giggles, informing me, not for the first time, that I was a mad *gaijin* before pouring me more tea.

One morning, as I was doing a spot of bike maintenance in the shade of a concrete wall, a man in a reversed baseball cap, creaking along the narrow street on a rusty bicycle, stopped beside me. He spoke good English.

'Do you have a problem?' he asked.

'No, I'm just making sure things are tight and working.'

'You are American person?' he asked.

'No, English.'

'Ah so, *desu-ka*? My name is Takuya.'

Leaning forward on his handlebars, Takuya chatted to me for a while – occasionally stopping to wipe the sweat from his face with a yellow towel draped round his neck. He told me he was thirty-one and worked eleven or twelve hours a day, six days a week, in his father's liquor store.

'It is too hard work,' he said. 'I don't enjoy, but I must help my father.'

We talked a bit more before he had to get off to work. Later that day I bumped into him on one of his delivery rounds and he asked me if I would like to visit his home that evening – apologizing that he lived with his parents. He seemed like a nice boy so we arranged he would come round to the *minshuku* at 8.30 and walk me back to his house.

When Takuya called at the front door at 8.25, Mrs Fairyland came galloping up the stairs and into my room scarcely able to contain her excitement that a Japanese boy had called round for the *gaijin*. Downstairs I found Takuya smiling, smelling of soap, in a grey T-shirt and a pair of baggy bright yellow and black 'Body Glove' shorts. His sockless feet were, rather worryingly, crammed into a dainty pair of women's heeled and pointed grey shoes, his heel hanging into thin space over the back. Takuya must have noted my look of surprise because as we walked – or more like, as I walked and he tottered – he explained that, as he lived just around the corner, he had slid into the first shoes that came to foot – his mother's.

After a few twists and turns up narrow and friendly alleys we entered a modern concrete apartment block where Takuya's mother, wrapped in kimono, greeted me by bowing almost as low as the floor. She asked me one question which Takuya needn't have translated as it was one I understood from a thousand times over: was I not lonely? Then she gave me a bowl of pickled pink shallots and a tall glass of *oolong-cha*.

Takuya lived self-contained in his own room with adjoining kitchenette. A large poster of James Dean covered one wall, against which was propped a soprano saxophone.

'I love jazz,' said Takuya and, pulling a CD from a selection of hundreds, flicked on Dizzy Gillespie. We sat on the *tatami* drinking first the tea, before progressing to a few bottles of Kirin beer. Takuya again told me how hard he worked, saying that although a recent law had been passed for a forty-hour week his father continued to make him work over a seventy-hour week which, Takuya said, put his father in breach of the law. I asked him how many days' holiday he had a year.

'Forty-six,' he said, which at first I thought was not bad at all, until he explained that this included not only national holidays but Sundays as well. In effect, he got nothing. For all this effort, Takuya earned 200,000 yen a month (about £1,300).

'I am Osaka University student,' he told me, 'and I live for bright light again. Next year I hope maybe for going to Kyushu – you have been to Oita? – where I work with my cousin in his business of landscaping.'

'He's a landscape gardener?' I asked.

'Yes, certainly. And the money make me very happy man – 500,000 yen [£3,300] in one month. The boss I understand makes 1,500,000 yen [£10,000] in one month only. Fine money for many happy day!'

As I folded and unfolded my legs to keep the pins and needles at bay, Takuya continued to tell me about his life which, he said, was indeed comfortable but he was fed up with people always 'acting as one' – no individualism.

'Japanese people,' he said, 'always same, same, same. Same short hair, same clothes, same idea, same opinion. I think this is boring lifestyle indeed. Once I grow a . . . *kuchi-hige* – excuse me, in English I do not have knowing this name . . .'

'Moustache,' I said when he indicated the channel above his upper lip.

'*So desho.* And my father, he get very angry man – he make me cut it away because he say I try to look like a different man, to be noticed, to . . . how you say . . . ?'

'Stand out from the crowd?'

'Yes, yes, and he say this is very bad – it is Japanese tradition for Japanese people always looking and speaking similarity together.'

'Do you think this might have its good sides – its advantages?' I asked. 'Could this help make Japan safer, say, than England?'

'Mmmm,' he said thoughtfully, 'maybe safety country indeed. In Japan, if someone take CD from store, owner will hit stealing person maybe like this . . .' and he demonstrated on himself with a biff across the ears.

'Is that all?' I asked, astonished, sceptically thinking that, if that was the sole punishment delivered to shoplifters in Britain, then there wouldn't be much left in the shops. 'Wouldn't the police be contacted?'

'For store owner police are too much trouble and money for involving. But for stealing man, the dishonour of being catched is usually indeed enough to stop him stealing in similarity style again.'

On the way out Takuya's mother handed me a pack of lacy *hankachifu* ('*Purezento*') while papa managed to bow mid-slurp of his *miso* soup. We walked back, chatting all the way, to the *minshuku* where, on the steps, Takuya suddenly went very quiet and then, looking as though he was about to kiss me, lunged instead without warning for my hand, giving it a vigorous shake. He mumbled something about how nice it was to meet me and, if I decided to stay longer in Koniya, I must give him a ring. I thanked him before turning and stepping into the *minshuku*, quietly sliding the door shut behind me.

I left Koniya the following morning but I didn't plan my departure very well as I'd only been going an hour or so before I got caught up in a severe and sudden storm. I made it to a small village, where I dived beneath the corrugated iron roof of a school's bike shelter. At one point a gust of wind blew with such strength that it ripped off a piece of the roof, flinging it across the road as if it was merely made of cardboard.

When the sun reappeared the land steamed and my sweat flowed. I dropped down a mountain into a small fishing village full of bonneted and aproned women tootling along on identical small-wheeled tricycles, all of them trailing seaweed from the plastic-coated baskets loaded on their rears. I gave the top of my head a sort of Stanley Laurel scratch and thought: how endearing, yet how bizarre.

Despite the struggle of the gradients, the quiet road which dog-legged its rollercoaster way over the mountains was a joy. The jungle forests that carpeted the slopes were full of the vivid green of summer while the silver-blue brilliance of the sea sparkled upon a jagged coast of rocky inlets and bays; and in the distance – across the narrow straits – the peaked magnificence of 'Habu Isle'.

A small flat-bed van pulled alongside and a workman's arm extended out of the window, attached to the familiar blue can of a Pocari Sweat. The driver tooted.

'*Ganbatte*!' he cheered before buzzing away.

A little later the same sort of thing happened with a pick-up truck, its cab packed with a group of people of widely ranging ages. Round a couple of bends I found the truck had pulled over: the occupants – a wife and husband, their two boys aged three and five, the wife's sister and the husband's parents – were all waiting for me.

'America?' I was asked.

'No, English.'

'Ah so, *desu-ka*? You are one person?'

'Yes.'

'Gaa! You are not lonely?'

'No.'

'Gaa! *Sugoi*! – That's great! You are hungry?'

'Umm, well, no, I'm fine – really.'

'Nonsense! You must be – come, we will eat!'

So I was ferried across the road to a disused quarry pit where, despite the advancing rumbles of thunder, a large square of blue tarpaulin was laid on the ground on top of which was placed a fine feast of food and drink, fit to sink any further ideas of claiming any more mountains that day. No sooner had shoes been kicked off and the feasters had stepped on to the tarp, hunkering down on our heels among the food, than the first fat drops of storm-cloud rain splashed on to the mat with an inauspicious ferocity. These drops were joined by more, then more, until a veritable deluge was bulleting on to our heads. Had this been an English gathering we'd have aborted the mission and dived for cover, but this oriental picnic-party was made of sturdier stuff – no wild-whipped storm was going to stop them sharing fun and food with the a tomfool of a *gaijin.* A canopy of umbrellas mushroomed over our heads, the wife's sister holding one for me as if I was royalty. As the lightning cracked and the rain ricocheted off our nylon domes, we tucked into our stomach-swelling assortment of riceballs, fried tofu with vegetables, raw squid, mini shrimps, fishy-flavoured bulgher mixed with what looked and tasted like rubber bands, and hairy hunks of pigs' trotters which were definitely not born to be tackled with chopsticks. Any left-over food was packaged up in foil and tupperware and presented to me, making it the largest doggie-bag I've ever had the good fortune to force into my panniers. To wash it all down I was cajoled into accepting a two-litre plastic bottle of *mugi-cha* (barley tea), a container of *shochu* (a potent alcoholic brew of sugar cane and rice), and four cans of *ryoku-cha* (green tea) with the words 'I like nature' embossed on the side.

The storm passed and the heat rose. A heavy stomach and a *shochu* mind are not the best combination for tackling an afternoon of switchback mountains. The snakes woke me up, though, and kept me on my toes – one looked a bit like Postman Pat with a magnificent crimson stripe running its length. Perversely, it was the dead snakes that proved more of a hazard than the live ones. Lying squashed on the corners of hairpin bends these remnants of snake would prove as lethal as an oil patch or banana skin, if happened upon on a speedy descent. I almost came a cropper on more than one occasion.

I carried on, never quite knowing where I was but never really caring. A small fishing village was preparing for a festival with people busy putting up stalls, hanging the narrow street with pink-and-white striped lanterns, and festooning a fishing boat with flowers and plastic wind-wheels.

More mountains, more snakes, more sweating, more *mugi-cha* down the hatch and then, towards evening, I plunged back down to the coast of the East China Sea – rocks, tunnels, hamlets, hills. A handful of flat brown houses clutched the slopes surrounding a harbour of concrete. At the roadside, in front of a grey cement wall, sat an old woman in a scarf and black wellies quietly watching the sea or the world or the *gaijin* fly by. So peaceful . . . until the wailing approach of the 'Fresh Food' delivery van – an ear-shattering mixture of screeching electric guitars and distorted shockwaves of shrieking sugar-pop vibrating out of the loudspeakers attached to its roof before bouncing off the steep cliff walls. The racketing noise, so repellent, so unnecessary, filled me with despair. How could such a din be allowed? What was the point? Didn't people mind having the sounds of the sea and the wind drowned into megaphoned oblivion? Seemingly not; the children continued playing with some beetles, the women continued weeding through a pile of stones and men continued sitting on the concrete slab of quay picking away at their tangle of nets – all behaving as if the cacophonous reverberations of the Pot Noodle-selling Fresh Food van didn't even exist.

I hurried along the coast in the growing darkness, anxious to find a place for the night before a storm front, its clouds as black as squid-ink, rolled in over the sea from the west. Hamlets diminished. The road, squeezed in between the mountains and the ocean, offered no hope of a camp-spot. My anxiety grew. I didn't fancy being caught between the storm devil and the deep dark sea. Adrenalin surged me onward, upward, over yet more mountains and rocky promontories, until at last I arrived in the little town of Yamato-son. With no space making itself even remotely obvious for a tent I pulled my bike into a bus shelter, tidying it up to make it my home for the night. But when a bunch of excitedly chattering ten-year-olds stumbled upon me I uprooted myself with a sigh, heading off back down the alleys, looking for an alternative spot to turn horizontal.

Towards the back of the village I found a school and contemplated tucking my tent at the foot of a potentially camouflaging bush that bordered the end of the playing field. As I was wondering whether just to whip up my tent quickly without all the palaver of seeking permission (something I wasn't sure I had enough energy for, let alone time before the storm arrived), I heard a sudden sound of frenetic splashing followed by some high vocal yelps of excited cheering. Cycling down the lane to the source, I peered over a gate to see the last heat of an *al fresco* swimming race taking place in the fast-dying light. A fit-looking schoolmaster in a blue nylon tracksuit stood watch over a clutch of pre-pubescent boys and girls in black costumes, caps and goggles. I stood for a moment mesmerized by the sight of these children, all looking so sleek and so uniformly appealing. Had it been your typical average British school swimming class of youngsters, the sizes and faces and hair and body weight of the children would have been all over the place – a higgledy-piggledy mish-mash. But here in this Japanese class, as the glistening-skinned children stood in a row on the side of the pool, they resembled streamlined oriental water-sprites.

Needless to say, spotting a *gaijin* head over the fence caused quite a stir. I gave a quick wave and then, not wanting to cause more of a scene than I already had, I backed off in retreat. But the schoolmaster, equally intrigued, called over to me, asking whether I needed any help. The pool nymphs, overcome by excitement at the sight of this strange being on a bicycle, broke rank to gather in a giggling clump around the gate. The schoolmaster, adopting a stern face, shooed them away to get changed before turning back to see to my needs.

'I'm sorry to disturb you,' I said, 'but I'm looking for a place to put my tent for the night. Do you know if it is possible to camp in the corner of the playing field?'

'But it is dangerous – there are many *habu*. And tonight there is maybe a typhoon!'

'Ah so, *desu-ka*?' I replied, thinking I'd heard that one before.

The teacher, who introduced himself as Syouichi Motoshita, then ran the usual gauntlet of questions over me concerning country of birth, status, mission in mind, factor of loneliness . . . until his clothed charges reappeared with expectant expression. After quietening them down Mr Motoshita then turned back to me, Oh Honourable *Gaijin*, asking whether I would mind handing out some sort of swimming diplomas.

'*Pas du tout*,' I said, or something similar in Japanese, and handed each little bowing-bodied cherub the aforementioned certificate. By the time this spontaneous ceremony had ended it was dark and I realized that, touching though the swimming episode had been, I was no closer to laying myself to rest. This was where I was wrong.

I was preparing myself to return to the bus shelter for a possibly breezy night of typhoonery when Mr Motoshita invited me to follow him. Because of the speed of his Japanese, I couldn't quite grasp where it was he wanted me to follow him to, but that didn't seem to matter and, with thirty or so swimming champions swarming after us, we passed through the weaving, dark, narrow streets of the town. Every so often Mr Motoshita would bark out an instruction and one of the chattering children would break away from the pack and disappear through the brown-rimmed sliding door of their home – a home which looked just like everyone else's.

Finally, there was only one child remaining, who scampered along at our heels like a playful kitten until we reached a pale block of concrete flats set at the back of Yamato's low huddle of houses which hunkered down behind the concrete sea-wall of the town. We walked across clean grey gravel chippings – identical to those that surrounded every water-fountain in Japan – and along to a ground floor apartment which I took to be the girl's home. I was right. It was her home, but so too was it Mr Motoshita's.

Poking his head through the open door he called, 'Yoko, come quickly. I have an honourable guest!'

Seconds later, a handsome woman appeared on the step. As the sounds of the approaching storm rolled in, the girl (who by now had told me her name was Yukiko) scampered happily up to the woman, repeating, '*O-kaa-san*, we have a *gaijin* to stay! *O-kaa-san*, we have a *gaijin* to stay!'

O-kaa-san (Mama), who introduced herself as Yoko, took this sudden news remarkably well. She shuffled over to me in her plastic outdoor slippers, bowing and smiling and welcoming me with a liberal dose of '*Dozo, dozo* – please, be my guest.' At her guidance I was led around the back, where my bike was tucked into a corner beneath the washing line. As I stepped inside with my last pannier, the storm threw itself with a vengeance upon the small fishing community and I thought: phew, close thing.

The apartment, about the size of an American's double-bay car port, consisted of a tiny kitchen leading to a tiny six-mat living room, two tiny matted bedrooms and a bathroom the size of a broom cupboard. One thing in this tiny *apaarto* was huge: the television, which continuously blathered away on high volume. Within moments of my entering her home, Yoko was serving me *mugi-cha* and a saucer of 'interesting'-tasting green elastic goo bound up in little packets of vine-type leaves.

Yukiko, the only child, sat cross-legged beside me, her bare knees touching mine, enthusiastically talking me through her school books and then, pulling out her atlas, asked me to point out the countries in which I had cycled. Every time my finger came to rest on a country and I would say '*Koko* – here', Yukiko would emit a high-throated series of disbelieving sooorrr, sooorrr, ah sooorrrs and call out through the open paper doors to the kitchen, where Yoko and Syouichi were both busy preparing a tasty-smelling supper, saying:

'*O-kaa-san, Otochan* – Jodie-*san* has been to Italy! *O-kaa-san, Otochan* – Jodie-*san* has been to Iceland! *O-kaa-san, Otochan* – Jodie-*san* has been to . . .'

After a little more kitchen-clattering Yoko appeared, inviting me to take a bath and insisting I give her all my washing for her to drop in the machine. Before I disappeared into the bathroom I made for the door across the narrow corridor behind which sat the toilet. Yoko, who spoke a few words of English and seeing where I was heading, suddenly went all a bit flustered, apologizing profusely that they didn't have a Western-style toilet.

'Oh, please don't worry at all,' I said. 'I prefer the Japanese style anyway,' and without further ado I stepped into the 'Cool Kid Cat' toilet slippers and closed the door. Mid-squat, a light knocking was heard accompanied by the anxious tones of Yoko.

'Jodie-*san.* Harrow! Harrow! You okay?'

'Yes, thank you, Yoko,' I replied, wondering in what way I couldn't be okay. 'Everything seems to be under control.'

When I emerged Yoko was still standing there looking deeply perplexed.

'Jodie-*san*,' she said in hushed tones, 'you can sit in toilet squat really?'

'But of course,' I said, 'I'm just like you. It's easy. It's natural. It's what I do all the time when I'm camping.'

Yoko looked as if I was not of this world.

'In fact,' I said, 'if I have a choice like in a *minshuku* or *depaato* I always choose the Japanese-style toilet to the Western style. They're much more sensible, much more hygienic – much more comfortable!'

When I emerged from the bath, octopus-red of face, I found the Motoshita family plus two new faces sitting on their heels around a low lacquer table heaving with food. The newcomers, Yoko explained, were the principal of the school (where Syouichi taught) and his wife. They were their good neighbours, she said, and she had invited them round to supper, thinking they would love to meet me. When we were introduced the kneeling wife, who was wearing a short silk jacket over an incredibly expensive-looking silk dress, bowed so low that her nose touched the *tatami.* The principal's face was set in a constant grin.

As we picked at platefuls of various fish and unidentifiable creatures from the deep (fried, grilled and raw), bowls of rice, eggy soup and seaweed and a green paste rolled up in a leaf which shot the roof off my mouth, we talked about Hokkaido (where Yoko once lived), Kagoshima (where Syouichi was brought up), school life (hard), school postings (all over the place), what I thought of Japan (confusingly complex), the difference between the cool-climed people in the north and the hot-headed ones of the south (lots!), a few other things (which I've forgotten about) and the weather (the principal informing me that it had just been Japan's hottest July on record). All the time the television babbled away, first through a dance competition, then a samurai home drama and then the ubiquitous games show in which, accompanied by a chorus of audience hysteria, a *gaijin*, dressed up in a gorilla outfit, and a Japanese boy put on a large elasticated plastic nose and a ginger wig.

During supper I had to excuse myself twice to go to the toilet and each time I did so Yoko would become highly concerned, believing that 'Japanese food is making you sick?'

'No, no, I'm fine!' I said, trying to reassure her, 'I've just been drinking too much!'

Finally, after the principal's wife had presented Yoko with a watermelon the size of a beach ball and Yoko had sliced it into juicy great chunks for all of us to finish off with, it was 11.30 and, after a further series of low-level bows, the guests returned to their home.

Forbidden to help with the washing-up, I was led by Yoko to her bedroom where she had earlier placed a futon for me beside her own (on which Yukiko was now deep-breathing). Despite the heat (it was still hot enough to sweat in the air-conditioned room), Yoko equipped me with a pair of red-and-green checked fleece pyjamas, thick enough to keep me warm for a night on a Pole, which, out of politeness, I felt obliged to wear. I lay down beside Yukiko listening to the washing-up clatter and chatter of Yoko and Syouichi in the kitchen and the howling gale hammering against the double-sealed and shuttered windows. I wondered if Syouichi was going to sleep with us girls but he didn't – he slept on a makeshift futon in front of the television.

Needing a pee during the night, I managed to crawl in slow motion across the floor of futons and creep to the toilet without waking either Yoko or Yukiko. But, on my return, Yoko suddenly sat bolt upright, tugged on the light and said anxiously, 'Jodie-*san* – you are sick?'

'No, no,' I said, 'I'm fine. I always have to go to the toilet in the night.'

Yoko looked relieved. 'I am making terrible dreaming,' she said. 'Japanese food is in my dreaming sicknessing you!'

At 6.30 I was wrenched from my sweaty pyjama'd slumber by a screeching wail emitting from the town's loudspeakers calling all Junior High School students to a bout of vigorous Sunday morning exercise in the playing field. Chided by Yoko, a sleepy-faced Yukiko rolled off the futon, pulled on some clothes and trudged outside into the wild rain. When she returned, looking not much more enlivened than when she'd left, she told me that these exercise classes were something she had to do every day, including Sundays and school holidays, and she showed me her card which was stamped for attendance. Failure to acquire a sufficient amount of stamps resulted in punishment.

Breakfast proved as magnificent as supper the night before and consisted of watermelon, orange segments, sliced tomatoes, *miso* soup, a block of warm tofu with soy sauce, rice, strips of *nori* seaweed and a tub of *natto* (fermented beans) which Yoko was amazed that I could eat, because even Yukiko turned up her nose at *natto*.

'What would you rather have for breakfast?' I asked Yukiko.

'*Makudonarudo*!' she cried.

Rifling through my panniers, hoping to come across something I could present to Yoko for having me to stay, all I could find was a dented box of Fortnum and Mason English Breakfast Tea and a small silk scarf I'd kept in my gift reserve which I had forgotten about. I felt a bit abashed with my meagre offering, even more so when Yukiko gave me a pair of 'Hello Kitty' socks and a pair of locally made earrings, Syouichi two Fuji films for my camera, and Yoko an expensive-looking canvas sun hat. They urged me to stay another day or two, especially as it was still blowing a gale (it turned out to be yet another tail end of a typhoon, this one having veered off along the north coast), but, not sure whether I was up to another day of being the focus of their boundless generosity – it's hard work smiling and saying thank you all the time – let alone another sweltering night in polar pyjamas, I opted to head off into the rain.

The wind was so strong, buffeting me backwards and all over the road, that it took nearly six hours to 'ride' and occasionally walk the twenty-odd miles back to Naze. Along with the hazardous fun of being one moment sucked towards the swaying underbellies of passing trucks and the next blasted clean off the cliff-face, I was also threatened by the wind tearing at the palms, sending their razor-sharp fronds scudding like fans of knife-blades dangerously close overhead.

On the outskirts of Naze a tanker pulled over up the road. In most other countries in which I've cycled, such a sight would cause inner alarms to stir. Uh-oh! I'd think. Potential flasher material ahoy? But, in Japan, it seemed my anxieties were of another sort: the worry that someone was going to be nice to me. And I was right. As I approached I watched the tanker driver jump down out of his cab, wave to me, dash across the road to the vending machine before darting back to put a can of chilled Boss coffee in my hands.

'*Ganbatte!* – Good luck!' he said, before bowing, clambering back into his cab and driving away.

Before I'd even had time to take a gulp, a white car came to an erratic halt just in front of me – the woman driver springing out of one door and her young son (in an 'American Car are born to Liberate' T-shirt) leaping out of the other.

'*Konnichiwa*! *Konnichiwa*!' cried the woman excitedly. 'We read about you in the newspaper – it is great!'

With that, she sprinted across the road to the well-customed vending machine to buy me a choice of four cans (coffee, tea, apple juice and Pocari Sweat) before foisting 500 yen upon me. In somewhat bewildered state I watched them accelerate off down the road. No sooner had I packed a pannier with my assortment of light refreshments than yet another vehicle pulled up, the occupants (a woman with her three small daughters) hopping excitedly around my feet and writing out their address for me in a jumble of giddy ideograms, urging me to come and stay. Worried that they would most likely be too nice to me I declined the offer, saying I had a ferry to catch. And then the woman did as I feared: she went across the road to the fast-emptying vending machine.

'Jodie-*san,*' she called as she went, 'what would you like?'

'Nothing, thank you.'

'Nothing?' she cried. 'What nonsense!'

And she dropped in 500 yen for five cans of caffeines and juices and fizzes. I never would have imagined that I could become reluctant to accept generous offerings – but I did: a sort of curious reaction to an overkill of kindness. In most countries, I travel with that all-pervading anxiety and awareness that someone somewhere might do something unpleasant to me. In Japan, the stress is reversed: not only someone but nearly everyone is going to do something overwhelmingly nice. And niceness, although nice, can be hard work to take.

TOKUNOSHIMA

SUGARCANE ISLE

* Cyclad: adj. ('saiklad) clothed Bicycle

CHAPTER 20

Spicy Your Mama

The ferry terminal in Naze was closed. Propped against the door was a large blackboard awash with a white swirl of chalked *kanji*. As I was studying it (thinking: '?'), a man approached. He walked up to the bank of vending machines alongside, dropped in a couple of coins for two cans of Boss coffee and wandered over to hand me one and read the blackboard.

'Where are you going?' he asked.

'Tokunoshima – I hope.'

'There are no boats,' he said. 'Typhoon warning.'

'Ah so, *desu-ka*?' I replied, thinking: huh! bloody typhoons. 'Does the notice say anything else?'

'Not really,' he said, 'but come with me. I work in the shipping company across the road. I can find out the latest weather forecast.'

So I followed the man to his office, where he showed me a satellite reading of the typhoon's latest position.

'Mmmm,' he said, 'maybe it is not so good.'

Another man in the office, who was heading over to the 'downtown' office of the A-Line ferry company (which sailed to Tokunoshima), told me to hop on board his van and he'd give me a lift over because 'my friend there speaks some English. Maybe he has fresh information.'

Over in the A-Line office I was introduced to an extremely fat man who stood up to bow to me in greeting, but when he sat down he completely missed his caster-footed chair, sprawling back like a cartoon character on to his ample behind. For a stunned few moments he lay flailing on the floor like a giant, upturned cockroach. I was surprised that the surrounding staff, although they couldn't have failed to notice the clattering mishap taking place under their nose, paid no attention to him whatsoever. Maybe missing his seat was a nothing-out-of-the-ordinary daily occurrence. Either way, I asked him if he was all right (he was). After picking himself up off the floor (no mean task for one of such wide-berthed stature), he dabbed the sweat from his brow with a square of folded *hankachifu* and politely informed me that all ferry sailings from the island had, for now, been cancelled.

'Have you any idea when the first boat to Tokunoshima might be?' I asked hopefully.

'If typhoon is keeping to present coursing then maybe ferry sailing in morning 5 a.m.'

Willing the typhoon to go and play havoc elsewhere I went to camp in the town park, tucking myself out of the worst of the wind behind a concrete building. When it was dark I fastened myself into my nylon sweat den and lay splayed on my back, listening to a bunch of youngsters setting off fireworks for hours. Every now and then a strong gust of wind would pummel my tent, contorting the poles to such an extent that the sides would momentarily cave in so close to my face that I felt as good as zipped into a body bag.

Just before midnight the skies burst, releasing a particularly ferocious variety of rain which hammered down so hard that I was led to worry: is this just a bad storm or is it a typhoon? Unsure as to what my chances of survival would be in either, and fed up with my wind-buffeted tent biffing me in the nose, I hurriedly packed up, diving for cover into the park's concrete toilet block.

For over three hours the storm swirled with a vengeance outside the open door, the rain drumming deafeningly on the roof as I sat on the edge of the sink-unit reading Pico Iyer's lyrical *The Lady and the Monk* – a brilliant account of his time spent living in Kyoto and the intriguing relationship he formed with a married woman called Sachiko.

Soon after 4 a.m. the storm blew off into the Pacific and I emerged from my slumberless hovel to find a *biro* (betel-nut palm tree) snapped in two – the top half having landed on the precise spot where my tent had been.

Doubting any ferry sailings I nonetheless decided to ride round to the harbour to check, thinking: well, better the devil I know than the devil I don't.

It was still dark as I rode through the city along roads awash with torrents of greasy water. Happily I found the docks buzzing beneath the dazzling glare of spotlights, with forklift trucks loaded with teetering towers of pallets and containers madly scurrying around like an industrious invasion of ants. Out in the blackness, where the sea was virtually indistinguishable from the sky, a low rumble of engines could be heard vibrating across the water and before long the twinkling-lit bulk of A-Line's *Naminoue* ferry could be seen slowly sliding shorewards.

When the sun finally dawned on me I was sprawled on the scrubbed wood decks of *Naminoue* and I stared up into a pinkening sky, feeling very much like you tend to feel when a night has passed you by. I fell into an exhausted drugged-like stupor and when I awoke an hour or so later the sun was searing the decks, the heat melting my mind.

It was still only breakfast time when I rode down the ramp and on to the small, tear-shaped island of Tokunoshima. In search of a map I entered the bustling ferry terminal, a shabby building with paint-peeling walls. No sooner had I stepped inside than a young man approached me.

'Excuse me,' he said in English, 'but are you visiting for sightseeing island?'

Tetsuhito ('call me Tetsu') Izumi was a strong, lean

twenty-four-year-old who had lived on Tokunoshima all his life, apart from going to college in Kagoshima and taking an elongated break in America. Along with his beguiling wide eyes and long, dark lashes the other thing that I first noticed about Tetsu was that he had a phenomenal sixteen pockets located in only two articles of clothing, most of them situated in a sort of sleeveless safari jacket that he wore over a 'New Orleans' T-shirt.

From Tetsu's opening question and from the official papers he was carrying, I took it that he was a tour guide of some description. But my surmisings couldn't have been further from the truth: he was the senior managing director of his father's funeral firm and he had come to the port to pick up some containers of dry-ice off *Naminoue* which he needed for storing bodies. Because of the storms and subsequent delays of the ship, Tetsu was anxious to get the dry-ice as soon as possible; from what I could gather, his father was concerned about the welfare of a particular corpse. Not wanting to deny any body their right to be chilled to the bone I made a move back to my bike, but not before Tetsu had quizzed me on just what it was I was up to and given me his address, urging me to come and stay with him and his family that evening.

'Really I am living very close,' said Tetsu, 'in Kametsu only.'

From where we were standing in the port of Kametoku, Kametsu was merely a mile down the road. Meeting his family was a nice idea but frankly, in my delicate state, I fancied camping. So, thanking him, I explained that I was planning on sleeping on a beach.

'Then you must be visiting in our house when returning to Kametsu. Okay?'

'Okay,' I said, 'thank you.'

'And if any problem time for you – hmmm . . . for example, maybe you are needing explanation for hard understanding, you must telephone my number here okay any time day time night time no problem really.'

'Thank you, Tetsu, you're very kind.'

'No, no. Ah! And one more extra excuse me. In Tokunoshima "thank you" is not *arigato* properly because Tokunoshima people are having speciality word and are saying *oboradaren.* This will be so great for you speaking because even Japanese people do not know this word – and I am thinking, ha! ha!, it will be so great for you speaking this word to Tokunoshima people. Ha! ha!'

'Oh, okay,' I said, fishing out a scrap of paper. 'Can you write it down for me, please, before I forget it?'

So on the back of my ferry ticket Tetsu wrote *oboradaren* (pronounced 'o-bolla-da-len') and as I practised saying it he said, 'Yes, yes – so great! Ha! ha!'

I left Tetsu to his sixteen pockets and corpse ice and rode through friendly and ramshackle Kametsu which, despite being Tokunoshima's main town, was so small that I had passed on through scarcely realizing that that was it. Life felt soporifically slow – the sort of pace where 'hurry' has no place in the vocabulary; the sort of place where it's okay to yawn in public. Every now and then a car would pass me – not fast, no rush – just dreamily drift on by.

I floated southwards with the hot wind rolling along the coast past huge-leafed plants, banana trees, blood-red hibiscus, tumbling bougainvillea spilling over walls like waterfalls and the odd abandoned car left to rust and ruin an otherwise flawless beach of powdered bleached sand slaked by an indigo sea. As I pedalled onward in a trance, a chirpy 'toot toot' made me start and, turning, I saw a compact forest-green Carol Autozam Minica come buzzing broadside. At the helm sat a beaming Tetsu, signalling for me to stop. Obediently I did so and Tetsu jumped out with a Tokunoshima tourist pamphlet in his hands which had the words 'I WANT TO IMPRESSION' printed on its cover.

'For you!' he declared, adding, 'My father says okay possible for me to today giving you sightseeing visiting tour of island by driving style because you are a bip. Hop in for pleasurable motoring – okay?'

'Well, *oboradaren*!' I said, 'but, excuse me, Tetsu, what is a "bip"?'

'Yes, bip.'

'Yes, but what exactly is a "bip"?'

'Hmmmm, my father he call you a bip because we think you as very important person!'

'Oh, you don't mean a VIP, do you?'

'Excuse me?'

'In English VIP is short for Very Important Person.'

'Ahhhh so, *desu-ka*? Yes, yes of course, VIP.'

'Well, it's a nice gesture,' I said, 'but I'm going to have to disappoint you as I'm only a cyclist.'

'No problem really!' he said, before again inviting me to hop in his Carol for a spot of pleasurable motoring.

Touched as I was by Tetsu's kind offer to act as my tour guide for the day, driving round an island with a running commentary in an air-conditioned car when I could have been cycling in silence was frankly not my cup of *oolong-cha*. So as best I could I politely declined his invitation and after a bit more of a chat we went on our separate ways.

About an hour later the Carol Minica Autozammed its way alongside me again. I pulled over into the verge and Tetsu, still beaming, popped out to deliver a map of Tokunoshima into my hands.

'Fine indication of sightseeing!' he said.

Although the map was printed in *kanji* Tetsu had carefully written the names of the major places of interest in *romaji*, as well as awarding them a quota of stars:

*	–	fine sight indeed!
**	–	a must stop beautiful scene!
***	–	Number One marvell Top spot!

Again I thanked him and again we chatted for a while, this time beneath the shady canopy of a banana grove. Pasted upon a nearby concrete telegraph pole was a poster where, among a wild whirl of ideograms, were the words:

Voltage Climax
Dondon Festival

'That sounds like an interesting sort of festival,' I said. 'What exactly goes on there?'

'Ahh,' said Tetsu, 'this is summer night in Matsubara port for *hanabi* – you are knowing *hanabi*?'

'Yes – fire-flower, which is much more descriptive than "fireworks".'

Fireworks. Sounds like cement-works, gas-works, road-works. But fire-flower – that's exactly what they were: flowers of fire. Tetsu and I discussed this point for a moment, with me saying how much more lyrical imagination seemed to be used in Japan for the naming of words compared with the name-it-straight speakers of English. Tetsu came up with another example: bow tie, which to the see-it-as-it-is English language is just that – a tied bow. But in Japanese it's a *chonekutai* – a butterfly tie.

Going back to the night of 'Voltage Climax' Tetsu said, 'Could I ask you to join me for a pleasure evening of fire-flower?'

'You could,' I said, 'but the trouble is I'm not sure if I've got the energy to ride all the way to Matsubara by tonight.'

'No problem indeed,' replied Tetsu, 'I will find you!'

'But I don't even know where I'll be camping.'

'Really this is very fine. I will find you so maybe you can care to be my motoring pleasure guest to festival, okay?'

'Okay – thank you,' I said, feeling more than a little dubious about just how Tetsu was going to find me when I couldn't even find myself.

Late that afternoon I followed a sandy track down towards the beach where, tucked amid an airy copse of pines, I found a small shabby building selling fried food and *aisu-kuriimu*. Apart from a mother with her two small children picnicking beneath the trees, there was no one else around except for the family who owned the place. The *okusama* seemed happy enough to let me fill up on water, use their toilet and camp anywhere I liked. So I set up my tent on a soft, sandy bed of desiccated pine needles, my door nosing out on to an alluring mile-long, brilliant white sand beach and a pellucid blue sea. Without dillydallying, I dug into a pannier for my swimming goggles and spent an hour floating above the coral and the scintillatingly harlequinned and striped fish of the reef.

When I returned to my tent I discovered a picnic table had been placed beside my tent and moments later the *okusama* brought me out a trayful of food containing aubergine, fish and chicken *tempura*, riceballs and seaweed, and tea. '*Dozo, dozo*,' she said with a smile before shuffling back to her kitchen from where the redolent and unexpected but not too out-of-place strains of a Caribbean steel band merged with the song of the wind in the pines.

I was just in the midst of polishing off the last of the rice when Tetsu popped out from behind a pine tree with a couple of cans of chilled 'I like Nature' green tea.

'How did you find me?' I asked, surprised.

'Ahhh – easy! Tokunoshima is small island,' he said, 'and a *gaijin* here has very great rarity, specially indeed on *jitensha*. Maybe all Tokunoshima people are knowing you are here!'

'Oh,' I said, 'and I thought I had tucked myself away rather nicely!'

Tetsu laughed and I looked at him in his black, back-to-front NY baseball cap and thought again how un-Japanese he looked with his wide eyes and thick long lashes. The people of Nansei claim to be born of a son of the sun, who gave birth to the male and female deities who created the Japanese archipelago beneath which the giant catfish rattles. Although the inhabitants of Nansei are lumped together as Japanese they are an ethnic people who, with their large eyes, thick eyebrows, swarthy skin, small bones and naturally wavy hair are much closer to the southern physical type of Pacific and South East Asian people than to the Mongolian light-skinned, narrow-eyed, thick-boned

Japanese themselves with their high, broad cheek bones. Because these island people (whom the mainlanders tend to bunch all together as Okinawans) have over the centuries been controlled by the domineering powers of China, Japan and America, they seem to have developed an open and easy-going aptitude for getting along and are noted by the Japanese as *shurei-no-tami* ('people who treat others with respect'). I could see this agreeable trait in Tetsu. He was full of an endearingly solicitous laid-back charm. That's not to say, of course, that the people I had previously met had been anything other than caring and sharing, but there was something distinctly different about Tetsu. I liked him a lot.

As we sat at the picnic table drinking our green cans of 'I like Nature' green tea into the fast-encroaching subtropical night, with a sultry wind whistling through the pine tops and the pacifying lull of the waves breaking on the distant reef, Tetsu told me about the *bosozoku* – motorcycle gangs, or literally 'Speed Tribes', with names such as the Edokko Racers, the Kanto Warriors, the Crazies, the Midnight Angels, the Hit and Runners and the all-women's Lady Bombers. In my lost and early days I had seen some of these gangs, mainly around the Tokyo–Yokohama area, cruising around on their poxy-engined bikes that they had customized beyond belief: ludicrously shaped handlebars and modified fairings elevated into the air on extended chrome stalks, fancy mirrors, severely misshapen seats, tune-blaring horns, wildly out-of-control paint-jobs, and triple-header pipes which increased the tinny din of the exhaust to head-crunching level. When a tribe of twenty or so passed, the roar of the engines was like the overpowering clamour of a thousand feverish chainsaws in a tunnel of tin. The young gang members, with their punch-permed hair, mirror-shades and kamikaze head bands, paraded around on their absurdly modified machines flying flags with the old militarist ensign of the flaring, red Rising Sun.

Tetsu told me that the *bosozoku*, by fighting so stridently against society, bring huge shame on reproachful 'ordinary' Japanese.

'Have you ever been tempted to join a tribe?' I asked Tetsu. 'Though I don't suppose there's a whole lot of opportunity on sleepy, palm-swaying Tokunoshima, is there?'

'No, no,' laughed Tetsu, 'that is so. Myself I am preferring the challenge pursuit in judo – my most deep passion!'

Tetsu, it turned out, was a 'black belt' and taught pupils at the local Junior High. He told me there had been two occasions on which he had turned to his judo in self-defence. The first time was after his whirlwind tour of America (one night San Francisco, one night San Diego, one night New Orleans, one night . . .) when on arriving in Jamaica for a reggae festival ('I love dreglocks') he was set upon by a couple of aggressive drug-dealers.

'Very frightened moment indeed,' said Tetsu, 'two black gentleman and I say "please go away I am black belt judo". And they go. Yes, really so great so easy!'

The second occasion on which Tetsu turned in a time of need to his judo was decidedly closer to home, just down the road from where we were sitting, where he caught a man stealing his mother's car. With one deft judo throw, Tetsu incapacitated the offender before handing him over to the police. This story surprised me. I told Tetsu I wouldn't have imagined anyone would have the audacity to steal a car on such a small island where everyone seemed to know each other.

'Ah, that is so,' said Tetsu, 'but the policemen they have explanation that this man is very strange man in his head and now he live in special hospital for strange head in Kagoshima.'

As we talked, *okusama*'s father shuffled towards us across the sandy pine needles to give us each a can of Pocari Sweat. He said something to Tetsu which I didn't understand. Tetsu translated.

'This man,' he said, 'he is having much worry for you as one person because soon he is closing to leave for night sleeping. He is worry because maybe danger for you one person sleeping only.'

I turned to the wiry old man, thanking him as best I could for his concern and trying to assure him I was sure I would be fine. The man nodded, smiling doubtfully, before he once again said something very fast which Tetsu translated.

'He has explanation that he will leave noodle house light on for you as technique of safety.'

It was a touching gesture but, frankly, I would have preferred to have been left in the dark; that way the building's lights wouldn't silhouette my tent and reveal my tent spot to any nocturnal undesirables – in the unlikely event that Tokunoshima should have any. But instead of airing my thoughts I just said '*O-bolla-da-len*' to the old man, who almost swallowed his teeth with surprise.

'Ha! ha!' laughed Tetsu, with evident delight. 'See! So great word!'

Tetsu said to me after he'd gone that the old man had also been concerned for me because of the *habu*.

'You are knowing *habu*?' asked Tetsu.

'I'm getting perhaps a little too familiar – people keep warning me about them,' I said.

'For sure they are danger snake,' said Tetsu, 'but no problem if you keep in high respect.'

He went on to tell me how he caught *habu* by hand and sold them for about 5,000 yen (£33) each, depending on size.

'Is this treating with respect?' I asked, but he didn't catch my gist. Instead he went on to say how, at just over four metres, the biggest *habu* ever had recently been caught on Amami-Oshima – whence I had just come. Thoughts of snake hunting put me in mind of an incident which I had recently read about in the paper: a Chinese hunter was fatally shot by the very snake that he was trying to catch. The man, named Li, was with his brother when they came across the snake while returning from a hunting trip on a mountain near Li Bian village in Huang Jin county, Shanxi province. Li, attempting to add the snake to his hunting bag, placed the butt of the gun on its head. The snake then coiled itself around the gun and lashed the trigger with its tail. Li was shot in the buttocks and died on the way to hospital.

By now time was getting on and Tetsu and I realized we had spent so long talking that we had missed the 'Voltage Climax' festival. Tetsu offered to drive me over there anyway just in case there was something still going on, but after a long day and the previous stormy and sleepless night I was more than looking forward to turning horizontal on my soft, sandy bed of arboreal needles. Tetsu left and I fell asleep with the all-pervading resiny scent and the soaring sounds of the surge of the surf.

I hadn't been lost in my dreams for long when something suddenly woke me. I opened my eyes and there, clinging to the inner netted side of the tent a mere foot from my head, was the shocking profile of a tarantula-like creature. Because of the fall of the noodle house's light that glared over my tent, sending the said multi-limbed creature (which spanned my hand) into silhouette, I was unable to decipher whether it was attached to the inside or the outside. Were it the latter, I could hopefully just flick it away without further ado, but be it the former there was a distinctly off-putting possibility of it falling on my face. For a short moment I lay on my back as rigid as a concrete girder, trying to will myself into levitation beyond this most unpleasant situation and back to the safety of my cool-sheeted bed at home. But such fanciful and unproductive thoughts aren't particularly useful at times such as these, especially when the multiple-legged shadow in question started crawling slowly towards the tent's apex. Not daring, even for a nano-second, to take my eyes off the spidery form, lest it drop into my bags or dart beneath my mat, I very, very slowly reached for the mini Petzl torch I kept beside my head and, after getting to grips with myself, beamed it on to the beast. Dazzled, it stopped in its creeping tracks, giving me time to ascertain that neither was it inside my tent nor was it a hairy tarantula. It was simply nothing more than an audacious old hermit crab, taking a rather ambitious mountaineering perambulation on the North Face of my tent.

A couple of hours later I awoke to yet more trouble. This time the cause was not so much a hard-bodied decapod as a soft-headed anthropoid – namely a couple of obviously well-inebriated men figure-of-eighting their pick-ups in the parking area at the end of the track in a manner that clearly demonstrated a distinct lack of grey matter. This backward behaviour continued for nearly half an hour – slithering and skidding and sliding round and round, the air menaced by the screeching revs of the over-stressed engines and the demented shrieks of the men.

Cursing powerfully under my breath, I put in a request to God to either get rid of or exterminate these men without delay before they spotted me cowering in my flimsy piece of crustacean-encrusted nylon. God obviously had more pressing matters to attend to because just as I poked my head under the gap at the bottom of my tent to survey the scene for the umpteenth time, I was concerned to see the pick-ups lurching to a halt and the men falling drunkenly out of the doors. They staggered around for a good (which was really a bad) five minutes amid wails of eerie and uncontrollable laughter. One of the men then pitched towards me across the sandy ground before coming to rest beside a tree a mere twenty yards from my tent. Propping himself against the trunk with one hand, his other fumbled around in the vicinity of his flies.

Uh oh, I thought, here we go again. Fearing that he would soon be working himself up into a lather, I was therefore pleasantly surprised to discover that his mission was only one of urination. Once zipped up, he then staggered an uneven course back to his truck and together with his accomplice sped erratically away, leaving me to plot the course of a hermit crab shuffling along like an old man beneath the ground sheet of my tent.

After Tetsu had made an early morning appearance to bring me a doggie-bag of breakfast from his mother, I cycled on around the island which turned gradually more mountainous the further north I headed – not big mountains but relatively rugged compared with the flat-topped variety of the interior, and inspiring that sense of spine-tingling awe like all mountains do.

Dutiful sightseer that I was, I stopped off at the highlighted points of one, two and three-star interest that Tetsu had recommended to me on his map. I paused to wipe my sweating face beneath the statue of a certain Mr Shigechiyo Izumi (who had finally popped his *geta* at the ripe old age of 120 – apart from that I knew nothing else about him except that he shared the same surname as Tetsu); I moseyed out to Cape Inutabu, a rocky promontory severely disfigured by a giant A-shaped structure built in the all-invasive concrete. And I also paused for thought (and several mouthfuls of banana) at the three-star ('Number One marvell Top spot!') Innojoh Futa sea arches – and very 'marvell Top spot' they were, too, though not as good as Durdle Door.

The villages I passed through were all more or less indistinguishable from each other – the low shanty houses held together with what looked like mainly a mixture of concrete and corrugated iron with bamboo reed mats propped up at forty-five degrees against the windows to help keep the heat of the sun at bay and out of the rooms, and surrounded by luxuriant gardens like wildly tumbling jungles.

In one of these villages a woman with long, tousled black hair darted out of her grocery store and into the road calling to me in English.

'Good morning, excuse me, you are from sheep?'

Perplexed, I said, 'From sheep?'

'Ah so, from sheep,' she confirmed.

Hmmm, I thought. I've been called a few things in my time but never a sheep. Was this, I wondered, the Japanese equivalent of an old cow? Or maybe it was just the Tokunoshima interpretation of a 'foreign devil'. Either way, I was still none the wiser and still in a state of bafflement.

'Sheep?' I said. 'What do you mean "from sheep"?'

'*Hai, hai*!'

'Sheep?' I tried again, 'a baaaaa sheep?'

The woman, cocking her head like a cocker spaniel, gave me a look that told me that my bovine impersonations were in need of a spot of fine tuning. Then she repeated 'You are from sheep?'

And I repeated, 'Sheep?'

Then, with cranium material creaking into operation, it suddenly hit me.

'Ahhh, *ship*!' I said. 'Sorry I'm a bit slow. Yes, I am – I'm off the ship.'

The woman, who told me her name was Hideko Oku, explained to me in Japanese that Tetsu had earlier pulled up at her store to ask if she had seen the cycling *gaijin* off the ship. As she talked she gave me a can of apple juice, after which she let me use her squat toilet. Up until this moment every toilet I had patronized in Japan had been made by the omnipresent Toto – but I remember Hideko's toilet well, manufactured as it was by a company called Janis.

An hour or so later, Tetsu, who appeared to be popping out of the woodwork, caught up with me, this time not in his Janis – I mean Carol – but in the company hearse, *sans* corpse. In the passenger seat sat his father, a cheerful man with a perpetual smile whose only words of English were 'Thank you velly much!' – a phrase which he insisted on repeating over and over to me, no matter whether or not I had done anything to justify thanking.

Tetsu seemed happy to find me – he'd had a bit of trouble, he said, with tracking me down and was worried that I might have been got by the *habu*. Ha! ha!

'I think most likelihooded explanation you are taking diversion tactic to maybe fine sightseeing location.'

'Ahh, that is most probably correct,' I said, though I didn't tell him I could just as well have been poised above the Janis.

Tetsu, reaching into the hearse's boot, gave me a pack of three small yellow towels ('for combating much sweating day!') which were embossed with the funeral company's logo on each corner.

'Maybe see you later for certainty!' said Tetsu, a touch enigmatically, before he and his father (who was leaning out of the passenger window with a cheerful 'thank you velly much!') drove away up the road.

That night I ended up in a place on the coast curiously called B&G. With a swimming pool, water slide, showers, toilets, *aisu-kuriimu* booths and picnic tables, it was obviously something of a daytime seaside leisure complex and was full of families having a splashing good time. I asked a woman with a baby on her back if she thought it would be all right for me to camp there for the night.

'Mmmm, maybe it is danger,' she replied.

'Danger?' I said. 'How much danger?'

'Mmm,' mmmmed the woman, 'maybe fifty per cent danger.'

So, hoping I could locate myself on the side of the safe percentage, I popped up my tent in the shade of some jungly bushes and, flipping on my goggles, plunged into the glorious and improbably clear blue sea to admire the fish.

By the time I emerged from my elongated dip the sun was

sinking into a liquid horizon and most of the B&G-ers were drifting back to their cars. A few people stayed behind, lingering on into the evening to cook their suppers on charred grill racks balanced over fire-pits. One such party invited me to join them and shuffled along on their reed mat to make way for me. The group consisted of an interesting mix of an aunt and her grandmother; a cheerfully drunk fisherman who, from what I could gather, lived with the aunt; the aunt's nephew, who lived in Kagoshima but was currently at Tokyo University; and the nephew's friend, a Tokyoite in the same class at the university. I asked the boys, who spoke a few words of English, what subjects they were studying and after running through a few different possible English translations they came up with the study of human science. They wanted to be psychiatrists, they explained, and to learn how 'people have reaction to different colour'. Was university hard work? No, they admitted, it was basically just one big party.

The aunt, a round and jocular woman with a heavily sweating face, kept slapping on to the grill rack an endless amount of fish and squid and octopus and aubergine and cabbage and shallot and green peppers and noodles and, piling upon my willing stomach, riceball after riceball.

The red-eyed fisherman, who was working with speed through several cups of *shochu*, dissolved into raucous laughter every time I playfully slapped his arm whenever he tried to slip it round my waist. Aunty's reaction was to catapult chunks of cabbage at him, implying to me that he was just a dirty old man and that I should ignore him.

'Don't worry,' I said, 'I've had worse in my time.'

The grandmother, a lovable old dear, was as thin and brittle as a chopstick and so tiny that she was as tall as I was when kneeling. She chatted away to me excitedly, no matter that I could only understand a fraction of what she said. The boy from Tokyo laughed, explaining that I wasn't the only one who was having communication problems.

'Okinawa people,' he said, 'they should speak Japanese!'

The aunt then expressed concern about camping in B&G – not because of the possibility of the fifty per cent danger but because there had been a typhoon warning.

'Don't worry,' I said, 'I can always sleep in the toilet. I've had plenty of practice.'

Filling my bowl with yet more noodles, the aunt then went on to tell me how excited she was to meet an 'honourable *gaijin*'.

'What was the nationality of the last *gaijin* you met?' I asked.

She thought hard for a moment before saying that she couldn't remember – it was so long ago.

'How long?' I asked.

'Mmmmm, maybe twenty years,' she said.

The fisherman, leaning overly close towards me with *shochu* breath, drunkenly explained that every fish I had eaten that night had been caught by his fair, or more like 'wandering', hand that very afternoon. I was about to commend his efforts when he farted so loudly it was impossible to ignore.

'Hark!' I said, cupping my ear in my hand, 'I hear the typhoon approaching' – a comment which deserved perhaps a snigger at most but which had the effect of sending the gathered ensemble, grandmother included, rolling around on the mat with guffaws of laughter, earning me a further two riceballs and tentacle of octopus.

After the barbecuing parties had dispersed for home, leaving me with enough doggie-bags to sink the sun, I crawled into my airless sweat zone and tried to go to sleep. But it was too hot, so instead I tuned into the World Service and heard a short report about how the LA police on Huntington Beach, in a new drive to try to prevent the escalating problem of drug-related shootings, had recently instigated a 10 p.m. curfew on the beach – a curfew which was promulgated by the Huntington Beach Police Patrol who strutted up and down the seafront announcing chummily into megaphones, 'Okay, everybody, it's hometime. Come on now folks – it's time to head on home.'

If anyone was just asking to have a hole put in the head, then surely it was they.

With such musings I fell into a feverish sleep, only to be awoken an hour or so later by the sounds of noisy rustlings not far from my tent. Fearing an invasion of hermit crab snatchers, I quietly unzipped my tent and peered out into the shadowy moonlit night. As I scanned the vacated domain of the picnicking area my gaze came to rest, with some trepidation, upon an indistinct figure crawling most disconcertingly through the undergrowth towards the rear of my tent. As the figure erratically crept along, moving ever closer towards me, I saw that it was a man, possibly the drunk fisherman, but I couldn't be sure. Still on all fours he then changed direction, lurching unsteadily in a wide circle towards the mouth of my tent, which put me in mind of the fifty per cent danger zone that I must now be in. Feeling like a sitting duck, I decided it was high time to rustle up some hasty form of self-preservation in order to combat whatever the crawler might have lurking up his trouser leg. Thus, when he crossed my far-too-close-for-comfort zone, I hastily set my scare tactic into operation which, for want of something better to do, involved entwining my body in my sheet sleeping bag and bounding out of my tent shrieking like a banshee. Happily, such pantomiming pranks produced the desired effect of scaring the prowler to such a degree that I never saw him again.

For a while I was left to wonder just what the crawler's intentions had been, but then I put the matter to the back of my mind and more or less forgot about it until, several months later, I read a copy of Alex Kerr's entertainingly informative *Lost Japan*, in which he mentioned the following:

> Another custom with roots in the distant past is *yobai*, a folk tradition once prevalent all over Japan, which has died out everywhere except on a few remote islands and in hamlets like Iya [situated in the central mountains of Shikoku]. *Yobai*, or 'night crawling', was the way

the young men of the village wooed their maidens. The boy would crawl into the girl's room at night, and if she did not reject him, they would sleep together. By dawn he had to leave the house, and if matters went well, he would visit the girl regularly at night until they got married. Some villages also extended the privilege of *yobai* to travelers, which may have been a way of preventing too much inbreeding in remote areas.

The next morning I took life easy, floating in the translucent sea before sitting in the shade of a concrete wall (beneath a poster advertising 'Hound Dog Special Soul of Island ¥ 3700') to write letters and catch up on my diary.

When the hordes arrived, two women with four small children set up a picnicking base beside me and before long I had been invited on to their shoeless mat to partake of a feast of fine fare which, among a heap of riceballs, slithers of stacked omelettes, *tempura* and fried bean curd, included fourteen different varieties of sea creatures.

After giggling hugely at my cack-handed attempts to fillet one of the fish with a pair of chopsticks – resulting in a fine display of how to get a mouthful of bones – one of the women showed me the way to do it. With a deft twist, off comes the tail. Then use the sides of the chopsticks to loosen the flesh by pressing down on each side of the body half a dozen times. This should enable the head to be pulled away from the body, the spine trailing close behind in one tidy piece. *Voilà*! The woman, courting disaster, handed me another eight-inch fish to try again. My tail came off good and proper. For that all-important spot of flesh-loosening my fish's sides received a nice gentle pummelling with the edges of my sticks. So far so *yoi* (good). But sadly, I fell at the spine, decapitating the fish in one easy step and sending the head catapulting into a neighbouring family of fish-eaters.

As I was preparing to leave, a woman with no front teeth scampered up to me and, chattering excitedly, explained that she had passed me on the road the previous day. She was wearing a white, long-sleeved shirt, the pocket of which was embellished with the words:

Permission Very Beat
collegian can't tell a person by his
appearance alone, the just day.

She then dug into her bag and handed me a can of White Water (although a more fitting name would perhaps have been Sugar Fizz) and warned me about the . . . don't tell me – *habu*.

I followed the undulating road northwards, passing fields of hooded and aproned workers digging up loads of strange root vegetables. Some waved, some called '*Ganbatte*!' and some beckoned me to join them for a cup of *mugi-cha*. Most of the few houses that I passed had a vast golden sea of monkey nuts drying in large, wide wicker baskets on the roadside. At one of the homes where I pulled over to admire the nuts, an old woman shuffled out from behind a wall and gave me a couple of handfuls wrapped in a sheet of newspaper to take away with me. When I asked her if they were ready for eating she said no, no – they must first be cooked or else I would be poisoned.

'Ah, like the *habu*?' I asked. And the old woman laughed.

After fighting through sticky cobwebs as thick as elastic when taking a short hike through the low-lying palms of the Kanami Cyclad Jungle (a three-star 'Number One marvell Top spot!') and after stopping off to buy a bag of curly cucumbers as thin as chipolatas from a help-yourself wooden roadside stall full of homegrown produce (everything an amazingly cheap fifty yen), and after meeting a woman who told me I was in the town (San) where there lived a *gaijin* teacher who was known as Mr Big (the woman explained she couldn't take me to his house as he had recently left to holiday in England), I bowled down the eastern coast back to Kametsu where I gave Tetsu a ring from outside the Green *supaa.* Within thirty seconds he was beside me, leading me back across the road to his house where he lived with Kazuomi (his fifty-three-year-old 'thank you velly much' father), Chiyoko (his fifty-two-year-old mother), his twelve-year-old sister Ryoko and tubby eleven-year-old brother Hiroki, and seventy-eight-year-old *obaasan.*

The house was new and modern and, by Japanese standards, incredibly big. After having tea with the family around a low lacquer table cluttered with an assortment of papers and dirty glasses and used tissues and monkey nut shells, Tetsu gave me a tour of his three-storey home. Downstairs was the funeral company office, two *tatami* rooms (one of which was the client entertaining 'lounge' that tonight doubled up as my windowless, air-conditioned room), a shower and a Japanese-style toilet.

'Don't worry,' said Tetsu, 'we also have Western-style toilet upstairs for you ease of use.'

'I'm not worrying,' I said. 'A Japanese-style toilet is fine by me.'

Tetsu's long-lashed eyes almost popped out of his head. 'You are meaning you are having ability to toilet Japanese-style?' he asked, truly surprised.

'But of course,' I said. 'Squatting comes quite naturally.'

'Is that so?' said Tetsu, and I assured him that, yes, it was very so indeed.

Upstairs in the kitchen, Chiyoko displayed peculiar enthusiasm for showing me the contents of her fridge (crammed with bowls of strange-looking foods) and talking me through the use of every one of her intriguingly-shaped Japanese knives. On the small table in the centre of the kitchen sat an array of dirty plates, chopsticks, a bowlful of crunchy miniature dried fish tossed in oil and covered in *goma* (sesame seeds), a large vat of white *udon* noodles and a stuffed toy called Sliced Bread Man (apparently a popular cartoon character in Japan) which belonged to the yappity small pet dog – a relative newcomer to the family, purchased for the Year of the Dog, and a dog that I soon gathered puddled everywhere and chewed anything in sight (including my ankle) if it wasn't fed Sliced Bread Man on demand.

Over on a counter sat an electric rice-cooker that was kept constantly full with the polished grains. Every home I had stayed in had had its own electric rice-cooker, which was used for rice and rice alone. When an American cake-mix company tried to market a form of cake-mix that could be used in rice-cookers at a time when very few Japanese possessed ovens, it met with overwhelming resistance from consumers and the project fell by the wayside. In the Japanese diet, rice is more important than bread or potatoes are for Europeans or Americans. The company had failed to take account of this and of the Japanese belief that the rice, which they feel has mystical qualities, would be contaminated if the cooker was used for anything else.

If perfect paddy fields carved out of the mountainside (to increase the area of land under cultivation) and bowlfuls of glistening rice seem quintessentially Japanese, then that is testimony to the impact rice has had on Japanese civilization. But rice was not native to Japan. It was an import, most likely from southern China, arriving in Japan some three thousand years ago.

For hundreds of years the precious grains were the currency in which the lords paid their samurai, leaving the 'commoners' to subsist mainly on rougher grains such as barley. These centuries of deprivation are said to have left a mark on the Japanese character, with people retaining a special respect for rice.

Being the staple food in the diet, rice is eaten by the majority of Japanese three times a day. No matter how many other dishes are served with a meal, rice always appears and is given undivided attention. The mystique that surrounds this indispensable grain is such that when rice is served with purely Japanese food it is called the honorific *gohan* – a word which is often used to mean simply 'meal'. But when it is served with a Western or Chinese dish it reverts to a more lowly *raisu*. Never once did I see brown rice (*gemmai*). As is common with other Asians, Japanese polish the raw grain until pristine white, removing in the process all vital vitamin B. In *Black Rain* (Ibuse Masuji's novel about Hiroshima after the bomb) the poignant evidence of the national fixation with 'pure', 'clean' white rice is affirmed whereby the protagonists, although practically on the verge of starvation, meticulously polish their miserable rice ration grain by grain as a way of maintaining their dignity.

Tetsu continued with his grand tour and from the kitchen we paid a visit to his parents' air-conditioned bedroom, where his father was found to be reading on his bed – no futons, just a couple of wide single beds. A glance in Hiroki's room was all that was needed to tell me he was a baseball fan – mitts, bats, posters and a Giants baseball jacket slung over a chair. Ryoko's room was pink, crammed with school books, and on her bed huddled a profusion of cuddly toys. Excitedly she showed me a CD of her favourite sugary pop singer – a woman called Maki Ohguro. I removed the CD sleeve to look at the lyrics, which were all in Japanese except for the words: 'High tension', 'love power' and 'Spicy your mama'.

The last room to visit was Tetsu's, where we sat on the *tatami* surrounded by the jacket of his judo suit, various clothes and books and comics, a rolled-up Bruce Lee poster and dozens of CDs. I picked up a few at random: U2, Madonna, Ace of Base, the Eurythmics, some Mexican *mariachi* and loads of Japanese pop. Again the lyrics of the ones I looked at were all in *kanji*, apart from one group called TMN, whose song *We Love the Earth* had the lines 'We are just creatures of the earth/good vibration/stay with me tonight'. Another of their songs, titled *Love Song*, was again all in Japanese except for the words: 'wow wow wow/exit/love train'.

I asked Tetsu if he read many books.

'No, never!' he said, before adding, 'Hmmmm, maybe sometime I am reading Japanese mystery story but always usual I am reading *manga*.'

And his room bore testimony to this fact: piles of these three-inch thick tomes lay heaped around the floor. Sifting around for a moment beneath the flotsam and jetsam of his *tatami*-covered belongings he extracted a photograph album containing the snaps of his time in America, which he talked me through one by one. Of more interest was the verse printed in gold italics on the shiny red cover of the album:

CHIRPY
I never want to lose
the innocense of my heart
refreshing times flow gently.

Of the many magazines littering the floor, the one that caught my eye was entirely devoted to the *bosozoku* motorcycle gangs.

'Ah,' I said with a smirk, 'a closeted enthusiast!'

I flicked through the pages, full of photographs of these bizarre youngsters clad in army fatigues, strategically ripped salaryman suits with customized additions of studs and badges and chains, and school uniforms with chunks cut off. The bikes were equally bizarre; one showed a fairing fixed to steel rods so improbably long that it sat suspended twenty foot above the Speed Tribe member's head.

After going out to supper at a conveyor-belt *sushi* bar with Tetsu and his siblings where, much to their merriment, they lured me into trying some Japanese mustard which produced the desired head-combusting results, I sat talking to Tetsu in his funeral firm's office. Seeing as we were surrounded by funereal matters I asked Tetsu what the average annual death-rate was on Tokunoshima and he told me that last year out of a population of 30,000, three hundred people had died.

'We are the most biggest funeral company in Tokunoshima,' said Tetsu, 'so we are servicing for most of the funerals and graves. This is very great for business – we like dead people!'

Intrigued to know a few more facts and figures I asked Tetsu what was the average amount that people spent on a funeral including the gravestones.

'Eight to nine million yen,' said Tetsu. (That meant up to £60,000!) 'But many people are spending many billion of yen.'

Apparently people went totally overboard for those who had gone under, lavishing upon the deceased the most garishly grandiose ceremonial 'altars' abounding in ornamental gold-plate and an abundance of flowers so perfectly arranged that they looked like tawdry imitations. Cemetery space is so limited in Japan (in the past, people have been buried standing up to help combat this problem) that apparently the trend is to reserve your space and set up your fancy gravestone before you die, rather than leaving it to your next of kin to realize that there is nowhere left to put you.

Tetsu was a prime example of this and he proudly showed me the photographs of his extravagantly ornate black marble grave (complete with gold-engraved obelisks) where the remains of him and his family would be 'laid to rest' down in the local cemetery. Tetsu asked me if I liked it, in much the same way as if I were to cook something for someone and ask them whether they liked it. What could I say when I thought the absurd expense and the pompous ostentatiousness of the whole extravaganza of death was nothing more than a vulgar waste of time, not to mention money? Surely a simple stone on a hillside or ashes scattered on the sea would be so much more poignant than an ornate extravagance that stares you in the face with sky-high expense.

'Well, frankly,' I said to Tetsu in reply, as if I had just popped a strange morsel of food into my mouth, 'it's not quite my taste.'

But there was no putting off Tetsu, whose business was an ever-expanding art form of acquired technique. Not long after I arrived home from Japan I received a letter from Tetsu who, after the usual Japanese-style opening paragraph of chit-chat about the weather and how the seasons were doing, went on to apologize for not writing sooner.

> The fact is I'm bad corresponded. a lots of things have happened to me since I saw you last. I was in Kagoshima since one year. Because I was working another funeral company to get many skill. I trained to make flower altar and to decorate the room by curtain. The general manager of the company said 'you'll take at least 5 year to master of these technique'. But I master just one year, and come back here in Tokunoshima last December. Now I'm busy doing the funeral business and also stone company. I am looking forward to your letter.
>
> As ever
>
> Tetsu

Enclosed with the letter were seven photographs: four of them showed his 'here's-one-I-prepared-earlier' elaborately decorated Shinto and Buddha altars; one was of me looking very hot and grinning inanely outside his house with my bike and surrounded by his family and friends on the morning I left; and the remaining pictures were of a couple of Tokunoshima's two-star 'a must stop beautiful scene!'

In the funeral office I asked Tetsu if he was religious.

'Maybe a little Shinto and sometime a little Buddhist,' he said, 'but really I am having of no particular interest.'

He told me how at school he had studied Zen – how he was made to sit for an hour or more in the lotus position and that if he moved he would receive a hefty whack across the shoulders with a long ruler-type stick.

'Always my legs so much painful,' he said.

Perhaps the reminder of this pain stirred up some earlier memories because the next thing he told me about was how strict his father had been with him in his youth – hitting and punishing him whenever he misbehaved.

'Always I remember one time occasion so bad when my father make me remaining on my knees without movement for two hour.'

When he was finally allowed to get up he found he was totally unable to stand up as his legs had succumbed to severe cramp.

By now it was almost three in the morning and, feeling hungry, we sauntered through the heated night down a festively lantern-lined street to Tetsu's all-time-favourite noodle house. A few men in overalls were sitting crosslegged at low tables in the raised floor *tatami* section, noisily slurping their noodles. They looked more than a little surprised to see me.

Tetsu and I sat at the bar in the shoes-on area and watched the corpulent *mama-san* whisk up a huge steaming bowl of *udon* noodles for each of us, topped with a generous handful of beansprouts and a slice of pink-dyed *kamaboko* processed fish 'cake'. As I tried my best to suck up the noodles as noisily as possible, a man came in to use the pink phone at the bar. I noticed that the last two fingers on his left hand were bandaged together.

'What's happened to your hand?' the *mama-san* asked him suspiciously once he had finished his phone call.

'Oh, that's nothing,' he said, 'just a small accident at work.' And after he had polished off a beer he walked out.

Tetsu said he suspected it was more than 'just a small accident' as he knew the man had seedy connections with the *yakuza. Mama-san* confirmed this.

'If he comes in here again,' she said to Tetsu, 'I'll fry his balls off!'

The *yakuza*, which roughly translates as 'worthless', are Japanese gangsters – the self-styled samurai of the underworld – and control everything from gambling and prostitution to pornography shops and 'protection' for businesses. Much of their funds are also gained through house conveyance and (because of Japan's strict laws on the possession of firearms) gun-running. They run massage parlours for Japanese tourists in Hawaii, organize the notorious 'sex tours' to South East Asia (salarymen travel there under the guise of a golfing holiday) and they recruit South East Asian prostitutes to work in Japan on tourist visas. Nowadays *yakuza* involvement in the smuggling and spread of drugs is affecting a far larger proportion of the population than ever before.

Unlike the Mafia and other organized crime elsewhere in the world, Japanese gangsters are very much a product of society and are unbelievably open with their dealings and whereabouts. Some gangs regularly publish an illustrated magazine for their members, others place the name of their gang on the front of the building that serves as their headquarters – the address even being listed in the telephone directory. They allow journalists to interview them in order to gain an insight into the workings of their mafia-style families. Occasionally the local news shows some footage of a 'godfather' returning in hula-swinging mood from his Hawaiian vacation.

The *yakuza* may be gun-toting gangsters, but compared with their notorious Italian counterparts they're still quite a prim and proper lot at heart – paying tax on their illegal earnings. It is said that one bunch of gangsters, entering a house to beat up its owner, even remembered to remove their shoes.

Walking back through the streets of Kametsu, Tetsu, referring back to the man with the bandaged hand, explained to me the *yakuza* pastime of finger-chopping. Like the samurai of old, Japanese gangsters believe in absolute loyalty and discipline. Disobedience and wayward swaying of orders are punishable by the ancient *yakuza* code of *enkozume*, or 'shorten finger'. Under the code a first offence is punished by lopping off the end joint of the little finger of the offender's hand. Such treatment is usually sufficient to mend the person's misguided ways, but if they persist in their wrongdoing another joint, and even a third, may be cut off. In order to 'show his spirit', it was not so long ago that the offender was required to do the digit-removing himself. But now, in these more spineless and swordless times, someone else tends to do the cutting while another (often a friend of the victim) helps to hold the hapless hand steady.

By the time Tetsu and I arrived back at his house, where Sliced Bread Man lay flaked out and dog-gnawed on the kitchen table beside the bowl of noodles, it was 4.30 a.m. Not much point in going to bed, really, as I had to be up soon after six to catch the *Queen Coral* to the tiny jewel island of Yoron.

Chiyoko arose early specially to prepare me breakfast before I left. No Japanese-style breakfast this (apart from the sacrosanct rice): it was toasted thick white-bread sandwiches filled with tuna and egg mayonnaise, and a vat of sweet, gritty coffee. After trying (and failing) to persuade me to 'Please, Jodie-*san*, stay another night, or even a week', she shuttled around the kitchen rifling through her drawers for anything she could possibly give me. Here, please, take this small traditional Japanese knife. Well thank you but, really, you keep it. How about this laquered rice bowl? No, really not, it's far too special. This saucepan? Thank you but I have nothing on which to cook. Ah so, *desu-ka*? – well now . . . this Japanese doll? It's very nice but I'd only be sure to break it on my bike. Really I don't need anything. Mmmmm, let me see . . . I know, Tetsu says you are a cook – then please accept this book of traditional Japanese recipes. Thank you, but with that on board (it was the size and weight of a concrete flagstone) I don't think I'd make it out of Kametsu, let alone to the other end of Japan. Ah so . . . then let me see . . . how about . . . And so on and so on.

But as she was obviously so anxious for me not to leave without an offering from her home, I finally relented by accepting an easily stowable and lightweight wicker hand fan with the words TOKUNOSHIMA TOPSHELLS dyed in fluorescent pink and green across its arc, and eight 500 yen phonecards (I know a useful gift when I see one).

After the obligatory snapshot session of me and surrounding family members poised beside my bike on the front door step (would I, I wondered, be put out to graze in the 'CHIRPY – refreshing times flow gently' photo album?) I made to cycle off to the port. This caused a momentary flurry of consternation.

'What? – you can't possibly cycle,' clucked mothering Chiyoko. 'Tetsu will take you in the car.'

'Of course!' chimed in Tetsu. 'It was my duty plan – my father says okay for me to starting working later hour today special.'

'But the port is only a mile down the road,' I protested. 'I'll be there in five minutes.'

'It is my pleasurable honour to take you as speciality guest,' said Tetsu, 'also too my brother and sister are having much excitement to join us for out of ordinary experience.'

Hmmmm – this was certainly a new angle of approach. Now I may know a useful gift when I see one but I also recognize an absurd idea and spending fifteen minutes to dissect my bike and dismember my packs just in order to cram the whole kit and caboodle into the bubble-sized Minica as a way of making life more complicated for everyone involved struck me as a very fine example of absurdity indeed.

So, honorary duties not withstanding and being the bullheaded and saddle-bottomed soul that I am – I rode there, beating the Autozammers by ten minutes (yes, even the sleepy backwaters of Tokunoshima have traffic-jamming roadworks).

As I was walking into the ferry terminal to buy my ticket, a small, slim woman with a wide smile intercepted me and said, in perfect and rather plummy-sounding English, 'Ahhh, American I presume?'

I felt like saying: no, David Livingstone actually. But instead I said, 'You presume wrong – I'm English.'

Handing me her name card, Chieko Sigeta said, 'How smashing! My son went to Oxford University. He speaks first class English!'

Chieko was a Jehovah's Witness and, wasting little time, set about debriefing me that Japan now had a grand total of 200,000 Jehovah's Witnesses, forty of whom resided in Tokunoshima.

'We have a new convention hall,' she said, 'really, it is very smashing for us all. Please, do come.'

I once went out with a Scouser whose mother was a devout Jehovah's Witness and my encounters with her ideas and the stories that I heard about the Witnesses, retailed to me by her unholy son, persuaded me to give any Kingdom Halls a very wide berth.

'Thank you, but I've got a boat to catch,' I said.

'Then perhaps you might care to take this,' said Chieko, handing me a magazine whose cover didn't exactly inspire confidence: a crucifix superimposed over a billowing mushroom cloud.

'Certainly I'll take it,' I said, 'but I can't promise I'll read it – specially as it's in Japanese!' Good, I thought, that should let me off the hook. And, 'smashingly', it seemed to as she drifted off round the corner, just as Tetsu and siblings arrived on the scene.

'Sorry, I haven't had a chance to buy my ticket yet,' I said to Tetsu, 'I've been a little waylaid.'

'No inconvenienced problem really,' said Tetsu, handing me my ticket, 'please accepting with pleasure.'

'What? You can't possibly buy my ticket for me.'

'Yes, no problem really.'

'Tetsu, don't be silly. It's expensive. Here, how much do I owe you?'

'Please my pleasure offering,' said Tetsu, 'from my mother.'

Our yes-yes, no-no ritual was interrupted when Chieko appeared again, offering me a bag of sweets and a crisp 2,000 yen (£12) note. This was more than I could take, in more ways than one.

'Really, you're very kind, but I can't possibly,' I said in a surely-this-isn't-happening tone.

'Please,' said Chieko, 'it is nothing.'

'It's a lot. Really, thank you, but I'm okay for money. Cycling's cheap!'

Tetsu, still standing beside me, leaned towards me and said quietly in my ear, 'It's okay – you must be accepting custom of Japanese-style giving here.'

So, pulling on a brave face, I turned back to Chieko and said, 'Thank you. You're very kind. I'll put it to good use.'

When the bulk of the *Queen Coral* glided into the dock, Tetsu went all quiet before saying that he would love to come with me. I told him he was better off sticking with his corpses.

'I tend to have a dubious habit of crashing into anyone I go cycling with,' I said. 'I wouldn't want you filling up your grave space sooner than your time.'

As I rolled towards the car deck I just caught sight of Tetsu trotting up the ramp for foot passengers at the side of the ship. We met up in the reception foyer where I persuaded him (not without trouble) into letting me buy him an 'I like Nature' can of green tea before we stood on the deck in the already sweltering shade watching the passengers clamber on board and waving to his brother and sister standing on the quay. Tetsu looked sad and I must admit I felt a fleeting *Brief Encounter* pang shoot through me. But I knew this was silly. I was just an old maid compared with this young and frisky whippet beside me. Tetsu, looking somewhat bashful, asked if he could hold my hand.

'Of course,' I said, touched by the innocence of it all. This was definitely no 'quick-hands-down-your-pants' man, that was for sure. But there again, this was Japan, where fast-forward public displays of behind-the-bike-shed type of behaviour are not *de rigueur* – at least not in Tokunoshima.

When a dapper ship steward finally gave a few hefty blows on the ship's gong, all passengers not travelling began to file off board. Tetsu was the last to leave.

As the *Queen Coral* slid slowly towards the mouth of the harbour, the monolithic engines throbbing deep down in the bowels of the hull, I hung over the balustrade energetically waving a 'Hello Kitty' *hankachifu* as Tetsu nipped up to the end of the quay in his zippy little Autozam, his brother and sister popping out of the sunroof to throw me handfuls of peace signs. Tetsu jumped out of the Carol, running right to the edge of the pier where it met with the *tsunami* sea-break of concrete kisses, and with arms flapping above his head like the sails of a windmill he shouted up to me. But his words were snatched by the wind and thrown out to sea, spinning into oblivion.

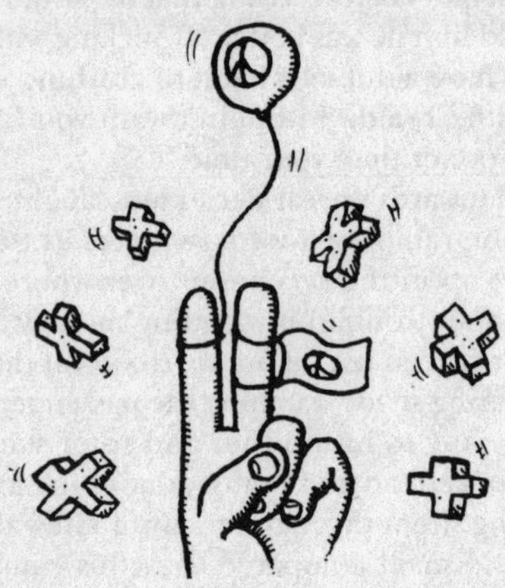

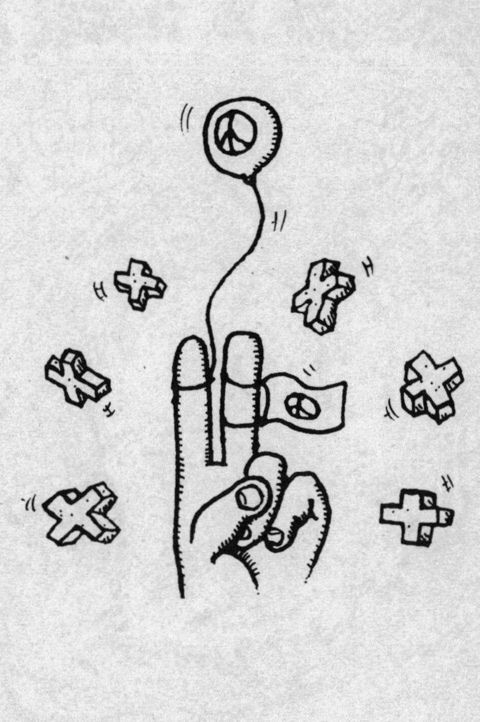

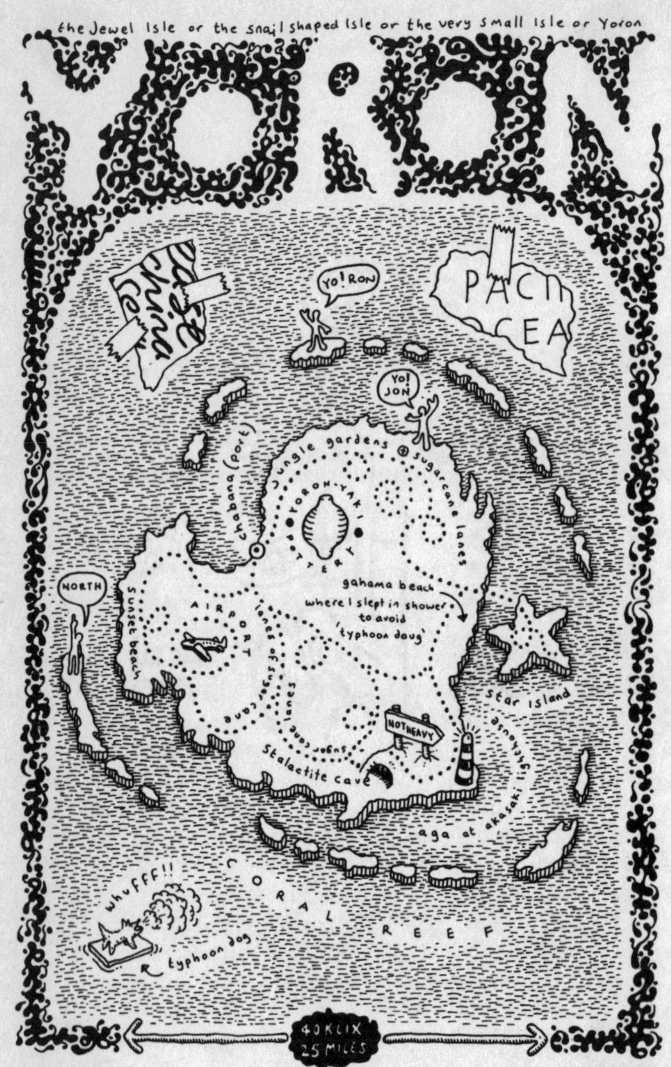

the Jewel Isle or the snail shaped Isle or the very small Isle or Yoron
YORON
PACI
CEA
YO! RON
YO! JON
jungle gardens
sugarcane lanes
chabana (port)
YORON-YAKI POTTERY
NORTH
sunset beach
AIRPORT
lanes of sugarcane
gahama beach
where I slept in shower to avoid 'typhoon doug'
star island
NOTHEAVY
sugar cane lanes
Stalactite cave
akasaki lighthouse
aga at akasaki
CORAL REEF
whufff!!
typhoon dog
40 KLIX
25 MILES

CHAPTER 21

Stateside Japan

Inside the *Queen Coral* the atmosphere smelt of air-conditioned bodies – bodies that lay enwrapped in brown blankets, heads propped on the standard brown plastic pillows of brick. Televisions blared – here a puppet form of samurai drama, there a show of violent cartoons. Unable to stand more than ten minutes of this I instead chose to plant myself outside in a shady nook on the hot, people-free deck. The combination of lack of sleep, intense heat and absurd humidity drained my blood of energy. I moved as if in a somnambulant trance. At one point, as I mixed up some of my left-over food supplies into a highly unattractive but tasty mixture in my plastic lunch box, I was vaguely aware of being observed with interest by a woman and a gaggle of giggling and whispering schoolgirls who had stepped outside for a breath of hot air. I could see that they thought I was some strange species – possibly escaped from the zoo.

They stared at me for some time before the woman, who spoke a little English, said, 'Excuse me – please, what are you making?'

In no mood to mince words I said, 'The dog's dinner.'

'Ah so, *desu-ka*? Mmmm, please this dish is having explain.'

'Well, it's very simple – you just throw anything you've got festering in the bottom of a pannier into a bowl – give it a good stir and it's ready to go.'

'Ah so, *desu-ka*?'

Feeling a bit bad for allowing my peevish mood to surface, I made a momentary attempt to be chatty by asking her if she was going to Yoron or on to Okinawa.

'Yoron,' she said with a smile and then explained that she was a tour leader of eighty-four twelve-year-olds (oh horror of horrors) who were having a week's holiday on the island. Knowing that Yoron was not much bigger than the size of a dinner plate, I felt a selfish twinge of gloom that they weren't going on to Okinawa. Would there, I wondered, be any space to hide?

It was mid-afternoon by the time the *Queen Coral* deposited me on the neck of the tiny tortoise-shaped island of Yoron. Standing on the concrete quay the heat was so great that it was almost too hot to breathe. I pushed my bike over to take stock in the shade of a solitary, fresh-out-the-mould giant polyhedron sea-break from behind which emerged a man in a T-shirt emblazoned with the words:

BLACKPOOL & BRIGHTON
Since 1894

He nodded to me, commented about the heat and the load on my bike, climbed into a flat-bed truck and drove away. Before I had a chance to move I was surrounded by an excited gaggle of young women trainee staff from A-Coop supermarket who wanted to take a series of photographs of me in their midst. All of them carried identical canvas holdalls with 'YORON IS FOR LOVERS' printed on the sides.

Wanting to find out the times of the ferries to Okinawa, I left my shady lump of concrete to tramp over to what I presumed to be the ferry terminal set behind the quayside car park but which turned out to be some sort of office – nothing to do with the boats. I asked a woman, sitting at a desk in front of a computer, if she knew where the shipping-line offices were and she told me it was a small building located in Chabana – Yoron's main and only town – about two kilometres along on the seafront. Instead of just leaving me to find the office myself (a task which I'm sure would not have been beyond even my navigational capabilities) the woman said she would take me there in her car.

'Don't worry,' I said, 'I'm on bicycle – I'm sure I'll find it fine.'

'Okay,' she said, 'I'll drive slowly – come on.'

So, in the grilling heat of the sun, I chased the rear of her white Nissan Sunny ('familee car') along the coast road to the office. Here she waited for me while I did what I needed to do before taking me along to the town office where she introduced me to her English-speaking friend, Kazushi Takeshita, who she thought could provide me with further information about the island.

Kazushi, a native of Yoron, had ten years previously spent a year living in Los Angeles. He told me, among other things, how much he loved football and that he was off that night to Amami-Oshima to take part in a football tournament between the islands. He said how disappointed he had been that Brazil hadn't won the World Cup.

'I sat up all night for watching it,' he said, 'and in the morning I was *suimin-busoku,* which means sleepy during the day after no night sleeping.'

'Ah,' I said, 'today I'm a prime example of *suimin-busoku.*'

Kazushi told me that if I wanted to camp I must go to the wonderful campground at Gahama Beach.

'Ask for Mrs Yamashita,' he said, 'she's in charge.'

After stocking up on food supplies in Chabana – a villagey town that seemed mainly to be full of coral gift shops – I rode along empty winding lanes lined with stone walls over which tumbled an exquisite profusion of wild flowers, fiery hibiscus, papaya and banana plants. Every now and then a small reed-thatched home would be just visible in a jungle-thick garden. In between lay fields of sugar cane, which reminded me of Tetsu's warning 'Don't sleep in the sugar cane,' he had said, 'there are very many *habu* – they like to eat the mouses.'

Gahama Beach campground was an appealingly shady affair tucked into a breezy thicket of pines and overgrown yucca plants, a mere shell's throw from the blinding white beach and perfect turquoise brilliance of the coral-reefed sea. The camping area comprised one pit-toilet, one shower, some long-semi-covered sinks for dish-washing and eleven raised table-top mounds of baked dry earth – each specially constructed to support a tent. As there was no Mrs Yamashita to be found I selected the best of the last three unoccupied mounds and put up my tent. Surrounding me on various mounds were: a friendly family of four; three student cadets who seemed to enjoy dropping plastic bottles and bags into their fire to watch them pop; five eighteen-year-old students (four boys, one girl) from Tokyo – all dentist trainees living in one cramped tent; a waiter from Okinawa called Kazuo, riding an eye-catching black and sun-glinting chrome Yamaha Virago and who had spent a year working in a Japanese restaurant in Christchurch, New Zealand; and, my closest neighbour, a lad from Kobe who, compared with the majority of rush-around little-holiday, hard-working Japanese, seemed to be leading a what's-the-hurry sort of life – working half a year in Hokkaido as a mono-ski instructor while the other half was spent travelling around Japan.

The dentists invited me to join them for their barbecued feast of fish and cabbage and onion and carrots and pepper and strange strips of jelly-type potato and beansprouts and long, thin mushrooms shaped like inverted exclamation marks. Later that night, after a moonlit dip in the ocean with Kazuo and the mono-ski man, I finally clambered into my mound-top tent, flicking away a deluge of hermit crabs and fist-sized beetles before tuning in to my trannie. The first station I found was the service-boys' Far East Network. Here, set to the 'Yee-haa' twangs of Country, was an advert warning about the harmful effects of the sun:

> I'm-a-takin' one big chance
> gettin' skin cancer
> if I spend too much time out here with you baby,
> coz you gotta protect your body,
> app-ly suncream;
> wear a hat, use your head,
> pro-tect your body
> app-ly suncream . . .

Thank you – that's quite enough of that. Flick of switch; turn to silence; fall asleep.

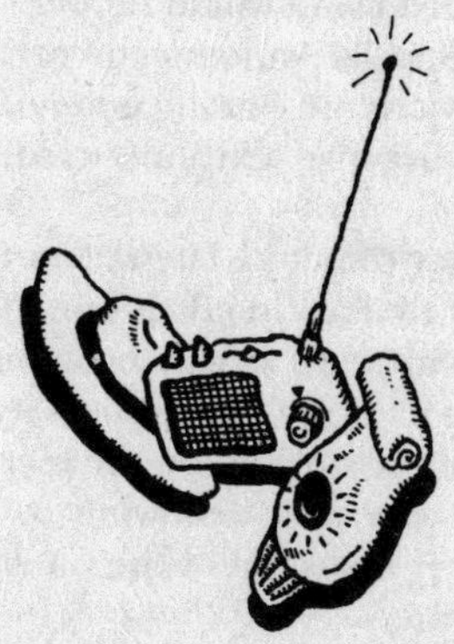

I spent a few days on Yoron doing nothing more gruelling than swimming with the multi-coloured fish out to Star Island (a submerged 'beach' consisting of peculiar star-shaped sand grains), cycling and walking around the island and eating other people's barbecues. Keeping my base-camp at Gahama Beach, I visited gardens and potteries and marvelled at cemeteries where the wooden graves decked in colourful banners looked like ships' sails. I helped cut sugar cane with a bunch of giggling *obaasan* in cancer-shielding sunbonnets who told me that I had no need to worry about snakes in the grass as Yoron, together with Miyako, were the only islands in the whole of the Nansei chain to be *habu*-free.

When my cheap swimming goggles broke I rode back to the sugar-refinery chimney-dominated town of Chabana to look for a new pair. The cheapest I could find cost an extortionate £18 and, when I asked the friendly shop assistant if she had anything *motto yasui* (cheaper), she said, '*Dozo* – please, pleasure *o-miyage* – souvenir – good Japanese memory, you have strong leg strong heart ha! ha! Please – my pleasuring!'

By the time I got around to thinking about moving on to Okinawa there were typhoon warnings in the air. Every so often the Far East Network would report:

'This is a FEN Special Announcement: . . . Sea Condition Yellow . . . strong winds are causing potentially dangerous sea conditions . . . practise extreme caution until 9 a.m. Sunday . . .'

A few hours after came the latest report:

'Sea Condition Red . . . in effect until 9 a.m. Monday . . . water-related activities are strictly prohibited. Strong gusty winds are creating extremely dangerous sea-conditions . . .'

As the sound of the surf out on the reef increased from a soothing low thunder to a bellowing roar, the fishermen began hauling their boats out of the water – a sign of rocky rough times to come.

Typhoon 'Doug', reported the FEN Special Announcements, was charging north from the island of Ishigaki (a little too close for comfort), having already done battle with the Philippines and Taiwan. I cycled over to the A-Line ferry office to enquire how likely it was that there would be a sailing tomorrow to Okinawa. It wasn't and, instead of a ticket, I was given a lurid green *aisu-kuriimu.*

As the wind increased the campground cleared. The only people left were Kazuo and the mono-ski man. Rather than be blown into oblivion I had tried every *minshuku* on the island but, not surprisingly, everything was full. With the palm trees bending over backwards in the wind, Kazuo and Mr Mono-ski left by motorbike for a multi-yen priced hotel in town. Meanwhile, I packed up to spend the night with my bike and bags, battening down the hatches in my small concrete bunker of the shower.

Though the furious sea careered way up over the top of the beach, though the wind screamed and roared and though a number of trees and corrugated roofs were ripped from their moorings, the main bulk of Typhoon Doug passed us by and I emerged from my showery shelter with a very large sigh of relief.

Despite tumultuous seas the A-Line ferry stopped by Yoron, on its way to Okinawa, to pick up a smattering of passengers who felt their stomachs could take five hours of upheaval. Surprisingly, mine held up pretty well, mainly because, unlike those who tried to weather the storm planted in front of the television, I wedged myself into a windswept cranny on deck to ride the waves.

It was from this position that I first set eyes on Naha, the prefectural capital of Okinawa, which, with a population of over 350,000, was the largest city I'd had to contend with for weeks. Bombed into oblivion by relentless American air attacks during the Second World War, Naha appeared to be virtually indistinguishable from a large sprawling chunk of Tokyo.

It was dark and stormy by the time we docked and the thought of having to negotiate six-lane freeways, fast flyovers and traffic swooshing out of the sheeting rain from all directions did not foster a sense of well-being. Blinded by neon, I wove my way through miles of featureless concrete, emblazoned with walls of blipping and flashing signs.

Following the Battle of Okinawa, when the Americans used the island as an operations base for bombing the rest of Japan, the Occupation Forces bulldozed the flattened city of Naha and then Americanized it into super-wide boulevards, highways and bypasses. It didn't take long for Okinawa to become one of America's largest military bases in the Far East, leaving the exact status of the island as undetermined. The one issue during the 'sixties which united all political and apolitical sides alike in rare agreement was for the return of Okinawa from America's possession to Japan. However, the Americans were not so keen, the Pentagon viewing Okinawa as essential to its task of actively confronting the forces of Communism everywhere. The massive Kadena air force base, situated fifteen or so miles north of Naha, was used for bombing sorties against Vietnam and was irreplaceable as a strategic outpost in the northern Pacific. In protest at America's intransigence, students, housewives and workers joined forces in large-scale demonstrations, uniting in a people's movement against a host of targets both inside and outside Japan. 'Oppose the War, Oppose the Treaty, Return Okinawa' ran the common slogan of the time.

In 1972, after twenty-seven years of occupation and intense political agitation, the US finally handed back Okinawa and it once again became a sovereign part of Japan. It was a euphoric time for the Japanese, even though the Americans kept the Kadena air base and other facilities (but stocks of nerve gas had to be removed).

Under the auspices of a mutual defence pact, the US military still maintains an enormous presence with naval, marine, air force and army contingencies firmly entrenched at bases throughout Okinawa. Despite the perennial source of tension with the civilian population (and the added anger over the rape of a twelve-year-old girl by American servicemen which occurred soon after I left), Okinawa is still one of the largest US military bases in the Far East.

OKINAWA
THE WARTORN OR JAPERICAN ISLE
Cape Hedonomisaki (concrete desolation)
very blue sea
very red sands
YUK!
TRAFFIC FREE
Okuma Beach (US military campground)
Ie Jima
Ernie Pyle monument (famous WWII correspondent killed at end of the war)
Shoshi Utaki pants garden!
jungle / snakes
Aha - moon dancing grannies (not a Norwegian dancing boy group)
motobu
motor bus
Nago
Taira Bay
Arume Bay
Cape Bun
motoboat
Nago bay
Kushi
Oura bay
MILITARY AREA
Camp Hansen (Hank's camp)
cape zanpamisaki
Ginoza... home town of school master who gave me 20 bottles of 'Guromsun Oral Liquid Tonic', 6 mangoes + 1 elephantine watermelon + who was also the cause of causing this book's longest map reference note.
Ishikawa
(next of) KIN BAY
NOISY
DIRTY
BUILT-UP
land riddled with war memorials
N
Naha
Cactus park
Cape Arasaki
SITES
funny
Kin blue beach: underwater scrabble + 3-person inner-tube race
Spotted first (?) racing cyclist asleep in the road
sad
Cave of the Virgins: 200 school girls + teacher commit suicide during Battle of Okinawa
Imperial Navy HQ: 200 men commit suicide with hand grenades
40 KLIX
25 MILES

Needing a cheap place to stay, I rode through the rain up Kokusai-dori (International Boulevard), Naha's long, broad street that slices through the city, crowded with banks, businesses, fast-food joints and a myriad of souvenir shops and army surplus stores selling, among the usual surplus paraphernalia of the military, hand grenades and bullets fashioned into key rings.

Talking to a couple of motorcyclists from Fukuoka on the boat, I'd picked up the name of the overly cheap-sounding Ichi (one) Dollar Minshuku. Giving me the telephone number, they had told me it was in a back street, somewhere near the Mitsukoshi department store. I found the *depaato* easily enough and, slipping down some side streets, had a quick scour around before I stopped by the Dairy Queen *aisu-kuriimu* booth to see whether the boy behind the counter could shed any light on the whereabouts of the Ichi Dollar. Sorry, he said, but he'd never heard of it. Did I have an address?

'Only a telephone number,' I said.

'Let me try it for you,' said the Dairy Queen boy, keeping a couple of plump girls waiting at the window of the counter. A lot of very fast Japanese into the mouth-piece ensued after which he held the receiver aside to tell me that the Ichi Dollar had closed down.

'Ah so, *desu-ka*?' I said, to which he replied, 'But lady says she has *minshuku* near Golden Orion cinema.'

'Where's the Golden Orion?' I asked.

'I don't know,' he said, at which point one of the Dairy Queen girls beside me, who was still patiently waiting for *aisu-kuriimu* chirped in that she knew where the Golden Orion was. After reaching for the telephone to get directions from the cinema to the *minshuku*, she said, 'Easy! I'll take you there!'

Not wanting to drag a couple of girls on a wild goose chase through the streets in the rain, after already having held up the pleasures of their *aisu-kuriimu* consumption, I said, 'Don't worry – just give me directions and I'm sure I'll find it.'

The Dairy Queen girls wouldn't hear of it and so I offered to buy them their *aisu-kuriimu*, which they likewise wouldn't hear of. I ended up not only being bought a Dairy Queen special of my own but also being escorted past McDonald's and A&W Root Beer, right to the door of the requisite *minshuku*.

Through the glass-plated entrance and up some stairs I found Mrs Ota, the tiny wizened owner of the *minshuku*, who told me the authorities had made her close down the Ichi Dollar because it suffered from swaying walls and had more than its fair share of cockroaches.

Mrs Ota's new *minshuku* was just a small first-floor flat that, since the death of her husband, she'd converted into rooms for renting out to lodgers or passers-by. Two rooms were already full – one with three Japanese girls, the other with a workman who was chain-smoking Larks. I had a choice between a 1,700 yen (£11) windowless cupboard crammed with a hospital bed, or sleeping with a Hope-smoking taxi-driver (who'd been there six months) in a row of capsule beds at 1,000 yen apiece – a wall of wooden 'coffins' whose ends were covered in short curtains patterned with penny-farthings floating among the words:

> Fresh wind I am reminded of my good old days. Cross are two bridges walk against the wind with to bicycle.

Despite the cycling theme, I chose the cupboard room as I didn't fancy being smoked out by the taxi-driver's Hopes.

Mrs Ota lived off the hall in a miniature internal room – even smaller than my cupboard – the end of which adjoined a small kitchenette. She too had a hospital bed though she was so tiny that, when she was standing, the bed was almost on a level with her chin. She lay on this bed almost constantly throughout the day, fanned by the wind of a large electric *senpuki* attached to the foot of her bed, while watching a wailing television planted beside it which remained on continually.

Despite her friendliness to me, Mrs Ota appeared decidedly bitter with life. Originally from Osaka, she hated Okinawa but had only come to Naha because of her husband's work. But then he had died on her, leaving her with no means of re-establishing herself in Osaka; her son, who still lived in Osaka, never came to see her so she was bitter about that too; and she didn't like the work her *minshuku* involved but, don't you know, you have to live somehow; and she hated the typhoons – in fact, she just hated outside, she never went out – well, maybe once a week to buy some food, but for never more than an hour as she hated Naha, hated the crowds, hated the noise.

'I prefer television watching,' she said. 'Life better that way.'

I wished I could make her lot a little brighter for her so, adopting a 'Little Miss Helpful' mode I asked if there was anything she needed from the market. But, of course, she wouldn't hear of it so I bought her a bunch of flowers from the flower shop next door and it was nice to see her smile.

For breakfast the taxi-driver gave me a beer and an offer of Hope and, although not included in the price, Mrs Ota presented me with two bowlfuls of tofu-and-seaweed soup, three hard-boiled eggs and a plate containing a shoal of tiny dried and bright pink fish with red eyes.

Of all the sixty islands of Nansei, Okinawa is by far the largest, stretching a respectable seventy-five miles (120 kilometres) in length but only three to twelve miles (5–20 km) in width. The unusual shape of this island (like a man on the brink of a dive, with stunted arms swept back behind him into the East China Sea, his face and extended donger poised into the might of the Pacific) influenced my plan of action, which was to ride north from his ankles, up round his Moon Beach buttocks, out along the Motobu Peninsula of his arms, up to the northern-most point of his head at Cape Hedonomisaki, through his eyes at Ada, skirting his caved-in stomach at Yaka to career around his crucial department near (gosh!) Gushikawa, round a toe or two at Umino, before rolling back up to Naha along the Achilles tendon of Itoman.

I was packing up my bags, ready to leave, when Mrs Ota called to me from her hospital bed. She had just seen the weather forecast, which she warned me did not look good: Okinawa was at present sandwiched between Typhoon 13 bearing down from the East China Sea and Typhoon 14 from the Pacific. Itchy to get going I ran downstairs, peered up through a cliff-face of neon overhangs into a small rectangle of dreary sky and decided to risk it. But by the time I'd finished at the bank I was in a quandary again – the man behind the counter, interested to learn where I was going, insisted on dialling the telephone weather service, only to report that a typhoon was definitely on its way but there was uncertainty as to which part of the island it would hit.

Unsure as to whether I should head north or south, or just simply scarper back to Mrs Ota's in retreat, I hovered for a while in the wonders of Heiwa Dori – a huge covered maze of a market bursting with strange and tantalizing foods. Leaving aside the surplus of fish and slippery sea creatures which were being happily slapped around on chopping boards – many being filleted alive as they wriggled and squirmed beneath the blade – and leaving aside the stalls overflowing with pigs' feet, knuckles, knees and ears (*mimiga* – sliced pigs' ears with vinegar – being a local delicacy, to those with pork-friendly taste buds), I finally emerged with a couple of mangos as big as melons and a bunch of *shima* – the small, red and addictively sweet variety of local bananas.

Despite the threat of the weather, and impatient to get going, I set off out of the city on a northward course, passing block upon block of local attractions such as Kentucky Fried Chicken, Mos Burger, McDonald's, Mister Donut, A & W Burgers, Lotteria, Shakey's Pizza, Dinner Bell Pizza and the particularly appetizing Rawhide Restaurant advertising its 'Stake & Robster' speciality on a sign outside, with plastic replicas of the dishes displayed in the window – which only had the effect of reinforcing the uncertainty engendered by the sign's English translation.

As I was washed northwards along National Route 58 – a thundering six-lane highway lined with the likes of Toys 'Я' Us mega-town America – the heavens burst with apocalyptic force. I raced through the doorway of the Happy House Shopping Mall to take refuge from the storm. For nearly two hours the rain hammered down, the wind whipping heavy-duty shopping trolleys around the parking lot as if they had a mind of their own. Was this, I wondered, a taster of the typhoon to come?

Just as I was thinking the Happy House might have to be my 'Happy Home' for the night, the rain eased off. After a quick phone call to secure a youth hostel bunk I raced up the spectacularly ugly Route 58 that ripped its way through a seemingly endless succession of cities. As soon as I could I turned off for Cape Zanpamisaki on to what looked on my map like a quiet lane winding its way through 'Yomitan Village'. In reality it was just another traffic-laden highway blasting through an urban sprawl – more city than town, with more concrete than it knew what to do with.

I made it to Maeda Misaki *yusu hosuteru* just as another storm, which had been chasing me the last few miles along the coast from Cape Zanpamisaki, burst forth so I dived through the doors, thinking: made it!

The next morning, having been informed by the hostel's *parento-san* that the typhoon had sheered off back into the East China Sea, I sallied forth beneath unpredictable skies to continue rolling up the 58 – now a coastal highway crowded with endless resorts: Moon Beach, Tiger Beach, Manza Beach, Seragaki Beach, Miyuki Beach, Inbu Beach, Kariyushi Beach, Kise Beach and . . . what's this? . . . Nago Paradise . . . paradise made of concrete?

Fed up with a coastal route which could have been so pleasant had it not been so awful, I veered off into the mountains of the Motobu-hanto Peninsula, along a quiet and winding road that led me first through what my map interestingly identified as the 'Pineapple Gordens Zone' before taking me past the odd hamlet consisting of a handful of traditional wooden houses, many of which had their panels of sliding doors thrown wide open to the shady side of the empty green valley. In one house an old man dressed only in a white vest and *suteteko* (baggy cotton underpants) was stretched out asleep on the *tatami*; the only sounds emanating were those from a gabbering television. A bent-backed woman, protected from the sun, dug away in her small vegetable plot with a curious digging tool – a small spade-head attached at right angles to a short wooden handle – giving me the impression that, if any tool was meant to break your back, then surely that was it.

I hit the coast again at Toguchi from where I jumped on a ferry for the afternoon forty-minute crossing to the monkey-nut shaped island of Ie Jima. The boat deposited me into the small and only town of Ie, an ugly place comprising little more than a community of squat ferro-concrete boxes. Just along from the harbour I paid a visit to the Ernie Pyle Monument, commemorating the life of one of the most famous war correspondents of the Second World War. After his four-year coverage of the Allied campaigns in North Africa, Sicily, Italy and France had brought Indiana-born Ernie a Pulitzer Prize, he went (in 1944) to join the US forces in the Pacific, in Iwo Jima and Okinawa where, owing to his dedicated reporting of the horrors of the war as seen through the eyes of the servicemen, he became known as the 'GI's spokesman' – by living the life of a GI. During the Battle of Okinawa he went to Ie Jima when, on 18th April 1945, the jeep he was travelling in came under attack from the fusillade of a Japanese machine-gun, turning the jeep over into a ditch. Still alive, Ernie Pyle lifted his head only to be killed by another burst of fire from the Japanese gun.

After rolling past fields of sugar cane, pineapple and tobacco where small figures stooped, bent over, busying themselves with the land, I cut down a track crowded with wild flowers to a secluded beach. Here I spent a peaceful night beside the sea, thinking about the very different scene it would have been fifty years before.

Back over on the Motobu-hanto Peninsula I followed the coast around through another curious-sounding place which my map identified as the Shoshi Utaki Pants Garden – a name which conjured up some interesting ideas of botanical smalls. That evening, looking for a place to camp, I followed what on my map looked like a quiet road out to Cape Akamaruzaki, but which turned out to contain a private JAL resort bang next to a large guarded and fenced-in private campground for US military and their families.

I was about to retreat when I met a *gaijin* family out for a walk who said they could smuggle me past the gate attendant easily enough. Feeling a shower was on the cards I gratefully took the Oveda family up on their offer. So, adopting the persona of a far-flung distant relation, I joined Hank and Lynn and their troop of offspring – Megyn, Morgyn, Mellysa and Trynity (eleven, nine and seven, and the baby of seven months) – plus a stray dog, as we wandered nonchalantly past the guard and into the camp. Half-Mexican Hank, a marine with cropped hair and a stocky power-pack of muscle, told me, as we walked past rows of interestingly shaped tents, that the US military had once owned the whole of this white-beached peninsula but had finally relented and given a slice to Japanese airlines to 'help cool relations'.

The campground was chock-around-the-block full of Americans. It was a very odd experience to be suddenly confronted with so many *gaijin.* I couldn't stop staring. Everyone looked so . . . well, weird. All arms and legs and flailing movements and jarring loud voices – voices which I could actually understand. I should have felt at home, being among people who, for the first time in months, didn't look at me as if I had ten heads. But I didn't. Despite the fact that I knew I was 'one of them' (a big-nosed barbarian) I felt uncomfortable. I probably wouldn't have felt quite so odd had there been a few Japanese mingling among the *gaijin,* but there were none as they were not allowed to use the campground or to use the beach or the land. Their land. Their land in their country. And it was this experience of sudden segregation that made me feel uneasy.

Lynn and Hank invited me to join them for their campfire supper of hamburgers and beers, which seemed to be more or less the standard fare of all the surrounding campers. I asked Hank, who was based in Okinawa for three years, how he liked Japanese food. He didn't.

'I keep mainly to pizzas and burgers,' he said. 'That way, I know what I'm eating!'

It was hot and humid and windless – prime time for a mosquito attack. Morgyn's agitated voice arose from out of the family's plastic-window-panelled tent:

'Mom, Mom, where's the flashlight?'

'Where it normally is, honey.'

'But I can't *see* it,' she wailed.

Once found, Lynn explained to me that the Okinawan mozzies are killers.

'Literally,' she said. 'Last year two people died from having gotten brain disease. Isn't that right, honey?'

'Sure,' said Hank, as he sprayed me with a triple-strength solution of DDT – so strong that I felt I was melting.

'You gotta be real careful.'

I asked Megyn, who was perched on a log beside me, how she liked living in Okinawa.

'Oh – it's okay,' she said. 'I miss my friends back home but the beaches are cool.'

'Do you go to an American school here?'

'Sure,' she said.

'Are you taught Japanese?'

'Well, maybe an hour a week,' she said, 'but I can't remember any!'

Hank had a month's holiday a year which he said he took in one big burst so that he could really relax and 'chill out'. Lynn told me that most Americans they knew that lived on base never went anywhere, just so they could stash away their cash in order to have, in Harry Enfield's words, 'LOADSA-MONEY' to spend when back in the States.

Lynn thought this 'real boring. I mean, jeez, talk about great memories to take home of a foreign country.'

At some point mid-barbecued burger, I mentioned I had been to see Ernie Pyle's memorial and wasn't it just rotten luck that he'd lifted his head for a peep of the action. And so near to the end of the war too. Lynn hadn't heard of Ernie but she liked the story, if 'like' is the right word – which it isn't – of his jeep flipping over and of his untimely end. Flicking back her long flaxen locks (the likes of which had been passed on genetically to her golden-headed daughters) she called inside to the tent where her crewcut husband was tending to a sudden wailing outburst from Trynity.

'Hank, honey,' she said, 'when didchasay the war ended?'

'Forty-five, hon,' came the reply.

'Oh yaah?'

Oh yaah.

Despite going overboard on the DDT, this particularly fierce species of Okinawan mosquitoes was still managing to spear my skin through a sweat-soaked armour of clothing. For a brief respite I asked if anyone fancied a dip in the East China Sea.

'It's not allowed,' said goldilocked Morgyn. 'There's no swimming after six or before nine.'

'That's right,' confirmed Hank.

So that was that.

The campground was segregated into an area for families, another for couples and another for singles – where in reality I should have been had I not been adopted by the Ovedas. It was in this singles section where all hell was running wild, thanks to a party of severely drunk servicemen shrieking with exaggerated movements around their campfires with some equally inebriated women. All night they howled with laughter and larked about like a bunch of adolescents bunking off school. At one point, sometime around 2.30 a.m., they embarked on a game of football which involved kicking around the prodigious amount of beer cans which they had drained earlier that evening. Several stray kicks resulted in missiles of crumpled aluminium pinging off my tent, which made me feel they were all just asking to have their heads stuck up a dead bear's bum. I should have shrieked blue or even deep purple murder at them, but instead my English reserve pulled me back and I seethed in silence. I was in such a sour mood that, sometime around four o'clock, when I dragged myself over to the toilet block for a pee, I felt extremely satisfied when I heard one of the severely drunk women whimpering from a nearby cubicle while another was being violently sick.

From the military camp at Okuma Beach it was an exuberant ride beside the clear waters of the East China Sea up the people-free coast to Cape Hedonomisaki, the northernmost point of Okinawa which, like most beauty spots in Japan, was marred by a concrete bunker of a tourist centre. Ignoring it as best I could I picked my way among the discarded cigarette butts and cans of pop, clambering up on to the craggy, melodramtic sea cliffs to peer over the edge into the belligerent blue ocean thundering on to the rocks over 300 feet down below.

Whereas the north-west coast had been flat, the east was decidedly mountainous. But to make up for all the leg-trembling effort there was a distinct lack of traffic – about one vehicle every half hour. Large rocky outcrops littered a reddish sand coast along which, every now and then, I'd spot a small knot of fishermen. The air, so humid, lay heavy around me like a wrung-out dishcloth.

Sweating up towards Mount Ibe while lost momentarily in a heat-dazed world, I was suddenly jolted back to the here and now by a young boy, barrelling along out of the blue on a nippy, drop-handlebarred bike. Being the first racing-inclined cyclist I had seen since arriving in Japan, I was naturally a trifle surprised to see one in such an unlikely area. But he was too fast for me and after he vanished up the steep dog-legging road of the mountain I let the matter slip from my mind (thanks to the heat it was far too much effort to give any subject much thought for long). I didn't think about the matter again until, several pint-loads of lost sweat later, I saw the boy again – this time not pounding the pedals but splayed spreadeagled at the edge of the road, his bike lying in an ungainly heap across the baking hot bitumen, just asking to be run over. The scene was such that my automatic reaction was to presume he'd bitten the bitumen – either that or he'd been had by a *habu* or a heart attack. But no, I was wrong on all fronts. When I stopped to check his wherewithal I discovered he was merely asleep. I admit that lying with your legs half in the road, your head in the verge, is an unusual position in which to take a nap but then, if your legs call it a day, they call it a day, come what may. However, I did my motherly bit by moving his bike and shifting his legs out of the road and then, noticing he had no water bottle on his bike, left him a couple of cans of Pocari Sweat.

The weather moves fast in Okinawa and before long the late afternoon sun had been obliterated by a smudgy ridge of cloud storming up over the mountains behind me. Keen to find a place to camp before it deposited its load upon me, I put my lacklustre legs into gear (something that comes surprisingly easy when you've got a potentially stinging great storm on your tail) and heaved my way with uncharacteristic speed over the final climb of the day. Hurtling down the other side towards the small fishing village of Aha (complete still with some traditional thatched-roof houses) the first fat raindrops rocketed from the sky, each one so bloated it produced a sizeable puddle on impact.

By the time the rest of the storm had caught up I was safely ensconced in the village store and being pampered by the chatty owneress (speaking not a word of English) who insisted on towelling down my arms and legs and giving me a block of fried bean curd and a bunch of bananas. While the storm threw itself with forceful rage upon the village, she expressed her concern over what might have become of me had I not made it to shelter.

'You might have died!' she said, a tad dramatically in Japanese.

'Ah so, *desu-ka*?' said I.

I was about to tell her I was more concerned for the fate of the sleeping racer-boy when I saw him go past the window sitting in the back of a white Noddy van.

By six-thirty the storm had passed and I asked the owneress if she knew of a little space where I could tuck my tent for the night.

'But you can't sleep in a tent in this wind – you might be blown out to sea! Here, come and sleep in the village hall,' she said, and led me next door to the hall.

'It's never locked,' she remarked as she slid open the door into a spacious, floor-boarded room, the walls of which were festooned with framed certificate-like diplomas.

'Oh, excuse me, I forget,' said the woman apologetically, 'I'm afraid tonight is dancing night. Ah, but this is all right, you can sleep after the class is finished.'

'What time will that be?' I asked, feeling weary.

The woman seemed uncertain, rattling off a selection of times that left me totally confused. When I asked her if she could write the approximate start and finish time down on a piece of paper she gave me a jar of pickled plums instead.

Rather than loiter around withoutent waiting for the dancing class to materialize, I pitched my tent in a narrow gravel alley that ran alongside the hall which, apart from the occasional gust transforming it into a turbulent wind tunnel, made for a fairly sheltered camp-spot. The chatty village store woman appeared suitably impressed with my instantaneous erection of nylon but said if the weather turned on me during the night I must sleep in the hall – otherwise I might die. Thank you, I said, I will; even though I knew the weather would have to be something little short of a typhoon for me to find the energy to uproot myself mid-slumber to enter a room no doubt rife with cockroaches.

Before I dropped off to sleep I caught the end of a report on the World Service about Woodstock 94, which was taking place twenty-five years after the original. This time the festival appeared to be three days of rain, mud and drugs but no alcohol – oh, and two deaths to date. A long-haired hippie who wore nothing apart from a pair of sandals and a layer of mud was asked by the reporter if the rain was spoiling things.

'The rain?' said the hippie with a breezy 'gee-I-hadn't-even-noticed-the-rain' tone in his voice. 'Man, what's the rain when I'm living free for three days of my life?'

'What do you usually do?' asked the reporter.

'Usually?' said the hippy. 'Well *usually* I go to law school.'

I had been asleep maybe a couple of hours when I awoke to the chest-stirring sound of hand-drums – a three-beat, five-beat rhythm accompanied by a chorus of women's voices singing a weird type of warble.

Slowly I unzipped my tent door. By pressing my head right against the side of the tent, I was able to lie on my stomach unnoticed among the darkened shadows of the alley and silently observe the curious scene taking place in front of the hall. A group of around forty middle-aged to elderly women had formed themselves into a large circle which, by a most peculiar form of dance – synchronized steps shuffling forwards, shuffling back, arms twisting and spiralling gracefully like half-flamenco, half-*habu* above their heads – slowly rotated clockwise. For nearly two hours the drums beat on while, beneath the silvery beam of the moon, the women – some dressed in aprons, others in kimono – shuffle-stepped and coiled and clapped and chorused with bewitching ululations as the circle of steps moved slowly round and round and round.

From my concealed ringside abode I lay propped up on my elbows, head cupped in hands, mesmerized – almost hypnotized – by the entrancing moonlit scene. Every so often I dozed off, the drums and lamenting strains accompanying me into fanciful and momentary dreams. Finally, just before midnight, a faction of women broke away to disappear into the hall while the rest, still in a circle, sat kneeling on the ground to laugh and chat in between bursts of exotically rousing song. And every so often the spine-tingling beat of the drums drifted into the night.

I wanted to remain unobserved, to see and not be seen. But I was forced to move position, firstly by two mean-faced crabs the size of small rocks that, no matter which way I tried to redirect them, appeared intent on making my home their home, and secondly by the call of nature. Slowly I slid from the mouth of my tent and cat-crept as noiselessly as possible down the shadowed and narrow-walled alley that ran behind the hall. Ducking down below the light of a window from where the sounds of chattering voices and a tinkling of cups emanated, I felt like a sneaky, good-for-nothing prowler, but all I was after was to reach the outdoor lean-to toilet undetected. I knew that, were I to be discovered, a hub of excitement would break out and shatter the dance instantaneously.

I made it to the toilet and was on the verge of leaving when I heard what I had hoped not to hear – the sound of approaching feet stopping just outside the lean-to. Then another set of feet approached and joined the waiting pair, the voices attached to the feet breaking into indecipherable chatter. Drat and double drat, I thought, realizing that there was nothing else for it but to reveal myself, so to speak, to the awaiting couple. So out I popped, bidding them a cheery *konbanwa* in the process. Not surprisingly the sight that greeted them came as something of a shock to the two tiny, twig-thin old dears. Hoping their hearts had not skipped too many beats I tried as best I could to assure them that, despite my unexpected and barbarian appearance, biting off their heads was really not on my agenda.

Expressions of surprise soon turned to smiles and I was led around to the front of the hall where, amid much merriment, the old dears' find was proudly displayed among the gathered group of sing-songers.

'*Doko kara*? *Doko kara*?' ('Where from? Where from?') everyone wanted to know. I was about to say 'England', but feeling in a puerile mood I said, 'The toilet!' and all the women fell over themselves with giggles.

After a few more whimsical moments I explained I was travelling alone by bicycle.

'Alone?'

'Yes, alone.'

'One person?'

'Yes, one person.'

'You really mean alone?'

'Yes, really alone.'

'You have friend?'

'No, no friend.'

'You are frightened?'

'No.'

'Gaaa, this is dangerous?'

'No, no – very safe.'

'Where do you sleep?'

'Usually in a tent.'

'A *tento*?'

'Yes, a *tento.*'

'Gaaa, but this is dangerous.'

'No, I think it's okay.'

'Tonight, where are you sleeping?'

'Over there, down the side of the hall.'

'Gaaa – *sugoi*! This is great!'

'Well, it's been very *sugoi* listening to you.'

'But are you not frightened?'

'Frightened? Here? No. Hot maybe, but not frightened.'

'You are student?'

'No.'

'Married?'

'No.'

'Lonely?'

'No.'

'How old?'

'Forty-five.'

Gasps of horror.

Out of all the identical questions I was asked on a daily basis, this latter was my least favourite. During my first few days in Japan I would give people my truthful age: *ni-ju-hachi* – twenty-eight. But as no one ever believed me I instead chose to either inflate it to an absurd level or drop it to around the age that would qualify me for Junior High or, if I was feeling more sensible, I would slide my age on down the scale until I hit upon a figure which did not make the questioners' eyes pop out of their heads. Generally I would settle for '*ni-ju-ni*' – twenty-two, as it was not only usually accepted without further expressions of disbelief but because the words, pronounced knee-joo-knee, tripped off the tongue with pleasurable ease. And that, in foreign tongue, is after all what it's all about.

Finally, interrogation over, I found a welcome cup of chilled *oolong-cha* being offered at the same time as the two women beside me launched into a spontaneous and stirring folk song. When they had finished everyone looked at me (gulp) and I was cajoled into singing a ditty from my motherland. As tinkering with bits of bicycles is more my forte than airing my vocals, I was understandably more than a little daunted by this request. Racking my brains and moistening my lips, the best (only) song I could think of on the spur of the moment was a very inappropriate and very unmotherlandish snatch of Chuck Berry:

> Ridin' along in my automobile
> My baby beside me at the wheel
> I stole a kiss at the turn of a mile
> My curiosity runnin' wild.
> Cruisin' and playin' the radio
> With no particular place to go . . .

Despite being out of tune, out of time, out of place and out of words, I was given not only a guttural chorus of appreciative 'ahhh-sooo *sugoi*!' but also a cheery demand for more. Plucking at strings in my (non-existent) repertoire the only ditty to run to my rescue was:

> My old man's a dustman,
> He wears a dustman's hat;
> He took me round the corner
> To see a football match.
> Fatty passed to Thinny;
> Thinny passed it back;
> Fatty took a rotten shot
> And knocked the goalie flat!

After which I excused myself and scuttled off to my hermit-crab hovel. I fell asleep as the women sang on and when I awoke in the morning I found two cans of coffee and a strip of *bashofu* – the locally made and famous pale yellow cloth produced from banana fibre and used in the manufacture of kimono – sitting in a carrier bag outside my tent.

After packing up I adjourned to the village store where, after a chat with the owneress, I sat outside in the shade eating my breakfast at the picnic table while watching Aha's morning rush-hour unfold before me. This consisted of a fisherman on a mini-tractor dragging a trailer-full of nets; a white flat-bed truck containing six workmen in baggy khaki trousers, black canvas split-toed boots and hard hats; an *obaasan* walking barefoot down the road with a large kettle in her hand and a U-shaped straw basket on her back attached to a tump-line around her brow; and, apart from a housewife who turned up at the store wearing a T-shirt which declared: PORTERSVILLE FLOWER ASSOCIATION TULIP BRAND, that was the whirring, blurring extent of Aha's 'downtown' rush-hour.

Bracing myself against the heat, I mounted up and took off across the Aha River and up into the hazy and empty jungle-clad mountains that my map indicated as being part of the Mount Yonaha Natural Protective Area, Noguchigera Preservation Area and the Yanbaru Kuina Preservation Area, which sounded almost too preserved to be true. For hours all I saw was a lot of hot uphill, the odd vehicle every hour or so, a plethora of various-sized snakes and, at one point, a spiky-leaved swathe of pineapples growing from fields of Devon-red earth.

Early afternoon, I arrived on the outskirts of Futami where, as it was the children's holidays, I stopped to rest in the shade of one of the buildings of the local Junior High school. But just because the children were on holiday didn't mean to say the teachers were (I later discovered that teachers rarely have any time off) and I hadn't been slumped, dripping with sweat, in the shade for long before I was happened upon by a teacher. As I had been caught helping myself without permission to a soupçon of private property (I had filled up my bottles from the outdoor tap, laid down my mat and surrounded myself with a wild profusion of plastic bags containing assortments of food) I felt, having acted like a typically brazen *gaijin*, a trifle abashed. But I had no need to be. The woman, a genial dame in a tight cream jacket and black and cream-checked skirt, took the fact that a dishevelled foreigner had taken the liberty of setting up a temporary base beneath her window as quite a normal and everyday event. Was there anything she could get me? Something to eat or drink maybe? Would I prefer to sit inside where it's cooler?

No, really, I'm fine. I'll be off in a tick. I'm sorry to have helped myself to this private spot of shade – didn't realize it was a school (ho! ho!).

The woman clucked over me for a few more moments, telling me to take my time, before she disappeared inside. No sooner had I thought: ah so, *desu-ka*? than the woman popped back out with a bowlful of what she described as 'typical Okinawan bean soup' and a carton of lime sorbet, both of which she sat and watched me eat with considerable pleasure.

After I'd appreciatively lapped up the last of the fast-melting sorbet I was invited inside to take tea with the school principal – an invitation which had me desperately trying to smooth down my crumpled and sweaty stuck-to-back T-shirt, scrubbing off the oily chain stain streaked across my starboard calf in a futile attempt to make myself even something far short of respectable.

I followed the check-skirted teacher into the principal's office where, after the standard patter of questioning, the principal – a slim man in maybe late forties who wore a black leather bootstrap tie – told me he was originally from Miyako (the island further south which I was planning as being my next port-of-call), where he had lived for thirty years. Now he and his family lived about twelve miles down the road in Ginoza-son.

'But Miyako is where I die,' he said, with a finality that sounded as if he had booked the precise time, day and spot for his death. Writing his name and address on a scrap of paper for me in unsteady *romaji* script, Mr Keifuku Takaesu then asked me if I would like to see his school, which was situated on the other side of the bay.

'But I thought this was your school,' I said, surprised.

'No, no. I am the principal of the Senior High School but I come here often to help with work.'

'Ah so, *desu-ka*?' I said, before adding that, yes, I would like to see his school. He seemed happy and offered me a lift in his car but I said I would meet him there, seeing as I was on my *jitensha* anyway.

When I arrived I found Mr Takaesu waiting at the gates in front of his school – a large white lump of concrete which, as far as lumps of concrete go, was actually by Japanese standards quite an old one – 110 years, to be precise, said Mr Takaesu, who before becoming the school principal had been a teacher of social studies.

As we ambled around the grounds, he told me his school had eighty pupils and eleven teachers and was the top school in the prefecture for sports.

'We are Number One girl and boy running 800 metre,' said Mr Takaesu. He asked me if I would like to have a look at the classrooms but, thanking him, I said I had better get going as it had been a long, hot day and I wanted to find a place to camp before it got dark.

'You can camp here,' he said in Japanese and led me round to a grassy area full of tropical bushes and weird flowers and several hundred platoons of mosquitoes. As I didn't fancy becoming an involuntary blood donor for the night I said I thought I'd try and find a windy beach where clouds of *ka* were unlikely to be flocking in search of a foreign-blooded feast.

Mr Takaesu walked with me back to my bike where, after a few pleasantries in Japanese, he suddenly said (turning once again unexpectedly to English), 'I think you very cute excuse me.'

As I wasn't quite sure how to take this I opted just to let it ride on by and, after exchanging an interesting mix of nod, bow and handshake, rode off up the road.

Supposing that that was the last I was likely to see of Mr Takaesu I was therefore surprised when, just after passing the US military base of Camp Schwab, I found him gesticulating at me in the entrance of a side road where he had temporarily parked his car. As gesticulation struck me as a pleasant alternative to other forms of hand play that lone men at the roadside have all too often 'dared' to foist upon me, I opted to stop to see just what it was he was so enthusiastically waggling at me.

Since our brief interlude, his knowledge, or at least his confidence, of English had improved hugely and as I ground to a halt at his feet he greeted me with, 'Ahh, Jodie-*san*, please fine muscle-tuning *purezento* indeed! Great spirit of strengthening for arduousness style travel!'

And with that truly magnificent opening gambit Mr Takaesu presented me with not one, but two packs of ten 20ml bottles of 'Guronsan Oral Liquid – Tonic, Nutritive in Physical Fatigue', which felt about as heavy as a couple of bricks and a lot more smashable. As the directions were all in *kanji* I asked him what was the dosage of the potion.

'One bottle only with one day,' he said, so a quick mental calculation told me that I would be cycling around with a slowly diminishing number of glass bottles on board for a sizeable three weeks.

'Do I need to take with a meal or is now okay?' I asked, feeling enthusiastic not so much because of the fact that I was eager for a 'fine muscle-tuning' boost, but because I was anxious to begin lessening my load as soon as possible.

'Certainly now okay fine,' said Mr Takaesu, so a couple of sucks later on the mini straw and I was left with only nineteen bottles to go. Things were looking up.

I had no idea what the ingredients were but they tasted suitably disgusting to do me good. I don't know if it was just a figure of my tonic-induced imagination, but the next dose of hefty hills to lie in my path struck my legs as nothing more than a mild breeze of a sneeze and the thought of plodding along with a pannier full of weighty and delicate glass suddenly didn't seem like such a fretful ordeal.

Rolling into the town of Ginoza, my attention was diverted from the sight of two cars having smashed into the fronts of each other by a recognizable voice calling my name. Mr Takaesu, who seemed to be popping out of the (road)works, was gaily semaphoring to me from the late afternoon shade of a pavement fruit-stall which, along with boulder-sized watermelons, was selling mangoes the size of small torpedoes. Here, after being introduced to the stall-owner (an androgynous person in a red Goofy T-shirt who I put at anywhere between the ages of twelve and thirty-five and couldn't work out whether he or she was the son or daughter or wife or friend of Mr Takaesu), I was presented with six phenomenally large mangoes and one elephantine watermelon. The sum weight of these edible offerings was so great that when I planted them on the rear rack of my already severely overladen steed it reared upon its hindquarters like a frisky stallion.

Mr Takaesu invited me home to stay with him and his family but, feeling more in need of a peaceful night with the wind and the sea rather than a wearying one of chatter and welded smiles, I declined his offer and, after a peace-pose picture or two (*hai, hai*! I assured him, of course I would send him a copy) I set off for Kanna Beach at a fast canter.

Kanna Beach had been recommended to me by Hank the Marine but when I skidded to a halt there just before dark, I discovered a crowded dump of uneven and litter-riddled ground. What's more, an axe-faced woman in a dusty apron and scuffed, plastic brown sandals, demanded 600 yen (£4) for the pleasure of prising myself among the vociferous masses. I should have said, '*Arigato*, but no *arigato*,' but as searching for somewhere else to camp in the dark in a populated area seemed like a bit of a tall order for my fast-ebbing energy, I instead, feeling cheapskate of mood, did a very un-Japanese thing and haggled with the woman about the price until she agreed to reduce it by half. Small things please small minds.

Despite spending all night under aerial attack from a continual bombardment of fireworks and despite drunken youths stumbling over my tent and playing football with a beercan (obviously a trick they had appropriated from the Single's Camp at Okuma Beach), during which my tent (inadvertently, of course) appeared to serve as an intermittent goal, and despite what felt like the equivalent of Colditz tunnelling away beneath my sleeping mat (thanks to a small regiment of subterranean hermit crabs), I slept like a top.

Soon after six the next morning I was in the midst of packing up when a most inconsiderate stormy rain cloud sailed in off the ocean to sit, depositing its tumultuous liquid offerings over my tent for a persistent five hours. This, as far as my career as a camper has gone, would ordinarily have been time considered well spent for a morning of inner-tent activities (short-patching, sock-darning, pannier-modifying, trannie-listening, letter-writing, postcard-fashioning, diary-sticking, leg-stretching, food-consuming, book-reading, map-planning, floor-cleaning, bag-reorganizing, nail-clipping, foot-inspecting, insect-watching, weather-listening, thought-thinking or, hell, maybe even snoozing) but sadly Japan, and in particular Okinawa, was just too hot for such cocooned carryings-on.

So instead I packed up (getting soaked in the process) in the shelter of the toilet block (praise be for toilet blocks) to gaze out at the rain and Pritt-stick a load of *nansensu* into my notebook.

By 11 a.m. the sun was back on beam and doing its utmost to incinerate every form of life (particularly head-hot *gaijin* on *jitensha*) that came within range of its fiery tentacles. I rode on past an ever-increasing assortment of crewcut Stateside servicemen residing in nearby Camp Hansen (Hank's Camp), which appeared to be surrounded by a fortress of pizza, burger and Mexican taco joints. Opposite Pee-Jay's Hi-Fi Plaza sat a bonneted woman beneath a big, faded parasol selling what her hand-painted board described as 'Ice Clean'. A poster pasted to the concrete girth of a telegraph pole was advertising the extravaganza of next week's 'AT&T's Super Sunday at [nearby] Kin Blue Beach . . . open islandwide to SOFA status people and all participants in the events will get a free t-shirt'. What was Super Sunday? Well, it was a day forecast to be full of 'slammin' entertainment attractions [which] include Three Person Volleyball, bands Shock Tacy, Unlimited Edition, and Angela Burton and Passion, the Shelly Hines Aerobic Dancers, a Tattoo Contest, Underwater Scrabble and Sunken Treasure Hunt'. And what's more 'Sports aficionados can take part in the Bench Press, Three Person Inner Tube Race or Beach Biathlon'.

Hmmm. Perhaps it was just as well I was a week too early.

Life turned busy and roads became clogged as I skirted the 'awa' cities – Ishikawa, Gushikawa and Okinawa – so, not warming to what I saw, I opted to veer off east to Ikei Island, where Kazuo (the Yamaha Virago biker on Yoron) had recommended I camp.

On my map Ikei Island looked stuck out on a limb, or more like (if applying the analogy of the diving man-shaped island of Okinawa) stuck out on a prick in the ocean. Despite its name, Ikei Island was not strictly an island; it was connected by a five-kilometre causeway to the Katsuren penile peninsula. It looked like it should be a pleasant 'getting-away-from-it-all' type of ride, but, *chotto matte kudasai* how could I forget? This might be the far-flung isle of Okinawa but it was still very much Japan, Oh Land of Fast Ruination. The causeway, which I had imagined would be a narrow and little-used road to nowhere, was about as busy as the M25. This Okinawan road was worse still, thanks to the fact that extra lanes were being built – no mean task, since because it was a causeway there was no land on which to build them. But reclaiming the sea has never stopped the dig-it-here, build-it-there Japanese in the past and on this sweltering Mother of all Summer days, it certainly didn't seem to be stopping them now. Stampeding up and down the causeway like an unleashed and furious herd of Pamplona bulls charged a mad, hurly-burly succession of fat and multi-tonned, cyclist-flattening dumper trucks loaded with phenomenal boulders each the size of your average house.

Added to the fun of fighting with the slipstream-sucking trucks was the wind, which was so strong it felt like battling into the teeth of a typhoon. Although I knew I should have given up the whole cock-eyed idea of ever reaching Ikei Island – which I felt certain was going to be a terrible disappointment anyway – I couldn't seem to stop myself. Not for the first time in my life on the saddle did I find I was forcing myself to do something which I had absolutely no need to do. Wasn't I hating every moment? Well, yes. Weren't the barrelling trucks making life hell, not to mention stupendously dangerous? But of course. Judging from the amount of traffic funnelling on to tiny Ikei Island, wasn't it plainly obvious that the scene to greet me the other side would be little more than a mad scrum of cars? Indeed, most likely. And being an 'island' with only one road to get on and off, didn't that mean I would only have to retrace those life-snuffing truck tracks? Most certainly. So, why then was I doing it?

Because . . . because . . . I felt impelled to. I felt that I couldn't turn round now, that I must keep going come what may, that I would feel sick with myself if I gave up, and that even if whatever greeted me was exceedingly unpleasant I would feel inwardly satisfied that I had seen it and wouldn't be left with that gut-niggling feeling of defeat or forever wondering what it was like, and because pushing myself to do something painfully pointless made the rollercoasting ride of internal sensations that much more extreme and hence, in the long run, that much more enjoyable. That's the theory. . . I think.

Thus I pressed on, cursing everything that came my way: the road, the wind, the trucks, the traffic, the noise, the heat and, most of all, my mind. But I made it to the other side and on to Ikei Beach-side Campground, which was appalling, packed with people and cars and litter and the head-crunching din of screaming jet-skis and megaphoned bop. Despite what Kazuo had told me, Ikei Beach-side Campground wasn't actually a campground but a dayground and cost 1,600 yen (£10.50) for the pleasure of being compressed into a zone of noise, scrums, fast-food and overflowing garbage dumpsters.

With head pulsating, I turned tail and rode off in search of peace. And surprisingly I found it – in the slow, sleepy, narrow twisting lanes and alleys of Ikei village. Here, despite being no more than a pedal-revolution or two away, there were no packs of body-flaunting GI slickers or over-alcoholed and high-volumed groups of Japanese youth. Instead there was not a soul apart from the odd fisherman bouncing along on a scooter and a cluster of ancient women sitting on some legless old armchairs with a basket of fish, chatting or dozing beneath the shade of a big banyan-type tree.

No one seemed in the least surprised when I tucked my tent into the corner of the little village green, overlooked on all sides by houses. Later, unprompted, a diminutive hunched-over woman, who looked at least 180, brought a thermos of *mugi-cha* and four hot, bacofoil-wrapped riceballs to the door of my tent – not quite the sort of room service for which I imagined Ikei Beach was known.

Although southern Okinawa is a chaotic mesh of overpopulated towns and cities, I felt drawn into its whirring hub to stand on the land where only fifty years before scenes of unimaginable horror took place.

Peaceable throughout their history, the Okinawans, after having been treated as foreign subjects by the Satsuma regime before being exploited, dominated and severely discriminated against by the Japanese during the pre-war militaristic period, suddenly found themselves caught between the might of the American war machine as it slammed its way down upon the fanatically resistant Japanese in the closing stages of the Second World War. After a bombardment of American air attacks which destroyed Naha, the spring of 1945 brought the beginning of the bloody eighty-two-day Battle of Okinawa – the only land battle of the war to be fought on Japanese soil.

While kamikaze pilots plummeted like giant demented wasps into the sitting-duck warships of the US Navy, Japanese soldiers and local civilians alike (the latter who, young and old, fit and feeble – considered as expendable by the mainlanders – had been forced to arm in a hurry and pressed into fighting) perished in their thousands under the Americans' ceaseless onslaught of intensive aerial and naval bombardments, followed by relentless assaults by bayonet combat troops and tanks using flame-throwers, satchel charges, white phosphorus and small-arms which wiped out anything that moved in the path of the advance.

Rather than surrender, most of the Japanese fought to their last man, as was their custom, or committed *seppuku.* By the time the guns of the bloodiest battle of the Pacific War finally fell silent on 22nd June 1945 and the stars and stripes of the American flag could be seen fluttering in the midsummer sun, some quarter of a million Japanese soldiers and civilians lay dead along with 12,500 Americans.

Apart from the fact that the Battle of Okinawa had literally transformed the landscape, reducing its towns and villages to rubble and had obliterated the island's economy and destroyed all the precious cultural assets that had been created over the centuries by the people, one of the main tragedies to result from the war, or 'Typhoon of Steel' as it later came to be called, was the appalling loss of civilian life. More than 150,000 (a quarter of the population) were killed. While many were blown to pieces by the intense bombardment of steel and fire from the air, land

and sea, others either simply perished from hunger, disease (mainly malaria) or untreated wounds or else were mercilessly executed by their own 'friendly troops' on unfounded charges of spying. By way of propaganda, the Imperial Army's military leaders managed to convince the Okinawans that *gyokusai* (dying honourably rather than risking the disgrace of capture) was the way to go rather than surrender to the American troops, who (they had been told) were blood-thirsty brutes hell-bent on butchering, rape and torture.

Such indoctrination persuaded large numbers of desperate and psychologically damaged civilians to commit mass suicide (mothers, clutching their babies, leapt off cliffs to their deaths) or to killing their own family members by slitting their throats, strangling, clubbing, poisoning, hanging, or simply by blowing each other up with grenades.

I rode around Nanbu, the colloquial name for southern Okinawa, in sombre mood. It was hard to be anything but when riding through a land riddled with war memorials: Yuhi River, remembered as 'Death River'; Arasaki, where a group of student nurses and civilians killed themselves; Mabuni Hill, where General Ushijima and his chief of staff, General Cho, committed *seppuku*, thus marking the end of the battle; Garabi Cave, where the sick and the wounded were left behind to blow themselves to pieces with grenades; Maya Cave, in which large groups of children were given poison shots to evade the foreign 'barbarians'; Kyan Point – or 'Suicide Cliff' – where countless civilians threw themselves on the rocks far below; Himeyuri-no-to – 'Cave of the Virgins' – where 200 schoolgirls committed suicide with their teachers; Maehira village, where the slaughter of the civilians by Japanese troops was a premeditated and well-organized plan.

I arrived at the Peace Memorial Museum just as it was closing, but the caretaker, a cheerful man who appeared flabbergasted that I was travelling alone, not only insisted I come in but also invited me to sit with him and his friend in the entrance hall while they plied me with questions and blackcurrant juice.

'Alone?'

'Yes, alone.'

'One person?'

'Yes, one person.'

'Really one person?'

'Yes, really one person.'

And so on, *ad infinitum.* Finally, not wanting to keep the man from closing later than he had already, I told them I could easily come back in the morning to look around the museum. Of course he wouldn't hear of it and told me to take my time as he was quite happy having a drink with his friend.

Along with the wartime memorabilia of maps and charts and documents and stained, bullet-holed uniforms and personal belongings and weapons and various utensils used by soldiers and civilians during the battle, there were walls of enlarged photographs showing horrific scenes along with videos of some of the US National Archive's movie footage taken during the actual battles.

Refugees and Japanese troops hid in the Okinawan tombs – huge structures with a surrounding semi-circular wall – and, more famously, in the *gama* or natural caves, which run underground throughout the south of the island. As the Japanese military had planned to use these caves as their last positions to protract the battle, it was here that desperate troops used their weapons against civilians, young and old, women and children as well as men – ordering them to leave, demanding their food and even executing recalcitrant occupants who were either too slow or loth to move.

Later, as they discovered that the Americans would not throw charges into caves occupied by civilians, some Japanese troops 'detained' civilian refugees in their caves, threatening to kill them if they tried to leave. (When attacking a military cave position, the Americans would cautiously approach the cave entrance from above. Once a foothold was gained, they would either throw satchel charges into the cave to seal it, or pump hundreds of gallons of gasoline into it and set off the explosion with tracer bullets or phosphorus grenades.)

The most heart-rending exhibits in the museum were the many enlarged and printed pages of testimonies of survivors displayed on various lecterns around the rooms:

Yukoh Tamaki (Male, Home Guard, then 44)

. . . There were three young Okinawan-born soldiers [in the cave]. They all got tetanus and when they died, they cried, '*Anmahyo*! my dear Mother!' *Yamatunchu* (mainland) soldiers were no different. None of them actually cried, 'Long live the Emperor!' when they died (as true-bred Imperial soldiers were supposed to do). Most of them simply cried 'Mother!'

There was one soldier who said he was going to commit *hara-kiri*. I asked why, and he said he had fought hard for the Emperor and the country, but nobody would care for him when he was so badly wounded. Said he would put an end to his own life by his own hand, rather than just wait to die unattended. We tried to talk him out of it, but he cut his belly with a knife anyway.

He writhed in pain, rolling over here and there. So the medics and the surgeon put him on a stretcher, tied his arms and feet to it, and threw him under our beds. He died in three or four hours.'

Toyo Gima (Female, then 19)

. . . There was a little boy about four or five years old [in the cave]. He was crying because he couldn't find his mother. Then, one of the soldiers said if the boy kept crying the enemy would hear him crying and they'd find us. The soldier angrily said someone should take care of the boy and asked if there were his parents in the cave. No one said anything. So they took him deeper into the cave and killed him. There was some light from [a] hole in the ceiling, so you could see it. They took him inside and tried to strangle him with a triangle bandage, the kind you used for dressing a wound.

I heard one of them say the cloth was too thick and they couldn't choke him to death with it. They tore the triangle cloth and made a finer string and strangled him to death with it. All the civilians who saw it were crying. I actually saw them put the string around the boy's neck, but it was so horrible I couldn't watch it to the end.

There were yet more sobering scenes of war in store for me when, just south of Naha, I stopped off to visit the Former Japanese Navy Underground Headquarters, which consisted of a network of tunnels constructed by navy personnel using only pick-axes and hoes. It was in this subterranean warren where, following the Battle of Oroku Peninsula (during which the Naval Base lost 4,000 men), Naval Commander Rear Admiral Ota, together with his remaining men, awaited orders from his commander, General Ushijima. The American forces, advancing with overwhelming fire superiority, forced Admiral Ota into sending a desperate telegram to the Vice Minister of the Navy on 5th June 1945:

'Detachment under attack. Cannot retreat. Will fight to last.'

The next day he sent another, commending the self-sacrifice and cooperation displayed by the civilians of the island and recommending that 'the Okinawan people [are given] special consideration from this day forward'.

Sensing things were not looking too promising, he then

sent General Ushijima a death poem: 'Even if my body perishes in Okinawa, the noble Japanese spirit within my soul shall defend Japan forever.'

Finally, at 0100 on 13th June, Admiral Ota and nearly 200 of his men committed suicide in the tunnels by blowing themselves up with grenades.

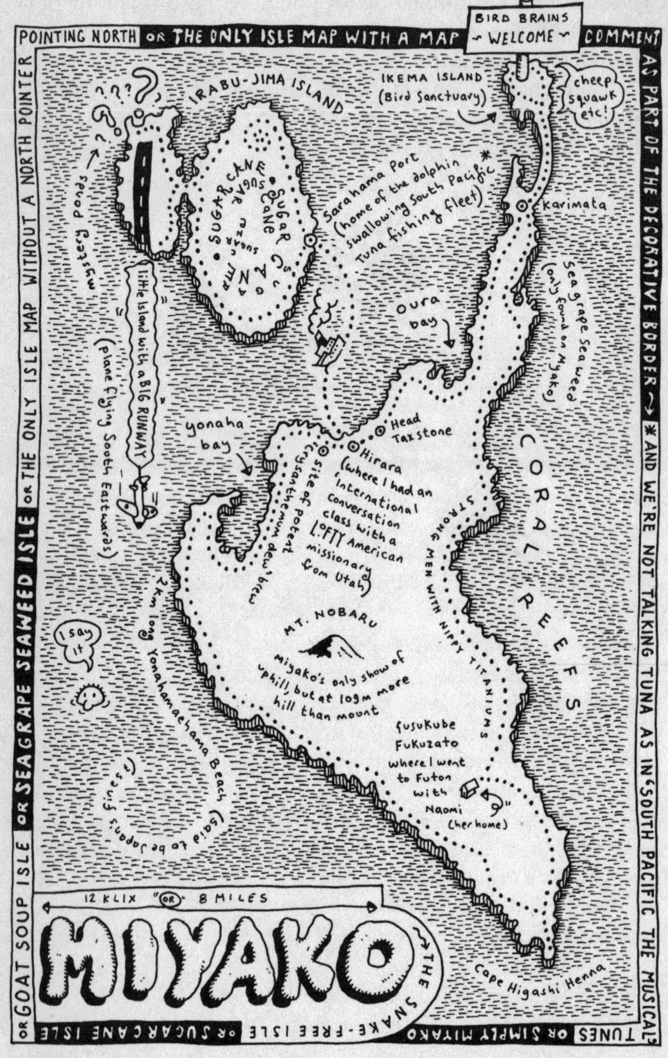
POINTING NORTH OR THE ONLY ISLE MAP WITH A MAP COMMENT AS PART OF THE DECORATIVE BORDER *AND WE'RE NOT TALKING TUNA AS IN 'SOUTH PACIFIC' THE MUSICAL'S TUNES OR SIMPLY MIYAKO OR THE SNAKE-FREE ISLE OR SUGARCANE ISLE OR GOAT SOUP ISLE OR SEAGRAPE SEAWEED ISLE OR THE ONLY ISLE MAP WITHOUT A NORTH POINTER
BIRD BRAINS WELCOME
IKEMA ISLAND (Bird Sanctuary)
cheep squawk etc!
IRABU-JIMA ISLAND
SUGAR CANE
mystery ponds
little island with a BIG RUNWAY
(plane flying South Eastwards)
Sarahama Port (home of the dolphin swallowing South Pacific Tuna fishing fleet)*
Karimata
Oura bay
Sea grape Sea weed (only found on Miyako)
Head Tax stone
yonaha bay
Hirara (where I had an 'International conversation class' with a LOFTY American missionary from Utah)
site of potent crysanthemum dew brew
CORAL REEFS
STRONG MEN WITH NIPPY TITANIUMS
MT. NOBARU
Miyako's only show of uphill, but at 109m more hill than mount
I say it
7km long Yonahamaehama Beach (said to be Japan's finest)
Gusukube Fukuzato where I went to Futon with Naomi (her home)
Cape Higashi Henna
12 KLIX OR 8 MILES
MIYAKO

CHAPTER 22

High Hopes and Hot Dreams

Down at Aja Port I spun on to the Arimura Line night ferry for the 300-kilometre crossing to the island of Miyako along with Fumio, a chirpy young motorcyclist from Kagoshima, who was riding a decidedly hip and hefty bike in a pair of impressively un-hip SURF JOY flip-flops.

Having had a bad night the night before when camping in unbearably clammy heat in a noisy park on the edge of Naha, I was looking forward to a good slumber on the ocean wave. But alas, this was not to be. Thanks to stormy conditions I was prevented from sleeping out on deck and forced instead to lay myself down with the air-conditioned masses in one of four smoke-filled rooms allocated to passengers. Each room, which consisted of a small patch in which to kick off your shoes and a raised carpeted floor the size of a couple of pingpong tables on which to lie supine with your allocated brown blanket (caked in long, coarse black hairs) and brown plastic brick 'pillow', was packed with people lying shoulder to shoulder, head to head, foot to foot. I ended up crammed in the corner, which at least had the advantage that I was only bordered on one side by human form, thus avoiding being stepped over and upon by others' constant comings and goings. A television, suspended from the ceiling on the opposite wall, gabbled and wailed away to such extremes that, had my brick-pillow been an actual brick, I would have gladly hurled it through the screen. But strangely, no one except for me seemed in the least bit rankled by its insane and noisy gibberings. In fact no one (except for me) seemed in the least bit perturbed that everyone was forced to sleep on top of each other. In a far from equanimous state, I sat squashed in the corner contemplating the chaotic scene around me. In this country of obsequious efficiency, were we, I wondered, really expected to be packed in like this? Feeling there must surely be some mistake, I extricated myself from the room of tangled limbs and ventured forth to investigate the matter.

I found a ship steward with a polished, hard-set face like the *Thunderbirds*' Mr Tracy and, producing my ticket, asked him if I was in the right cabin. He peered at my ticket and said, '*Hai, hai.*'

'And my cabin is non-smoking?' I asked.

'*Hai.*'

'Oh. Now there's a funny thing because it's full of people smoking.'

'*Hai,*' replied Mr Tracy, who was obviously a man of many words.

Cocking my head and furrowing my brow in a suitably quizzical manner I said, 'Excuse me, but is my cabin smoking or non-smoking?'

'*Hai, hai*!' came the two-for-the-price-of-one reply.

Feeling I was being sandwiched somewhere between a concrete wall and a stirring storm in a Japanese tea cup, I opted to let one smoking dog lie before lighting up a new one.

'Excuse me, but is the ferry full?' I persevered, despite already knowing the answer to be a negative (the woman who sold me my ticket at the ferry terminal had said that, due to the threat of typhoons, the boat would be carrying well under half of its capacity of passengers).

'*Hai, hai*,' said Mr Tracy.

At this point Fumio slip-slopped along in his fetching SURF JOYs. He spoke a few words of English and asked if I was okay.

'I was just asking this man if the ferry is full, because I have a feeling it's not.'

Fumio gave me the sort of baffled look that would be more at home on the face of a Baffin Island puffin. I plumped for a spot of rephrasing.

'Would you mind asking this man whether the ferry is or is not full, because he doesn't seem to understand my Japanese?'

Obligingly Fumio said something exceedingly fast and exceedingly lengthy to Mr Tracy, after which Mr Tracy replied with a monologue of equal length and rapidity.

Fumio turned to me and said, 'This man say ferry is maybe no full for certain.'

'Maybe or definitely?' I asked, nonplussed.

'Yes.'

'Would you mind asking him?' Feeling in a Difficult Foreigner sort of mood, I intended to get to the bottom of this little conundrum. Fumio, bless him, still smiling enigmatically, dutifully translated the goods – or not-so-goods.

'This man,' he said, 'is believing ferry to be not full most certainly yes.'

'So why are all the few passengers that there are packed like peas in a pod in only four small smoky cabins?'

'Yes.'

'Yes?'

'Mmmmmm.'

Distant voices within me were telling me to let things be – this is not your country, they were saying, just accept things as they are. But I couldn't stop myself. I had reached the point of no return.

'Fumio,' I said, 'does the room where you sleep have lots and lots of people?'

'Yes,' said Fumio.

'So what I want to know,' I said, 'is why are so many people forced into such a small space when there is obviously plenty of room around the ship where we could sleep in comfort?'

'Ahhh sorrr,' said Fumio, beginning to see the light, or there again he might have just switched it off.

'Please ask this man,' I said, 'why these double doors into this cabin are locked.' (Curtains were drawn across the windows of said doors, making me suspect that us squashed passengers were not supposed to see something that we were not supposed to see – such as a nice large empty cabin.)

Fumio, making of my request as best as he could, posed the question to Mr Tracy, who by now was shuffling in uneasy fashion from foot to foot.

'This man,' said Fumio, 'has explanation that this door has not possibility for entrance.'

'Why not?' said the Difficult Foreigner.

'Yes,' said Fumio.

Feeling like a pressure cooker, I decided it would be wise to curb the steam billowing from my ears and call it a day.

'Thank you,' I said, with astounding reserve, 'that's all I wanted to know.'

And, after an exchange of bows, I strode off huffing and puffing, and out on to the rain-lashed deck to release a considerable amount of pent-up vexation.

Despite the weather, the air was still incredibly hot and I wandered around the empty deck clad only in my daily landlubbing uniform of patched stripy shorts and threadbare vest, lapping up the joyous sensation of wild wind and rain upon my skin.

After a while I decided to put the fact that I was wet and in swimmingly buoyant good spirits to good use by carrying out a spot of outer-deck detective work. Perambulating down the side of the ship I blithely peeped through the windows, ascertaining what it was that lay behind the glass: kitchens here, staff quarters there, and – what's this? – row upon row of drawn curtains. I stopped at one window across which the curtains were not properly pulled and peered into the unlit dimness beyond.

The sight that greeted me came as no surprise – a room the size of two tennis courts, empty save for rows of neatly folded brown blankets and plastic brick pillows. It was the same old story on the lower deck. Whereas the comparatively few passengers that there were could have been slumbering in spacious comfort, we were instead corralled forty to the dozen in cramped and pitiful pens. For a fleeting moment I felt galvanized into kicking up more of a foreign-devil fuss. But then I thought: Hey ho, never mind – this is Japan. And feeling okay I walked back inside.

After changing into a dry vest and spare (albeit identical) pair of shorts, I stepped out of the toilet and into Fumio. What with our little encounter with Mr Tracy I thought he might turn the other cheek, but with no ship's steward on the scene he was just as chipper as when I had first met him in the terminal.

I apologized for putting him on the spot with Mr Tracy before telling him about the empty tennis-court rooms which were kept locked and empty for no apparent reason other than keeping us out.

'I think everyone should complain!' I declared back on the trouble-making war-path, 'then maybe something would be done!'

'Yes, thank you,' said Fumio, thanking me for no apparent reason, 'all people should be standing for complain. But big problem is Japanese people do not have method of complain. So we say *shikata ga nai*? – what can you do?'

Realizing that life was probably just too short to spend the next few hours of it moaning, I instead resigned myself with remarkable resilience to a cramped and smoky night. If everyone else could live through it then surely so could I, even if I was an awkward barbarian at heart.

By now it was just after 10 p.m. and my cabin of compressed cattle was still a light-glaring, TV-blaring hive of activity. An endless stream of snacks and cans were being popped open while people were coming and going, chatting, joking, smoking, giggling or reading doorsteps of *manga.*

Picking my way carefully among the seething seas of flesh, I tip-toed back to my corner where I found my immediate neighbour – a young woman in her twenties – sitting back on her heels in her allotted coffin-sized space while studying, with worried expression, a book called *Teach yourself English.*

When I sat down in my coffin, my body all of two millimetres away from hers, she smiled at me shyly and I smiled back.

'Harrow,' she said.

'Hullo,' I replied.

'My nem is Naomi,' she said, so I told her mine.

'America?' she said.

'No, England.'

'Ahh sorrr, *desu-ka?*'

Naomi, a twenty-four-year-old beauty with long raven hair, was, I discovered, suffering from a severe bout of *doki doki,* because in four days' time she was off to Los Angeles to meet her fiancé, Christopher Fauver, a twenty-two-year-old US marine based in Oceanside, California. She had met him on base in Okinawa before he had been posted back to America.

'But I have much fright about everything,' she said. In a hushed voice, Naomi explained to me how she had been working for several years in Naha as a social worker for young children. It was in Naha that she had met her fiancé while competing in a 'ballet-ball' (volleyball) tournament. When he had asked her out for a date she was far from keen, knowing only too well the notorious reputation of the marines.

'Always very many sex, girl and drinking problem!' she said.

But lured on by her friends she gamely took him up on his offer and was pleasantly surprised with what she found.

'Very nice boy with much time for thought and kindness.'

They hadn't been going out for long before he proposed to her. The idea was that, once married, they would continue living in Japan, but when Chris was unexpectedly posted off to Oceanside, Naomi had to give up her job and return to her parents on the small island of Miyako where, apart from her short stint in Okinawa, she had lived all her life. Problems with acquiring a US visa resulted in her having to wait there for weeks. Although she had managed to pick up some temporary work as a school nurse, she spent most of her time worried about her relationship with not only Chris but also her parents, who were far from happy about her marrying a *gaijin* – especially a US marine.

'They think a foreigner is bringing shaming on to family name,' she said, looking downcast.

The following morning it was still raining fishing-rods as we slid into the port at Hirara (Miyako's main town) on the dot of six-thirty. I sank several fathoms into the bowels of the ship to collect my bike from the car deck, leaving Naomi to be met by her mother. As I emerged on the harbour front I saw Naomi scampering excitedly towards me. 'Jodie-*san*! Jodie-*san*!' she panted, as she galloped broadside, 'my mother she send you hopes to join my family as speciality guest for tonight please in our house okay?'

As Naomi's mother hadn't even met me, this struck me as a particularly genial invitation – especially for a woman who I had gathered was not exactly enamoured with *gaijin*. But then I suppose I had a slight advantage in that I wasn't planning on marrying her daughter.

I arranged to meet Naomi that evening on the other side of the island in her home town of Gusukube Fukuzato. This gave me the day to take a perpendicular spin around Miyako, an almost triangular island which, thanks to its lucky stars (and not stripes) sparing it from the ravages of wartime bombardment that pelted down on Okinawa itself, there survives a soupçon of traditional Ryukyu culture and architecture. But from what I could tell, such vestiges of the past appear all but smothered by the Japanese soft spot for its modern hard stuff: concrete and more concrete.

One relic that still remains from bygone days is the Jintozei Seki, or 'Head Tax Stone' – a kinked (and once much disliked) finger of rock which stands all of 1.4 metres high. After the southern Kyushu kingdom of Satsuma had invaded the islands during the fifteenth century, the Satsuma, not wanting to let their heavy-handed tactics turn fruitless, laid in with the juice by demanding that any islander who reached the height of the stone should pay taxes to the central government. Sometimes, but only sometimes, it pays to be vertically challenged.

Scarcely had I set foot and wheel upon Miyako than, on the spur of the moment, I decided to step back off, thanks to the skipper of a small post-boat, who offered to give me a ride for the wave-bouncing, spray-soaking fifteen-minute trip over to the tiny island of Irabu. Despite its tininess, Irabu is home to the hefty and dolphin-swallowing South Pacific Tuna Fishing Fleet. I sat for a while in Irabu's port at Sarahama transfixed by the comings and goings of these pristine and ultra high-tech vessels while eating a breakfast on the hoof in a bus shelter, waiting for the squall to blow over.

Before long the sun burst forth, heating the already steaming hot day to extremes. The wind was so strong I bowled round one side of the island in about ten minutes flat, while the other took me not much short of a strugglesome couple of hours. But such are the capricious joys of cycling.

Carpeting the island lay rustling seas of wind-swaying sugar cane dotted with small knots of stooped and bonneted women of samurai strength swiping at the canes with ferocious neck-slicing sabres. Every so often, jarring horribly with the fresh green waves of cane and the deep blue backdrop of the sea, I passed heaps of hardcore household refuse left to rust and ruin an otherwise arcadian scene: fridges, futons, electric fans, tables, a drum kit, a moped, a bicycle (which I would have swiped had I had anywhere to stick it), telephones, a computer, TV, chairs and shelves and kitchen appliances and so on and so on – all of which looked in pretty good nick with plenty of life in them yet, except of course for those who 'need' the latest.

Feeling fed up with the wind, I stopped beneath a palm for a rest and a riceball, which I consumed while overlooking Shimoji – the islet that lies barely a sugar-cane throw off the south-west coast of Irabu. I was in the midst of a dazed state, thinking how pleasantly quiet and far away from everything I felt, when a stratosphere-shattering great airliner suddenly roared out of the blue, grazing the cane heads on course for what appeared to be a certain crash landing. Bracing myself for a devastating impact I was pleasantly surprised to witness no such calamity. The airliner simply and silently disappeared from view behind the trees. Mystified, I wondered where it went. Into the sea? Into thin air? Into a disorientated Bermuda Triangle? No. On investigating the matter I discovered the aircraft had landed as intended on a swathe of runway so vast that it literally swallowed the face of diminutive Shimoji. Why such a massive plane for such an out-on-a-limb untouristy spot? Because, of all places, far-away Shimoji was the site where JAL and ANA (All-Nippon Airlines) trained their 737 pilots.

Back on easy-rolling Miyako (where there are no hills higher than the 109-metre Mount Nobaru) I spent the rest of the day wheeling through fields of yet more sugar cane and racing with the wind along the spectacular eastern coast crowded with necklaces of coral and dazzling white beaches. All along this stretch of coast I kept passing (or more like being passed by) steely, compact-muscled Japanese running hell for lycra along a special track at the side of the road, and calf-rippling piston-pedalling cyclists on titanium racers. Later I discovered that triathletes from all over the world flock to Miyako for the annual Strongman Challenge, a gruelling race involving a three-kilometre swim, a 136-kilometre cycle and a 42-kilometre marathon. The rest of the year a steady stream of Miyakan Strongmen and Strong-women are to be found building up for The Day.

I met Naomi at the appointed time of 7 p.m. outside the small A-Coop supermarket in Fukuzato where, despite my remonstrations, she insisted on knowing what sort of food I liked to eat before treating me to a trolley-full. When I had told her that I found most Japanese food tasty as long as it was dead, Naomi (despite having a foreign fiancé) refused to believe that *gaijin* could enjoyably eat her native fare. Maybe Chris had a Hank-style diet: burgers, tacos and pizza.

'What did Chris eat when he was in Japan?' I asked.

'Ahh Chris,' said Naomi, 'is typical American junky.'

Ah so, *desu-ka*?

Naomi's concrete-bunker home was similar to most of the other houses on Miyako – small and hunkered down close to the ground to protect itself from the ravages of the savage typhoons that annually rake the area. Over the neighbouring concrete wall I came face to face with a small herd of cows – only the second lot I had seen since leaving the green, grassy, BSE-riddled land of home, and the sight and unmistakably bovine bouquet of them on this far-flung Far Eastern island struck me as oddly misplaced.

After a much-needed shower I met Naomi's father over a bowl of noodles. His small, wiry chest was concealed behind a tight, grubby white vest while his *suteteko* baggily reached to the top of his sinewy calves. Other than 'America?', and a few slurping grunts, he said nothing. I suspected his aloofness might be because he assumed I was from the same side of the planet as the much-frowned-upon fiancé, but Naomi later explained that this was what he was always like when he came home from Tokyo. I asked her what he had been doing there.

'He is a house construction.'

Ah so, *desu-ka*? 'He builds houses?'

'That is so.'

'How long has he been away?'

'For one year only.'

'And now he's back to stay?'

'No, he is here now for six day vacation.'

'He is only home for six days a year?'

'That is so.'

What's more, I discovered that his 'vacation' was something of a misnomer: it involved six murderous days of continuous toiling in the fields from 5.30 a.m. to 7 p.m. in order to cut the cane. No wonder he communicated only in grunts.

Naomi had plans. Every Tuesday she drove off to Hirara to have an English lesson with an American called Ken.

'Jodie-*san*,' she said, 'please come for my guest of surprise. Maybe we make fine fun for international conversation class!'

Sportingly I belted myself into Naomi's car – the first car I had been in for months (not a pleasant experience) – and we took off at a snail's lick across the island to Hirara: despite empty roads, Naomi drove no faster than twenty miles per hour.

Ken, it turned out, was more of a mouthful than his easily truncated name suggested. Handing me his business card (which, what with him being a teetering six-foot-six giant, necessitated elevating myself heavenwards in order to reach) I learnt he was Elder Kenneth R. Albrechsen ('The surname's Danish,' he enlightened me) from North Logan, Utah, and a member of the Church of Jesus Christ of Latter-Day Saints.

Ahh so.

What with this and the fact that we had met Elder Ken for our 'international conversation class' in an ante-room of a church hall, I began to put two and two together – or, more like, Ken and God together.

'Are you a missionary?' I asked.

'Why sure,' he said. 'Didn't Naomi tell you? I'm here to Spread The Word.'

Now don't get me wrong. It's not that I have anything particularly against Spreaders of Words (apart from the ones from bygone days who succeeded remarkably well at killing off countless millions of indigenous peoples around the world by introducing them to deathly Western diseases – not to mention all the other wholly unholy things that they did). It's just that I find people who go round knocking on doors inviting you to be saved at inopportune times, such as when you are elbow-deep in pastry or when you're trying to extract the hamster from the hoover, just a trifle trying to take.

Elder Ken and his male 'partner' Sue (pronounced Soo-ay) Hideyuki, Naomi and myself sat around a table in a darkened room and sipped green tea. Wanting to know more about the life of an American missionary in Japan, I asked Oh Lofty One how he came about ending up in Miyako, of all curious places.

He had been a Christian all his life, he said. 'I always wanted to do missionary work, and now that I am it's proving to be the most fulfilling years of my life.'

'Years?' I said, surprised, imagining that he was here for maybe just a season or two. 'How many years?'

'Two,' said Ken. 'I'm living a two-year high.'

I asked him why he chose to come to Japan.

'I didn't choose,' he replied. 'Jesus sent me.'

'I see. So you could have been sent anywhere in the world?'

'Sure,' said highly-peaked Lofty. 'You have no say on what country you get posted to, nor on how often you change city or town. That's the beauty of it. You go where Jesus needs you.'

'Have you lived anywhere else in Japan other than Miyako?'

'Why, sure I have. Let's see now . . . I started in Tokyo

before moving to Osaka and then to Okinawa. But Miyako sure is the most spiritually rewarding.'

Lofty Ken retailed how, the night before he left Utah, he had received the Holy Spirit – a 'mind-blowing' experience by all accounts, which involved the laying-on of hands. Once in Japan he was partnered up with missionary Sue, to whom he must stick like a limpet for twenty-four hours a day. Everything that they did, stressed Ken, they had to do together. This involved not only the obvious tasks of a missionary like the door-knocking, God-recruitment rounds, but also eating, shopping, reading, studying, walking, socializing and sleeping (it was compulsory to be in bed by 10.30 and up no later than 6.30). Knowing how much I prefer to do things alone, this stiflingly symbiotic relationship sounded like purgatory.

I asked (knowing that they lived in an eighth-floor flat) what happened if, on leaving their apartment block, they had got all the way to the bottom of the stairs only for one of them to realize they had forgotten something – say, for sake of argument, their Bible. Surely they don't both have to go lumbering back upstairs in a togetherness?

'Why, sure we do,' said Ken. 'It's no trouble. It becomes second nature real soon.'

Ken was almost at the end of his two-year stint. In just over three months he would be back in Utah. I asked him how he felt about heading on home.

'Well, I guess I've got mixed feelings,' said Ken. 'It'll be kinda strange to be back to a regular life – a life that among other things will include dating!'

'Can you not have a steamy date while in mid-mission?'

'No way. No dating means no distraction. We gotta focus full on Spreading the Word.'

'I see,' I said.

There was a moment's silence before Ken said, 'Say, what does Jesus mean to you, Josie?'

Gulp. Well, I guess the inevitable had to be slipped in somewhere along the line. Being the sort who is neither holy nor unholy, I instead answered Ken with a typically non-committal, 'Well, let's just say, my bike is my God.'

Flippant as it may sound, this is in a way very true. After all, I'll make no bones about it: my bike is the Light of my Life (and I'm not talking flashy LEDs). It harms no one and does only good. It leads me onwards and upwards and downwards, and even sometimes backwards. It makes life worth living. It gives rise to love and hell, hope and pain, fear and joy. It causes one to suffer, plunging thy spirits into the murky depths of despair before catapulting them to inexplicable heights of sheer heaven. It provides a means for seeing and appreciating this wonderfully topsy-turvy world that we live in – slowly, quietly and efficiently. And what's more, it also gives me a bloody good appetite for more. And I thank Thee for that.

With the conversation swinging round to the introduction of Christianity to the islands – the Portuguese arriving, St Francis of Xavier, the number of churches on the islands compared with the rest of Japan and so forth – I mentioned the intriguing sight of the graveyards and cemeteries, an influx of simple white crucifixes enscribed with *kanji* dotted among the costly and elaborately marbled Buddhist headstones. Surprisingly, Ken appeared to know next to nothing about the arrival of Christianity in Japan. As I knew precious little about it myself, I chose to say no more and that was that.

Back at Naomi's house I got something of a shock when, stepping through the sliding door, I found her parents dead on the *tatami*. At least, that was what I assumed when I spotted them sprawled some distance from each other in an ungainly gunned-down position, with the television still blaring out a demented games show. In fact, Naomi's mother had collapsed in such a way that she was half-blocking the doorway from the kitchen to the corridor, which necessitated my stepping over her in order to get a glass of water from the tap. She was wearing a simple flimsy nightgown while he was still clad in his long voluminous pants and grimy white vest. Naomi was not in the least bit perturbed about the deceased state of her parents, assuring me that they were nothing more than merely asleep. She told me that by the end of the day they were always so utterly exhausted that they usually fell asleep before they had even found the energy to clamber on to the futon.

Naomi led me into her room and showed me where I was to sleep – in the futon with her. Although I couldn't imagine meeting a Japanese girl on, say, the Calais to Dover crossing and then a few hours later inviting her to climb into bed with me, Naomi's sleeping arrangements struck me as nothing to raise an eyebrow or two about. In fact it all seemed so natural, and that was one of the many delightful things about Japan – to be shot of my deep-seatedly prudish Western taboos.

Naomi asked me if I would like to see a photo of her distant sweetheart.

'*Hai, hai*!' I chirped eagerly.

But before revealing the snap, Naomi issued me with a sheepish warning.

'Sorry, no handsome boy,' she said.

'Ah, but, Naomi,' I said, doing my best to adopt a bolstering air, 'looks aren't important. It's a handsome heart that counts. Many handsome boys have cruel hearts and many girls.'

'Ahhh, that is so,' replied Naomi. 'Chris have friend who is velly handsome boy. In one week many girl.'

We chatted lying side by side on top of the futon in the buzzing draught of the electric fan, which whipped a wind of humid air over our scantily clad skins. Despite this stirred-up breeze I was still sweating profusely, unlike Naomi, whose blanched flesh unveiled a dearth of perspiration. Naomi said that was because Japanese people had a lower body temperature than the likes of *gaijin* – a disputable fact but one which, from my previous observations of these comparatively less sweaty people, I was willing to believe.

As the crickets dementedly chirruped in chorus to the odd mooing of cow, Naomi told me of her fear of going to America, a fear which lay in strong contrast with her eagerness to marry before she reached the age of what for Japanese women is, though less so than it was, considered the sell-by date of twenty-six.

I hadn't been lost in Japan for long before I had discovered I was a 'stale Christmas cake'. This uncomplimentary term for unwed women aged twenty-six or older is used by many Japanese, who consider that single females, like Christmas cake eaten after the 25th, have lost their flavour, their fruitiness and their chance of titillating a taste-bud or two. But I was not alone. Stale Christmas cakes are on the increase in Japan: in 1970, only 18% of women aged between twenty-five and twenty-nine were single. A generation later this figure had risen to 40% and is fast-rising because, for Japanese women today, marriage and child-rearing often mean a lost career, less money, less freedom, more housework and, worst of all, an unhelpful husband.

By now it was well after midnight and what with the previous sleepless night's fiasco on the sardine ferry, we were both well-weary. It was so inexorably hot and sticky that I was all for lying on top of the futon to reap maximum effect from the frenzied whirrings of the fan. But Naomi had no such intention. Putting her lower-body-temperature theory into practice, she pulled on a pair of blizzard-proof pyjamas before snuggling down under the copious and weighty covers, as if in preparation to hibernate through an imminent Ice Age. Despite our previous topic of conversation about feeling the heat, I just couldn't hold myself back.

'Naomi,' I said, with torrents of sweat coursing down my temples, 'excuse me for asking, but don't you find it, you know, just even a little bit hot?'

'Hot?' said Naomi, as if no such word was currently a part of her vocabulary, before adding enigmatically, 'My sleeping temperature is making regular time.'

Then, before either of us knew it, she had dropped off into her refrigerated dreams, leaving me flaked out and panting on top of the covers, furiously flannelling off my feverish brow as a commune of suction-footed geckos noisily clucked their way across the walls.

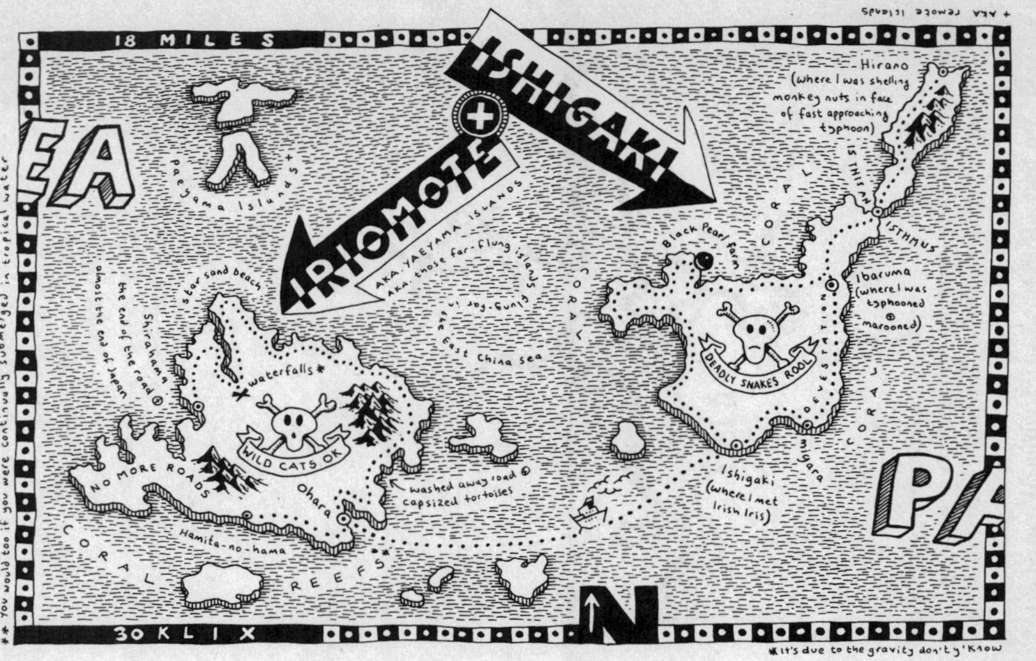

+ AKA remote islands

* It's due to the gravity don't y'know

** You would too if you were continually submerged in tropical water

CHAPTER 23

Typhoon Moon

Two days after 'sleeping' with Naomi a typhoon was upon me. I was on the island of Ishigaki ('Stone Fence') at the time, camping on a beach. The first I knew of its imminent approach was from a fisherman who woke me around 4 a.m. warning me to seek shelter. Although over the past few weeks I'd had enough near-encounters and tail-ends of typhoons to make me dangerously blasé, I had more than a sneaking suspicion that this ancient fisherman knew what he was talking about and I took the warning seriously.

With his thick island dialect, communication was not easy between the two of us but I managed to ascertain that the typhoon was still a good few hours away. Time enough to find a roof over my head. Deciding to leave any further slumber to a safer date, I packed up, being careful to shake out both shoes and tent as Ishigaki is, out of all the islands of Nansei, a veritable haunt for *habu*. Indeed, as I wheeled off into a ferocious headwind the road was littered with almost as many tyre-squashed snakes as an English byway is with squirrels and rabbits and pheasants and foxes and badgers and deer and hedgehogs and frogs combined. Not all the *habu* were lifeless, though. One, a six-foot monster with a body as thick as a drainpipe, snaked its way from out of a cane field, but rippled back whence it had come when it caught sight of my startled form bearing down upon it.

Ishigaki resembled the rough shape of a deep ladle. I found myself battling north into the escalating gale up the handle – a narrow peninsula pounded on either side by huge and heaving seas, to reach the small hamlet of Hirano where the fisherman had informed me I would find a *minshuku*. But all I found was a ghost town of small, squat concrete houses huddled down behind heavy concrete walls with all their windows boarded up and not a soul in sight.

Apart from the raking wind whining through the hamlet and the sound of a loose door banging back and forth on its hinges, the whole place was eerily quiet, like a Wild West town long deserted by its cowboys and railroad. Having spent many a fractious hour fighting into the teeth of the gale to get this far, exhaustion finally caught up with me and I slumped jelly-legged on a kerbstone out of the worst of the wind and, for want of something better to do (or eat), I started to shell some monkey nuts. But no sooner had I placed Nut Number Five into my mouth when an almighty thunderclap made me momentarily lose all contact with my skin. This terrific detonation was enough to shake the ground like a mild earthquake, and awakened me to the fact that perhaps perching on the pavement blithely shelling peanuts in the face of an impending and potentially catastrophic typhoon was unwise. Hurriedly I tried knocking on a few boarded-up doors in search of a *minshuku*, but there was no sound from within. So feeling that I still had time on my side, I turned tail to race with the wind the sixteen-odd kilometres back down the ladle's narrow handle towards the junction at Ibaruma, where I felt certain I would find more life.

Charged up with a gushing surge of adrenalin, my legs spun me southwards as the menacingly louring sky detonated with head-shattering cracks around me. Not one vehicle passed apart from a man in a van who shouted something at me with urgent expression (probably 'What the bloody hell do you think you're doing?'). Half-way down the rain began – but no ordinary rain this. It alternated between torrentially vertical and torrentially horizontal and struck my skin like shards of glass. Within moments the road was hopelessly awash. As forking bolts of lightning cracked the black and bedevilled sky to pieces, I charged onwards.

At a point where the peninsula was little more than a kilometre wide, I found myself sandwiched by seas so inconceivably mountainous that they threatened to break clean across the waist-thin isthmus, sweeping me off into the East China Sea. By now the thunderous sky had merged forces with the furious ocean, blacking out altogether the low ridge of mountains that formed the peninsula's spine.

The only shelter I came across on my mad-hatted dash down to Ibaruma was nothing more than a makeshift open-sided roadside stall into which I dragged myself to take stock of the situation. Inside I found row upon row of heady-smelling golden-sweet *painappuru* – small 50 yen (33p), medium 100 yen, large 150 yen. Despite the fact that I had a typhoon hot on my tail, the thought of passing such cheap pineapples by was just too much. Of course the most sensible thing would have been to pack a pineapple on board for consumption at a later and safer date, but, in my wild and storm-lashed state, judicious moves did not rate high. Dropping 100 yen into the box, I pulled out my knife and carved open the sweet, oozing flesh. Sucking on the delicious juice while soaked to the core, I stood on the edge of a rampant typhoon that was angrily beginning to tear pieces of shanty clean off into the wind. It was a sensational thrill, bearing on dangerously carnal. Before leaving, I piled a pannier knee-deep with fruit and then took off into the storm.

Five kilometres from Ibaruma the wind picked up to such a buffeting pace of a gale that it was virtually impossible to walk, let alone cycle. By the time I limped into 'town' – a small cluster of houses lining the roadside – the late morning sky had caved in, turning the day to tunnel-dark and any objects which weren't weighted down were being tossed across the road. I narrowly missed decapitation by a metal sign torn from a lamp post and was momentarily winded by an airborne bucket taking me from behind.

Having long since sobered up from pineapple intoxication, I now recognized the beast-grey conditions as the terrifying elements that they were. Never mind looking for a *minshuku*, never mind the boarded-up houses, never mind if I never set mouth on a pineapple again; I had to get inside – and quick.

Fighting my way into the wind, while ducking the odd airborne missile, I scarpered up to the nearest boarded door, hammered on the wood with a no-nonsense degree of urgency and moments later I was being dragged through a narrow crack by a small, dumpy *obaasan* with gold teeth. Her spontaneous urgency to help me was such that, only when I was standing dripping and storm-shocked in her concrete-floored entrance way, did she pause to assess just what curious flotsam it was that the gale had washed up on her mat.

Surprisingly, despite my dishevelled and alien appearance, Mrs Dumpy didn't seem in the least bit disappointed with her waterlogged catch. Within moments she took me under her ample and motherly wing and led me down a dark corridor to a small *tatami* room on the corner of the house. A folded-in-three futon was dragged out of a hole in the papery wall together with a hard-husk pillow, and then, after showing me to the hot-tub, she insisted she do all my washing. When I emerged from a revitalizing soak I found the low table in my room set with tea things and a lacquer tray of *tempura* and rice. On the *tatami* beside the table stood a Dalek-like thermos filled to the brim with piping hot water.

To prevent the glass from being smashed, every window in the house was boarded up with sturdy wooden slats that slotted into hefty steel girders built into the window's frame. Attractive architecture is not what Japanese buildings are famous for, but the low, squat, concrete and metal homes that lie like wartime pillboxes, hugging the ground around Japan's southern-most islands, make houses elsewhere in the country appear positively charming in comparison.

By now the storm had whipped itself up into such a fearsome tempest that what I had earlier taken to be a Herculean battle of the elements was nothing more than a damp and breezy sneeze in the face of the monstrous forces currently hurling themselves upon Ibaruma. The terrific noise and violent velocity of the wind made me feel as if I was pinned to the side of a tunnel with a never-ending express train hurtling past my head.

Every now and then, a gusty giant of a wind-devil slammed into the side of the house like gunshot. My flimsy walls of *fusuma* doors rattled with an incessant and quaking insanity. At one point when I peeped out of the window through a slit in the slats, I watched a sheet of corrugated iron sail through the air like a piece of rice-paper before slicing a tree in two. Rather the trunk than my throat, I thought.

When the electricity went off, Mrs Dumpy appeared with a supply of candles, one of which she lit – the gleam of the flame dancing off her golden teeth. She also brought me another thermos of hot water. Feeling grateful, but lacking any suitable offering, I gave her a couple of my least storm-damaged *painappuru*, which of course she wouldn't accept. (Seeing as much of Ishigaki consisted of a spiky whorl of pineapple fields, I suppose it must have been rather like *sore wa honeori zon desu* translated by my usefully useless *Japanese in 3 Weeks* phrasebook as 'carrying coals to Newcastle'.)

What with being unable to open the windows (lest the floods came in) and what with no electricity to switch on the fan (whose base was embossed with the words 'High Velocity Louver'), the air in my den was suffocatingly humid. Despite sitting in a near-naked state, sweat oozed freely from every pore, crease, nook and cranny.

As the ominous dark of the day turned into night the intensity of the wind increased to such a banging and bellowing howl that in particularly slamming moments I felt certain the roof would be ripped clean off the house. All manner of unidentifiable objects continued to crash and smash outside my barricaded windows. At one point I padded along the corridor to see how Mrs Dumpy was faring and found her lying like a beached whale on the *tatami*, fast asleep in front of the dead television. Entering a land of oblivion appeared to be her chosen method of weathering the capricious nature of a ravaging typhoon.

All night the storm raged, causing such a vociferous clatter that it was impossible to sleep. Even when I turned my Walkman up to full volume, only the dimmest strains of Pergolesi could be heard, fighting a losing battle with the ferocity of the unremitting wind.

By morning the clattering roar of the wind banging incessantly into the side of the house had increased to such an extent that it now felt as if my head was strapped to a Jumbo's engine on take-off. Outside all sorts of hefty-sized objects were being tossed around more than ever, and whenever something was sent crashing into the side of the house I braced myself, waiting for the windows to implode or the walls to explode from the force or the pressure. Monitoring the conditions through my weather-window slit in the slats, the dark and violent scene was of a cloaked and furious world caving in on itself.

When I shuffled along the corridor by torchlight to check up on Mrs Dumpy she was nowhere to be seen so, trusting she hadn't been sucked up into oblivion, I felt that, as the phone was dead, there was little I could do other than pad back to my leaking den to sit alone as the hurly-burly world collapsed around me. As I sat marooned on my island of futon in an ever-dampening sea of *tatami* I wondered whether, by Ishigaki standards, this typhoon was bad, very bad or bloody disastrous. Pondering this for a moment, I suspected that it was probably no more than just bad because in order to qualify for 'very bad' I felt that the roof would have been ripped off by now, and for 'bloody disastrous', well, I suppose I would have been sucked into orbit by the extraneous forces. Or there again, simply pinned beneath a pannier without my porridge.

Things hadn't yet turned quite that dire. I still had two and a half handfuls of oriental oats left, and eighty-five monkey nuts, fifty-two raisins (which for rationing's sake I counted carefully), four small curly cucumbers that an old woman had given to me from her garden, a quarter of a squeezy tube of honey, eight dwarf bananas, a can of tuna, two riceballs, two cans of Pocari Sweat and of course, a lorry-load of *painappuru*. Water still issued from the bathroom taps so, after filling up the bath as a reserve, I felt I was just fine in the liquid department.

By now I was getting into the swing of storm fever and, apart from the moments that I thought I might die, was really quite enjoying myself. It's not every day you find yourself sitting like a lonesome duck in the middle of a typhoon scrupulously counting raisins and peanuts by candle-light with neither dicky-bird nor human form within sight.

So, as the storm continued to work its way into a frenzy, I decided that the best thing I could do was to spend my time productively. My first project involved emptying all my panniers to check them for wear and tear before mending and patching and reinforcing the webbing and the fabric and giving the whole lot a thorough once-over. Ditto my tent. I darned and patched all of my clothes that needed darning and patching (which was virtually everything). I sorted out a small pile of things that I had been meaning to send home in order to lessen my load such as pamphlets and cuttings and maps and films and touching little trinkets (which kindly souls had given me). I spent hours lost in my diary going into detail about the most trivial things which I had never felt the inclination to go into before. I wrote reams of letters, filling them with pages of nonsense and half-hearted collage, and I cut out as many postcards as I could from the available materials that I kept stored on board my bike. I allotted time every couple of hours to do a series of stretching exercises to keep my muscles up to scratch lest they thought they were in for a bit of a holiday. I also brushed up on a few Japanese phrases from my usefully useless *Japanese in 3 Weeks* phrasebook ('Hands off!'; 'I should like to be taken full length'; 'These are quite damp yet'; 'I have been tolerably well'; 'You kill my cat and I'll kill your dog'; 'The mountains will be in labour; an absurd mouse will be born'; 'I am love sick for you'; 'Bless me! How you happen to be here?'; 'Well, by gosh, I am from Missouri'; 'Don't tread on one's corns'; 'Call me sweetheart', and so on). I savoured the three books that, at my request, my mother had sent out to me (Gabriel García Márquez's *Love in the Time of Cholera*; Roddy Doyle's *Paddy Clarke Ha Ha Ha*; and William Least-Heat Moon's *Blue Highways*). From time to time I stretched out on the futon to uncreak my back and allow myself the pleasurable indulgence of thinking about nothing in particular. At one point I was struck for some reason to compile a mental list of my Top Five Least Favourite Words which were, at that time of typhoon, as follows:

1. Genre
2. Scenario
3. Clique
4. Knee-jerk
5. Key Issue

And once I'd got that off my chest I felt a whole lot better.

In between all these inactive activities I had plenty of time to study my sparsely furnished surroundings: *tatami* which needed a good hoover; a sliding wall of papery doors patterned with forests of bamboo; a Toshiba calendar pinned to a wall which for August displayed a most unfetching photo of a red life-ring intertwined with a bouquet of watermelon and bananas and hibiscus with a wishy-washy focused frond of pine adorning a ruffle of silk. Below this hung another calendar stuck on July (making me unsure whether I was coming or going) with a picture of Jesus, his arms held out in an encapsulating welcome beneath the words: 'Let the children come to me'. Once, after having studied this scene for the umpteenth time, I finally managed to tune into a chaotically static World Service and fleetingly caught the wonderfully lugubrious vocals of the inimitable Morrissey:

> . . . and if a double-decker bus
> crashes into us,
> to die by your side
> such a heavenly way to die
> and if a ten ton truck
> kills the both of us
> to die by your side
> the pleasure and the privilege is mine
> . . . there is a light that never goes out . . .
> there is a light that never goes out . . .

And I wondered if Morrissey and His Holiness were trying to tell me something.

Night Two was no different from the first – sleepless, death-defyingly windy with the prospect of my penned-in den dwelling being shredded to pieces. But then, around 2 a.m., something strange happened. Unable to sleep, I was lying in a sweaty daze futon-flat on my back, staring up into a never-ending blackness, when, for the first time in thirty-eight hours, a complete and utter silence fell upon Ibaruma. I sprang up, slid back a window, knocked aside a hefty wooden slat of boarding, and peered out expectantly. Not a dicky-breath of wind. Not a droplet of rain. Where had it all gone – and so suddenly? After having become used to the tumultuous noise, the silence, though welcome, hit me as distinctly eerie. A searchlight suddenly fell on my face. I looked up – it was the moon, coming and going as slithers of cloud drifted across its pearly face. Evidently the skies were clearing, something which I had imagined to be simply impossible only moments before. The storm had gone, had had enough, blown itself out, just like that. A neighbour's dog barked and broke the deafening silence. Then a voice, calling to it, some way away. It was a tremendous relief to discover that there was a world around me after all. Life had not been sucked away. Realizing that I could be back in the saddle by morning my spirits soared, and I padded back to bed leaving the window wide open.

Weary after all the encapsulated hours of clamorous excitement I drifted off immediately, but no more than twenty minutes ticked by when THWAAAM! The storm returned with a renewed vigour, slamming with such fearsome ferocity into the side of the house that the sliding partitions of my room collapsed on top of me from the force of the pressure. Once resurfaced, I realized that the storm, although back, was different. In the lull of only half an hour the wind had completely changed tack and swivelled 180 degrees.

Strange and powerful things, typhoons. Produced in tropical low-pressure areas of southern oceans close to the Equator, they generally have wind speeds at the centre of more than 100 miles per hour. The thirteenth-century skilled seafarers of Japan may have called the typhoon that thwarted the invading fleet of Kublai Khan the 'divine wind', but to me typhoons certainly seemed to spell more destruction than divinity – an unforgiving force to be reckoned with.

For the rest of the long night and even longer day the typhoon tugged and fought and wrestled with the island until finally, with only eight raisins, four peanuts, half a pineapple and a spoonful of honey to go, the seemingly endless storm gradually lessened its hold until it was no more than a very murky and savagely squally day.

After seventy-three hours of captivity, I emerged from my damp and wind-battered den to step once again into the Big Outdoors.

With the comparable calming of the elements Mrs Dumpy had materialized. Judging from her soporific appearance, she had simply hibernated through the entire typhoon.

The ride back to Ishigaki (Ishigaki's main town) was like negotiating an assault course. I had to drag my bike through mud and floods and fallen trees and fencing and poles and an inordinate amount of crumpled sheets of corrugated iron. In one small village, people stood around surveying the damage inflicted on their properties, which included several houses having completely caved in on themselves. Vehicles lay pinned beneath trees and concrete poles and toppled walls.

I continued to haul myself through the post-storm flotsam and jetsam splayed across the road while wrestling into a relentless headwind. By the time I passed a sign heralding my arrival into 'Ishigaki DT' (downtown), I was feeling knock-kneed weary. After stocking up on food supplies in a store near Jean Shop Town Boy, I sought out a *minshuku* run by a doting three-foot *obaasan* who gave me a half-price room, where I flaked out on the *tatami* in the revitalizing breeze of a dementedly burring green King Fan.

The following morning I sailed down to the port to see what my chances were, weather prevailing, of catching a boat over to Iriomote, the last main island of the Nansei chain. It didn't take me long to establish that those chances were minimal, the churned-up waves being just too unpredictable for the ferries to run. However, a hardy handful of smaller vessels were setting out regardless and the skipper of one, overhearing my enquiries, heaved my loaded bike on board, lashing it down in the cockpit before turning the bow into the mountainous seas.

To say the crossing was rough and rocky is a bit like saying a typhoon's a breeze. It was an exuberantly terrifying boat ride. Despite the short distance across the channel, I was only rarely able to catch sight of Iriomote (easily visible from Ishigaki) not because of misty conditions – the skies were clear – but because the turbulent ocean was towering above us like a Manhattan skyline. Thanks to the reassuringly placid expressions of the captain and crew – not to mention their masterly craft-handling in unforgiving conditions – I could sit back (or more like cling on) and enjoy the ride for what it was: a hilariously fun near-death experience.

Although not as severe as on Ishigaki, the typhoon had definitely gone to town on Iriomote as well. As I left the tiny town of Ohara, the road was awash with storm debris – driftwood, fishing-nets, glass floats, polystyrene and plastic containers of every shape, size and form, corrugated iron, chunks of trees, dead fish and in one place two capsized tortoises. On top of that, whole segments of road had collapsed or been washed clean out to sea.

Compared with all the other islands of Nansei I had rolled around, Iriomote had a distinctly different feel and flavour – a feeling that made me fancy I was not so much in Japan as in South East Asia. Carpeted in a dense mountainous jungle where leeches sucked and wild cats roamed, the island was wonderfully untamed and uncultivated. Strange *sakishimasuo* trees, supported by a writhing tangle of limb-like root buttresses, rubbed foliage with thickets of mangrove. With just one road on Iriomote, running around the perimeter of only half the island, vehicles were few and far between. The only traffic I saw south of Ohara comprised an old man in a lampshade hat riding a cart pulled by a languorously plodding water buffalo. In places lay the odd field of sugar cane and the cloying sweet-smelling spiky-swirl of pineapple.

I spent several days on Iriomote wandering up the wide and winding gravy-brown Urauchigawa River and walking for hours, happy and lost, into the steamy jungle, where I stumbled across bountiful waterfalls, sparkling rock pools, huge eagle-like birds, electric-blue-tailed lizards, no wild cats and two clinging leeches.

From Iriomote I fancied sailing off for the tiny island of Yonaguni – the western-most point in Japan – which sits almost in the lap of what the Portuguese named Ihla Formosa (Island Beautiful), otherwise known as Taiwan. But what with no sailings owing to monstrous seas, together with the news that another typhoon was kicking up its heels on course to hit the Nansei Islands, I changed my mind and scampered back to Ishigaki, from where I hoped to make a speedy retreat to Naha to pick up the boat to Kagoshima.

It was down near the harbour in Ishigaki that I met my first *gaijin* in weeks. Dispersing with my Japanglish, I tuned in to my English tongue and discovered that young, peach-skinned Irish Iris was in Ishigaki on a JET teaching programme which, out of all the places I had so far seen, struck me as a fine place in which to be posted. But Iris was not so sure. Despite having only been in Japan for three weeks, she told me she was bored and couldn't wait for school to start as she was desperate for someone with whom to speak English. It beat me how she could possibly be bored in such an intriguing place and it beat her how I could possibly enjoy travelling by myself for so long.

With typical Irish (and Japanese) warm-hearted and spontaneous hospitality, Iris insisted I come and sleep on her small patch of floor – an offer which, had I not had a boat to catch, I would happily have taken her up on. She asked me where I was going and when I said Naha, she mentioned she was thinking of going there next weekend to meet up with a group of other *gaijin* JETs and could I tell her how often the ferries ran? Happy to help, I pulled out my Arimura Line timetable – a confusing swirl of *kanji* which, during my hours of typhoon captivity, I had had plenty of time to decode and decipher mostly by way of reading upside-down and back-to-front.

To save on the cost of accommodation in Naha, I presumed Iris would favour a night crossing.

'Oh, no,' said Iris, 'I want to use the boat ride to kill a day.'

And I thought: crying shame.

My boat was scheduled to leave that evening at 6 p.m. but when I ambled along to the ticket office that morning to check up on times and connections back to Kyushu, I was told that the sailing had been brought forward by six hours in order in outrun a typhoon rearing up fast from the South China Sea.

The ferry, *Hiryu 3*, was the same dismal tub that I'd had the misfortune to cross on with Naomi to Miyako on that sardine-crammed night. However, this time, despite a similar scene of four smoky, TV-blaring, packed-out cabins (along with the locked, out-of-bounds large empty rooms), I was determined to sleep outside. Fortuitously, unlike the inclement weather of the original crossing, the rain was kept at bay. But before slumbering, I first had half a day on my hands. Leaving the chaotic scrums of air-conditioned bodies inside, I armed myself with groundsheet, Karrimat and food supplies and hit the deck in search of a place to roost. This was easier said than done. Unlike the mightily impressive European and North American ferries that I have travelled on which offer tables and deckchairs and furlongs of seats spread among a multiplicity of levels, this Japanese barely buoyant blundering old bucket offered no such choice. The only place outside where passengers were permitted to air themselves was a narrow strip of deck running on either side of the ship upon which were perched the ship's sole *al fresco* seating: a couple of wooden and backless benches of peeling paint. It was impossible to find a spot out of the wind and sun, but it was a big improvement on staying fugged up inside.

People rarely ventured out, even for a breather. However, one man propped himself against the railings and spent a good twenty minutes glaring at me without a word before disappearing back inside. A short time later he re-emerged to take up the same staring position. Despite my rising hackles, I tried smiling at him but, judging from his vacuous expression, it was a smile well wasted.

Finally he said in English, 'Why you no sitted inside?'

'Because I like to see where I'm going.'

'But sitted here is very hot and much winding.'

'Yes, but I prefer to sit here with my nose in the wind rather than in an air-conditioned armpit feeling sick.'

'Ahh so. What now writing do you?'

'My diary.'

'You major in subject what please?'

'I didn't go to university.'

'No university?'

'No, no university.'

Long pause.

'Why no university?'

'Because I didn't have university in me. I wanted to cycle.'

'Excuse me?'

'I opted to cycle rather than take exams.'

'What nature for working job have you?'

'Cycling and cooking.'

'Mmmmm. But where is precisely your college of study?'

'I don't study. I haven't studied since I left school at sixteen.'

Longer pause.

'How long staying time in Japan?'

'Maybe five or six months.'

Elongated intake of sucking air through teeth.

'Sor. You are teacher of English language?'

'No, I'm travelling around Japan by bicycle.'

'Is that so?'

'Yes, that is so.'

'You are student?'

'No.'

Pause.

'You have experience at working practice.'

'Well, of sorts.'

'Excuse me?'

'Yes.'

'What nature please your method at making money for so long-range travel?'

'I make money from cooking and cycling and a bit of writing.'

'You are writer?'

'No, not really. I'm more a cook.'

'A cook of food?'

'Yes, a chef.'

'A chef? Ahh so. You are Fanny Claddock! Ha, ha!'

'Ha, ha!'

'You are chef in restaurant?'

'No.'

'What location you chefing?'

'Oh, just here and there.'

'Here? You are chefing in Japan?'

'No, no. I'm cycling here. I mainly do chefing in England.'

'England?'

'Yes, England.'

'Excuse me, why chefing in England?'

'Because England's my home.'

'Ahh so. No America?'

'America? No, England.'

'Ahh so. That is great.'

'Thank you.'

'So you are chefing of famous bread and butter? – Ha, ha!'

'Yes, ha, ha! And a few other things besides.'

Then, inquisition over, the man bowed, turned, walked inside and that was that until, towards evening, he reappeared, gave me a can of *oolong-cha* and two riceballs and said, 'Why no sitted inside?'

'Because I like to hear the sea rather than sick sounds.'

'Excuse me?'

'I prefer fresh air.'

'Ah so, *desu-ka*? You like Japanese food?'

'Yes.'

'In England how you say "map"?'

'Map.'

'And how you say "mop"?'

'Mop.'

'Ah so, *desu-ka*? Great similarity! Thank you!'

And with that the man disappeared inside for good.

When it grew dark I managed, despite the strength of the wind, to anchor myself down in a small corner of the deck and fell asleep to the deep solid reverberation of the engines. Some hours later I awoke, aware that the reassuring rumble of said engines had died to almost nothing. Checking it wasn't my imagination, I peered over the side. We were scarcely moving. More like bobbing. Wondering what was going on I wandered off along the deck only to discover a number of the crew casually fishing off the stern. This led me to muse whether we had in fact left Ishigaki six hours early not so much to outpace the rumoured typhoon, but in order for the crew to indulge in a spot of deep-sea angling.

Shortly after 2 a.m. I was rudely awoken by the chief steward shouting at me to get up and go inside.

'You cannot sleep outside!' he yelled.

'Why not?' I asked.

'Because you cannot sleep outside.'

'Well, I feel sick inside,' I said.

'You cannot sleep outside!' he bellowed, obviously stuck on autopilot.

Feeling that this man was getting all shirty under the collar over a molehill, I chose to dislike him.

'It's too stuffy, too smoky, too noisy and too cramped to sleep inside,' I said. 'Anyway, why don't you unlock the large rooms so that the passengers don't have to sleep on top of each other?'

'You cannot sleep outside!' he reiterated, demonstrating perhaps the limit of his English.

Another member of the crew, overhearing the hubbub, climbed down some steps to intervene. He was calm and polite and pleasant. The unpleasant man stood bowing for a moment before disappearing inside. The pleasant man apologized for the behaviour of the unpleasant man and explained that, although sleeping outside was unusual, it was not forbidden.

'But sleeping must take place on seat only.'

'But there are only two benches on the whole ship,' I said. 'both placed in the windiest position possible.'

'Yes,' said the man.

Yes what? I thought. However, as I liked the pleasant man and didn't want to cause further flutter on board, I scooped up my bedding and obediently followed him to one of the two benches.

'Sorry, but sleeping is allow here only and alternative choice for indoor.'

Despite the bench-bed feeling as if it was lying in the maws of a maelstrom, I chose to remain outside. But to do so necessitated lassoing myself with bungees to the narrow plank along with weighing down my sleeping bag with two hefty panniers so as to avoid being swept clean off to China.

Arriving back in Naha, I weaved my way through the bumper-to-bumper traffic of Kokusai-dori to Mrs Ota's *minshuku* where I had based myself some weeks before. I wanted to collect a package of odds and ends that I had left with her and to present her with a small offering which I had bought in Ishigaki.

When I walked through the door I found her crawling around on the floor on her hands and knees. Apparently she had fallen off the window shelf and sprained her ankle. Any sympathy I expressed she waved aside.

'I am really very pleased,' she said. 'Now I don't have to go outside. I hate outside!'

I helped her into her high-rise 'hospital' bed situated beneath a big poster of Snoopy.

'Snoopy – urgh! I really don't like!' she said, making me wonder if there was anything that she did.

'Well, at least it's a good time to be indoors in all this typhoon season,' I said.

'Tchhh!' said Mrs Ota, 'I really don't like having *minshuku* but I think maybe is better than nothing for indoor life style.'

There was no time to hang around. The weather reports indeed showed a typhoon storming great guns up from the south so, not wanting to get marooned in Naha, I scuttled off to the port to see whether the Kagoshima ship was still scheduled to sail. It was. With just over a couple of hours until departure I took off to take a quick look around the nearby 'Teahouse of the August Moon' before going to eat a *nori*-covered fish-filled riceball in Wakasa Park. A heavily pregnant South East Asian-looking woman came and sat down beside me. I said hello, but she said nothing. Instead, after chain-smoking four cigarettes on the trot, she wrenched at her short, flowery-blue billowing dress and revealed her breasts. People stared then looked away. I tried to pretend that her behaviour was nothing to write home about and asked her if she was okay.

'He screwed me, he screwed me!' she cried in a strong American accent, before dropping her head between her bare nail-scratched knees and sobbing uncontrollably. She reeked of alcohol. Passers-by glanced at this embarrassing scene before pepping up their pace.

I didn't know what to do. I'm always hopeless in this sort of situation – always say the wrong thing or put my foot in it. So, deciding not to say anything, I just put my hand on her forearm and sat with her. After a while she broke into a torrent of abuse, fortunately not at me, but at the man who had apparently 'screwed' her. In a momentary lull I took the opportunity to ask her if she was all right, when she obviously wasn't. Seemingly, the effect of my words motivated her into getting up and smashing a half-empty bottle of whisky into the fountain before lurching out of the park, which left me to think what a lucky thing it was that I wasn't an agony aunt.

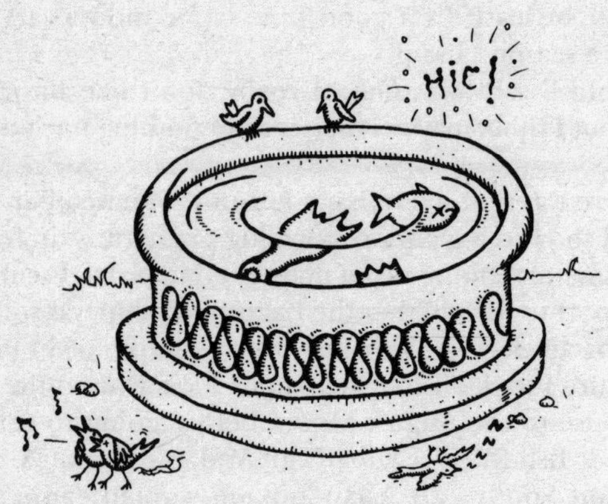

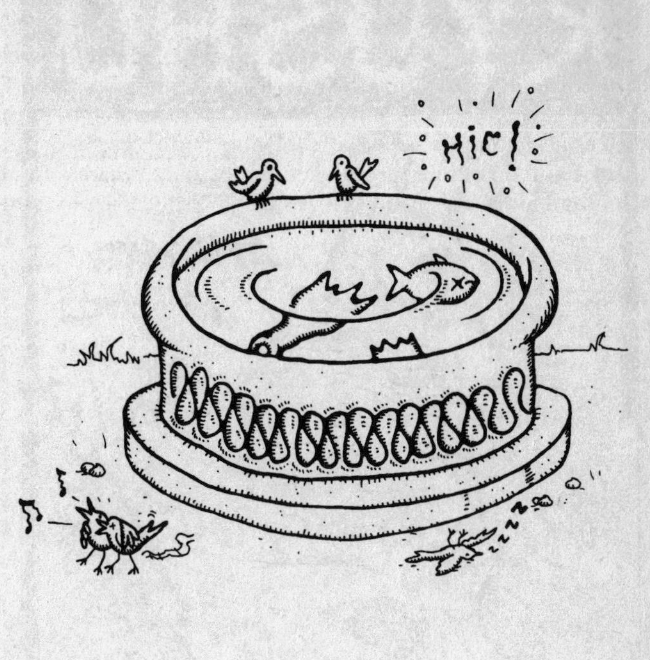
HIC!

* I could of used a knife & fork but the availability of a uniformed utility added an extra something to this gastronomic adventure.

CHAPTER 24

Dog-box Man

The *Queen Coral*. On board another ferry. How many ferries? I was losing count. Along with bicycles and trains, boats are the way to go. Drifting gives rise to dreams; seas to stretched horizons; horizons to distant lands. Slowly. That's how travel should be. Slowly creeping across the continents and watery masses of the world. Unhurried, unrushed. Gentle with time. Gentle with my mind.

As I sat on deck in dreamy mood preparing my picnic lunch, a student from Fukuoka trotted excitedly up to me and said, 'America?' In her hands she held a canvas bag printed with the words:

ELEPHANT FAMILY
Elephant family are popular with us.
Their humming makes us feel happy.

'No, English,' I replied.

'English? Ahhh, Oxford University very fine!'

'Well actually . . .'

'What subject you are please majoring?'

Seeing as the girl's questions were of a presumptive nature and seeing as I was feeling flippant of mood and seeing as I obviously resembled a prime example of a 'very fine' Oxford University graduate, clad as I was in oil-stained stripy-patched cycling shorts and threadbare T-shirt, I said, 'Well actually I majored in bicycle maintenance.'

'Excuse me?'

'I majored in bicycle maintenance,' I repeated.

'Is that so?' said the girl, looking blank.

'Yes, that is so,' said I.

As the girl's questioning seemed to have hit a momentary hiatus and as I was feeling decidedly peckish, I took the opportunity to pop a piece of fried tofu in my mouth. This action spurred the Elephant Girl on to a new topic.

'Excuse me,' she trumpeted, 'what please have you eating?'

'Tofu,' I said.

'Tofu?'

'Yes, tofu.'

'You like tofu – really?'

'Yes, really.'

'Hoaaaaaw,' hoaaaaawed the Elephant Girl with considerable throatiness, evidently well impressed. 'But tofu is Japanese food.'

'Well, funnily enough,' I said, 'I eat tofu in England too.'

'Hoaaaaaw – really Japanese food in England?'

'Yes, really. This is not so odd. After all, Japan is full of American food.'

Long pause to consider this deeply philosophical point.

'Ah so. Thank you very much. Bye bye,' said the girl. And with that truncated conclusion she ambled away.

Thanks to a starry night and an amicable crew, I spent the night without incident on the spacious upper deck, falling asleep beneath the golden gaze of a cat's-eye moon. Just before six I was awoken by a member of the cheerful crew relaying an invitation from the captain to join him in the wheelhouse for a spot of *nihon-cha.* Feeling a bit of a wreck, I thought the occasion might be a trifle daunting. But it was not to be. The moment I stepped through the door, a grinning man greeted me before placing a china cup of green tea in my hands and the captain's cap on my head. Everyone made a fine show of complimenting me on my haphazard Japanese, which reminded me just what a polite lot the Japanese are. After the captain instructed one of his lesser mortals to take several photographs of him and myself at the helm, he showed me the ropes – or, rather, the ultra-computerized control panel: a long row of one-armed bandit-like machines that wouldn't have looked out of place on Bognor seafront.

Arriving back in Kagoshima felt oddly reassuring and very familiar. It was still raining ash from the dark-billowing Cherry Volcano as I rode past the 'Fishes Market' and a garage with a huge neon sign proclaiming: FORD; ENJOY CAR LIFE. CLEAN CAR.

Major excitement of the day was returning to the bosom of the Hondas' Young In Kagoshima – Mrs Honda greeting me as if I was of her own flesh and blood. But above all, what really boosted my pulse rate was collecting my first wodge of letters in four months, Mrs Honda having touchingly acted as my *poste restante.*

That night I rang home and received some news which put paid to my plans of continuing to ride for several more months around Japan before crossing over to South Korea and from there . . . well, maybe down into South East Asia and on to that favourite old onion of Oz. Much as I would like to give a sensational reason for my sudden need to fly back to base – such as being ill, or penniless or pregnant or dead (not that I'd care to be any of those things, mind) – I'm afraid I can't. I just had to go home. But not before a whirlwind two weeks of two-wheeling around steamy Kyushu.

In order to see as much as possible and travel as far as I could in the fast-diminishing days before reaching Tokyo in time for my flight, my life, rather worryingly, had to be meticulously planned. And as planning doesn't come naturally to me, this was to be no mean feat. Instead of collapsing with weary pleasure on to my futon on the floor of Young In Kagoshima, I fretted in sweat into the early hours while poring over copious maps calculating distances down to the last kilometre. The idea was to have no days of rest, no loitering with intent at spots of roadside or non-roadside interest, no veering at a whim off course – in short, no dilly-dallying and no wild goose chases for packets of porridge as I was wont to do.

The legs were willing, but the mind was weak. First stop south of Kagoshima my plan went to pot when, cruising into Ibusuki, I swayed off track and ended up being buried into a shallow grave on the black sand beach. Judging from a nearby sign, it seemed I had somehow fallen by the wayside into . . .

> SUNAMUSHI – NATURAL SAND STEAM BATH
> A unique experience you should never miss clothes yourself in Yukata, a cotton kimono, walk down to the beach, rest your body in the sand heated by hot springs below you. It's a natural sauna. You'll feel completely

> relaxed and refreshed after sweating out all the fatigue. This natural therapy, utilizing 85°C hot springs of alkalic saline contents, has been noted as an effect remedy against such ailments as neuralgia and rheumatism, disorder of digestive system or female organ, along with its effectiveness for health and beauty treatment.

Ah so, *desu-ka*? Not one to miss a chance encounter of being buried alive, I had dutifully embalmed myself mummy-fashion in the obligatory orange *sunamushi* (*suna,* sand; *mushi,* steam) *yukata,* and slip-slopped along the seafront in the compulsory blue flip-flops before offering myself to one of a clutch of chatty little gravediggers – all mealy-biceped grannies in snow-white scarves and sky-blue aprons. Joining a row of decapitated heads topped in towels and shaded from the devilish rays of the sun by diminutive umbrellas sprouting from the sand like a kaleidoscope of colourful toadstools, I submitted myself to the hands of a giggling old barefooted gravedigger who gleefully covered me with dumpy shovel-loads of fiery-hot, black sandy gravel.

Buried beneath what felt like the entire contents of Bournemouth beach and a lorry-load of embers, I was so hopelessly immobilized that the only part of my anatomy that I was able to move was my eyeballs. As the minutes sizzled slowly by, I lay on my back submerged in the burning sand trying to convince myself it was doing some good (though as for my 'female organ' I was not so sure), while wondering how the devil I could go about attracting the attention of the gravedigger to come and dig me out.

Later, looking far worse for wear than a boiled octopus, I dragged myself in my glowing, geothermically cooked, sand-scorched skin back along the seafront. On the way I had the good fortune to bump into a man on a bicycle who led me past the Café Teria and the Cocktail and Talk Club to a friend of his who owned a most appealing *minshuku,* old and wooden with a leafy courtyard that led on to its own steamy *onsen* of healing waters.

Mr Yoshimoto, the owner of the *minshuku*, was a fresh-faced and friendly man with a dazzling teenage daughter called Nagisa. Despite her initial reservation, Nagisa became highly animated at the prospect of having a foreign octopus come to stay. We spent some time together, she giggling at my Japanese and I at her English, stumbling over ourselves to correct each other. I later received a letter from her:

Dear Josie
Hello, How are you? I'm fine.
Autumu is here in Japan.
Kagoshima is little cool now.
When you came to Kagoshima,
I speaked to you and you wrote your address at my note book.
Do you remember me?
I'm fourteen. I like to eat and play.
– Bye the way –
I write letter to you again

love Nagisa

Having returned to life again after my near-death burial, I found that the kilometres peeled away as the pace hotted up. I swooped south before accelerating north, hugging the coast all the way. The humidity was so intense it hung on me like an extra layer of clothing, causing my knees to sag. But with not a minute to waste, I pushed on through a whirl of sweaty skin-glazed days – heavy and dazy days that seemed to congeal together in a series of hot and sporadic memories. Kaimon-dake (known as Satsuma Fuji owing to its towering mount of conical perfection), where, in a dark and dripping old disused tunnel, I became caught between a couple of coiled and colossal tongue-spitting snakes – the sort of deathly-fanged serpents that looked as if they would eat you first and ask questions later. The city of Sendai, where a sign in English advised motorists to 'DRIVE WIDE AWAKE' and where my *minshuku* provided a surprising array of bedside-reading soft porn material in place of your average British b&b's Bible – one particularly well-thumbed offering was entitled *Oldies But Good Nudies.*

More ferries. More islands. The hills turned greener, the sea clearer, the roads emptier. Old wooden farmhouses floated among shimmering watery-green fields of rice, their eaves fringed with drying bundles of garlic and onions, the burning dust laid with golden baskets of beans.

Hideki Araki, a round and jovial postman, invited me home to stay with his wife Soyoko and their two young children. Hideki was not only a postman but also a fisherman. Did I like fish? he asked. *Hai, hai*! I said. And with that he took himself off with a rod and a net and a friend and an hour later there were four squirming eels running amok in Soyoko's kitchen sink.

'Watch this!' said Hideki as he skinned them alive.

Fifty minutes later there were several furlongs of juicy and barely grilled eel wriggling on down towards my lower duodenum. I patted a content and well-replete stomach.

'*Oishii*,' I said. 'Very delicious.'

In the morning Soyoko packed me a snack for the road – dried *ika* (squid) which she informed me was to be dipped into a garish glob of canary-yellow sauce that she spooned into a small plastic pot with 'Hello Kitty' on the lid. Another bag was filled with a *bento* of last night's eel (by now definitely dead); grilled salmon; fried tofu; *wakame* seaweed; something very rubbery which I couldn't tell was animal, vegetable, mineral, or edible; some interesting fungi that resembled a cross between a UFO and an octopus; a mound of the never-leave-home-without-it sacrosanct rice; a pickled plum and pickled radish; a mini fish-shaped sachet of soy sauce; and a chunk of watermelon. My bottles were filled to the brim with iced *oolong-cha.*

It was still early. Miki, the daughter, clad in her grey sailor-uniform, had already left to walk down the mountain to Junior High. Young crop-topped Hidekudzo was being harried by his mother to finish his breakfast of *miso* soup as out of the window she could see his eight-year-old classmates skipping down the road to school.

Postman Hideki, adeptly chopsticking up the last of his polished rice grains, suddenly became galvanized into action by a sudden idea.

'Jodie-*san*!' he exclaimed 'you must visit the one and only other *gaijin* currently on Nagashima Island.'

Frankly there were other things I would rather be doing (like slurping my way through another bowlful of seaweedy soup) than slogging over mountains in order to seek out fellow *gaijin* – after all, I was going to be back in *gaijin*-country in a few days' time so I didn't need another one to add to my plate just yet.

'Is this *gaijin* your friend?' I asked Hideki.

'No, no, but everyone on Nagashima knows where she lives. She is from America. Ga!'

Which I gathered was good enough reason to go banging on her door at 7.25 a.m. Hideki, I hasten to add, did the banging. He had also done the driving as he refused to let me cycle, so, after putting my mount into the back of his nippy little post van, he transported me up and down a helter-skelter of mountains to the *gaijin*'s front door.

I felt a trifle daunted. What was I going to say to her, apart from 'Hello, I hope we haven't woken you'?

Finally the door was opened by a very white, middle-to-cruiserweight woman wrapped in a towel. Her hair and skin were soaking. I guessed, without too much demand on my grey matter, that she had been rudely pulled from the shower. Her expression, not surprisingly, was one of mild surprise. Unfortunately Hideki said nothing – just smiled and bowed. I did my best to imitate him, and failed miserably. I also could not think of anything to say. The woman, whose daunting girth was about five times the size of your average Japanese, was now standing in a little pool of water that had collected around her feet. Fortunately she took the initiative.

'Hi, guys!' she boomed with a big but forced grin, 'how're ya doin'?'

Considering the circumstances, her demeanour was admirable.

Finding my tongue, curiously in the same place as I'd left it, I said, 'Oh, hello. I hope we haven't woken you?' before realizing that, unless she had a tendency to sleep in the shower, it was a pretty daft question. Then, thinking it best to pass the buck to Hideki, I asked her, 'Sorry to bother you, but do you know Hideki?'

'Hideki?' said the woman, nonplussed, as Hideki pricked his ears.

'Ummm, yes. This gentleman here.'

'Why, I've never seen him in my life,' she replied, and I had no reason in the world to doubt her.

Hideki continued to beam and wag his tail.

'Oh, really?' I said.

'Yah, right.'

Thinking it might be a nice idea to try to be a touch more conversational, I told the woman that I didn't know Hideki either; he had just kindly invited me to stay as I was passing on through.

'Gee, that's swell,' she said. 'Folks round here are real a-comma-datin'.'

She asked me what I was doing in Japan, so I told her.

'You mean to say you're biking round Japan? You've gotta be kiddin'.'

'Well, that's the idea,' I replied, suddenly realizing that my steed was standing proud about ten feet away, tethered in the back of the post van.

'Cool. But I guess, to put it mildly, it must be kinda hard. I mean, jeez, Japan's all moun'ain!'

'Hmmm, it is a bit. And it's a bit hot, too.'

'Tell me about it,' she said, but I chose not to. 'You having fun?'

'Yes, lots of very confusing fun,' I said, before asking her what brought her to Japan.

'I'm organizing events for the JET programme.'

'So you speak Japanese?'

'Yah, but I sure should do after all this time. I graduated in Japanese at school in South Carolina.'

'Oh, that's handy,' I said, just as a telephone started ringing from somewhere behind her. 'Well, I suppose we'd better leave you to it. It's nice meeting you. Sorry about the early morning call.'

'No problem. Say, you have yourself a good time now. Enjoy!'

'Thanks,' I said, as Hideki and I turned back to the van and the door slid shut behind us.

I had hoped to make it to Nagasaki – I got within a whisker, thirty-eight kilometres to be precise – but what with a galloping-tight schedule to reach Tokyo, time just wasn't on my side. So instead I battled with the thundering traffic as I charged north-eastwards across the Amakusa Five Bridges which straddle the islands of Shimabara-wan that itself leads into the Ariake Sea – an almost enclosed mass of water heavily cultivated to produce prawns, pearls, seaweed and commercially grown fish.

Not far from the fifth bridge, a red van pulled over and a man in an orange boilersuit jumped out and waved me down.

'Welcome at Japan,' he called, 'you are having maybe a requiring to be lifted? Hop in as pleasure guest!'

And then, noting my face of surprise, he added, 'Please no worried. Only joke. Ha, ha! Maybe you like my improvement suggestion as invitation to take drink for so hotting in sporting activity. One minute only please!'

And with that he accelerated off down the road to a vending machine. True to word, after 'one minute only', he reappeared with a couple of cans of chilled *mugi-cha*.

'Thank you,' I said.

'America?' asked he.

'No, I'm . . .'

'Ahh, you are Kiwi. All Kiwi person travel so far!'

'Well, actually, I'm English.'

'English? Ahh, Jodie Foster. Very fine. Please, your most favourite suggestion for movie?'

'Movie?'

'Yes indeed. For myself most pleasure movie is *ET*. Ha! So fine! You like Whitney Houston?'

'She's all right, I suppose.'

'You see my car I have box for dog containment.'

Looking into the back of his van I saw two large wooden crates.

'Are there dogs in there now?' I asked.

'Dog?' said the man, looking mystified. 'Dog? You are wishing to see Japanese driving licence?'

'Driving licence?' I said, while thinking: Is it me or him that's lost it?

'Excuse me?'

'What?' Help. Then, realizing this dog-box man was truly off his rocker, I said, 'I'd love to see a Japanese driving licence,' because I thought: hell, why not?

So the dog-box man pulled out his wallet, flipped it open like a cop showing identity and said, 'Japanese driving licence. Very fine. You are liking?'

'Very nice,' I said. And then, spotting a well-thumbed photo of a kimono'd woman tucked behind the wallet's plastic-window sleeve, I took the presumptive liberty of asking, 'Your fine wife?'

'Ahh, this is my very soon wife. We are at presently fiancéed. She is my Number Three wife. Ha, ha! I have many problem marriage but now I hope future maybe certainly fine. You have marriage history?'

'Umm, no.'

'Ahhh so. Maybe I find opportunity for you invitation as my Number Four wife. Ha, ha! Only joke!'

'Ha, ha! Well, you never know, I might just take you up on your invitation – when I become desperate.'

'Excuse me?'

'Not today, thanks.'

'Ha, ha!'

'Ha, ha! Well, suppose I'd best get going. Thanks for the *mugi-cha.* Mind those dog-boxes. Have a happy wedding. *Sayonara*!'

'Bye-bye, Jodie Foster. Ha, ha!'

Late afternoon in Kumamoto, Kyushu's third largest city, famed not only for Suizen-ji Koen (its surreal 300-year-old exquisitely crafted gardens) but also for its almighty, multi-tiered (albeit a ferro-concrete reconstruction) castle. Oh, and for its *uma-sashi* – wafer-thin sliced raw horsemeat.

Way up on a hill overlooking the city I found a place to stay – Higogi *minshuku*, whose toilet had a notice on the wall which said:

> TO OUR FORIEGN GUESTS
>
> No worries when you use our western toilet – to make you feel more comfortable we have provided wet paper towels which you may wipe the toilet seat with – please use them if you like . . . just wipe and off you go!!!
>
> HAPPY TIMES
>
> The management

The owner, Nobuya Baba, was a kindly, shiny domed man who, together with his ample wife, not only pampered me to extremes (something I did little to resist) but also took to calling me their *musume* (daughter). Despite the notice in the toilet there were no other 'foriegn' guests staying – only a cheery woman from Fukuoka who gave me three rotary pens housed in a posh-looking pouch, a pack of Fuji films and something that she called a 'good heart card'. She also took to putting her motherly arm around me a lot, which struck me as a public show of affection quite unusual for the Japanese. Later a manager of a sweet factory arrived from Kita-Kyushu who gave me two 1,000 yen telephone cards (worth £12), both of which were printed with the address and photograph of his sweet-toothed factory – which he invited me to visit to fill up my panniers for free.

Two incidents of note occurred during my short stay in the City of Raw Horsemeat. The first was during an exploratory wander when I happened upon a tucked away shrine where, in a state of considerable complexity, I observed a priest clad in traditional garb (long luscious silk robes, hefty high-rise headwear and big, glossy black clogs as high as bricks) blessing a fresh-off-the-production-line silvery-sleek Lexus saloon which a salaryman (watched over proudly by his family) had carefully reversed on to the shrine's forecourt. The method whereby the priest 'blessed' the car (nowadays a common procedure in the hope of protection from breakdowns and accidents) was curious. In his hands he held a long pole, like a broom handle, topped with a rustling head of slithers of virginal paper that he enthusiastically shook both inside and outside the Lexus, as if giving it a good feather-dusting. This bizarre coalescence of ancient and modern proved an elaborate and lengthy procedure, involving a lot of meaningful murmuring and magic-wand waving. Finally, after a fair bit of bowing and graciously beaming grins on the part of the Lexus family, they clambered into their super-safe vehicle, the father casting me a now-we're-invincible wave – and promptly drove into a concrete wall. Actually he didn't, but in a thoroughly un-Christian (and no doubt un-Shinto) spirit I rather wish that he had.

Not long after this incident Kiyoko Nishimura, a young and vivacious reporter from TKU TV news, got wind of the fact that a 'one person only' female cycling *gaijin* was in town, and sought me out. Kiyoko spoke tip-top American-accented English after having spent two years at school in Ohio before living for a year in Boston.

'It was my best time ever!' she told me. 'Life was so free, so great. Always I could do exactly what I like without worry about what other people are thinking. This was really new experience at freedom for me. In Japan, everybody want to know what is your business. No time for privacy never! But suddenly in Ohio I speak anything I want and always this is so fine. Here, if people express strong opinion they are made to feel . . . you know . . . kind of really different. Japanese people are thinking to have opinion is very disrespectful to Japanese tradition. Always we must think as one in similarity.'

Kiyoko went on to tell me how she would love to return to America but there was no chance of this as getting hold of a Green Card had proved to be impossible. Also, with Japan being stuck in a recession, she must hold on to her job while she could. It was a good job, she said, despite the fact that she had only five days' holiday a year.

'Japanese people,' said Kiyoko, 'don't know how to holiday. They only know how to work.'

That evening, on returning to my 'no worries western toilet' *minshuku*, I found that Nobuya and his wife had organized a little gathering of friends and food for me in celebration of my buffoonish stint of trying (but spectacularly failing) to look mean and moody while riding through downtown Kumamoto for a two-minute flash of laughable stardom at the end of the news. Everyone guffawed and giggled at the sight of not only me but also the Babas, who featured fleetingly when I was filmed shouldering my mount clumsily down the steps of their *minshuku*.

The following day the *Kumamoto Nichinichi Shimbun* (*Kumamoto Daily News*) had a picture of me in full cycling swing loaded to the hilt with panniers. Thanks to this and my gallivanting snippet of TV, any thoughts of cycling out of the city without further incident were promptly blown to the *kaze*. Half of Kumamoto appeared to recognize the bicycling *gaijin*, which was bad news for wanting to extract myself swiftly to the mountains from the chaotic clutches of the city, but good news for being showered with offerings from all and sundry. Cars screeched to a sudden halt in the middle of the road long enough for gifts of food and drink or towels or maps or hats or T-shirts or 'Hello Kitty' socks and telephone cards (and, twice, even money) to be proffered by way of an extended arm; youngsters ran alongside or cheered from the sidelines; and several taxi-drivers operated their automatic doors to open and close alternately like the waving wings of a saluting aircraft. One woman, emerging from a ladies' outfitters, took one look at me and spontaneously dipped into her carrier bag to hand me her latest purchase – an oxblood-red silk shirt. Round the corner a young man, crossing the road at the lights, looked up, saw me and, in a state of considerable excitement, delved into the bag he was carrying to give me apparently the first thing that his hand fell upon – a shop-sealed kitchen knife complete with protective sheath. This was getting too much! The generosity of these city people knew no bounds. I had to hit the mountains before utter absurdity set in. But before I had a chance to do so, a schoolgirl on a bicycle reached into her basket and tried to give me her text books – all in Japanese.

'No, no.'

'Yes, yes.'

'No, no.'

'Yes, yes.'

'No, no . . .'

And so it went, on and on and on . . .

Pulling out the stops, I heaved my weighty steed up to the wonders of Mount Aso, the collective name of five separate volcanoes (all of them extinct except for turbulent Nakadake) which rear up out of the centre of the mostest (hold on to your hats – it's superlative statistic time again), bestest, greatest, finest, largest crater basin in the world, measuring a phenomenal twenty-four kilometres long, nineteen kilometres wide and 120 kilometres in circumference. Unlike calderas elsewhere in the world, which tend to be unpopulated and pongy sulphurous lunar landscapes, the mighty Mount Aso (ahhh so!) is home to nearly 100,000 people and contains a busy mosaic of roads and railways and towns and farms. The startlingly lush rich hills lay dotted with the arresting sight of herds of beef-cattle and horses (the luckless nags providing the pink horsemeat that would be eaten raw and as thinly sliced as *sushi*) and plump-uddered cows grazing on the rich green grass. Because cows were such a rarity in Japan, locals were cashing in on the fact that they had a bunch of oriental fat Daisies and Buttercups on their hands by selling glassfuls of milk from stalls and tourist-luring wooden cabins erected at the side of the road.

Once over the Takamori Pass I lunged twisting and turning through verdant and sparsely populated valleys, at one point pausing for a spot of lubrication at a vending machine on which was splayed a magnificent moth the size of a dinner plate.

Following a perambulating deviation in which I wandered down into the sheer chisel-walled wonders of mossy Takachiho Kyo Gorge before paying a visit to the cave of the sun goddess Amaterasu, I veered off Route 218 – a route stampeding with traffic towards Kyushu's east coast – and sought out instead the joyously empty and narrow ribbon of road that wound its way sandwiched between the Takachiho mountain railway and the Gokase River rapidly rushing along at the foot of the gorge's towering, forest-clad cliffs.

At a point where the Gokase River joined forces with the Hinokage River, I crossed a small stone bridge beside a huddle of endearingly ramshackle houses clinging precariously to the rocky walls above the water. All along this stretch of river I had noticed that the trees on both sides of the gorge, high above the water-line, were all lying like thousands of giant matchsticks, dead and decidedly flattened. As I pondered the scene I heard a woman's voice calling to me from behind. I turned round to see an *obaasan* leaning against a witch's broom that she was using to brush the road in front of her house – a house that clung to the shadows beneath the cool, dripping walls of rock and whose sliding front door opened directly on to a well-ordered and compact kitchen. The *obaasan,* propping her brush aside, invited me in for a bowl of iced noodles and tea. As we sat at the table looking out through the open door that led to a fetching view of the river, I asked her what exactly had happened to cause the woeful sight of crumpled trees.

Ahhh, she said, eight months ago there was a truly terrible typhoon, the worst she had ever experienced, which triggered an evacuation of the village as the river rose to phenomenal heights and flattened the trees with ease.

Gradually, as I continued along the river, it turned from a fast froth to a becalmed ivy-green, its surface straight-faced, almost rippleless. As the river broadened, fishermen in lampshade hats appeared, standing statue-still in the bows of their pencil-thin craft, stirring only occasionally to pole themselves along like gondoliers.

With barely a minute to spare I made it to Hyuga-shi, a remarkably unremarkable city straddled across the notorious National Route 10 which I'd had the misfortune to experience many a blue-mooned week earlier. Without further ado I charged on board the *Pacific Express* for the twenty-hour voyage to Kawasaki.

Unlike the dilapidated and cramped quarters of that surly old tub, *Hiryu 3,* which had ferried me from Ishigaki to Okinawa, the spiffy *Pacific Express* was a magnificently plush and spacious vessel. One of its most memorable features was the sumptuous washing facilities, which included a big communal bath. Any qualms or reservations I may have nurtured about baring myself to mass nudity during my first few days in Japan had long since been well blown to the divinest of winds. Nowadays it was: show me a bathful of buxom back-scrubbing women and I'm out of my clothes in a jiff. Apart from the raucous banter of this sea-faring brood, the most comical thing about taking the plunge on board the ocean wave was that, owing to the considerable swell of the sea, one didn't just sit in the bath but slid all together as one – toddlers, children, pubescents, two-toned cyclists, *okusamas, mama-sans, obaasans*, great-*obaasans* alike – from one end of the swimming-pool bath to the other, a guffawing and spilling surge of colliding flesh.

Expressing myself across the *Pacific*, I woke up on deck in the morning and was approached by a grinning man in pebble specs and a T-shirt that declared:

Mr Junko Jnr
STABILITY
I like things
straight but
still I'm a bit
dangerous
our adventu
rous world

Mr Junko bowed before bending down to give me two rice *bisuketto* and a Pocari Sweat. Taking my hand and shaking it as if wringing the neck of a chicken, he said, 'Thank you velly much.'

Then he walked away and I never saw him again.

Entering Tokyo Bay was like sailing into a thick brown soup of boats. The coastline – a coastline that I found hard to believe I had kamikazed through and survived – was an endless frenzied stretch of putrid-smoking and flame-licking chimneys and factories and petrochemical plants and monster cranes that lay heavily cloaked beneath a brooding sepia cloud of humid thick pollution. Above this filthy, lung-decimating cloud the sky was clear and fresh and blue, but as the mighty *Pacific Express* slid into dock at Kawasaki we entered an atmosphere of browny-grey that hung heavy, like a suffocating and filthy drowning skin.

Rather than lose myself back into the interminable concrete beast-grey sprawl of Tokyo, I opted to hop across the bay on a ferry that dodged its way through a chaotic flotilla of tugs and tankers and containers and fishing-boats and ferries. My ploy was to scoot back up Chiba's Boso-hanto Peninsula to Narita. With only sixty miles to go, I thought I'd make it back to the airport in time to catch my flight, no sweat – or more like a lot of sweat but no trouble.

In the event I was wrong. My last night on the soil of the rising land saw me pitching my tent on a sunless and watery ledge bordered by concentric squares of paddies not far from the spot that my map curiously marked as King Field. As I lay inside, flaked out on my mat, my skin slippery with sweat, I tuned into the Far East Network (being back in GI territory) and heard a voice urgently warning me to 'secure all outside items . . . gather together emergency supplies . . .' because, despite thinking I was almost home and dry, Typhoon Kinner was storming its way towards me. All military installations on the Kanto Plain had been placed into a 'state of readiness 1' which, as far as states of readiness go, sounded suitably serious to me.

The typhoon announcer gave the latest update on wind speed, direction of approach, area of destructive force, number of helpless cyclists it had in its sights, etc. etc. so, with trusty head torch strapped to a heavily beaded brow, I unravelled maps, synchronized watches, ate a banana (hopefully not my last) and attempted to calculate how long it might take for the Killer Kinner to Tie me in a Phoon if it held to its present course. A spot of compass-work combined with arithmetic (the latter being nothing too taxing, mind: many a long-division ago I failed my 'O'-level maths – though I hasten to add that I put this down more to the fact that I spent the entire exam trying to coax a big hairy-legged spider into galloping up the desk of a particularly swotty neighbour than to my inability to distinguish my roots from my ratios) resulted with my concluding that I could, if lucky, catch a three-and-a-half-hour nap before I had best pack up and scarper.

Thus, shortly after 2 a.m., I found myself wearily stumbling over ankle-twisting tent pegs as I tried to dismantle my home in the blowy dark without measuring my length in the paddies.

Although heavy rain and whiplash winds caught me at dawn on the final leg to Narita, they were only Kinner's sidekick as the typhoon had (as typhoons are wont to do) performed a whimsical arabesque and tacked off out to sea.

As Finnair jetted me off for the 7,837-kilometre flight to Helsinki (en route for London), I found myself strapped into a seat beside a robust American called Chad. Chad hailed from St Louis, Missouri – a revelation that, in a moment of reduced-oxygen excitement, prompted me to reach for my useless but lovable *Japanese in 3 Weeks* phrasebook and blurt out, 'Ah so, *desu-ka? Yareyare, boku niwa ikko wakaran,* – Well, by gosh, I am from Missouri.'

And you know what Chad said? He said, 'Well, by gosh, I *am* from Missouri!'

Actually he didn't. But I'd have guffawed if he had.

Instead, he said, 'Jeez, I sure am glad to be sittin' here. I mean, don't all that bowing just drive ya nuts?'

With highly impractical phrasebook-speak still swirling round my head, I turned to peer out of my porthole upon the last few alluringly high-peaked glimpses of Japan and thought: Cut your capers! Call me sweetheart – the mountains will be in labour; an absurd mouse will be born.

And I knew then that the rising lure of the land would woo me back. Soon. Very soon.

A Gaijin's Glossy Glossary

Some Japanese translators use a phonetic system of vowels with a bar over the letter to indicate pronunciation or stress. In this book such vowels have been doubled (e.g. *chiizu*, *depaato*).
[Note: 'lit.' = 'literally']

abunai: (it's) dangerous, unsafe; look out!
Ainu: the original inhabitants of Japan, said to be of Caucasian stock because of their rounded eyes, hirsute appearance and naturally wavy hair
aisu-kuriimu: ice-cream
ama: woman diver
ama-san: nun
ame: rain
ano ne!: (interjection) why!; well!
ao: blue
aotake: (lit. 'blue bamboo') green bamboo
apaato: apartment, flat
ara!: (interjection) oh dear me!; good gracious!
arigato gozaimasu: thank you
awamori: local *sake*-type brew, very potent distilled spirit, that used to be made from *awa* (millet); entered Japan from trade with Thailand

baka: fool
banchi: building number
bango: number
banzai!: (lit. 'ten thousand years') cheers!; hurrah!
Basho: Japan's greatest *haiku* poet (1644–94)
basho: sumo tournament (usually prefixed by spring, summer etc.)
basho: place, spot, location
basho: banana tree
bashofu: banana-fibre cloth
benjo: (older word for) lavatory, toilet (room), water-closet
bento: lunchbox, usually containing rice and fish, often sold at railway stations
beya: stables (sumo)
bifubaaga: beefburger
biro: betel-nut palm-tree
biru: beer
bisuketto: biscuit
bonkei: art form involving creation of a miniature landscape on a tray
bonsai: the art of growing dwarfed ornamental varieties of trees or shrubs in small shallow pots by selective pruning (*bon*, basin, bowl; *sai*, to plant)
boshu uchiwa: traditional flat and round hand-fan made in area of Narita
bosozoku: speed tribes, hot-rod or motor-cycle gangs (noisy but usually harmless!)
burakumin: (lit. 'village people') traditionally outcasts associated with lowly occupations such as leather work
bushido: 'the way of the warrior' – the code of ethics followed by the samurai. A term popularized during this century to designate traditional Japanese ideals of conduct. Doctor Inazo Nitobe, in *Bushido, the Soul of Japan*, itemizes as *bushido*: rectitude or justice, courage, benevolence, politeness, sincerity, honour, loyalty and self-control.
butsudan: ornate freestanding Buddha shelf; Buddhist altar in the home

cha: tea
chagama: metal pot hanging from *kagi* over an *irori* for boiling water for tea
-chan: a suffix denoting affection
chanko-nabe: nourishing stew eaten in vast quantities by sumo wrestler
chanoyu: tea ceremony. The tea cult is the traditional way of drinking tea in accordance with set rules of etiquette.
chiizu: cheese
chikan: sexual pervert, particularly one who rubs up against women on crowded subways and trains and who (in my mind) deserves a good solid kick in the crucial department
chinpira: a punk; trainee *yakuza* gangster
chizu: map
-cho: city area (for large cities) between a *ku* and a *chome* in size; also a street or a town
chochin: paper lantern, usually collapsible
chojo: mountaintop, summit
chome: city area of a few blocks
chonan: the older (eldest) son
chotto: a little
chotto matte kudasai: just a moment, please

daijobu: fine, safe, all right, certainly, surely
daikon: giant white radish (up to 40 cm long with circumference of 25 cm or more), usually grated and served with many dishes, or sliced and pickled
daikon-ashi: radish-legs (describing a person's long gangly legs resembling giant radish)
daimyo: feudal lords during Tokugawa shogunate who had virtually complete control over their domains
dakara: so, therefore, because, since, as
dame: no way, useless, no go, in vain
danchi: public apartments built by government; collective zone
densha: train

denwa: telephone
denwa bango: telephone number
depaato: department store
deshi: pupil, disciple, Zen pupil
desu-ka?: is that so?; really? (usually preceded by 'ah so' or 'ahhh so'. Circumstances of conversation dictate how long the ahs are)
desu-ne: that is so; yes it is
do itashimashite: you're welcome; that's all right
dohyo: sumo ring
dojo: exercise hall, training place for martial arts (lit. 'way place')
doki-doki: palpitate, beat, throb; palpitation (heart)
domo: thanks; sorry; good to meet you
domo arigato gozaimasu: thank you very much
donjon: central main building of a castle
donko: name for local trains in country areas
dori: road (also *tori*)
doro: road, way, street
dozo: please (when offering something); go ahead; be my guest

eki: railway station
ema: small wooden plaque depicting divine horses (*uma*), upon the back of which one writes a personal message or 'wish' before hanging it up in a shrine's grounds
en: garden
engawa: traditional verandah of a house overlooking the garden
enkozume: gangster finger-chop punishment (*tsume*, finger-nail, toenail, claw; 'ts' changes to 'z' when joined to another word)
erebeta: elevator
esukareta: escalator
eta: a pariah class in pre-Meiji times; the rarely publicized untouchable caste of Japan. Traditionally they held menial jobs, usually dealing with animals and leather.

They are looked down upon by Japanese society and few can marry out of their stigmatized class. Officially they no longer exist. Also *burakumin*

ettorrr: umm, err, well

femunisuto: feminist

fu: urban prefecture

fude: brush used for calligraphy

fukugi: species of tree

fundoshi: traditional male underwear; type of loincloth now mostly seen only at festivals or worn by sumo wrestlers

furigama: Japanese script used to give pronunciation for *kanji*

furisode: (lit. 'swinging sleeve') type of kimono with voluminous sleeves

furo: bath, bathroom, bath tub

furoshiki: (lit. 'bath spread') a piece of cloth (usually one metre square) used for bundling up articles for carrying or storing away. *Furoshiki* have long been used in Japan and the word itself dates back to the early Edo era (around the seventeenth century). The name comes from one of the first uses of this cloth: to carry a change of clothes to a public communal bath-house. *Furoshiki* come in various sizes and materials: there are large cotton ones with arabesque patterns for binding up quilts, and dainty silk ones patterned with a family crest or with flowers and birds

furu kosu: full course

fusuma: (sliding) screen – sliding paper doors used to divide the open space of a house into rooms and corridors. Both sides of the wooden framework are covered with several layers of strong paper, making them heavier than *shoji*. Sometimes decorated with colourful mural paintings depicting traditional or natural scenes

futon: thick padded quilt-like mattress, easily rolled up and stowed during the day (the stuffing ranges from rice hulls to foam rubber); eiderdown

ga!: expression of surprise, amazement
gaijin: (lit. 'outside person') foreigner; e.g. *gaijin-san*, 'Mr (or Ms) Foreigner'; alien
gama: natural caves in Okinawa
ganbarimasu: I shall do my best (often said in reply to '*ganbatte!*')
ganbaru: to do one's best
ganbatte!: do your best!; have strength!; good luck!
ganbatte kudasai!: please do your best! (more respectful term, addressing older person)
garasu: drinking-glass
geisha: (lit. 'person of the arts') professional female entertainer or companion, skilled in traditional performing arts. She does not dispense sexual favours as part of her normal job, which is to comfort and entertain her guests.
gekiga: 'strong' comics; television animation
gemmai: brown rice
genkan: (lit. 'hidden barrier') entranceway or foyer where shoes are removed or replaced when entering or leaving a building
genki: (lit. 'original spirit') vigour, energy, vitality; spirits; courage; healthy
geta: traditional raised wooden clog-like sandals with toe-thong
gimu: official duty; social obligation
giri: loyalty
go: game on a square board marked with a grid having 361 intersections, played with black and white stones – as subtle and complex as chess. The game was introduced to Japan from China in the eighth century and was originally played only by the aristocracy
gohan: steamed/boiled rice (cf. *raisu*); meal
goma: sesame seed
gomen: contraction of *gomen nasai*
gomen nasai: I'm sorry; I beg your pardon
goraiko: sunrise (only used when one climbs a mountain specially to view rising sun – otherwise use *hinode*)

gun: county; army, force
gurepu furutsu: grapefruit
gyokusai: dying honourably (rather than surrendering)

ha!: (interjection) ha!; aha!; yes!; indeed!
habu: poisonous snake found in Okinawa area
hachi-ji: eight o'clock
hai!: yes!; okay!; understood!; fight! (lit. 'yes', but actually, in certain contexts, it can mean only passive acknowledgement that the addressee is paying attention). Note that *hai!* is not equivalent to 'yes' in the English sense, which can sometimes (often in my case) lead to misunderstanding and misinterpretation
haiku: seventeen-syllable poem containing a *kigo* or season-word
haji: shame, disgrace
hakama: loose trousers worn by men with kimono
hakui: white robe, such as worn by doctor, nurse, pilgrim
hakui no tenshi: nurse (lit. 'angel in white robe')
Hakuin: Zen monk of the seventeenth century, famous for his use of the phrase 'the sound of one hand clapping'; one of the principal figures of the Rinzai school of Zen
hama: beach
hamu eggu: ham and eggs
hanabi: (lit. 'fire-flowers') fireworks
hanami: cherry-blossom viewing
handikyappu: handicap
handobaggu: handbag
hankachifu: handkerchief
hanko: seal or stamp, used to authenticate a document (in Japan, it carries much more weight than your signature)
hanto: peninsula
happi: light coat made of silk or cotton, like a short kimono
haragei: (lit. 'belly language') non-verbal communication used to convey true intentions; often aggressive in business context

hara-kiri: (lit. 'belly slitting') vulgar word for ritual disembowelment (suicide according to the samurai code) – polite term is *seppuku*

hashi: chopsticks; also (depending on intonation) a bridge, or the edge or border of something

hashiwatashi: the indelicate act of passing food back and forth via chopsticks

heiwa: peace

henro: pilgrims on the Shikoku Eighty-eight Temple Circuit

heya: room

heya wa arimasu-ka?: do you have a room?

hibachi: charcoal brazier of iron or ceramics traditionally used as a heater in winter

hinin: contraception or birth-control. If a woman says '*Hinin shite*' she is not, boys, saying 'You're a little s***' but 'Use a condom!'

hinkaku: prestigious and spiritual aura

hinode: sunrise

hinoki: Japanese cypress (often used in shrine architecture)

hinomaru: the national flag; the Japanese sun flag (*hi*, sun; *maru*, circle)

hiragana: cursive phonetic syllabary of the fifty sounds of the Japanese language, used to connect *kanji* and to write Japanese words phonetically

hitori: alone, one person

honedu meron: honeydew melon

honne: a person's private 'face'; original feeling; truth; the reality that lies behind superficial utterances

honto: true, real, genuine (e.g. 'that's very true'); Okinawa, being the largest of the so-called Okinawa islands, is referred to as the *honto*, while the outer islands are the *rito*

hosutesu: (from the English word 'hostess') a woman employed in a drinking establishment to attract customers. The primary purpose of a hostess is to encourage customers to patronize a place regularly and spend a significant amount of money

hoteru: hotel

hotto doggu: hot dog
hysteri: nervousness and instability (generally used of women)

iada: nasty
ichi: one
ichiban: number one, the best; first, most
Igirisu: England, Britain
Igirisu-jin: English person
ii: good, nice, fine
ijime: bullying, relentless teasing
ika: cuttlefish, squid
ikebana: traditional art of flower arranging
ima: now
intanashionaru: international
inu: dog
ippai(**no**): full
irasshaimase: welcome (as a greeting), heard when entering homes, shops, restaurants and even lifts – there is no need to respond
iro onna: sexy woman
iro otoko: sexy man
iroppoi: lit. 'colourful', but used to mean sexy. The *iro* (colour) referred to is pink, which is directly associated with sex
irori: traditional open fireplace pit in a lowered section of the floor in the middle of a room
irori no jizai kagi: wooden pot hanger over an *irori*
itadakimasu: (lit. 'I will receive', 'I will partake') expression used before starting a meal
ittaikan: feeling of unity, of being one body, of belonging to one kind
Izanagi and Izanami: brother and sister deities and lovers who created the islands of Japan when they descended to earth at Amanohashidate

jamu: jam
jigoku: 'hells' or hotsprings

jikatabi: traditional split-toed boots worn mostly by builders, carpenters and workmen
Jimmu Tenno: the first semi-mythical emperor of Japan
jinja: Shinto shrine, easily spotted by the *torii* gate at its entrance
jirowashi: sea eagles
jitensha: bicycle
jitenshaya-san: bicycle shop
jizo: guardian deity of children
JNTO: Japan National Tourist Organization
josei: woman; feminine
JR: Japan Railways
JTB: Japan Tourist Bureau
juku: private school, crammer

ka: mosquito
kabuki: classical dramatic art form that evolved from *noh*, which has been a favourite among the Japanese since the seventeenth century. Music and dancing are fundamental to the *kabuki* performance. The typically Japanese melodies are played, mostly on several *shamisen* (a three-stringed instrument of the lute family) and other instruments peculiar to Japan. Differing greatly from modern drama, which lays primary emphasis on reactions, *kabuki* is a formalized art in which the significance of omissions, exaggerations and many of the actors' movements are pre-defined. All roles, including those of female characters, are played by men. The actor is considered more important than the play; he does not change his acting style to fit the play, but the play is changed to fit his particular skills.
kado: card
kaeru: frog
kamaboko: processed mashed fish combined with rice and flour (and no doubt half a hundredweight of chemicals), dyed fluorescent pink and found floating in circular swirls atop bowls of soup and *soba*

kami: head, source; Shinto term for deity, god, divinity, spirits of natural phenomena
kamikaze: (lit. 'divine wind') name given to the typhoon that sank Kublai Khan's invading armada in the thirteenth century; also name adopted by suicide pilots in Second World War in their effort to duplicate this fortuitous storm
kampai!: traditional salutation or toast before drinking, commonly used in both formal situations and casual parties, when proposing a toast and when raising glasses for the first drink of the evening(lit. 'dry glass' – on these occasions it is the equivalent of 'bottoms up!')
kana: phonetic alphabet used in writing Japanese
kanai: wife (one's own)
kane: money
kanji: Chinese calligraphic characters (ideograms) used in Japanese script. Used along with *kana* to write Japanese.
Kannon: Buddhist goddess of mercy, comes in many renditions throughout Japan
kare raisu: curried rice
karoshi: death from overwork (*karo*, overwork; *shi*, death)
kasa: umbrella; sedge hat
katakana: script used primarily to transcribe foreign words into syllabic Japanese
katsu: bonito (tuna fish)
katsuobushi: dried and flaked flesh of any of various similar or related fish species, such as *katsuwonus pelamis* (oceanic tuna)
kawa: river (also *gawa*)
kawaii: cute, sweet, pretty, lovely, dear, charming
kaze: wind, breeze
keiki: cake
kekko desu: no thank you
-ken: prefecture
kendo: (lit. 'the way of the sword') oldest martial art
kenpeitai: military police
ki: spirit, life force, mind, heart, feelings, will

kiipuseiku: keepsake

kimono: clothes, garments, dress; traditional outer garment made of different fabrics, designs, patterns and cuts in accordance with the occasion – formal or informal. There are various types of kimono and the designs and colours differ according to the marital status of the wearer. Japanese women tend to wear kimono during the New Year holidays, or on such occasions as the coming-of-age ceremony, college graduation parties, wedding ceremonies and receptions, as well as funeral services. Men wear kimono mostly at home to relax in. On formal occasions they may wear *haori* (a half-coat) and *hakam* (divided skirt).

ki-o-tsukete: take care

kissaten: tea room; coffee shop

-ko: lake

koan: illogical Zen Buddhist riddle, used as meditational tool to achieve enlightenment

koban: police-box, usually sited on a corner. The officers in this local sub-station keep a careful eye on their neighbourhood and tend to be very helpful (as long as you can understand their answers).

koen: park

kogane gumo: large striped fighting spider

kohii: coffee

koinobori: big carp banners like windsocks, flown from the rooftops of Japanese homes in honour of the household sons to celebrate Boys' Day in late April/early May. Boys' Day is the final holiday of Golden Week. Boys' Day has now become Children's Day, so the carp can signify the celebration for girls as much as for boys.

kokeshi: traditional wooden dolls made in the north-eastern region of Japan. The doll consists of a cylindrical torso, turned on a lathe. A round head is fitted on the torso and a girl's face drawn in. Two or three colours, such as red, blue or yellow, are used to paint lines or a chrysanthemum design on the body.

koko: here
koku: province
kokumin kyuka mura: government-sponsored national holiday village, a complex offering cheap accommodation for vacationing families, and groups of friends
kokumin shukusha: peoples' lodges, situated in scenic areas, similar to holiday villages but not offering as wide a range of facilities
kokusai: international
kokutai: national structure
kokutetsu: (lit. 'national line') word for Japan Railways (JR)
kome: uncooked rice
konbanwa: good evening
konjo nashi: (lit. 'lacking in spirit or courage') when used by a woman to a man, equivalent of saying, 'You haven't got any balls!'
konnichiwa: (lit. 'this is the day') good afternoon, hello
koppu: cup
kore-wa nan-desu-ka: what is this?
kori: ice
koseki: household register of families
kotatsu: low wooden frame standing formerly over a brazier sunk into the floor; nowadays over an electric heating element covered with a quilt and a loose table-top, at which one can sit to warm the lower half of the body (in summer the electric flex and quilt are removed, leaving a *kotatsu* that can be used as an ordinary table)
koto: thirteen-stringed instrument, made of paulownia wood, that is played flat on the floor
kotsu kosha: Japan Travel Bureau (JTB)
-ku: ward, district, area
kuchi-hige: moustache
kudasai: (lit. 'to give') please (added to the end of a request)
kuni: country, land, state, nation
kura: thick-walled store-house, traditionally used to store furniture and decorations
kurejitto kado: credit card

kusai: bad/foul-smelling, stinking, offensive, '*Wah*! *Kusai*!' is the equivalent of saying, 'Pooh! What a disgusting smell!'
kyakuma: drawing-room or parlour, where guests are entertained
kyanpu: camping
kyanpujo: campsite
kyoiku mama: Education Mother, a woman neurotically concerned with pushing her children through the education system
kyuri: cucumber

-machi: town; city area (for large cities) between a *ku* and a *chome* in size; also street or area
mah!: (interjection) oh!; oh dear!, dear me!; my!
mai-peisu: (lit. 'my pace') in one's own time, at one's own speed
Makudonarudo: McDonald's
makura: pillow
mama-san: owner or manageress of a *mizu shobai* establishment
manga: a comic (contents often include soft porn)
manju doryaki: soya bean cake
masshurumu: mushroom
mayoi-bashi: form of bad chopstick manners
mawashi: sumo wrestler's silk loincloth
Meiji: (lit. 'enlightened government') the throne name of Mitsuhito, Emperor of Japan, who ushered in the Meiji Restoration of the 1860s whereby Japan was roused from its long dormancy and feudalism and entered into the modern age. The Meiji Era was the period of the Emperor's reign (1868–1912).
meishi: the all-important business or calling card, used extensively in Japan. Etiquette calls for the lower-ranking or younger person to offer his card first. When the card is extended, it should be turned so that the other person can read it as he accepts it. It is considered impolite to use a damaged card or one that bears a memo not intended

for the receiver. In *kanji*, *meishi* is written in two characters: one meaning 'name' and the other 'thorn' or 'needle'. The use of the latter character appears to be related to the fact that ancient Chinese signed their names with needle-like splinters of bamboo or other wood.

mibun: social rank, standing

michi: way, road, street

mikan: tangerine, mandarin

mimi: ear

mimiga: sliced pig's ear in vinegar

minshuku: authentic Japanese-style guest-house – good family-run budget accommodation

misaki: cape (geographical promontory) (also *saki* and *zaki*)

miso: thick brown paste made from fermented, mashed, salted soya beans and used like bouillon; can also be made from barley or rice. Basic to many dishes.

miso shiru: soup made from *miso*, forms part of traditional Japanese breakfast and often contains *wakame* (large flat seaweed) and tofu. A wide range of differing types of *miso* is used, from *shiro miso* (light, sweet, and lightly salted) to *hatch miso* (pure unadulterated bean paste).

miyage: see *o-miyage*

mizu: water

mizu shobai: 'water trade', colloquial name given to one of Japan's largest and most conspicuous entertainment trades encompassing cabarets, nightclubs, bars, assignation inns, 'love hotels' (specializing in short-time room rentals), 'soaplands' (bath and massage parlours) and geisha houses. The primary ingredients of the *mizu shobai* are alcoholic drinks and attractive women.

mizugo: (lit. 'water child') aborted foetus

mizuwari: (lit. 'water-divided') referring to a 'whisky and water'

mondo: question-and-answer technique used by Zen masters

moningu saabisu: 'morning service', a light breakfast included in the price of a cup of coffee at many *kissaten*

moshi-moshi: hello (on the phone)
motto yasui: cheaper
moyashiko: the new 'Beansprout Generation' of tall, young, well-pampered Japanese
mu: concept of 'nothingness' which lies at the core of Zen
mugi-cha: tea made from barley, usually served chilled in summer
muko: over there (anywhere outside Japan)
mura: village
mushi-atsui: sultry, close, muggy
musume: daughter
muzukashii: difficult, hard

nansensu: nonsense
natto: a bitter, sticky, glutinous gloop of fermented soya beans
ne!: (interjection) I say!; I see!; I suppose!; isn't it?; don't you?; dear!
neko: cat
nekutai: necktie
nemaki: nightwear
nigo: (lit. 'number two') colloquial term referring to 'wife number two', i.e. mistress. The honorific suffix *-san* is usually added: *Nigo-san*, 'Mrs Number Two'. A second mistress is known as *Sango-san*, 'Mrs Number Three'.
Nihon or **Nippon**: Japan (lit. 'Land of the Rising Sun' or 'Source of the Sun')
nihon-cha: Japanese tea
Nihongo: Japanese language
Nihon ryori: Japanese food
Nihon-sei: made in Japan
ni-ju-hachi: twenty-eight
ni-ju-ni: twenty-two
ninjin: carrot
Nisei: an American born Japanese
noh: classical drama (Japan's oldest theatre form, dating from fourteenth century) performed on a stark stage. The principal characters wear masks and effect extremely

symbolic movements to the accompaniment of monotonic music. The *noh* singing, called *yokyoko*, is also practised as an independent art.

noma: lake

nombe: drunkard; one who drinks to excess

nomimono: a drink; something to drink

nomiya: (lit. 'drinking shop') a generic term for bars and taverns, usually referring to unpretentious neighbourhood places

noren: cloth hung from the eaves as a sunshade; since the Edo period (early seventeenth to mid-nineteenth century) typically as a trade sign in front of a shop-keeper's house, bearing his name or trade name

nori: Japan's most popular seaweed, dried in paper-thin sheets and used to wrap around *sushi* and riceballs. *Nori* has been cultivated in Japan's gentle bays and narrow inlets for over 300 years. Harvested during the cold winter months, it is carefully washed and then slowly and evenly dried in square forms, much like the traditional method of paper-making.

nusa (gohei): small papers (at one time cloth) given as offerings at Shinto shrines and seen festooned on trees, shrubs, fences or any likely spot all over shrine compounds

o-: prefix used in polite speech as indicator of respect for the thing or person in question (see *-san*)

obaasan: affectionate name for an old woman; grandmother; sometimes used with a hint of condescension

obi: sash or belt worn with kimono

oboradaren: thank you (on the island of Tokunoshima)

ohayo: morning

ohayo gozaimasu: (lit. 'it's early') good morning

oishii: delicious

ojii-san: grandfather; old man (grandfatherly type)

ojo-san: young unmarried woman (equivalent to Miss)

oka: 'cherry-blossom' missiles that the Japanese sent slamming into US battleships

o-kaa-san: mother (*kaa*, mother, with respectful prefix and suffix)
okusama: madam
oku-san: wife (someone else's); madam (e.g. what a woman is called by a shop assistant)
o-kyaku-san: guest (*kyaku*, guest, with respectful prefix and suffix)
OL: 'Office lady' – standard female employee of large firm, usually a clerical worker
omen: mask made of wood or, more commonly, papier-mâché
omiai-kekkon: an arranged marriage
omikuji: prayer papers sold at Buddhist temples – they are attached in their thousands to any likely spot (trees, shrubs) on the temple grounds
o-miyage: almost socially mandatory souvenir gifts brought back from holidays and trips to give to family and friends (lit. 'local manufacture'), commonly used with the honorary '*o*-' prefix
on: a favour; obligation; kindness; a debt of gratitude
onbu: (lit. 'carrying on the back') depending on people; in particular, causing strangers to bear one's expenses, to pick up the bill; also the custom of carrying a baby strapped to the back
onigiri: round or triangular riceball sprinkled with sesame seeds or wrapped with dried seaweed, usually filled with fish or spicy vegetables – very popular for picnics and snacks
onsen: hot springs; spa. Usually surrounded by various guest accommodations.
oolong-cha: Chinese tea
origami: art of paper-folding
oshibori: finger-cloths, usually offered in restaurants; served cold in summer, hot in winter
oshi-ya: professionals employed to pack more passengers into trains
osoroshii: terrible, dreadful

otearai: toilet; washroom
otera: Buddhist temple, usually much more ornate than a Shinto *jinja*
otochan: daddy (also *papa*)
otoshidama: New Year gifts
otsue: pilgrim's staff
oya: parents; also (interjection) oh!; my!; bless me!; by George!; by Jove!
oyasumi-nasai: (lit. 'please take a rest') goodnight

pachinko: pinball played on vertical machine
pan: bread
painappuru: pineapple
parento-san: youth hostel warden
purezento: present, gift
puraibashi: privacy

rabu hoteru: love hotel – an establishment (usually gaudy and gimmicky) that rents rooms to couples for short periods of an hour or more
raisu: white rice served with Western or Chinese food, or on flat plate; called *gohan* when served in a bowl
ramen: white Chinese noodles adapted to Japanese palate, served in big bowls in a chicken stock with vegetables and/or meat; can be eaten hot or cold
resutoran: restaurant
rikishi: sumo wrestlers
ringo: apple
rinjin: neighbour
rinko bukuro: bicycle bag, for transporting your partially dissembled bike in when travelling by train or bus, available in Japan's well-stocked bicycle shops. To save money (and weight), wrapping your bike in your tent's groundsheet can, with a bit of ingenuity, work just as well.
Rinzai: type of Zen Buddhism
rito: Okinawa's outer islands
romaji: script in roman letters, Latin alphabet

roshi: Zen master; also the *sensei* or high priest at a temple
rotenburo: open-air bath, naturally occurring hotsprings
rubabu: rhubarb
ryokan: traditional Japanese inn
ryoku-cha: Japanese green tea (of various sorts)

saikuringu terminaru: cycling terminal – lodgings similar to youth hostels, designed for the growing number of people touring Japan by bicycle
saisen bako: offertory box at shrines and temples
sakana: fish
sake: potent rice wine with 15–16% alcoholic content, usually served warm in *ochoku* (thimble-sized cups). Although it can be made anywhere in Japan, famous *sake* are produced in regions that have a supply of good water, or good quality rice. One of the many sayings about *sake* is that it has ten merits: it is the best medicine, a prolonger of life, a meal for the traveller, a friend to those who live alone, a convenient excuse to visit without invitation, a disperser of sorrow, a social leveller, a relief from work, a harmonizer of all men, and an overcoat against the cold. Another saying is that one should drink *sake*, not be drunk by it.
saki: cape (geographical promontory) (also *misaki, zaki)*
sakura: cherry-blossom, the flower that symbolizes the nation of Japan
salaryman: standard male employee of a company; white-collar worker
samisen: three-stringed instrument of the lute family with the shape and sound of a banjo
samurai: warrior aristocrat in feudal Japan – a privileged class permitted to wear two swords as a sign of their caste. Below them were the common people: farmers, artisans and merchants. The samurai were abolished after the Meiji Restoration.
san: mountain (also *yama, zan*)
-san: suffix used in polite speech as an indicator of respect for the person to whom it is attached

sashi-bashi: bad chopstick manners which involve spearing food with the tips of the sticks
sashimi: bite-size pieces of very thin slices of fresh raw fish (sometimes beef, poultry or horsemeat) served with soy sauce, *wasabi* and thinly shredded ginger
sayonara: goodbye
seiza: position of kneeling, sitting back on one's heels, required on formal occasions and in many traditional arts, such as tea ceremony and sometimes calligraphy; sitting still, sitting quietly
seko: bullfighting trainer
seku hara: sexual harassment
semi: cicada
sencha: Chinese-style tea ceremony
sengu-shiki: shrine removal
senpuki: electric fan
sensei: a teacher or master; also very common as a generic title for almost any person of authority, either genuinely or as a form of obsequiousness; often added to the end of a person's name as a sign of respect
sensu: folding hand-fan
sento: public baths found in all cities and towns
seppuku: suicide by disembowelment (less vulgar term than *hara-kiri*). In feudal times this ritual was the exclusive privilege of nobles and samurai.
senko: joss stick, incense
senpai: one's elder/senior/superior, typically at school and at one's place of work
seubei: rice cracker
shakuhachi: oriental wind instrument played like a recorder with a deep soulful sound; conventionally made of bamboo
shanpu setto: shampoo and set
shashin shu: photograph album
shi: city; four
shiitake: type of large, flat, dark mushroom with strong flavour

shikata ga nai: what can be done?; it can't be helped; it has to be

shiken jigoko: 'Examination Hell' – pressurized selection process that young Japanese are put through in the hope of gaining entrance to good schools and universities

shima: island; also small, sweet, red Okinawan bananas

shimenawa: sacred rope

shinkansen: the evil-eyed, swift-moving Bullet Train (lit. 'new line', since new railway lines were laid for these high-speed trains, which travel in excess of 200 kilometres per hour)

Shinto: the polytheistic indigenous religion of Japan, which propounds that all living and even inanimate objects have souls. Ancestor worship and purity are two basic tenets. State Shinto, prevalent from the Meiji era to the end of the Second World War, was a bastardized form that made the Emperor an omnipotent living god. Shinto in Japan is called *Kami-no-Michi* (The Way of the gods).

shisa: ceramic lion-dogs placed on Okinawan rooftops to ward off evil sprits

shishi: lion-dog

shochu: distilled spirit (average alcohol content 30%) often made from sweet potatoes and also from sugar cane and rice. Much more potent and rougher than *sake.* Was once considered a low-class drink and even used as disinfectant in Edo period.

shoda: (lit. 'way of writing') calligraphy

shogun: warlord, military ruler of old Japan to whom all *daimyo* and *samurai* owed allegiance. In pre-Meiji times the shogun was the actual ruler of Japan; succession was hereditary as long as a family could remain in power. The shogun was always invested by the Emperor.

shogunate: the office or rule of a shogun

shoji: sliding room-divider panels made of thin translucent sheets of rice paper pasted on lightweight wooden frames. The traditional purpose of *shoji* was a screen to block the view rather than a door to bar entrance. Modern *shoji* may have panels of frosted glass rather than rice paper.

shojin ryori: vegetarian meals, usually served at Buddhist temples
shoyu: soy sauce
shu: sect
shukubo: temple lodgings
shunga: (lit. 'spring picture') explicit erotic drawing or print
shurei-no-tami: people who treat others with respect
Sir Goy: see *sugoi*
soba: long noodles made from buckwheat, with squared corners, and colours that vary from grey to brown. They are served with a sprinkling of shredded pork, beef, chicken or egg with leeks and mushrooms in a bowl of fish stock. They may also be served cold with an accompaniment of soy sauce, freshly chopped onions, ginger and minced horseradish.
sode: sleeve
so desho: oh really; is that so?
so desu: you are right
sokkusu: socks
sopurando: Soapland, a combination of bath and massage parlour whose speciality is catering to the sexual needs of a primarily male clientele. They are found in all Japanese cities, in what is obviously an acceptable arrangement with vice-control authorities.
sore wa honeori zon desu: like carrying coals to Newcastle
soroban: abacus
Soto: type of Zen Buddhism
sudare: bamboo blinds
sugi: cryptomeria wood, very common Japanese cedar tree
sugoi: wonderful, amazing, great
suido: straits
suika: watermelon
suimin-busoku: sleepy during day after no night sleeping
suimono: clear soup
sumimasen: excuse me, I'm sorry, I apologize; thank you, I'm grateful

sumo: Japanese wrestling
sumotori: sumo wrestler
sunamushiyu or **sonayu**: natural sand steam-bath on beach geothermically heated to 80°C (176°F), famous in Beppu and Ibusuki in Kyushu
supaa: supermarket
sushi: lightly vinegared rice, seasoned with salt, sugar and *mirin* (sweet rice wine) and moulded into bite-sized mouthfuls, overlaid or mixed with raw fish, shellfish, seaweed, vegetables or omelette
suteteko: men's baggy cotton underpants
suzumushi: pet insects

tabi: white or (sometimes) dark blue split-toed socks, worn with *geta* as part of traditional Japanese dress
tabun: maybe
tada: free
tadaima: now; at present; typical as an exclamation, by way of greeting, when returning home
taiko: Japanese drum
taka kura: thatched wooden store-house on stilts
takai: expensive
tako: colourful kites; octopus
takoyaki: stall foods; fried dough balls surrounding bits of octopus and seasonings
takuan: yellow pickled *daikon*
tanuki: folklore character (badger/racoon/dog-like creature) frequently represented in ceramic figures
tataki: slipper/shoe-changing area
tatami: floorcovering on which shoes are never worn, made of plaited rush cover on top of a straw pallet reinforced with yarn, and sunk into the floor. *Tatami* mats are used as a unit of room measurement.
tatemae: public 'face'; the way things seem to other people. An attitude adopted in order not to offend.
temawarihin kippu: special ticket required to carry a bagged bike on a train

tempura: fritter-like dish consisting of various kinds of fresh seafood, meat and vegetables (green pepper, carrots, aubergines, mushrooms, lotus root) coated in a batter of egg and flour (*koromo*) and quickly deep-fried in sesame or pure vegetable oil until they turn a translucent glaze. These morsels are dipped into *ten-tsuyn* – a sauce of *mirin* (sweet *sake*), fish broth and soya sauce to which grated *daikon* with pimento powder and/or fresh grated ginger are added to taste. *Tempura* is served with a bowl of rice and a small dish of pickled vegetables.

tenki: weather

tenno: emperor

Tenno Heika: His Majesty the Emperor; Heavenly King

tento: tent

tenugui: small towel or flannel provided at many *sento* and *onsen*

teppo: sumo wrestler's wooden-pole 'punchbag'

toge: mountain pass; height

togyu-jo: Japanese bullfight

toiret: toilet

tokonoma: decorative alcove found in most Japanese homes, in which an *ikebana* flower arrangement, a *kakemono* scroll painting or other artworks may be displayed. An honoured guest is usually seated in front of the *tokonoma*.

Tokugawa, Ieyasu: the military leader of Japan who controlled the nation at the turn of the sixteenth century. The word *shogun* is synonymous with this man. The Tokugawa era begun by him lasted from 1600 until the Meiji Restoration in 1868. Feudal Japan, with the *samurai* and their *bushido*, was at its height during this time.

tomodachi: friend

tori: road

torii: entrance gate to a Shinto shrine

toruko: Turkish bath

tsubo: traditional unit of land measurement, defined as one square bay or two tatami mats (3.3 square metres)

tsukin jigoku: commuter hell

tsunami: tidal wave, usually following sea-centred earthquake
tsuyu: rainy season ('plum rains')

udon: long white and slightly thick type of noodle made from wheat and served with a sprinkling of shredded pork, beef, chicken or egg with leeks and mushrooms in a bowl of fish stock
uma: horse
uma-sashi: raw horsemeat
umeboshi: very sour picked red plum served with many dishes as a condiment
umi: sea (also *kai, nada*)
unagi: eel
ura dori: backstreets
utsukushii: beautiful

wa: peace, team spirit, social harmony
wa doka desu-ka?: which way is?
wagamama: selfishness, egotism
waifu: wife (used mostly only by the younger generation)
wah!: expression of surprise or disgust
waka: thirty-one syllable poem
wakame: large flat seaweed sold either fresh or dried, used in salads and soups
wakizashi: dirk
wanko: lacquered bowl
waribashi: cheap, disposable, separable chopsticks made of plain wood, found in homes and restaurants
wasabi: very powerful green horseradish
washi: handmade paper
washoku: Japanese-style food
waza-waza: especially, on purpose

ya!: (interjection) oh!; ah!; dear me!; well!; hello!; so long!
yabusame: horseback archery
yakitori: pieces of chicken (white-meat, leg, heart, gizzard, etc.) and vegetables threaded on bamboo skewers and

dipped into a specially prepared sweet soy sauce before being grilled

yakuza: professional criminal gangs (Japanese equivalent of the Mafia) or a member of such a gang. They are prominent in *mizu shobai* businesses and have powerful connections in both legitimate business and politics at all levels of government in Japan.

yama: mountain (also *san, zan*)

yamakago: old-style people-carrier for ferrying travellers up and down the Hakone mountain area during the Edo period

Yamato: traditional name of Japan, meaning 'Mountain Road' (euphemism for 'conquest')

Yamato-damashi: pure (Japanese) spirit; the soul of Japan

yamete!: stop!; leave me alone!

yareyare, boku niwa ikko wakaran: well, by gosh, I am from Missouri

yata-no-kagami: the Eight-pointed Mirror, one of the Three Sacred Treasures

yo!: (interjection) hello!; bravo!; well done!; good!

-yo: suffix added to give extra emphasis to a word

yobai: 'night-crawling'

yoi: good, fine, nice

yoma: Eastern-style room

yopparai: a drunk

yokozuna: sumo grand champion

yoshoku: Western-style food

yubin bango: postcode, zip code

yubinkyoku: post-office

yukan: evening newspaper; brave

yuki tsuri: structural support for trees to hold the load of snow during winter without breaking

yusu hosuteru: youth hostel

zabuton: small cushions used for sitting on, usually in *tatami* areas

zaki: cape (geographical promontory)

Zen: Japanese school of Buddhism, introduced in the twelfth century from China, which teaches the achievement of enlightenment through inner contemplation
zenzai: rice cake with sweet soya-bean paste

A Bare and Basic Bicycle Glossary

bureki reba: brake lever
chen: chain
chenhoiru: chainwheel
chen sute: chain stay
direra waia: derailleur cable
furemu pompu: bicycle pump
furonto direra: front derailleur
handoru sutemu: handlebar stem
handoruba: handlebars
kamu reba: front-wheel quick-release
mae bureki: front brake
mae habu: front hub
mae hoku: front fork blade
pedaru: pedal
ria direra: rear derailleur
rimu: wheel rim
sadoru: saddle
sharin: wheel
shifuto reba: gear lever
shita paipu: down tube
shito posto: seat post
shito sute: seat stay

supoku: spokes
tate paipu: seat tube
taiya: tyre
taiya barubu: valve
ue paipu: top tube
ushiro bureki: rear brake

APPENDIX 1

Equipment Department

Bicycle

Frame	Custom-made 18″ ROBERTS bronze-brazed, touring angles, pink. Built in 1988 by Chas Roberts, traversed several continents and still going strong.
Wheels	Saturae 26″ H × 22 rims. DT stainless steel spokes. Hand-built by Red'ed of Icelandic fame.
Hubs	Campagnolo Nuovo Record 36-hole large flange.
Tyres	Avocet Cross 26 × 1.5.
Headset	Campagnolo Nuovo Record.
Handlebars & stem	Cinelli.
Brakes	Shimano Deore XT Cantilever.
Brake levers	Campagnolo Super Record.
Cranks	TA 150mm.
Chainrings	Chris Bell's precision-made, nigh-on indestructible round 'EGGS': 24/36/40.
Chain	Sedisport.

Freewheel	Suntour 13-32.
Derailleur (front and rear)	Shimano Deore XT.
Gear levers	Campagnolo Nuovo Record.
Pedals	Campagnolo Gran Sport.
Bottom Bracket	Specialized S1.
Seat post	Strong.
Saddle	Terry.
Racks (front and rear)	Blackburn.
Waterbottle cages	Blackburn.
Mudguards	Milremo.
Brake blocks	Scott Matthauser.
Brake hoods	Modolo.
Handlebar covering	Titus – padded leather.
Toe clips	Cateye, nylon.
Toe straps	Christophe.
Computer	Cateye ATB.
Bike light (rear)	Vistalite LED (Light Emitting Diode), attached to rear rack.
Bicycle bell	Make unknown – found at the side of the road on Vancouver Island, BC.
Panniers	Tika – red, canvas, adapted to take Karrimor (old style) clips.
Front	CT17 Expedition International.
Rear	CT10 Expedition Standard.
Handlebar bag	CT30 Delux (plus shoulder strap). Tika are durable and nearly (but not quite) waterproof bags that have stood up well to extended touring in both Western and Eastern Europe, Canada, America, Mexico and Japan.
Rack pack	Cannondale – second-hand, bought for $1 in Durango, Colorado. Useful for cramming extra food supplies on board.

Sleeping Arrangements

Tent	The North Face –Tadpole 1.85kg (4lb 1oz), with no-see-um insect netting side walls and door. A lightweight, capacious and fast-to-erect, pitch-it-anywhere, free-standing tent.
Pegs	8 × The North Face Super Tent Peg (virtually indestructible). 2 × Chouinard T-stakes (indestructible). 1 × small spare aluminium inner sleeve in case of breakage.
Groundsheet	The North Face, made-to-measure for Tadpole tent. Super-lightweight, fast-to-dry. Picked up in a sale bin in REI, the camper's seventh heaven outdoor store, in Los Angeles. 1 × cheap plastic sheet cut to size to fit door storage area.
Sleeping bag	1 × The North Face Kazoo 1kg (2lb 2oz), three-season goosedown bag. Works a treat. 1 × home-made cotton sheet sleeping bag (5oz). Easy to wash and good for keeping the very-not-easy-to-wash Kazoo clean. Also adds a little extra warmth, if needed. Conversely, it's vital in hot conditions when the last thing you want to go to bed with is a blood-boiling down-feather bag.
Sleeping mat	1 × Karrimor Karrimat Expedition, ¾ length, yellow (10oz). I used to take a Therm-a-Rest Ultralite ¾ length self-inflatable mat, but the Karrimat, being a 'closed-cell' foam pad, is lighter and puncture-proof and far more adaptable. What's more, at the end of a long day in the saddle, the Karrimat saves waiting around for things to inflate.

Kitchen Department

Stove None. I went stoveless to Japan because I felt like being clobber-free on the cooking front. I'm quite happy gnawing on raw food day in, day out and rustling up inedible-looking mixtures with any unlikely ingredients I can lay my oily hands on.
1 × plastic food container – doubles up as a 'bowl' for mixing the above mish-mash, while the lid acts as a chopping board.
1 × big plastic mug – also gets used as a bowl and, at a push, a bath.
2 × plastic screw-top containers into which I decant jars of honey etc.
1 × small and serrated Kitchen Devil sharp knife with home-made reinforced protective blade sheath.
1 × Swiss-made Kuhn Rikon vegetable peeler. Lightweight, strong and sharp. Without a doubt, the best peeler I've ever peeled with (and, being a cook by trade, I've peeled with a few in my time). It's so good it even makes peeling 45 kilos of potatoes a pleasurable experience. In some countries (i.e. ones in which crops are treated with heavy doses of 'night soil'), I peel everything that can be peeled in the hope of preventing some mysterious and potentially lethal disease-causing bacterium from running amok in my gut.
1 × lightweight stainless steel spoon.
1 × lightweight stainless steel knife.
1 × Permaware durable plastic teaspoon.
1 × pot scourer, cut in half.
1 × 7cm^2 tea towel.
1 × lighter – used mostly for burning toilet paper.
3 × water-bottles (to fit my bicycle frame-mounted bottle cages).
1 × Ortlieb 4 litre waterbag. Lightweight and collapsible and easy to store. Also works well as a pillow and cushion.
Plastic bags – all conceivable (and inconceivable) shapes and

sizes and amounts. Without at least a dozen bags full of plastic bags I'm lost.

Rubber bands – most of which I make from an old pair of rubber gloves that have sprung a leak (a prepared-before-the-programme top-tip I picked up from *Blue Peter* circa 1974) and used to seal my plastic bags full of all and sundry.

Clothing

1 × Rohan fully waterproof jacket with hood.

1 × pair Rohan waterproof trousers. Both of these items were prototype one-offs (which I was testing for a new cycling range of clothing that Rohan was planning to launch) and worked very well. Unfortunately, despite a short, sharp burst of producing a range of excellent cycle clothing, Rohan got second wind and decided to revert to supplying their more traditional mellow-toned hiking and rambling and bird-spotting gear. I now bundle myself up against the elements in a North Face Stowaway II Gore-Tex jacket.

1 × Rohan Polartec Fleece top. Lightweight and warm and is almost dry as soon as it's washed.

1 × Bell cycling helmet, white (which, because of the heat, did not see a lot of contact with my head). I now use a Specialized Banshee.

1 × sun visor (bought for $2 in a hippy shop in Hawaii in 1992). Saves my nose from multiple peelings.

1 × pair Nike trainers.

1 × pair flip-flops (bought in Katmandu in 1988 for about ½p). Essential for use in showers to avoid picking up all sorts of undesirable foot infections, etc.

1 × pair black cotton-lycra leggings.

2 × pairs stripy cotton-lycra home-made cycling shorts (material bought cheaply from a stall in Berwick Street Market, London W1).

1 × pair baggy cotton shorts (bought in a kite shop on the island of Molokai, Hawaii).
2 × cotton vests (sleeveless T-shirts).
1 × cotton T-shirt.
2 × bras (make excellent insect traps during downhill descents).
3 × pairs M&S knickers (wear one, wash one, keep one spare).
3 × pairs white ankle socks (ditto the above).
1 × swimming costume.
1 × pair swimming goggles.
1 × bandanna.
1 × big cotton scarf – good not only for blocking out neck draughts but also for make-shift slings, bikini tops, blindfold (when trying to sleep in brightly lit places), emergency towel and shopping bag.
1 × pair lycra-backed, leather-palmed and padded cycling mitts (though most of the time it was too hot to wear them).
1 × mini towel – one of the few advantages of having a mini body means you only need a mini towel.

Washbag/First Aid and Other Paraphernalia

Washbag – small, lightweight stuff-sack filled with toothbrush, toothpaste, shampoo, soap etc.
Dental Floss – not only good for teeth, but for making washing lines, tying up parcels, mending panniers, strong thread, make-shift guy ropes, making trip-wires around tent to forewarn of any unsavoury characters prowling around at night.
Lip-salve stick with sunblock.
Sun-block cream – gave up on this after a while. Japan was just too humid – cream refused to be absorbed into such sweaty skin.

Insect repellent – or, judging from the amount of mosquitoes I attracted, was this simply mis-labelled insect fodder?

Tiger Balm – good for headaches, pulled muscles and making your eyes water.

1 × 10ml bottle Hypercal tincture (Ainsworths Homoeopathic Pharmacy) – heals cuts in a jiffy.

1 × small phial each of Arnica tablets (for injuries, shock, etc.) and Arsen Alb (for food poisoning).

Face moisterizer cream – decanted into small plastic bottle.

1 × small container of multi-vitamins and minerals to hopefully reach the parts that a diet of seaweed and octopus tentacles didn't reach.

1 × 10ml bottle Tea Tree essential oil (good antiseptic).

1 × 10ml bottle Lavender essential oil (good for everything from burns to insect bites to soporific pillow aromas).

1 × packet Puritabs (in case I found myself faced with suspect water supplies).

1 × hefty supply of the all-essential toilet paper (collected in small doses from various sources en route).

1 × pair Boots Travel Bands – worn on wrist acupressure points to help control 'motion sickness' – although to have any effect on a plane I should perhaps try wearing some on my ankles and neck as well.

1 × pair washable foam earplugs (essential when bedding down *en masse* with several hundred ferry passengers all of whom seem intent on doing anything but sleep).

Small selection of plasters and bandages.

Assortment of safety pins, needles, extra strong 100% polyester thread.

Mini nail clippers and file, ultra lightweight plastic clothes pegs. Waterproof card clearly stating blood group.

Cut-off pencil, half a rubber, airmail paper and envelopes, permanent black marker pen, biro, mini Pritt Stick and Sellotape.

1 × small black notebook (usually an Alwych from Waverley with an 'All-Weather' cover) that acts as my never-far-from-reach diary.

Calculator – credit card size, solar powered (good for currency calculations and for those all-too-frequent moments when the simplest of calculations goes clean out of head).

Oxford Minidictionary – good for those all-too-frequent moments when the simplist – whoops, I mean simplest – of spellings goes clean out of head. Also never fails to prove an intriguing read.

Mini Japanese dictionary.

Japanese in 3 Weeks (ha!) phrasebook. (Cut your capers!; You kill my cat and I'll kill your dog; Well, by gosh, I am from Missouri).

Books – vital in order to enter another world (preferably fictitious) at least twice a day. In Japan, where books in English were non-existent outside of the cities, I carted around a weighty library on board my bike for fear of running out of the all-essential reading material.

Maps – even if you don't know where you are it's nice to think you do.

Mini compass – if in doubt head north. Or should that be south?

Mini thermometer – for dangling off handlebar bag. Even if it's not very pleasant to know it's 115°F inside your tent, it's still quite an interesting fact to log in the diary and to bore friends with on postcards.

1 × mini folding hand-fan.

1 × mini mirror (50p-sized) – indispensable for hoiking airborne insects out of eyes.

1 × Swiss Army knife – with scissors – vital for fashioning makeshift postcards out of cardboard boxes.

1 × mini address book – crammed full of mini words and mini names and mini numbers.

1 × money pouch – with traveller's cheques, cash (dollars and yen), Visa card (in Japan far more places take Visa than Mastercard), BT Chargecard (a boon for phoning home), insurance, driving licence, international driving permit, plane/ferry tickets. YHA membership card,

passport, spare passport pictures. (Photocopied details of passport, traveller's cheques, credit card theft information etc. stored elsewhere in my baggage along with supply of emergency money.)

1 × Dog Dazer – battery-operated, ultra-sonic dog deterrent – helps to spare a shin or two from ending up as a bicycle-chasing dog's dinner.

1 × Petzl Micro head torch – not only suffices as bicycle light, but v. useful for sparing the hands for inner (or outer) tent activities.

1 × Mini-Maglite Solitaire torch.

1 × collapsible rucksack – useful for a jaunt in the hills and for cramming last minute food supplies on board overladen mount before setting up camp.

Oakley sunglasses and spec case – protects eyes from sun, wind, rain, grit, dust and winged insects.

Sony Walkman Sports personal stereo plus four cassettes of custom-made compilations – for that moment when you need a good blast from the past (or the present).

Sony mini shortwave radio – can't leave home without it as I find I'm addicted to tuning in to anything from the World Service to Radio Moscow to Radio Ouagadougou (?) – or something like that.

Cheap digital Casio watch – with alarm.

Canon Sureshot camera – for quick, easy, no-messing snaps. Highly recommended as it's still going strong after twelve years despite being full of Saharan sand, doused in several rainy seasons, frozen and boiled, dropped on multiple occasions and involved in various bicycle head-on collisions.

Canon AE1 Programme with Tamron 70-210 lens – also standing the test of time miraculously well after spending seventeen years bouncing around on my bike.

Padded bicycle-crash-proof camera case.

20 × Fujichrome Sensia 100 film (36 exposures) – good all-rounder.

1 × mini Minox tripod (essential for taking self-timered, self-posing snaps).

Leica 8×20 BCA mini binoculars. Immensely useful for spying on all sorts of things. Also a boon for homing in on distant out-of-eyesight signposts (especially ones at bottom of hills) to prevent having to cycle all the way down to it and then all the way back when you discover you've gone the wrong way.

Bicycle Tools and Bicycle Bits

1 × spare tyre: Michelin Hi-Lite Express 26 × 1.50. Folds in three for easy storage.

1 × spare inner tube.

3 × plastic tyre levers plus puncture repair kit including talcum powder to prevent tube sticking to tyre.

Spare spokes, brake, gear and straddle cables.

1 × mini cross-head screwdriver.

1 × mini flat-head screwdriver.

Allen keys – to fit all allen bolts on bike.

1 × Park cone spanner (for removing pedals).

1 × mini adjustable spanner.

1 × 8/9mm open spanner.

1 × 10/11mm open spanner.

1 × 15mm TA crank spanner.

1 × TA crank remover.

1 × chainlink tool (plus few spare links in case chain breaks).

1 × block remover.

1 × spoke key.

Few spare nuts and bolts, mini oil container, camera film cannister of good quality bike grease, piece of picture wire, spare pannier clip and Fastex clip, spare piece of big and small webbing, curtain rings, rag, rubber gloves, gaffer tape, insulating tape, short length of 4mm rock-climbing chord.

2 × karabiners.

6 × plastic cable ties – indispensable for the fix-it department.
1 × mini Leatherman knife with pliers (pliers prove very useful for making things out of roadside rubbish).
1 × bicycle pump.
1 × mini bicycle pump (as emergency back-up).
1 × cable lock and padlock.
1 × Ortlieb waterproof map case (only fault with this was that the manufacturers placed the Ortlieb logo in the middle of the case which inevitably was just in the position that I wanted to be on the map).
3 × bungie cords (essential for lassoing ten tons of superfluous kit and several hundred kilos of Japanese grandmothers' home-grown giant radishes and cabbages onto rear rack).

APPENDIX 2

Japanese Historical Periods and Chronology

10,000–300 BC	JOMON PERIOD
300 BC–AD 300	YAYOI PERIOD
300–710	KOFUN PERIOD
710–794	NARA PERIOD Nara was the capital for most of this period, which marked the highwater-mark of Chinese influence on Japan.
794–1185	HEIAN PERIOD – Entrenchment of Japanese Values. In 794 the capital was established at Kyoto, which was at the time called 'Heian-kyo'; it remained the capital until 1868.
1185–1333	KAMAKURA PERIOD – Domination through Military Rule. The government passed into the samurai headed by a hereditary line of shogun who established their headquarters at Kamakura, near contemporary Tokyo.
1333–1576	MUROMACHI PERIOD – Country at War. A new line of shogun took over, governing from the Muromachi quarter of Kyoto. In

	the 15th and 16th centuries much of Japan was racked by civil war.
1576–1600	MOMOYAMA PERIOD – Return to Unity. During this period the great leader, Nobunaga Oda, became the first Japanese to effectively use firearms in battle. The son of a *daimyo*, Oda seized power from the Imperial court in Kyoto and used his military genius to initiate the process of pacification and unification in central Japan. For ten years he waged war, but his efforts were cut short when he was assassinated by one of his own guards in 1582. Oda was succeeded by his most able general, Hideyoshi Toyotomi, whose legendary bad looks earned him the moniker of 'Saru-*san*' (Mr Monkey).
1600–1867	EDO or TOKUGAWA PERIOD – Peace and Seclusion. After the Battle of Sekigahara in 1600, Ieyasu Tokugawa established a new line of shogun in Edo. The succeeding centuries were a period of economic and urban growth but in the 19th century the deteriorating economy and the growing threat from Europe and America lead to the collapse of the shogunate and to the Meiji Restoration.
1868–1912	MEIJI RESTORATION – Emergence from Isolation.
1868	The Meiji Restoration brought about a nominal restoration of power to the Emperor Meiji and ushered in a period of intense Westernization.
1889	The promulgation of the Constitution.
1894–5	The Sino-Japanese War.
1904–5	The Russo-Japanese War.
1910	Japan annexed Korea.

1912–26	TAISHO PERIOD This era coincided with the reign of Emperor Taisho, who was mentally unstable and little more than a figurehead.
1914	Japan declared war on Germany and acquired German possessions in the Far East.
1925	Universal suffrage for men.
1926–89	SHOWA PERIOD The era began with the accession of the Emperor, whose given name, Hirohito, was rarely used in Japan. 'Showa' was the name given to his reign.
1937	War with China broke out. In December thousands were massacred in the Rape of Nanking.
1941	The attack on Pearl Harbor and the sinking of two British battleships initiated the Pacific War.
1945	Atomic bombs dropped on Hiroshima and Nagasaki precipitated Japan's surrender.
1946	A New Constitution was promulgated establishing the foundations of a parliamentary democracy and extending the franchise to women.
1952	Following the Treaty of San Francisco, the Occupation came to an end and Japan resumed her independent status.
1989–	HEISEI PERIOD Emperor Akihito ascended the throne upon the death of his father. When he was officially crowned on 12th November 1990 he took the name Heisei, which translates as 'Perfecting Peace'.

An Inconsequential Index